My Scrap Paper Diary

My Scrap Paper Diary

FROM SNAKE BITE TO
POW 1941 – 1945

—⋘—

Pte Vic Petersen WX 571

Compiled and researched by Anthony W Buirchell
with assistance and permission of the Petersen family

Copyright © 2025

The moral right of the Author of the work has been asserted by them in accordance with the Copyright, Designs and Patents Act 1988. All rights reserved. No part of this book may be used or reproduced by any means, graphic, electronic or mechanical including photocopying, recording, taping or by any information storage retrieval system without the written permission of the publisher except in the case of brief quotations embodied in critical articles and reviews.

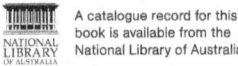 A catalogue record for this book is available from the National Library of Australia

Creator: Anthony William Buirchell with Vic Petersen's Writings

Title: My Scrap Paper Diary Pte Vic Petersen WX 571

Target Audience: Youth and adults.

Printed and Channel Distribution

Publishing Consultants "Pickawoowoo Publishing Group"

Publisher

Cric Croc Enterprises, www.criccroc.com.au

For enquiries, write to: rights and permissions via publisher.

Lightning Source/ Ingram Aus.

Artist: Cover designed by Laila Savolainen

ISBN 978-0-9756230-4-6 (paperback)
ISBN 978-0-9756230-5-3 (hardback)
ISBN 978-0-9756230-6-0 (e-book)

A Tribute

The value of diaries to history are immeasurable. The methods of maintaining a diary during wars can be no more brilliant than that used by Private Vic Petersen.

Vic wrote his daily notes on scraps of paper from 9th June, 1941 to 7th May 1945 a total of 1440 entries. He hid the writings in his clothing and belongings. The information of day-to-day happenings and the "OIL" on the wider events of the war offers blow by blow and day by day accounts.

Although the author never had the privilege of meeting Vic he has come to admire the man and the way he conducted himself through times of adversity and his resilience. The work at Tymbakion, the 10 days in a cattle carriage while the temperature plummeted below zero and the 4 years as a POW are unimaginable. On top of his negative experiences in life he showed he cared for his fellow man shown when he wrote a letter to my own mother, Clem, the wife of a fellow inmate, my dad William Buirchell, to let them know of his health. This kind and considerate act was played out several times by Vic. Sharing Vic's Diary is a way of paying tribute to a fine and brave Australian.

There is a Tribute Website where people can pay tribute to others who served. If you have someone in this category, go to:

www.prisonersofwarcrete.com
Anthony W Buirchell

Contents

Foreword · 1
Introduction · 7
Acknowledgements · 9
Background · 11
Personal and Pre-War Data Vic Petersen WX517 · · · · · · · · · · · · · · 13
Army Records for Vic Petersen WX517 · 15
Overseas Service ·17
The Battle of Greece 1941 · 19
Battle of Crete 1941 · 21
Year of 1941 Olive Trees ·29
Year of 1942 Parachutes and Train to Stalag. · · · · · · · · · · · · · · · 51
Year of 1943 Stalag VIIIB ·144
Year of 1944 Railway Maintenance · 258
Year of 1945 Survivor and Liberation · 430
Trials & Tribulations · 508
Obituary for Private Charles Amos George Victor (Vic) Petersen ·572
Map of Vic's Journey from Perth to Palestine 1940 · · · · · · · · · · · ·575
Map of Crete ·576
Map of Vic's Movements from Crete to Stalag VIIIB · · · · · · · · · · ·577
German Town Names ·579
Glossary ·581

Foreword

From an early age I was aware of the 2nd/11th Battalion of the Australian Infantry Forces and its nickname The Perth Battalion. When the Second World War was declared many men bravely walked to the nearest recruitment office and signed up to fight for King and Empire. One of these intrepid souls was C A G V Petersen WX 571 and a country boy. I knew of others through my father who enlisted after many of his mates and relations signed their Attestation Sheet.

After five bitter years the men who were returned home spoke little of their experiences from thousands of kilometres and often out of touch with family and home. The few letters that were exchanged told only snippets of the real life of our towns people so far away in foreign lands.

I had heard of a Soldier's Diary that had surfaced in Perth and was reputed to belong to a West Australian by the name of Vic Petersen. He had been in the 2nd/11th Battalion and set out to keep a diary about his experiences. He kept the diary on scrap pieces of paper. Each scrap of paper was listed by date and then stowed away on his person and belongings.

How Vic Petersen managed to write a daily comment on pieces of scrap paper is an incredible story in itself. The names of the men in the book, I researched and wrote, Spirited Away, continued to turn up throughout Vic's diary, until the end of the war.

After his capture on the south coast of Crete on 6th June, 1941 Vic began writing notes for his Scrap Paper Diary. He soon found himself in a different war from the start. He was made to march from Tymbakion, Crete, over the mountains without food and water to Retimo on the northern side. While sleeping under vines he was bitten by a snake and nearly died. At one time he was in a ship that was being stalked by a British submarine. The submarine fired two torpedoes at the ship narrowly missing and as Vic breathed a sigh of relief he remembered that he couldn't swim. He spent 12 days in a hellhole called Salonika then had to suffer ten days crammed in a rail carriage usually used to move horses across country.

The weather was below freezing and many of the men with Vic suffered from frost bite. He finally reached the stalag he was to remain incarcerated in. He had some luck when he was selected to spend 4 years as a railway maintenance worker for the Germans.

I immersed myself in books and diaries about World War II as I wanted to find out more about the POWs and Vic. The men proved to be gallant in the field and their mateship knew no bounds. I soon found there were many diaries written in book form and piecemeal. Then there was one I found special. It was the one belonging to Vic Petersen. It was a War Diary made up of 1440 pieces of paper and these were crammed in every nook and cranny in his clothes and belongings.

Together and in chronological order they presented to the reader a smorgasbord of what Vic was doing every day; World News; progress of the war all over the World; The daily weather; news about family and friends at home and life in the stalag and work as a POW.

He was a leader.

The news is written each day and so a reader does not have to read from page 1 to the end. Vic's persistence and determination will amaze and outline to the world what life was like behind the wire and for over four years.

Unfortunately returning men spoke little about their own experiences and official records had missing information so as a researcher I was often in the dark trying to determine what had happened to those bravest of the brave incarcerated in Crete and Germany. Once I found Vic's Diary the whole period opened and discovery became a flick of a page or two.

As the Presenter my position was to keep the original notes authentic, as Vic wrote them, including the nuts and bolts, errors in spelling, tense, grammar and punctuation. This was my tribute to the 'Man of Notes' who battled with messages that were written secretly and quickly well away from prying eyes.

Vic Petersen has filled many holes in the vast knowledge of life as a POW in Crete and Germany. I feel privileged having his name broadcast widely through the two books

- Spirited Away (written and researched by myself)
- Scrap Paper Diary 1941 – 1945

I have been involved in having these published.

Anthony W Buirchell

Private Charles Amos George Victor (Vic) Petersen WX571 War Diary

Introduction

As a member of the 2/11th Bn A.I.F Army number WX 571 and being in that unit during the Battle of Crete on May 20th, 1941 against the Germans, and our Battalion fought at Retimo, and the Island of Crete was captured by the Germans and on being told by our Commander to make to the other side of the island in the hope of getting away, and in doing so to smash our rifles to make them of no use to the enemy.

The Crete Battle finished at the end of May and on reaching the other side. There were Battalions of different troops being Australians, New Zealanders and English troops as well as Air force personnel. We hid among the hills and got what food we could by scrounging or buying from the local inhabitants until the evening of June 6th, 1941 when members of the German Army arrived and from that night we became Prisoners of War under the Geneva Convention and for us were told the war was over, and the following diary is my day to day events that happened during my term as a Prisoner of War and the facts, figures, and news being as best I got them from the limited sources at my disposal whether right or wrong in their content.

Acknowledgements

Sue Petersen, Vic's daughter-in-law for the unfettered use of the diary which will have historical value in the future.

Vic's daughter-in-law, Jackie Petersen for her patience and skill in taking the 1440 pieces of scrap paper and typing these into a document. Using her stenographer skills, she placed the notes in chronological order for this diary to be presentable to the public.

Grant Petersen, Vic's Grandson the custodian of the diary.

Background

The following gives an insight into Vic Petersen, the man and the soldier. It sets the scene for understanding his persistence in wanting to write about his 5 years incarcerated as a Prisoner of War and his perceptions of the war, day by day.

Personal and Pre-War Data Vic Petersen WX517

Date of Birth: 27th August, 1913
Place of Birth: Bridgetown, Western Australia
Next of Kin: Alice Mary Petersen (Mother)
Employment: Labourer
Religion: Church of England
Recruitment Date: 9th November, 1939
Recruitment Place: Harvey
Rank: Private
Service: Australian Infantry Force, 6th Division
Regiment: 2/11th Field Ambulance
Service Number: WX571

Australian Electoral Roll 1903-1980 showing place of abode

1936 Manjimup, Western Australia
1937 Manjimup, Western Australia
1949 Armadale, Western Australia
1954 Gosnells, Western Australia married to Merle Constance
1958 Gosnells, Western Australia married to Merle Constance
1963 Gosnells, Western Australia married to Merle Constance
1968 Gosnells, Western Australia married to Merle Constance
1972 Gosnells, Western Australia married to Merle Constance
1977 Gosnells, Western Australia married to Merle Constance
1980 Gosnells, Western Australia married to Merle Constance

Army Records for Vic Petersen WX517

9th November, 1939	Taken on strength Perth
7th December, 1939	Embarked for concentration Eastern Command from Fremantle
22nd February, 1940	Previously shown enlisted 7.11.39 corrected to 9.11.39 Perth
2nd March, 1940	Evacuated to P. Henry Hospital Ingleburn
2nd March, 1940	Admitted to CDS mumps Ingleburn
2nd March, 1940	Admitted to P. Henry Hospital (not diagnosed) Ingleburn
2nd March, 1940	Evacuated to P. Henry Hospital (measles) Ingleburn
15th March, 1940	Discharged from P. Henry Hospital Little Bay
15th March, 1940	To area camp Inglewood 5 days no duty Paddington
30th March, 1940	Pre-embarkation leave and returned to camp Claremont
20 April, 1940	Embarked for overseas in Y3
19th May, 1941	Disembarked Kantara
10th April, 1941	Embarked for service in Greece Middle East
4th June, 1941	Missing transferred to X list Crete
8th June, 1941	Believed Prisoner of War Crete

19th February, 1942	Official report incarcerated Stalag VIIIB POW no. 4538 Germany
29th May, 1945	Deplaned UK as recovered POW UK
30th May, 1945	Marched in and taken on holding strength UK

Overseas Service

—m—

(Written and researched by Anthony W Buirchell)

Vic was one of many who volunteered for service at the outbreak of WWII. He enlisted November, 1939, trained at Northam Military Camp, Western Australia. He was a Private in B Company, 2/11th, City of Perth Battalion, Australian Imperial Forces (AIF) 1939 – 1945. Three weeks later the newly formed 2/11th Battalion was transferred to Rutherford, New South Wales (NSW) and shortly afterwards up the road to Greta, NSW to continue army training. In March, 1940, the battalion returned to Perth for pre-embarkation leave. This was the last opportunity for the soldiers to visit their families and friends before sailing to the Middle East.

Farewell marching through the streets of Perth, embarked ship 2/11th Battalion departed Fremantle on the 20th April, 1940, on-board the hospital & troopship HMHS Nevasa with one of the escorts ships being the Royal Sovereign Class Battleship HMS Ramilies. Arriving in Egypt via Suez Canal, the battalion continued training and acclimatising to desert conditions in Gaza and Egypt, North Africa campaign.

The 2/11th Battalion was part of the 6th Division under General Mackay and Allied Armies General O'Connor. Commencing 3rd January, 1941 the first Australian military engagement was against the

Italian Army who was holding positions along the North African Coast. This was a victory resulting in gaining control of Bardia and Tobruk in Libya and the capture of 90,000 Italian soldiers. A handover was made to troops' fresh from Australia who were to garrison at Tobruk whilst completing their own desert training, these included West Australians of the 2/28th battalion. There was a football match between the 2/11th and 2/28th Battalions. The spirit of this football match continued after the war, with annual cricket matches, and as the 'diggers' & 'rats' grew older, it became lawn bowls.

The Battle of Greece 1941

The next action the 2/11th Bn was against the German Army in northern Greece. The Yugoslav and Greek armies, which had earlier held off Italian army attacks, collapsed against an intense German attack, which resulted in the Germans having to provide direct support to the Italians.

Australian, New Zealand and British (British Expeditionary Force) were continuously attacked by German Stuka dive bombers using machine guns and bombs. There were Panzer tanks and battle experienced SS troops from April, 1941 a night time embarkation from Greek ports of Nauplion and Kalamata to Crete was made, thus allowing the bulk of Commonwealth forces to escape.

This daring evacuation of 50,000 Commonwealth forces from Greece is recorded as a major achievement of WWII, logistically more successful than the earlier Dunkirk evacuation. This finally resulted in the Greek Army negotiating an armistice only to Germany, refusing to surrender to the Italian forces.

Battle of Crete 1941

On the island of Crete, 42,500 Commonwealth Forces dug in waiting for the expected German invasion from the sea.

The Germans continually bombed Crete until 20th May when they then commenced the largest ever aerial invasion consisting of parachutist and gliders supported by 1209 aircraft and 63 small ships to carry three infantry divisions. After many fierce battles there were huge losses on both sides, the Germans captured Crete, on 1st June, 1941.

At the evacuation Vic and many of his mates had followed the thousands over the mountains headed for the tiny village of Sfakia on the south coast. Here a number of British Warships were taking Allied soldiers off Crete and moving them to the safety of Alexandria in Egypt. At the surrender all Allies were given the option of surrender or take to the hills. Vic and several mates joined a group that headed for the Mesara Bay area near the town of Tymbakion.

When they arrived at Mesara Bay they searched for boats and LCMs to use to escape. Unfortunately, a German patrol captured them. They were caught soon after reaching Tymbakion and told, 'The War for you is over'. The German patrol offered them 24 hours to make up their minds to either surrender of fight.

Having been given this ultimatum Vic began to keep a diary which many years later he called Memoirs: Prisoner of War Days World War II.

It is an amazing day by day account of Vic's four years as a POW and begins on the 6th June, 1941. There are many people that Vic meets and for ease of identification these will be listed alphabetically. If the reader wants more information they can contact this website through the email. He also visits many places and these will also be listed. In the case where Vic stayed for a long time the place will be noted only at the start of the placement.

The diary was written on scraps of paper in pencil and hidden in his clothing. Considering his final entry was 6th May, 1945 a quick sum gives a total of 1440. The accuracy of the diary has been used to verify and research many aspects of the men who fought in the Battle of Crete, those who escaped and the POWs who ended up in a Stalag in Central Europe.

Vic along with many others surrendered on the evening of 6th June. The group was marched back over the mountains to Heraklion and then west towards Retimo. This started Vic's incarceration as a Prisoner of War (POW).

The group was marched 150 miles over 4 days without food and water. He nearly died on the return march to Suda Bay. On the evening of June 10th, the column he was in went to sleep under grapevines near Retimo airstrip. Later in the night he awoke screaming in pain. He sought out the guards who ignored his pleas until he dropped unconscious in front of them. He was taken by truck to a German doctor who treated him and explained he had been bitten by a snake and was barely three minutes from death.

The German doctor saved Vic, saying, "Another three minutes and we could not have saved you." Later an orderly stated, "Your life was saved but it was very difficult". Vic had great respect for German doctors and orderlies after this experience.

This resulted in Vic being separated from his mates in the 2/11th Battalion who were transported to Stalags in Germany.

Three months later, when Vic's health was restored, he and other prisoners were taken to Suda Bay and embarked on the ship the Norburg. This ship took them to Iraklion (port of Heraklion). From here over 150 men were loaded into trucks and taken across the mountains to a transit camp near Tympaki. Vic was surprised he was back where he had been captured nearly three months earlier.

At this camp, which became known as Tymbakion, the POWs were forced to dig up 80–100-year-old olive trees so that the Germans could build an airfield. This was hard work and as the Germans provided very little food causing Vic's weight to drop from 11.5 to 8 stone.

Thankfully the local Cretan people would sneak food to the prisoners. Vic was given POW number 4538/Kreta.

Vic's diary lists day by day activities which resulted in grubbing out the olive trees. There are weather reports and some POW movements. At one time 50 air force prisoners were evacuated. Another 50 POWs were brought into the camp, rounded up from the hills and a few left and taken to the north side of Crete.

On the 29th December, 1941 the entire camp was abandoned and the Allies were trucked back to Heraklion and then further west to Suda Bay. (The work building the aerodrome was left to the 7000 local

Cretans). Vic's ordeal to this point was about to show that things could get worse, markedly so.

The entire group was loaded on a Bulgarian ship the Citta and it sailed for Salonika a transit camp in Greece. From the wharf at Salonika the men were marched to Salonika Prison or Stalag 183. It was an old brick school two stories high and was to become Vic's hellhole.

The buildings surrounded a quadrangle where the men were lined up frequently as part of the discipline. All entrances were gateways guarded or wired up with barbed wire. It was almost impossible to escape although some tried through the latrine plumbing only to get caught and shot. The latrines were open air seats of four rows of ten with a pit beneath. Unhygienic and reeking.

Food was very poor in terms of amount and nutrition. Lice pervaded every crack and bedding they could find coming out at night to play havoc biting the inmates.

Anyone causing a problem of breaking the night curfew would create a problem for his other mates. Everyone would be made to stand at attention on the quadrangle and remain so for hours on end. A rifle butt or boot was used to rouse those collapsing. At one stage two prisoners became so mentally traumatized they ran for the barbed wire fence and upon climbing part way up were shot. Their bodies remained hanging for the rest of the day.

After six days the group that Vic was part of was marched through the town to the railway station. It was during this march that Vic was amazed at the bravery of the Greek women folk. They lined the streets and as the men passed, they bustled into their midst and stuffed food into their clothing and hands. While they were doing this the guards ran about pushing and shoving them and resorting to bash them with rifle butts in the backs, arms and breasts. The women melted away leaving the grateful men to continue their march to the railway station.

At the Salonika station an engine with several cattle trucks in tow waited. The prisoners were crammed in at 35 to each. The floors had straw strewn around and the two small air holes at either end was covered in barbed wire. Once crowded inside it became obvious that there was little room for everyone to sit or lay down and so they had to work out a roster. The most humiliating part came when one wanted to defecate. This was a matter of squatting over a piece of material and once finished the corners were folded together and the parcel pushed through the barbed wire covered air holes. The partner of the person needing to relieve himself had to straddle his mate until the deed was finished. With dysentery and diarrhea rife it was a difficult and continual activity.

Food was issued at the start of the journey and was expected to last for the week or as long as the trip would take. Those who rationed their food did better than those who ate everything straight away. Anyone trying to escape at stops would be shot.

As the train moved north into Germany and Poland the temperature plummeted to below freezing. The men had very little to keep warm and frost bite was prevalent. Some of the men froze to death. Outside the truck the ground was covered with snow and the sides were iced up.

On 29th January, 1942 Vic and his mates reached the Lamsdorf railway station. They were lined up and marched for half an hour to Stalag VIIIB one of the largest German prisons and one that was dreaded. Tens of thousands of men from the Allies armies and including thousands of Russians were crammed into this camp.

Vic's initial reaction to this prison was one of shock and wondered what the future held. He spent several weeks acclimatizing and meeting others he knew.

The Germans were using the prisoners as labour in their industries through work parties. The conditions weren't ideal but did stop the boredom that saw the time pass by ever so slowly.

Vic was placed in a work party called E 388. The object of the men in this party was to keep the train lines open at all times by doing maintenance and sweeping the snow from the tracks.

Vic found the jobs along the railway lines easy enough to carry out and there was shelter, food and a relative amount of freedom. The only problem he faced was the amount and nutrition of the food. He was constantly hungry and his weight spiraled down and took away his strength.

However, in comparison with other parties he was lucky and even more so when he was never called upon to change industries to work in.

Apart from a few arguments with the guards and the engineer about long days and lack of food the days, weeks and months moved along.

Vic busied himself by taking on the many responsibilities that were available and joined in the activities the men enjoyed. He became the mailman handing out the letters, cards, cigarette parcels and Red Cross parcels to those who were named. He took part in the kitchen assisting with preparation of food, buying groceries and cooking various meals.

Vic was well liked and held in esteem by his fellow prisoners. He even wrote letters home to some of their wives in an effort to placate personal problems. He stood up to the guards in individual arguments. His one main disappointment that he mentions over and over in his diary was the lack of communication from his family. He knew all their birthdays and wrote regularly to them but rarely did anyone of them return the favour. He felt lonely and alone too often.

Year of 1941 Olive Trees

Private Vic Petersen has been in German hands since June 6, 1941. He is about to add another year to his already 6 months. Vic Petersen Diary 6th June, 1941 to 31st December, 1941. (In the original as written by Vic)

Friday 6th June, 1941
(near Tymbakion, Crete) This morning three German officers came at 1000 hrs where we were waiting on the beach on Crete, to see if we were going to surrender to them or fight it out, and gave us till the following morning to make up our minds. A Major McNab went as hostage to guarantee that we would surrender the following morning. Our midday meal consisted of a bit of meat, tin of bully, fried onions and potatoes most of which we were buying from the Greeks or Cretans. At 1800 hrs the German soldiers appeared on the scene, evidently doubting our giving up the following morning, and thus we became Prisoners of War, and to their way of saying for you the war is over, so began something that we had no idea of what was ahead of us or for how long, and that night they kept us on the march till midnight before we rested for the night. As the night was dark and very hilly with boulders and trees around one could have possibly slipped away in the darkness, but my one thought if I stay eventually my parents will know where I am, instead of roaming the hills or perhaps being killed. A cloudy and windy day.

Saturday 7th June 1941
At a place called Idecca, where we had camped at midnight after marching the previous evening from 1800 hrs having been taken a Prisoner of War of the Germans and on the march all day from the morning till 2300 hrs, and everybody very footsore. No food given to us all day by the Germans. The Cretans handing us out a bit of bread and a few cherries. Fine and warm.

Sunday 8th June, 1941
At Heraklion on Crete as a POW) given some bread by the local inhabitants and also plenty of raisins. At 1300 hrs moved to some barracks and at 1500 hrs was given our first meal by the Germans which consisted of two biscuits and some cheese, and given a hot drink which tasted like herbs grown in the hills nearby. At 1800 hrs had boiled rice and raisins. Fine day.

Monday 9th June, 1941
At Heraklion on Crete as POW of the Germans and up at 0530 hrs to a meal of raisins and mint tea and on the march again, doing about twenty miles for the day. At 1300 hrs rested for a while and had bread and raisins, and stopped for the night at 1730 hrs but no rations. Fine day with cool night.

Tuesday 10th June, 1941
On island of Crete between Iraklion and Retimo as POW at 1200 hrs issued with a loaf of bread that was to last three days, and that night camped amongst the grapevines not far from Retimo which had been our area of fighting during the battle of Crete. That night about 2230 hrs woke up from the effects of a bite on the neck and got severe pains, which from later on when I met up with some of the boys who were there reckon you could have heard me screaming five miles away, and which eventually became so severe that I became paralized and I collapsed at the German guard's feet, being unable to use my arms and

legs, They realized something was wrong as before they said I was only putting on a show, and rushed me off to the Retimo Hospital where they froze and lanced where I had the pain on the neck and was told I had been bitten by a snake, and the Doctor said another three minutes and we could have done nothing for you. I thought I had had it, and throughout my mind went all of the snakes in Australia one had to come to this part of the world to get bitten and was given needles and oxygen to keep the ticker going. Fine and warm.

Wednesday 11th June, 1941
In hospital at Retimo Crete suffering the effects of snake bite, the evening before while a POW of the Germans and not feeling too good and had a bad relapse during the day. Quite a few German soldiers in the hospital with a few of the Allied troops. Fine day.

Thursday 12th June, 1941
As Prisoner of War in Retimo Hospital suffering from the effects of the snake bite, and still getting severe pains in legs and had to have needle to ease the pain. Fine day.

Friday 13th June, 1941 to Sunday 22nd June, 1941
In hospital at Retimo on Crete Island as POW of the Germans getting over the effects of snake bite. Treatment very good and good food and being a fair amount of it. One thing I must say the German soldiers in the hospital were very kind and could not do enough for me, and as the German orderly said the first morning I was there, "You're life was saved but it was very difficult." Fine weather during this period.

Monday 23rd June, 1941
At Retimo Hospital as POW on Crete and today my clothes were returned to me, minus steel mirror, razor blades and badges on my coat, and my watch which I explained I had seen taken from my trousers when I went into hospital, having pinned it inside when I became a

POW and I was lucky enough to get it back as the rest meant really nothing compared to it, and was moved to another lot of barracks where there were a few of our troops but were mostly Greeks and Cretans. Fine day.

Tuesday, 24th June, 1941
On Crete at Retimo Crete as Prisoner of War in compound with many Greeks and Cretans and about nine Allied troops. Fine day.

Wednesday 25th June, 1941
On Crete at Retimo as Prisoner of War in compound with Greeks. Had severe stomach pains today, possibly still from the effects of the snake bite. Fine and cloudy.

Thursday 26th June, 1941 to Friday 27th June, 1941
On Crete Ialand at Retimo as German POW in compound with Greeks and still suffering from some pain. Not much to eat rice or beans done with olive oil which takes a bit of getting down. Have asked the cookhouse to take ours out before the olive oil is put in. Fine weather.

Saturday 28th June 1941
At Retimo on Crete Island as a POW in compound with many Greeks and Cretans. Had pains in chest and legs and feeling pretty weak on the legs. Day terribly long with nothing to do. Fine day.

Sunday 29th June, 1941—Monday 30th June, 1941
Prisoner of War at Retimo on Crete Island in compound with Greeks. Had bad pains in my stomach on several occasions during the two days. Fine weather.

Tuesday 1st July - Thursday 3rd July, 1941
On Island of Crete as POW at Retimo. Food still nothing much. Fine weather.

Friday 4th July 1941 – Sunday 6th July
Same as the previous three days and weather getting warmer.

Monday 7th July, 1941 - Wednesday 9th July, 1941
Prisoner of War at Retimo on Island of Crete in compound with Greeks who really make you sick at times to seen the way they carry on although things are rough and hard. Still suffering stomach pains. Have read several books to fill in the time, dont know where these appeared from. Fine weather these three days.

Thursday 10th July 1941 to Sunday 13th July, 1941
At Retimo on Island of Crete as a POW in a compound with Greeks. Read a few more books and feeling a little better the last couple of days. Fairly warm.

Monday 14th July, 1941 to Friday 18th July, 1941
On Island of Crete as POW at Retimo still managing a few books to read to while away the time. Hear that an ammunition dump had blown up at Suda Bay. Very warm weather these few days.

Saturday 19th July, 1941
At Retimo on Island of Crete as POW in compound with Greeks. Four Australian, one English and one Maltese came onto camp today. Fine day.

Sunday 20th July, 1941
Prisoner of War on Island of Crete at Retimo, same routine, except for some reason or another had a roll call.

Monday 21st July, 1941
Same as previous day and roll call again. Fine weather.

Tuesday 22nd July, 1941
Prepared to go to Chania but only got 300 yards so everything as previous day.

Wednesday 23rd July, 1941
On Island of Crete as Prisoner of War at Retimo and the usual routine nothing to do and getting bored. Heard revolt in one of the prison camps on the island. Fine and warm.

Thursday 24th July, 1941
On Crete as Prisoner of War our move to Chania working party again cancelled because of revolt in one of the prison camps. Roll call, two men missing but told they had been captured and would be shot. Plenty of activity by German troops and told our troops were attempting a landing on South Coast. Fine and warm.

Friday 25th July, 1941
On Island of Crete as Prisoner of War at Retimo in company large contingent of Greeks and Cretans. Still plenty of activity by German troops, told the attack on the South Coast by our troops had failed. Some of the boys out on working party today. Fine day.

Saturday 26th July, 1941
At Retimo on Crete as POW and left here by truck to a camp at Suda Bay arriving at about 0830 hrs. 16 of us, camp was small and dirty and the Greeks were very filthy and camp joins Bay so can go in swimming to get clean. Very hot day.

Sunday 27th July, 1941
On Crete Island as a Prisoner of War in camp near Suda Bay. Was given a dixie of meat and vermicilli. First meat seen for some time. One Greek tied to a post out in the hot afternoon sun, dont know for what punishment. Brother Bill's 21st birthday. Fine day.

Monday 28th July, 1941
At Suda Bay on Island of Crete as POW. On working party in morning. Dinner time a very dirty Greek washed in the sea with scrubbing brush and broom. Fine and warm.

Tuesday 29th July, 1941
On Crete Island at Suda Bay as POW. Working party during the day handling British ammunition. Very warm day.

Wednesday 30th July, 1941
At Suda Bay on Crete and today we were moved from here to another camp on the other side of Chania. This camp was very dusty and windy. Ray Blechynden in this camp. Given bucket of grapes and pears by the civilians. Very warm and dusty.

Thursday 31st July, 1941
On Island of Crete as POW in camp at Chania very handy to beach and some showers. Had porridge for breakfast, bread and drink of tea for dinner and mixed stew at night and some grapes. Have to watch the figure or will be putting on weight. Dusty and warm.

Friday 1st August, 1941
Prisoner of War on Island of Crete at Chania. Did some work at NZ R.A.P. Living in tents at this camp. British planes bomb Maleme aerodrome and some machine gunning and some planes hit as well as a bridge and three Germans wounded. Very warm.

Saturday 2nd August, 1941
At Chania on Island of Crete as Prisoner of War. No work. Concert in evening. Jerries take searchlights and A/A guns up to Malame aerodrome. Hot and fine day.

Sunday 3rd August, 1941
On Island of Crete at Chania as POW. Searchlights and A/A guns taken back from Malame aerodrome. Fine day.

Monday 4th August, 1941
Prisoner of War on Island of Crete. Queens birthday and also Bess Pearce. Warm day.

Tuesday 5th August, 1941 - Wednesday 6th August, 1941
At Chania Prisoner of War camp on Island of Crete. On working party at German Headquarters camp. Aussies played English in cricket and winning outright by six runs. Warm and fine.

Thursday 7th August, 1941 - Saturday 9th August, 1941
Prisoner of War on Crete at Chania camp. No working parties allowed out on account of quarantine on account of infantile paralysis. Weather warm.

Sunday 10th August, 1941
Doreen B and Edna H birthdays. On Crete Island at Chania as a POW. Nothing much to do. Cloudy morning with some rain.

Monday 11th August, 1941 - Thursday 14th August, 1941
On Island of Crete at Chania as POW. Everything quiet except for a little work at German cookhouse, which was always looked forward to for a little handout, and a dump went up in flames with some ammo. Days warm with nights starting to get a little colder.

Friday 15th August, 1941 – Saturday 16th August, 1941
Not feeling too good these couple of days as POW in Chania camp on Island of Crete. Getting giddy turns when wake up in the morning, which our Doctor says is a reaction setting in of the bombing we went

through. Heard Mr Menzies going to London and Australia getting worried about the International situation. Fine and warm with exception Saturday morning being very dull. Wrote home.

Sunday 17th August, 1941 - Saturday 23rd August, 1941
On Island of Crete at Chania camp as POW of the Germans. All days quiet and not much to do. Our rations which were on Crete, bully beef now run out, and now using Jerry food and very tasteless, especially that needing sugar. Fine weather.

Sunday 24th August, 1941 – Monday 25th August, 1941
At Chania camp as POW on Island of Crete. On working party 25th and heard some of our planes over during early morning of the 25th. Fine weather 25th being very warm.

Tuesday 26th August, 1941 - Wednesday 27th August, 1941
The latter day being my 28th birthday what a way to spend it as a POW on Island of Crete, and not feeling the best, having a continuance of giddy turns. Heard news of our troops going through Iran. Boys making hats and trousers out of tent as clothes wearing out. Roll calls on both mornings. Fine weather.

Thursday 28th August, 1941 - Saturday 30th August, 1941
In Prisoner of War camp at Chania on Island of Crete. Fair amount of enemy air activity. Heard that four stukas were brought down by our fighters, we dont know from where? Mr Fadden new Prime Minister of Australia and Menzies goes to London. Fine and fairly warm.

Sunday 31st August, 1941
Prisoner of War on Island of Crete in camp at Chania. Heard that some of us were moving this coming week to Araklion. Windy and dusty day.

Monday 1st September 1941 - Tuesday 2nd September, 1941
In Prisoner of War camp at Chania on the Island of Crete. Played NZ at cricket and won by 2 runs. Due to move to Araklion. Both days windy, dusty and a little rain.

Wednesday 3rd September, 1941
Two years since Australia went to war against the Germany. Pulled down tents ready for moving. Tents went but we did not. Cloudy, windy, dusty with some rain.

Thursday 4th September, 1941 - Friday 5th September, 1941
On half hours notice for moving which did not eventuate, but Friday 5th September at up at 0550 hrs roll call and breakfast 0630 hrs. Paraded at 0715 hrs and on trucks about 0800 hrs and moved to Suda Bay, getting on a boat about 0900 hrs and pulled away from wharf to midstream about 1200hrs. Dinner and tea consisted of half a packet of biscuits and quarter of tin of bully beef. Dull and cloudy day.

Saturday 6th September, 1941
Prisoner of War on ship Norburg at Suda Bay waiting to go to another camp on the Island of Crete. Breakfast six to a tin of bully and three to a packet of biscuits. Hard to know what to do to pass the time away. 10th Anniversary of Grandmothers death. Dinner and tea consisted of M & V. Dull day with a few spots of rain.

Sunday 7th September, 1941
On board boat Norburg in Suda Bay as Prisoner of War on Island of Crete, awaiting movement to new camp. Meals four to a tin of bully and two to a packet of biscuits. Cloudy but warm.

Monday 8th September, 1941 - Tuesday 9th September, 1941
Prisoner of War on boat Norburg in Suda Bay on Island of Crete awaiting transhipment to new working party. Rations slightly better, latter day three cargo boats and two escorts pulled in. Fine and very hot.

Wednesday 10th September, 1941
Brother Clarrie's birthday. Left Suda Bay on board boat Norburg as Prisoner of War for Araklion at 0600 hrs. At 0800 hrs bit of excitement on board as Torpedo from British submarine narrowly misses boat, and for once I cursed our navy as I could not swim. A sub chaser drops depth charges. Roll immediately called, and one man missing from our Battalion who had got off the boat in Suda Bay the night before, and the Germans reckon he was a spy and had warned the submarine we were coming out. I dont think with 200 allied troops on board. Arrived Araklion about 1330 hrs and were going to leave us aboard for the night, but changed their minds, and marched us about twenty minutes to prison barracks, which I have been in about13 weeks previously. Not long after being in the barracks there was a loud explosion down at the harbor, and it turned out that the submarine they had said they had sunk, had evidently followed the boat to the harbour and torpedoed it at the wharf, and where the torpedo hit was the hatch that we had been on, so the second lucky escape for the day. But what a time the guards gave us after it, the barracks we were in was practically standing room only, and we were not allowed outside for toilet use, and some of the guards were drunk from drinking wine, so it was not apleasant night for us. Plenty of Jerries around Araklion. Fine day.

Thursday 11th September, 1941
Prisoner of War on Island of Crete in barracks at Araklion, and only allowed outside for a wash. Explosion of previous evening confirmed torpedoing of boat in harbour that we were on, as they took some of the boys to work on the boat during the day, and officer of the guard a little worse for drinking in the evening. Fine and warm.

Friday 12th September, 1941
In barracks as a POW at Araklion on Island of Crete and leave here for a new camp site by truck at 1330 hrs. A fair way from Iraklion, and very winding road through the hills. Plenty of grapes growing and the local

population give us a wave. Arrived at the new camp site about 1700 hrs and put up tent for the night. A warm day.

Saturday 13th September, 1941
Prisoner of War on Island of Crete at our new campsite, which is near Tymbakion and not very far from the place I was taken POW early in June. Busy during the day putting up tents and cleaning up the area, and well fenced with plenty of barbed wire about seven of eight foot high, and our water supply is a drain, running along just inside the camp fence, evidently coming in by gravitation from the hills, and Jerry for a change pleased with our effort of cleaning up the camp and lines. A fine day.

Sunday 14th September, 1941
Prisoner of War on South Coast on Island of Crete at place called Tymbakion, practically same as day before but no tents to erect and did some washing of what there was? Fine day.

Monday 15th September, 1941
In a camp near Tymbakion on Island of Crete as POW. Today started our first days work on a new job, having to march about three miles. Job grubbing out and chopping down olive trees to make way we believe for an aerodrome, the only a bit of level ground left on Crete. Dusty and windy day.

Tuesday 16th September, 1941 to Thursday 18th September, 1941
Brother Jack's birthday 16th. The same work as Monday and our pay is thirty dracmas a day, don't know in English how much that is, and cigarette issue of five every two days or a cigar. Thursday a few showers.

Friday 19th September, 1941 - Sunday 21st September, 1941
In Tymbakion camp as a POW on Island of Crete, and the same as earlier, except no work on Sunday. Weather warm except Sunday being cool, windy and dusty.

Monday 22nd September, 1941 to Thursday 25th September, 1941
Prisoner of War on the Island of Crete at a camp near Tymbakion where we are grubbing down old olive trees, some 100 years old, and it is heartbreaking to see what it is doing to the local population, as this is their livelihood and the trees are loaded with olives. Greeks hiding food in holes by the side of trees ungrubbed out overnight. No issue of cigarettes for a week. Weather cloudy, windy and dusty, and nights with mornings getting cold.

Friday 26th September, 1941 - Sunday 28th September, 1941
On Island of Crete as POW in camp at Tymbakion, grubbing out olive trees. Greeks brought us down plenty of food on the 27th from the hills. No work on the Sunday and wrote letter to Bess and Grace P. Three Pecco planes landed on new drome. Snow on mountains first time for the winter. Thunder and lightning 26th.

Monday 29th September, 1941 - Sunday 5th October, 1941
At Tymbakion on the Island of Crete as a POW and grubbing out olive trees for aerodrome to be built. One of the days the Greeks brought us down plenty of food and beans done in olive oil at dinner time. This seems to be on on special occasions in their church. Warm and dusty.

Monday 6th October, 1941 to Thursday 9th October, 1941
Prisoner of War on the Island of Crete in camp near Tymbakion, and grubbing out olive trees to make way for aerodrome. Greeks not allowed to bring us any more food these few days as some parcels have been seen to contain letters. All RAF personnel taken off job and flown to Athens. Araklion still being bombed by our planes. Would very much like to get some news of the worlds doings. Hear a lot of rumours but unable to confirm them. Monday and Tuesday windy otherwise fine with cool nights.

Friday 10th October, 1941
On Island of Crete as POW near place called Tymbakion, and today they had us levelling some of the ground out that we had cleared said it was to be used to plant grapes for German buyer. Must think we are very dumb, finished off piece marked out and back to camp. Fine and warm.

Saturday 11th October, 1941
In camp at Tymbakion, as POW on Island of Crete. Did not go to work today because of our protests of the previous day, when we said we were doing war work, which was not allowed under the Geneva Conventions, and a bit of arguing going on about it. About a dozen English prisoners captured in hills today. Did some washing and wrote to Grace Hamilton, but do not think our letters are getting away. Weather fine.

Sunday 12th October, 1941 to Tuesday 14th October, 1941
Prisoner of War Tymbakion camp, on Island of Crete at camp near Tymbakion, doing work of grubbing out olive trees. Few extra cigarettes on the 13th. All days dull with occasional showers. On the 12th Jerries brought some Greek woman into camp on 12th to do boys washing.

Wednesday 15th October, 1941 to Saturday 18th October, 1941
On Island of Crete at camp near Tymbakion as POW, grubbing out olive trees. Told have to get one tree down a day and finished for the day,. Heard rumours of Jerries being pushed back by Russians and Italy kicking Musso out and refusing to fight. Fine except for early Thursday morning.

Sunday 19th October 1941
As above no work today and wrote home. Fine and cool.

Monday 20th October, 1941 - Wednesday 21st October, 1941
Prisoner of War on the Island of Crete in a camp near Tymbakion, and grubbing out olive trees. Another fifty men brought into the camp

today. Fine but cool at night especially as have practically nothing as bedding to keep warm.

Thursday 23rd October, 1941 - Saturday 25th October, 1941
Prisoner of War at camp near Tymbakion on Island of Crete working at grubbing out olive trees. Heard two rumours during this period of Australian troops doing some mopping up in Libya and British Motorised Divisions linking up with Soviet Divisions. Most of these rumours came from Greek sources. The Greeks gave a bullock to the camp today. Must mention all of our meals were midday a bit of bread and salami sausage and night time a bowl of lentils, like split peas. Fine weather.

Sunday 26th October, 1941
As above and no work today. Wrote to Mabel P. Paid 600 dracmas by Jerries today. Played cards and lost 630 dracmas on the day.

Monday 27th October, 1941 to Tuesday 28th October, 1941
At a camp near Tymbakion on Island of Crete as POW. No work today (Tuesday) as the Jerries search the camp. Played pontoon in the afternoon and managed to win a bit. Dull day with heavy rain and thunderstorm at night.

Wednesday 29th October, 1941 to Thursday 30th October, 1941
Prisoner of War on Island of Crete in camp near Tymbakion, grubbing out olive trees to make way for an aerodrome. Weather dull with some rain each night.

Friday 31st October, 1941 - Sunday 2nd November, 1941
On Island of Crete as a POW camp in a place near Tymbakion, grubbing down olive trees. Wrote to Poppy J on the second also played a few rubbers of bridge, and playing pontoon each night, but unable to win anything. Cloudy days.

Monday 3rd November, 1941
Prisoner of War in camp at Tymbakion on the Island of Crete grubbing down olive trees. Greek population brought us down quite a bit of food today, being one of their church celebration days. Fine day.

Tuesday 4th November, 1941 to Friday 7th November, 1941
Melbourne Cup Day if held (4th). On Island of Crete as a POW in camp near Tymbakion, working at a road work over the river. Three English letters arrived in camp. Weather dull with attempts to rain.

Saturday 8th November
Practicably same as above

Sunday 9th November, 1941
Same as above but no work. Fine day but cold.

Monday 10th November, 1941
Same procedure as 4th and 7th. Fine day but very cold.

Tuesday 11th November, 1941
On Island of Crete as a POW in camp at a place near Tymbakion. Armistice Day and had two minutes silence at 1100 hrs. On road work. Dull and cloudy.

Wednesday 12th November, 1941- Saturday 15th November, 1941
Prisoner of War on Island of Crete at camp near Tymbakion. In camp with a festered hand. Road finished and again working on aerodrome, under protest, and threatening to shoot ten men if we refuse to work, and of course men with rifles prevailed, as we did not want to see any lives lost. Weather fine but dull.

Sunday 16th November, 1941 to Friday 21st November, 1941
On Island of Crete in camp near Tymbakion as a POW, and working on aerodrome shifting earth. St Mary's Day on the latter day and the

local population gave us a hand out of food which was very welcome. Receiving extra 1/6 loaf of bread from the engineer, all working on the aerodrome. Weather been cold at nights with dusty days and cold wind.

Saturday 22nd November, 1941 to Sunday 23rd November, 1941.
Same as previous day except worked for four hours on the Sunday which is usually free. Fine day and warmer.

Monday 24th November, 1941
Prisoner of War on Island of Crete working on aerodrome near Tymbakion. Bombing heard from camp about 1600 hrs. Fine day.

Tuesday 25th November, 1941 - Saturday 29th November, 1941
Prisoner of War on Island of Crete at Tymbakion camp, doing work on aerodrome. Had three-day period of heavy thunder, but not much rain. The weather was very cold with winds and falls of snow on the mountains. Very heavy transport by plane, going on to Libya, said to be Alpine Troops, going over to fight. Had another hand out of food on Tuesday from the local population. A couple of Greeks escape.

Sunday 30th November, 1941
Prisoners of War at camp near Tymbakion on Island of Crete, no work today. Did some washing of what was holding together. Received a parcel from Greek Relief including a pair of socks, a few cigarettes, handkerchief and a waistcoat jacket. Fine day but very cool.

Monday 1st December, 1941
Prisoner of War at camp near Tymbakion on Island of Crete, doing work on aerodrome. Bread ration cut down to ten men a loaf. Heavy fall of snow.

Tuesday 2nd December, 1941
Same as above 1st, and only two special duty men on today. Rumours of shortage of petrol and diesel on island, and Jerry having a bad time in Libya, and Greek prisoners to be released in near future. Wrote to Merle S. Weather very windy and dusty day.

Wednesday 3rd December, 1941
Prisoner of War at camp near Tymbakion on Island of Crete, working on building aerodrome. One Greek accidentally shot in stomach during morning. Cold windy and dusty day.

Thursday 4th December, 1941
On Island of Crete, as POW in camp near Tymbakion working on aerodrome. Very cold and windy in the morning, which set in with rain about 1200 hrs, and getting heavier and knocked off work at 1400 hrs, setting in for the rest of the day. Transport planes busy carting water and food to Libya. A miserable day.

Friday 5th December, 1941
Prisoners of War on Island of Crete, in camp near Tymbakion doing work on aerodrome. Everything very wet and muddy this morning from previous night's rain. Cold, windy day.

Saturday 6th December, 1941
On Island of Crete, as POW in camp near Tymbakion doing work on aerodrome. Things a bit drier today but plenty of snow appearing on the mountains. Cold, windy day but fine.

Sunday 7th December, 1941
Prisoner of War on Island of Crete at camp near Tymbakion doing work on aerodrome till 1300 hrs. Plane crashed on mountain side during storm of three days before, all being killed. Played pontoon during afternoon. A fine day.

Monday 8th December,1941
Same as above and working on aerodrome, and rumoured news and enemy in disorder on Russian Front, and fighting still going on in Libya. A dull day, rains setting in at 1800 hrs.

Tuesday 9th December, 1941
Prisoner of War on Island of Crete as a POW, at camp near Tymbakion doing work on aerodrome, but returned to camp at 1200 hrs owing to rain. Told by Jerry that Japan has come into the war. Cold morning with rain at midday.

Wednesday 10th December, 1941.
Same as previous day, and returning to camp at 1300 hrs because of rain. Very cloudy with rain.

Thursday 11th December, 1941
At camp near Tymbakion on Island of Crete as a POW, and working on the building of aerodrome. Heard that America had declared War on Germany and that Japan had made an attempt to invade the Philippines. A fine day.

Friday 12th December, 1941
Same as above, except news items and todays news was: 13 000 Jerry prisoners taken in Libya, Germans retreating all fronts in Russia, and Japanese attack on Phillipines had failed. 3 Jap warboats and 2 American sunk and that Prince of Wales and Repulse of Royal Navy sunk. 4 Greeks escape. A fine day.

Saturday 13th December, 1941 - Sunday 14th December, 1941
Same as previous day, except news items: new guards no good and another Greek escaped. Commandant very wild with guards. On Sunday, the same, and no work today. Fine days.

Monday 15th December, 1941 - Thursday 18th December, 1941
On Island of Crete as a POW in camp at place near Tymbakion, and working on aerodrome and laying stones, and also digging drains. Engineer tries to make us work till1700 hrs reckoning there is a war on and very annoyed we should knock off at 1600 hrs. Six English letters arrive in camp today. Rumours going on in War in Libya being finished with many German and Italian prisoners being taken, and also the Sydney. Weather fairly good except for the 15th.

Friday 19th December, 1941 - Saturday 20th December, 1941
Prisoner of War on Island of Crete in camp near Tymbakion, doing work near aerodrome, grubbing rushes. Ten Greeks escape today, and commandant in one hell of a rage. Jerries say they sank eight British submarines in the Mediterranean and sabotage at Araklion had caused four transport planes to be destroyed, and rumour of Commandos being landed on Island thirty five miles from Crete. Fine first day, then dull.

Sunday 21st December, 1941 - Monday 22nd December, 1941
At Tymbakion camp on Island of Crete as a POW working on aerodrome ½ day on the Sunday and rain set in at 1600 hrs same day.

Tuesday 23rd December, 1941 - Wednesday 24th December, 1941
On Island of Crete as a POW of the Germans in camp near Tymbakion working on aerodrome, Tuesday being a quiet day. On the Wednesday went back to camp with a good many cans of wine also many packets of sultanas and various other items, given to us by the Greek population for Christmas. Received ten cigarettes in evening. Fine with cool wind.

Thursday 25th December, 1941
On first Christmas as a POW on the Island of Crete at camp near Tymbakion, and what's in store by the next one, who knows? Made some fritters of rice, lemon sultanas and paresen fried in olive oil,

rice and raisins for dinner, given a dozen mandarines each, also got an overcoat, also had a 2 gallon can of wine between seven. Greek civilians hand in several small parcels of things during the day to the camp. For tea at night, beef, cabbage, beans, gravy and plum pudding. Barrel of wine came in evening and had a bit of a spree in the Greek lines and everybody feeling merry for a change and so ended Christmas day

Friday 26th December, 1941
Boxing Day. Nobody out too early today, after the effects of such a whopping Xmas Day, tea and eggs for breakfast, tea and Greek bread for dinner. Stew with pork, cabbage, beans and peas for the evening meal. Issue of wine during the day. A cold and wet day.

Saturday 27th December, 1941
Prisoners of War on the Island of Crete at a camp near Tymbakion. Did not go to work today as weather looking very doubtful, but eventually came out fine day.

Sunday 28th December, 1941.
On Island of Crete as POW at a place near Tymbakion. 0800 hrs told to pack up as we were shifting camp, moving Araklion, and one of truck drivers said we were going to Germany and this meant plenty of work, and plenty of food. Reached Araklion about 1400 hrs and in the barracks for the third time in six months and slept here for the night. Had rice and raisins for tea. Cold but fine day. Raid on aerodrome at night.

Monday 29th December, 1941
Prisoner of War on Island of Crete at Araklion, where we slept overnight and ready to be on the road again at 0800 hrs and waited out in the rain for nearly an hour. On trucks that went about 10.30 hrs and still raining, and at 1100 hrs eventually on the move, through Retimo

and to Suda Bay, where arrived about 1700 hrs raining nearly all the way and very cold. Camp very wet, and had to sleep in tents on damp ground, about 15 men to a tent. Other prisoners in here recently captured in Libya. Had ¼ tin bully and ¼ loaf of bread for day.

Tuesday 30th December, 1941
On Island of Crete as a POW in camp at Suda Bay waiting to go on board ship for Europe. Not much to eat, under very primitive conditions. Air raid at night. Dull but fine.

Wednesday 31st December, 1941
Prisoner of War on Island of Crete in camp near Suda Bay, waiting to get on boat eventually Germany. Made a move about 1000 hrs but heavy rain set in, and back to the camp again, and not leaving today. Made us throw away all our tent canvas and anything German, Couple of biscuits for dinner with a piece of cheese and rice for tea. Dull and rainy and some snow down to the waters edge, giving us a taste of winter to come.

Year of 1942 Parachutes and Train to Stalag

An amazing sight never to be forgotten. Private Vic Petersen has been in German hands since June, 1941 He is about to add another half year to his already 6 months. Vic Petersen Diary 1st January, 1942 to June 30th, 1942 with the Account of being moved as a Prisoner of War from Crete to Salonika then taken by train to Stalag VIIIB.

Thursday 1st January, 1942 New Year's Day
New Years Day and wondering whats in store for the days ahead as a POW on the Island of Crete in camp near Suda Bay, and awaiting transhipment to parts unknown. In camp until 1000 hrs and then made a move to the wharf, and on-board ship at about 1200 hrs and given 6 biscuits and half a tin of meat to last for three days. Jerries celebrated coming of the New Year with plenty of shooting night before. In harbour for the night. Snow on mountains here for the first time in ten years, and very cold day with rain and snow.

Friday 2nd January, 1942
On board Italian ship in Suda Bay as POW Island of Crete. Left Suda Bay about 1200 hrs and heard we are headed for a Greek port somewhere. Sea very rough and cold windy day.

Saturday 3rd January, 1942
Prisoner of War on board Italian ship travelling from Island of Crete to Greece, and eight ships in the convoy. Arrived Pireaus Harbour, the port of Athens, about 1400 hrs and got off boat and stood on wharf in the cold till dark, and then marched back on the boat for the night. Given cup of tea and some bread to eat. Fine but very cold.

Sunday 4th January, 1942
On board Citta-de-Savona as POW in Pireaus Harbour. Off the boat about 0800 hrs and standing around in the cold with snow on the ground. Had a bit of porridge. Re-embarked on another ship. Found out Ray Blechyden was amongst us. Had rice soup for dinner. Evening meal macaroni soup with good sized dixie of tea. Fine but cold day.

Monday 5th January, 1942
Prisoner of War on board Bulgarian ship in harbour near Athens. Air raid alarm during early hours. Pulled out from harbor about 0630 hrs went a few miles and then anchored again. For breakfast three salty fish, drink of tea and loaf of bread for three days. On the move again in the afternoon and past numerous islands and plenty of snow to be seen. Sleeping in hold with not much room but plenty of fleas and lice to accompany us. Raided ships hold below us and got raisins, currants, lard and mint tea. Fine but cool day.

Tuesday 6th January, 1942
As a Prisoner of War on board Bulgarian ship somewhere around the Greek coastline and headed for Salonika. Anchored about 0100 hrs till daylight not far from shore, plenty of snow right up to the waters edge. Breakfast three fish and a loaf of bread between twelve, also mint tea. Made a bit of porridge ourselves. Still passing along Greek coast in the Agean Sea and drizzling rain right up to 1030 hrs and then anchored somewhere along the coast about 1200 hrs for the rest of the day. Dull with rain.

Wednesday 7th January, 1942
On board Bulgarian ship as a POW of the Germans somewhere in the Aegean Sea on way from Crete to Salonika. Left during early hours of morning from previous days anchorage. Plenty of snow covered mountains to be seen and down to the waters edge. Breakfast four fish and a mug of tea. Made a little porridge and continuing on our way past numerous headlands. Dull day with drizzling rain.

Thursday 8th January, 1942
Prisoner of War on board Bulgarian ship going along the Greek coast in the Agean Sea on way to Salonika, and about 0600 hrs this morning ran aground on mudbank in heavy fog and misty rain. Destroyer attempted to pull us off, but the rope broke, and no luck in trying to reverse off, and still there at 1230 hrs. Three fish for breakfast and a cup of tea, and 2/3 loaf of bread for 2 days. Tug arrived about 1330 hrs and the destroyer attempt to get us off the mud bank, but up to 1615 hrs no success. Further attempts during the day also failed.

Friday 9th January, 1942
On board Bulgarian ship off the coast of Greece as a POW en route to Salonika, where we aground from previous day and eventually further attempts with strong winds enabled us to get off, but it was 0930 hrs before we were safe enough to proceed, 1000 hrs are told is about is about 2 hrs from Salonika. One little note down the coastline through us getting raisins and sultanas from the hold, you could have probably followed the ships trail, from the boys sitting on the side of the boat and just going practically straight through us. Arrived Salonika about 1200 hrs and went off in in barges and about ½ hrs walk to barracks. All our gear was searched and we were all separated. Saw some of the boys in hospital there but did not know any of them. Plenty of Jerries about the place and the British Sgt-Major in charge of the camp was a real bastard, worse than any German we had run into yet, called us names and insults as if we have no right to be here. I believe many of

the English boys told him he would not see England again for the way he treated us. One Greek grabbed for handing out cigarettes—into the rooms about 1600 hrs which were originally Turkish Barracks and prison. A fine day for a change but cold.

Saturday 10th January, 1942
Prisoner of War in barracks at Salonika in Greece. Check parade 0800 hrs. Medical inspection at 1000 hrs, coffee and quarter loaf of bread. Medical did not eventuate. 1200 hrs coffee and bean soup. During afternoon received Red X food parcel which contained 15 articles of food. 1630 hrs check parade, 1700 hrs coffee and bean soup. Everybody having a real meal from their parcels, not having seen such luxuries for months. Cold wet morning with fine afternoon.

Sunday 11th January, 1942
Prisoner of War in barracks at Salonika Transit camp in Greece. Check parade 0800 hrs then coffee and bread. Everybody busy washing clothes and shaving to try and make ourselves look a little respectable. Dinner of thick barley soup, 1400 hrs parade by English Sgt- Major on discipline. 1700 hrs coffee and barley soup. Wet morning, fine afternoon.

Monday 12th January, 1942
0800 hrs check parade, coffee and bread roll. Roll called on account of some not having put their names in. 1200 hrs barley and lentil soup, also same as 1700 hrs with coffee. On Mess fatigue for the day. A miserable day wind and rain.

Tuesday 13th January, 1942
In Salonika Transit camp in Greece as a POW of the Germans. Check parade coffee and bread 0800 hrs. 0940 hrs fall in and march about 4 ½ miles for short shower and delousing parade, taking all day. Missed

dinner but had double tea about 1800 hrs. Cold wind and all pools of water along the road frozen over.

Wednesday 14th January, 1942
Prisoner of War at Salonika Transit Camp in Greece. Check parade, coffee and bread 0800 hrs. Inspection by Jerries at 1000 hrs for shirts, socks and trousers. 1200 hrs bean soup, 1630 hrs check parade 1700 hrs coffee and bean soup. Very dull and cold day.

Thursday 15th January, 1942
Prisoner of War in Salonika Transit Camp in Greece. Check parade, 0800 hrs, coffee and bread, also got a new shirt. Packed up ready for moving at 1115 hrs, but owing to rain returned to room. 1145 hrs barley soup. All out at 1300 hrs and had to hand in after roll call and search all table knives and forks. 1530 hrs on the way to the station, and into trucks 39 in each, and closely packed in for the night with straw on the floor to lie on. No tea. Left some time during the night. Dull wet day.

Friday 16th January, 1942
Prisoner of War on train having left Salonika the previous night heading into unknown parts and eventually to Germany. 0900 hrs, toilet ritual, and got rations for the day. 1/3 loaf bread each and six to a tin of meat. Cannot see much out of the truck so laid down and read a book. 2330 hrs reached some station and given coffee and staying here the rest of the night. Plenty of snow about and a dull day.

Saturday 17th January, 1942
Prisoner of War heading for Germany on train from Salonika Transit Camp in Greece, and going through Bulgaria so were told, but did not travel very far, as heavy blizzards and snow was blocking the lines. Cold and dull day.

Sunday 18th January, 1942
Prisoner of War on train in Transit to Germany and today was one of the coldest days I have put in for a long time. Lay in bed in the truck all day. Snow everywhere and ice flowing down the river. ¼ loaf bread, meat, currants and a sweet for days rations. A very cold day.

Monday 19th January, 1942
In Transit on train to Germany as POW somewhere in Europe. Plenty of snow feet thick and could hardly see the houses. Very cold and lay in bed. Days rations at 1400 hrs.1/3 loaf of bread meat and coffee. Water bottles frozen, and ice on all the bolts inside of the wagon. Another very cold day.

Tuesday 20th January, 1942
Prisoner of War on train somewhere in Europe travelling to Germany, having come from Crete 1st January to Salonika in Greece, and today was even colder than yesterday, lumps of ice hanging on to the steel in the trucks. Several of the boys collapse because of the cold and snow which is everywhere, yards deep, and did not get our rations until about 1645 hrs, bread frozen hard and hardly cut it. For the 24 hours to 1800 hrs was about the best travelling we had done. Had coffee about midnight. Cold freezing day.

Wednesday 21st January, 1942
Snow everywhere and colder than ever. Cannot touch anything in truck, because of being covered in ice, and of course when it melts, well we get wet with dripping water. Rations late again and one chap in our truck died during the night because of the cold.

Thursday 22nd January, 1942
On train travelling to Germany as a POW. Snow everywhere again. Had to change trucks, which proved to be very cold, with the numerous cracks in it and no lights. Cold day.

Friday 23rd January, 1942
Prisoner of War on train travelling in Europe on way to a POW camp in Lamsdorf. Today we reached Graz in Austria and marched to a Red X place for hot soup and coffee. Snow everywhere. Rations as usual. Slept very cold during the night, all inside of truck being frozen. Several chaps taken to hospital because of the cold. Cold and bleak.

Saturday 24th January, 1942
Prisoner of War travelling through Austria to Germany, en route from Crete. Still plenty of snow about and very cold. Got coffee about 1700 hrs. Did not travel very far today. Rations same as usual. Water bottles frozen. A cold day.

Sunday 25th January, 1942
Prisoner of War travelling through Austria to Germany. Snowing heavily and very cold. Did not travel very far again today. A bit warmer this evening. Plenty of trucks of petrol in station, also drums. Had to carry on extra rations, also got tea.

Monday 26th January, 1942
Travelling through Germany by train as a Prisoner of War to prison camp at Lamsdorf. Still plenty of snow about and very cold again. Rations about 1300 hrs also tea.

Tuesday 27th January, 1942
Prisoner of War on train travelling through Germany, to prison camp from Crete. Still very cold and plenty of snow about. Passed through several big towns. Rations a bit short today. Tea with rations and hot soup at 2330 hrs. Cold bleak day.

Wednesday 28th January, 1942
On train as a Prisoner of War travelling to camp in Germany ex Island of Crete January 2nd 1942, and travelling practically from 0001 hrs to

1400 hrs without much delay and continued travelling till 2359 hrs. Rations short again today. Cold and plenty of snow.

Thursday 29th January, 1942
Prisoner of War on train enroute to camp in Germany and still plenty of snow about. Had hot soup about midday Arrive destination camp Lamsdorf which was Stalag VIIIB, about 1930 hrs and had to march about ¾ hour from the station to the camp, which is a very large one. And barracks very cold, and searched as usual and allowed two rugs each. A cold day.

Friday 30th January, 1942
Prisoner of War in Stalag VIIIB Lamsdorf Germany, which proved to be a camp of enormous size with thousands of prisoners and from here they eventually go out on working to various parts of Germany. Some of the boys went through fumigation and de-lousing today. Indians hand us out some food had plenty of soup. Check parades at 0730 hrs and 1700 hrs. Saw Jock Taylor and heard experiences of other boys. Fine but cold day. Must mention now that after being on Crete and not getting the right food one wants, I am now down to eight stone in weight from the 11 ½ stone when taken prisoner, and also the snow and cold we are going through in Europe coldest winter for twenty one years.

Saturday 31st January, 1942
Prisoner of War in Stalag VIIIB Lamsdorf. More of the boys being deloused today, also received a Canadian Red X food parcel which contained 1 lb butter, ½ lb sugar, ½ lb tea, tin of jam, pkt biscuits, raisins, dates, salt, tin bully beef, tin of pork, tin of milk, soap, 2 tins of fish and some chocolate. Very acceptable and made good use of, after the days we have just had. Jerry rations 2 lots of tea, soup, potatoes and five to a loaf of bread. Barracks warmer today. Myself got a bad cold.

Sunday 1st February, 1942

Prisoner of War in prison camp Stalag VIIIB. Check parade 0800 hrs. Tea: potatoes, stew and usual bread. Fatigue ration of bread. Making good use of the food parcel and feeling the best for about five weeks. Nothing much doing today, except for shaving hair off our bodies and head for de-lousing tomorrow. Had 13 weeks of hair on my head and oh how cold. Three or four chaps die today through fumigation of barracks and several very ill. Check parade 1600 hrs. Fine but very cold.

Monday 2nd February, 1942

Prisoner of War in Stalag VIIIB in Germany. Through the process of fumigation and de-lousing today and one of the greatest reliefs to have your louse-ridden clothes taken away and given a clean issue after our check parade at 0800 hrs. Tea, soup, potatoes, 1/5 loaf bread and a little honey. Made a hot dish of potatoes and bully beef. One of the hut fireplaces blew up today. Wrote home and a cold day.

Tuesday 3rd February, 1942

Prisoner of War in Stalag VIIIB and usual check parade at 0800 hrs. One of the Jerry Commanders goes off the deep end about the untidiness of the barracks, and burning of bed boards, barracks broken into, and says no Red X food parcel or cigarettes and confined to barracks till person responsible comes forward. No delousing today. Tea: potatoes, soup, a ration of butter cheese and honey. Not much. Red X issue of brush, soap, shaving soap, and some razor blades and a couple of camp newspapers with plenty of Jerry propaganda. Cold day with slight falling of snow.

Wednesday 4th February, 1942

Prisoner of War in camp Stalag VIIIB Germany. Check parade at 0800 hrs. Tea: soup, potatoes, twice today bread ration. Moved from 6 Barrack to 10 Barrack. Saw several chaps from 2/7 Field Ambulance. Cold dull day snowing slightly.

Thursday 5th February, 1942
Check parade 0700 hrs. Tea: soup, potatoes, and bread ration. Saw Noel Lumby today and SM Curtis of the Bn. Saw how potatoes and swedes are kept during the winter months. Head feeling very cold after the 13 weeks hair taken off, and made a hat of old socks to keep it warm. Feeling plenty empty as rations are very poor. No Red X parcels in. Cold bleak day.

Friday 6th February, 1942
Prisoner of War in Stalag VIIIB Germany with check parade at 0700 hrs. Today received from Red X 2 tins bully beef, ¼ lb butter, and ½ tin sardines. Search on by Jerry for any extra rugs. Soup powder from canteen not bad. Todays rations tea potatoes, soup twice bread and honey. No issue of clogs or boots yet as promised. Fairly cold and snowed during the night.

Saturday 7th February, 1942
Prisoner of War in Stalag VIIIB Lamsdorf Germany. Check parade 0700 hrs. Saw the Bn Padre today. Todays rations potatoes, soup, tea twice, 1/6 bread, bit of cheese, honey and butter. Snowed during early hours of morning and slightly all day, and fairly cold.

Sunday 8th February, 1942
Check parade 08.30 hrs. Medical inspection for lice at 1000 hrs. Chipped at for not shaving. Wrote a card to Aunty Nell and Virgilia. Todays rations: soup, tea, potatoes twice, usual bread, a bit of sausage meat, honey and margarine. Twenty nine from barracks go to concert party. Fairly cold with a bit of sunshine.

Monday 9th February, 1942
Stalag VIIIB Lamsdorf Germany as a Prisoner of War. Check parade at 0700 hrs and 1700 hrs went down for boots clogs and underclothes. About fifty men return to camp tonight from working in the sugar

beet factory for 4 months. No Red X parcels yet. Usual rations. Dull and very cold day.

Tuesday 10th February, 1942
Prisoner of War Lamsdorf Germany. Check parades at 0700 hrs and 1700 hrs. Got a few soup powders from the canteen and the usual small rations and feeling bit on the hungry side with the little we are getting. Cold as usual.

Wednesday 11th February, 1942
Prisoner of War Germany with the usual check parades, rations and five to a tin of meat. Heard rumours of Red X food parcels arriving so may see something before the week is out, but they say is very remote. Cold day with snow in evening.

Thursday 12th February, 1942
In Germany as POW in Stalag VIII at Lamsdorf. Check parades usual, British Army officers trying to be a bit officious and bringing too much discipline in camp. Bulk issue came in today and consisted of a little chocolate, condensed milk, cheese, butter, jam, bully and beef steak. Some of the boys using monopoly money to buy tea from the Indians, so games taken away. Cigarette issue today. Usual rations with a very good macaroni soup. A Cpl Williams gave a 2 ½ hour talk on his doings as a tramp, which proved very interesting. A sunny day but cold.

Friday 13th February, 1942
Prisoner of War Stalag VIIIB, Germany. Check Parades 0700 hrs. Called for volunteers for work and immediate rush, but compound commander gave talk, and advised us not to go out yet, so only five volunteered. Not allowed out of compound because of chaps going out improperly dressed. Paper chits used at canteen for value of 1 & two Reichmarks and 10 & 50 Phennig. Soup powders of 100 grams 60 Phennig, salt and pepper 10 Phennig, soup containers 60, housewives

70, note books 20, matches 50, cigarettes 100, tobacco cigarette papers, saccharine tablets 15 pkt. Did a bit of poetry writing, and the usual rations of not much. A bit of sunshine today.

Saturday 14th February, 1942
In Germany at Stalag VIIIB as a Prisoner of War. Check parade 0700 hrs and day started a little warmer. Today had more bulk Red X Issue and helped to go and draw it, of which comprised two 1lb tins prunes, tin of M&V and tin of milk. Todays rations as usual of tea, soup, twice, potatoes, bread, honey and some swine flech. Boiled some rice for tea. Fairly warm and with some snow during afternoon.

Sunday 15th February, 1942
Prisoner of War Stalag VIIIB near Lamsdorf. Three check parades and barracks inspection. Church parade at 0930 hrs. Big crowd there. Medical inspection for lice 1330 hrs. Wrote to Mrs Forrest. Received camp newspaper with the usual Jerry propaganda. Played housie housie, usual rations but a little light on the potato issue. None too warm today.

Monday 16th February, 1942
Prisoners of War Stalag VIIIB Germany. Snowed heavily during early hours of morning and again between 1000 hrs and 1200 hrs. Check parade 0700 hrs. Barrack commander gets control of barrack room from Germans and issues more orders going the wrong way for us colonials. Our turn will come. News broadcast throughout camp, but think a lot of it propaganda. Usual rations. Cold dull day.

Tuesday 17th February, 1942
At Prisoner of War camp Lamsdorf Germany. Check parade 0700 hrs. Item read out about having anything to do with German women. News over German transmitter in camp, mentions fall of Singapore and rejoicings in Tokyo and Thailand. Shifted a bit of snow. Cigarette issue of 40, and the usual scrimpy rations. A cold day.

Wednesday 18th February, 1942
In Prisoner of War camp at VIIIB Lamsdorf Germany. Check parade 0700 hrs. Very cold this morning. Helped to get another bulk issue of Red X food, which consisted 1 tin bully, 1/5 tin of butter, 1/6 tin of steak, half packet of apricots and five lumps of sugar. A few of the hut go out working. Party arrived in the camp, who were being repatriated, got as far as France, some on boats and then had to come back. Check call on 1800 hrs. A rather cold day.

Thursday 19th February, 1942
Prisoner of War Stalag VIIIB Germany. Check parade 0700 hrs. All N.C.O's move out of the barrack today, expect us privates will be out on working party soon. Managed to get packet of cards from the canteen today. Heard of one of the Bn in Repat crowd who returned. Usual issue of days rations and played cards in evening. A cold day.

Friday 20th February, 1942
Prisoner of War in Stalag VIIIB Germany, with usual check parade 0700 hrs. News today says Germans have accounted for ten million Russians. War with Japan has cost Britain 1,000 million £'s and Britain now controlled by Americas gold, and the usual miserable rations to dampen things further. Played bridge in evening. Cold day.

Saturday 21st February, 1942
Prisoner of War in camp at Stalag VIIIB near Lamsdorf. Check parade at 0700 hrs. On working party in morning shovelling snow. Bulk issue Red X today which consisted of 1 tin M&V, 4 to a tin of milk, some jam and six to a tin of meat. Todays rations tea, soup twice, potatoes, bread, cheese and honey. Sun came out in afternoon and thawed snow, making conditions somewhat damp, otherwise cold day.

Sunday 22nd February, 1942
Stalag VIIIB Lamsdorf as a Prisoner of War. Check parade at 0800 hrs. Church service at 0930 hrs. Washed bed boards. Saw Sgt Rendavey today looking fit and well. Medical inspection for lice. Wrote cards to Mrs W and Nurse H. Had a bit of a concert in evening. Usual tea, soup and potato ration with bread, jam, margarine and sausage meat. Sunshine again today and snow thawing out.

Monday 23rd February, 1942
Prisoner of War Stalag VIIIB Lamsdorf. Had a bad night, coughing, no sleep, and aches in the joints. Check parade at 0700 hrs. Usual rations. Conditions outside very wet, owing to snow thawing out, otherwise best day of the winter.

Tuesday 24th February, 1942
Prisoner of War in Stalag VIIIB Lamsdorf, Germany. Check parade at 0700 hrs. Went on sick parade this morning with coughing and bad back. Issue of thirty cigarettes. Usual tea, soup, potatoes, bread, honey, margarine and cheese. Conditions slightly wet, as it was raining and snow thawing out.

Wednesday 25th February, 1942
In Stalag VIIIB Lamsdorf Germany as a POW. Check parade at 0700 hrs. Snow shovelling in afternoon and received a ticket to a camp concert in the evening, there being about fifteen people in the show and eight different instruments, which rendered well known tunes and a few songs were sung, and a pleasant evening was spent. Bulk issue of 1 ½ ozs chocolate, 3 ½ ozs cheese, ¼ lb butter and a 1/3 tin of tinned tongue. The usual German rations. Snowed a bit during the afternoon.

Thursday 26th February, 1942
In Stalag VIIIB Germany as a Prisoner of War. Check parade 0700 hrs. On snow shovelling party in afternoon and went cleaning out Jerry

canteen, and concert hall. Heard that we may expect a food parcel next week. Heres hoping! The usual rations, but managed to get extra soup for the work of snow shovelling in the afternoon. A dull and cold day.

Friday 27th February, 1942
Prisoner of War in Germany at Stalag VIIIB near Lamsdorf Germany. Check parade 0700 hrs. Snow shovelling in morning for which received extra soup, and also snow shovelling in the afternoon. Usual daily ration. Fairly cold day.

Saturday 28th February, 1942
In Germany as a Prisoner of War. Check parade as usual. Snow shovelling during morning. Red X bulk issue of tin of M&V, 2 to a tin of jam, four to a tin of condense milk, and five cubes of sugar. Todays rations tea, soup, potatoes twice, bread, margarine and ten to a small tin of meat. Fairly warm.

Sunday 1st March, 1942
Prisoner of War Stalag 8B near Lamsdorf Germany. Check parade 0800 hrs. Church parade 0930 hrs, a very good service. Boxing exhibitions during the day in camp, but was not interested in them, also medical inspection of the feet, and some very dirty feet were seen. Todays rations: tea twice, soup, cabbage, potatoes not too good bread margarine, jam and sausage meat. Fine sunny day but cold.

Monday 2nd March, 1942
Prisoner of War Lamsdorf Germany. Check parade 0700 hrs. Cleaning up to No 10B Barracks today and washing down tables. Todays rations tea twice, soup twice, potatoes, bread and honey. Dull day.

Tuesday 3rd March, 1942
Prisoner of War Stalag VIIIB Germany. Check parade 0700 hrs and one of working party to be deloused at 0800 hrs and moved into

Barrack 30 at 1500 hrs. Todays rations tea twice, soup potatoes, bread, margarine, jam and milk cheese. Red X food parcel between four so did not get too much as most food parcels were of 10 lbs weight and issue of 40 cigarettes. For the time being till a later date at Stalag VIIIB Germany so will not mention it each day.

Wednesday 4th March, 1942
Check parade 0730 hrs. In block 30 waiting orders to move out to a working party. Saw Fred Whitehurst this morning, one of our Bn boys. 1400 hrs had to go and change our clothes. 1700 hrs a TB needle. Rations soup twice, potatoes, bread and honey. Dull cold day.

Thursday 5th March, 1942
Check parade 0730 hrs. News this morning mentions Britain bombed Paris and many civilians killed. German planes bomb Alexandria through cloud and rain. Issued with cake of Jerry soap, shaving soap and soap flakes. Rations tea twice, potatoes, bread, margarine and sausage meat.

Friday 6th March, 1942
Up at 0400 hrs this morning to go out on working party. Issued with 40 cigarettes, and rations of 1/3 loaf bread, small tin of meat between two. Left Barrack 30 about 0515 hrs to another barrack and here waited about half an hour, and were taken in and searched. About 0700 hrs marched to Arnahorf station and got into truck 50 of us and four guards. Started on journey 0900 hrs through plenty of snow country, which made it look very desolate, passing through a couple of towns by the name of Glatz-H, and Olberg. Saw several other parties of our troops working, and reached our destination in Sudatenland at a place called Bodisch about 1700 hrs and quartered in a room about twenty foot wide and fifty feet long with a small area next to the kitchen with tables for our meals and bed bunks three tiers high with a rug and straw mattresses, and at the other end another room with big stove

in the middle and more tables for our meals and entertainment area with a storeroom attached which kept the Red X food parcels in, and the toilet was a big hole out in the yard with a ten foot fence around and about 20 yards wide and fifty yards long. At night time the toilet was inside when the barracks were locked. The barracks were quite close to the railway on a little bit of a hillside and was about 200 yards from the railway station and from the barracks look out over valleys and pine plantations below. At about 1800 hrs had a hot bowl of stew after the days train trip. There is a German woman in the cookhouse. During the evening organizing ourselves into sections of ten for the issuing of the meals and Ray Blechynden of the 2/II is in charge of the section that I am in and also have a Kim Hannd of the 2/II on the party which consists of English, New Zealand, Australian, a couple of Spanish and a descendant of Fletcher Christian from Pitcairn Island in the New Zealand group. The Sergeant in charge of the work party is from Mt Lawley WA, who was a POW at Lamsdorf in the First War and again at Lamsdorf this war. His name is Sol Burcove but being of Jewish extraction has changed his name to Burton. The water is brought up in a big cart and about 100 yards away and has to be pulled up by the boys, which we found out in the morning, to wash in the Winter had to break through about six inches of ice.

Saturday 7th March, 1942
Until further notice our POW address will be stationed on working party E 388 at Bodisch, Sudatenland, now annexed by Germany - up at 0700 hrs given slice of bread and cup of ersatz coffee. Went to work about 0830 hrs and our job was shovelling snow from the railway line after a walk of about 50 minutes which made us very warm walking through the snow. Two buglers one at each end of working party to warn us of us of approaching trains. The bloke in charge of job a fair cow, and I think even the guards were sick of him before the day was out. 1300 hrs returned to camp. For dinner 2 bowls of stew. 1700 hrs 1½ slices bread and a cup of coffee, and even on this first day there were

complaints of the rations for the work we were doing. Fairly warm with some snow.

Sunday 8th March, 1942
No work today. Did washing and wrote letter card to Cousin Vic Fisher. Drew bread ration, margarine and cheese very small amount. Dinner a very good potato stew. Breakfast and evening meal consisted of slice bread and cup coffee. Played bridge in evening and fairly warm day.

Monday 9th March, 1942
Up at 0715 hrs and to work at 0815 hrs close to the camp and 1300—1700 hrs working hours. For dinner: bowl and half stew and breakfast and evening meal slice bread and cup coffee. Bread ration 13-1kg loaves for fifty men for three meals. Work a lot easier today as not pushed so much, but rations still not enough. Not too cold with sunshine.

Tuesday 10th March, 1942
Up at 0500 hrs to go to work today, leaving by train at 0600 hrs, 25 of us going one station by the name of Weckelsdorf, changing trains then going about four stations through the hills, arriving at a place called Ober-Adersbach about 0645 hrs, and started work shovelling snow about 0710 hrs. Between 0900 hrs and 1000 hrs had a rest for something to eat, then worked till 1315 hrs, and left by train at 1410 hrs to return to camp, arriving at 1500 hrs and on return journey in day light, saw that we were passing through some beautiful scenery of pine forests and rocks, almost as if they had been packed there. Saw plenty of farm houses, with fowls and evidently stock inside the sheds because of the Winter conditions. Two bowls of stew on return to camp. Tonight got a few extra potatoes, 7 ½ loaves of bread and 2 lbs margarine as extra rations for the party. Played cards 500 in the evening. A cold day with cold wind.

Wednesday 11th March, 1942
Same job as yesterday except that at times altered slightly and on finishing at job walked towards next station for return and back in camp at 1500 hrs and two bowls of stew, and extra potatoes for tea again, also coffee. Received bread, margarine and cheese to do us for two meals. Today some books were received from Stalag VIIIB, so will now be able to do some reading. Played bridge in evening cold frosty day.

Thursday 12th March, 1942
Same job as yesterday except went two stations further and getting off at Johnsdorf-Hottendorf and still shovelling snow from the railway lines to enable the trains to get through, and returning to camp at 1500 hrs and the two bowls of weak stew on arrival. Tea: ½ dozen potatoes and cabbage and usual bread and margarine for two meals. Played bridge in evening. A cold day with cold wind and occasional falls of snow.

Friday 13th March, 1942
To same places as yesterday only working other direction the temperature being 21 degrees below freezing, the coldest I have been yet, and standing in snow did not help, and back at camp to 1500 hrs to the two bowls stew, and the usual evening ration of bread, potatoes and milky cheese. Camp newspaper in from Stalag and mail but no luck myself. Clayton Buckley received nice clothing parcel from home NZ. Sunny day, but the coldest I have experienced since being in Germany.

Saturday 14th March, 1942
On the same job as yesterday at Johnsdorf-Hottendorf, and continuing work towards next station of shovelling snow which was Rodowenz, which was clinging very hard to the rails at ten degrees below. Back to camp at 1500 hrs with the usual stew and evening issue of rations. In evening had first bath since being on the working party. Sunny day but very cold.

Sunday 15th March, 1942
No work today wrote card home and played bridge in afternoon. The guards inspected our boots, good rations today: bowl and ½ mashed potatoes, 1/2 bowl soup of good fatty meat stew, ½ bowl cabbage and coffee for tea and the usual bread ration for two meals. Did some washing today and weather not so cold.

Monday 16th March, 1942
Out on the usual job of snow shovelling, getting off at Radowenz with work at 0715 hrs and crib time 0910 hrs to 1000 hrs and knocking off at 1300 hrs and camp at 1500 hrs and usual stew of two bowls. Coffee, potatoes for tea with usual bread ration, cooked a few potatoes that I scrounged from potato patch by railway line. Fairly warm day and things starting to thaw out a little bit.

Tuesday 17th March, 1942
Out at the usual time catching train 0600 hrs and to Radowenz shovelling snow, and finishing at 1300 hrs and walking to next station called Qualisch to catch a train back to camp 1500 hrs and 2 bowls of stew, coffee and potatoes for dinner and the usual 2 meal bread ration, and margarine. Fairly warm day.

Wednesday 18th March, 1942
On early workshift again going to Qualisch shovelling snow and back in camp as usual 1500 hrs and a change from stew of roast meat, gravy, mashed potatoes and cabbage, and the usual evening ration bread, potatoes, margarine and coffee. Not quite so warm today and tried to rain in the morning.

Thursday 19th March, 1942
Early shift at 0600 hrs to Qualisch and shovelling snow starting at 0715 hrs. Crib time from 0930 to 1010 hrs finishing work 1330 hrs and in camp at 1505 hrs for the usual, and coffee, potatoes and bread in

evening. Some of the railway lines we're working are in a bad state, it's a wonder the train stays on them. Fairly warm day and settling in with a little rain at 1300 hrs and continuing in the afternoon.

Friday 20th March, 1942
At the same place as yesterday with the same times, and the usual rations. Cigarettes very scarce in camp so doing a little trading for potatoes with some of my ration. Fairly cold with some snow falling.

Saturday 21st March, 1942
Did not go out working today, doing inside camp work, and helping in the kitchen. Two bowls of stew at 1500 hrs. Coffee, potatoes for tea, with usual bread, margarine and some jam. Must mention at this stage, having been starved for so long on Crete without salt, the party of 50 was using a gallon bucket of salt a day. Stalag newspaper in and some mail Ray Blechynden receiving a letter. Beautiful sunny day, best day yet in Germany.

Sunday 22nd March, 1942
No outside work today, carted water for the camp and peeled potatoes in the kitchen in the morning. Afternoon did washing, had a bath. Wrote card to Cousin Ethel, letter card to Auntie Em. Todays meals ½ bowl soup, ½ bowl of steak and gravy, bowl of potatoes, ¼ bowl of cabbage, and other usual rations of the day. Played bridge during the afternoon. Beautiful sunny day.

Monday 23rd March, 1942
On the second shift today, and going in the opposite direction to what we had been going leaving 0700 hrs and going through a big junction called Halbstadt, and then Heinzensdorf, and starting work at 0730 hrs picking and shovelling metal stone ballast from between sleepers. Ballast well frozen, in crib 0940hrs to 1010 hrs. Dinner between 1200 hrs and 1300 hrs of soup and bread. Finished work 1635 hrs and

back in camp at 1720 hrs and then having two bowls of stew, potatoes and coffee and usual bread and margarine for two meals. A beautiful sunny day.

Tuesday 24th March, 1942
Opposite direction again today, on early morning shift, cleaning out drains by the railway line at Johnsdorf, and back in camp at 1500 hrs to the usual midday meal of two bowls of stew, with the evening meal of coffee, potatoes bread and margarine. Got a couple of new rigs today. Fine morning, dull afternoon.

Wednesday 25th March, 1942
On second party today. Dinner one hour to get down one laddle of soup, and back in camp at 1730 hrs to mashed potatoes, soup, meat, and gravy, and usual issue of bread and margarine. Received fourteen marks pay this evening. Snow beginning to thaw out now, and can see the ploughed fields and green grass and crops that have been underneath all Winter. A lovely day.

Thursday 26th March, 1942
On early shift to Adersbach on usual work and back in camp at 1500 hrs to the proverbial two bowls of stew, and evening meal of the usual rations. Change over of interpreters tonight at the camp. Fairly warm day.

Friday 27th March, 1942
On second shift today, both parties going out at same time, one to Heinzendorf, and the other one further on, but returned to camp at same time 1730 hrs. Meals for the day soup for dinner and two bowls stew on returning to camp. Coffee, bread, potatoes and margarine. Camp newspaper in, but it always gives everything going right for Germany and news of Stalags and camps, also mail in Ray Blechynden getting two letters. Beautiful day.

Saturday 28th March, 1942
Both working parties out at 0700 hrs and the party I was on went to Braunau, cleaning up street by railway station and railway yards. Ladle of soup for dinner. Finished work 1620 hrs and back to camp 1730 hrs. Two bowls stew. Coffee, potatoes, cabbage and usual bread and margarine for two meals. Braunau a fairly large place. And the people seemed to be friendly. One of the Sudaten towns. Some goods in from the town of Weckelsdorf, which comprised suitcases, knives and spoons, also pocket knives, combination knife fork and spoon, cigarette papers and holders, razors, matches, pipes, notebooks, pencils, locks, wallets and toothpaste. Had bath and did some washing. Dull cold miserable day

Sunday 29th March, 1942
No work today. Wrote home to Cousin Alison. Helped Ray Blechynden with the canteen orders. Dinner: bowl soup, bowl mashed potatoes, ½ bowl meat and gravy, ½ bowl cook and uncooked cabbage. Very good. Coffee, bread, margarine for tea. Played bridge during evening. A little mouth organ music in the evening also fine sunny day with cold wind.

Monday 30th March, 1942
On railway work in Sudatenland starting 0745 hrs at Heinzendorf, Crib time 0900 hrs to 0930 hrs and midday break 1200 hrs to 1300 hrs with a ladle of soup. In camp 1730 hrs and two bowls of stew and the usual potatoes, bread, coffee and margarine. The Hun is now trying to push us on the job and heard that there will be no potatoes for tea in future. Paid 8 marks tonight. Cold morning and sunny afternoon.

Tuesday 31st March, 1942
My sister's birthday. POW working party in Sudatenland and going to Braunau with the usual starting times, crib, dinner and back to camp at 1730 hrs with two usual bowls of stew, tea instead of coffee tonight

and usual potatoes with some cabbage, bread and margarine. More goods from the stores today, but Braunau had very little of anything. A beautiful day.

Wednesday 1st April, 1942
At Braunau again today on railway work, taking away gravel and ballast from the side of railway line working from 0800 hrs with crib dinner times the same and bowl of soup and at camp 1730 hrs, where received soup, meat and gravy with mashed potatoes, and the usual for the evening meal. Dull day with some rain becoming heavy about 1700 hrs.

Thursday 2nd April, 1942
Prisoner of War in Sudatenland doing railway work, and on party at Heinzendorf fixing sleepers to railway lines for track laying. Getting the boss a little annoyed, but making out we dont understand the Duetsch language. Having the usual working times as yesterday, and in camp at 1730 hrs with the usual rations for the day. Seargeant Major goes to Weckelsdorf and gets more canteen goods, and also managed to get two tins of tobacco for ten marks and some tea from another working party camp not far away. A fair cow of a day cold, wind, sleet, and rain.

Friday 3rd April, 1942
Good Friday. POW on working party stationed Bodisch Sudatenland doing railway work. No work today. Helped in the kitchen carting water, peeling turnips and parsnips and cutting them up for soup. The rumour goes that from Monday we will be on heavier rations because we will be doing heavier work. Wait and see, also getting 34 Phennig for every working hour which is about 5 pence. Two bowls of stew for dinner and the evening ration of potatoes, bread and margarine. Played bridge in evening. Dull, windy day with some light falls of snow.

Saturday 4th April, 194
Easter Saturday. On railway working party to Braunau today, with usual crib, dinner and back to camp times and usual bowls of stew and evening ration with a little cabbage and jam added. Received nine cigarettes each from Turkish Red X, and a ten gallon keg of beer for Sunday. Sunshine and cold wind.

Sunday 5th April, 1942
Easter Sunday. In Sudatenland as POW. No work today. Helped the cook in the kitchen, as the girl who usually helps was on holiday, and the old woman cook goes off about the small meat ration allowed for us from the German authorities. Had bath and did some washing, and wrote letter card to Bill and Grace Pearce, and card to Cousin Betty. Barrel of beer in camp but did not like the taste very much being very light colour. Dinner: soup, stew, mashed potatoes and some cabbage with the usual evening ingredients coming up. Cloudy and cold day.

Monday 6th April, 1942
Easter Monday. POW working party on railway work in Sudatenland. No work today, and nothing much of note and doing some reading. Two bowls of stew and cabbage for dinner. Evening bread ration increased slightly for section of ten men, and margarine and cheese. Dull some sunshine and rain.

Tuesday 7th April, 1942
On railway work in Sudatenland as a POW. On Heinzendorf job today, starting work 0800 hrs and with usual crib and dinner time breaks and two bowls of stew which was sent out on the train from the camp. In camp again 1730 hrs, very poor tea only bread ration, margarine and cabbage, and everybody very dissatisfied with the ration. Rumours were going around of a British and American landing in France, but as all rumours start from nothing at the latrine this proves false. Dull, but warm day.

Wednesday 8th April, 1942
Working today at Ruttersdorf shovelling mud from near station, not much was done, because of nothing for breakfast. Crib time as usual and ladle of soup for dinner. In camp 1730 hrs one and half bowls, and meat and gravy, and two loaves of bread to ten men and usual margarine. Loaf bread was about a kilo or 2.1/5lbs in weight. Had a bit of a stink tonight with the guards who tried to take two mens rations because they did not work, but they eventually gave in and we all said we wanted to go back to the StalagVIIIB, but they said, 'No'. Dull, cloudy day.

Thursday 9th April, 1942
On the same job as yesterday except conditions were muddier today because of overnight rain with the usual times and rations. Dull day with a little sunshine

Friday 10th April, 1942
Did not go out on working party staying behind to help dig hole for latrine, also cut up bad turnips and scrubbed them. Giles managed to get away with loaf of bread today from the rations. Some cigarettes turned up today and the boys are happy. Must mention when cigarettes were around the boys were OK but when there were none you dare not speak to them as they would bite your head off. More rumours today that American and English troops had landed in France, and that the Germans were calling on the French to resist the invasion of Europe. Todays meals bowl and half stew for dinner, and ½ bowl stew with coffee, bread and margarine for tea also 1 kg loaf bread to 5 men. Cold, windy day with attempts to try to rain.

Saturday 11th April, 1942
On railway work party stationed Bodisch Sudatenland and on party going to Braunau shifting earth from side of railway line, and with the usual crib and dinner times and back to camp 1730 hrs, ladle of

stew for dinner, but on arrival at the camp for the meal there was a big row on about what we were to eat, which we refused, and the railway engineer was sent for, to see it. After plenty of talking, more bread was promised, fats, cheese and meat, and also make up bad vegetables, and finally finished up with our usual rations for tea with promises. Mail and camp paper in but not in the luck myself. Bulk issue of Red X food parcel supposed to be here by Monday. Miserable day with showers.

Sunday 12th April, 1942
Prisoner of War attached to working at Bodisch ex Stalag 8B Germany. In camp today, wrote home and card to Muriel. Had a bath and did some washing. Played bridge in evening, for dinner had soup, boiled potatoes, meat and gravy. Coffee for tea with bread and margarine. Barrel of beer and lemonade. Dull, cloudy miserable day.

Monday 13th April, 1942
Prisoner of War on working party at Bodisch in Sudatenland ex Stalag VIIIB. On Heinzendorf working party today, digging holes, very rocky and water running in holes. Midday bowl of stew, sent out in bulk from camp by train. Finished work 1630 hrs and in camp at 1730 hrs, and bowl of soup. Coffee for tea with usual bread and margarine some cheese and jam. Received some games from the Stalag today, being draughts, snakes and ladders, dominoes and cards. Dull, cold day trying to rain.

Tuesday 14th April, 1942
Prisoner of War attached to working party at Bodisch Sudatenland ex Stalag V111B, doing railway work. On job to Braunau today, shovelling earth into railway tucks and putting it to another place alongside of railway line. Started work 0730 hrs, crib time 0900 hrs to 0930 hrs. Dinner time 1230 hrs to 1330 hrs very watery stew. Back to camp by 1730 hrs to a bowl of soup, coffee, 5 to a loaf of bread and 1 lb margarine

to ten. Received pay of five marks. Not feeling too energetic these days and losing weight and condition from not enough to eat. Sunshine with cold day, and a couple of attempts to snow.

Wednesday 15th April, 1942
Prisoner of War attached to working party at Bodisch. Ex Stalag V111B and doing railway work. Both parties going to Braunau today, shovelling out earth from railway line and putting in metal ballast. Usual working times and meal times. Camp 1730 hrs to cabbage and swede soup, coffee and cabbage bread and margarine. Played bridge in evening. Snow during early darkness, and a little during the day. Temperature zero 0700 hrs.

Thursday 16th April, 1942
On working party at Bodisch Sudatenland as a POW ex Stalag V111B doing railway work, the same as yesterday, and same times, and the usual rations. Some Red X food and received issue of ½ bar chocolate, ½ lb cheese, tin of M&V, 1 tin of jam, 1 tin of condensed milk, ½ lb butter, and some dried fruit, and 28 gold flake cigarettes and four dravas. Some of the bulk issue missing. A dull day.

Friday 17th April, 1942
Prisoner of War attached to working party at Bodisch Sudatenland, and doing railway work, same working times, and on return to camp at 1730 hrs. Bowl of watery soup, bread and margarine. Four of the boys going back to Stalag tomorrow, Engineer on the job today and I think a bit disgusted with amount of work being done, but have not the energy to do the work. Beautiful sunny day.

Saturday 18th April, 1942
On working party as a POW at Bodisch Sudatenland doing railway work. Same work as yesterday with the usual times, and the usual rations with the evening soup a little thicker than usual, mashed potatoes

and sausage meat. Mail and camp newspaper in. No luck myself, a lovely day with beautiful sunshine.

Sunday 19th April, 1942
Prisoner of War at Bodisch Sudatenland on railway working party. No work today. Had bath and did some washing. Made a pudding of rice, prunes, margarine and condensed milk and a little bread. Wrote card to London, and letter card to Auntie Em. Went for a walk to the pub to get barrel of beer, but only had lemonade myself. Dinner had soup, boiled potatoes, meat, gravy and cabbage. For tea: coffee, usual bread and margarine. Played bridge in evening. Dull miserable day.

Monday 20th April, 1942
On working party in Sudatenland on railway party as a POW. Two years today since embarked on boat for overseas. Flags flying on all buildings today for Hitlers birthday. Some of the Heads on the job today and reckon some of the boys are not doing enough, and talking about putting them in strafe otherwise clink. Day with sunshine and sprinkle of rain.

Tuesday 21st April, 1942
Prisoner of War in Sudatenland on railway working party. To Braunau and same work as previous days working and meal times and usual watery rations. Dull morning with sunshine in afternoon, rain 1700 hrs thunder and lightening in evening.

Wednesday 22nd April, 1942
On railway working party as a POW at Bodisch Sudatenland. Did not go out today because of cramps in the legs. S/Major had more arguments about the food rations again with the guards and the old bugger in charge of the food store. Two years today since left for overseas. Usual daily rations unusual police activity on trains today. A dull day but fairly warm.

Thursday 23rd April, 1942

Prisoner of War attached to working party on railway work in Sudatenland. Today to Braunau and working party split up a little. Usual working hours, and the usual rations, bowl of soup for dinner, and on return to camp soup with cabbage extra coffee for tea with bread and margarine. Heard today of escape of French General and 24,000 Reichmarks offered for his capture dead or alive. Dull day with little sunshine.

Friday 24th April, 1942

Prisoner of War attached to railway working party at Bodisch, Sudatenland. Ex Stalag V111B. Working parties split up again today, went to Braunau-Older, unloading rails, finished at 1230 hrs then waited an hour for train to return to Braunau to do ½ hours work. Reasonably good stew for midday meal for a change. Back to camp 1730 hrs to bowl of soup, and usual tea issue of bread and margarine with some milky cheese. Issue of 30 English cigarettes. Nice sunny day.

Saturday 25th April, 1942

Anzac Day to us. Working party as a POW in Sudatenland on railway working party, and at Braunau with usual working and meal times. Stew for dinner, return to camp boiled potatoes and sausage meat, with bread, and margarine, and a little jam evening meal. Christian received personal parcel and Sgt Casson tobacco parcel. Dull and cold day.

Sunday 26th April, 1942

Prisoner of War on railway working party at Bodisch, Sudatenland. No work today. Had bath and did washing cleaned out barracks. Dinner soup meat and gravy, potatoes and cabbage. Usual bread, margarine evening meal. Bulk issue of Red X food. Wrote card to Joyce H. Dull but fine day.

Monday 27th April, 1942
On railway working party as a POW stationed at Bodisch, Sudatenland. On job at Braunau with the usual times and meal times. Stew for dinner and soup 1730 hrs and bread and margarine. Jerry Officer came round today to inspect camp, and orders some changes to take place. Played bridge in evening. Cold morning, sunny afternoon.

Tuesday 28th April, 1942
Prisoner of War stationed at Bodisch in, Sudatenland on railway working party. On party of eight to Ottendorf, and did ¼ hours work in the morning and returned to Braunau for dinner which consisted of bowl of stew, bowl of soup on return to camp 1730 hrs, and usual bread and margarine issue with mint tea. Dull day with cold wind, and slight attempts at trying to snow.

Wednesday 29th April, 1942
In Sudatenland on railway working party as a POW stationed at Bodisch. Same working place and meal times, usual midday stew and bowl of soup on return to camp, meat and gravy with boiled potatoes, margarine, bread and a little jam. Guards trying to do the bounce today, reckon too many are staying in camp sick, and they say only those with fever to stay behind. Talking about using the whip, but not much notice taken of their threats. Very dull cold windy day, snowed previous night.

Thursday 30th April, 1942
Prisoner of War railway working party at Bodisch Sudatenland. On job at Braunau today. Times and meals as usual. Guards reckon because the little blokes can do the job set them during the day that everybody can do the job. A very windy and bitterly cold day with attempts at trying to snow.

Friday 1st May, 1942

At Bodisch, Sudatenland as a POW on railway working party. On job at Braunau again with the usual times, except that they tried to get us to work until 1800 hrs but the guards said no. Usual midday meal and on return to camp the usual bread and margarine ration. An issue of thirty English cigarettes. Snowed during the early hours of the morning and continued slightly during the day.

Saturday 2nd May, 1942

Prisoner of War at Bodisch Sudatenland on railway working party. Holiday today, except they called for twenty men to go to Halbstadt to unload three trucks of coal, finishing around 1100 hrs. Had hot shower afterwards, and a pot of beer at railway station. Remainder of camp also went to Halbstadt for shower. Bowl of soup for dinner with boiled potatoes and sausage meat later and coffee for tea with usual bread margarine and some jam. Bulk issue today, getting a tin of jam, 2 tins of M&V and one piece of cheese, and two pieces of chocolate also extra tin of M&V between two. Buckley receives cigarette parcel of 200 cigs. Roy B had a slight feverish attack this week. A dull day with slight attempts to rain.

Sunday 3rd May, 1942

At Bodisch as POW in Sudatenland on railway working party. No work today. About forty of us marched to Weckelsdorf today to have our photos taken, and on the way back had a pot of beer at roadhouse. Mail in today, but no luck myself. Ray B had one though and heard the Sunday news that Bessie P was married and camp newspaper also in. Had check on clothing. Todays rations coffee for breakfast, dinner soup, meat and gravy with boiled potatoes. Coffee for tea with usual bread, margarine. Wrote home. Very nice day.

Monday 4th May, 1942

Prisoner of War on railway working party at Bodisch Sudatenland. On job at Braunau, but went out to Braunau Olberg for three hours to unload some sleepers. Today started long day, working until 1800 hrs to get Saturday afternoon off. Stew at midday with bowl of soup on return to camp, with coffee bread ration and margarine as usual. Heard rumours that Russian and English planes are continuously over Germany, and that Russians are pushing Jerries back. Dull and very cold day with some rain.

Tuesday 5th May, 1942
At Bodisch Sudatenland as a POW on railway working party. On job at Braunau with the usual times and rations. Ray B visits doctor and is told to go back to Stalag for two or three weeks. A dull and cold day.

Wednesday 6th May, 1942
On railway working party as a POW at Bodisch Sudatenland. On party at Braunau. Long hours and times as usual. Engineer says we are not doing enough. Cloudy but warm day.

Thursday 7th May, 1942
Prisoner of War at Bodisch Sudatenland on railway working party. On job at Braunau. Guards and boss tell us that we have to clean out dirt from under six sleepers and replace with metal ballast and stamp down tightly between two for days by six o'clock or stop there till it is done. We are so weak, hardly able to lift pick little along swing it. Very long and tiring with not enough to eat. Stew midday with bowl soup on return to camp and bread and margarine ration. Sgt Major goes shopping and buys each section a pot of potato salad. A beautiful day.

Friday 8th May, 1942
At Bodisch Sudatenland as a POW on railway working party. Had today off for working last Saturday. Helped peel potatoes in morning. Guards and bloke in charge of rations, and reckons our rations are being cut down, because we are not doing enough work. Camp newspaper in and some mail. Bowl of soup for dinner and same on return

of men to camp with coffee, bread and margarine. Dull day otherwise fine.

Saturday 9th May, 1942
Prisoner of War on working party at Bodisch Sudatenland only worked till 1200 hrs today, having afternoon free. Return to camp, bowl soup 1700 hrs sausage meat with boiled potatoes coffee, bread and margarine. 1800 hrs to Halbstadt for hot showers and return at 2100 hrs. Attempted to rain today.

Sunday 10th May, 1942
Prisoner of War on railway working party at Bodisch Sudatenland. In camp today. Levelled off some ground to put down some tables. Clothes inspection and search for Reichmarks and civvy clothes. Soup for dinner with boiled potatoes meat and potatoes. Coffee for tea with usual bread and margarine. Wrote card to Merle S and Joyce H. A lovely day.

Monday 11th May, 1942
At Bodisch Sudatenland on railway working party as a POW. On job at Braunau. Finished six sleepers by 1615 hrs and returned to camp on 1630 hr train. Bowl of stew for dinner with bowl of soup on return to camp, followed by bread, margarine and some cabbage. Picked up duck egg on way to work this morning so had poached egg on toast tonight. Sgt Casson receives another cigarette parcel. Fair amount of German air activity. Fine and warm day.

Tuesday 12th May, 1942
Prisoner of War on working party stationed at Bodisch Sudatenland. On job at Braunau digging out earth between sleepers and replacing with metal ballast, but was upset in our plans by rain in the morning but after a bit of fast going managed to finish our quota by 1615 hrs. Crib and dinner time as usual, very weak stew for dinner, with some

with boiled potatoes on return to camp, with bread, margarine and white cheese. A couple of German officers around this evening and some of us get an issue of new boots. R Dumurgue receives a personal parcel. A wet day.

Wednesday 13th May, 1942
Prisoner of War in Sudatenland stationed at Bodisch on railway working party. Mums birthday. On job at Braunau with the same work and times as previous day. Soup for dinner, with boiled potatoes, meat and gravy on return to camp with bread, lard in place of margarine and some jam. Another officer visits here today to see about parcels on return to Stalag, but says the railways are the chief hold up, being needed for the war. A very warm day.

Thursday 14th May, 1942
On railway working party as a POW Bodisch Sudatenland, with the usual work and times and rations of the day before. A fairly warm day with a little rain.

Friday 15th May, 1942
Prisoner of War on railway working party stationed at Bodisch in Sudatenland. On job at Braunau. Crib, midday meal at usual times and back to camp 1735 hrs and usual bowl soup followed by coffee, bread and lard. The soup being very watery. Buckley received another cigarette parcel. Started to rain in afternoon and all wet when left for home, and continued raining throughout the night.

Saturday 16th May, 1942
In Sudatenland stationed at a camp near Bodisch as a POW on railway working party and today working at Braunau till 1200 hrs when returned to camp. Went for showers to Halbstadt at 1445 hrs and returning by 1720 hrs. Bowl of soup on return at midday, sausage meat and boiled potatoes, followed by coffee, bread lard and some jam.

Ray Templeman and SE Davis received food parcel each. Rained early morning hours and on and off till 1200 hrs which caused some of the creeks and gullies to flood but otherwise warm day.

Sunday 17th May, 1942
Prisoner of War on railway working party Bodisch Sudatenland. In camp today. Bulk issue of Red X food arrived from Stalag V111B today and we received tin of steak and kidney stew, 18 biscuits each, four to a tin of honey. More to be given out later. Wrote letter card to Cousin Alison. Rations soup, meat and gravy with boiled potatoes and coffee, bread and lard. Received 31 English Cigarettes. A very nice day for a change.

Monday 18th May, 1942
On railway working party as a POW stationed at Bodisch in Sudatenland. On job at Braunau with the usual working, crib and midday hours. Bowl stew at midday with bowl soup to return to camp which was terrible stuff not fit for pigs, and we complained to an officer who was around. He reckons the Jerries have to have the same and of course usual bread and margarine ration. Received some more bulk issue of food, some sugar, 4 to a tin of honey and a chocolate each. Another nice day.

Tuesday 19th May, 1942
Prisoner of War on railway working party stationed at Bodisch in Sudatenland. On Braunau job with the usual work and meal times. A hard days work. Very weak soup midday and return to camp, with boiled potatoes on return to camp with bread, lard and some milk cheese. Fine day till 1500 hrs with a sudden thunderstorm and rained heavily for twenty minutes, then fine again.

Wednesday 20th May, 1942
Stationed at Bodisch in Sudatenland as a POW on railway working party. On job at Braunau, but first of all going on to next station to

load some old sleepers and then having to walk back to the main job, which made me very tired. Soup for dinner, with meat and gravy on return to camp followed by potatoes, coffee usual bread etc with some jam. Bulk issue ¼ lb butter and ¼ lb cheese. Fine but cloudy day. 12 months since invasion of Crete.

Thursday 21st May, 1942
Prisoner of War on railway working party at at Bodisch in Sudatenland. On job at Braunau with the usual work and meal times. Heavy showers of rain 0900 hrs. Soup at midday, with boiled potatoes with stewed tripe and gravy, followed by coffee usual bread and lard. Camp newspaper in and mail and received my first letter since being a POW and from Verna and written on January 22nd 1942. Doug Lee gets a cigar parcel. Cloudy and fairly warm.

Friday 22nd May, 1942
Stationed at a camp in Sudatenland near Bodisch as a POW on railway working party. On job at Braunau with digging out earth between sleepers and replacing with metal ballast. Same time as usual, with bowl of soup for dinner with boiled potatoes and barley soup on return to camp followed by coffee usual bread and lard for tea. Not feeling too good today. Buckley and Dalziel received cigarette parcels. Cloudy but very warm.

Saturday 23rd May, 1942
Prisoner of War at Bodisch Sudatenland on railway working party. Did not go to work today owing to bad stomach and feeling very weak as well. Only ½ days work. Soup at 1315 hrs. To Halbstadt at 1445 hrs for showers, returning at 1730 hrs to camp, and got boiled potatoes and sausage meat with the usual bread issue and lard. Issue of thirty English cigarettes each and five tins of tobacco for the camp. S/M went shopping and brought back a dozen fish which we boiled and they were very acceptable for a change. Dull day with occasional showers.

Sunday 24th May, 1942
Prisoner of War in Sudatenland on railway working party. No work today, so not out of bed too early. Midday meal bowl of spinach each with boiled potatoes meat and gravy and the usual bread and lard later. Received bulk Red X issue of 1 tin of steak and kidney each, ½ tin jam and cigarette, tin of sugar. Tried to get some beer and lemonade for camp today but unsuccessful. Mail in again today received two letters from Verna and one from Mrs Walker. Grace Pearce engaged. Cannot understand why no letters from home, and camp paper is also in and Sgt Casson receives cigarette parcel. Wrote card to Audrey, Vic, Mrs Walker and Verna. Warm till about 1730 hrs when a sharp thunderstorm and rain came up.

Monday 25th May, 1942
On party at Bodisch as a Prisoner of War. No work today being Whit Monday. Todays meals dinner spinach, meat, gravy with boiled potatoes with coffee bread and lard for tea. Carter receives personal parcel today. A fine day.

Tuesday 26th May, 1942
On railway working party as a POW stationed near Bodisch Sudatenland. On job at Braunau usual work crib, dinner and knock off times. Bowl of spinach soup midday, with boiled potatoes meat and gravy on return to camp, coffee bread and lard with some very nice cheese for a change. Doug Lee receives cigarette parcel. Days starting to get long, being just on 2200 hrs before it gets dark. Beautiful sunny day.

Wednesday 27th May, 1942
Prisoner of War at Bodisch, Sudatenland on railway working party. On same job at Braunau. Usual times as previous day with bowl of soup for dinner and boiled potatoes meat and gravy on return to camp, tea bread and lard. A severe electric storm came up about 1900 hrs with

some bad lightning and heavy thunder and heavy rain for about half an hour, otherwise a fine day.

Thursday 28th May, 1942
Prisoner of War stationed near Bodisch Sudatenland on railway working party. Same times working and rations as previous day. A glorious sunny day, the best I have seen in Germany yet.

Friday 29th May, 1942
Prisoner of War on railway working party in Sudatenland on the usual job at Braunau. Soup for midday meal, with boiled potatoes, meat and gravy and spinach on return to camp at 1730 hrs, with bread margarine. Lunam and Check receive personal parcels. Issue of eleven Turkish cigarettes. 1300 hrs electrical storm and rain simply poured down, with another storm and rain at 1930 hrs.

Saturday 30th May, 1942
On railway working party as a POW near Bodisch, Sudatenland. Half days work knocking off at 1200 hrs. Bowl of soup on return to camp at 1315 hrs. At 1415 hrs went by train to Halbstadt for showers, returning at 1730hrs then having potatoes and sausage meat with coffee usual bread and lard. Jam still not having turned up. Mail and camp newspaper in but none myself. Sgt Casson gets a cigarette parcel. A very dull morning looking like rain, but turned out a beautiful afternoon.

Sunday 31st May, 1942
Prisoner of War Bodisch Sudatenland. No work today. Received bulk issue of tin of steak and kidney, ¼ lb butter, ¼ lb cheese and chocolate, also issue of 40 English cigarettes. Boys busy with oven making pies and cakes. C Clark gets a personal parcel and Lee and Blee get cigarette parcels. Todays rations spinach, potatoes, meat and gravy followed by coffee usual bread and lard. Wrote letter cards to Aunty Nell, Carmel and home. Fine morning followed by cloudy afternoon.

Monday 1st June, 1942
Stationed near Bodisch Sudatenland as a POW on railway working party. Anniversary of fall of Crete Island to Germans. On job at Braunau with the usual working times. Bowl of soup for dinner, with meat and meal mixture, boiled potatoes, coffee bread and lard ration. Doughty receives cigarette parcel. Heard today that there had been a food riot in Zeckoslavakia, many men and women being shot as the result. Dull and cloudy day.

Tuesday 2nd June, 1942
Prisoner of War on railway working party at Bodisch, Sudatenland. On job at Braunau. Crib, dinner and knock off times as usual. Spinach soup for dinner with spinach and potatoes on return to camp, bread and lard with coffee. Photos came today, but have to go to Stalag first to be stamped. Farmers cutting some of the grass around the fields for hay. A very nice day.

Wednesday 3rd June, 1942
Prisoner of War at Bodisch on railway party working at Braunau, and the usual times. Spinach soup for midday, with spinach meat and gravy with potatoes on return to camp, usual bread lard and some cheese tonight. Sgt Major bought some honey toothpaste and boot polish for the camp. SE Davis receives food parcel and Dalziel a tobacco parcel. Heard that many British planes are visiting the Ruhr valley in Germany. Pay day. Dull but fairly warm day.

Thursday 4th June, 1942
Stationed in camp near Bodisch Sudatenland on railway working party at Braunau. Usual work and meal times. Bowl of spinach soup for midday, with potatoes bowl of spinach on return to camp, with bread and lard. Received cake of soap from Red X, and Dalziel and Lee get parcels. A perfect day.

Friday 5th June, 1942

Prisoner of War on railway working party in Sudatenland and on job at Braunau with usual times of work, and return to camp at 1730 hrs with watery floury soup at midday and return to camp meat gravy and boiled potatoes, usual bread and lard. Fine morning, followed by clouds and windy afternoon.

Saturday 6th June, 1942

On railway working party as a POW. Twelve months today a Prisoner of War. Half days work today. Bowl of soup on return to camp and to Halbstadt in afternoon for showers, and on return getting boiled potatoes, sausage meat and bread ration cut down from five to six a loaf, and smaller lard ration. C Clark gets tobacco parcel. Mail in and camp paper. Two letters myself from Wickepin and one from Jean but still none from home. A fine day.

Sunday 7th June, 1942

Prisoner of War on railway working party at Bodisch Sudatenland. No work today. Bulk issue of food from Red X, which consisted of tin of steak and kidney, ½ tin honey, ¼ lb butter, ¼ lb cheese and tobacco tin of sugar. Wrote cards to Jean and Eileen. Made a pie of steak and kidney with potatoes which proved very good, day very long, getting light about 0330 hrs and not dark till 2130 hrs. A perfect day.

Monday 8th June, 1942

Prisoner of War on railway working party stationed near Bodisch Sudatenland. On job at Braunau, Crib, dinner and knock off times as usual with bowl of thin soup for dinner, with meat and gravy, boiled potatoes on return to camp and issue of bread and lard. No parcels for anybody today. A dull day finishing off with some heavy rain about 1500 hrs.

Tuesday 9th June, 1942

On railway working party as a POW in Sudatenland, stationed in camp near Bodisch. On job at Braunau, working on train job. Previous days working times. Midday meal bowl of thin soup with boiled potatoes, meat and gravy on return to camp, with bread and lard ration. Local inhabitants very busy cutting grass for hay. Potato crops showing up well now. Told off by W Pedersen today over cigarettes. A dull day.

Wednesday 10th June, 1942

Prisoner of War on railway working party in Sudatenland stationed in camp E-388 near Bodisch, on job at Braunau on work train. Usual working hours with thin bowl of barley soup for dinner with potatoes meat and gravy on return to camp and bread and lard ration. Buckley and G Smith receive personal parcels. Buckley's being a very nice parcel from home in New Zealand. Dull day with showers of rain in the afternoon.

Thursday 11th June, 1942

On railway job at Braunau as a POW stationed in camp near Bodisch Sudatenland. The usual times existed with practically the same as previous day for meals except for some lettuce and milky cheese. A dull day with rail setting in at 1900 hrs.

Friday 12th June, 1942

Prisoner of War on railway working party near Bodisch. Did not go to work today because of a bad back, and time goes very slowly at the camp. Bowl of spinach soup at midday with potatoes, spinach, meat and gravy with coffee, bread and lard. Red X food parcels arrive at station today, so will probably get an issue of one this weekend, also 3 weeks cigarette supply with them. Dull but fine until 1830 hrs when rain set in.

Saturday 13th June, 1942

Half days work today, shovelling earth from near railway line. Bowl of spinach soup for dinner. Went to Halbstadt for showers at 1500 hrs, and returning 1730 hrs to camp and getting potatoes, spinach and sausage meat, coffee, bread and lard. Twelve more men arrived from Weckelsdorf today to reinforce our party. Brought big supply of bulk supplies with them. Planted 20 lettuce plants, 15 cabbage plants, 5 sauerkraut and one tomato plant. Dull and cloudy, setting in with some rain during afternoon.

Sunday 14th June, 1942

Prisoner of War Bodisch, Sudatenland. No work today. Received bulk issue of Red X goods being ¼ lb butter. ¼ lb cheese, ½ tin jam, tobacco tin of sugar and a cut for a few extras, getting ½ tin of steak and kidney. Twelve men got about 35 biscuits, 1 lb sugar, 1 lb butter, 2 tins bacon, tin of steak and onions, 1 ½ pkts cheese and cigarettes. We also received 25 cigarettes, taken from the new arrivals supply. Did not receive Red X food parcel today, our first issue being next Sunday, so roll on. Three of the new party receive cigarette parcels and one a personal parcel. Todays rations spinach soup midday with potatoes meat and gravy at 1730 hrs with some lettuce and sauerkraut with usual bread and lard. Sunny day.

Monday 15th June, 1942

On railway working party as a POW at camp near Bodisch Sudatenland. On job at Braunau with usual working and the usual rations for the day. Photos came back from Stalag today and not too bad. English mail in today and Buckley x New Zealand receives cigarette parcel. Dull and cloudy till 1500 hrs when rain set in for the afternoon.

Tuesday 16th June, 1942

At Bodisch camp E-388 as a POW. Did not go to work today, owing to a crook stomach, and lay in bed most of the day, not being too warm on account of rain. Usual rations, and makes one feel hungry with the new men who arrived with all their bacon and steak. Smoky Smith gets cigarette parcel. A miserable day raining practically all the time.

Wednesday 17th June, 1942
On railway working party as a POW near Bodisch Sudatenland. On usual job but getting off at Braunau-Older. On usual times today with bowl of soup for midday, but as one party goes out later and works till 1800 hrs, so did not get the evening meal till about 1900 hrs with potatoes meat and gravy and usual bread etc. Blee NZ gets food parcel Lee a cigarette parcel and Goodwin NZ a personal parcel. A dull day.

Thursday 18th June, 1942
Prisoner of War on railway working party near Bodisch Sudatenland. On usual job Braunau, and same times, bowl of very poor soup at midday, and evening meal of potatoes, meat and gravy and usual bread and lard. Today Red letter day as received Red X parcel of each of English and Scottish cigarettes, so everyone happy and issue of thirty five English cigarettes. Five men returning to Lamsdorf, 2 of original party, and three from the new party. Fairly fine day.

Friday 19th June, 1942
Prisoner of War on railway working party near Bodisch Sudatenland. On train gang job at Braunau today, unloading cinders along side of railway track, and also loading sleepers. Usual work times. Watery soup at midday with the usual potatoes, meat and gravy on return to camp, lettuce, bread and lard. Five of the new party get cigarette parcels. Under-officer gets annoyed when we want to get something to eat out of our Red X issue, but gives in, and says will only issue stuff twice a week. Must explain here that all our Red X issue is kept in a separate room, and only given out with the tins punctured, and the Under-Officer and our S/Major have two different keys to the room to

prevent anyone pilfering the food, so both have to be there when we get anything out. Dull morning with fine afternoon.

Saturday 20th June, 1942
At a camp near Bodisch Sudatenland as a POW on railway working party. On job at Braunau loading sleepers. Only half days work. Came for showers at 1500 hrs and on arrival twelve men were needed to unload five trucks of coal, and get Monday free. Back from showers at 1730 hrs. Todays rations bowl of soup at midday boiled potatoes, sausage meat and lettuce evening meal and usual bread and lard. (1/5 loaf bread). A fine day.

Sunday 21st June, 1942
Prisoner of War on railway working party near Bodisch Sudatenland. No work today. Some of the boys go and get photos taken. At 1700 hrs with eleven others volunteered to go to Halbstadt and unload coal, did two hours work for which we were given Tuesday off. Special carriage came up to the camp to pick us up for work. Wrote home and sent photo of myself. Having arguments with the Jerries over our rations. Today made a steamed pudding with bread, sugar, raisins and lard and had hot with golden syrup, and not too bad. Todays rations soup at midday with meat, potatoes and gravy at night and usual bread and lard - Did a bit of sewing. A fine day with cold breeze.

Monday 22nd June, 1942
Prisoner of War in camp near Bodisch Sudatenland, on railway working party. On train job at Braunau loading sleepers. Usual working hours, with midday meal of soup and return to camp: potatoes, meat and gravy with bread, lard, milk cheese and fish cheese, a very gluey and unsavoury smelling stuff. Jerries say we can't get food stuff from our parcels till Wednesday. Casson gets a cigarette parcel and one of the new arrivals a personal parcel. More arguments about the food and midday soup is going to be cut out and will get 1/5 loaf of bread

a day with 1/8 loaf bread on Sunday, and potatoes, meat and gravy at night. A fine day.

Tuesday 23rd June, 1942
At camp near Bodisch Sudatenland on railway working party. Not working today, as having the day off for unloading coal on Sunday. Read book called 'The Exile', and also author of the 'Good Earth', also played cricket. Bowl of soup midday with potatoes, meat and gravy, some lettuce and bread and lard. Sgt Casson did some shopping today and bought a knife and tin opener. Also mentioned again about the rations with no soup at midday. No mail again today. Heard that Tobruk had fallen and 25000 prisoners taken by the Germans. A fine day.

Wednesday 24th June, 1942
On railway working party as a POW near Bodisch Sudatenland. On job at Braunau loading sleepers-usual work hours. Change of rations today, no soup at midday, but came home to soup with more potatoes in it, also some lettuce. Kept some of todays potatoes for tomorrow when we will get meat and gravy at night with extra potatoes. Midday soup being out, usual bread and lard, being 1/5 loaf of bread and got the rest of the food out of our Red X parcels tonight. Mail up today, and received letter from Sigrid, and still awaiting the first one from home. Camp newspaper in, and plenty of Jerry victories and propaganda. A very warm day.

Thursday 25th June, 1942
Prisoner of War on railway working party on train job at Braunau loading sleepers. Usual working hours. No midday meal with potatoes meat and gravy on return to camp, with bread, jam, no lard. Making tea and cocoa from food parcels, better than the coffee from the cookhouse which is made from wheat browned up and crushed. More mail and camp paper today, but no luck myself. A dull day with slight shower midday with heavy rain 1500 hrs.

Friday 26th June, 1942

On railway working party as a POW in camp at Bodisch. On job at Braunau, loading sleepers, bolts, plate and screws and washers. Todays meals were soup on return to camp, with 1/5 loaf bread and lard and fried some meat loaf from food parcel. A fine day.

Saturday 27th June, 1942

Prisoner of War on railway working party in Sudatenland. Half days work. To Halbstadt at 1500 hrs for showers returning 1730 hrs. Todays rations potatoes, sausage meat, with usual bread and lard. Mail and parcels in received in by Lee – book, Stephenson – book, C Clark – personal, Dalziel – personal, plenty of chocolate in them: Casson, Heggie and Phipps -cigarette parcels, while Goodwin received invalid parcel. Dull cold and windy day.

Sunday 28th June, 1942

Prisoner of War in camp near Bodisch on railway working party. No work today. Issued with 17 cigarettes and Red X food parcel. Todays rations boiled potatoes, meat and gravy, with usual bread and lard. Everybody making tasty little dishes and steamed puddings from food parcels. Wrote letter card to Sigrid, and cards to Mabel Bernice and Roslyn. Cannot stop from getting hungry, not enough variety and vegetables in the food we are getting. Too much of boiled potatoes. Dull windy and cold day.

Monday 29th June, 1942

Prisoner of War on railway working party at camp near Bodisch Sudatenland. On train gang job loading and unloading earth from alongside of railway line. Usual times crib 0930 hrs, dinner 1230 hrs and return to camp 1630 hrs. Todays rations soup on return to camp with bread and lard. Had a tin of pork and beans and fried them with some potatoes and very tasty. A little mail came in, but no luck myself. Change of Under-Officer in the German guard. A dull day interspersed with sunshine and attempts to rain.

Tuesday 30th June, 1942
Prisoner of War stationed near Bodisch Sudatenland on railway working party. Same job as yesterday and same times. Rations meat and gravy with boiled potatoes on return to camp from work, bread and strawberry jam in place of lard. Made some fish patties out of salmon bread crumbs and potato, had some spring onions and lettuce to go with them. Weather same as yesterday.

Wednesday 1st July, 1942
On railway job as a POW near Bodisch, Sudatenland. On job packing sleepers, with the usual times. Rations soup on return to camp with bread and lard, which I must state had to be part of our breakfast ration with the usual ersatz coffee. Tried some boiled fat-hen today and found it very nourishing. A weed that grows by the wayside. Dull, warm day when rain set in at 1900 hrs and came down very heavy for about ¾ hour.

Thursday 2nd July, 1942
Prisoner of War on railway working party in camp near Bodisch, Sudatenland. Same job as yesterday and same times involved. Meat and gravy with boiled potatoes with a bit of lettuce bread and lard. Made a tasty pie of potatoes with ham and veal loaf. Had another row about rations tonight, trying to do us out of our bread ration lard and jam. A fine day.

Friday 3rd July, 1942
On railway job as a POW stationed near Bodisch, Sudatenland. On job at Braunau shifting metal in morning and afternoon loading sleepers at Ottendorf. Times as usual. A thick soup on return to camp with

bread and lard. Made a cake this evening with bread crunbs jam, sultanas, cocoa, margarine and sugar. Mail in with Camp Newspaper from Stalag, but out of luck again. A warm day.

Saturday 4th July, 1942
Stationed near Bodisch Sudatenland as a POW on railway working party. Half days work today doing odd jobs. To showers at Halbstadt 1500 hrs, and returning to camp at 1730 hrs. Rations: potatoes, sausage meat, ¼ loaf bread, lard and jam. A fine day.

Sunday 5th July, 1942
Prisoner of War at Bodisch Sudatenland. No work today except for twenty men, who went to Halbstadt to unload coal and stones. Must mention on these occasions of these Sunday jobs, they run a carriage and engine to the camp to pick us up and return. Red X food parcel issue today, and seventeen English cigarettes. Played cricket and cards during the afternoon. Wrote cards to Ethel B and Doreen B. Cigarettes up from Stalag, and also supposed to be a bag of other parcels, will know tomorrow. Meat and gravy with boiled potatoes, 1/5 loaf bread and lard. Had stewed prunes with sultanas and bread. Very good and now getting to an occasional meal of fat hen when we can pick it. Beautiful day.

Monday 6th July 1942
On railway working party stationed at Bodisch Sudatenland. On a job at Bodisch today loading trucks of earth. Finished early and had rest of the day off. Picked big handful of wild strawberries today, so will have strawberries and prunes for breakfast tomorrow. Todays rations thick stew at 1800hrs with 1/5 loaf bread and lard. Made a pie of potatoes and liver pate. Yesterdays bag of parcels were for 2 cigarettes Pritchard, 2 cigarettes Domurgue, 1 cigarette Casson, 1 cigarette Phipps, Myers and Goodwin. A fairly warm day with fair amount of winter in it.

Tuesday 7th July, 1942

Railway working party as a POW stationed near Bodisch Sudatenland. On a job at Oldberg today loading and unloading earth with the usual work times involved. Potatoes, meat and gravy on return to camp with ¼ loaf bread and lard, also a little lettuce. Fine and sultry till midday when had a slight shower, settling in with a thunderstorm and rain at 1630 hrs and heavy rain at 1700 hrs.

Wednesday 8th July, 1942

Stationed near Bodisch, Sudatenland as a POW on railway working party. One of a party of ten loading earth on trucks at Halbstadt. Earth very wet and sticky, usual working times and back to camp 1730 hrs. Thick soup on return to camp with 1/5 loaf bread and usual lard issue. A dull day setting in with a thunderstorm and rain at 1630 hrs, some very vivid lightning.

Thursday 9th July, 1942

Prisoner of War on railway working party at a camp near Bodisch, Sudatenland. Some of the boys up at 0430 hrs to load a couple of trucks of earth at Bodisch, and then have to go to Oldberg to load four more. Did not go to work myself as had a crook stomach, but U/Officer said I had to go unless I had a temperature, so went from 1230hrs to 1600 hrs. Rations: potatoes, meat and gravy, very good tonight and some lettuce, ¼ loaf bread and lard. A fine day.

Friday 10th July, 1942

At camp near Bodisch Sudatenland on railway working party as a POW. On job at Oldberg clearing out earth between sleepers, with the usual times except that did not knock off till 1800 hrs. Work getting very solid. Thick soup on return to camp and bread and margarine and jam. Drinking plenty of tea and cocoa from our parcels while we have it. Mail parcels and camp newspaper in, personal parcel for Myers and cigarette parcel for Casson, Myers, Buckley, Gillon, Goodwin and Clark. Hot, sultry day.

Saturday 11th July, 1942

Prisoner of War on railway working party in Sudatenland. Throwing earth away from railway line at Olberg. Boss gets annoyed because some of the boys did not do enough work and reckons some of them would have stayed behind, had there been another guard, being only half days work. Party at Halbstadt have to work the afternoon, and quite a stink about it, and three of the boys coming home with us. To the showers at 1500 hrs and returned 1730 hrs. Potatoes with sausage meat, 1/5 loaf bread, lard and jam. Red X parcel between 2 men, and ten men get a bulk issue. Dull cloudy day

Sunday 12th July, 1942

Prisoner of War near Bodisch, Sudatenland on railway working party. Working today and getting Monday off-loading old sleepers. Some of the party unloading metal ballast and coal trucks. Potatoes, meat and gravy with ¼ loaf bread and lard. Wrote letter card to Auntie Em. Dull day with attempts to rain.

Monday 13th July, 1942

On railway working party as a pow near Bodisch. No work today having the day off for working yesterday. Played poker, and did nothing but eating contents of Red X food parcel. Hell of a row over the three men refusing to work on the Saturday afternoon. Reckon it was sabotage. Cloudy and cold with attempts to rain.

Tuesday 14th July, 1942

Prisoner of War stationed near Bodisch, Sudatenland on railway working party. One of party of sixteen working at Halbstadt loading earth. Did not leave till 0900 hrs and work till 1800 hrs. Others go to Braunau and Olberg. Buckley and Lee to return to Stalag tomorrow through sickness. More Stalag cigarettes up, also a bulk issue of Red X food. Potatoes, meat, and gravy with ¼ loaf bread, lard and 3 oz sugar. Cloudy and cold day.

Wednesday 15th July, 1942

Prisoner of War near Bodisch in Sudatenland on railway working party. On jobs at Heinzendorf loading rails, and at Halbstadt shovelling earth. Soup on returning to camp with lettuce, 1/5 loaf bread, butter and cheese. Red X food parcels arrive today with an issue of parcel between 2 and thirty six English cigarettes, and drew ½ tin of tobacco. Buckley and Lee left us today to return to Stalag having to be up at 0415 hrs to walk to Halbstadt for train connection. A cold day with some rain.

Thursday 16th July, 1942

On railway working party, camp near Bodisch as a POW. On job at Heinzendorf laying rails from side of line to centre ready for loading on trucks. Fairly easy day finishing work at 1510 hrs, but unable to return to camp till 1700 hr train. Rations: Potatoes, meat and gravy, 1/5 loaf bread and butter. Mail and camp papers in, received letter from Verna, but still that elusive one from home. Personal papers for Harry Davis and Hampton. Book parcels for Thorpe, Myers, Stewart Davie and Casson and cigarette parcels for Goodwin and Dalziel. A dull cold day.

Friday 17th July, 1942

Prisoner of War in camp near Bodisch Sudatenland on railway working party. On job at Heinzendorf loading rails and necessaries. Worked till 1800 hrs, otherwise usual work times for the day. Soup on return to camp with ¼ loaf bread, lard and jam. Debenham to return to Stalag tomorrow, and I have taken over Canteen job. Rumours of a shortage of food in France. Dull, cloudy day but fairly warm.

Saturday 18th July, 1942

On railway working party as a POW near Bodisch Sudatenland. On Heinzendorf job, but owing to trucks not turning up for loading rails, and on shovelling earth for ½ days work, which otherwise would have been a full day. Missed showers today, because not enough room on train. Got some canteen goods today. Issued with Red X food parcel today, ½ pkt biscuits, and thirty English cigarettes. Rations: Potatoes, sausage meat with 1/5 loaf bread, lard and cheese. Dull, cloudy day with some rain 1000 hrs.

Sunday 19th July, 1942
Near camp Bodisch Sudatenland as a POW on railway working party. No work today, except for ten men wanted for unloading coal at Halbstadt. Clothing parade. Busy with canteen orders and everyone busy making tasty dishes with food from parcels. Wrote to Mrs Forrest and Verna M. Potatoes, meat and gravy, ¼ loaf bread and lard. Dull but fine day.

Monday 20th July, 1942
On job at Halbstadt, 3 of us loading truck of coal for Lager, rest of party to Olberg. Usual times for the day, and on return to camp the inevitable soup ration with 1/5 loaf bread and lard. Busy trying to straighten out canteen list, with orders filled and unfilled. Dull day with some rain.

Tuesday 21st July, 1942
Prisoner of War on railway working party near Bodisch in Sudatenland. On sleeper loading job at Olberg, and some working at Heinzendorf loading rails, and some at the Lager unloading coal and earth. Times as usual with usual rations of meat and gravy with potatoes, 1/5 loaf bread with lard, and 3 oz sugar. Going through the Canteen book and find a deficiency of nearly forty Reichmarks from the previous person doing the job. Some of the boys play poker in the evening. Dull day with a little rain.

Wednesday 22nd July, 1942
On railway working party near Bodisch in Sudatenland as a POW. On sleeper job at Olberg. Usual times, work pretty heavy and back

not feeling the best. Soup on return to camp and with loaf ¼ bread, lard and milk cheese. Cigarettes up from Lager V111B, and personal parcels for Gracie, Ross and Horsborough. Book parcel for Thorpe and cigarette parcels for Armstrong, Barker, Stevenson, Galletly, and Phipps 2 cigarette parcels, so plenty of cigarettes about, put the boys in good heart. A day of cloud and sunshine.

Thursday 23rd July, 1942
Prisoner of War on railway working party near Bodisch in Sudatenland. This morning all of us on shifting railway lines bolted to sleepers ready for track laying, and in afternoon eight of us staying in Halbstadt, and the rest on to Braunau. Had to load earth, and shift earth from metal ballast. Usual times and worked till 1800 hrs. Meat and gravy with potatoes, 1/5 loaf bread, lard and small piece of cheese, and a bit of lettuce. A wet, miserable day.

Friday 24th July, 1942
Prisoner of War on railway working party stationed near Bodisch in Sudatenland. Usual times and rations of soup on return to camp with ¼ loaf bread, lard and jam. Hope I never see soup again, after I leave this part of the world. Dull day but fine.

Saturday 25th July, 1942
On railway working party as a POW near Bodisch in Sudatenland. On job at Olberg, and being half a day, had to clean out earth from under and in between three sleepers and refill with metal ballast. To Halbstadt for showers at 1500 hrs and returning to camp at 1730 hrs with potatoes, sausage meat with a bowl of cabbage, 1/5 loaf bread and lard. Eightly more Red X food parcels up today. Received a bulk issue this evening and got 1. ¼ biscuits, 3 round pkts of cheese, 2 tins of jam, 1/3 pkt prunes, ¼ lb butter, tin of steak and onions, 1½ tins of bacon, ¼ lbs sugar and 1 oz of tea. A fine day all round.

Sunday 26th July, 1942

In camp near Bodisch in Sudatenland as a POW on a railway working party. No work today. Boot parade in morning. Mail and camp paper up, but no luck again from home, getting a little disheartened and disgusted when you see others getting so much. Wrote home. Todays eats roast beef and gravy (so we were told) boiled potatoes, 1/5 loaf bread and lard. Got well and truly stuck into the bulk issue food today, dont know what we would do without it, making tea, biscuits and cheese and jam every couple of hours, and made a bacon pie. Another 200 Red X food parcels in today. Fine and very warm.

Monday 27th July, 1942

Prisoner of War on railway job near Bodisch on sleeper job at Olberg today. Usual times and rations of soup, 1/5 loaf bread, lard and a little lettuce on return to camp, and made a salad of vinegar, sugar and condensed milk to go with the lettuce. Brother Bills 22nd birthday today. More Red X parcels up and cigarettes. Dull sultry day with some rain between 1430 hrs and 1600 hrs.

Tuesday 28th July, 1942

On railway working party as a POW near Bodisch in Sudatenland, and on sleeper job at Olberg, and usual working hours with the all-familiar potatoes, meat and gravy on return to camp, ¼ loaf bread and lard and 3 ozs sugar. A few more Red X food parcels up. Personal parcels for Phipps and A Davies. Book parcel for Casson. Cigarette parcels for Pierce, Pritchard, H Davis. Dumurgue, Casson and Horsborough, also from Stalag ten tooth brushes and cigarettes from Turkish Red X. Dull and miserable day.

Wednesday 29th July, 1942

Prisoner of War at Bodisch, and on the sleeper job at Olberg, which is cleaning out earth and replacing rails and sleepers with metal ballast. Usual times, crib, (lunch fresh air) and 1730 hrs to camp with rations of soup, potatoes, 1/5 loaf bread, and a double ration of lard and cheese for a change. Fine but dull.

Thursday 30th July, 1942
Prisoner of War in Sudatenland on railway working party. One of eight on party working between Halbatadt and Heinzendorf, picking up old sleepers, fairly easy day for a change, and worked till 1800 hrs, and on return to camp, potatoes, meat and gravy with, 1/5 loaf bread and lard. Eating well cannot seem to satisfy myself, nearly ½ lb cheese with plenty of jam and tea to wash it down. Dull day with occassional showers.

Friday 31st July, 1942
Prisoner of War railway working party near Bodisch in Sudatenland, and on party between Halbstadt and Heinzendorf picking up sleepers and loading earth, with usual work hours and soup on return to camp with 1/5 loaf bread, lard and jam. A fairly dull day.

Saturday 1st August, 1942
On railway working party as a POW in Sudatenland and at job near Halbstadt loading earth into railway trucks. Half day and finished at 1215 hrs and then able to get our showers before returning to camp, and did not have to come down in the afternoon. Did some washing. Mail and Stalag Camp paper in, but no luck in the mail again. Farmers busy cutting second crop of grass hay, crops starting to ripen off, and some ploughing being done. A nice day.

Sunday 2nd August, 1942
Prisoner of War on railway party at Bodisch in Sudatenland. No work today. Issued with Red X parcel today. Wrote to cousin Betty and Mrs Walker, fixing up canteen book and playing poker. A very warm day.

Monday 3rd August, 1942

In Sudatenland near Bodisch on railway working party as a POW. One of party of eight working at Halbstadt, taking plates off old sleepers, and loading the sleepers on to trucks. Usual working hours and return to camp at 1730 hrs with soup bread and lard. A dull day with occassional showers of rain, culminating in a severe electric storm at 2000 hrs.

Tuesday 4th August, 1942

Prisoner of War near Bodsich in Sudatenland on railway working party. On same job as previous day loading old sleepers and a couple of trucks of earth, with usual times and ration of potatoes, meat and gravy with bread, lard and about 3 ozs sugar on return to camp. Peas got in for our rations were condemned but managed to get a few by picking them over. Dull sultry day.

Wednesday 5th August, 1942

In Sudatenland near Bodsich as a POW on railway working party, and on Halbstadt job and loaded four of trucks of earth. Camp at 1730 hrs with potatoes compressed meat, peas, cabbage, parsnips and carrots (gone mad). Mail in, but still waiting for that one from home. Sultry day with a few drops of rain.

Thursday 6th August, 1942

Prisoner of War railway working party Sudatenland. On job at Halbstadt loading earth, wanted eight men to load three trucks in the afternoon, but we only put about two barrow loads in third truck. Worked till 1800 hrs. Meat, gravy and boiled potatoes on return to camp with bread, lard and a little milk cheese. Made a meal of baked potatoes with tin of stewed beef and vegetables and some boiled peas. Sultry day with some rain.

Friday 7th August, 1942

Prisoner of War on railway working party stationed near Bodisch in Sudatenland. On job at Halbstadt loading earth and cleaning up generally. Usual times of working, and rations on return to camp, soup, lettuce, bread, lard and jam. Parcels up tonight and received by Phipps and Casson book parcel to Thorpe, tobacco parcels to Goodwin, Heggie and AJ Clark. Very fresh morning, coming up dull later in the day.

Saturday 8th August, 1942

Prisoner of War working party on railways near Bodisch, Sudatenland. On job at Halbstadt loading earth and instead of finishing at midday day being Saturday worked till 1500 hrs and thereby will get next Saturday morning off. Other boys go to showers at 1500 hrs and returned to camp at 1730 hrs with rations boiled potatoes, sausage meat, also some cabbage, usual bread and lard. Camp newspaper up. Issued with Red X food parcel in evening. Fairly cool morning, coming up dull and sultry later in the day.

Sunday 9th August, 1942

Stationed in camp near Bodisch Sudatenland as a POW on railway working party. Some of the boys working at Olberg today, and return about 1600 hrs. Allowed out around the camp for an hour during the morning and afternoon to pick raspberries, got quite a few and made come jam with some. Wrote home. Days in a camp no good, as want to be eating all the time, when you have not got it. A fine and warm day.

Monday 10th August, 1942

Prisoner of War on railway working party near Bodisch in Sudatenland. On job at Halbstadt loading earth and usual work times, with soup on return to camp at 1730 hrs with usual bread and lard ration and about three ozs sugar. Bravo cigarettes up from Stalag with an issue of 40 per person. Doreen B birthday. Cloudy but very warm day.

Tuesday 11th August, 1942

Prisoner of War on railway working party in Sudatenland. On job at Halbstadt loading earth, and cleaning up. Usual times, returning to camp at 1730 hrs, with rations of meat and gravy with boiled potatoes and usual bread and lard. Played poker after roll call, and heard rumours of Russians retreating but costing Germany many men. A very warm day.

Wednesday 12th August, 1942

Same routines as yesterday and rations as usual with some cheese ration for a month, about a mouthful a day. A fine beginning to the day, coming up very sultry and with a couple of heavy showers of rain.

Thursday 13th August, 1942

Prisoner of War on railway working party in Sudatenland. On job at Halbstadt with usual times and rations of potatoes, barley soup and usual bread and lard. Fine but thunderstorms in evening.

Friday 14th August, 1942

Prisoner of War railway working party stationed near Bodisch, Sudatenland. Same as day before except that I hurt a muscle in my back and did not work after 0900 hrs, otherwise usual times and rations on return to camp with a little jam as extra. Parcels and camp paper in. Parcels received by personnel Hogg, Xmas, Blee, Hunter, Barker, Davis, Carmona, Heggie. Cigarettes for Ross and tobacco for Myers. Fog early, rain later.

Saturday 15th August, 1942

Prisoner of War railway working party Sudatenland. No work today because of a bad neck, but had to go to Halbstadt, so had shower at midday. Half days work for others, and go to showers st 1500 hrs, and return at 1730 hrs and rations of cabbage, potatoes, sausage and usual bread and lard. Dull but fine day.

Sunday 16th August, 1942

In Sudatenland as a POW. No work today, except for six men who went to Halbstadt to unload a truck of coal. Red X food parcel issue, and forty seven English cigarettes. Made a pudding of bread, raisins and creamed rice. Wrote to Verna and Sigrid. Parcels up from Stalag. Personal for Galletly, SE Davis, Goodwin and RA Petersen, and cigarettes for Galletly. Rations barley soup, meat and gravy some good potatoes for a change, with usual bread and lard. Dull start to day but turned out nice day.

Monday 17th August, 1942

On railway working party as a POW in Sudatenland. Did not go to work today because of a strained muscle in neck and shoulders, 8 men to go to Olberg and the rest to Wittelsteine. Getting around with neck doubled up on shoulder. Managed to get a few potatoes and a cabbage extra today, so had a good tuck in. Seven more parcels arrive today.

Tuesday 18th August, 1942

Prisoner of War in Sudatenland. Practically the same as yesterday. Six more parcels in today, so both bags opened today. Personal parcels for A Davies 2, SE Davis, Blee Galetly, Goodwin, Templeman, Check, Armstrong. Cigarettes: Casson, Pritchard, Dalziel, Davies. Farmers very busy cutting hay and ploughing fields. Evening soup, potatoes, bread and lard, and soup at midday for those working. A fine warm day.

Wednesday 19th August, 1942

Prisoner of War stationed near Bodisch Sudatenland on railway working party. Went to the doctor this morning and given six days rest and to have a neck and shoulders rubbed. Got some new potatoes and cauliflowers. S/Major Burton to return to Stalag tomorrow, and Sgt Casson to take over. Personal parcels for Dumurgue and Barker. Cigarette parcel S E Davis. Rations: soup at midday for those working and on return to camp, cabbage soup potatoes and usual bread and lard. Warm, sultry day.

Thursday 20th August, 1942
Prisoner of War at Bodisch Sudatenland. In Lager with bad neck. S/M leaves 0900 hrs for Stalag V111B. Rations for those out working soup at midday and on return to camp for all, cabbage, meat and gravy, potatoes with bread and lard. Warm sultry day.

Friday 21st August, 1942
Prisoner of War on railway working party at Bodisch in Sudatenland. Still on sick list with bad neck. Under Officer dragged us to Birkight and Weckelsdorf during the day. Rations: soup midday for those working, and night soup with boiled potatoes, bread and lard and some jam. Personal parcels for Gillon and Armstrong, cigarettes for Gracie, Pritchard 2 and Templeman. Hot sultry day.

Saturday 22nd August, 1942
Prisoner of War on railway working party in Sudatenland. Still got bad neck and shoulders. Boys only half days work today. To showers at 1500 hrs and returning 1730 hrs. Cabbage, potatoes, sausage meat, bread and lard. Foggy morning, turning out very warm.

Sunday 23rd August, 1942
Prisoner of War Bodisch, Sudatenland. Still got a bad neck and at times causing severe pain. Red X parcel issue and thirty seven English cigarettes. Boot parade. Wrote to Auntie Nell. Rations potatoes meat and gravy, bread and lard. Foggy morning, but fine day.

Monday 24th August, 1942
On railway working party as a POW in Sudatenland. No working again today. Parties at Olberg, and Mittelsteine. Soup on return to camp of working parties and boiled potatoes, bread and lard. Muggy day with some rain.

Tuesday 25th August, 1942
Prisoner of War at Bodisch Sudatenland. Went to the Doctor again today and given another five days off. Went by train but had to walk home. Parcels in today but not issued. Cabbage, potatoes, meat and gravy, and the usual bread and lard to fill our empty tummies. A hot day.

Wednesday 26th August, 1942
On railway working party as a Prisoner of War near Bodisch Sudatenland. In camp with bad neck. Working parties at Olberg, and Mittelsteine. Soup at midday for those working, and on return to camp for all soup, potatoes, bread and lard and a little cheese. Mail and parcels received letter from Verna, but the one from home still eluding me. Personal parcels for Pascoe, Myers, Hampton, Ross, Gracie and cigarettes for Clark C, Goodwin, Pritchard, Blee, Myers, A Davies, Lunam and Hogg. Argument at work today, and Carlos goes Gaffer. Hot day.

Thursday 27th August, 1942
Prisoner of War stationed near Bodisch in Sudatenland. 29th birthday today. Still off work but Parties at Olberg and Mittelsteine. Potatoes, meat and gravy with usual bread and lard. A hot day.

Friday 28th August, 1942
Prisoner of War Bodisch. Working parties and rations as previous day with a little jam. Very warm day.

Saturday 29th August, 1942
On railway working party near Bodisch, Sudatenland as a POW. Still on sick list, and working parties out half day. Showers at 1500 hrs and returning at 1730 hrs. Rations at midday, potatoes, sausage meat with bread lard and a little cheese at night. Red X parcel issue with 38 cigarettes. Farmers very busy with hay. Warm day again.

Sunday 30th August, 1942

Prisoner of War Bodisch, Sudatenland. No work today except nine men went to Halbstadt in afternoon to unload coal. Mail and was lucky enough to receive five, 3 from Verna, one from Sigrid and Cousin Joyce. Wrote 2 cards to cousin Joyce. Very hot day.

Monday 31st August, 1942

Near Bodisch in Sudatenland as a POW on railway working party. Went to work today on party to Mittelsteine, but did not do much, as shoulder still not the best. Knock off time not till 1600 hrs. Some very nice country here, and farmers busy getting in the hay. Some more parcels up today with personal parcels to Gillon and S E Davis, and cigarettes to Kirkpatrick and Pritchard. Also some books from the Stalag. Cabbage and potato soup at midday, and same on return to camp with boiled potatoes, bread and lard and a sugar ration. Hot muggy day.

Tuesday 1st September, 1942

Prisoner of War Bodisch, Sudatenland. One same job as yesterday and same times and rations soup midday with potatoes, cabbage, meat and gravy, bread and lard. Foggy morning, later coming out warm and finishing with an electrical storm in evening.

Wednesday 2nd September, 1942

Prisoner of War Bodisch Sudatenland on railway working party. On same job as previous day, but did not do much as not feeling too good. Same times, and the usual rations midday and on return to camp. Personal parcels received by Kirkpatrick, Pritchard and Dalziel. A fine day.

Thursday 3rd September to Wednesday 9th, 1942

No diary written for these 7 days.

Thursday 10th September, 1942
On railway working party as a POW near Bodisch. Did not go to work today because of a bad stomach. Soup midday for those at work. Evening meat and gravy with potatoes, bread and lard, with an issue of fish cheese which you could smell long before you saw it. Heard general air raid alarm during night. A dull day.

Friday 11th September, 1942
Prisoner of War Bodisch. On railway job at Mittelsteine today digging out earth between sleepers with the usual work hours, soup midday and soup and sauerkraut on return to camp with bread and lard and a small jam ration. A very hot day.

Saturday 12th September, 1942
Prisoner of War on railway party near Bodisch Sudatenland. On party at Olberg, but did not get ½ day off as had to unload ballast metal, so we all get next Saturday morning off. Had showers at Halbstadt on way home from work. Soup at midday, with potatoes, sausage meat and usual bread and lard. Red X food parcel issue and 38 cigarettes. A fine day.

Sunday 13th September, 1942
Prisoner of War at Bodisch, Sudatenland. In camp today. Wrote home and to Alison. Busy taking in canteen orders and cigarette money. Soup potatoes meat and gravy with the usual bread and lard and some salad. A fine day.

Monday 14th September, 1942
Prisoner of War near Bodisch Sudatenland as a POW on railway working party. On job at Mittelsteine with usual work times. Midday soup, with thick stew on return to camp, potatoes and the usual other issues with sugar. Mail and camp paper up. 99 Canadian Red X parcels in. Usually being English parcels. Cool morning with fine day.

Tuesday 15th September, 1942

Prisoner of War near Bodisch Sudatenland on job at Halbstadt today unloading slack and cement, and loaded a couple of signal posts. Usual crib and lunch breaks and home at 1715 hrs. Midday soup and return to camp with stew potatoes, bread and lard. Another 140 Red X food parcels today, also bulk to arrive. Fine day but not too warm.

Wednesday 16th September, 1942

Prisoner of War near Bodisch, working party E388. On the job at Mittelsteine in morning, coming back to Halbstadt in afternoon to load signal equipment. Usual breaks and work times with midday soup and on return to camp soup potatoes bread lard and some very nice cheese. Rest of Red X parcels up today making about 260. Mail in, but no luck. Jacks 28th birthday today. Cold morning sunny later.

Thursday 17th September, 1942

Prisoner of War near Bodisch in Sudatenland. On railway working party to Mittelsteine, then to Halbstadt in afternoon loading signal posts etc. Home by early train. No soup midday, on return to camp soup, meat and gravy potatoes, bread, lard and potato salad. Parcels and camp paper in. First Australian personal parcel in and received by E Juon, other personal parcels to Thorpe and Casson and cigarette parcels to Barker, Nobby Clark, Casson, Lunam, Ross and Templemen. No soup at midday, but soup at night with meat and gravy, potatoes, bread and lard, also some potato salad. Cold morning with sun shining later but cold day throughout.

Friday 18th September, 1942

Prisoner of War near Bodisch on railway working party in Sudatenland. On job at Mittelsteine, usual times but not much work done though. Cabbage soup midday, with soup on return to camp, potatoes, bread and lard. Truck of flax went up in flame in yard today. Cass went shopping. Cold morning otherwise fine.

Saturday 19th September, 1942

Prisoner of War near Bodisch on railway working party. 18 men to Mittelsteine, rest free until 0900 hrs when 12 men needed to go to Halbstadt to load signals. One party finishing 1100 hrs then having showers. Rest of party go at 1500 hrs and return 1615 hrs. Cabbage at midday, with potatoes, sausage meat, bread, lard in evening also a sugar ration. Six more parcels up today, these and yesterdays were opened. Personal parcels Kerr, Hunter, Buckley, Dalziel, Stevenson, Balsarini, Clark C and cigarettes to Kerr 2, Davies and Park. First Red X Canadian food parcels issued, also Australian and New Zealand, but packed in Canada and very good parcels. Played poker in evening and also dished out canteen goods. Fresh morning otherwise lovely day.

Sunday 20th September, 1942

In camp at Bodisch as a Prisoner of War. No work today. Some of the boys go to get photos taken otherwise nothing of importance. Wrote letter card to Sigrid. Rations: meat and gravy with potatoes and spinach, bread and lard. A lovely day.

Monday 21st September, 1942

Prisoner of War Bodisch, Sudatenland on railway working party. On group at Mittelsteine laying rails. Home by 1715 hrs otherwise times as usual. Cabbage at midday with soup on return to camp and potatoes, bread and lard. A warm day.

Tuesday 22nd September, 1942

Prisoner of War Bodisch on railway working party. On job at Mittelsteine, laying rails, home by 1715 hrs train, otherwise usual crib and lunch times. Cabbage midday with meat gravy, potatoes on return to camp with bread and lard ration. Seven parcels up and received by personnel SE Davis, books 2 by Myers, tobacco 2 by Parks and cigarettes RA Petersen and Pascoe. Fairly windy day otherwise fine.

Wednesday 23rd September, 1942

On railway working party as a POW near Bodisch Sudatenland. On job at Mittelsteine laying rails. Home by early train otherwise times as usual, with cabbage at midday, and return to camp with thick soup, potatoes, bread and lard. A cool dull day.

Thursday 24th September, 1942

Prisoner of War near Bodisch. On job at Mittelsteine laying rails. Home by late train with the usual work times. Meals cabbage at midday, with soup on return to camp with meat gravy and potatoes, bread and lard. Mail and camp paper up, received letter from Verna. Dull but fine.

Friday 25th September, 1942

On railway working party as a POW in Sudatenland. On job at Mittelsteine, but home by early train, but working times as usual, with soup at midday. Stew on return to camp with potatoes, bread and margarine for a change, also jam. Bulk issue up today with plenty of bully, biscuits cheese, sugar, tea, honey, jam and cigarettes.

Saturday 26th September, 1942

Prisoner of War at Bodisch party E388. Did not go to till 0900 hrs and starting work 1015 hrs knocking off again 1140 hrs being half days work. Showers at 1500 hrs and return 1730 hrs. Sauerkraut midday with potatoes, sausage meat for ten, bread and margarine, issued with Canadian Red X food parcel and 40 English cigarettes being Players, State Express, and Craven A. A fine dull day.

Sunday 27th September, 1942

Prisoner of War Bodisch. No work today – clothing parade. Wrote cards to Ethel and Mavis. Sectional table tennis tournament on. Potatoes, soup meat and gravy, bread and margarine. Dull windy day.

Monday 28th September, 1942
Near Bodisch in Sudateland as a POW on railway working party. On Arbeit Zug today at Mittelsteine. Home by early train otherwise usual times. Soup midday with soup on return to camp and potatoes, bread and margarine and a sugar ration. One of the guards going away tomorrow, so took up collection of cigarettes for him. Raffled cap for Hospital Fund and collected 27 marks. A very hot day.

Tuesday 29th September, 1942
Prisoner of War Bodisch. On rail laying job at Mittelsteine. Home by early train otherwise times as usual, with cabbage midday potatoes, meat and gravy in evening with usual bread and margarine. A dull and windy day.

Wednesday 30th September, 1942
On usual job at Mittelsteine. Times as yesterday. Cabbage midday, with soup on return to camp, potatoes usual bread, margarine also jam. A very hot day.

Thursday 1st October, 1942
Prisoner of War stationed at Bodisch on railway working party. On rail laying job at Mittelsteine. Home by early train otherwise usual meal and work hours. Gaffer very angry because a bit behind time and might hold up trains. Cabbage midday, potatoes meat and gravy on return to camp with bread and margarine. Twenty three parcels up today and received by personnel Ellwood and Balsarini, cigarettes by Pritchard 3, Phipps Gracie, Lunam, Heggie, Check Hampton, Buckley, Kirkpatrick, Horsburgh, Blee, Clark C, Dalziel Casson, Davies, Hogg, Dumurgue, Park and books by Myers. A hot day.

Friday 2nd October, 1942
Prisoner of War in Sudatenland on railway working party. On party at Mittelsteine stomping sleepers, and swindled them out of twenty

times as yesterday. Cabbage at midday, with potatoes soup, bread and margarine on return to camp. No mail up for ten days now. Dull day with a few spots of rain.

Saturday 3rd October, 1942
On railway working party near Bodisch as a POW. On party at Braunau this morning, only half days work. To showers at Halbstadt at 1500 hrs, returning 1730 hrs. Mail and camp newspaper up today, none from home, but received one from Doreen and Carmel. Red X parcel issued and forty cigarettes. Cabbage midday with potatoes sausage meat, bread and margarine at night. Dull but warm day.

Sunday 4th October, 1942
Prisoner of War stationed near Bodisch on railway working party. No work today. Wrote to Doreen. Played game of cricket in old gravel quarry. Rations of meat and gravy with potatoes and boiled pumpkin and soup with usual bread and margarine. A fine day.

Monday 5th October, 1942
Prisoner of War Bodisch. On party of eight at Braunau plating sleepers, did 267 in morning, then had to unload some rails in the afternoon. Usual working times and early train home. Cabbage midday, with soup on return to camp potatoes, bread and margarine. The gafrighter leaves us today. Nights starting to get dark earlier, and fairly dark in morning on being wakened up. Farmers busy ploughing up the ground, will not be many fields of grass left soon. A fine day.

Tuesday 6th October, 1942
On railway working party near Bodisch as a Prisoner of War. At Braunau today unloading metal and plating sleepers. Machine broke down and had easy day. Cabbage midday, with potatoes meat and gravy on return to camp and usual, bread and margarine. A dull day.

Wednesday 7th October, 1942
Prisoner of War on railway party near Bodisch. On job at Braunau plating sleepers, and had to make up for loss of yesterday and had to do 450 sleepers which we did easily enough. Usual work hours, no midday meal today, but soup and potatoes on return to camp, usual bread and margarine and a jam ration. Parcels up today and received by books Myers and cigarette parcels Myers, Petersen RA, Parks, Pascoe, Kirkpatrick, Templeton, Goodwin, Buckley, Ellwood, Xmas, Casson 2, Galletly, Barker and Phipps. A warm day.

Thursday 8th October, 1942
On railway working party in Sudatenland as a Prisoner of War. On job at Braunau plating sleepers, did 310 today, with the usual work times, and again no soup at midday, but soup, meat, gravy, potatoes, bread, margarine and some sugar on return to camp. Foggy morning with fine day.

Friday 9th October, 1942
Prisoner of War Bodisch Sudatenland. Went to Mittelsteine today, unplating and shifting old sleepers, with the usual work times, no midday meal, but soup potatoes bread and margarine on return to camp. Cold dull wet day.

Saturday 10th October, 1942
Prisoner of War Bodisch. On job at Braunau this morning loading sleepers for Mittelsteine. Did 305. Half days work, and to showers at 1500 hrs returning at 1730 hrs. Soup midday, with potatoes, sausage meat, bread and margarine at night. A bulk issue of Red X food, which included five tins of bully, one of honey, one round pkt of cheese, ½ pkt biscuits, some tea and sugar. A very dull cold day with attempts to rain.

Sunday 11th October, 1942
Prisoner of War near Bodisch in Sudatenland. No work today. Wrote to Carmel today. Had a parade for clothing in morning. Doing up canteen books. Soup potatoes meat and gravy, bread and margarine. Dull wet miserable day.

Monday 12th October, 1942
Prisoner of War railway working party. On party at Braunau plating sleepers. Did 272 singles and twenty four doubles. With the usual working times. No meal midday but soup, potatoes usual bread and margarine on return to camp. No mail up for nine days. A dull and cold day.

Tuesday 13th October, 1942
Prisoner of War near Bodisch, Sudatenland on railway working party. On job at Braunau plating sleepers. Did 300, with the usual work times, no midday soup but potatoes meat and gravy, bread and margarine on return to camp with a sugar ration as extra. Casson went shopping today. A frosty morning followed by dull cold day.

Wednesday 14th October, 1942
On railway working party as a Prisoner of War near Bodisch. On job at Braunau, plating and loading sleepers, and with usual work hours, no midday meal, but the usual soup potatoes, bread, margarine and a cheese ration on return to camp. Dull cold day with a bit of sunshine.

Thursday 15th October, 1942
Prisoner of War, Bodisch Sudatenland. On railway party, Braunau loading sleepers 321, and plated 100 with usual times. Cabbage midday with the usual evening rations. A frosty morning with a cold cloudy day. Air raid alarm at night.

Friday 16th October, 1942
On railway working party near Bodisch as a Prisoner of War. On job at Braunau plating sleepers 360 and usual times, with cabbage midday meal, and evening rations same except for jam ration. Six parcels up tonight but not given out. Cold and cloudy day.

Saturday 17th October, 1942
Prisoner of War Sudatenland on railway working party. On job at Braunau and loaded 300 sleepers. Half days work, and visit to the showers 1500 hrs and returning 1600 hrs. Some mail up but received none myself. Parcels received by personnel Horsburgh, Pritchard, and F Smith, cigarettes Casson and Ellwood. Canadian food parcel issue and forty Player cigarettes. Soup midday with potatoes, sausage meat bread and margarine. Very dull cold day with drizzling rain.

Sunday 18th October, 1942
Prisoner of War Bodisch Sudatenland. No work today. Parade in morning of clothing. Ration of meat and gravy with potatoes, soup, pumpkin, bread and margarine. No cards or letter cards issued today. Snowed for the first time today for the coming winter. A very cold day, starting with drizzling rain, then some snow.

Monday 19th October, 1942
Prisoner of War in Sudatenland on railway working party. Went to Braunau for plating, but civvie with keys for engine did not turn up, so went to Mittelsteine and unplated old sleepers. No soup midday and home by late train, otherwise usual work and meal times. Soup on return to camp with potatoes, usual bread and margarine. Dull and cold day.

Tuesday 20th October, 1942
Prisoner of War stationed at Bodisch Sudatenland. On railway job at Braunau today plating sleepers doing 125 singles and 169 doubles. A

bit of a row today with civvies working in shed and Gestapo called in. Pay day drew 9 Reichmarks and 10 Phennigs. Usual working times, rations cabbage midday with meat, gravy and potatoes on return to camp usual bread and margarine, also sugar and milky cheese. Very frosty morning, but followed by a fine day and cold frosty night.

Wednesday 21st October, 1942
Prisoner of War on railway party at Bodisch. On job at Braunau plating sleepers during morning doing 224. In afternoon took engine and equipment down to Tuntchendorf for plating sleepers there. Civvies get told off more than we did about yesterdays affair. Usual times except home by late train. No meal midday, but stew on return to camp with potatoes, pumpkin and bread and margarine. A dull cold day.

Thursday 22nd October, 1942
Prisoner of War on railway working party in Sudatenland. On plating party to Tuntchendorf. Did not do the usual amount as had to go to Mittelsteine for more screws. Home on early train but otherwise usual hours. Cabbage midday with meat, gravy potatoes on return to camp with bread, margarine and a jam issue. Mail hanging off again. Dull day.

Friday 23rd October, 1942
Prisoner of War stationed at Bodisch. On plating job at Tuntchendorf. Engine not going too good and rain made sleepers slippery. Usual times and home by early train, with cabbage midday meal and soup on return to camp and bread and margarine. A wet and miserable day but not cold.

Saturday 24th October, 1942
Prisoner of War railway working party in Sudatenland. On job at Mittelsteine today, digging out between sleepers and half days work. To showers at 1500 hrs returning at 1530 hrs. Bulk issue of Red X food

today consisting of 5 tins bully, 1 tin of honey, one round pkt cheese, some sugar and forty Players cigarettes. Soup midday, with potatoes, sausage meat and the usual bread and margarine. A dull day.

Sunday 25th October, 1942
Prisoner of War stationed at Bodisch. No work today, except for ten men unloading coal at Halbstadt. Parade at 1100 hrs. Wrote letter card home. Meat, gravy with potatoes pumpkin and soup, bread and margarine. A very dull day.

Monday 26th October, 1942
Prisoner of War on party in Sudatenland on railway work. On party at Mittesteine laying rails, with the usual work hours. Cabbage midday with soup potatoes, bread and margarine on return to camp. News item attempt by NZ, Australian, Greek and Indian troops to land at Mersa Matruh. Fine day.

Tuesday 27th October, 1942
Prisoner of War on railway working party near Bodisch in Sudatenland. On job rail laying at Mittelsteine. Usual times with cabbage midday meal, meat gravy and potatoes, on return to camp bread and margarine. Mail and Camp Newspaper in with personal and cigarette parcels. Received letter from Bernice Allwood. Personal parcels to Alty, Hunter and Caroma, cigarettes Barker and Heggie. Not too well today

Wednesday 28th October, 1942
On railway working as a POW in Sudatenland. Did not go to work today, because of crook stomach. Cabbage soup midday, with soup, potatoes, bread and margarine on return of workers to camp. Mail camps and parcels up again today. No mail myself. Personal parcels by G Smith, books by Stevenson, cigarettes or tobacco by Casson, Ross, F Smith, Pascoe, H Davis, Heggie, Hunter and Pritchard. A fine day.

Thursday 29th October, 1942

On railway working party as a POW in Sudatenland. Did not go to work again today, because of a bad stomach. Rest working Braunau and Mittelsteine. Cabbage midday for those working. On return to camp meat gravy, potatoes, pumpkin, bread and margarine with a jam and sugar ration. A dull cold day.

Friday 30th October, 1942

Prisoner of War on railway working party near Bodisch in Sudatenland. Still no work today, being off with a crook stomach. Cabbage midday for those out working, soup on return to camp, potatoes, bread and lard and margarine. Mail and parcels in today, and received letters from Alison, Aunty Nell, Verna and two from England, but still that elusive one from home. Received personal parcels by Alty, Casson, and Thorpe. Cigarette parcels Buckley, Petersen NZ, Kerr, Phipps, Casson, Pritchard, Check and Kirkpatrick. A fine day.

Saturday 31st, October, 1942

Prisoner of War on railway working party. Out working today, but not feeling too good, loaded a few rails and sleepers and shifted boody (hut), half days work. To showers at 1500 hrs returning at 1615 hrs. Soup midday with potatoes, and at night potatoes sausage meat, bread and margarine. Issued with Canadian Red X food parcel and 40 English cigarettes. Had a concert in the evening for opening of new portion of barracks, and have also got a piano in. A very good evening having beer, some items by Under Officer and finished up with supper. Lights out at 2245 hrs. A fine day with some wind.

Sunday 1st November, 1942

Prisoner of War near Bodisch in Sudatenland. No work today. Parade at 1100 hrs. Playing cards and writing out poems. Wrote to Gladys Thorpe and Mrs L Thorpe in England. Still not feeling too good.

Rations: potatoes, meat and gravy, soup pumpkin bread and lard. Fine morning followed by a dull day and rain in the evening.

Monday 2nd November, 1942
On railway working party as a POW near Bodisch Sudatenland. On party unloading sleepers at Braunau, erecting boody (hut) at Tuntchendorf, and cleaned out six sleepers of metal. Home by early train. No midday meal but stew on returning to camp with potatoes and the usual bread and margarine. Still not feeling too good. Cool, cloudy day.

Tuesday 3rd November, 1942
Melbourne Cup Day. Prisoner of War near Bodisch on railway working party. At Tuntchendorf, cleaning metal out from sleepers, home by late train, otherwise times as usual. Cabbage midday meal, with meat gravy and potatoes on return to camp with bread and margarine. A cold miserable day.

Wednesday 4th November, 1942
Prisoner of War near Bodisch in Sudatenland. One of party of twenty up at 0430 hrs, leaving at 0600 and going out Weckelsdorf line to Parschnitz past where we were snow shovelling last winter, to dig a drain for signals to be put in. Finished work 1300 hrs, leaving on 1317 train back to camp, arriving back at 1500 hrs. Some very nice scenery, big electricity works there, and saw some very solid pillboxes on the old Zeckoslavich border. Parcels in and received by personnel Heggie and Kirkpatrick, cigarettes by Casson, Pritchard, Xmas, Gillon, Hogg, Lunum, Phipps, Goodwin and A Davies. Soup on return to camp, again at 1730 hrs potatoes bread margarine and a sugar ration. A cold and dull day.

Thursday 5th November, 1942
Railway working party as a POW near Bodisch Sudatenland. On same party as previous days to Parschnitz and returning to camp 1500 hrs.

Soup on return, with meat potatoes gravy at 1730 hrs bread and margarine. A wet morning early, but otherwise cloudy day and not too warm.

Friday 6th November, 1942
Prisoner of War near Bodisch Sudatenland. On same party as two previous days and the same times. Stew on return to camp, with stew potatoes ay 1730 hrs bread margarine also some jam and cheese. A drizzly and cold day.

Saturday 7th November, 1942
On railway working party near Bodisch Sudatenland as a POW on same job as yesterday and no half day off for anybody today. Returned 1500 hrs and continued on to showers at Halbstadt returning at 1730 hrs and meal of soup, potatoes, sausage meat, bread and margarine. Bulk food issue of 5 tins of bully, tin of jam, one of cheese, chocolate and forty cigarettes. Another 483 Red X food parcels on way for us and 13 pkts cigarettes. Heard rumours today that Jerry retreating in Russia and African front, and Americans take some land off Japanese, and Zchecks begin to wonder how many British ships actually left because of the number stated by the Jerries as having been lost. Nights getting dark early, because of the clocks being put back one hour, darkness setting in at 1600hrs. A dull day.

Sunday 8th November, 1942
Prisoner of War at Bodisch on railway working party. No work today. Wrote out poetry, played cards and reading, and section knowledge test in evening. No 4. followed by 2. Wrote to Lily Thorpe letter card and cards to Aunty Nell and Bernice. Soup, meat, gravy, potatoes, pumpkin, bread and margarine. A cold day with some drizzling rain.

Monday 9th November, 1942
Prisoner of War on working party near Bodisch. Working on signal job at Parschnitz. Out at 0430 hrs and returning to camp at 1500 hrs.

500 English Red X food parcels and 13 cigarettes parcels arrive for us today and busy from 1530 hrs till 1715 hrs carting them up from the station to the barracks. Personal and cigarette parcels up, personal for Galletly, Goodwin and Clark and cigarettes for Galletly, Pritchard, Blee, Phipps, Gracie, H Davis and SE Davis. Camps up but no mail. Soup on return to camp with soup again at 1730 hrs potatoes, bread, and margarine. Dull day till midday, then some sun till 1400 and dull again.

Tuesday 10th November, 1942
On railway working party as a Prisoner of War near Bodisch. On party at Parschnitz, putting in underground electric cables. Finished there today. Same times. Soup on return to camp at 1500 hrs at 1800 hrs meat gravy potatoes, bread, margarine and sugar ration. Heard news that British troops occupied Mersa Matruh and taken 40,000 prisoners. American troops occupy Morocco and Algeria and pushing towards Tripoli and Benghasi and Tobruk being bombed. Snow fell during evening. Dull day with some rain and snow.

Wednesday 11th November, 1942
Prisoner of War near Bodisch in Sudatenland on railway working party. On party today via Weckelsdorf to Qualisch putting up snow fences, and returned to camp by 1500 hrs soup on return to camp with stew, potatoes, bread and margarine at 1800 hrs. Snow laying on ground all day from previous night. Temperature at zero on going to work. Casson 25 today. Very cold wind and misty dull day.

Thursday 12th November, 1942
Prisoner of War on railway working party near Bodisch Sudatenland. On same job as yesterday and same times. Soup on return to camp 1500 hrs and meat, potatoes and gravy at 1800 hrs also bread and margarine. News that German troops had occupied unoccupied France and that American troops had landed in two of the important places

in West Africa. A very cold day with a little snow and snow of previous couple of days being frozen on ground.

Friday 13th November, 1942
Prisoner of War in Sudatenland. On same job as previous day, with the same times, and the usual meal times and rations the same. A dull day and not quite so cold.

Saturday 14th November, 1942
Prisoner of War on railway working party in Sudatenland. On job at Qualisch putting up snow fences same time as previous day, except instead of returning to camp 1500 continued on to Halbstadt for showers and back to camp 1745 hrs. Soup with potatoes, sausage meat, bread and margarine. News item Bardia and Tobruk in our hands again and 20,000 prisoners. Item of two previous nights of Americans taking two places was one place taken and the other being bombarded. Americans use 500 freighters and 200 war boats in their expedition. Jerries sink 11. Russian and Japanese fronts quiet. English Red X food parcel issued and forty cigarettes. A cold day with snow falling.

Sunday 15th November, 1942
Prisoner of War stationed at Bodisch no work today, parade at 1345 hrs for inspection of boots, overcoats, Caps and gloves issued. Wrote cards to Merle, Jean and Nurse H. Parcels up again and received by personel C Clark, Check, Hogg, Pierce and SE Davis. Cigarettes by Kirkpatrick, Alty, Horsburgh, Pritchard 3 and Templeman. Stayed in bed till 1230 today. Pay day received 8.40, Reading and Writing. Soup with potatoes, meat, gravy, bread and margarine. Not too warm a day.

Monday 16th November, 1942
Prisoner of War in Sudatenland on railway working party. On party one station this side of Parschnitz, cleaning grass away from metal along railway line with the usual times. Personal parcels received by

Ross, Hogg, A Davies, Buckley, Myers and Templeman. News item: Our troops pushing on towards Benghazi, and troops other side of Tripoli, pushing on through Algiers and Tunisia, towards Tripoli. Tunis in the meantime being heavily bombed. Soup on return to camp and soup again at 1700 hrs, bread and margarine. Fairly cold day with snow falling.

Tuesday 17th November, 1942
Prisoner of War at Bodisch in Sudatenland on railway working party. On party to Qualisch putting up snow fences, with usual times and back to camp at 1500 hrs. Soup on return with potatoes, meat and gravy at 1800 hrs, usual bread, and margarine. Parcels up and received by Petersen RA, Xmas, Hunter, Horsburgh. Cigarettes by Hampton. Armstrong returns and brings news of doings in Stalag V111B. A day of sunshine and falls of snow.

Wednesday 18th November, 1942
Prisoner of War at Bodisch. On party putting up snow fences, getting off at Radowenz and then walking towards Johnsdorf – Hottendorf with the usual working hours returning to camp by 1500 hrs. with soup on return and soup potatoes, bread and margarine at 1800 hrs. News items: Benghazi fallen, Derna evacuated, German – Italian troops land in Tunis to assist French troops and big battle raging. Jerry claims to have sunk 58 ships in the Mediterranean. Big battle raging around Solomon Islands, and Jerries not doing too good in Russia. Germans say we have had more experience in the desert and more planes is why we have advanced in the desert. Cass went shopping. A fine morning, followed by clouds and some snow, heavy fall of snow previous night.

Thursday 19th November, 1942
Prisoner of War at Bodisch on railway working party. On party putting up snow fences, getting off at Hottendorf and working towards

Ober-Adersbach. In camp at 1500 hrs having plenty of snow fights amongst the snow. Soup at 1500 hrs with potatoes meat and gravy, bread, and margarine at 1800 hrs. Fairly warm day.

Friday 20th November, 1942
Prisoner of War on railway working party in Sudatenland. On job at Addersbach putting up snow fences, with usual times returning to camp by 1500 hrs, with soup and soup again at 1800 hrs with bread and margarine. Mail and parcels up, and received my first letter from home since being a POW, dated June and it is now November, and six others from other people. Personal parcel received by Dumurgue and cigarettes by Gracie and Myers. News items: Spain mobilises. American troops in Corsica. Admiral Darlan (French) hands himself over to British authorities and French navy go to British ports, and attack on Tunis still being pushed forward. Germans retreating slightly from Stalingrad, and Russians take a couple of small towns. A fairly cold day.

Saturday 21st November, 1942
Prisoner of War stationed near Bodisch on railway working party. On gang putting up snow fences at Petersdorf, very muddy job as working on muddy ground. Continued on to Halbstadt for showers on returning at 1500 hrs and back to Lager at 1800 hrs. Soup, with potatoes sausage meat bread and margarine. Issued with Red X food parcel and fifty English cigarettes. Fairly warm with a little snow.

Sunday 22nd November, 1942
Prisoner of War near Bodisch, Sudatenland. No work today, so not out of bed too early. Parade 1315 hrs for inspection of boots and clothes. Wrote to Gladys Thorpe. Had euchre tournament in evening and I managed to win first prize (15 cigarettes). News flash: British troops landed in Sicily. Fairly cold day.

Monday 23rd November, 1942

Prisoner of War on railway working party near Bodisch. On party at Petersdorf putting up snow fences, and heavy snow storm all the morning. Same work times and back to camp by 1500 hrs with soup ration, with soup again at 1800 hrs bread and margarine. News: Solomon Islands recaptured, fighting continues in the desert and around Tunis, and 24 Jap cruisers sunk. Spanish government restless, and demanding Gibraltar back, and Britain replies no, so Spain appeals to Axis powers and mobilises. Mail up and received letter from Nurse Hamilton. Cold windy day with snow practically all day.

Tuesday 24th November, 1942

Prisoner of War stationed near Bodisch on railway working party. On party at Petersdorf, putting up snow fences, and having to re-erect some of Saturdays and yesterdays fences, because of the heavy wind and snow blowing them down. Had crib in farmhouse, and they looked as if they just get enough to live on by the look of them. Usual times except train late as a result of being held up by snow, thereabouts being three and four feet deep. Soup on return to camp, with meat gravy potatoes bread and margarine at 1800 hrs and a sugar ration. Will probably be starting on snow shovelling again soon so therefore will probably be getting our rations cut down. News: Russians encircle Jerries, north and south at Stalingrad and have now driven the Jerries 30 kms from Stalingrad taking 15,000 prisoners, and 15,000 dead. Cyrencia in British hands and British forces co-operate and Americans in Sth Africa, Genoa and Turin raided in Italy, also Stuttgard in Germany. Batavia again in British hands as Japs evacuate. Plenty of sabotage going on in the continent. Fairly cold windy day.

Wednesday 25th November, 1942

Prisoner of War near Bodisch in Sudatenland. On party at Petersdorf, erecting snow fences. Usual times, except returning train an hour late. Soup on return with soup again and potatoes bread and margarine at 1800 hrs. Reading and playing cards during evening. News: Jerries surrounded near Stalingrad and 120,000 taken prisoner. Cold but no snow.

Thursday 26th November, 1942
Prisoner of War near Bodisch. On party to Petersdorf putting up snow fences, returning to camp at 1500 hrs with the usual rations on return and later. News: Last nights flash misinterpreted and proved to 36,000 prisoners and forty-one thousand dead. Fairly warm day, there being no wind or snow.

Friday 27th November, 1942
Prisoner of War Bodisch. On party to Qualisch, putting up snow fences, being fairly easy day. Usual times returning to camp at 1500 hrs with soup and soup again at 1800 hrs bread and margarine. Not much news, except that Jerries now 60 kms from Stalingrad. Fairly warm day but cloudy.

Saturday 28th November, 1942
Prisoner of War stationed near Bodisch, Sudatenland. On working party to Qualisch, putting up snow fences, with the usual times but went straight on to showers at Halbstadt at 1500 hrs and returned to camp at 1615 hrs with rations of soup, potatoes, sausage meat, bread and lard. Five parcels up and received by personnel Buckley and Barker, and cigarettes by C Clark, G Smith and Pritchard. Red X food parcels issued and fifty cigarettes. News flashes: Around Stalingrad about 100,000 dead and prisoners taken by Russians, and 4,000 tanks captured and Russians continue to advance. In France parts recently occupied by Jerries French troops mutiny and much sabotage. Northern Africa Jerry troops land in Port near Tunis, and French ships in these ports, fled to English occupied ports or sunk themselves also mutiny amongst the French troops. Japanese start to retreat in Burma. A fairly good day with some sunshine.

Sunday 29th November, 1942

Prisoner of War stationed in Sudatenland. No work today, except for twelve men unloading coal at Halbstadt. Not feeling too good today. Wrote to Mrs Henderson, (Tas) and Mrs Burchell (Kojonup). A new game by the name of Bagatelle. Meat, gravy, potatoes, pumpkin, soup, bread and margarine. A miserable day with nasty wind and snowing.

Monday 30th November, 1942

Prisoner of War on railway working party near Bodisch. Putting up snow fences at Qualisch, also unloaded a few sleepers. Usual times. A few fights amongst the snow at times, using the shovels. Soup on the return to camp at 1500 hrs with same again at 1800 hrs with bread and margarine. Played cards in evening. Fine morning till 0900 then snow.

Tuesday 1st December, 1942

Prisoner of War stationed at Bodisch on railway working party putting up snow fences at Johnsdorf-Hottendorf, and also did a little snow shovelling and usual working times. Parcels up and received by Armstrong, Phipps, Clark AJ, books by Casson, Smith and Stevenson. Tobacco by Parks. A bit of a row at works today, some of the boys wanting to carry one pole, instead of two and Under-Officer reckons too many sick, still staying away from work. The absence of mail being felt. Soup on return to camp, with meat gravy and potatoes, bread and margarine and sugar ration. Cold breeze with sunshine.

Wednesday 2nd December, 1942

Prisoner of War stationed near Bodisch. Finished on early job at 0430 hrs, and on party at Braunau today, shovelling snow and taking plates off sleepers. Some working at Tuntchendorf. Plenty of snowballs being thrown about. Freistig at 0930 hrs Mitlegessen at 1215 hrs and to return to camp at 1730 hrs. Soup at midday, and again at 1800 hrs with bread and margarine and jam ration. Cold morning with some snow.

Thursday 3rd December, 1942

Prisoner of War near Bodisch, Sudatenland. On party to Braunau, taking off plates till 0900 hrs then twelve of us went to Halbstadt to unload coal, having seven trucks in all, and had to work pretty hard till 1500 hrs to get it finished, and feeling very stiff after it all. No soup turned up till 1600 hrs so had no dinner, had bath after unloading coal but had no soap or towels. Camp at 1615 hrs so had dinner on return to with potatoes, meat and gravy, bread and margarine. A day of snow interspersed with sunshine.

Friday 4th December, 1942

On railway working party as a POW. Did not go to work today because of stiffness and pains from previous day of unloading coal. Gangs working at Braunau and Tuntchendorf. Personal parcel received by SE Davis, and cigarettes by Casson also two parcels of reading books up. Soup midday with soup again at 1800 hrs potatoes, bread and margarine. A fairly cold day.

Saturday 5th December 1942

Prisoner of War stationed near Bodisch on railway working party. On party to Braunau loading rails and plates. Six men to Halbstadt, twelve men at home from unloading coal previous Sunday. Worked till 1500 hrs and had showers on return coming through, getting home 1745 hrs. Mail up and received three letters myself. Bulk issue of food, seven tins beef, two of cheese, one of jam and honey. Received notice from Geneva of cutting down of parcels, owing to transport problems. Rations: soup, potatoes, sausage meat, bread and margarine. News item: Italy being bombed, unrest there, and two major armies in Tunis now coming in contact with each other. A fairly good day being no wind. Stashee goes away today, gave him 320 cigarettes, pair of socks and seven cakes of soap, one of our very popular guards, and a new guard arrives.

Sunday 6th December, 1942

Prisoner of War stationed near Bodisch, Sudatenland. Owing to snow falling overnight, 15 of us had to go snow shovelling and six men went to Halbstadt to unload coal. Shovelling the snow between Bodisch and Weckelsdorf. Fairly good job till sleet commenced to fall and got pretty wet. In Lager again at 1230 hrs coal shovellers return at 1315 hrs. On the hot water during the afternoon also reading and doing up canteen book. No cards or letter cards today. Rations Potatoes, meat gravy pumpkin usual bread and margarine. A fair cow of a day, sleet falling and a thaw set in.

Monday 7th December, 1942

Prisoner of War on railway working party. On party at Tuntchendorf, digging out metal, parties also at Olberg and Braunau. Boss a bit annoyed because dont quite finish the job. Under Officer goes crook about blokes joking about us wearing the yellow bands and the civvies being in our place. Came to Braunau on 1530 hrs train and returned to camp with others at 1745 hrs. Fixing up canteen order in evening. Soup midday and again at 1800 hrs bread and margarine. A fairly good day, thawing out heavily.

Tuesday 8th December, 1942

Prisoner of War stationed near Bodisch, Sudatenland. At Tuntshendorf shifting metal between sleepers, others working at Halbstadt, Braunau and Olberg. Usual times returning to Braunau 1530 hrs and camp 1745 hrs. Potatoes, meat gravy bread and margarine and a sugar ration. News items: Naples bombed, few ships of the Italian Navy sunk in Mediterranean, battle going well in Africa, and Russians also doing a good job. A fairly good day, being a heavy thaw overnight, which caused local river to rise slightly.

Wednesday 9th December, 1942

On railway working party as a Prisoner of War in Sudatenland. On party working at Truntchendorf cleaning metal from between sleepers.

Same times as previous day. Soup at midday and again at 1800 hrs, bread and margarine with a jam ration. Mail and camps up received two letters. Weather same as yesterday.

Thursday 10th December, 1942
Prisoner of War in Sudatenland. On working party at Tuntchendorf cleaning out metal from between sleepers and given 14 to do today, and the old chow gets a bit annoyed because a couple didn't finish their quota. Usual times, soup at midday with meat, potatoes, gravy, bread and margarine on return to camp. Played cards in evening. Heavy fog in morning sunshine about 1200 hrs till 1330 hrs, and then heavy fog came up again. Plenty of air activity throughout the day.

Friday 11th December, 1942
On railway working as a POW in Sudatenland. On party at Tuntchendorf, cleaning out metal between sleepers and taking plates off sleepers. Same times, mail and camps up received a couple of letters. English and Canadian food parcels issued to last 14 days, for two men and 25 cigarettes. Unrest still in Italy some refusing to work and many arrests made. Turin heavily bombed. Surrounded army of Jerries in Russia being supplied by aeroplane. Soup at midday and again at 1800 hrs with bread and marg. A frost in morning and turning out a beautiful sunny day.

Saturday 12th December, 1942
Prisoner of War on railway working party in Sudatenland. Did not go to work till 0900 hrs because of work on previous Sunday. Went to Braunau and shifted earth. Other party at Tuntchendorf. Finished work at 1500 hrs and stopped at Halbstadt on way home for showers, getting to camp at 1745 hrs. Soup on return to camp with potatoes, sausage meat, bread and margarine. News flash: All Japanese driven out of New Guinea. Big tank battles in Libya and Tunis. Unless chaining up offf German prisoners discontinues in England by morning of

the 12th, all British prisoners will be chained up. A couple of German Generals in Russia relieved of their duties. Cold dull day.

Sunday 13th December, 1942
Prisoner of War near Bodisch. No work today by anybody. Sent Christmas card to Mum and wrote to nurse H. Reading and playing cards, boys getting very playful pulling everybody out of bed, and one side going the other in evening. A fairly good day.

Monday 14th December, 1942
On railway working party as a prisoner of War in Sudatenland. On party at Tuntchendorf, unplating sleepers with the usual times. Soup midday and again 1800 hrs with bread and margarine. A fairly fine but cold day.

Tuesday 15th December, 1942
Prisoner of War Bodisch. Same as previous day. Casson goes shopping for canteen goods. Soup midday with meat, gravy, potatoes, bread and margarine at 1800 hrs. A dull day.

Wednesday 16th December, 1942
Prisoner of War near Bodisch on railway working party. Same job as Monday and Tuesday, same times and rations. Dished out canteen supplies in evening. News: Heavy tank and aerial battles around Tunis. Naples bombed again. Russians still doing well. Fairly cold and dull day.

Thursday 17th November, 1942
Prisoner of War near Bodisch on railway working party at Tuntchendorf unplating sleepers and pulling them up the bank by bridge. Usual work times. Personal parcel received by Casson, books by Thorpe and cigarettes by Ross, Dumurgue and Armstrong. News: Result of tank battle in Libya, enemy pushed further west, and fall of Tripoli expected

soon. Also big battle still raging in Tunisia, Tunis being bombed heavily. In Italy, Genoa, Naples and some other place bombed, especially Naples receiving attention day and night. Sixth German Army still surrounded in Russia, and Russians still doing well. Soup at midday with potatoes, meat and gravy on return to camp with bread and margarine. Doing canteen work in the evening – fairly nice day with some sunshine. Gets dark at 1600 hrs now, and no light in morning till 0730 hrs. Time some mail was up again.

Friday 18th December, 1942
Prisoner of War on railway working party, Sudatenland. On party at Mittlesteine, unplating sleepers and pulling them up the bank. Times as usual. Liar not in too good a mood, reckons some of the boys are showing him up too much. Reckons those that do not work too well, will be made to do jobs on Sunday and will receive no pay. Issue of 25 cigarettes and Canadian food parcel between two. Soup at midday with soup, potatoes, bread and margarine at 1800 hrs. News: Things going well in the desert, Rommells Army now cut in two and Tripoli badly threatened. Two big towns in Italy evacuated Florence being one. Russian advance held up because of the enormous amount of material left behind by the Jerries, German Troops mobilise on the Spanish frontier. A fairly nice day.

Saturday 19th December, 1942
Prisoner of War railway working party in Sudatenland. On party at Rappersdorf, putting in iron pegs for fixing wire for signal post for station, also cleaning up road nearby. Finished 1315 hrs. Walked to Halbstadt for showers. About ten minutes before return to Lager, 3 trucks of coal came in and had to be unloaded and went home with other boys at 1730 hrs. On return to camp soup, potatoes, sausage meat, bread and margarine. Doing up canteen book in evening. A fairly good day.

Sunday 20th December, 1942

Prisoner of War near Bodisch. No work today except for twelve men to go to Halbstadt to unload coal at 1500 hrs and return at 1900 hrs. Parade for inspection of clothing at 1100 hrs. Some of the boys decorating Christmas tree in barracks, and making arrangements for Christmas Day. Wrote cards Verna, Poppy and Donald. Marked some clothes and doing canteen work. Potatoes with meat gravy bread and margarine. Fairly good day with a lot of fog in evening.

Monday 21st December, 1942

On railway working party as a POW in Sudatenland. On party at Mittelsteine unplating sleepers, pulling them up the bank and stacking the plates. Missed home train at 1500 hrs and came on goods to Braunau, only to see our train pulling out, just as we got there, so did not get back to Lager till 1915 hrs. Soup midday with same on return to camp and potatoes, bread and margarine. Staschee our guard returns to Bodisch. No mail up for ten days. News: Rommels Army now cut in two in Tripoli, one part retreating towards Tripoli, and the other some other place, and also Tunis and some other place in Tunisia being bombed. Naples and Turin bombed in Italy. Evacuation of some large towns in Italy, including Milan. Russians still doing well around Stalingrad. Some of the British troops in Burma now within 50 miles of the Burma Road. A fairly good day.

Tuesday 22nd December, 1942

Prisoner of War in Sudatenland, on party to Mittelsteine cleaning up metal out of drains and on side of bank near railway line. Usual times. Three cigarette parcels up and received by Pritchard 2 and Casson. Soup midday with the same on return to camp: potatoes, bread and margarine. Frosty morning with nice day afterwards but getting cold again 1500 hrs.

Wednesday 23rd December, 1942

On railway working party as a POW near Brodisch in Sudatenland. On party at Mittelsteine cleaning metal out of drains with the usual hours and soup at midday with same on return to camp with potatoes, bread and margarine and sugar ration. News: Russians capture 25 towns around Stalingrad and Jerries lose 40,000 men, and also Russians now again in part of the Ukraine. Frosty morning followed by dull and cold day with snow in evening.

Thursday 24th December, 1942

Christmas Eve. Prisoner of War near Bodisch. At Braunau today loading old sleepers and had to load 700 for the day, finished them by 1200 hrs so came home on the 1230 train, had soup on return to camp with potatoes, meat gravy, bread and margarine at 1800 hrs with a jam issue. Had room decorated in evening and had a sing song around the pianos and allowed in recreation barracks till 2200 hrs. Issued with Red X Christmas parcel which contained cake, biscuits, chocolate, pudding, sweets and other articles. News: Russians still doing well, with 15,000 Jerries being killed in one place and one Army still encircled and 66 transport planes being shot down in dropping supplies to them. Fairly cold day.

Friday 25th December, 1942

My first Christmas in Germany as a Prisoner of War on railway working party near Bodisch, Sudatenland. No work today, all being in Lager E388 at Bodsich and a day enjoyed by all. Cup of tea at 0800 hrs. and a church sevice at 1000 hrs. Tea again at 1030 hrs. Bagatelle competition and won by Dumurgue. 1300 hrs dinner provided by Jerry which consisted of soup, macaroni, meat and gravy with mashed potatoes, pumpkin, providing tea ourselves. Afternoon was spent in competitions and games, there being a whist drive and knowledge test. Afternoon tea at 1630 hrs. Tea at night 1830 hrs consisted of braised steak and macaroni from our Christmas parcels with mashed potatoes, then followed by our Christmas pudding. During the evening beer was drunk and several toasts, and also several mixed items were given with songs, recitations and humorous items, and the evening finishing off with tea cake, biscuits and cheese, and the singing of Old Lang Syne and The King. The room included a Christmas tree decorated and had candles on the tree and looked a great sight when the lights were turned off. Everyone declared it a Christmas we will always remember. (under the circumstances). Fairly cold day.

Saturday 26th December, 1942
Boxing Day. Prisoner of War Bodisch Sudatenland. No work again today, so did not get out of bed till about midday when potatoes, meat and gravy were had for dinner and the usual bread and margarine ration. During the afternoon did a little washing, reading and playing cards. A little bulk issue dished out today and received two tins bully, ½ tin jam and about six ounces of cheese. A fairly cold day.

Sunday 27th December, 1942
Prisoner of War of the Germans near Bodisch. No work today except for ten men to Halbstadt to unload coal at 0900 hrs returning 1315 hrs. Wrote to Alison but will not post till next weekend when an Air Mail will start. Reading and playing cards. News: Admiral Darlan assassinated. 550 ships have arrived at Algiers with supplies. British and NZ troops in Burma. Potatoes, meat, gravy, bread and margarine rations for the day. Day not too warm, ground being very hard.

Monday 28th December, 1942
Prisoner of War in Sudatenland. On railway working party. Back to work again after three day break for Christmas holidays. On party to Mittelsteine, cleaning metal out of drain other party at Braunau loading old sleepers, and usual working hours with soup at midday and soup, potatoes, bread, margarine, a sugar ration on return to camp. Wrote out some poetry in evening. News: Russians still doing

well. British in Rangoon. Romells Army in Tripoli not doing too well. Few Italian ships sank in Mediteranean. Italian towns continue to be bombed also places in France, Holland, Belgium and Western Germany. Frosty morning and a cold day.

Tuesday 29th December, 1942
Prisoner of War near Bodisch Sudatenland. Same work and same times as yesterday with rations midday soup and evening meal soup, potatoes, bread and margarine. News: Russians still doing well and many Germans dead and prisoners and also aerodrome taken. In Tripoli events much the same and Admiral Darlans successor announced. A very cold day with some snow in evening.

Wednesday 30th December, 1942
On railway working as a Prisoner of War of the Germans near Bodisch. On party at Mittelsteine only got off between Tuntchendorf and Mittelsteine to clean out drains. Did not finish job as had to go and erect boody (hut) and do some stomping. Arbeit Zug down so did not knock off till 1600 hrs, otherwise times the same. Midday soup with soup, potatoes, bread and margarine on return to camp. Played cards in the evening. News: Berlin getting done over as only trains with anything to do with the war allowed out. Fairly cold with some sunshine.

Thursday 31st December, 1942
Prisoner of War near Bodisch. On party at Mittelsteine stomping sleepers. Usual times, and the same rations as per previous day. Mail and parcels up. Received one from home with the news that Bill passed away in the Middle East. Personal parcels received by Pierce, Gillon, Gracie, F. Smith and Pritchard. Snowed during the day and a very cold and windy day.

Year of 1943 Stalag VIIIB

A Prisoner of War working on the railway line at Bodisch.

Private Vic Petersen has been in German hands since June, 1941. He is about to add another year to his already two years and 6 months.

Friday 1st January, 1943
Prisoner of War on railway working party near Bodisch. Army authorities wanted us to work today, but railway authorities did not want us to so did little jobs around the Lager to say that we did something. I helped with working, while others did snow shovelling cleaning out air raid shelter and chopping wood, and washing out barracks. Issued with English food parcel and 50 cigarettes. Played cards during afternoon and evening. Potatoes, meat, gravy, bread and margarine as rations. A reasonable day with some snow.

Saturday 2nd January, 1943
Prisoner of War in Sudatenland on railway working party. On party at Mittelsteine stomping sleepers, gang of 12 and 15 loading old sleepers, rest at home as result of working last Sunday. Home to Halbstadt on 1500 train for showers, returning to camp 1730 hrs. Potatoes, meat, gravy, bread and margarine. Played cards in evening. News items: Russians doing well, there being many Germans surrounded, aerodrome and many planes captured. American planes bombing

West Germany and France. Italian ships sunk in Mediteranean and a German convoy attacked. Cold day with snow.

Sunday 3rd January, 1943
Prisoner of War near Bodisch. No work except one of party of ten to Halbstadt to do snow shovelling. Finished 1115 hrs and back in camp 1315 hrs. Hit truck on way to work in train and 15 others had to go down and clean up gear. Rations: meat, gravy, with potatoes midday with a few, potatoes, bread and margarine ration at night. Reading and playing cards during afternoon and also did up canteen book. No mail cards up today. Fairly windy day with some snow.

Monday 4th January, 1943
On railway working party near Bodisch Sudatenland as a POW. On party at Mittelsteine cleaning out drains and some stomping of sleepers and gang at Braunau shifting snow, usual times. No work train. Wrote cards to Ethel and Mrs Walker, sending them by Air Mail. Played cards in evening. Soup midday, potatoes, bread and margarine on return to camp. News Items: Tunis and Crete heavily bombed. Three places not known heavily bombed. Slow retreat of Italians and Germans in Tripoli continue. British subs sink 10,000 ton, German ship. Big night air battles over England and 200 German planes shot down. Sir Neville Henderson dead. American output of planes for December, 5,000. Russians continue to have great successes many dead and prisoners being taken and important towns and places. Naval battle of New Guinea and Japs lose 11 ships. Cold day with some snow.

Tuesday 5th January, 1943
Prisoner of War Bodisch. On job at Mittelsteine stomping sleepers. Usual times. Ernie Juon goes back to Stalag today. Played cards in the evening. No issue of Red X parcel food as key is lost. A fairly cold day with a bit of snow.

Wednesday 6th January, 1943

On railway working party as a POW in Sudatenland. With a party of 16 shifting snow at Bodisch, rest at Braunau. Parcels up today and received by cigarettes Galletly, Ellwood and Casson. Personal parcels by F Smith, Balsarini, Caroma, H Davis and myself and being the first one from home and posted on August 1942. Soup midday and again at night with potatoes, bread and margarine also a sugar and cheese ration. Stalag cigarette issue of 122 cigarettes each. Calm day with a little snow.

Thursday 7th January, 1943

Prisoner of War near Bodisch, Sudatenland. On same job as yesterday and other gangs the same. Midday soup with potatoes, meat and gravy, bread and margarine at night. News Items: Russians still carrying on capturing small towns, prisoners and much war material. Crete and Tunis bombed. 30 planes shot down over the Mediteranean. Romells Army still retreating and Japanese lose 9 ships off Burma. Fairly cold day.

Friday 8th January, 1943

Prisoner of War of the railway working party in Sudatenland. On party at Bodisch shovelling snow from railway line and along bank, and rest at Tuntchendorf loading old sleepers. Usual times and midday soup, with same again at 1800 hrs with potatoes, bread and margarine. A little mail up but no Australian, also camp magazine. English Red X food parcel issued one for a fortnight. Fairly mild day.

Saturday 9th January, 1943

Prisoner of War Bodisch. Did not go out today, having the day off for work previous Sunday. Some snow shovelling and some putting up sign posts along railway line. To showers at 1500 hrs returning 1615 hrs. Rations: cabbage potatoes, sausage meat, bread and margarine and a jam ration. 18 parcels up and some playing cards from Stalag. Personal parcels to Dalziel, Blee and G Smith. Cigarettes by Casson 5, Pritchard 2 Kerr, Blee, Clark C, Armstrong, Kirkpatrick, Hogg, Horsburgh and Buckley. Reading, playing cards and making gloves. Fair day with a little snow.

Sunday 10th January, 1943
Prisoner of War near Bodisch, Sudatenland. No work today, except ten men went out at 0700 hrs but returned at 0815 as they were not needed. Parade at 1345 hrs. Played cards and general knowledge test, our section winning. Wrote letter card home. Soup, potatoes, meat and gravy with bread and margarine. News Items: 13 Jerry tankers sunk on way to Nth Africa, and America and Britain declare war on Northern China. A fairly cold day.

Monday 11th January, 1943
On railway working as POW in Sudatenland. On party shovelling snow from railway line, one party cleaning drains Braunau and one at Tuntchendorf putting up sign posts. Usual hours with midday soup, and soup again at 1800 hrs – Potatoes, bread and margarine. Collected cigarette money and doing up canteen books in evening. A frosty morning, with temperature at 18 degrees below followed by a sunny day and turning cold again at 1600 hrs. The temperature 14 below. Ice in boots when we knocked off.

Tuesday 12th January, 1943
Prisoner of War on railway working party in Sudatenland. On party at Bodisch shovelling snow off railway line, having to go over again of the previous day because of drifts caused by high winds, others working at Braunau and Tuntchendorf. Usual job times and rations the same as previous day. A little mail up, but received none myself. A very cold day, with bitterly strong cold wind.

Wednesday 13th January, 1943
Prisoner of War near Bodisch. On snow shovelling at Bodisch, going over some of yesterdays in morning because of drifts caused by high wind. In afternoon went down past Birkyht and cleared line of drifts. Usual times. Gofreight goes today, taking over job at Weckelsdorf and an old guard takes his place. Usual rations for the day. Cold miserable day.

Thursday 14th January, 1943
Prisoner of War railway working party in Sudatenland. At Bodisch cleaning out drain, and going over yesterdays place again on account of drift caused by strong winds. Down to Birkyht and cleaned up around station in afternoon. Usual work hours. Camps up today and five letters. New Under Officer taking over guard today old one being shifted. Played cards in evening. Usual rations except for extra sugar and cheese ration. Dull day with strong bitterly cold wind.

Friday 15th January, 1943
Prisoner of War in Sudatenland. On party working around Bodisch shovelling snow from railway line and cleaning out drains, others at Braunau. Usual hours. Major Padre comes from Stalag and stays the night. Church service during evening. Jerry who speaks English with him and a very nice chap. Soup midday and again at 1800 hrs with potatoes, bread and margarine and a little jam ration. Little warmer today and less wind.

Saturday 16th January, 1943
Prisoner of War Bodisch. On snow shovelling job at Bodisch and Birkyht. Finished days work 1430 hrs and then to Halbstadt for showers returning on the 1600 hr train. Played cards in evening. Soup, potatoes, cabbage, sausage meat, bread and margarine rations for the day. Fairly good day being a little warmer.

Sunday 17th January, 1943
On railway working party as a POW stationed near Bodisch. Were going to go and have our photos taken today but coal unloading at Halbstadt intervened being amongst gang of twelve, going at 0900 hrs and returning at 1315 hrs. Clothes inspection at 1415 hrs. Wrote cards to Gladys and Lily Thorpe. Midday rations potatoes, meat, gravy, at night few potatoes, bread and margarine. A moderately warm day.

Monday 18th January, 1943
Prisoner of War stationed near Bodisch. On party working around Bodisch, shovelling snow from railway line. About eight letters up but got none myself. Soup midday and again at night, with potatoes, bread and margarine. Bit of news: Russians still doing well, taking much material and taking many prisoners. German Sixth Army still said to be surrounded, and in a bad plight. 900 bombers over Berlin, Sicily bombed and German bombers over London. Fairly good day cold at 1500 hrs.

Tuesday 19th January, 1943
On railway working party near Bodisch as a POW. On gang working Bodisch and Birkyht, shovelling snow. Others working at Braunau. Usual times and easy day. Taking canteen orders at night and a little reading. Usual rations. News: some of the British advance in to within 25 kms Tripoli. Russian drive extends from Leningrad as well as in the southern sections. Soup midday, and at night potatoes, meat, gravy, bread and margarine. A frosty morning, being reasonable day except coming up very cold 1500 hrs.

Wednesday 20th January, 1943
Prisoner of War in Sudatenland. On party around Bodisch snow shovelling from railway line; others at Braunau and Tuntchendorf. Usual hours. Parcels up and received by Park, Myres and Clark SB. Cigarettes

or tobacco by Pritchard, Gracie, Dalziel, Phipps 2, Xmas 2, Balsarini, Heggie, Petersen RA, Davies H, Ellwood, Templeman, Pascoe 2, Ross and Kirkpatrick. Usual midday soup, with soup, potatoes, bread and margarine with sugar ration at night. A fairly good day with little icy snow and a little wind.

Thursday 21st January, 1943
Prisoner of War in Sudatenland near Bodisch. Party E388 on party working shovelling snow off railway line between Halbstadt and Ruppendorf. Finished early and home on 1615 train otherwise times as usual. Camps and little mail up. Soup midday and again 1800 hrs with potatoes, bread and margarine. A fairly good day.

Friday 22nd January, 1943
On railway working party as a POW in Sudatenland. On party working around Bodisch and Birkyht shovelling snow. Usual hours. Red X parcel issue for a fortnight and 25 cigarettes. Casson went shopping. Soup at midday with soup, potatoes, bread and margarine at night and a jam ration. A bit of wind otherwise mild day.

Saturday 23rd January, 1943
Prisoner of War Sudatenland. Did not go out today having day for working last Sunday. Parties working at Braunau and Bodisch. Did not go to showers because of a bad neck and shoulder. A little mail up again. Gave out canteen orders and a little reading. Soup midday, with soup, potatoes, bread, margarine and a little sausage meat at night. A mild day with a little sprinkling of rain in the afternoon.

Sunday 24th January, 1943
Prisoner of War at Bodisch. No work today, so reading and playing cards. Rations: soup midday with meat, gravy, potatoes, bread and margarine. Wrote to Virgilia. Parade 1430 hrs for boots and trousers inspection. Reasonable day.

Monday 25th January, 1943

Prisoner of War Bodisch Sudatenland. On party at Bodisch cleaning out drains and shovelling snow from railway line. Went to work but came back immediately because of pains in neck and left shoulder, others working at Olberg and Braunau. Soup midday with soup at night with potatoes, bread and margarine. News: Heard of the fall of Tripoli, and Rommells Army being hunted along coast road towards Tunisia. Berlin bombed heavily again. Russia still attacking all along the line and German 6th Army still surrounded and continuing to fight. Frost in morning followed by a fairly cold day.

Tuesday 26th January, 1943

Prisoner of War at Bodisch. Went to the Doctor this morning with bad neck and given five days off. Usual parties out at Bodisch, Olberg and Braunau. 16 parcels up but not given out. Soup midday, with potatoes, meat and gravy at night and, bread and margarine. Some potato salad costing 20 Phennig available through canteen. Reading and playing cards. Frosty morning, followed by cold day and some snow.

Wednesday 27th January, 1943

On working party as POW in Sudatenland. In barracks with bad neck. Usual parties out. Allan Burt (Kiwi) arrived today bringing strength up one. Yesterdays parcels given out: cigarettes received by Check, Davis SE, Dumurge, Ross, Pierce, Alty, Barker, Gilllon, Davies 2, Casson, Goodwin, Smith G, Myers and Buckley. Admission in Jerry papers that troops on Russian front have been there two winters and one summer, because not enough men to relieve them, as Russians have more material, but Jerries saying they are withdrawing to their schedule, that German 6th Army has put up a great fight, which will go down in history and that Tripoli was evacuated according to plans. Soup midday, with soup again at night, potatoes, bread and margarine and sugar ration. Fairly cold day with some snow.

Thursday 28th January, 1943

Prisoner of War stationed near Bodisch, Sudatenland. In camp with bad neck and shoulders. Usual snow shovelling parties at Olberg and Braunau and gang at Braunau unloading coal. Letter cards up to send to people who send personal parcels, telling them what not to send. News: Crete and Sicily bombed also cities of Florence and Turin, British subs sink 300,000 tons of enemy shipping, German planes visit England but beaten back by fighters, losing 18 planes. German 6th Army have fixed their last rounds, and now at the mercy of the Russians. Canadian troops land in Persia, Aden and Karachi. Russians still continue to meet with success. Soup at midday with meat, gravy, bread, margarine at night also jam ration. Doing up canteen books and playing cards. Fairly mild day thawing out a little.

Friday 29th January, 1943

Prisoner of War in Sudatenland on railway working party. Still in camp with bad neck and shoulders but improvement on yesterday. Work parties at Bodisch and Braunau. Reading and playing cards - Soup midday, with barley soup potatoes, bread, margarine at night. A fairly mild day. 12 months since arrived at Stalag V111B.

Saturday 30th January, 1943

Prisoner of War stationed at Bodisch. Still in camp with bad neck. Parties working Bodisch and Braunau. Some of the boys go to showers at 1445 hrs returning at 1600 hrs. Soup at midday with soup again at night potatoes, sausage meat and bread and margarine. Twenty parcels up today and received by personnel Casson, Templeman, Davis SE. Cigarettes or tobacco received by Park, Pedersen 2 (his first parcel) Clark C, Davis H, Galletly, Pritchard, Hogg, Heggie, Horsburgh, Lunam, Goodwin, Alty, Hunter, Blee, Casson, Check and Templeman. Cigarettes from Stalag 120 each. Reading and writing during day. A fairly mild day with some wind.

Sunday 31st January, 1943
Prisoner of War in Sudatenland. All quiet except for ten men to Halbstadt to unload coal, returning at 2130 hrs. Reading and writing out poems, also collected Stalag cigarette money. Wrote cards to Sigrid and Mavis. Soup with potatoes, meat, gravy, bread and margarine. A fairly mild day.

Monday 1st February, 1943
On railway working party near Bodisch Sudatenland. To doctor again this morning with bad neck, and get another five days off. If I have to go again it will be Stalag. Parties at Braunau and Bodisch. Those at Bodisch go to Halbstadt in afternoon to unload coal, and did not get home till 2045 hrs. Soup at midday and again at night potatoes, bread and margarine. A black frost this morning otherwise a fine day.

Tuesday 2nd February, 1943
On working party as a POW near Bodisch. In camp with bad neck, and copying out poetry. Those on coal yesterday did not go to work till 1300 hrs at Bodisch other gang at Braunau. Soup midday with the usual again at night. News: British 8th Army still advancing in Tunisia and within the central Southern sector. Russians still doing well and now have the 11th German Army surrounded. In one place Russians made 10 attempts to take it but failed, but eventually took it and many prisoners. De Gaulle and Giraud in Nth Africa not hitting it off too well. A fairly good day with sunshine.

Wednesday 3rd February, 1943
Prisoner of War in Sudatenland. On railway working party but did not go to work today because of bad neck and shoulders. Parties at Bodisch and Braunau. Copying out poetry and reading. Played cards in evening. Soup midday with soup at night on boys return to camp. Potatoes, bread and margarine and sugar ration. Head of Italian staff

resigns. Fairly nice day with sunshine not much snow about but a little commenced to fall at 1100 hrs.

Thursday 4th February, 1943
Prisoner of War on railway working party in Sudatenland. Still in camp with bad neck and shoulder. Only 2 men working Bodisch rest at Braunau. Reading and playing cards. Usual soup midday with potatoes, meat, gravy, bread and margarine at night. A fairly good day.

Friday 5th February, 1943
Prisoner of War near Bodisch in Sudatenland. Still in camp with bad neck and shoulders. Parties out as previous days. Going over canteen book and playing cards. 19 parcels up and received by personnel Heggie, books Stevenson and Park, cigarettes or tobacco by Luman 2, SB Clark, Hunter, Galletly, Balsarini, Pritchard, Barker, Kirkpatrick, Horsburgh, Armstrong, Alty, Dumursque, Myers, Check and myself, first cigarette parcel from Red X. Soup midday and again at night with potatoes, bread and margarine and jam ration. News fairly good – fairly good day with slight fall of snow.

Saturday 6th February, 1943
Prisoner of War stationed at Bodisch. To the doctor again this morning and ordered back to the Stalag. Only 15 men out today others having day off as the result of previous Sunday work, and some worked late last night. Playing cards and no luck, and some reading. A few English letters up but no Australian or Kiwi mail up. Soup midday with potatoes, sauerkraut in evening, bread and margarine. A fairly good day but snowed a bit.

Sunday 7th February, 1943
Prisoner of War on railway working party in Sudatenland. One party of 16 men out at 0700 hrs, 12 men on coal at 0900 hrs. These men returned at 1315 hrs and 12 more men went out at 1500 hrs. Under

Officer running around and seeing everybody had bag for coal. Reading and playing cards. Wrote to Aunty Em. No parades today. Soup, meat, gravy, potatoes, bread and margarine days ration. A fairly nice day.

Monday 8th February, 1943
Prisoner of War near Bodisch on working party E388. Still not at work because of bad neck. All men working at Braunau today. Reading. Not much of note today. Usual midday soup, with some again at night with potatoes, bread and margarine. Nice sunny day and cold night.

Tuesday 9th February, 1943
Prisoner of War Bodisch. Still at camp, waiting to go to Stalag on Doctors orders because of bad neck and shoulders. Gangs working at Braunau. No mail or parcels up. Soup midday with meat, gravy potatoes, bread and margarine for evening meal. Jock and I packed up gear and searched – ready to go to Stalag tomorrow. Gave the food parcel a hiding tonight. A fine day.

Wednesday 10th February, 1943
On railway working party Bodisch. Up at 0440 hrs breakfast and on train for Stalag 0515 hrs. A fairly cool morning. Passed through Mittelsteine at 0600 hrs. At Glatz at 0650 waited about half hour and then on to Kamez, waited here about ¾ hr, then proceeded to Neisse. After leaving Kamez followed alongside of ranges on the right and river on the left, passing through tunnel and coming into Frankenberg, country getting very flat from here on. Arrive Neisse at 0950 hrs waited in Red X room till 1320 hrs before proceeding. Had a nice bowl of soup here. Plenty of Jerry soldiers about and saw them on exercises from Neisse to Lamsdorf. Stalag V111B. Got off at station past Lamsdorf arriving Stalag about 1400 hrs and then searched again and into barrack F1. Saw Ernie Juon in evening and Fred Roberts.

Thursday 11th February, 1943
Prisoner of War in Stalag V111B at Lamsdorf, having come in from working party with bad neck and shoulders. Went through Delouser at 0800 hrs and then to the Doctor who said I have to have an Xray tomorrow. Cyril Harper came in this morning. Saw Bill Topia. Moved to barrack 25A after dinner. Issued with ½ Canadian parcel (Tuesday issue) and sixty five cigarettes. Collected bed boards at 1500 hrs. In afternoon saw Ernie Juon again also from Bn Mal King, Paddy Kempton, Jack Edwards, Frank Flood and Evans, also Curtis and Regan Brothers, old boys from Tymbakion on Crete. Chick Howes and one of the Tommies from the Tent of the ships Cat, also saw Johnny Warburton ex 2/11. Heard all sorts of tales about SM Burton. In evening out with Ernie and delivered a note to one of the boys. Everything going really well in here and able to move about compounds pretty freely, but some of them still getting chained up. Soup and potatoes at 1100 hrs bread and marg, honey with tea at 1630 hrs. A nice day.

Friday 12th February, 1943
Prisoner of War in Stalag V111B Lamsdorf with bad neck and shoulder. This morning saw Jimmy McGann, Snowy Whitehurst, Firpo and Don Golding from Bn, also Christian ex388 party and Rocky Branch who was going to hospital with spot on lung, and saw Jim Prentice 2/11 in afternoon. At 1400 hrs went to Lazarett for Xray and had to go through several formalities and with the result that it was 1730 hrs before I got back to Barrack. In the evening tried to see Vince Park and Sgt Lawrence but they were not in. Saw one of the medical orderlies from Tymbakion, his two mates in Poland looking after wounded Russians. Also, in evening a tale by a chap of the Royal Navy on his experiences, but he did not have time to finish them. Told us how Italy came in when we had our backs to the wall and had the Germany followed up after France fell. We could not have stopped them. Heard that most of the French fleet was in Oran and some in Dakar. The Hood,

Warsprite, Resolution and Valiant Oran Harbour about two miles and steamed up. French asked them not to fire, but eventually learnt that French sailors fled, dropped a couple in the town, and killed a good many, destroyer and cruiser attempt to escape but were blown out of the water. Italy declared they had the eastern Mediterranean closed up to our navy but they proved it different. On the trip up the Adriatic Sea to Trieste, Brindisi and Toranto, with Sydney and Australia with them. New ships came out and bring convoy through the narrows for Middle East, the Illustrious and Southhampton with them. Two Italian destroyers came out to tackle them, but turned tail, one escaped to Sicily and the other one blown up. On being recalled our destroyers on turning around hit a mine and had the front part blown off with the sailors who were having breakfast, the part floated but all sailors were killed. At ten in the morning reported that planes were on the way from Sicily to intercept the fleet, but the convoy for Middle East had gone on and got there safely. Ten planes dropped tin fish, but missed and then 400 dive bombers attacked and continued for four hours dived practically straight down. Punctures in fingers of Jerry airmen. Two o'clock in the afternoon Illustrious hit, well into the hangar, so had to flood the hangar to put out fire and about 80 men drowned. Illustrious called out of line and Jerry attacked it alone and caused another fire, so they put into Malta, but Jerry followed her up, and with the result of the bombing Maltese would not work on her, so had to take it to Alexandria. Same day Southhampton only 36 hours in the Mediteranean collected 5 bombs, attempted to tow it, but not worth trouble. So had to put four tin fish in her to sink it. Helping Wavell in the desert by shelling all the coastal towns. Next job after that the bombardment of Tripoli, The Mole, Town, ammo and petrol dump. First ones inland blew up Jewish church, sub leads them into harbor, finish job unmolested from shore guns, and submarines and planes return to Alex. Tea at 0630 hrs. M&V stew with potatoes 1130hrs. Issued with ¾ Canadian parcel. Fairly good day.

Saturday 13th February, 1943
Prisoner of War in Stalag V111B in convalescent barracks. Saw chap name of Preen from 2/7 Field Ambulance, also Singleton from Tymbakion Camp in Crete. In evening saw Kim and Sgt *(unreadible)* and he mentioned having heard that *(unreadible)* had sent money to England to send Wot boys cigarettes, and saw in news where Sgt Curtis 2/11 had got the MM and D McLeod and Les Morgan mentioned in dispatches. Heard news of Tick Whiteaker from the chap who was on the same party as him. Heard that Blackford had got the MM for escaping. Ernie was to have gone out on party today E165 but now goes on Monday. Clark from 2/7 knows Wally Pedersen also Moran from 2/7. Soup midday with tea 0600 hrs and 1400 hrs potatoes, also midday 5 to a loaf of bread with margarine white cheese and honey. A bit of hail and snow otherwise fairly good day.

Sunday 14th February, 1943
Prisoner of War in convalescent barracks Stalag V111B. Wrote cards to Doreen and Carmel. Looking up Bn chaps and saw Jim Kelly today, otherwise a quiet day. 80 English airmen arrived in today including some parachutists who landed and blew up ammunition and food dumps. 36 hours raid and first wave of 1000 bombers at 6000 feet. Bit of reading during evening. Very cold and windy day.

Monday 15th February, 1943
Stalag V111B convalescent barracks as a POW. Still waiting result of Xray taken on neck and shoulders, which are still not too good. Went on dental parade today to get false teeth fixed so now without any top teeth for a few days. Got a new overcoat, pair of trousers and changed pullover and puttys. Ernie Juon went out on working party today, and he received another cigarette parcel, 4th in about six weeks. Saw Don Cross this evening from the medical branch of our battalion and a chap from 2/7 Field Ambulance from Kellerberrin. New prisoner airman, reckon finish of war not so far away. Issued with 50 cigarettes

and won section tin of tobacco. Stew midday and potatoes and for tea, bread, paste, and honey.

Tuesday 16th February, 1943
Prisoner of War in convalescent barracks Stalag V111B Lamsdorf, waiting result of Xray, for bad neck and shoulder. Went around seeing anyone I know and saw Prestage and Sgt Lawrence for the first time since Crete. Issued with Canadian food parcel between 2. Some English mail in, but Australian and Kiwi lacking. Quite a few of the 2/7 Field Ambulance about. Bit of reading between times. Tea at 0730 hrs swede soup and potatoes 1100 hrs with soup bread at 1600 hrs and some meat paste. News seems to be more of a withdrawal along Russian front by Jerry. Fairly good day except for cold wind.

Wednesday 17th February, 1943
Prisoner of War in Stalag V111B Lamsdorf in convalesence barrack with bad neck, and shoulder. Did not get out too early today, having a quiet day and played whist in evening. Tea at at 0800 hrs soup at 1100 hrs with potatoes and at 1600 hrs bread, margarine, sausage meat and honey. Fine day but cold.

Thursday 18th February, 1943
Prisoner of War in Stalag convalesence barrack V111B. Not out too early. Some mail up today had one from Gladys and Lily Thorpe, Jean and Verna. Reading during afternoon, and to a concert in eveninmg and certainly a great show put on considering we are in a POW camp. Tea at 0800 hrs, potatoes and swede soup at 1100 hrs with bread, fish, cheese, marg and honey. A very nice day with sunshine

Friday 19th February, 1943
Prisoner of War in Stalag V111B convalescence barrack with bad neck and shoulder, and things very quiet. Did a bit of reading. Issued ½ Canadian food parcel each. Quite a few returned to Stalag today and

rumours of anothaer1700 coming in from Poland tomorrow. Rumour of Jerry evacuating Poland and Norway. Tea at 0800 hrs, soup and potatoes midday, soup, bread 1600 hrs. A perfect day, with some wind and cloudless moonlight night.

Saturday 20th February, 1943
Prisoner of War in convalescence barracks at Stalag V111B. Not much doing today, except plenty of rumours flying about. Saw SM Burton today looking a bit thin in the face. Went too musical concert, followed by lecture with the US marines in Nicaragua given by Pte G Ayres. Stud poker very popular card game and many cigarettes change hands in a few minutes. Received tin of bully beef taken from parcel. Les Barndon in camp but have not seen him yet. Change over in camp guard. Tea 0800 hrs with potatoes, soup midday and usual other evening meals rations. Very good day with perfect night.

Sunday 21st February, 1943
Prisoner of War at Stalag V111B Lamsdorf in convalescence barrack. Wrote card home and letter card to L Thorpe. Saw Leo Barndon today with Cyril Harper, visited several of the Bn boys. Watched a bit of soccer and rugby. Heard talk in evening by a New Zealander, about what it's like on an Australian station. Tea 0700 hrs, sauerkraut soup midday, with bread and bits & pieces. A beautiful day.

Monday 22nd February, 1943
Prisoner of War in convalescence barrack Stalag V111B, Lamsdorf. Not much doing today. Issued with 50 cigarettes. Did a bit of reading and playing whist in the evening. Tea at 0800 hrs. Soup and potatoes midday bread and margarine in evening. Frosty morning and perfect day.

Tuesday 23rd February, 1943
In convalescence barrack as a Prisoner of War Stalag V111B, Lamsdorf. Bulk issue today of tin of margarine, tin of jam, ½ pkt biscuits and

sugar. Received Australian Red X tobacco parcel 1 lb tobacco. Wrote home, Ethel, Joyce, and Gladys Thorpe. Had shower during afternoon, so will have some washing to do tomorrow. Reading to pass time away. Trucks busy bringing in food parcels. Frosty morning fine day.

Wednesday 24th February, 1943
Prisoner of War in Stalag V111B, Lamsdorf with bad neck and shoulder. Visited some of the boys today, otherwise reading. General visits the camp today. Tea at 0730 hrs M&V stew midday, with potatoes, sausage meat bread and margarine and honey evening meal. Foggy day and not too warm.

Thursday 25th February, 1943
Prisoner of War in convalesence barrack Stalag V111B. A quiet day. Received a letter from Verna. Some Aussies received mail of January. Said to be plenty of Aussie Personal parcel chits out tonight for tomorrow. Played whist in evening. A little reading, eyes a bit sore. Tea at 0730 hrs swede soup and potatoes midday, bread, margarine, cheese and chocolate. More sick in today. Cold foggy day.

Friday 26th February, 1943
Prisoner of War in Stalag V111B in convalesent barrack with bad neck and shoulders. Not much doing. Reading most of the time. Plenty of parcel chits about, one Canadian gets seven parcels of 2000 cigarettes each. Locked up early tonight. Speech on. Tea 0800 hrs M&V stew at midday with potatoes, porridge 1630 hrs and bread etc. Rumours today of repats going. Nice sunny day.

Saturday 27th February, 1943
In convalesent barrack as a POW Stalag V111B Lamsdorf. Issued with a tin of salmon each. Everything pretty quiet. Plenty of personal and cigarette parcels about, some of them playing two up with their cigarette chits, and as many as 2000 cigarettes in the ring at times, and

some of them even gambling their next cigarette and even food parcels to recoup their losses. Not much mail about today. Two rats killed in compound. Wrote cards to cousin Joyce and Jean H. Played whist in evening, and partner and I won 30 cigarettes each. Tea 0800 hrs swede soup and potatoes midday with bread & margarine 1630hrs. Reading most of the day, fine but cold wind.

Sunday 28th February, 1943
In convalesent barrack as a POW with a bad neck and shoulders at Stalag V111B Lamsdorf. Wandered around and saw some of the Bn boys today, and watched football match between RAF and AIF. Ground too small and rough. Tea 0800 hrs sauerkraut soup and potatoes midday, tea 1600 hrs and bread. Saw a bit of a concert during the evening. Fairly dull day with some wind blowing.

Monday 1st March, 1943
Prisoner of War in Stalag V111B Lamsdorf. Post Office busy today and issued out about 5000 cigarette parcels. Letter from Doreen and Verna. Passed day quietly today. Played whist in evening. Tea 0800 hrs. Soup, bread and usual eats. Dull cold day with cold wind blowing.

Tuesday 2nd March, 1943
Prisoner of War in Stalag V111B convalescent barrack with bad neck and shoulders. Visited Jerry Doctor in afternoon. Received eight letters today 3 from Verna, one Ethel, one Carmel, one Sigrid, one Jean and Mrs Forrest. Post Office getting ready for big parcel issue again next Monday. Received ½ English food parcel minus M&V. Usual daily rations. Usual daily rations. Dull cold and windy day.

Wednesday 3rd March, 1943
Prisoner of War in convalescent barrack at Stalag V111B. Received orders today to move to a working compound. Jock comes up from hospital today. Quite a bit mail about. Received letter from Verna

4th December. Met chap from Manjimup by name of Archie Tickley 2/7 Field Ambulance and knows lots of people I know. Mal King to go out on paper factory. Usual daily rations. Dull cold day with some snow.

Thursday 4th March, 1943
Prisoner of War Stalag V111B in working compound. Found out today that Don Golding and Jim Kelly knew my Uncle Dick when in Pemberton. Mal King goes out to work today, and pushing others out fast. Dave Anderson has letter from Ray Sandover and Hawley. Issued English parcel today. Heard in evening a talk from a chap from Royal Navy on the sinking of the Bismark. Tea 0730 hrs, swede soup at midday with usual bread etc at night. Cold morning and sunny afternoon.

Friday 5th March, 1943
Prisoner of War Stalag V111B in working barracks awaiting orders to return to work party E388. Not much doing watch soccer and rugby during afternoon. Received letters by air mail in two months date of stamping, one from Ethel and one from Sigrid. Quite a few go out on working parties. Got teeth back yesterday. Usual daily rations, cold morning otherwise reasonably fine day.

Saturday 6th March, 1943
Prisoner of War in working party barracks at Stalag V111B. Received letter from Allan today, dated September. Watched football in afternoon. Played whist in evening. Rumour landing of 600,000 troops in France. Tea 0630 hrs with swede soup midday, usual bread etc in evening. Miserable day with cold wind rain and some snow.

Sunday 7th March, 1943
Prisoner of War in Stalag V111B in working party compound. Wrote letter card to Gladys. Went to Aussie football match in afternoon. and saw Sgt Rees and Jim in evening. Not too good today, having bad

headache and cold. Tea 0730 hrs sauerkraut and potato soup midday with usual bread etc at night. A fine day.

Monday 8th March, 1943
Stalag V111B Lamsdorf as a POW still got a bad headache and cold today, so pretty quiet on the day. Laid out in the sun for a while in afternoon. Played whist in evening Proposition tonight of changing with RAF blokes. Photo taken today. Nearly sent out on wrong working party. Tea 0630 hrs pea soup and potatoes midday, with usual bread etc at night. Frosty morning but nice day.

Tuesday 9th March, 1943
In working party barrack in Stalag V111B Lamsdorf as a POW. Not feeling too good again today with bad headache and cold. Issued in bulk today on one tin of cheese, tin of salmon, pkt sultanas and six ounces of sugar. Nearly out on to another party again today. No news rumours. Plenty of local plane activity here, supposed to be a fair few day and night fighters here. Usual daily rations. Frosty morning but nice day.

Wednesday 10th March, 1943
At Lamsdorf in Stalag V111B as a POW in working party barracks. Suffered with bad earache all night, and not to good this morning. On sick parade and left ear badly inflamed. To get it cleared out tomorrow. To Stabstadt in afternoon. 200 NCO's get ready to leave here Friday. Jock Taylor and Cyril Harper on party. Big cigarette parcel day again. Did some washing in evening. Same daily rations. A beautiful sunny day.

Thursday 11th March, 1943
At Lamsdorf as a POW in Stalag V111B, went to Doctor this morning for treatment to ear, and in afternoon had to move back to convalescent barrack. Letter from Gladys. Some of the Stalag NCO's kicked out

of those going away, also straffe chaps, Jock Taylor being one. Played whist in evening but had terrible cards. Usual daily rations with some biscuits and jam. A very nice sunny day.

Friday 12th March, 1943
Prisoner of War in convalescent barrack Stalag V111B, Lamsdorf. Letter from Gladys. NCO's move out at 1300 hrs. Reading during the day. To Air Force Concert in evening, a very good show. ½ tin milk issued today. Found out that Archie Tickley knew Vic and Alf Fisher my cousins. Tea 0700 hrs M&V, potatoes midday with porridge, soup and bread at night. A lovely day.

Saturday 13th March, 1943
Prisoner of War in convalescent barrack at Stalag V111B in Lamsdorf. Issued with tin steak and kidney pie. Two chaps here from Stalag V111C for repat commission. RSM Brown of 2/11 in charge of the camp. Saw photo of Jimmy Linto, Cracker Bennett, and Bill Dawson. Watched football in afternoon, and visited some of the boys during the evening. Wrote cards to Verna and Mrs Forrest. Usual rations for the day. A nice fine day.

Sunday 14th March, 1943
Prisoner of War in Stalag V111B in convalescent barrack. Watched football in afternoon, and saw a chap by name of G Wiseman from 8 Mile Well who knew dad and several others that I know. Also Jim Kelly knew Vic and Alf Fisher. Lumby in from working party. Went to Military Band Concert in evening, and a great show. Tea 0800 hrs with potato and sauerkraut soup and potatoes midday and bread etc in evening. Fine day but cold.

Monday 15th March, 1943
Prisoner of War in convalescent barrack in Stalag V111B. Not much doing. Issued with 50 cigarettes. Received two letters and snap from

Lily Thorpe. About 30 to 40 airmen brought in today, shot down over Essen. NZ Sgt came to see me about changing with his nephew in the Air Force. Played whist in evening and won 2nd prize. Tea at 0800 hrs pea soup midday with potatoes and bread etc 1600 hrs. A very nice day.

Tuesday 16th March, 1943
Prisoner of War in convalescent barrack at Stalag V111B. Issued with ½ English parcel today. A quiet day. Stayed in during evening waiting for a visitor. Heard that a division of Aussies in England. Usual rations. A nice fine day.

Wednesday 17th March, 1943
Prisoner of War in Stalag V111B. Visited Doctor this morning about my ears. Went visiting a few of the boys during the day. Managed to get a book to read. Tea 0800 hrs M&V stew at midday, and potatoes, bread etc 1600 hrs. A perfect spring day.

Thursday 18th March, 1943
In Stalag convalescent barrack at Lamsdorf. Visited Doctor again. Read most of the day. Issued with ½ English parcel with the M&V taken out. The usual rations for the day. Sunny day but a cold wind.

Friday 19th March, 1943
Prisoner of War in Stalag convalescent barracks. Slept in till late this morning. Visited some of the boys and reading. Tea 0730 hrs. M&V stew and potatoes midday, semolina and raisin bread soup at night. Dull cloudy with cold wind blowing.

Saturday 20th March, 1943
In convalescent barrack at Stalag V111B as a POW. Fairly quiet day. Watched a good soccer match during afternoon. Talking to G Wiseman in evening. Very sore throat this morning. Tea at 0730 hrs,

swede soup and potatoes midday, with usual bread and dry rations at 1600 hrs. Fine sunny day.

Sunday 21st March, 1943
Prisoner of War in convalescent barrack at Stalag V111B, Lamsdorf. Wrote to Allen today, watched football in afternoon and to concert in 29B during evening by LM Makers. A very good show. Getting sick of the camp life and want to get out on working party again. Tea 0800 hrs, sauerkraut and potatoes soup midday, with usual bread and dry rations in the evening. Dull day with a fairly cold breeze.

Monday 22nd March, 1943
Prisoner of War in convalescent barracks Stalag V111B. Issued with 50 cigarettes, tin of milk, and 4 oz bacon. Reading most of the day and evening. Usual days rations. A fine day.

Tuesday 23rd March, 1943
In Stalag V111B convalescent barracks as a POW. Had letter from Gladys. Reading and visiting some of the boys. Issued with biscuits, ovaltine tablets and sugar. Tea 730 hrs potatoes, swede soup midday, bread and soup with usual dry rations at 1600 hrs. A nice sunny day.

Wednesday 24th March, 1943
In convalescent barrack Stalag at Lamsdorf. Getting properly bored in the camp with nothing to do. Did a bit of reading. Usual daily rations. Fine day.

Thursday 25th March, 1943
Prisoner of War in Stalag V111B, Lamsdorf in convalescent barrack. Went and saw Max Barr and Paddy Kempton. Also saw Frank Dyson of the Tymbakion camp days on Crete. No mail today as none in camp. Roll call outside this evening. Had to hand in three extra bed boards.

Still plenty of wild rumours about. An issue of cheese, margarine and salmon. Tea at 0730 hrs, soup, potatoes midday, tea bread and other rations at 1600 hrs. Fine day but very windy and dusty.

Friday 26th March, 1943
In Stalag V111B Lamsdorf as a POW in convalescent barracks. On Dr's parade this morning, and afternoon moved to working barracks. Reading most of the day. Some more RAF men arrive. Tea 0730 hrs. M&V stew at midday with potatoes, porridge, ¼ loaf bread and the usual dry rations. Cloudy and fairly sultry day.

Saturday 27th March, 1943
Prisoner of War in working barracks at Stalag VIIIB. Notified intention of returning to old working party E388 Bodisch, Sudatenland. Saw Bill Bee and latest news sheets. Bulk issue of tin meat roll, and ½ lb dates. Watched soccer matches in afternoon. Received two letters from home 9th and 17th November and also snaps. Tea at 0700 hrs, swede soup and potatoes midday with tea and dry rations at 1600 hrs. Dull and sultry with a few spots of rain.

Sunday 28th March, 1943
Prisoner of War in Stalag working barracks V111B, Lamsforf. Wrote card home and to Lil and Tom. Party of Aussies arrive from Bavaria, and saw the following 2/11 Bn boys, Griffiths, White, Ash, Sullivan, Sgt Nesbit, Bishop and Norm B Coy HQ, Mc Namara, Cant, Whiteaker, and a few others I did not know. All looking well on it. Tea at 0730 hrs soup and sauerkraut soup midday with potatoes, and tea and bread and dry rations 1600 hrs. A nice day and fairly warm.

Monday 29th March, 1943
In Stalag V111B in working party barracks as a POW. Joyce C's 22nd birthday. Went and saw the new arrivals again this afternoon. To RAF

show 'Out of the Blue' in evening and a very fine show. Issued with 50 cigs. Tea 0730 hrs, pea soup and potatoes midday, soup and dry rations 1600 hrs. Practically rained all day and everything very wet.

Tuesday 30th March, 1943
In working barracks as a POW in Stalag V111B Lamsdorf. 0800 hrs helped to unpack and puncture tins of food parcels for compound. Issued ½ English parcel each. Afternoon and evening visiting. Received four boatmail letters from Mrs Walker, Nurse H, Jean and Wave. Tea 0700 hrs swede soup and potatoes midday with bread, soup evening meal and bread and dry rations. A Jerry guard dies today. A very nice day after yesterdays rain.

Wednesday 31st March, 1943
Prisoner of War in working party barracks Lamsdorf. Florrie's birthday. Not much doing today. No books to read. Tea at 0730 hrs, M&V stew with potatoes midday with tea, bread and dry rations at 1600 hrs. Dull windy day with some rain.

Thursday 1st April, 1943
Prisoner of War in working party compound waiting to go out on working party. Afternoon went down for clothes ready for going out to party. Visiting some of the boys in the evening. Issued with ½ food parcel. The usual daily rations. A cold and windy day.

Friday 2nd April, 1943
Prisoner of War in working party compound at Stalag V111B. Waiting on orders to go out to working party, so hanging around barracks. Heard about 1600 hrs in the afternoon and moving out tomorrow, so moved into Barrack 25B. In evening went around and collected notes for the party. Tea at 0730 hrs M&V stew at midday, semolina porridge, ¼ loaf bread and jam at 1600 hrs. Wet cold windy day.

Saturday 3rd April, 1943

Prisoner of War at Stalag V111B in barrack 25B ready for moving out on party. Up at 0600 hrs moved down to be searched at 0700 hr. Left Stalag 0730 hrs, catching train at Annahoff 0810 hrs. Fairly easy search. Waited at Neisse about 1 ½ hours. Soup from Red X. Plenty of German Army activity here. Did not stay long at Kamez, ½ hour at Glatz, 1 hr Mittelsteine, arrived lager E388 Bodisch at 1600 hrs. Bad train smash in Halbstadt yards. One of the party attempts to escape. Cabbage and potatoes at night. A very nice day.

Sunday 4th April, 1943

Prisoner of War back on railway working party E388 Bodisch Sudatenland. Roll call at 0600 hrs. Went for photos to Weckelsdorf at 0930 hrs, returning at 1240hrs. Clothing parade 1430 hrs. Received Red X food parcel. Wrote letter card to Ethel. Whist drive in evening. Soup at 1300 hrs with mashed potatoes meat and gravy. Potatoes again at 1800 hrs 400 grammes of bread and margarine ration. Some of the boys playing football in the afternoon. A very nice day.

Monday 5th April, 1943

Prisoner of War on railway working party near Bodisch Sudatenland. On train gang party, first work for ten weeks, and still feel the strain on the neck. Loading and unloading metal. Crib 0930 hrs, swede soup midday, with soup again at 1800 hrs with, potatoes, 1/5 loaf of bread. Two new guards here to take place of two going away. Reading and writing during evening. Cold morning but lovely day.

Tuesday 6th April, 1943

Prisoner of War stationed at Bodisch on railway working party. On gang working at Arbeit Zug, between Heinzendorf and Olberg. Fairly easy day. Times same as yesterday. Mail up. Swede soup midday, potatoes and gravy at night with bread and margarine. Fine day.

Wednesday 7th April, 1943.
Prisoner of War stationed at Bodisch. Same job as yesterday, same times and rations. Cold windy day with some rain and snow.

Thursday 8th April, 1943
On railway working party as a POW in Sudatenland. On train gang loading and unloading earth between Olberg and Heinzendorf, with the same working times. Eight parcels up and received by Kirkpatrick, cigarettes by Pritchard, Lunam, Armstrong, Park, Petersen RA, Casson and Check. Swede soup midday with meat, gravy, potatoes, bread and margarine ration at 1800 hrs. Fairly cold day with snow practically all day.

Friday 9th April, 1943
Prisoner of War near Bodisch, Sudatenland. Sam Blee returns to Stalag today with heart trouble. Same job as yesterday and same times. Issued with 50 cigarettes and Red X food parcel in evening. Usual soup midday with potatoes, meat, gravy 1800 hrs bread and margarine. Changeable day with wind, snow and sunshine.

Saturday 10th April, 1943
Prisoner of War stationed near Bodisch on railway working party in Sudatenland. Stayed in today with cold and sore throat. Boys have showers today some home at 1600 hrs others 1715 hrs. Soup midday, with cabbage, potatoes, bread, margarine at 1800 hrs. A dull day.

Sunday 11th April, 1943
Prisoner of War Bodisch, Sudatenland. On party unloading sleepers and metal, and another in afternoon for unloading coal. Played soccer in afternoon. Wrote cards to Joyce and Wave. Parcels up. Personal parcels to Heggie, Pierce, Goodwin and cigarettes to Kirkpatrick, Lunam, Casson, Pritchard, Horsburgh, Pascoe, G Smith, Phipps, Alty, Ross and

myself, third parcel of 200 and book parcel received by Myers. Played monopoly in the evening. Usual rations. A dull day with a little rain.

Monday 12th April, 1943
On railway working party as a POW in Sudatenland. On Arbeit Zug, loaded and unloaded 112 concrete posts, also cinders and some earth. Fairly easy day. Had to unload coal in evening and not in camp till 1900 hrs. Swede soup midday with soup and potatoes on return to camp usual bread and margarine. A dull day.

Tuesday 13th April, 1943
Prisoner of War in Sudatenland. On Arbeit Zug, unloaded cinders, also loaded and unloaded earth. Usual working times. Got into a row at station at Halbstadt, and again on getting to Bodisch, on getting out on wrong side as train started off, before all boys were out. Swede soup midday, with barley soup and potatoes and bread ration at night. Frost in morning but a lovely day.

Wednesday 14th April, 1943
On railway working party as a POW. in Sudatenland. On Arbeit Zug, between Heinzendorf and Olberg loading and unloading earth with the usual working hours, and the usual daily rations. A beautiful day.

Thursday 15th April, 1943
Prisoner of War near Bodisch on railway working party. On Arbeit Zug gang loading and unloading earth, also some metal and cinders usual work times. Swede soup midday, with meat gravy potatoes bread and margarine and a sugar ration at 1800 hrs. Plenty of aerial activity. Dull morning but turned out a beautiful day.

Friday 16th April, 1943
Stationed near Bodisch on railway working party as a POW. On Arbeit Zug, loading and unloading metal and earth with the usual hours.

Mail and camp newsletter up. Received two from Verna, one Joyce, one Betty, Sigrid, Home, Gladys and Lily. Issued with 50 cigs and Red X parcel. Swede soup midday, with potatoes, meat, gravy, bread and margarine and a jam ration at night. A very warm and nice sunny day.

Saturday 17th April, 1943
Prisoner of War near Bodisch. On party of five today at *(unreadable)* loaded 360 sleepers. Finished work at 1215 hrs but did not go back then, as had showers on way back, getting to camp 1520 hrs. Soup midday, with cabbage, potatoes at night, with usual bread and margarine and some sausage meat. Local farmers busy. News good. A dull but warm day.

Sunday 18th April, 1943
Prisoner of War at Bodisch. No work today, parade today and clothing cards re-checked. Wrote to Sigrid and Gladys. Two soccer games in the afternoon one and four section, four winners: two and three section 3 winners. Some of the boys visit Birkight party in evening, the party breaking up, and we were making arrangements to take over their wireless and food boxes. Soup with mashed potatoes, meat and gravy, and potatoes again at night, with bread and margarine. A fine warm day.

Monday 19th April, 1943
On railway working party as a POW near Bodisch. On Arbeit Zug loading and unloading earth with the usual work hours. Plenty of friendly waves from the local population. Usual daily rations. News fairly good. A warm sunny day.

Tuesday 20th April, 1943
Prisoner of War near Bodisch, Sudatenland. Adolf's 54th birthday. Flags flying from practically every building, house and all stations. Loading and unloading earth between Olberg and Heinzendorf, also

unloaded cinders with usual work times. Boys went down to Birkight in evening and brought back 50 boxes for putting food in. News item: Biggest aerial battle of war over Sicily and seventy-eight troop carriers shot down. Swede soup midday, with potatoes, meat, gravy, spinach, bread and margarine at 1800 hrs. Hot sultry day with rain during afternoon.

Wednesday 21st April, 1943
Prisoner of War near Bodisch on railway working party. On Arbeit Zug, unloading metal, with usual times. Previous Under Officer returns today. Casson gets wireless up today from Birkight. Harry D gets his number taken for not working, fully expected to get mine taken. Parcels up and received by Pritchard 3, Baldwin 3, Kirkpatrick 2, Alty 2, Kerr 2, Templeman, Davies, Galletly, Goodwin, Check, Dalziel, Gillon, Phipps, Gracie, Heggie, Hampton, Clark, Pascoe, and Casson. Usual daily rations. Frosty morning but beautiful day.

Thursday 22nd April, 1943
On railway working party as a POW Sudatenland. On Arbeit Zug unloading metal, cinders and earth with the usual times and the usual daily rations. Dull and cloudy but warm.

Friday 23rd April, 1943
Good Friday. Prisoner of War in Sudatenland. On working party on Arbeit Zug, loading and unloading earth and usual times. Issued with 50 cigarettes and Red X food parcel. Mail and camp paper up and received four myself: Two from Alison, one from Sigrid, and one from Verna. Swede soup midday with barley soup, potatoes, bread, margarine and jam ration at night. Cool morning but a hot day.

Saturday 24th April, 1943
Easter Saturday. Prisoner of War stationed at Bodisch, Sudatenland. Only 28 out today, being on Arbeit Zug, unloading metal, and cinders

being ½ day and getting to camp 1315 hrs, returning to Halbstadt at 1500 hrs for showers and back again at 1615 hrs. Mail and parcels up, received letter from Betty and Verna, also cigarette parcel from Red X, and cigarettes received by Davis S, Davis H, Davies, Clark C, Pedersen, Goodwin, Barker, Armstrong, Dalziel, Pritchard 2, Gracie, Templeman and Hunter. Have wireless installed by extension from guards room. Soup midday with potatoes with a little lettuce, sausage meat usual bread and margarine in the evening. Fine morning, coming out very warm, which culminated in a thunderstorm at 1800 hrs and some heavy rain and hailstones fell.

Sunday 25th April, 1943
Easter Sunday and Anzac Day. Prisoner of War near Bodisch in Sudatenland. Parade in morning at 1100 hrs. Afternoon two soccer matches 3 section v 4, and 1 section v 2. Wrote cards to Betty and Alison. Rations soup potatoes mashed with meat and gravy, and potatoes at night with bread and margarine in the evening. Dull cold and windy day.

Monday 26th April, 1943
Easter Monday. Prisoner of War near Bodisch in Sudatenland. No work today so in bed reading. Later in day played table tennis. Heard today that hostilities ceased in Tunis and Nth Africa Saturday 24th April. Barley soup midday with potatoes with other rations at night. Cold windy day.

Tuesday 27th April, 1943
On railway working party near Bodisch as a POW. On Arbeit Zug, loading and unloading earth and shovelling over side of bank. Some unload coal. Usual times and usual rations. Cold windy day and some rain.

Wednesday 28th April, 1943
Prisoner of War Sudatenland. On party on Arbeit Zug, loading earth and shovelling over side. The chow gets a bit annoyed with some of us

for not working. Usual times and rations. Cold windy day. Interspersed with sunshine and heavy showers of rain. Got a stiff neck again.

Thursday 29th April, 1943
Prisoner of War working on railway working party near Bodisch. On Arbeit Zug, loading and unloading earth also cinders. Usual hours, and midday soup with potatoes, meat, gravy, bread etc at night. Cold windy day.

Friday 30th April, 1943
Prisoner of War near Bodisch on railway working party. No Arbeit Zug today, shovelling earth back from line, and also metal, after metal train had been along. A fairly easy day. Swede soup midday with barley soup, potatoes at night, bread, margarine and jam ration. Red X food parcels up for about nine weeks and also camp paper and some mail, but received none myself. Issued with food parcel and 50 cigarettes. Dull cloudy day with showers of rain.

Saturday, 1st May, 1943
Prisoner of War near Bodisch Sudatenland. 'May Day'. No work today. In morning two games of soccer played, 3 section playing 1 and 4 section playing 2 section, first mentioned winning. A good many cigarettes being bet on the latter game, over a thousand changing hands. Afternoon to showers, but had to walk home because of no train. Had four French girls following us up. Enjoyable walk through woods spare time reading. Potatoes, spinach, sausage meat, bread and margarines as rations. Nice sunny day.

Sunday, 2nd May, 1943
Prisoner of War near Bodisch Sudatenland. No work today. Did some washing in the morning, and no clothing parades today. Wrote letter card home and card to Bernice. Reading and playing monopoly.

Mashed potatoes, meat and gravy midday with potatoes at night with usual bread and margarine. Fine sunny day but cold breeze.

Monday, 3rd May, 1943
Prisoner of War on railway working party in Sudatenland. On party to Heinzedorf until 0930 hrs, then on to Braunau doing odd jobs getting ready for laying points at Braunau tomorrow. Usual work times. Casson and Ron also out today. Parcels up and personal parcels received by G & F Smith, books Thorpe, cigarettes by Davis, Barker, Pedersen, Hampton. Buckley, Pierce and Hunter. Ron gets word tonight going back to Stalag. Played monopoly in evening. Swede soup midday with soup again 1800 hrs, potatoes, bread and margarine. Frost in morning with sunshine later. New guard arrives and pretty dopey looking, and not to good at speaking Jerry language, and first night on duty prowls around the barrack nearly all night.

Tuesday, 4th May, 1943
Prisoner of War near Bodisch Sudatenland. All of party at Braunau today, working with civvies in laying down railway points. Worked till 1800 hrs today. Inspector on job also. Casson also out. Swede soup midday with potatoes, meat, gravy, some spinach, bread and margarine at night. Frosty morning coming out fine with a few clouds.

Wednesday, 5th May, 1943
Prisoner of War railway working party Bodisch. On Arbeit Zug today, unloaded four trucks of cinders also put on and unloaded some sand blocks and wedges for boys digging out tomorrow. Then went to Braunau and picked up their tools, where they were working and dumped them at Heinzendorf. Fertig 1630 hrs. New person out to take Rons place. A little mail up but none myself. New Under Officer takes over today. I take over Canteen books again. Frosty morning turning out to be a beautiful day. Days stretching out again not dark until nearly 2100 hrs.

Thursday, 6th May, 1943
Prisoner of War at Bodisch Sudatenland. Today on party of eight stumping sleepers at Olberg, also party on Arbeit Zug, and some digging out. One of the new guards out and not a bad sort, another and him chased fish in the creek. Liar in a pretty good humour. Fertig 1600 hrs Swede soup midday, with potatoes, meat gravy, bread and margarine at night. Quite a few Russian women working around here. Fine sunny day with some clouds and a little sultry.

Friday, 7th May, 1943
On railway working party in Sudatenland as a POW. On Arbeit Zug today, loading and unloading earth and also unloaded two trucks of cinders, and the rest of the boys digging out except for two or three at camp doing odd jobs painting and fixing up fence. Usual times. Jock arrived back today. Issued with 50 cigarettes and Red X food parcel. Two new guards had scrap today and surprised at the stuff we get in parcels. Swede soup midday with potatoes, barley soup, bread and margarine 1800 hrs. Fine morning turning sultry and breaking out with hail and rain at 1500 hrs clearing the air and making it cooler.

Saturday, 8th May, 1943
Prisoner of War on railway working at Bodisch. Got off at Halbstadt to go on Arbeit Zug, but had to finish up walking Heinzendorf, and just started there, when Zug arrived, so then went loading and unloading earth. Fertig 1445 hrs. In Halbstadt 1500 hrs, then had showers and returned to camp at 1600 hrs. Everybody in good humour tonight as they heard that Tunis has definitely fallen and Russians doing well. 25 ships sunk off Tunis, and some Japanese ships sunk off New Guinea. Ten men returned to Halbstadt at 1630 hrs to unload two trucks of coal returning 1900 hrs. Usual rations for the day. At present got a bad rash on my face and feeling very sore and itchy. Cloudy but fairly warm.

Sunday, 9th May, 1943

Prisoner of War at Bodisch Sudatenland. At 0900 hrs all called out to go to Halbstadt and unload 13 trucks of metal at Heinzendorf. Finished 1220 hrs and back in camp at 1315 hrs. Afternoon played soccer and drew, watched 7 a side game between NZ and England, scores 4 – 5 as teams mentioned. Wrote letter card to Lil and Nurse H and card to Poppy. In evening played some table tennis. Twenty parcels up and received Pritchard, cigarettes by Balsarini, Smith F, Check, Kerry. Ross, Alty, Parks, Phipps, Templeman, Dalziel, Heggie, Horsburgh, Hunter and 200 myself. Myers 2 and Myers books. Heard Italian police force doubled to quieten down population who are restless. Potatoes, meat and gravy 1300 hrs, potatoes usual bread and margarine 1800 hrs. A very nice day with a few clouds in afternoon.

Monday, 10th May, 1943

Prisoner of War on railway working party at Bodisch in Sudatenland. On gang at Heinzendorf, digging out. One gang at Halbstadt planting sleepers and Arbeit Zug at Mittlesteine. Tom and I go very slow and Liar calls us swindlers for leaving some earth under sleepers; others have to help us to finish to get home with other boys. Arbeit Zug not home till 1900 hrs. News: Now 100,000 prisoners taken in Tunis including four Generals and mopping up operations continue. Churchill in America. Heavy bombing of Corsica, Sardinia, Sicily and Southern Italy. Reckon that the death knell is ringing for Italy. Swede soup midday with soup again at 1800 hrs with bread, margarine also sugar ration. A dull morning with rain clouds about midday, but eventually cleared up and fine sunny day.

Tuesday, 11th May, 1943

Prisoner of War stationed at Bodisch Sudatenland. On party at Heinzendorf spreading metal and stomping sleepers. One party at Halbstadt, and Arbeit Zug at Mittlesteine. Polsih girl near where we are working and very friendly. Usual work times. Swede soup midday with potatoes, meat and gravy at night with bread and margarine. Dull morning followed by fairly fine day.

Wednesday, 12th May, 1943
Prisoner of War on railwy working party Bodisch Sudatenland. On Arbeit Zug working between Olberg and Heinzendorf picking up rubbish on side of railway line. Rest of party except on duties in camp, digging out at Heinzedorf. Usual times and the usual rations. Still isolated fighting in Nth Africa, and 48 ships sunk in trying to evacuate troops from Tunis and enormous quantity of material seized. Corsica and Sicily getting well raided. Dull morning but turned-out perfect day.

Thursday, 13th May, 1943
Prisoner of War stationed at Bodisch Sudatenland, on railway working party. Mum's birthday. Started digging out at Heinzendorf, then had to go and unload five trucks of metal. Afternoon dig out between eight sleepers, but had to get help to get them on time. One gang also planting sleepers at Halbstadt. Camp newspaper and eight letters up. Swede soup midday with potatoes, meat and gravy at night with bread and margarine ration. Played monoply in evening. News Items: Desert prisoners now total 150,000. Bombing continues in Mediteranean and Russians doing well. A fine morning and nice day overall.

Friday, 14th May, 1943
Prisoner of War near Bodisch, Sudatenland. Started digging out at Heinzendorf, and then six trucks of metal had to be unloaded and then returned to the digging out. Arbeit Zug and gang at Halbstadt plating sleepers. Old Liar not in too good a mood wanting to get sleepers dug out, so as to get rail laying done. Usual work hours. Busy at night with canteen orders as Casson going shopping early tomorrow. Usual day and evening rations. News Items: Prisoners in desert now

total 163,000 with seventeen generals with 15 of them supposed to be German, and majority of prisoners being German. A very warm day, most of us working without shirts.

Saturday, 15th May, 1943
Prisoner of War on working party near Bodisch. All home today as the result of working last Sunday except for ten men who went to unload metal in the morning returning at 1300 hrs. At 1430 hrs another 25 men called out to unload more metal, and did not get back to Lager till 2045 hrs, getting Monday free for the days work including myself. Nineteen parcels up, and received a permit parcel from Virgilian Corner from Boans, quite a surprise and included pack of cards, bridge scoring pad, housey-housey and a book, also received parcel of nine books from Albert and Son on behalf of Sigrid. Did not get a list of other parcels. Casson went shopping this morning but did not have time to give articles out. No time for showers today. Soup midday, with potatoes, sausage meat and usual bread and margarine at night. Another very nice hot day.

Sunday, 16th May, 1943
Prisoner of War at Bodisch. Dad's birthday. Out with a party of 15 this morning to finish unloading yesterday afternoons trucks of metal, finishing at 1130 hrs having showers and returning to camp by 1315 hrs. Next Saturday off for this. Wrote cards to Merle and Mrs Walker. Gave out canteen goods in afternoon. Reading and playing monoploy. Mashed potatoes, meat, gravy at midday, with potatoes, bread and margarine at night. Day started dull, then came out fine, but finished up showers of rain 1730 hrs.

Monday, 17th May, 1943
On railway working party in Sudatenland as a POW. Everybody home today for Saturdays extra work. Laid in bed reading all the morning. New Under Officer arrives, also Sgt Major of guards Coy here. A few

letters up but missed again, the fourth time now. In afternoon doing up the canteen book, and playing housey-housey. Face feeling very sore as result of sores on it. Not enough vitamins. Soup midday with potatoes, bread, margarine at night. A fairly sunny day with cold wind blowing.

Tuesday, 18th May, 1943
Prisoner of War near Bodisch on working party E388. Gang at Halbstadt plating sleepers, some digging out and the Arbeit Zug. Started digging earth away from sides, and five of us had to go on the Arbeit Zug, to unload seven trucks of metal. While train in station, guard got lousy, because some of us were a bit slow starting work when we were told. Told when finished unloading metal would be firearm. Finished at 1500 hrs and went back to Liar's gang and he said we had to finish digging out sides but we said 'no' and both him and the guard got annoyed, especially with me as I refused to shift, but eventually did in case everybody was kept till 1800 hrs. Train gang also called in to help to dig some out and then another argument, but they did not dig out all they were given and finished at 1800 hrs and in camp 1915 hrs. Soup midday with potatoes meat, gravy, bread and margarine at night. News: Prisoners in desert 175,000; 1500 tanks and 1000 guns. Fine day but cold wind blowing.

Wednesday, 19th May, 1943
On railway working party near Bodisch as a POW. Went to Doctor today with sores in ear and had the day off. Boys working at Heinzendorf and Arbeit Zug. Another row on the job today about the Arbeit Zug gang working on contract. Buckley goes out to it, and had to get the Doctor to the barracks and also Greasy 'The Engineer'. Camp papers up and about a dozen letters, received three myself, one from Eileen, Mrs Walker and Gladys. Pay night. Swede soup midday, same again at night, with potatoes usual bread and margarine and sugar ration. Fine morning, but turning out dull later with cold wind.

Thursday, 20th May, 1943

Prisoner of War at Bodisch, Sudatenland. On Arbeit Zug today unloading metal and spreading cinders. Lang some (slow) Arbeit Zug today. Rest of the boys laying rails at Heinzendorf. Casson also out today. Home by the early train. Swede soup midday, with potatoes, meat, gravy at night, usual bread and margarine. Beautiful day with cold breeze frost in morning.

Friday, 21st May, 1943

On railway working party as a POW. Working on Arbeit Zug one gang laying rails at Heinzendorf. Unloaded some sleepers, also loaded some metal and sleepers at Braunau for points at Olberg. Home by early train. Issued with 50 cigarettes and Red X food parcel. Usual daily rations. Fine day with fairly cold breeze and blowing.

Saturday, 22nd May, 1943

Prisoner of War Bodisch. In camp today, having time off for last Sundays work, as a result of winning cut. Some of the boys home 1215 hrs and others at 1400 hrs. No showers today as boiler broken down. Reading, playing monopoly and doing canteen book. Heard tonight that some of the boys going back to Stalag. Talk in evening over wireless by Jerry who has been in the desert 27 months. About some time more parcels were up. Swede soup midday, potatoes, sausage meat, bread and marg at night. Fine day with cool breeze. Sunset 2030 hrs.

Sunday, 23rd May, 1943

Prisoner of War Bodisch Sudatenland. In camp today, except eleven other men and myself to unload coal at 0900 hrs returning at 1215 hrs by special train, as train services cut down on Sunday. Afternoon played cricket for about three hours. Barrel of beer in. Collected cigarette money. Letter card to Pearce's. Not allowed to take book to work. Potatoes, meat, gravy midday with potatoes, bread and margarine at night. Fairly fine day.

Monday, 24th May, 1943

Prisoners of War in Sudatenland. On gang at Heinzendorf laying rails and nine on Arbeit Zug. Fairly easy day. Home by early train. Twenty one parcels and received by Underhill, cigarettes, by Pedersen, Balsarini, Gillon, Clark, Ross, Galletly, Casson, Kirkpatrick 2, Balsarini, Gillon, Davis H, Hampton, Gracie, Ellwood, Check, Lunam, Xmas, Petersen RH, book parcel received by Thorpe and myself. Two books from Mrs L. Thorpe, England. Swede soup midday, with swede soup at night and potatoes, bread and marg. Dull day but came out warm in afternoon.

Tuesday, 25th May, 1943

Prisoner of War railway party in Sudatenland, on gang at Heinzedorf laying rails, nine men on Arbeit Zug. Rained all day so finished work early and allowed to come home on 1445 hr train. Rain did the crops a lot of good which was badly needed. Midday soup with potatoes, meat, gravy, bread and margarine at night. A wet day with everybody getting clothes wet.

Wednesday, 26th May, 1943

Prisoner of War at Bodisch. On gang at Heinzendorf, nine men on Arbeit Zug. Home on usual train. A few letters up but received one myself, also camp newsletter. Heard that Russia is going to turn Democracy. Big raid on Dortmund, and many thousands killed. Swede soup midday with soup again at night potatoes, bread and margarine. Dull cloudy day with heavy shower of rain at 1530 hrs.

Thursday 27th May, 1943

On railway working party as a POW in Sudatenland. On gang at Heinzendorf laying rails and nine men on Arbeit Zug. Home by early train. Not much doing, everything going fairly smoothly. Latest: British raid on Dusseldorf. Tables all done up with flowers, looked rather nice. New Under Officer arrives and new guard arrived this evening, as old Under Officer and one guard leave us. The tall Polish chap came up and said 'goodbye' before leaving. Swede soup midday with potatoes, meat, gravy, bread and marg at night. Fairly dull day with attempts to rain.

Friday 28th May, 1943
Prisoner of War in Sudatenland on railway working party. On gang at Heinzendorf and usual Arbeit Zug gang. Home early train with usual daily midday and evening rations. Reading. Czeck people seem very pleased about something tonight. Dull cloudy day.

Saturday 29th May, 1943
Prisoner of War Bodisch. Did not go out today, having the morning off for previous Sundays work. Some of the boys home at 1210 hrs and the others at 1400 hrs. Shower house still out of order so no showers again today. In bed most of the day and reading. Macaroni soup midday, with potatoes, sausage meat, bread and margarine. Essen again raided. A dull day.

Sunday 30th May, 1943
Prisoner of War Bodisch. No Sunday work, so made good use of the bed again and did a little reading. Wrote cards to Eileen and Sigrid. Mashed potatoes at midday with meat, gravy aand boiled potatoes at night with bread and margarine. Cold dull day with showers of rain.

Monday 31st May, 1943
On railway working party as a POW in Sudatenland. On Arbeit Zug today 11 men, rest on digging out. Went down Mittlesteine way, loading rails, plates and screws. Very nice down this way now, trees looking lovely and green, some nice barley crops down here too. Going by the waving of the people not many Germans working on the farms, but people from the occupied countries also unloaded truck of cinders at Braunau. Home early train. Usual midday and evening rations. Cold morning with a few clouds, but later turning out a beautiful day.

Tuesday 1st June, 1943
Prisoner of War near Bodisch. On Arbeit Zug down at Mittlesteine loading rails, plates and screws, others working at Heinzendorf. Fairly heavy days work and home by early train. Swede soup midday with potatoes, meat gravy, bread and margarine at night. Ross goes into Stalag for operation. Casson also goes into Stalag on business. A fine day turning out very warm about 1400 hrs. Quite a few fish poached from the stream nearby, one man getting nine. Two years being a prisoner of war most of them here.

Wednesday 2nd June, 1943
Prisoner of War Bodisch. On Arbeit Zug at Mittlesteine picking up rails etc, also laid a couple of rails at Ottendorf. Others at Heinzendorf. Charlie Clark gets thumb taken off while loading rails, and being cold the time did not realise that it had happened. Home by early train. Casson returns from Stalag 2100 hrs. Some of the crops lying down with the rain. 20 parcels up but did not get list received. 200 cigarettes from Red X myself. Usual daily rations. Raining on going to work, but fine about 1000 hrs and afternoon a nice day.

Thursday 3rd June, 1943
Prisoner of War near Bodisch Sudatenland. On job at Heinzendorf today, heating up crib and dinner, also shifted a few stones and did a bit of weeding along the line and nine men on Arbeit Zug. Home by early train. Boys catch a few more fish. Midday swede soup with potatoes, meat, gravy at night and bread and margarine. News Item: Russians doing well, and French coast again raided. Dull morning with some sunshine midday, then few isolated showers setting in steady rain 1600 hrs.

Friday 4th June, 1943
Prisoner of War on railway working party in Sudatenland. At barracks unloading truck of wood and carted it to the Lager and sawed it up a

little. Gang at Heinzendorf and nine men on Arbeit Zug. A little mail and camp newsletter, received letters from Ethel, Mavis, Verna and Lily. Swede soup midday with potatoes, meat, gravy, bread and margarine at night. Wet morning but came out fine in afternoon.

Saturday 5th June, 1943
Prisoner of War stationed at Bodisch. On party Heinzendorf doing odd jobs, nine men on Arbeit Zug. Half day and finished work about 1125 hrs, in Lager until 1215. Halbstadt showers still out of action, so had bath in camp. Pay day. Playing monopoly and reading. Boiled potatoes with sausage meat, usual bread and margarine. News Item: Rumour: American troops in Turkey and German troops in Spain. Dull morning turned out fairly good.

Sunday 6th June, 1943
Prisoners of War stationed at Bodisch, Sudatenland. Two years a prisoner of war today. Wrote letter cards home and to Gladys, enclosed photo in each. 5 men to Halbstadt for unloading coal, and home in special carriage at 1300 hrs. Playing monopoly, reading and doing canteen work. Large and small barrel of beer. Played cricket for about 2 ½ hours in afternoon. Plenty of friendly women about the scrub near the camp and guards keeping a watchful eye on us. Midday mash potatoes, meat and gravy with mixed preserved vegetable salad, potatoes, bread, margarine at night. A very nice day.

Monday 7th June, 1943
Prisoner of War stationed at Bodisch. On job at Heinzendorf laying rails, nine men on Arbeit Zug and two in camp sawing wood. Building over bridge today and behind in work all day, but finished in time. Home by early train. Swede soup midday, soup at night with potatoes, bread and usual margarine. Rain about 0830, dull till 1630 hrs then a little sunshine.

Tuesday 8th June, 1943
Prisoner of War stationed near Bodisch, Sudatenland. On same job as yesterday and nine men on Arbeit Zug, ready to come home on early train, but guard discovered one of the boys had escaped so had to wait till Casson and Under-Officer came out, so home on late train. Oberfield-Wabel arrives about 2130 hrs, and asks when did the man disappear. Swede soup midday, with potato, meat and gravy at night with bread and margarine. Took Tunics and overcoats away and searched gear before bed at midnight. Dull day with spots of rain.

Wednesday 9th June, 1943
Prisoner of War on railway working party in Sudtenland. On job at Heinzendorf laying rails, and nine men on Arbeit Zug, usual times and home by early train. The Bull arrives on job, and goes off the handle because we did not stand up. A little mail and camp newsletter up, but none myself. Swede soup midday with soup, potatoes, bread and margarine at night. A warm morning with a little rain after midday, setting in with heavy rain at 1600 hrs.

Thursday 10th June, 1943
Prisoner of War stationed at Bodisch. On Arbeit Zug today and gang laying rails at Heinzendorf. Went down past Tuntchendorf and picked up some stones, and unloaded them also sand and cement and also unloaded some cinders. Had fairly easy morning. Afternoon loaded and unloaded some metal. Talking to a lad of about 14 who came from Dortmund in the Rhineland which had been bombed. Vince Park recaptured today and two Air Force blokes who had been out for five days. These two went onto Trautenau and Vince stayed night here. Received card from Stalag regarding mail. Swede soup midday with potatoes, meat, gravy with usual bread and margarine, and also sugar ration. Dull and sunshine but fairly warm.

Friday 11th June, 1943

Prisoner of War in Sudtenland. On Arbeit Zug today and gang laying rails at Heinzendorf, unloaded a little cinders, and seven trucks of metal. Settled in with heavy rain 1400 hrs, and finished work 1500 hrs and back in camp on the 1610 hrs train. Vince goes to Trautenau. Received 50 English cigarettes and English food parcel. Swede soup midday with barley soup, potatoes, bread, margarine and jam ration at night. Fine hot morning, setting in with rain 1400 hrs for rest of afternoon.

Saturday 12th June, 1943

Allan's sixth birthday today. On Arbeit Zug and others doing odd jobs at Heinzendorf, also six plating rails at Halbstadt. Finished 1230 hrs and home 1350. Had bath and did little washing in afternoon. New Under Officer arrives in afternoon. Parcels late this week. Barley soup midday, with potatoes, meat, gravy, bread and margarine at night. Heard that two Italian Islands had been bombed into submission. Dull and occasional sun, but fairly warm.

Sunday 13th June, 1943

Prisoner of War Bodisch. Not out of bed too early today. Writing out list of letters when written and received. Wrote card to Joyce and one to Stalag to Australian Red X concerning mail. Played cricket during afternoon. Barrel of beer up. Had a sing song from 2100 hrs to 2215 hrs. Potatoes mashed, meat and gravy midday with potatoes, mixed vegetable salad, bread and margarine. Not too bright in the morning, but turned out fairly good afternoon.

Monday 14th June, 1943

Near Bodisch, Sudtenland as a Prisoner of War. Holiday today being Whit Monday. Did some washing, mending and a little writing. Played cricket in the afternoon. Small barrel of beer. Barley soup midday, with potatoes, lettuce, bread and margarine at night. Fairly good day, dull again at 1900 hrs.

Tuesday 15th June, 1943
Prisoner of War stationed at Bodisch. On Arbeit Zug today, one gang at Heinzendorf laying rails. Loaded some sleepers at Halbstadt in morning, and unloaded them in afternoon, also picked up truck of metal from Braunau and unloaded, also loaded some cinders and unloaded some earth. Home by early train. Two guards out today. Six parcels up and received by 2 book parcels Myers, cigarettes: Casson, Pritchard, Davis SE and Balsarini. Reading and Writing in evening. Usual daily rations. Dull and cold morning, but came out warm sunny afternoon.

Wednesday 16th June, 1943
Prisoner of War stationed at Bodisch. On Arbeit Zug and gang laying rails at Heinzendorf. Unloading and spreading cinders between Olberg and Braunau in morning. Afternoon picked up some metal and unloaded where laying rails. Home by early train. Vince Park arrives back this evening. Reading during evening. Swede soup midday, with soup again, at night potatoes, usual bread and margarine. Cold, dull morning coming out finer during afternoon and warmer.

Thursday 17th June, 1943
Prisoner of War in Sudtenland on railway working party. On Arbeit Zug and gang at Heinzendorf laying rails. Unloaded five trucks of metal in morning and loaded some earth and metal in afternoon. Vince Park ordered out to work in afternoon, but did practically nothing. Home by early train. Swede soup midday, with potatoes, meat gravy, with bread and margarine at night. Rained till about 1100 hrs in morning and thunderstorm in afternoon for about an hour.

Friday 18th June, 1943
Prisoner of War Bodisch. On party at Olberg digging out at points, and nine men on Arbeit Zug. Fairly long throw with the earth, but Arbeit Zug pulled in, making things a lot easier. Came home on 1600 hrs train. Camp and six letters up, but missed again. Parks & Charlie Clark to go back to Stalag. Swede soup midday with barley soup, potatoes, bread and margarine at night. Fifty cigarettes and Red X parcel issued. Items of interest: Churchill in Tunis. Two British Admirals in Turkey. Fine and fairly warm.

Saturday 19th June, 1943
Prisoner of War stationed at Bodisch. On digging out at Olberg, seven sleepers between four men, ½ days work, getting back to Lager at 1210 hrs. Arbeit Zug at 1350 hrs. Cigarettes and 340 Red X food parcels up. Bath in afternoon, and a little washing, also doing canteen book. Fine morning, dull in afternoon with a little rain at 1800 hrs.

Sunday 20th June, 1943
Prisoner of War on railway working party near Bodisch, Sudatenland. Gave the bed a good time during the morning as it was wet outside. Afternoon wrote cards to home, Verna and Aunty Em. Played Crib in evening. Barrel of beer up, and lost a bit through the top busting. Rations of mashed potatoes, meat and gravy midday, with potatoes at night and usual bread and margarine. Wet morning, but cleared up a little in the afternoon.

Monday 21st June, 1943
Prisoner of War stationed at Bodisch. Digging out at Heinzendorf, all finished about 1430 hrs so returned to Stalag by 1610 train, and Arbeit Zug of nine men returned at usual time. Three men to return to Stalag tomorrow. Five personal parcels up and received by Thorpe, Stevenson, Gracie, Myers, Armstrong. Plenty of chocolate in the New

Zealanders parcels. Played crib during evening. Swede soup midday, with potatoes, macaroni soup, also lettuce, mixed vegetable salad, bread, margarine at night. Very foggy morning and then coming out fine and very warm.

Tuesday 22nd June, 1943
Prisoner of War Bodisch. On Arbeit Zug today loading and unloading earth and metal, also moved digging out gang tools from Olberg to Heinzendorf. Digging out gang home early and Arbeit Zug usual time. Park, Kerr and Clark SB return to Stalag V111B today. Played crib in evening. Midday swede soup at night potatoes, meat, gravy, bread and margarine. Few clouds about but warm day.

Wednesday 23rd June, 1943
Prisoner of War Bodisch, Sudatenland on railway working party. At Heinzendorf digging out and nine men on Arbeit Zug. Home by early train, but Arbeit Zug gang home before us. Few fish caught. Five personal parcels up and received by Gillon, Barber, Petersen RA, Underhill and Clark SB returned to Stalag. Played crib in evening. Usual daily rations. Very hot sultry day, hottest for some time, turned cool again 1500 hrs, but warm again at night.

Thursday 24th June, 1943
Prisoner of War Bodisch. On job at Heinzendorf digging out metal from sleepers, sifting out, and putting it back again. Nine men on Arbeit Zug. Home by early train. Zug gang usual time. A little explanation regarding digging out gang, going home early, is by giving us a contract job of so many sleepers, and when finished if train available we go back to camp, otherwise we use 'go slow' tactics and they get more done this way by contract. Had a trout given to me today, and so had a nice fish meal. Soup at midday, potatoes, meat, gravy, bread and margarine and some lettuce at night. Dull and warm with some rain between 0930 and 1000 hrs.

Friday 25th June, 1943
On railway working party as a POW in Sudatenland. At Heinzendorf digging out metal from between sleepers, nine men on Arbeit Zug, and six men at Ruppersdorf, plating sleepers. Home on early train, and two other gangs as usual. Mail and camp paper up, received letter from Gladys. Issued with 50 cigarettes and Red X food parcel, all got a Scottish one tonight. Usual rations for the day, with little jam as extra. Fairly cool day, with fair amount of wind.

Saturday 26th June, 1943
Prisoner of War Bodisch. At Heinzendorf stomping sleepers. Did not start till 0930 hrs because of rain. Some on Arbeit Zug and some unloading coal. Home at 1400 hrs. Some go to showers. Casson goes shopping. Gave out canteen goods in afternoon. Barrel of beer up at night and at time of writing 2230 hrs Casson playing piano and having a sing song. Also played crib during evening. Potatoes and lettuce midday, with potatoes, sausage meat, bread and margarine at night. Rained till about 0930 hrs then cleared up a little but more rain in afternoon, thereby being a dull miserable day.

Sunday 27th June, 1943
Prisoner of War Bodisch. In barracks today except for five men to unload truck of coal at Halbstadt. Fairly quiet day playing crib, monopoly, reading and doing canteen book. Barrel of beer up. Mashed potatoes, meat, gravy midday, with boiled potatoes at night, bread and margarine. Came out a fine morning, but later in day got dull and cold with a little rain.

Monday 28th June, 1943
On railway working party as a POW in Sudatenland. At Heinzendorf on digging out gang, one gang at Halbstadt and Arbeit Zug. Finished in time for early train, and train gang later. Wrote letter card and sent

photo to Lil. Stalag cigarettes up. Reading and played crib in evening. Usual daily rations. A fairly fine day.

Tuesday 29th June, 1943
Prisoner of War at Bodisch. Digging out at Heinzendorf gang also plating at Ruppersdorf and the Arbeit Zug. Home on 1610 hr train, Arbeit Zug usual time. Five parcels up and received by Kerr, Pierce, Check, Dalziel and Balsarini. Cigarettes: Pritchard. Reading and playing crib in evening. Soup midday, potatoes, meat, gravy, bread and margarine at night. Mention of raid on Cologne, and historic places destroyed. Dull day with a few showers of rain.

Wednesday 30th June, 1943
Prisoner of War Sudatenland. On gang digging out at Heinzendorf, gang also at Ruppersdorf and Arbeit Zug gang. Home early train, others later. Four personal parcels in and received by Alty, Galletly, Davis H and Templeman. Played cards in evening. Soup midday, with barley soup, potatoes, usual bread and margarine at night. A dull day raining early and continued showers throughout the day.

Thursday 1st July, 1943
On railway working party in Sudatenland as a POW. On digging out gang Heinzendorf, gang at Ruppersdorf, and Arbeit Zug gang. Early time, and Arbeit Zug gang later. Reading and playing crib. Pay night. Fairly tame day. Cut in the rations. Soup midday, with potatoes, meat gravy, bread and margarine at night. Dull wet morning till 1000 hrs then cleared up a bit for the rest of the day.

Friday 2nd July, 1943
Prisoner of War stationed at Bodisch at Heinzendorf, putting in new sleepers at bridge over local creek, and home by early train, Arbeit Zug gang out and home their usual time. Issue 50 cigarettes and food parcel. Reading playing cards and doing canteen book. Mail late this

week. Midday soup, with soup at night, potatoes, bread, margarine a jam and sugar ration. Dull morning but fine later.

Saturday 3rd July, 1943
Prisoner of War Bodisch on railway working party. Six men home from last Sundays work, gang at Heinzendorf laying out rails and sleepers, ready for laying on Monday, and Arbeit Zug. In camp at 1210 being half day. Returned to Halbstadt 1445 hrs for showers, back to Lager 1600 hrs. Playing crib, reading and doing canteen book. Two barrels of beer up, and boys having a sing song around the piano at time of writing 2230 hrs. No mail again today, potatoes midday with potatoes, sausage meat, bread and margarine evening meal. A fairly fine day getting dull in evening.

Sunday 4th July, 1943
Prisoner of War Bodisch Sudatenland. No work today, so slept in late and three hours sleep in the afternoon. Reading, playing crib, doing canteen book and taking in cigarette money. Wrote card home, Carmel and Mrs Forrest. Mashed potatoes, meat, gravy midday with potatoes and other rations at night. Fine morning later dull and cold.

Monday 5th July, 1943
Prisoner of War Bodisch. At Heinzendorf rail laying, five men on Arbeit Zug, all home at 1740 hrs. No mail up now for ten days. Heard five more men coming to party tomorrow. According to German news we are losing a good many planes in raids over Germany and the Mediternean. Russians still attacking. Quiet evening. Midday soup with potatoes, soup, usual bread and margarine at night. A fairly dull day.

Tuesday 6th July, 1943
Prisoner of War stationed at Bodisch. At Heinzendorf laying rails, and seven men on Arbeit Zug. Finished in time for 1620 train and Arbeit

Zug later. Parcels up and received by Hunter, Davies, Xmas, cigarettes: Barker 2, Xmas, Balsarini, Pritchard, Kirkpatrick, Goodwin, Gracie, Davis SE, Galletly and myself. Also had an issue all round of 12 cigarettes by the Turkish Red X. Played some very exciting games of crib this evening. Soup at midday and at night potatoes, meat, gravy with usual bread etc. A dull morning with a little sprinkling of rain, later clearing up and being very warm.

Wednesday 7th July, 1943
Prisoner of War on railway working party at Bodisch. On rail laying job at Heinzendorf, and six men on Arbeit Zug. Home early train. Mail up, none from home for eleven weeks now, but received one from Gladys, Lil and Tom. Camp newsletter also up. Played crib in evening. Midday soup and at night potatoes, barley soup, bread, marg and a jam and sugar ration. Fairly dull day with shower of rain.

Thursday 8th July, 1943
Prisoner of War stationed at Bodisch. On rail laying gang at Heinzendorf and seven men on Arbeit Zug. Back on early train. Nothing much of note today. Played some more exciting games of crib during evening. Usual daily rations. Dull cool day with some rain in evening.

Friday 9th July, 1943
Prisoner of War near Bodisch Sudatenland. On rail laying job at Heinzendorf. Seven men on Arbeit Zug. Work times same as usual and Arbeit Zug later. Phipps goes to Weckelsdorf party and one from Weckelsdorf comes here. Issued with Red X food parcel and fifty cigarettes. Played crib in evening. Barley and flour soup midday and at night potatoes, barley soup, bread and margarine. Dull cold day.

Saturday 10th July, 1943
Prisoner of War Bodisch at Heinzendorf doing odd jobs, shifted boody. Half day and home 1210 hrs. Gang Arbeit Zug in at 1400 hrs.

To Halbstadt for showers at 1500 and returning at 1600 hrs. Played cards in evening two barrels of beer up. Midday cabbage and potatoes, with potatoes, bread and margarine evening ration. Fine morning but came out dull later and some rain.

Sunday 11th July, 1943
On railway working party as a POW in Sudatenland. No work today. Up early to get breakfast and back to bed till 1230 hrs. Everybody gave the beds a fair bashing today. Doing up canteen book in afternoon. Wrote to Virgilia, and enclosed photo. Heard over German wireless tonight that British and American troops had landed in Sicily by parachutes and boat, and fairly heavy fighting going on. Potatoes, meat, gravy midday with potatoes, cabbage, bread and margarine at night. Fairly dull day.

Monday 12th July, 1943
Prisoner of War Bodisch. At Heinzendorf on rail laying gang, and four men on Arbeit Zug. Back in camp at usual time. Mail and camp paper up. Received four letters, one from home. Verna and Nurse H, first from home for three months. Reading during evening. Battle still going on in Sicily. Cabbage and flour soup midday, with barley soup, potatoes, bread and margarine evening meal. Dull in morning with some rain, but very warm. Warm and came out fine in afternoon.

Tuesday 13th July, 1943
Prisoner of War Bodisch Sudatenland. On job at Heinzendorf laying rails and three men on Arbeit Zug unloading metal. Home by early train, but had to do a bit of running to catch it, but driver slowed down for us. Finished reading 'The Purple Robe' this evening a very good book by Joseph Hocking. Meat and potato soup midday with potatoes, cabbage, bread and margarine at night. Dull cloudy day, with showers of rain throughout the day.

Wednesday 14th July, 1943

Prisoner of War Bodisch. On job at Heinzendorf laying rails, and six on Arbeit Zug. Home early. Arbeit Zug have civvy police on in charge and rather annoyed about it. Cigarette parcels up and received by Pritchard 4, Horsburgh 2, Hogg 2, Check, Ballsarini, Ellwood, Casson, Lunam, Smith G, Armstrong, Pierce, Gillon, Davis H, Davies SE, and Templeman. Reprints of Photographs in, but have to go to Stalag first for stamping. Reading evening. Meal soup midday, with barley soup potatoes, bread and marg, sugar and jam ration at night. Day of dullness & sunshine with cool breeze.

Thursday 15th July, 1943

Prisoner of War stationed at Bodisch. On job at Heinzendorf and home by early train. Had civvies flat foot with us today. Arbeit Zug four men and usual times. Mail and camp paper up, but received none myself. Meat, soup midday, with potatoes, meat, gravy at night with usual bread and margarine. Dull morning, but later came out a hot day.

Friday 16th July, 1943

Prisoner of War stationed at Bodisch. Rail laying at Heinzendorf. Probably finished laying here, as may be going Trautenau line next week. Home early train, and Arbeit Zug as usual. Issued with 50 cigarettes and Red X food parcel. German news very quiet concerning Sicily and Russian Front. Flour soup midday, with barley soup at night, potatoes, bread and margarine. A very hot day throughout, hottest day for about two months.

Saturday 17th July, 1943

Prisoner of War stationed Bodisch, Sudatenland. At Heinzendorf, packing up boody and tools ready for working at Trautenau next week. Home by 1210 hrs. Return to Halbstadt 1500, back in camp at 1615 hrs. Under Officer away and heard the news from London in German.

Good to hear the lion roaring and National Anthem. News different complexion to Jerries. Barrel beer and everyone enjoying themselves around the piano. Potatoes, cabbage midday, and potatoes, beetroot at night, bread and margarine. Rye crops beginning to ripen up a bit now. A fairly warm day.

Sunday 18th July, 1943
At Bodisch as a prisoner of War. No work today. Up at 0700 hrs for breakfast, and back to bed till 1220 hrs. Played cricket in afternoon result of challenge match section 4 against the rest. The rest winning and won 60 cigarettes. Barrel of beer in afternoon. Wrote cards home, Ethel, Doreen, and Allan H. Pay day. Midday meal of potatoes, meat, gravy with potatoes, cabbage, bread and margarine. Italian Press says biggest display of might ever shown in Mediteranean as a result of the landing in Sicily. Russians doing well. Bit dull in morning, otherwise a good day.

Monday 19th July, 1943
Prisoner of War on railway working party in Sudatenland. Today went out to Trautenau way as far as Petersdorf to lay rails. It being done in three sections of two lengths at a time and iron sleepers being screwed to rails by a bolt. Left camp at 0550 hrs and on the job about 0730 hrs. Freestig (morning Tea) 0925. Mitag Essen (midday meal) at 1150 hrs and finishing at 1540 hrs leaving the job by special engine and carriage for camp at 1550, getting back at 1720 hrs. A very nice run out this way now, different to October when there is all snow. The trees being nice and green, now with many shady spots to walk in. On return saw many people in the two swimming pools about here, also talking to some of the boys at Adersbach Felsen, and saw Major Hiddelsteine at the party at Weckelsdorf. Crops do not seem to look as well out this way as they are our usual area. Cabbage, potato, meal soup midday with barley soup and potatoes, with bread and marg at night. News doing well in Sicily. A fairly warm July day.

Tuesday 20th July, 1943
War Bodisch. On job as yesterday but only laid four lengths of rails, owing to metal train working there. Same meal times and back to camp same time. No mail or parcels up. Potato, cabbage meal soup midday and at night potatoes, meat, gravy, bread, margarine. Dull morning but came out fairly warm 1100 hrs, but dull again 1500 hrs and shower of rain.

Wednesday 21st July, 1943
Prisoner of War Bodisch. On job at Petersdorf laying rails, but behind with the work today, but finished up same time and same times as Monday. Old Berker station master below our camp, reports on Casson and Chris Hampton down in barracks when women there, and reckon cooks mix too much with gefangers, so getting two new cooks. Bill Kerr returned this evening. Potatoes, cabbage meal soup midday, barley soup, potatoes, bread and marg with a sugar and jam ration at night. Fairly warm day.

Thursday 22nd July, 1943
Prisoner of War Bodisch, Sudatenland. Same jobs and times as yesterday, but home hour later, because carriage midday train derailed and held us up, till back on the line again. 22 parcels up and received by Smith G, cigarettes: Pierce, Pedersen, Gracie, Davies, Check, Dalziel 2, Myers, Hampton, Armstrong, Underhill, Galletly, Heggie 2, Hunter, Templeman, Pritchard, Goodwin, Casson 2, and myself. Some of the NZ parcels from Australian Red X. A quiet evening. Not any news of importance. Fairly warm day.

Friday 23rd July, 1943
On party at Bodisch as a Prisoner of War. On job at Petersdorf laying rails. Bit of an argument today, about the extra stopping on the run down from the finish of the rail laying. Usual times etc. Mail and camp paper in received letter from home. Stalag cigarettes up. Back in 19

days, photos return from Stalag. Issue of Scottish food parcel and 50 cigarettes. Cabbage, potato meal soup at midday, barley soup potatoes, bread and margarine evening meal. Another warm day.

Saturday 24th July, 1943
Prisoner of War in Sudatenland. On job at Petersdorf shifting rails, doing odd jobs, ready for next week. Left from work by Arbeit Zug about 1200, getting in Lager at 1315 hrs. To showers 1500 hrs and returned to camp 1620 hrs, Barrel of beer in evening. Bit of a stink because we do not line up in threes when ordered by Four-eyes., Potato, cabbage midday, with potatoes, bread, and margarine at night. News about Sicily very remote over German wireless. Very warm day.

Sunday 25th July, 1943
Prisoner of War Bodisch Sudatenland. Up early cooked and had breakfast, and back to bed till 1245 hrs, being a bit tired as the result of getting up early all the week. Played cricket in afternoon, and had a very enjoyable game. Wrote letter card to Merle. Potatoes, meat, gravy, midday with bread and margarine at night. German news mentions Hamburg having had terrrible raid and heaviest raid of the war, it still being dark eight o'clock in the morning as the result of the smoke from the fires. Today was the most beautiful day I have seen in this country from sunrise to sunset.

Monday 26th July, 1943
Prisoner of War stationed near Bodisch. On the job at Petersdorf laying rails, and usual time for work there. Plenty of sweating done today. Doing canteen book up in evening. Soup midday, with barley soup, potatoes, bread and margarine at night. News over German wireless: Fighting still going on in Scicily. Mussolini resigns, and Marshall Bagdolio takes over. King in charge of all forces, as the war goes on. Heavy fighting still on the Russian Front. Heavy raids over Kiel, Essen

and Hamburg by our planes last night. A pretty hot day with some heavy clouds about.

Tuesday 27th July, 1943
On railway working party as a POW in Sudatenland. Date of deceased brothers birthday (Bill). At Petersdorf rail laying with usual work and meal times. Nothing of note today. Played crib in evening. Midday soup, potatoes, meat, gravy, bread and margarine in evening. Heavy thunderstorm for half an hour at 1500 hrs and saw one birch tree that had been struck by lightning.

Wednesday 28th July, 1943
Prisoner of War Bodisch, Sudatenland. On job at Petersdorf laying rails, only laid four lengths today, shifting a couple of rails in the first shift, with the usual times. Three new arrivals this evening. Played crib in evening. Not much news. Cabbage soup midday, with cabbage soup, potatoes, bread and margarine at night. Heard ship sunk with 2000 children. A dull day but fairly warm.

Thursday 29th July, 1943
Prisoner of War Bodisch. On job at Petersdorf and Qualisch laying rails, with the usual times. Everything went very smoothly today and had time to spare after laying of rails. Played crib in evening. Time some mail and parcels were up again. Cabbage soup midday, with meat, gravy, potatoes, and cabbage, bread and marg at night. Nothing of note in the news. A few clouds, but fairly hot day.

Friday 30th July, 1943
Prisoner of War near Bodisch, today working at Weckelsdorf and between Matha-Mohren, taking up and laying new rails. Laid eighteen lengths. First time down this way. Fairly easy day. Started at 0615 hrs, and back in Lager at 1500 hrs. Had a feed of wild strawberries and raspberries, picked by side of the railway line. Had a beer this afternoon,

and very good after the days work. No mail parcels up yet this week. Another new guard today. Issued with fifty cigarettes and Red X food parcel this evening. Cabbage midday and at night potatoes, cabbage soup, with usual bread and margarine. Very warm day.

Saturday 31st July, 1943
Prisoner of War on railway working party in Sudatenland. Today went down to Matha-Mohren by train, then walked about a mile to take up eleven rails and replace with new ones. Valley widens out down here. Right on the Zceck border, the last rail being laid party in Germany and Zceckoslavia. Finished this job at 0815 hrs and waiting on the Arbeit Zug, to load the old rails but did not turn up, so had early morning. Flat Foot shouted some beer. Back in camp at 1215 hrs. To showers at 1500 hrs returning again 1615 hrs. Train schedule later tonight 1900 hr train not through till 2015 hrs. Barrel of beer up tonight. Potatoes, cabbage midday, with potatoes again at night, bread and margarine. Fairly warm day.

Sunday 1st August, 1943
Prisoner of War Bodisch. In camp today and not too well with a crook stomach. Some of the boys played cicket in afternoon. Wrote cards to Gladys and Lil. Barrell of beer for afternoon. New potatoes, meat aand gravy midday, with potato, bread and margarine at night. Heard that 50,000 people had been killed in raids on Hamburg, also that a good many Jerries on the Eastern Front were shooting themselves. Very hot and fine day.

Monday 2nd August, 1943
Prisoner of War stationed at Bodisch. Did not go to work today because of crook stomach. No guards to go to the Doctor. Party at Petersdorf and joined later by eight men who were loading rails between Weckelsdorf and Zceck-German border. Home usual time. Mail up and received one from Mum, one from Florrie & one from Carmel.

Camps also up. German news Russians still attacking. 125 four engine planes over Rumania bombing oil wells. Mussolini in Spain and Italians being recalled from Germany. Naples bombed. Cabbage midday, with mixed soup at night, potatoes, bread and margarine also this weeks and last weeks sugar and jam ration. Went through canteen accounts. A very hot and fine day.

Tuesday 3rd August, 1943
Prisoner of War Bodisch. Went to the Doctor today with bad stomach and stiff back. Party working at Qualisch and Arbeit Zug. Back at usual times. Nothing much of note. Cabbage midday with potatoes, soup, bread and margarine at night. A very hot day.

Wednesday 4th August, 1943
Prisoner of War on railway work in Sudatenland. In camp today with bad hip. Party working at Qualisch and Arbeit Zug with the usual hours. Reading and doing odd jobs. Tonight went to Weckelsdorf to see a variety of picture show, showing scenes of the Saar Valley, and people going about their work. Swimming and diving exhibitions, Trapeze work, Rodeo Thrills and a cartoon sketch, brought out from Stalag. Also got some mail delivered to us, received one from Jean. Came out from show at 2210 hrs, some marched home and eight of us waited for the train. A severe electrical storm at 2330 hrs with heavy rain. Cabbage midday with the usual potatoes, meat, gravy, bread and margarine at night. A hot day with bad heat at night.

Thursday 5th August, 1943
Prisoner of War Bodisch. In camp again today. Severe electrical storm 0230 hrs. Slept fairly well this morning after last night late night. Easy day. Party at Qualisch and Arbeit Zug. Usual work hours. Cabbage midday with potatoes, and mixed soup at night, bread and margarine, also beetroot and white cheese issue. German News: Orel evacuated

by their troops to a more favourable position. Still fighting in Sicily. A dull day but quite a change after the heat we have just had.

Friday 6th August, 1943
Prisoner of War in Sudatenland. Two new aarrivals to party at 0010 hrs. Out to work today at Qualisch. Laid two lengths of rails and engine of passing train derailed and causing hold up of rail laying for the day, so laying out sleepers and shifting rails. It was a little after midday before the engine was back on the rails. Caused delay in the schedule of trains, and did not get back from work till 1815 hrs. Issued with fifty cigarettes and Red X food parcel. Parcels up and received by Barker, Hunter, Horsburgh and Check and 2 book parcels by Check, cigarettes: Kerry, Hunter, Pritchard, Xmas, Alty, Gillespie, Hampton, Casson, Davis S 2, Petersen RA, Myers, Davis H 2, Balsarini and Underhill 3. Soup midday, and potatoes soup at night with bread and margarine ration. German news: still in our favour. Dull day with few spots of rain.

Saturday 7th August, 1943
On railway working party in Sudatenland as a POW. To Qualisch and laid three lengths of rails. One truck of metal train derailed, making late in getting back to camp, about 1415 hrs instead of midday, as half days work. More personal parcels up and received by Armstrong, Hampton, Smith G and Heggie. Cigarettes Smith G, Pritchard, Hall and Casson. Did not go to showers today because of late arrival back from work. Barrel of beer up in evening. Cabbage and potatoes midday, with sausage meat, bread and margarine at night. Dull day with some rain in afternoon.

Sunday 8th August, 1943
Prisoner of War Bodisch. No work today. Plenty of rest in the bed in the morning. Afternoon played cricket, and wrote letter card home

and to Florrie. Nothing outstanding to note. Meat, gravy, potato midday with the evening meal potatoes, bread and margarine. A dull day with some rain in evening.

Monday 9th August, 1943
Prisoner of War stationed at Bodisch. On party going as far as Parschnitz, a bit further than have been before along this line. Did not start before ten, and loaded twenty eight rails for the day, only doing about two hours work for the day. The flat foot refuse to allow us to talk to the Jews at Addersbach Felsen. Everything still going fairly well. Cabbage at midday, with potatoes, meat, gravy at night with the usual ration of bread & marg. A dull day with odd shower in morning, coming down fairly heavy about 1500 hr and again pretty heavy 2000 hrs.

Tuesday 10th August, 1943
Prisoner of War on railway working party in Sudatenland. On job at Qualisch rail laying with usual times and back to camp usual hour, and gang on Arbeit Zug. A few letters and Camp up today but nothing myself. Bulk issue of sugar and cocoa from Stalag, box broken open on train, two lots of sugar and all the cocoa taken, evidently by the civilians. Usual rations for the day. A fairly decent day.

Wednesday 11th August, 1943
Prisoner of War in Sudatenland. On job at Qualisch laying rails with usual times, also gang Arbeit Zug. Not much done this afternoon, laid in a field of peas and had a feed. Farmers now busy cutting their crops, pulling flax, and ploughing ground for next years crop, some still cutting grass hay. Seems to be a community affair with the gathering of each others crops. Two recent arrivals to return to Stalag tomorrow, only have been here a week. Reading during the evening. Soup midday, with new potatoes, meat, gravy, usual bread and margarine with jam ration at night. Sugar held over. A fairly reasonable day, after a

cool morning. Thunderstorm at 1100 hrs and thunderstorm in distance in evening.

Thursday 12th August, 1943
Prisoner of War Bodisch, Sudatenland on railway working party E388. At Qualisch digging out to depth of sleepers sifting metal and putting it back. 14 sleepers to two men, majority finished early. Bill Kerr and a mate did a bit of a swindling but were found out. Home usual time. A little mail up today received a letter from Verna. Soup midday, potatoes and barley soup, bread and margarine at night. German news: very tame. Dull morning, later coming out fine but fairly cold.

Friday 13th August, 1943
Prisoner of War at Bodisch railway party. On the job at Qualisch, digging out, Leir not out today, finished fairly early and home usual time. Civvies also digging out near the station. Issue of 50 cigarettes and Red X food parcels in evening. Four personal parcels up and received by Gillon, Kirkpatrick, Kerr and Templeman. Cabbage soup midday with barley soup, potatoes, bread and margarine at night. Cold morning followed by a dull day, not much sunshine.

Saturday14th August 1943
Prisoner of War Sudatenland on railway party. On job at Qualisch digging out. Finished at 0830 hrs latedt 0900 hrs, and then started to rain, retired to boody till 1200 and back in camp 1325 hrs. To showers at 1500 hrs returning 1610 hrs to camp. Arbeit Zug gang worked till 1700 hrs, thereby getting next Saturday off. Camps and a few letters up, but received none. Cabbage and potatoes midday, with potatoes, sausage meat, bread and margarine at night. Dull morning starting to rain 0900 hrs and occasional showers throughout the day.

Sunday 15th August, 1943

Prisoner of War Bodisch. On party of eight out at 0700 hrs to unload coal, and another fourteen at 0900 hrs and returning at 1205 hrs, and thereby getting next Saturday off. Reading, wrote cards to Sigrid and Mrs Walker. Barrel of beer in the evening. Passing trains by the camp plenty of thumbs up and waving by Zcecks. Breakfast this morning from food parcel, porridge, bacon, egg powder and tomatoes. Potatoes, meat, gravy midday with potatoes usual bread and margarine at night. Jerry claims to have badly damaged a convoy off Gibraltar, sinking 170,000 tons of shipping. Rained till about 1000 hrs then occasional showers till 1300 hrs when it fined up, turning out cool evening.

Monday 16th August, 1943

Railway party Bodisch as a POW. At Qualisch digging out, and nearly kept till six o'clock because Goodwin did not finish his job, a Kiwi and the biggest man on the party. Finished work before midday and home usual time. Stalag cigarettes up. Did canteen book in evening. Made the mistake of getting dressed at 0315 hr this morning. Paddocks full of stocks from cut hay. Cabbage midday with new potatoes, meat, gravy, bread and margarine ration at night. Fairly cool and dull day, till 1100 hrs when sun came out, and followed fairly nice day.

Tuesday 17th August, 1943

On railway working party near Bodisch as a POW. On job at Qualisch digging out, work a bit heavier today, but home usual time. Arthur Goodwin in trouble again today, and get order to return to Stalag. Reading and played crib in evening. Midday cabbage, with potatoes, meat, gravy and usual bread and margarine at night. Fairly dull till midday when sun came through.

Wednesday 18th August, 1943

Prisoner of War near Bodisch. On gang at Qualisch digging out and shifting rails also got six lengths of sleepers ready for laying tomorrow.

Home at usual time. Bull comes in evening and got told about waving to the civilian population, told they would be the ones to suffer. Mail camps and parcels up, none myself, but personal parcels received by Pritchard, Casson and H Davis. Cigarettes by Wilson, Casson, Pritchard, Kirkpatrick, Pedersen, Lunam Check and myself. Nothing of note. Midday cabbage and at night potatoes meat, gravy, bread, marg also jam and sugar ration. Dull morning, but later coming fine & warm.

Thursday 19th August, 1943
At Bodisch Sudatenland as a POW. On railway gang at Qualisch, and laid six lengths of rails and usual times. Home guard blokes on duty here at Lager and look pretty old. 314 Red X food parcels up, seven boxes of cigarettes and tobacco. Some of the civvies open their eyes when they see all the parcels. New Under Officer here for a few days, while other one goes on six days leave. Arthur Goodwin returns to Stalag. Cabbage midday and at night potatoes, and soup with bread and margarine. Warm dull morning, later coming out very hot and still very warm at 2200 hrs.

Friday 20th August, 1943
On railway party near Bodisch as a POW. On job at Qualisch and laid six lengths of rails. Working in cutting and very warm. Home as usual. Issued with 50 cigarettes and Red X food parcel. Seven parcels up and personal parcels received by Davies, S Davis and Lunam. Cigarettes Heggie 2, Pritchard and myself two books, pack of cards and another game, sent by Boans on behalf of Sigrid. Bit of reading during evening. Usual rations for the day. Warm morning and continued to be a very hot day and still pretty hot at 2200 hrs.

Saturday 21st August, 1943
Prisoner of War Bodisch Sudatenland. Nobody at work today because of last Sundays unloading coal. Most of us reading, sleeping or playing

cards. Some of the boys go to the showers at 1500 hrs while some of us go raspberry picking, had raspberries with sugar and powdered milk mixed for cream for tea. Finished reading the two new books sent by Sigrid and good reading. Cabbage, potatoes midday, with sausage meat, bread and margarine at night. Fairly warm day throughout.

Sunday 22nd August, 1943
Prisoner of War on railway party near Bodisch. No work today. During morning started to re write diary since taken POW. During afternoon played cricket and marched to the place of playing and back to the tune of the bagpipes. Barrel of beer on return from cricket. Wrote letter card to Nurse H. Had toothache badly all day. Fine and hot day.

Monday 23rd August, 1943
Prisoner of War on railway party near Bodisch. On job at Qualisch laying rails. Home late tonight as left job later. Everything fairly quiet, picked up on job circular asking railway blokes to give a little bit of their rations for those in Hamburg. Cabbage midday, with potatoes, meat, gravy, bread and margarine for evening meal. Fairly hot and fine till 0930 when it clouded over completely and came up very dull, culminating in a thunderstorm at 2100 hrs and lightning put lights out.

Tuesday 24th August, 1943
Prisoner of War Bodisch, Sudatenland. On job at Qualisch but only laid four lengths as metal train upset schedule. Home early. Smudge Smith returned to Stalag today and Tom Hogg to Trautenau to the bunker. New beds arrived today so busy cleaning down shelves tonight, ready for putting them in tomorrow. Midday cabbage with potatoes, barley soup at night and bread and margarine ration. Jerry news: Berlin bombed last night and 64 planes shot down. Russians still attacking. Bit of rain on going to work, but fined up later and fairly decent day.

Wednesday 25th August, 1943

Prisoner of War Bodisch out on the Qualisch job, laying rails and back to camp usual early time for this job. New beds put in today and make improvement in the room, everyone busy tonight putting things in place again. Cabbage midday meal, while at night potatoes, gravy, bread and marg. German news: Russians still attacking and in recent attacks lost 80,000 dead Charkov evacuated. Dull morning, but later came out fine day.

Thursday 26th August, 1943

On railway working party as a POW in Sudatenland. On usual job at Qualisch laying rails and in camp usual time. Setting out points ready to be laid. Fixing up beds and gear again in evening. Casson went shopping and gave out the stuff also. Did not get much. Camp paper and four letters up, also parcels received by Dalziel, Pierce, Gillespie and 60 cigarettes myself from Sydney from Nurse H. Cigarettes Pritchard 2, Balsarini, Hogg, Pierce, Davis SE, Check and Kirkpatrick. Midday cabbage, with potatoes, meat, gravy at night with bread and marg ration. Fairly warm day although dull.

Friday 27th August, 1943

Prisoner of War Bodisch. 30th birthday today. On job at Qualisch, laid three lengths of rails, then continued on building points section ready for Monday. Usual work hours. 50 cigarettes and Red X food parcel issued in evening. Under Officer returns. Same rations as yesterday. Fine on going to work, but came up dull later with occasional showers.

Saturday 28th August, 1943

Prisoner of War railway party at Bodisch. At Qualisch job finishing laying out and screwing up points ready for laying on Monday. Half days work and in camp 1315 hrs. To showers at Halbstadt 1500 hrs returning to barracks 1615 hrs. About ten letters up and lucky enough to receive letter and snap from Clarrie. Cabbage and potatoes midday with sausage meat, bread, margarine and jam ration issue at night, Jerry news: Nuremburg bombed, heavy damage and 60 planes shot down. Fairly cool morning, but came out nice and fine day.

Sunday 29th August, 1943
Prisoner of War Bodisch, Sudatenland. One of the twelve called out at 0900 hrs to unload coal and back again at 1200 hrs. Doing up canteen book and reading during the afternoon. Wrote card home. Potatoes, meat, gravy midday with bread, margarine evening ration. Dull old morning, turning into some rain in afternoon.

Monday 30th August, 1943
Prisoner of War Bodisch. At job at Qualisch laying railway points till 1000 hrs, then digging out 14 sleepers between four men and finished fairly early and back to camp usual time for this job. Parcels up and received by Petersen R A, cigarettes by: Gillon, Barker, Davis S E, Pritchard 3, Casson 2, Lunam, Petersen R A, Underhill, Armstrong, Balsarini, and myself. Cabbage midday with barley soup, potatoes, bread, margarine evening ration. Heard that British parachutists had landed in Italy. Russians still strongly attacking in all sections. Martial law declared in Denmark because of enemy agents, and sabotage activities. Dull day with a little rain.

Tuesday 31st August, 1943
Prisoner of War, Lager E388 near Bodisch. Stayed home from work and went to the dentist at Weckelsdorf Market and had a tooth out. Went by train and walked back, had beer on the way and got here about 1200 hrs. Afternoon reading, writing, and doing up canteen book. Pay day. Cabbage midday with meat, gravy, potatoes, bread and marg at night. Planes over Germany and Munich, also bombed Naples in Italy. Dull and fairly wet day.

Wednesday 1st September, 1943

Prisoner of War on railway working party in Sudatenland. On job at Qualisch digging out between sleepers. Finished about 1130 hrs had dinner and slept till time to come home at 1600 hrs. A little mail up and camp newsletter but received none myself. Rations as per previous day. News: Berlin raided again and other towns in West Germany. Dull cloudy day with some rain.

Thursday 2nd September, 1943

Prisoner of War Bodisch. At Qualisch digging out. Train late this morning, missing connection at Weckelsdorf so went by Arbeit Zug. To camp at usual time. Cabbage midday with barley soup, issue of old and new potatoes, bread, margarine and a sugar ration at night. Cook potatoes on job, burrowed from under the bushes, grown near railway line. Cloudy but fairly hot day.

Friday 3rd September, 1943

Prisoner of War Bodisch. Fourth anniversary of the start of the war. At Qualisch digging out between railway sleepers and not feeling too well today. Home as usual. Issue of 50 cigarettes and Red X food parcel. To bed tonight with flu. Usual daily rations German news: mentions our troops landing in Italy and mention after four years of war they have faced blacker times than they are at present. Dull sultry day and very warm.

Saturday 4th September, 1943

Prisoner of War Bodisch. No work today having the time off from working previous Sunday. Not too good, attack of the flu, and very stiff in the joints, so in bed nearly all day. Boys back from Qualisch 1245 hrs and go to showers 1500 hrs returning again 1615 hrs. Cabbage and potatoes midday, with sausage meat, bread and marg at night. News: Still fighting in the landed area in Italy. Berlin bombed again and also in daylight. Dull but reasonably warm.

Sunday 5th September, 1943

Prisoner of War railway working party near Bodisch in Sudatenland. No work today, still not feeling too good, from the flu so in bed most of the day. Wrote card to Carmel. Some of the boys played football in the afternoon and came back with bruised shins and bits of skin off. Potatoes, meat, gravy, midday with potatoes, bread and margarine for evening meal. Our troops still fighting in Italy. Changeable day with little rain.

Monday 6th September, 1943

Prisoner of War Bodisch, Sudatenland. Qualisch laying rails, and home a little later than usual. Myself with two others went to the Doctor and old Doctor away and this one didn't seem to know what to do. Feeling a bit weak from the effects of the flu. Casson gets word to go to Stalag in morning. Usual daily rations. News: Russians still attacking. Our troops capture a couple of small towns in Italy. Italian forces retreat in one place without any fighting. Couple of towns bombed in Germany and 27 planes lost. Reasonably fine day but not too hot.

Tuesday 7th September, 1943

Prisoner of War near Bodisch. At Qualisch and laid six lengths of rails with the usual working and meal times. Casson goes to Stalag today on business. No mail or parcels for a week. Nearly all the harvest in, fields getting ploughed up for next season. Potatoes very scabby this year, and very few outstanding crops. Evenings starting to draw in now and getting dark before 2000 hrs. Cabbage midday with the evening meal being potatoes, barley soup, bread and margarine. Foggy morning, but cleared later and a fine day.

Wednesday 8th September, 1943

Prisoner of War Bodisch, on job at Qualisch and laid six lengths of rails. A little late owing to goods train running late, but back at usual time. Tom Hogg returned today from bunker and quite enjoyed his stay there. 26 parcels up and received by cigarettes Pritchard 3, Davis H 2, Underhill 2, Alty, Balsarini, Armstrong, Pierce, Gillon, Gracie, Gillespie, Casson, Horsburgh, Hunter, Davies, Smith F, Templeman and Lunam, Kirkpatrick and Hogg. Midday cabbage and at night potatoes, meat, gravy, bread and margarine with weekly jam and sugar ration. Jerries evacuated Stalino on Black Sea. Germany bombed slightly (supplies). Our troops in Italy bombed. Bit of activity in New Guinea. Fairly warm muggy day with some rain in the evening.

Thursday 9th September, 1943
Prisoner of War near Bodisch, Sudatenland. On job at Qualisch, and laid six lengths of rails. Had argument with one of the boys about sitting down. Usual work times and back in camp as usual. A few old Jerries called up and about seventy in uniform at Addersbach-Felsen. Mail up and received one from Lil and Tom. Usual daily rations. News as such: Italy gives in, and Germany says Brenner Pass is well protected by guns, men and panzers. Russian troops further in Iran, couple of places bombed in England and eleven British planes shot down over Germany. Everyone pleased with events. Dull morning but later came out fine day.

Friday 10th September, 1943
Prisoner of War in Sudatenland. Clarrie's 27th birthday. At Qualisch and laid six lengths of rails, laid out four and did a bit of stomping, with usual times and everything running very smoothly today. Issued with 50 cigarettes and Red X food parcel in evening. Usual daily rations. News flashes: Italians and Jerries fighting in Italy. Jerries occupy Albania, Italian Troops in Athens lay down their arms and four raids of 500 planes each over Berlin. Cold frosty morning with fairly warm day later.

Saturday 11th September, 1943
Prisoner of War Bodisch. Half days work at Qualisch, some digging out and some shift the boody (hut) back at 1315 hrs. To showers at

1500 hrs and returning 1610 hrs. Four men on a job later unloading some metal. Reading and mending during evening. Cabbage and potatoes midday with sausage meat, beetroot, bread and margarine at night. News Items: Russians still seem to be doing well. Rommel in charge of Northern Italy. Some Italians still fighting there. French Southern Coast said to be well fortified. Reckon that Italy was sold by the king, Bogdaglio and his click. Fairly warm day with some clouds.

Sunday 12th September, 1943
Prisoner of War Bodisch, no work today. After having breakfast of porridge, potatoes, carrots, cabbage, eggs and curried rice and beef, back to bed again until nearing midday. Played cricket during afternoon and had a very enjoyable game. Did a fair amount of reading. Wrote letter card to Clarrie, and cards to Alison and Jean. Potatoes, veal, gravy midday with potatoes bread and margarine at night. For tea from the food parcel tin of beef casserole, potatoes, carrots, stewed prunes and peaches. News not much tonight. Barrel of beer up today. Dull morning, but came out nice afternoon.

Monday 13th September, 1943
On railway working party near Bodisch, Sudatenland as a POW. At Qualisch and laid second set of points, preparing through 1st and 2nd shifts, and laid during the third. A very heavy job with the result that took quite a time and the 1325 hr passenger train was held up for just over an hour, and were late getting back tonight. Twenty parcels up and received by books: Check, cigarettes: Dalziel, Alty, Balsarini, Kerr 2, Pritchard 2, Underhill, Gillespie, Kirkpatrick, Xmas, Hogg, Galletly 2, Casson, Hampton, Wilson and 2 myself from Godfrey Phillips and De Reske, of opinion that they are sent privately through the Red X, as nobody else here seems to get them. Had four from them now. Cabbage midday, with barley soup, potatoes at night and usual bread and margarine. A fairly fine day.

Tuesday 14th September, 1943

Prisoner of War Bodisch. On working party at Qualisch, digging out at the road crossing, and few extra sleepers. Finished myself at 1200 hrs. Everything going very smoothly. Midday cabbage with barley soup, potatoes and bread and marg at night. German news quiet. Fairly warm.

Wednesday 15th September, 1943

At Bodisch as a POW on party at Qualisch and laid four lengths of rails and laid out some sleepers. Laid over the road crossing today, and had the civvie gang helping us. A little mail up and received one from Doreen myself previous letter missing. No camp newsletter for two weeks now. Casson still away. Cabbage midday, potatoes, meat, gravy at night with bread, margarine and weekly sugar and jam ration. Dull day but fairly warm.

Thursday 16th September, 1943

Prisoner of War Bodisch. Brother Jack's 29th birthday. At Qualisch laid two lengths of rail and dug out five sleepers between two and finished at midday. Leir goes away for eight days holiday. Home usual time. A little mail up again but none myself also three "Clarions" up. Quite a few of the boys reckon the war will be over by Christmas, but very doubtful myself and took a bet of five to one, that it would not. Usual daily rations. News: Russians still doing well, said to be within 400 kilometres of Polish border. Naples in our hands. Said to be only six divisions of Italians fighting with Germany, Sardinia and Corsica also said to be in our hands. Our planes over Germany and France. Dull morning starting to rain about 1200 hrs and continued till 1700 hrs, then sunny again.

Friday 17th September, 1943

Prisoner of War stationed at Bodisch. At the Qualisch job digging out and finished at midday and home usual time. H Davis returns to

Stalag today. Issued with 50 cigarettes and Red X food parcel. Stalag cigarettes up. Usual daily rations. News Items: Nobresish evacuated by Jerries. Our troops still fighting at Palermo otherwise everything quiet. Very foggy morning, but came out fairly warm later in the day.

Saturday 18th September, 1943
At Bodisch as a POW. Our party at Qualisch digging out. Half day, seven sleepers between four men, finished at 0915 hrs, then had to wait till after 1300 hrs before we came home, because of metal train coming and Arbeit Zug used to help. In camp 1405 hrs to showers at Halbstadt 1500 hrs and back in camp at 1610 hrs. Reading during afternoon and evening. Orders out tonight that our civvie coloured pullovers and shorts have to be marked RGF and food from parcels to be emptied out of tins. News quiet tonight. Cabbage, potatoes, midday and at night sausage meat, bread and margarine. Nice sunny day with cold wind blowing

Sunday 19th September, 1943
Prisoner of War Bodisch. No work today so after having breakfast retire to bed till 1200 hrs. Afternoon played cricket evening wrote to Doreen, Florrie and Sigrid, also did some reading. News quiet. Potatoes, meat, gravy, midday and at night potatoes, bread and marg. Fine morning but a dull afternoon.

Monday 20th September, 1943
Prisoner of War stationed in Sudatenland. Woke up this morning to hear rain pelting down. At Qualisch digging out between sleepers and finished midday and home usual hour. Cabbage midday at night potatoes, meat, gravy and usual bread and marg. Reading during evening. News quiet. Dull morning, sitting in with rain at midday.

Tuesday 21st September, 1943
On railway working party as a POW in Sudatenland. At Qualisch digging out between sleepers and finished at 1045 hrs and then reading

and lying down in boody till left for camp at 1600 hrs. Seventeen parcels up and received by Hall and cigarettes Xmas, Gracie, Pritchard 2, Price, Hampton, Horsburgh 2, Davis DE, Underhill, Kirkpatrick, Myers, Davies, Balsarini 2, (Check books). Usual daily rations. Dull cold morning, continuing throughout the day.

Wednesday 22nd September, 1943
Prisoner of War stationed at Bodisch. At Qualisch digging out between sleepers and finished about 0915 hrs. No Arbeit Zug today so left Qualisch by the 1340 passenger train, and in camp at 1500 hrs. Reading and playing crib in evening. From tomorrow on 'locked up' barracks at 2000 hrs. Mail up but no camps, Received one from Doreen and one from Jean. News quiet. Usual daily rations. Dull morning setting in with rain at 1230 hrs.

Thursday 23rd September, 1943
Prisoner of War Bodisch, Sudatenland. At Qualisch job digging out between sleepers and finished at 1020 hrs. Home at usual time of Arbeit Zug. Reading and sleeping during the day after finishing work. Bit of a scramble getting out of the train this morning at Qualisch as school kids try to get in our carriage, when we got out. Some of next years crops already up and they lie dormant under the snow till it melts in the spring, and also seems to be a general digging of potatoes, and plenty of flax pulled and left out in the fields for bleaching. Roll call at 0800 hrs from tonight on. No German news because of wireless being switched off. Same daily rations. Very cold morning but lovely and sunny till 1100 when clouded over practically rest of day.

Friday 24th September, 1943
Prisoner of War Sudatenland. At Qualisch on digging out between sleepers and finished at 1020 hrs. Back in camp usual time. Issued with 50 cigarettes and Red X food parcel. Civilian police and Jerry girl come and give us the once over on leaving and again later and picked

out Jock and took him away, was wondering who she was going to pick on. German news seems to be in our favour. Cabbage midday and at night potatoes, soup, bread, margarine and weekly issue of sugar and jam. Frosty morning and turning out a beautiful sunny day.

Saturday 25th September, 1943
Prisoner of War Bodisch. Thirteen weeks from today to Christmas. Digging out at Qualisch and finished at 0815 being half day. Back in camp 1320 hrs. Did not go to the showers today so had to bath in camp in big old wooden tub. Snowy went shopping today so gave out our goods in afternoon. Playing crib and reading. Mail up and received one from Bernice and one from home. Three weeks camps missed now so looks as if they have gone out of existence. News still appears to be very good. Cabbage, potatoes midday with sausage meat, usual bread and marg at night. Fairly dull throughout the day.

Sunday 26th September, 1943
On railway working party as a POW near Bodisch in Sudatenland. No work jobs today. Reading, doing canteen book, writing up diary, and wrote cards to Gladys, Lil and Tom. German News: still seems to be in our favour, admit evacuation of one or two places. Potatoes, meat, gravy midday, with potatoes, bread and marg at night. Breakfast: porridge with bacon, eggs, potatoes, and toast with tea, mostly from the Red X parcel. Four-eyed guard returns. Dull miserable day with some heavy rain.

Monday 27th September, 1943
Prisoner of War Bodisch. At Qualisch today. Leir back on job today and laid six lengths of rails and laid out six lengths of sleepers for tomorrow. Gillespie and Price return to Stalag today and good riddance. News nothing of note. Parcels up and received by Alty and cigarettes by Pritchard 4, Underhill 2, Gillon, Pedersen 2, Davis SE, Dalziel, Petersen RA, Hampton, Gillespie and myself 2, and a book

parcel from London. Casson still away will be three weeks tomorrow. Usual daily rations. Fairly cold morning and continued dull all day.

Tuesday 28th September, 1943
Prisoner of War near Bodisch, Sudatenland. On Qualisch job and laid six lengths of rails and laid out six lengths of sleepers. Everything fairly quiet and no news. Pete has a go at going away this morning, but captured again fairly early. Four-eyes the guard. Four more men expected tonight. Cabbage midday, with soup, potatoes at night, bread and margarine. Dull day with cold wind.

Wednesday 29th September, 1943
Prisoner of War stationed at Bodisch. At Qualisch job and laid six lengths of rails and laid out a couple of lengths. Arbeit Zug derailed today and the 1330 hr train from Qualisch did not go till 1605 hrs and the 1530 train having to discharge its passengers at derailment and return as the 1605 hr and returned on this train to camp ourselves, thereby getting back usual time. Four men returned were Fred Earl in charge, Thorpe, Ross and Smith. Sgt Casson did not return, as the Red X personnel and Repat are being repatriation any time. Things bad in Stalag as 14,000 prisoners from Italy have arrived there and no beds are available. Fred Earl gives us a talk in evening of the 8th Army activities through North Africa, the capture of Sicily, and other doings of the war. Majority reckon the war will be over by February. Cabbage midday with meat, gravy, potatoes, bread, marg and weekly issue of jam and sugar. A dull day with light and heavy rain all day and heavy fog.

Thursday 30th September, 1943
Prisoner of War stationed near Bodisch in Sudatenland. At Qualisch and laying rails and home at usual time. Fairly quiet day. Mail up and received letter from Gladys. Have to have the meat tipped out of tins from Red X parcel. News very quiet. Same daily rations. Dull foggy day with misty rain.

Friday 1st October, 1943

Prisoner of War at Bodisch. At Qualisch job and laid four lengths of rails and prepared three for laying tomorrow. Took some picks down to be sharpened. Fairly easy day and in camp usual time. Isssued with 50 cigarettes and Red X food parcel. Some mail up and received one from Ethel, Verna and one letting me know of some farm books on the way from England. News quiet. Cabbage midday with potatoes and vermecilli soup with potatoes, bread and marg evening meal. Dull and cloudy till midday when sun broke through and finest evening seen for a week.

Saturday 2nd October, 1943

Prisoner of War near Bodisch in Sudatenland. On the Qualisch job and laid three lengths of rails and laid out six lengths of sleepers. Half day and in camp at 1245. To the showers at 1500 hrs and returning at 1610. Reading and playing crib in evening. Saw big Italian X train in Halbstadt. Usual rations. Dull cloudy day.

Sunday 3rd October, 1943

Prisoner of War Bodisch. In camp today. Slept in till 1000 hrs except for getting up for breakfast. Reading and playing bridge, doing up canteen book, sewing and wrote letter card to Bernice and card home, occupied the day. Barrel of beer up, but not many drinkers getting a bit too cold for it now. Potatoes, meat, gravy midday with potatoes, bread, margarine at night. Were to listen to Lord Haw Haw but Goebels speaking, so did not hear it. Dull with a little sunshine.

Monday 4th October, 1943

Prisoner of War stationed at Bodisch. No bolts available so no rail laying today and digging out instead and fairly heavy job, digging out 30 centimetres on inside, and going out 40 centimetres on the outside, and about one and a half yards wider, and not finished too early. Just started for home, went about two yards, when tender of engine derailed and had to wait on breakdown train from Trautenau. Left job about two hours late and back in camp at about 1920 hrs. The usual daily rations. News: Another couple of towns evacuated by Jerry. Bandits troublesome around Trieste, otherwise news quiet. Frosty morning turning out fine and warm day with cool evening.

Tuesday 5th October, 1943
Prisoner of War near Bodisch Sudatenland. At Qualisch job digging out by station, fairly heavy work but finished by midday and to camp usual time. Expecting a visit tomorrow of a couple of officers. Reading during evening. Cabbage midday with potatoes, and soup at night with bread and margarine. German wireless admits evacuation of Corsica because of superiority of enemy troops and fighting north of Naples and also five big towns and Trieste Coast bombed. Frosty morning with fine day but cold wind.

Wednesday 6th October, 1943
Prisoner of War in camp near Bodisch. On the job at Qualisch digging out and half days work today, returning at 1330 on account of visit by officers, and arrived at 1500 hrs. Arbeit Zug gang return at 1610 hrs and had tea at 1630 hrs. At 1730 hrs officer and Doctor visit here. Doctor gives us an examination. Many rumours going around as to the reason of it all. News quiet. Cabbage midday, with potatoes, meat, gravy, bread, marg at night with the weekly sugar and jam ration. A fine warm day.

Thursday 7th October, 1943
Prisoner of War on party E 388 Bodisch. At the Qualisch job digging out between sleepers. Finished fairly early. No Arbeit Zug so had to return on the 1330 hr train and arrive here at 1530 hrs. Bit of a scramble getting on the train as have to clear children out of carriage for us. Nothing up again ten days since had any parcels. Reading and playing crib. News quiet. Usual daily rations. Frosty morning but turned out fine day.

Friday 8th October, 1943

On railway working party as a POW near Bodisch, Sudatenland. On job at Qualisch digging out by the station, and very solid work today. Finished the digging out here now. No Arbeit Zug today so times as yesterday. Issued with a 50 cigarettes and Red X food parcel. A little mail up again and received from Gladys, Verna and Jean. Played crib during evening. Rations as usual. News: Raid over Stuttgart, heavy damage and nine planes shot own. Fine morning later coming up very dull and turning out very cold afternoon.

Saturday 9th October, 1943

Prisoner of War Bodisch. At Qualisch and laid three lengths of rails and returned by the 1130 hr train and in camp 1245 hr. To showers at 1500 hr and returning at 1615 hrs. Had a bit of an argument with conductress on getting on train at Qualisch. Played 500 in evening. Potatoes, gravy midday, with potatoes, sausage meat at night usual bread and marg. Germans admit evacuation of Cuban bridgehead, otherwise everything quiet. Fine morning but cold breeze and a bit dull during afternoon.

Sunday 10th October, 1943

Prisoner of War stationed near Bodisch in Sudatenland. No work today and in bed till late. Reading, washing, sewing during day, also wrote cards to Betty and Verna. Knowledge test during evening. Potatoes, meat, gravy midday with potatoes, bread and margarine evening ration. For tea had mashed potatoes, peas, bacon and eggs. Germans mention of many four engine bombers shot down in heavy raids over Germany and heavy loss of crews, also mentioned in news that Russia wants air bases in Egypt, and other places same as America, and no more Jews wanted in Abbysinia. A heavy frost this morning followed by a fine day but cold breeze blowing and again came up a frosty evening.

Monday 11th October, 1943

Prisoner of War Bodisch, Sudatenland. At Qualisch and laid four lengths of rails and shifted some rails ready for laying near station. No Arbeit Zug so returned by the 1330 hr train to Bodisch arriving 1450 hrs. Playing crib and writing up the diary in evening. News quiet except Russias attacking heavy with new material, and good many four engine planes shot down over West Germany. Flour meal soup midday with the evening meal being potatoes, meat, gravy bread and margarine. Very heavy frost with temperature at zero but followed by a beautiful fine day with cold breeze, cold again at night.

Tuesday 12th October, 1943

Prisoner of War in Sudatenland. At Qualisch today, first period went a couple of stations further on from Qualisch to pick up some rails. Laid four lengths of rails and prepared for tomorrows laying. Arbeit Zug out today and back in camp at 1715 hrs. Some mail up today and received one, and a photo from Carmel, Sigrid, Ethel, Verna and Gladys. Jack Kirkpatrick returned to Stalag today. Cabbage 'Ruben' soup midday while at night had potatoes, gravy usual bread and margarine. Frosty morning followed by a beautiful fine day. Go to work before sun up return when it has gone down, days closing in very fast.

Wednesday 13th October, 1943

Prlisoner of War at Bodisch. At Qualisch again today, finished laying rails between Qualisch and Radowenz, and moved back to station and finished laying points Petersdorf end. Should finish out there this week. Home late tonight as did not leave job until1630 hrs. Saw some of the tobacco Zcecks smoking in their pipes, it was just wood shavings. Had another row with conductress this morning, trying to bundle us into half a carriage. Had her practically in tears. Watery meal soup midday with potatoes, meat, gravy for evening meal and bread and margarine jam and sugar ration. Heard station master down below us get six months gaol, so we hear, kicked out of the Nazi party. Our gang was responsible for his predicament as he was reporting the guards as smoking English cigarettes, and they told us so we got him caught with English cigarettes one Sunday afternoon as he walked past our barracks, and had a guard hiding in the kitchen who saw him take them, and he was bundled down to the guards office and searched with the above result, but we had to watch him when he came back as he was out to get us. News: British and American troops in Northern Italy, and fighting East of Kiev on the Eastern Front. Frosty morning, temperature 2 below, but turned out a perfect day, except for cold breeze.

Thursday 14th October, 1943
Prisoner of War on railway party near Bodisch. On the Qualisch job and laid two lengths of rails, finished off the points at Radowenz, and did some stomping. Home usual hour. All the farmers busy pulling their sugar beet. Some of the trees looking very pretty now with the coloured autumn leaves. Plenty of air activity about. Still no parcels up for seventeen days. First snow of the winter fell at 1545 hrs. No soup midday, with barley soup, potatoes, bread and marg for evening meal. News rumour: That fighting has finished in Italy and that Italy has declared war on Germany. Frosty morning with dull, cold windy day with some snow falling 1545 hr to 1700 hrs.

Friday 15th October, 1943
Prisoner of War at Bodisch party E388. At Qualisch and laid eight lengths of rails near station in the one stretch. Should finish rail laying out here tomorrow. Home usual. Nights getting dark very quickly now. Issued with 50 cigarettes and Red X food parcel. A little mail up, but received none myself. Watery cabbage soup midday with potatoes, gravy at night bread and margarine. Frosty morning dull day but reasonably warm.

Saturday 16th October, 1943

On railway working party as a POW in Sudatenland. At Qualisch job, laid four lengths of rails, bit of stomping and loaded boody (hut) on wagon for Halbstadt, as finished rail laying out here. In camp at 1315 hrs, being half day. To showers at Halbstadt 1500 hrs, back in camp 1610. A few civvies around trying to exchange sacharine for cigarettes. Played crib and reading during afternoon and evening. Issued with a pair of sandshoes. Potatoes, cabbage midday with sausage meat, bread, margarine at night. Heard rumours that Portugal had granted Britain a port and air bases, otherwise German news not much except that saying recent raid when we lost 121 planes out of 250 and that in recent raids Air Force had lost 3600 personnel. Dull day with a little rain early, but later clearing up and a fine evening.

Sunday 17th October, 1943

Prisoner of War Bodisch. No work today, so did not get up till 0930 hrs, and then reading, writing up diary and mended boots. Ten parcels up and received by Thorpe & Earl 2, Ross, Smith G 2. Wrote letter card home and to Poppy. Played some bridge during the evening. Nothing of note in the German news. Midday with potatoes, meat, gravy and pumpkin and evening potatoes, bread and margarine. Had tea of own making mashed potatoes with cut up onion in it, bacon and tomatoes followed by stewed prunes and peaches, bread and a mug of tea. Dull day with a little sunshine.

Monday 18th October, 1943

At Bodisch as a POW, at Qualisch today in with gang of fifteen. The usual Arbeit Zug and the rest with Leir at Halbstadt. Should have been Arbeit Zug with us at Qualisch but none came so unplated sleepers. Freistag at 0930 hrs, Mittag Essen 1200 hrs and did not do any more coming home on 1330 train, and in camp 1500 hrs. 248 Canadians Red X food parcels and cigarettes for seven weeks arrived today. Started crib tournament in evening, but lost my game. Reading, writing and playing crib during the evening. News quiet. Usual daily rations, and fairly warm day with some sunshine.

Tuesday 19th October, 1943
Prisoner of War in Sudatenland. Work teams same as yesterday and at Qualisch myself, unplated a few sleepers and Arbeit Zug came from Trauentau and then loaded 29 rails for the day and going past Petersdorf, and to the next station. Had two hours for dinner. Back at camp 1715 hrs. Farmers now busy getting in their beet crops. Valleys and hills look very nice with the silver birch trees in their autumn leaves amongst the pines. Saw a plane passing over high, leaving a smoke trail, but no news of note. Crib tournament continued tonight, usual rations for the day. Fairly fine and warm day.

Wednesday 20th October, 1943
Near Bodisch in Sudatenland as a POW of Germany. Three gangs out. At Qualisch myself loaded a few rails, and unloaded thirty four, and also unloaded some bolts also plating sleepers and some unloaded. Fairly easy day and home by the Arbeit Zug. Reading and doing up the canteen book in evening. Crib tournament continues. Cabbage midday with potatoes, meat, gravy, bread, marg at night. Report of news regarding Portugal concessions to Britain were in the Azores. Concerning ourselves rumours of cutting down on some of our French cigarettes and boot wear. Dull morning, but turned out reasonably fine day.

Thursday 21st October, 1943
Prisoner of War Bodisch, Sudatenland. Three gangs out. At Qualisch myself loaded 120 sleepers and 72 rails for the day. Home by Arbeit Zug. In camp 1715 hrs. Fairly easy day, just plodded along with no set number to do. Some mail up today and received one from Allison and a snap. Parcels scarce again, probably due to the fact of change

of Stalags now being attached to Stalag V11A, instead of V111B. Crib tournament continues. Reading and doing canteen book in evening. Cabbage midday with the evening meal being potatoes soup, potatoes, bread and margarine. Cool morning with fog, but after sun broke through, turned out a perfect day and nice evening.

Friday 22nd October, 1943
Prisoner of War Bodisch. Three gangs out again today. At Qualisch myself and helped to load 28 rails, plates, bolts and lashings and unplated sleepers. Home by Arbeit Zug usual time. Issued with 50 cigarettes and Canadian Red X food parcel. Crib tournament finishes this evening and won by SE Davies, beating Galletly two straight games. Nothing of note in the German news. Evenings pass very quickly now, seem to be no sooner home, than it is time for roll call and bed. Dull cool morning with fair amount of wind but fair afternoon.

Saturday 23rd October, 1943
Near Bodisch, Sudatenland as a POW. Same gangs as yesterday again at Qualisch myself unplating sleepers till 0930 hr, then at by fire till 1100 hrs and came home on 1215 hr train, getting in camp at 1240 hrs. To showers at 1500 and back again at 1610 hrs. Played crib in evening and also a whist drive. News quiet. Cabbage and potatoes midday with pumpkin, sausage meat, bread and margarine with weekly sugar issue and jam for a fortnight for the evening ration. Cold morning turning out cold dull day.

Sunday 24th October, 1943
Prisoner of War near Bodisch, no work today. Six men return the piano during the day. Heard that the first lot of repats had arrived in England. Reading and doing canteen book and wrote cards to Mrs F, Mavis, and Allan. Played in euchre tournament, but beaten in first round, and also played some crib. Got up a committee to start arranging for Xmas emtertainment. Potato, suckling pig and gravy midday

meal, while at night had potato, pumpkin, bread and margarine. Cold morning but turned out a nice day.

Monday 25th October, 1943
Prisoner of War Bodisch, Sudatenland. Three gangs out but Arbeit Zug and Halbstadt gang combine after Freistig. On Halbstadt gang myself, going with nine others to Mittelsteine first and returning after picking up some tools there. Saw troop train go through. Leir got a swollen face and not at work. After Freistig unloaded some rails. Then went on Arbeit Zug to Olberg and loaded forty rails, plates, lashings, bolts etc. Saw a train load of new and old cars and trucks at Halbstadt and talking to Jerry who spoke English. Been in Russia since war started and pleased to be back in Germany. Looks as if this stuff had been evacuated from Russia he reckons things in the general living of the Russians are bad. In camp 1755 hrs. Midday rations of cabbage and evening meal of barley soup, potatoes, bread and margarine. Fairly warm morning with lovely sunny day and cool night.

Tuesday 26th October, 1943
Prisoner of War at Bodisch on railway working party. Gang at Qualisch, Halbstadt, unloaded a bit of earth early. And after Freistig (morning tea) with three others helped to unload 20 tons of coal, finishing at 1500 hrs, had showers and finished for the day. Talking to a couple of Russians, fairly young and well built for their age. Played challenge euchre match in evening and won, 15 mills on it winning the challenge. Cabbage midday with evening meal of mixed macaroni meal and potato soup, with potatoes, bread and marg. German news mentions fighting a thousand times stronger, in Russia and evacuation of some places. Dull cold day.

Wednesday 27th October, 1943
Near Bodisch as a POW. 15 at Qualisch, Arbeit Zug and Halbstadt gangs combine with the exception of three others and myself, staying

at Halbstadt unloading 4 ½ tons of briquets and stacked 160 sleepers, finishing at 1500. Evening return euchre challenge match this time being beaten and lost 25 mills. The Bull here this morning and again at night. Cabbage midday with potatoes, meat, gravy at night bread, margarine and weekly sugar ration. News fairly quiet, except for a number of huge encirclements of Jerries by the Russians. A dull cold day, setting in with heavy fog in evening.

Thursday 28th October, 1943
Prisoner of War Bodisch. 15 men to Qualisch, Arbeit Zug and Halbstadt gang combine. In morning carted 15 cylinders of carbide gas, unloaded some lashing and bricks. Afternoon with eleven others unloaded and stacked 375 sleepers, finishing about 1600 hrs. Started Yankee crib tournament in evening, being beaten in the first round. Read one of Horlers books and rather a good story. Usual rations for the day. Heavy fog till 1200 hrs then turned out to be a beautiful day.

Friday 29th October, 1943
In Sudatenland as a POW. 15 men again at Qualisch, with Arbeit Zug and Halbstadt gang combining, except for myself and two others who carted some sandstones, cement, cork powder and some coal to the inspectors joint, the others unloading stone and rails. In evening issued with 50 cigarettes and English food parcel. Continued Yankee crib tournament and beaten in second round. Nothing startling in German news. Midday cabbage with potatoes, meat, gravy, bread and marg at night. Frost and fog in morning wih a very nice day after 1000 hrs.

Saturday 30th October, 1943
Prisoner of War near Bodisch. At Qualisch today on gang unplating sleepers. Had very easy morning half day so in camp at 1245 hrs. Saw woman and child have very lucky escape from being run down by train. To showers at 1500 and returning at 1610 hrs. Myers and Fred Earl went shopping today, but did not get much so gave these articles

out in afternoon. Continued third, fourth and fifth round of Yankee crib tournament being beaten in third and fourth rounds. So have not broken ice yet. Have to have meals without top false teeth as they have cracked down the centre. Cabbage and potatoes midday with pumpkin, sausage meat, usual bread and margarine at night. Frosty morning but came out fine at Qualisch 0800 hrs but return to Bodisch fog still hanging around till 1300 hrs.

Sunday 31st October, 1943
At Bodisch as a POW with eleven others called out at 0900 to go and unload stone at Halbstadt, after waiting there for two hours, found out there was none, so walked back to camp getting there about midday. Continued Yankee crib tournament throughout the day, still no luck won only one game out of eight, also did some reading. Wrote cards to home and Donald. Potatoes, meat, gravy midday with potatoes, pumpkin, bread and margarine evening ration. German news mentions heavy fighting Russia and Italy. Reports by British papers of German atrocities in Italy and word of English troops in Italy good. Foggy morning but fine after 1030 hrs.

Monday 1st November, 1943
At Bodisch in Sudatenland as a POW. 15 men at Qualisch. Arbeit Zug and Halbstadt combine. At Halbstadt unloaded metal during the morning and loaded sleepers between Olberg and Heinzendorf the afternoon. Evening continuation of crib tournament and beaten again. Usual cabbage midday with potatoes, meat, gravy at night, bread and margarine ration. Latrine news rumours. British and American troops pushing in Yugoslavia towards Hungary. Unrest in Austria. Heavy frost this morning but came out a beautiful day.

Tuesday 2nd November, 1943
On railway working party as a POW in Sudatenland. Should be Melbourne Cup Day back home. 15 men Qualisch with Halbstadt and

Arbeit gangs combining again. Myself with four others unloading and stacking sleepers, also unloaded a few double sleepers and plates, rest loading sleepers between Olberg and Heinzendorf. Fairly easy day, just working along steadily all the time. Heard that new Stalag is fairly large with Serbs and other International prisoners there. Yankee crib tournament continued tonight and had a couple of wins. Same rations as yesterday. Jerry paper deals largely on the discussions going on in Moscow otherwise everything quiet. Cold frosty morning with a lovely day.

Wednesday 3rd November, 1943
Prisoner of War stationed near Bodisch. Fifteen men on railway job at Qualisch, and others also railway with Halbstadt gang and Arbeit Zug combine. Myself with five others unloaded and stacked 450 sleepers, rest away distributing coal and loading sleepers between Olberg and Heinzedorf. Old chow gets a bit annoyed because we go too fast up front when going to the station. Reports us to the Under Officer. Managed to get a mirror and a spoon today, also another 50 pkts of matches up. Read book called 'Sheriff of Dyke Hole', a good book. Continued crib tournament in evening another couple of successes tonight, but too late to win the tournament. Usual working times and usual daily rations except for weekly sugar and jam ration. Nothing in the news. Frosty morning and fine day but cold wind.

Thursday 4th November, 1943
On railway working party E388 as a POW near Bodisch in Sudatenland and attached to Stalag V11A. 15 men at Qualisch and the rest of us at Halbstadt. Did not start till 1015 hrs and then unloaded some iron sleepers by station, finishing at 1430 hrs and then with five others unloaded some iron sleepers, lashing bolts and screws finishing 1540 hrs. Armstrong and Gracie return to Stalag today. Continuation crib tournament another win tonight. Read 'The Saving Clause by Zapper' – short stories. Pay night. Parcels and mail overdue. Ruben soup midday

with potatoes and mixed soup at night, bread and margarine. Dull cold day with cold wind blowing.

Friday 5th November, 1943
On railway party Bodisch as a POW. 15 men to Qualisch, rest at Halbstadt, the two gangs again combining up till 0900 hrs loading coal for Lager and two other places. From 0930 hrs till 1100 hrs with five others stacked about 200 sleepers, 1200 hrs went to Heinzedorf, loaded a few sleepers in afternoon, ten of us pulling sleepers up railway embankment with rope. Did not do too much though. Received 50 cigarettes and Canadian Red X food parcel tonight. Bit of reading throughout the evening. Crib tournament continued lost game tonight. Ruben soup midday with potatoes, mixed soup, bread and margarine at night. Dull day starting to snow 0900 and continued for the day.

Saturday 6th November, 1943
Prisoner of War Bodisch. 12 men at Qualisch and 12 at Halbstadt. Loading and pulling sleepers up bank between Olberg and Heinzedorf. Finished about 1215 hrs then had a shower and returned to camp about 1400 hrs. Finished crib tournament in afternoon had a win and a loss myself. J Horsburg first 12 wins out of seventeen. J Barker 2nd in a play off, also reading during the afternoon and evening. Potatoes and marrow at midday with sausage meat, bread and margarine evening meal. German news not much but mentions bombing of Rome and Vatican City by RAF. A dull cold day with a sprinkling of snow.

Sunday 7th November, 1943
Prisoner of War Bodisch. Sudatenland. No work today and in bed till 1000 hrs and then got up and did some mending. Afternoon more mending a little reading and played cards in evening. Did not write any mail today waiting on some probably turning up this week. Potatoes, meat, gravy, pumpkin midday with potatoes, bread, marg evening ration. A cold dull day.

Monday 8th November, 1943
Prisoner of War Bodisch. 14 men on Qualisch gang, and 13 combine at Halbstadt. Myself at Halbstadt and first job helped to unload two trucks of sleepers then loaded some metal and unloaded by civvie working gang working on points. Next unloaded 5000 bricks and finished unloading and stacking 100 sleepers. Home usual time. Heard tonight that Stalag V111B still exists, but our working party is not attached to it, being nearer to the new oneV111A at Girlitz and being attached there, so the hold up of mail and parcels is caused by mail going to V111B and being returned to V111A and distributed from there. Also new regulations in writing mail if not written on day of issue cannot write or hand it back so tonight wrote home and to Sigrid. Usual daily rations. Dull cold day.

Tuesday 9th November, 1943
On railway party as a POW Sudatenland. Eleven men to Qualisch, and again two gangs again combining at Halbstadt. During morning myself with five others unloaded and stacked sleepers and seven others loaded 5800 bricks. In afternoon all of us went loading sleepers between Olberg and Heinzendorf. Finished usual time. Ruben soup midday with potatoes mixed soup at night with usual bread and margarine. German news: New material in battles in Italy. British bombers attack convoy in Mediteranean near Dedoconese Islands, but driven off. German planes over England. Still heavy fighting on the Eastern Front. Hitler says Germany will never capitulate, three million homes destroyed by our bombers, but that does not matter, will fight on till victory. Heard Kiev in Russian hands. Dull cold day with icy snow falling throughout the day.

Wednesday 10th November, 1943
Prisoner of War Bodisch, 15 men on Qualisch gang, and 14 on Halbstadt. During morning myself with 4 others unloading and stacking sleepers, the rest loading earth. Afternoon 2 men Braunau

unloading sand. Myself with 5 others unloaded 2 trucks of earth, and the rest loading earth. Reading during evening. Some of the locals not very enthusiastic about Hitlers latest speech. German news quiet. Soup midday with potatoes pumpkin, meat, gravy, bread, marg at night. Frosty followed by some sunshine but fairly cool day.

Thursday 11th November, 1943
Prisoner of War Bodisch. Armistice Day 25th Anniversary of finish First World War. 15 men gang to Qualisch rest to Halbstadt. Myself with 5 others unloading earth and 11 men loading up. Home a bit later today than usual, train being late. Old Fred seems to get a lot of abuse, every body going past having a pick at him. Reading during evening. Ruben soup midday with vegetable soup & potatoes, bread and margarine as evening meal. Dull day with bitterly cold wind.

Friday 12th November, 1943
On railway party in Sudatenland as a POW. 15 men Qualisch and same at Halbstadt. In morning unloaded some iron sleepers, rails and points, also bit of metal. Afternoon past Olberg to replace broken rail. Took the old one out and put in another one only to find a bit too short, so for the time being had to put the old one back. Train a bit late again tonight. Boys from Qualisch put swedes and Rubens for winter down cellar after being home early. Still no mail or parcels. Issued with Canadian Red X food parcel and fifty cigarettes. Ruben soup midday, with potatoes, barley soup and bread margarine at night. German news mentions heavy artillary action at Kiev, and other breakthrough healed over, also regained some high positions in Italy and attack on one of our convoys in Mediteranean, 6 ships being sunk and a good many damaged. Bit of snow about this morning, attempted a bit during the day, fairly dull and cold with light snow 1930 hrs.

Saturday 13th November, 1943
Prisoner of War Bodisch Sudatenland, 13 men Qualisch and 13 Halbstadt. Had to go to Qualisch today stacking sleepers and unplating. Very sloppy job, as snow was thawing out. Left on return at 1130 hrs and in camp 1245 hrs. To showers at Halbstadt 1500 hrs, returning at 1610. Reading during afternoon and evening. Commenced a Yankee whist tournament tonight, Bill Kerr and I together, winning our first match four games to one. Potatoes and pumpkin midday with sausage meat, bread, margarine evening ration. German news mentions heavy fighting against superior forces in Russia. Recapturing positions in Italy, also mentions of sea attack on island of Leros, and then parachutists dropped and battle now going on, between our forces coupled with Badaglios against the German troops. Fairly dull day with some rain, and fair amount of snow, now laying out Qualisch way.

Sunday 14th November, 1943
Prisoner of War Bodisch Sudatenland. No work today except for four men called out to do a job at crossing gate at Birkight. Reading, bit of sewing wrote cards to Mrs Walker and Virgilia. Continued Yankee whist drive, lost 2nd round but won 3 and 4 rounds, otherwise a day passed fairly quietly. Potatoes, meat, goulash midday, potatoes, bread and margarine in evening. Dull windy day with some rain, hail amd snow.

Monday 15th November, 1943
Prisoner of War near Bodisch. 14 men to Qualisch and 14 to Halbstadt. 3 at camp shifting rubbish. On gang at Halbstadt and to Braunau in morning unloading sleepers and points. In afternoon unloading earth and some loading. Had row with the Rat. Home late tonight as trains running late. New railway guard comes to the Lager. Ruben soup midday, potatoes, meat, gravy, bread and margarine for evening. Whist drive continues. Plenty of German news, but hard to take which way it means. Fairly cold and dull day.

Tuesday 16th November, 1943
Railway party as a Prisoner of War Bodisch. Fifteen men Qualisch gang, nine Halbstadt and five putting up snow fences at Ottendorf. At Halbstadt myself unloading earth and had a fairly easy day. Evidently row with the Rat yesterday upset him as the civvies were loading the earth today. Plenty of snow balls being thrown about today some of the local kids sending a few over. Ruben soup midday with potatoes, meat, gravy at night and bread and margarine. German news mentions some of our planes over Greece and fighting still continues on Leros, another sub sunk in Agean Sea. Heavy fall of snow early hours of morning, otherwise fairly good day except for cold breeze.

Wednesday 17th November, 1943
Prisoner of War stationed at Bodisch. 15 at Qualisch, 9 at Halbstadt and 6 at Ottendorf putting up snow fences. At Halbstadt myself loading and unloading earth. Reasonably easy day with plenty of snow balls flying about. Fred goes shopping but does not get much. Whist tournament finished tonight, Bill Kerr and myself winning by one point from Templeman and Hampton. Ruben soup midday with potatoes, meat, gravy, bread and margarine. German news mentions fall of Leros, capuring 200 English officers and 3000 prisoners and 250 Italian officers and 5000 prisoners. Nothing doing in Italy and quiet in Russia. Japs also claims great victories. American planes over Norway. Snow during the early hours of the morning with bit during the day otherwise fairly decent.

Thursday 18th November, 1943
On railway party near Bodisch as a POW. 15 men Qualisch and 14 Halbstadt, myself with 7 others loaded earth and 6 unloading earth. Afternoon went to Braunau and unloaded some railway points, returning to Olberg and loaded 100 sleepers. Nothing of note happened. Stalag cigarettes up. Month today since we had any mail. Usual daily rations. German news mentions fighting new places in Russia. Artillery

duels in Italy. Our planes over France, West Germany and Norway. 100 guns lost on Leros and 12000 tons of transport lost. Meat and bread practically unprocurable in Eritrea for workers and 2,000,000 dead in India as a result of hunger. Frosty morning and very cold just after midday otherwise not bad.

Friday 19th November, 1943
Prisoner of War Bodisch. Gang 14 men Qualisch and 15 at Halbstadt. Myself at Halbstadt and with 7 others unloaded two trucks of metal, stacked 120 sleepers, loaded and unloaded some coal, and loading earth. Rest of the gang unloading earth and carting coal that was unloaded. Reasonable easy day. The Bull and the Inspector here today. Issued with 50 cigarettes and English food parcel. Mail up today for the first time for a month and a day. Received five myself: 1 from home, Ethel, Sigrid, Mavis and Lil & Tom. Under Officer in good mood cutting with matches, as to whether nine or ten men go to Qualisch tomorrow. Usual working times for the day and the same old daily rations. How would we live without those Red X food parcels. German news mentions heavy rain in Italy, things quiet in Russia, our planes in daylight raids over Norway and raids over Western Germany and many planes shot down. Jap radio says that America admits only losing a cruiser and a couple of destroyers off Bouganville. Cold frosty morning otherwise fairly good day.

Saturday 20th November, 1943
Prisoner of War near Bodisch in Sudatenland. 4 men home from last Sundays Arbeit. A gang of 10 to Qualisch and 13 to Halbstadt. At Halbstadt myself and loading earth ½ day and had shower before returning to camp. Those at Qualisch did not return till 1500 hr train, and continued on to Halbstadt for their showers and returning 1615 hrs. Three 'Camp' papers up today. Commenced a euchre tournament this evening. Bill Kerr and I together but lost first two matches. Rations altered over weekends, but same during week, getting less

potatoes and more bread, so today had potatoes, pumpkin, sausage meat and 250 grammes bread for today and tomorrow. No margarine up for three days and weekly sugar and jam ration. Difference in rations said to be due to a poor potato crop, but good grain crop. No German news but heard from outside source of landing in Northern Italy by our troops up from Corsica. Cold frosty morning but otherwise fairly good day.

Sunday 21st November, 1943
Prisoner of War at Bodisch. No work today, out of bed about 0930 hrs. Fairly quiet day, reading and wrote letter card home and to Ethel. Euchre tournament continued, had first win out of about 6 matches. Potatoes, meat, goulash, midday with quarter loaf of bread. No margarine, sugar or jam ration as yet. German news mentions street fighting *unreadable*, more rebels cleaned up in Albania, Japanese claim small losses at Bouganville and Italy quiet. Fairly cold day with fog in afternoon.

Monday 22nd November, 1943
Prisoner of War Bodisch. 14 men Qualisch gang and the same Halbstadt gang. Myself at Halbstadt – early morning loaded old sleepers, taken out from where 'Rats' gang were laying points, and very dirty job. In afternoon with 6 others went to Braunau and unloaded two trucks of sleepers and on the way back unloaded some earth, between Olberg and Heinzendorf. Two 'Camps' up and 9 parcels on the way. Reading during evening and euchre tournament continued. No German news of importance. Ruben soup midday, with potatoes, vegetables meal soup at night with 1/5 loaf of bread, 2 days issue of marg, one day still to come, and last weeks and this weeks sugar and jam ration. Dull but reasonably warm day.

Tuesday 23rd November, 1943
At Bodisch as a POW. 13 men on Qualisch gang, and and myself 14 gang at Halbstadt. Early morning helped shift rails and sleepers for 'Rats' gang

for laying points, also unloaded the sleepers. After Freistig loaded earth till midday, then went to Braunau unloaded truck of sleepers. On way back unloaded two trucks of earth between Olberg and Heinzendorf. Usual work times for the day. Days start closing in about 1600 hrs now. Euchre tournament continued, had a couple of wins tonight. Potatoes and vegetables soup at night, bread and marg ration (very low). Nothing of importance in German news, except for our bombers over Berlin and the Rhineland last night. Dull but reasonably warm day.

Wednesday 24th November, 1943
Prisoner of War Bodisch. Usual gangs out to Qualisch and Halbstadt. At Halbstadt myself. Early morning shifted sleepers for 'Rats' gang to lay points. Afterwards with 6 others, unloaded and stacked sleepers till 1345 hrs them with rest of gang loaded earth by engine shed. Had a guard out with us today. New Under Officer here now, probably taking over on Sunday. Reading in evening and continuation of euchre tournament. Lost tonight. Rations potatoes, meat, goulash with bread. Nothing in the news except for our planes over Berlin, third successful night. Cool morning but came out a nice day.

Thursday 25th November, 1943
Prisoner of War Bodisch, Sudatenland. Usual gangs at Qualisch and Halbstadt with myself in the latter. Early morning unloaded points in yard, finished this and 4 men stayed Halbstadt to load and unload some sand, the rest of us went and unloaded 5 trucks earth between Heinzendorf and Olberg. Day went fairly quietly, and the usual knock off time. Euchre tournament continued and had fourth win tonight. Two boys from Weckelsdorf-Felsen stayed here for the night, going on to Stalag tomorrow. Usual rations, news quiet. Reasonably fine day.

Friday 26th November, 1943
On railway working party as a POW in Sudatenland. Usual gang at Qualisch and Halbstadt being in the latter party. At Halbstadt loaded

and unloaded some sleepers laying by engine shed, also some rails in morning, and afternoon at Olberg loading earth. Issued with Canadian Red X food parcel and fifty cigarettes at night. Some mail up today and received 7 letters: one from home, one from Florrie, Sigrid, Merle, Muriel, Verna and Gladys. Rations Ruben soup at night with potatoes and bread. German news mentions Berlin and Stuttgart bombed by our Air Force. Heard some of our planes going over last night. Reasonably fine day with a little snow at night.

Saturday 27th November, 1943
Prisoner of War Bodisch, Sudatenland. 11 men to Qualisch 10 to Halbstadt and 5 to Ottendorf. At Halbstadt myself and then proceeded to Olberg, loaded some earth and after crib loaded sleepers. While Zug at station chased trout up the stream and between 6 of us got 9, myself getting the biggest. Half days work, having showers at Halbstadt returning to camp at 1415 hrs. Those from Qualisch, continued on to showers and return at 1630 hrs. Reading and continuation of euchre tournament in evening, had a win and a loss putting us out of the winning question now. 'Camp' papers up and personal parcels up and received by Stevenson, Hunter, Hampton, Galletly, Ross, Check, Pritchard and books Stevenson. Cigarettes by Pedersen, Davis SE 2, myself 2, and a couple of others, names did not get recorded. Rations: Potatoes, pumpkin, sausage meat and bread. German news quiet, and Russian Front, also Italy. Stuttgart and Berlin done over again last night and Dresden daylight raid. Heavy damage admitted and ninety three of our planes lost. Beautiful day till 1100 hrs then clouded over, came up fairly cold with attempts to snow in evening.

Sunday 28th November, 1943
Prisoner of War stationed at Bodisch. 16 of us called out this morning to unload a truck of rails at Halbstadt. Finished 1015 hrs and walked back, getting in camp at 1115 hrs. No cards up today for writing. Passed the day, reading, sewing and euchre tournament continued. Quite a

few of the boys down with the flu and sore throats tonight. No German news of note today. Rations of potatoes, meat, gravy midday 1/5 loaf of bread and ¼ lb margarine to last till Friday. For breakfast 2 trout and very enjoyable. Invoice received for 37 Xmas parcels, also told will get the usual weekly parcel as well as the Xmas one and 50 extra cigarettes. Roll on Xmas! Fairly good day till 1100 hrs then came up dull.

Monday 29th November, 1943
On railway working party as a POW in Sudatenland. 12 men to Qualisch and 12 to Halbstadt, at Qualisch myself and getting back at 1500 hrs. From Qualisch had to walk to Petersdorf to stack sleepers. Thawing out and conditions very sloppy. 7 men crook today and Doctor calls at Lager and diagnosed their cases as flu, and another one goes crook tonight. Two of the old guards come in for a few minutes tonight. Reading, playing cards and euchre tournament, and lost again tonight and one round left to go. Made Secretary of the Bodisch Gefangers Race Club meeting for New Years Day. News fairly quiet. Japs claim heavy successes and again intensive fighting in Italy. Potatoes, Ruben, barley soup with usual bread. Dull day with some rain and fog.

Tuesday 30th November, 1943
At Bodisch as a POW. 11 men to Qualisch, and 11 Halbstadt. Good many sick again today. Myself at Halbstadt continuing between Olberg and Heinzendorf to unload some earth. After this loaded and unloaded 30 rails. Afternoon returned to Halbstadt loading earth, and 3 men unloading and stacking truck of sleepers. Only did an hours work myself in the afternoon owing to having jammed my thumb and the cold making it ache. Home 36 minutes late, because of late running of train. Len Xmas goes to Dr today and ordered back to Stalag with broken bone in foot. 20 of the Xmas parcels up today and each one got the name on who it is for. No German news. Ruben and meal soup with potatoes and usual bread. A reasonably fine day with snow in the evening.

Wednesday 1st December, 1943

Prisoner of War at Bodisch. Nine men on Qualisch gang and ten men to Halbstadt, there being about twelve home sick. Making the fire. Halbstadt gang and the rest unloading earth between Olberg and Heinzendorf, and loaded a bit of stone, also few sleepers. Afternoon unloaded a few sleepers and loaded earth Freistig about 1600 hrs. Xmas and Hall returned to Stalag today. No news tonight. Rest of the Christmas parcels up also 100 cigarettes each. Potatoes, meat, gravy, usual bread and sugar and jam ration up for a fortnight. Fairly mild day with some snow between 1500 and 1600 hrs.

Thursday 2nd December, 1943

Prisoner of War in Sudatenland at Bodisch. More men sick today and eight to each party at Qualisch and Halbstadt out of twenty nine workers. At Halbstadt myself and then went to Olberg unloading earth. After Freistig went to Ottendorf, changed one rail, and turned another one round. After dinner returned to Halbstadt unloaded the old rail then loading up earth by station finishing at 1545 hrs. Finished euchre tournament tonight with Pritchard and Smith G, the winners. Making arrangements for Xmas. Roll on Xmas! Ruben soup with macaroni, potatoes and bread. German news: mentions pushing the Russians back, and that Wilson says he will take the Island of Leros back. Fairly good day with cold front working up in evening.

Friday 3rd December, 1943

Prisoner of War Bodisch. Ten men to Qualisch and nine to Halbstadt including myself, many still being down with the flu. In morning unloading earth, frozen four inches through between Olberg and Heinzendorf. Afternoon returned to Halbstadt, and loaded earth by the station. Fairly good day throughout. Issued with 50 cigarettes and Canadian food parcel in evening. Received chit today that another 12 personal parcels on the way. No work tomorrow so had bath tonight. Reading during evening and wrote out canteen orders for tomorrows shopping. Frosty and foggy all day at Halbstadt, but no fog on returning to camp.

Saturday 4th December, 1943
Prisoner of War near Bodisch, Sudatenland. No work today owing to having worked previous Sunday morning. Went shopping today with Fred and Eric. Did not get much today as usual, nothing in but expected. Went out at 0900 hrs and returned 1210 hrs. The streets all done wiith stone and very slippery this weather. Place badly laid out, streets running all ways. Afternoon playing cards, reading also washed out trousers and made a cake. Ruben soup with potatoes and usual bread. Frosty morning, but nice day.

Sunday 5th December, 1943
Prisoner of War on railway gang near Bodisch, Sudatenland. No work today except for twelve men needed at Halbstadt 0950 hrs to unload trucks of metal returning at 1300 hrs. During the day playing cards, reading and writing out songs for Christmas. No letter cards again today, missed two weeks now. Also doing canteen book and sent in Stalag cigarette money. Rations: potatoes, meat, gravy, midday and bread ration. German news report: Japs claim another great victory near Bogounville, and German success on one of our harbours somewhere. A few planes over Germany and also the Soviets attacking without success. Cold frosty morning with perfect sunny day and frosty at night.

Monday 6th December, 1943
Prisoner of War Bodisch. 12 men to Qualisch and with myself 12 to Halbstadt. Morning unloaded metal, loaded some sleepers and unloaded them. Afternoon down Olberg and Heinzendorf way, picking up plates, bolts, screws etc. Had to pick them off the ground as they were frozen to it. Rats gang digging out, very hard picking as the ground is frozen down about five inches. Usual work hours. Heard

that two more arrivals due tomorrow. Photo arrives for Snowy Myers. Usual daily rations. On the news front: Germans mention many battles in Russia but the Soviets meeting with no success, but the Sebastapool was in Russia hands. Rain stopping anything of importance in Italy. 'Said in Cairo' that they will soon have the Japs where they will want to capitulate, and the Japs reply was, that would never happen while one Jap was alive. Japs claim more outstanding successes near the Marshall Islands. Heard that raids over Leipzig did a fair amount of damage and planes also over Vienna same night. Heavy frost in morning but came out beautiful day and beautiful moonlight night.

Tuesday 7th December, 1943
Prisoner of War stationed at Bodisch on railway party. 12 men to Qualisch and myself with gang of 12 at Halbstadt, and had a very easy day. Morning unloaded truck of metal then down to Braunau and loaded truck of sleepers, returning to Halbstadt and loading about a dozen rails. Usual working hours. Gracie and Hall return from Stalag today. Things are not too good in the new Stalag they say. Mail and parcels up today, received four letters one from Mrs Walker, Jean, Gladys, Lil and Tom, parcels cigarettes Pritchard, Underhill, Horsburgh, Smith G 2, personal parcels by Stevenson, Smith F, Dalziel and books by Underhill, Petersen RA and food parcel by Stevenson. Received word today that the Xmas food parcel will not be an extra issue now, as stated previously. Reading and writing during evening. Ruben soup, potatoes and bread rations. No German news as wireless not too good. Fairly mild day but not much snow.

Wednesday 8th December, 1943
Prisoner of War in Sudatenland. Gangs of 12 to Qualisch, and the same to Halbstadt including myself. Loading rails till midday, then went to Olberg and loaded more also plates and screws. Return to Halbstadt and loaded 130 sleepers. Some Jerry issue socks, clogs, gloves, shirt and underpants today. Reading during evening. Several of the boys

practicing for a bit of a band for Xmas. Potatoes, meat, gravy, usual bread 4 lb margarine between 9 men for five days. No German news again tonight. Dull day but very mild.

Thursday 9th December, 1943
Prisoner of War Sudatenland. Gang of 14 to Qualisch, and including myself 15 of us to Halbstadt. First job today was stacking sleepers, then unloading sand which was so frozen that we had to get picks and practically pick it out, then shifted an oven and a copper. Afternoon loading earth by station, and also frozen very hard. Everything fairly quiet. Reading during the evening. Usual rations. German news still mentions heavy fighting in Russia but Soviets gaining no successes. A little fighting in Italy, also our planes bombing some Italian towns in Northern Italy and one German ship hit with a bomb carrying some of our prisoners, some being killed and wounded. Cloudy day with cold wind.

Friday 10th December, 1943
Prisoner of War on railway working party in Sudatenland near Bodisch. 14 men on Qualisch gang including myself 13 to Halbstadt. Loading earth till 1230 hrs and afternoon unloading it between Olberg and Heinzendorf. Fair amount of snow about earth well frozen usual working times for the day. Issued with 50 cigarettes and Canadian Food parcel. Reading during evening German news quiet. Ruben soup with potatoes and usual bread ration. Fairly mild and snowed steadily practically all day.

Saturday 11th December, 1943
Prisoner of War near Bodisch on railway job. Owing to 12 men being home today from working previous Sunday the rest of us had to go to Qualisch today and continued on to Halbstadt from Bodisch for showers, getting in camp1615 hrs. Reading during evening. Mail and 'Camp' papers up and received a letter from Gladys. Usual daily

rations. German news claim successes, despite many Soviet attacks. Fairly mild day with the sun coming through occasionally.

Sunday 12th December, 1943
Prisoner of War stationed at Bodisch. Fairly quiet day with nobody being called out for work. Reading, writing and mending during the day. Wrote letter card home and Gladys. Potatoes, meat, gravy & bread. German news mentions bombers over Emden in daylight raid and a new place mentioned on Russian Front. Frosty and cold day.

Monday 13th December, 1943
Prisoner of War in Bodisch. Gangs of 15 men to Qualisch and myself included 16 to Halbstadt. During morning shifting rails and sleepers where the 'Rats' gang were laying points and gave hand to slide new points in. Afternoon shifted a few sleepers and rails and locking points on truck. Leir returned today after being away for seven weeks. Chow today on job at Bodisch. Wireless out of action for getting Jerrry news, but got the following BBS news from Jerry: 118 planes shot down during one of our raids over Germany. Churchill says the whole of Italy not wanted will stop when get to a certain point. No let up of bombing over Germany during winter, and biggest surprise of war yet waiting for Jerry. Reading during evening. Ruben soup, potatoes, usual bread and margarine for five days. Very cold frosty day and suffered badly from cold today.

Tuesday 14th December, 1943
At Bodisch Sudatenland as a POW. 13 men on gang to Qualisch and 16 men at Halbstadt including myself. Loading points, iron sleepers, bolts and lashings on truck to go to Breslau also gave the 'Rats' gang a help by shifting sleepers and metal. Fairly easy day. Reading during evening. Wireless still out of action, so no German news again tonight. Same daily rations. Frosty morning coming out milder about 0900 hrs and again cold in the afternoon.

Wednesday 15th December, 1943
Prisoner of War in camp near Bodisch. 15 men to Qualisch and 16 with myself to Halbstadt. First job here, then went to Braunau and unloaded truck of points. Loaded 100 sleepers and unloaded in different places in yard. Returning to Halbstadt and unloaded some earth near Olberg, having a very easy day. Reading and doing canteen book during evening. Potatoes, meat and goulash with usual bread. Frosty morning and dull cold day, ground fairly well covered with snow.

Thursday 16th December, 1943
Prisoner of War at Bodisch. 15 men on Qualisch gang, and 16 to Halbstadt. At Halbstadt first thing to Olberg and unloaded earth. Returned to Halbstadt loaded wooden and iron sleepers near station, then went and unloaded them. After this, 3 men stayed behind to unload a truck of sand by engine shed, and myself with 3 others unloaded truck of coal. Started about 1145 hrs. Rest of the gang went with Leir to Tuntchendorf. Guard in charge of Russians put in charge of us. Tried to get us four on the coal to try and unload second truck, and help unload the sand but got abused and went away. Later another bloke tried to get the seven of us but told him off and he disappeared. Five minutes later civvie inspector and engineer and shed inspector in conference and were left alone. Reading during the evening. No news, wireless out of action. Some rations. Fairly cold day with fog during the day.

Friday 17th December, 1943
Prisoner of War Bodisch in Sudatenland on railway working party. 15 men to Qualisch and with myself 16 to Halbstadt. On Arbeit Zug and went out to Olberg, releasing earth and stone out of drain by line and loading on trucks. Kept busy most of the day. Issued with 50 cigarettes tonight, 10 men get Canadian food parcel, 3 invalid parcels and 21 English, leaving a Canadian parcel each for Xmas week. Fairly quiet day and the usual daily rations. Wireless still out of action but heard

that the Innisbruck was bombed last night and Breslau only wireless station on the air. Heavy frost followed by beautiful sunny day, coming up heavy frost again at night.

Saturday 18th December, 1943
Prisoner of War in Sudatenland. 13 men to Qualisch, and with myself 16 of us went to Halbstadt. Myself with 5 others loaded eight ton of coal and then had showers. All of us then came back to Arbeit Zug to and unloaded the coal by barracks for use here. Finishing the day at 1115 hrs. Those at Qualisch go through to showers and return 1615 hrs. Reading, washing and mending trousers in evening. Ruben soup, potatoes, sausage meat, bread, margarine for five days, weekly sugar ration and fortnight's jam up and a cheese issue. Wireless still out of action so only news heard was BBC from the Jews. Heard that rebels had help for Yugoslavia, this party comprising English, Italians and Yugoslavs commanded by British Brigadier. Berlin raided again. Cold windy morning, otherwise fairly decent day.

Sunday 19th December, 1943
Prisoner of War stationed at Bodisch. Fairly quiet day no outside work. Passed the day reading, writing and sewing. Wrote cards to Jean, Verna, Carmel, Joyce and "Lil & Tom". Potatoes, meat, gravy and usual bread. No wireless back yet so no news. Fairly windy and cold.

Monday 20th December, 1943
On railway working party near Bodisch in Sudatenland as POW. Gang of 15 men to Qualisch, and gang including myelf of 16 to Halbstadt. First of all went by passenger train to Braunau and then loaded earth in the goods yards. Picked up all tools at Olberg and stored at Braunau. Loaded trucks of square stones at Braunau and then returned to Olberg and loaded earth during the afternoon. Usual work hours. Wireless back again, but did not get the news. Undone the boxes of Xmas parcels and took all the straw out ready for quickness in issuing

on Friday night. Ruben soup, potatoes and bread and potato ration cut down from 620 grams to 480 grams. Frosty morning followed by a good day.

Tuesday 21st December, 1943
Prisoner of War Bodisch. 13 men to Qualisch, and 16 to Halbstadt and went through to Braunau on passenger train and evidently what we were to do was changed and returned on next train to Halbstadt. Shifted some old rails and double sleepers on small wagon, also tools from the boody and put on Arbeit Zug, for Braunau. Afternoon to Braunau again and unloaded tools there, picked up truck of rails and points and returning to Halbstadt and unloaded them. Then unloaded the truck of square stones that we had loaded yesterday. Evidently our planes getting well over here now and not allowed to have lights on at barracks at night outside. Saw searchlights in the distance tonight. Four personal parcels and received by Kerr, Davies, Templeman and J Horsburgh. Cigarettes Underhill. 'Camp' newspaper in but no mail. Usual daily rations. German news report Russia still attacking, but without success. Patrol duels in Italy. Daylight raid over Bremen and night raid over Mannerheim, and two other places and German planes bomb London targets. Some of our planes shot down over the Mediteranean, and our Navy somewhere busy in the Adriatic. Fairly warm morning, and continued throughout the day, with sun shining fairly well.

Wednesday 22nd December, 1943
Prisoner of War stationed at Bodisch. 15 men to Qualisch and 8 to Halbstadt and myself with seven others at Braunau, stomping sleepers. Finished our job at 1500 hrs then returned to Halbstadt by train and joined other 8. Usual times working and back at camp. New Zealand food parcels up today and mail. Received eleven myself. Some of my Air Mail to Australia got their two months and ten days and mail from Melbourne dated 4th October received today per Air Mail, and August

boat mail. Received letters from Doreen, Poppy, Bernice, Merle, Sigrid, 2 from Verna, 2 from Nurse H, 2 from Jean. Potatoes, meat, gravy, with usual bread. German news much the same as last night. Cold morning with fine day, except very cold wind.

Thursday 23rd December, 1943
Prisoner of War stationed Bodisch in Sudatenland. Qualisch gang of 15 men, and 18 including myself in Halbstadt gang and then with 7 and myself went on to Braunau stomping sleepers. Finished stomping midday and then shifted some plates, on one of the loop lines. Returned to Halbstadt 1535 hrs and home with the others. Usual time. No German news but have heard Big Ben strike nine and the English news. Busy decorating up the room for Xmas Eve and Xmas day. Issued with extra Canadian food parcel tonight. RA Petersen broke bone in right hand. Reading tonight and odd jobs. Ruben soup with potatoes with usual bread, and half usual margarine for five days and keeping 4 lb for Xmas Day for mashed potatoes etc. Warm day with a little snow, fell about 0900 hrs then fairly good day with a fog at night.

Friday 24th December, 1943
Prisoner of War Bodisch, Sudatenland. Usual gangs out 14 Qualisch and 16 to Halbstadt. On Halbstadt gang had to unload four part trucks of earth to finish in time to get shower and get home by midday train. Had only half days work and had fairly easy morning except we had to go flat out from the word go, and there was no doubt about the verdict, but were nearly beaten because of passing trains running late and keeping us from getting out of the station, to unload, the first time they were late for months and had to be today. Any way we managed it and home by 1215 hrs. During afternoon the Xmas parcel was issued, and the beer was on tap. After tea had and evening of community singing, solos, recitations and music supplied by Eric

Thorpe and band, which comprised 3 mouth organs, 2 mandolins, guitar and a drum stick fixed up on a tin. Evening passed along nicely, supper being at 2130 hrs, then followed more songs and recitations and a few hymns to finish with. Under Officer and two guards sang in German 'Holy Night" and Lily Marleen. Evening finished about 2315 hrs. Three barrels of 50 litres of beer went by the board. Bottle of cognac won by Hampton and myself second prize 10 rm. Fairly warm day, but front in early morning.

Saturday 25th December, 1943
Prisoner of War Bodisch Christmas Day. Nobody out before 0700 hrs this morning and all late getting up, and roused out at 0800 hrs by the bagpipes. Breakfast then followed and many were the different foods consumed. At 1000 hrs a church service was held. Just before church the cook came in and wished us all a Merry Xmas and Happy New Year, shaking hands all round and also for the articles we had given her at Xmas, she repaid by sending in 2 plates of biscuits and 2 ½ long bun loaves and very much appreciated by all, when we realized the small rations that they are getting. 1100 hrs tea came in and this was washed down by Xmas cake and chocolate biscuits, then came the Jerry dinner at 1230 hrs, this being potatoes, meat goulash and gravy. Then followed some reading, some sleeping and some playing cards, and also more beer being consumed. 1530 hrs hot water up for tea or cocoa, and had with Xmas cake and chocolate biscuits, Canadian biscuits then followed more card playing. Before the evening meal an action was held of the Xmas and Menu cards done and painted by Fred Earl and Syd Stevenson, the money going to the Welfare Fund of Stalag V111A. The sale realised 482 marks and this was made to 500 Marks by Eric Thorpe with a donation. Xmas dinner at 1800 hrs and this was steak and kidney with macaroni mashed potatoes, followed by Xmas pudding. After cleaning away, beer was introduced and several toasts were drunk, with songs by different ones, also community

singing, and several musical items. About midnight when the party broke up. Had the Under Officer and two guards sitting with us for dinner and gave them a bit to eat from ours. Frosty morning followed by a mild day with some snow falling.

Sunday 26th December, 1943
Prisoner of War Sudatenland. Boxing Day and not too many out before 1000 hrs this morning the day being taken easy after Xmas Day festivities. During the day, reading, playing cards, sewing and wrote cards home and to Virgilia and Doreen, when not indulged in sleeping. Potatoes, meat, gravy and usual rations. Back to the meagre items after yesterday. German news reports that Soviets attacking without success, this being on Xmas Eve and Xmas day, also no gains to us in Italy and fighting on the streets of some towns in from the Adriatic and our so called American gang Air Force dropped some bombs over Berlin to disturb their festivities, and not lose theirs. Fairly mild day with some snow falling.

Monday 27th December, 1943
Prisoner of War Bodisch. Gang of 12 to Qualisch and 16 to Halbstadt including myself. On Albeit Zug first of all went down to Ottendorf and the rest of the day loaded earth and stone, then had to bore couple of holes and put new plates where a rail has cracked through. 'camp' papers in and reading during evening. German news items: a convoy of supplies to *unreadable*, wiped out. Soviets still attacking and fierce fighting, but no success. 'Scharnhost' battle ship sunk after firing its last shell, and a greater superiority of our ships attacking. Small local attacks in Italy and fighting still going on in the streets of some towns. Japs give fantastic figures for two months in the Pacific. Potatoes, swede and macaroni soup with usual bread etc. Very nice morning but dull and cloudy afternoon.

Tuesday 28th December, 1943

On railway working party in Sudatenland as a POW of the Germans. 12 men to Qualisch and including myself 16 to Halbstadt. First thing we did was to unload four trucks of earth near Ruppersdorf and then with four others unloaded truck of sand, while the rest of the gang loaded earth. At midday they found out the sand was for different stations, so in the afternoon we five had to lay it again. Usual working hrs and the usual daily rations. Reading during the evening. German news much the same, except that Otherno evacuated by the Germans and more positions occupied North of the town. Fairly mild day throughout.

Wednesday 29th December, 1943

Prisoner of War Bodisch.14 men to Qualisch and 16 with myself included to Halbstadt. First thing went to Olberg leaving ten men there shovelling earth over the bank. Myself and five others returned with the Arbeit Zug and unloaded sand at Heinzendorf, Ruppersdorf, Birkight, Bodich, and at three crossings also unloaded ten sleepers at Bodisch railway station, and some old wood for the Lager. Returned to Halbstadt and then on to Olberg and picked the other boys up, then on to Ottendorf, Tuntchendorf, Braunau and unloaded more sand, returning to Olberg and loading earth and stone from drains. Usual daily hours. Potatoes, meat, gravy and bread ration. News Items: Russians doing fairly well, Germans claim victories, doing fairly well in Italy, our bombers over Italy, British say in some raids they saw no German planes, while Germans claim 26. Over Western Germany our planes returned safely and for once Jerry claimed none. Japs pay surprise visit on Americans in New Guinea. American planes visit Rabaul and Japs claim 30 out of 50 planes. Fairly mild day, thawing out fairly heavily, and also light mist falling at times.

Thurday 30th December, 1943

Prisoner of War stationed at Bodisch. 14 men gang to Qualisch, while 16 of us went to Halbstadt. First thing loaded some carbide gas holders, and myself with five others went to Ottendorf and unloaded them, while the rest shovelled earth over bank by railway line at Olberg. On returning picked up the rest of the boys and went to Halbstadt. Loaded some earth, rails and lashings and taking them to Braunau. After midday went to Ottendorf and picked up the boys we had left there in the morning and brought them back to Braunau. Fixing in rails at Braunau ready for when they lay the new points. Home at the usual time. Heard tonight that one of our previous under officers had been caught in the protectorate, selling French cigarettes at a mark a time and now in the bunker. Reading and playing cards during evening. News: Germans fighting around Bitepz. Jerries claim rear guard victory, heavy shelling and mortar attacks. Keriston evacuated. Leningrad shelled with success. In Italy a hill taken from our troops. Berlin raided last night and Western Germany visited 23 planes shot down. Battle near Bay of Biscay Germans claim to have damaged this Enterprise, 'Glasgow' and sank six destroyers and a couple of small boats. Ruben soup, potatoes and bread. Mild morning with drizzling rain, fairly cold at 1500 hrs and at 1700 hrs snow commenced to fall.

Friday 31st December, 1943

Prisoner of War near Bodisch in Sudatenland. Gang of 14 to Qualisch and gang of 16 including myself direct to Braunau, where we took out a couple of rails, and replaced with two others, then returning to Halbstadt but did not have time to have showers. Those at Qualisch continue to showers and return to Lager at 1400 hrs. A little mail up and received one from Cousin Joyce and also 341 Canadian Red X food parcels up, giving us practically supply on present strength to end of March. Issued with NZ food parcel tonight the first I have seen from there. It contained corned mutton, butter, jam, sugar treacle, tea, milk, dried peas, emergency ration chocolate, raisins and cheese. At 1900 hrs room cleared in preparation for concert and New Years Eve celebrations, which commenced at 2000 hrs. There were several toasts drank during the evening, recitations, ommunity singing, solos and musical items and these continued till 2359 hrs. Supper during the evening and plenty of beer. Usual daily Jerry rations and frosty morning with fairly mild day, and some snow.

Year of 1944 Railway Maintenance

Private Vic Petersen has been in German hands since June, 1941. He is about to add another year to his already 4 years.

Saturday 1st January, 1944
Prisoner of War on railway working party in Sudatenland, working party E388, now attached to Stalag V111A and originally to Stalag V111B. New Years Day. On the stroke of midnight, honoured the old year out and in with the new of the singing of 'Old Lang Syne'. Under Officer and one of the guards with us, and the Under Officer said a few words to us, and then on with more singing and single items continued the programme until 0215 hrs. Did not get up till about 0930 hrs. Reading and playing cards for the morning. At 1415 hrs started the Bodisch Clubs race meeting of ten races, which kept us going during the afternoon till 1700 hrs, and a good afternoon sport was had, there being a couple of barrels of beer, and betting on the races, the profits going to the Welfare Fund of Stalag V111A. Playing cards in evening and some music given by the bagpipes. Potatoes, meat, gravy, bread as rations. News as such: Jerry defences crumbling before the Russian attacks and in some places close to the 1919 Polish border. A 2,000 km Front in Pacific, America advancing well and turning the Jap guns on the retreating Japs, living on their food for two days, and putting on dry socks belonging to them while giving their transport a

chance to come up. Fairly mild morning with snow settling in during the afternoon.

Sunday 2nd January, 1944
Prisoner of War Bodisch in Sudatenland. Ten men called out to clear railway points of snow at Halbstadt at 0930 hrs returning at 1400 hrs. Not up too early myself and during the day, reading and playing cards. Wrote cards to Aunty Nell. Nurse H, Mabel and Cousin Joyce. Parcels up and received by Gillon, cigarettes by Petersen RA, Hunter, Dalziel, Myers, Pearce, Pritchard 4, and Balsarini. Also received some of my spare kit from Stalag V111B. Fault in the electricity, and lights were only about quarter capacity, and had to use candles and no news as not enough power to enable the wireless to go. Potatoes, meat, gravy, bread and margarine for five days. Fair amount of snow about early, but fairly mild before the day was out.

Monday 3rd January, 1944
Prisoner of War Bodisch on railway working party. Gang of 12 men to Qualisch, and with myself 14 of us to Halbstadt. At Halbstadt and being the firemaker till midday, the rest loading earth by the points. Afternoon unloading earth between Olberg and Heinzendorf. Potatoes, ruben soup and bread. English news: Russians 15 miles from 1939 Polish border at the town of Novragradvelensk and town said to have fallen. Germans suffering severe losses West of Kiev, Berlin done over second night in succession, 1,000 tons of bombs dropped last night, plenty of night fighters encountered over last two miles and twenty-seven planes lost. Troops weather bound in Italy. Eighth Army doing well around the Adriatic rough conditions. Street fighting by bandits in towns in Yugoslavia and the Japs retreating before the Aussies in New Guinea. German news: No success to Russians on Eastern Front. Heavy fighting around Shitomer, Southern Italy quiet yesterday. Supply store blown up by Germans at Augusta. Terror raids by our planes over Berlin, 31 planes shot down. A very dull and windy day, thawing out very fast, not much of Saturdays nights snow left.

Tuesday 4th January, 1944

Prisoner of War Bodisch. Today 12 men to Qualisch and 16 to Halbstadt. At Halbstadt myself and loading earth in morning and unloading in afternoon between Olberg and Heinzendorf. Easy day and home the usual time. Underhill and Petersen get orders tonight to return to Stalag, but did not leave. Reading and playing whist during the evening. Rations of potatoes, vegetable soup and usual bread etc. English news: Russians continuing on past the town of Novragradvelensk near the Polish border, in one place 250 miles from Rumanian border. Conditions getting very difficult in Sofia for the German troops, and things fairly quiet in Italy. Bandits doing well in some towns in Yugoslavia. Planes over Germany and none lost. German news: nothing of importance usual Russian attacks failing, attack on convoy in Atlantic and ten destroyers sunk by U boats. Fairly mild day, thawing out and more snow falling.

Wednesday 5th January, 1944

Prisoner of War on railway working party Sudatenland. 14 men to Qualisch and 15 to Halbstadt. At Halbstadt myself and with three others unloaded 65 tons of briquets, and kept fairly busy, and eyes very sore tonight from the dust of them. Other men loading and unloading earth between Olberg and Heinzendorf. Usual hrs. Underhill and Petersen RA return to Stalag today and Len Xmas returned from Stalag to here. The usual daily rations. English news: Lt General *unreadable* takes over in Italy in place of Montgomery who goes to England to take charge of the invasion troops; RAF does over some important railway junction in Bulgaria, Berlin and West Germany done over, with bombs and mines. Germans admit the evacuation of certain Russian towns. Russian troops a few miles from Old Polish border. Spanish 'Blue Division' and Spanish Legion take their place. France being bombed continuous yesterday. Very cold windy morning, continuing windy through out the day and snow falling from 0900 hrs onwards.

Thursday 6th January, 1944

Prisoner of War near Bodisch Sudatenland. Usual gang out today, but myself went to the Doctor with bad eyes as the result of the dust from out of the briquets of yesterdays loading, and got three days off and on return did some washing and mended some socks as could not do any reading or writing – usual times for those working and the usual rations for the day. Six men arrive from Lamsdorf tonight to strengthen the party. English news: Russians now over the Polish border in one place. In Mediterenean 12 German ships sunk by five of our subs. German news: nothing much. Very cold morning with cold wind blowing all day.

Friday 7th January, 1944

Prisoner of War stationed at Bodisch. Usual work parties to Qualisch and Halbstadt, and returning usual times. In camp myself with bad eyes, so not out of bed too early. Doing canteen book in morning and washed out trousers and tunic in afternoon. Issued with Canadian food parcel and 50 cigarettes in evening. Balsarini to return to Stalag. Ruben soup, potatoes, bread and margarine for five days. No news of note either English or German. Frosty looking day with cold wind blowing and some snow.

Saturday 8th January, 1944

Prisoner of War Bodisch. Gangs out 11 to Qualisch and 8 to Halbstadt, others being in camp for work done last Sunday morning. Both parties home early. In camp myself with bad eyes. Some to the showers at 1500 hrs and return 1615 hrs. 'Camp' papers up. Played cards during day and evening. Potatoes, sausage meat and bread. News: Russians 15 miles over Polish border. News: Aircraft factory bombed by our plane, near Yugoslavia border. Russians doing well elsewhere 950 planes over France yesterday and three German towns down over and 42 German fighters shot down. Maoris in bayonet charge and take 400 prisoners. Aussies pushing in New Guinea towards Americans. Fairly cold frosty day with some wind.

Sunday 9th January, 1944
On railway working party as a POW near Bodisch, Sudatenland. No work today and fairly quiet day with everyone doing a little sewing, sleeping, reading or playing cards except for 14 men being called out at 1230 hrs to unload coal at Halbstadt. And returning at 1600 hrs. Wrote letter cards to R Doust and "Lil & Tom". Potatoes, goulash, usual bread as rations. News promising: mentions Russians thirty miles over Polish border. Very rough windy day with some rain falling and heavy thaw setting in.

Monday 10th January, 1944
Prisoner of War Bodisch. Parties out today with 12 Qualisch and 21 to Halbstadt, at the latter place myself. Five men return to Bodisch to do a job there, rest of us loading earth in morning and unloaded it between Olberg and Heinzendorf in afternoon with the usual working hours. Potatoes, meat goulash with bread rations for the day. News fairly promising again tonight in town over border only 30,000 of the original 100,000 once there. Russians also fighting thirty miles from German railway junction, supplying all the troops in the East. Bandits still causing trouble in Yugoslavia. Factories and aerodromes done over in France – Sofia again raided and caused a bit of a worry there. Frosty mild day with some wind and rain and sleet. Attempts to snow, thawing out heavily and very slippery.

Tuesday 11th January, 1944
Prisoner of War stationed at Bodisch. Work teams of 14 men to Qualisch and 19 to Halbstadt and Arbeit Zug. During morning loaded earth at Olberg. Afternoon with three others unplated some sleepers at Olberg, while the rest went to Ruppersdorf unloading earth. Usual daily times. Balsarini returned to Stalag today and Fred also went in on duties. Parcels up and received by Stevenson food and personal parcels received by Myers and Pedersen. Cigarettes Check, Gracie, Kerr and Alty. Usual daily rations. News: 5 German divisions done over by Soviets 35 miles over Polish border of 39. One place 20 miles from a

junction supplying East. In Italy west coast consolidated, advancing two miles yesterday. Canadians take the town of Othermo after one of the bitterest battles of the war. Bombardment from the sea. Sofia again bombed a second time in 12 hours by Wellington Bombers, escorted by lightning fighters who shot down nine German planes. Bombing over Burma and Solomon Islands Japanese Navy in hiding somewhere in port or afraid to come out. Polish borders to be modified with outlet to the Baltic. Cold morning till midday, then clouds, sunshine and wind.

Wednesday 12th January, 1944
Prisoner of War railway working party in Sudatenland. Gangs of 14 men to Qualisch and 19 to Halbstadt and Arbeit Zug. Went to Olberg loading earth in the morning and afternoon unloaded it at Ruppersdorf. Passed the evening reading. Fred not back yet. Potatoes, meat, and goulash with bread and margarine for five days. News Item: town at Novragrad-velonsk 23,000 dead and 400 tanks taken by the Russians. Flying Fortresses and Wellington do Pireaas over. Big air battle over Germany yesterday and Germans claim 136 planes. Americans say biggest battle of the war. Cold frosty morning later turning out very nice day and cold again in Evening. Fred Earl returned at 2345 hrs.

Thursday 13th January, 1944
Prisoner of War at Bodisch. 13 men to Qualisch and 19 to Halbstadt. Six men on oval unloading and 13 odd jobs in Halbstadt, yards during morning and afternoon loading and unloading earth in Olberg. Bull here tonight enquiring about cigarettes we gave to the Russians they only got 800 instead of 7 or 8 thousand as they stated. Fred brings back a new sanitor with him, and news of a few of our latest weapons in use. Ruben soup, potatoes and bread as rations. Not much in the news. Fairly cold day and tried to snow.

Friday 14th January, 1944
Prisoner of War at Bodisch, Sudatenland. 14 men to Qualisch and 21 to Halbstadt, and Arbeit Zug. On Arbeit Zug loading earth at Olberg

in morning and afternoon unloading. 'Camp' paper up. Owing to change over of issue of parcels, received a NZ parcel tonight and 50 cigarettes, we get another parcel and 50 cigarettes on Monday. Playing cards in evening. Ruben soup, potatoes, usual bread. News: Russians 50 miles over Polish border and doing well elsewhere and news fairly good tonight. Very mild day with slight rain falling throughout the day.

Saturday 15th January, 1944
Prisoner of War Bodisch. 4 men to Qualisch and 15 to Halbstadt and Arbeit Zug. On Arbeit Zug loading earth and unloading earth at Olberg during morning. Half days work. Had shower at 1230 hrs and returned to camp at 1350 hrs. Afternoon bit of reading, doing up canteen book and playing cards. Potatoes, sausage meat and bread. News: fairly good Russians 100 miles from the line where the Germans first started to push them back. Sofia and other districts evacuated. Mild morning, cold rain and now setting in at 1200 hrs.

Sunday 16th January, 1944
Prisoner of War at Bodisch. No work today except 0900 hrs, I was called out with 9 others to go to Halbstadt to unload coal, returning at 1400 hrs. Church service during afternoon. Wrote card home to Aunty Em and Merle. Whist tournament finished this evening with Check and Davies winning, with Xmas and Horsburgh as runner ups. Potatoes, meat and gravy and usual bread. Mild day with snow thawing out.

Monday 17th January, 1944
Prisoner of War on railway working party in Sudatenland on working party E388. 12 men to Qualisch and 20 on Arbeit Zug at Halbstadt. On Arbeit Zug loading earth in morning and unloading at Olberg in afternoon, also shifted boody down to where unloading earth ready for tomorrow for shifting earth beside of line. Usual work hours. Isssued with Canadian food parcel and 50 cigarettes on new day of issuing parcels. Mail up and received 5 letters myself: 2 from Verna, one

from Sigrid, one from Mavis, and one from Nurse H. Potatoes, ruben soup, margarine also fortnights issue of sugar and jam and a cheese issue. News again good tonight. Messerschmit factory done over. Russia an attack of the nerves, and Germans counter attack and push them back a little. Things fairly good in Italy. Eisenhower says he will carry out what he intends to do. Bulgaria says she will not do the same as Bagdolia. Fairly good morning with the sun breaking through about midday.

Tuesday 18th January, 1944
Prisoner of War stationed at Bodisch. 13 men to Qualisch 8 unloading coal at Halbstadt, the rest of us loading and unloading earth, and distributing sleepers for firewood to different houses along the line. Usual hours. Reading during the evening. Potatoes, barley soup and bread. News fairly good from all sectors. Germans expecting invasion and by their views, and say that when the attack comes it will be wholesale slaughter of American and English, and materials and leave them so weak as to give Germany the final victory. Frost in morning and still on grass at 1500 hrs. Fairly cold and dull.

Wednesday 19th January, 1944
Prisoner of War Bodisch. 13 men to Qualisch and 21 to Olberg. At Olberg myself and shovelling earth over bank by railway line. No Zug here today, going out with Qualisch gang and the boys from there, home later than usual. Pritchard and Wilson return to Stalag today. Reading during the evening. Usual daily rations. News: Russians advance well in Northern sector near Leningrad, coming through Jerry line, that has been on for 2 years. Fairly mild day with snow during the morning clearing away in afternoon.

Thursday 20th January, 1944
Prisoner of War Bodisch. 13 men to Qualisch and 21 to Olberg. At Olberg myself shovelling earth over bank by railway line. Fairly

easy day but outside earth frozen very hard. Fred goes shopping today and gave out the articles during the evening. Parcels up and received by Alty, Heggie, Hunter, Kerr, Pierce, Ross. Cigarettes by Horsburgh, Barker, Pierce, Davies SE. Ruben soup, potatoes, and usual bread. News fairly good. Fairly mild day coming up cool in the evening.

Friday 21st January, 1944
On railway working party in Sudatenland as a POW of the Germans on party E388 and attached to Stalag V111A. 13 men to Qualisch and 21 to Olberg where we were shovelling earth over railway embankment. Fairly easy day and home usual time. Played cards in evening. Mail up and received Barley soup, potatoes, and bread ration. News: Novragrad simply taken by storm, 25,000 German dead in seven days. Jerries said to be drowning civilians and prisoners of war on the Krim because of food difficulties. Progressing fairly well in Italy. Very mild day, thawing out heavy during the afternoon.

Saturday 22nd January, 1944
Prisoner of War Bodisch. In camp today from working previous Sunday, so not up before nine. Nine men at Qualisch and home1345 hrs and no showers for these as train was late. 13 men to Halbstadt and unloading coal, returning at 1210 hrs and already having had shower. Doing odd jobs during day and canteen book. Some new clothing given out to those who have only one pair of strides. Parcels up and received by Thorpe games parcel, Xmas and Templeman personal and cigarettes by Alty, Galletly, Gracie, Dalziel, Davies SE 2, Myers, Pierce, Pritchard and myself. Played first game of poker for nine months and won 31 ½ marks. Played euchre in evening. Potatoes, sausage meat and bread. News fairly good. Russians continue to do good in the north. Our bombers also busy over many places. Some German planes over England and a few shot down. We lost 53 planes over France. Fairly cool morning, followed by mild day but windy.

Sunday 23rd January, 1944

Prisoner of War stationed at Bodisch. In camp today except that 20 men were called out at 0900 hrs to unload metal at Halbstadt. Passed the day sewing, reading, playing cards, writing and wrote letter to cards to Alison and Gladys. Talk in evening of the New Zealanders actions after Crete to Tripoli. Rations: potatoes, meat and goulash, bread and margarine for seven days. News: Air supremacy over Italy. Three crack German divisons cut off by mile long landslide. All well Russian Front. Fairly mild day with some sunshine.

Monday 24th January, 1944

Prisoner of War Bodisch. No gang at Qualisch today, there being 16 at Braunau digging out being there myself and finishing at 1430 hrs. 15 being on the Arbeit Zug unloading metal at Braunau and 300 bags of cement at Halbstadt, returning to camp 1610 hrs. Issued with 50 cigarettes and Canadian food parcel. Reading during the evening. Rations: ruben soup, potatoes, and usual bread. News: fairly good. Generals Neame, O'Connor and Air Marshall Boyd escape from Italy to British hands after being prisoners of war since early 1941. Fairly mild morning and trying to snow during the day.

Tuesday 25th January, 1944

Prisoner of War stationed near Bodisch Sudatenland. Gangs of 18 men to Halbstadt being there myself and helping the Rat gang to lay new points and stomping, working till 1630 hrs. Other 15 men on Arbeit Zug, working at Braunau unloading metal and loading earth. See a few Junkers engines going through today. Reading during the evening. Potatoes, barley soup, and bread. Radio reception bad. No news tonight. Fairly mild day and trying to snow during the day.

Wednesday 26th January, 1944

Prisoner of War near Bodisch. Eighteen men to Halbstadt helping Rats gang laying points and stomping and finishing at 1550 hrs and came home on 1610 hr train. Others on Arbeit Zug and home usual time. Reading and writing during the evening. Under Officer returned tonight. Potatoes, meat, goulash, bread as rations for the day. News: Russians still doing well. Our bombers over France fairly often. Fairly mild day with some wind and attempts to snow.

Thursday 27th January, 1944
Prisoner of War stationed at Bodisch. 13 men on Arbeit Zug, and 17 at Braunau digging out - at Braunau myself and finished our job at 1445 hrs, and back in camp at 1610 hrs and Arbeit Zug usual time. Reading during the evening. Usual daily rations. News item: everything going down fairly well on Russian Front. Jerries giving heavy resistance in Italy. Japs lose fairly heavy in plane and convoy attacks near New Britain. Mild warm day with snow & rain.

Friday 28th January, 1944
On working party as a POW in Sudatenland. 13 men on Arbeit Zug at Halbstadt and Braunau and 17 at Braunau digging out. On the digging out gang myself and finished at 1215 hrs. All work finished by about 1400 so back in camp on the 1610 hr train. Fred went to Qualisch today to see about some of us getting our teeth fixed and have to go on Tuesday. Bill Kerr returned to the Stalag today. More food parcels on the way for us. Reading till supper time. Had an attack of billiousness tonight and had a blackout for a while. Oatmeal porridge, potatoes and bread as the days rations. News alright and going reasonably good. Fairly mild and fairly warm.

Saturday 29th January, 1944
Prisoner of War Bodisch. At home today with a crook stomach and 20 men home from working the previous Sunday so only 7 out working and being half day. 4 men go to Weckelsdorf to get food parcels, 416 arriving, giving us a supply to practically the end of June on present strength. Those out working returned at 1215 hrs. Mail and 'Camp'

paper up, received four letters myself being one from Alison, one from Carmel, one from Nurse H and one from Verna.

Personal and cigarette parcels up also and received by Davis SE, Heggie, Deeming, Gracie, Galletly and Pedersen. Cigarettes received by Davis SE 2, Hogg 2, Ross 2, Xmas 2, Ross and Davies. Potatoes, sausage meat and usual bread. Everything going fairly well in the news, including at the new landing in Italy. Very mild day, practically no snow about, except in isolated places, quite a contrast to this time last year.

Sunday 30th January, 1944

At Bodisch in Sudatenland as a POW. No work today except that 20 men were called out at 0700 hrs to unload coal, and on getting there had to wait around for tools and all the coal was not here. Bit of a mess up and the boys did a bit of complaining and had to walk back from the job. In bed myself still with a bad stomach. Did a bit of reading and playing cards in the afternoon. No writing material in today but managed to scrape up a couple of cards and wrote to Betty and Mavis. Talk in evening of the New Zealanders part in the battle from Tripoli to Tunis, until the person there was taken prisoner. Potatoes, meat, gravy with usual bread and margarine for 7 days. News fairly good, heard of the Free French, after taking hill, running out of ammunition and keeping the Jerries off with boulders and stones, also woman fighting with the bandits in Yugoslavia. Weather still mild some wind.

Monday 31st January, 1944

Prisoner of War Bodisch. Workers at Halbstadt and Braunau. Go to the Doctor with crook stomach and two others. Get three days off and to have coffee and soup. One to return to Stalag. Reading most of the day. Issued with food parcel and 50 cigarettes. Usual daily rations. News: everything going very well on new landing, and Russians heading towards Estonian Border. Our planes fairly busy over Hanover and Brunswick, lost a fair few planes but Germans also lost a quite a few shot down and damaged on ground. Fairly cold morning but came out a good day.

Tuesday 1st February, 1944
Prisoner of War near Bodisch, Sudatenland. Gangs working at Braunau and Halbstadt. Home myself but with 5 others go to Qualisch to get teeth fixed. Could not get repairs done to mine so have to get a new plate made, and the price is pretty tough. Top set costing me 175 marks. One with top set lower partial plate 265 marks, one bottom plate 180 marks. The six of us amounted to 1005 marks and payment was 700 R marks to him, and the rest in food – bribery! Have to go again in about 12 days time. Prices for articles 1 mark ten cigarettes, 25 for 1/4lb coffee, 16 for 1lb butter, 5 for tin of salmon, 30 for 2 ¼ lb raisins, 15 for 2 grams tea, 5 for cake of soap, 30 for chocolate, 10 for tin of bully. Returned home 1500 hrs. Bit more snow lying about Qualisch way and fair amount of water from the thawing out. Oatmeal porridge, potatoes, and bread. News progressing favourably. All Fronts in Italy meeting with heavy resistance but carrying on. Fair few of our planes over France and Germany. Russians press onward. Air bases near Venice being done over as used a fueling base in the Balkans. In the Pacific things going well. Fairly cool morning and later turned out nice sunny day.

Wednesday 2nd February, 1944
At Bodisch as a Prisoner of War. Arbeit Zug gang at Braunau, cleaning up station yards from mud, and home at 1615 hrs. In camp myself and did a little washing, reading and writing out poems. Usual rations with weekly sugar issue. News: Fair few of our planes doing their duty over enemy country. Russians coming on well, and things fairly good in Italy. Germans claim over 800 of our planes during January about 500 of them over Germany. Pacific Front going favourably. Fairly dull morning but reasonable afternoon.

Thursday 3rd February 1944

A Prisoner of War Bodisch in Sudatenland. 12 men on Arbeit Zug and including myself 17 of us at Braunau digging out and finished at midday all returning to camp 1615 hrs. A little reading during the evening. One of the old guards here tonight on a visit – 'One Eye'. A good many French got off the train at Braunau this afternoon and looked pretty thin, done up and unshaven. Usual daily rations. Great things tonight, the Russians having pushed forward over part of the 1939 Polish border, causing pincer movement and cutting off many Jerry divisions. Near the Leningrad Front going well also. In Italy Jerries pushing on very strongly but our men holding on. Planes from Egypt carrying material to men in Yugoslavia, where they estimate these to be about 300,000 giving Jerry trouble. Our planes over Germany and France. Big raids on Wilhelmshaven and U boat base. In Pacific things going well, capturing a small island by the Americans which will enable them later on to take the Phillipines and make visitations to Tokyo possible. Very mild warm day with some sunshine and attempts to rain, which set in late in the day.

Friday 4th February, 1944

Prisoner of War Bodisch. Gangs of 13 men on Arbeit Zug and 16 to Halbstadt to help the Rat lay points, filling in and stomping. At Halbstadt myself and during the morning 12 yard rail rolled on my left foot and so out of it for rest of day. Well swollen up tonight. In camp at 1615 hrs and Zug gang the usual time. Mail up & received 4 myself, one from Sigrid, Ethel, Gladys and Lil & Tom. SE Davies and Hall returned from Stalag today. Meal soup, potatoes and bread. Rained a bit during the morning and little snow, otherwise fairly good day.

Saturday 5th February, 1944

Prisoner of War stationed at Bodisch, Sudatenland. Went to the Doctor with bad foot and got 4 days off. Only 6 out working rest being free from last Sundays work. Men home at 1215 hrs being half day. Some parcels up today, Stevenson personal and 2 cigarette parcels from repatriated person. Dalziel tobacco and Fred Smith personal. In the evening held concert had two barrels of beer and closed up 2200 hrs. Bull here during afternoon and evidently somebody around here being spying or saying a bit too much, or some people are guessing a lot, maybe a bit of trouble to get the BBC now. Did not affect tonight though and everything still going well on Russian Fronts. Our planes still fairly active. Americans capture a couple of small islands in the Pacific. Usual daily rations. Set in with snow overnight and kept up slightly all day.

Sunday 6th February, 1944
Prisoner of War Bodisch. No work today and for a change nobody called out so some slept in till fairly late. No mail cards again today but used a couple of old 8B cards myself and wrote to Gladys and Lil & Tom. Also during the day reading, playing cards and writing out poems. Fred gave a talk during the evening of the Westinghouse Brake as operated on trains. Rations potatoes, meat, gravy, bread and weekly margarine ration. Plenty of news: Russians continue to do well, cutting off more men by leaving the main roads alone and cutting over the mountains. Cut of men attempting to get out losing tanks and men and planes shot down. Things also well in the Leningrad sector, our planes busy and not many lost. Our troops hard pressed in Italy on all fronts. Bandits still causing Jerry trouble in Yugoslavia. Resistance against American bombers weakened yesterday in Pacific. Rabaul bombed. Fair amount of snow about this morning, and continued to snow at various times during the day.

Monday 7th February, 1944
Prisoner of War in Bodisch. In camp myself today with bad toe. Some on Arbeit Zug and some at Halbstadt digging out. All home at 1615 hrs. Reading, playing cards and doing up canteen book during the day. News: Russians still pushing forward. Our troops still hard pressed in

Italy. In Pacific American Navy shelled two places on the Island of Korea. Usual daily rations. A dull day with snow falling.

Tuesday 8th February, 1944
Prisoner of War in Bodisch, Sudatenland. In camp again myself with bad toe. Some men at Braunau and some on Arbeit Zug. 3 men go to Doctor with the flu and some have sore throats, evidently change of weather responsible as was very stiff in the joints myself this morning and in bed for most of the day getting up to shave during the afternoon. Some of the boys home at 1615 hrs and the rest the usual time. Potatoes, macaroni soup and usual bread. News: Nicopol in Russian hands and 5 German divisions cut off there somewhere and advancing well on the northern sector. Enemy shelling the bridgehead of the landing in Italy with nine inch guns, and elsewhere they are holding out stiffly. A good many of our planes over France and Germany and very few lost. One of our hospital ships bombed, killing two nurses and wounding 68. A very nice day with plenty of snow lying about.

Wednesday 9th February, 1944
On railway working party near Bodisch in Sudatenland. Party E388 and attached to Stalag V111A. Went to the Doctor again today and two others also each of us getting three days off. Some working Braunau and some on Arbeit Zug, and all home at 1615. Bit of reading during the day. More with sore throats tonight. Potatoes, meat, gravy and usual bread. News: Our planes still doing plenty of bombing with very little losses, France being heavily done over again. Many different types of planes being used. In Italy things quiet except for artillery duels and and patrol activity. Plenty of our troops stationed around the bridgehead in Italy. Germans claim they evacuated Nicopol according to plan, but Russians say about 17,000 were killed or taken prisoner. Ten divisions still cut off. Photos in American papers of Korea show dead and debris, lying about. Fairly good day. Setting in with more snow during evening.

Thursday 10th February, 1944
Prisoner of War in Sudatenland. In camp myself with bad toe, bad back and the flu, and about seven or eight others down with the flu, with working ranks sadly depleted. Some at Braunau digging out, and some on arbeit zug. Those at Braunau home at 1615 hrs. Arbeit Zug brings coal for Lager, and a bit of an argument ensued as to whether they had finished when they had unloaded the coal here. Also an argument on job at Braunau. Passed the day away myself with mending socks, reading and sleeping. More men sick with the flu tonight. Owing to the arguments resulting today there was no news tonight. Did not get to sleep very early tonight as barracks very sultry. Potatoes, ruben soup and usual bread. Snow set in early hour of the morning and continued throughout the day, there being some places 2 and 3 feet deep.

Friday 11th February, 1944
Prisoner of War at Bodisch Sudatenland. In camp again today with sickness. Two more to the Doctor this morning with the flu. Some on arbeit zug, and some on Braunau shovelling snow and stomping. Both parties home at the usual time of 1740 hrs. Under Officer still not in a very good mood today as the result of yesterdays arguments. Reckon he has given us a good spin and this is the way we treat him. He says he will stand for no more of it. Passed the day writing and reading during the evening. SE Davis returned today after being away for a week. Things not the best in Stalag. Usual daily rations. No news again tonight. Fairly mild day with more snow settling in during the evening and more snow about now than during December and January.

Saturday 12th February, 1944
Prisoner of War in Sudatenland. Back at work again today, shovelling snow around the Lager, others working at Halbstadt and Braunau and home at 1400 hrs. Held race meeting today in aid of funds for

the Tooth Fund, realising 270 dollars and with raffle amounts to 409 Marks. Did some writing during the morning and part of the afternoon. A little mail up today but received none myself, now eleven weeks since any from home. Potatoes, sausage meat and usual bread. Snowed overnight, continued again about 1100 hrs and kept up practically all day, getting heavier during the evening, being about a foot thick for the day.

Sunday 13th February, 1944
Prisoner of War at Bodisch. Seven men including myself went to Qualisch to the dentist for a fitting of teeth. About an hours job, but being Sunday could get no earlier train than the 1325 train and back in camp at 1530 hrs. Except sick and two washers all go to Halbstadt this morning cleaning points of snow and return about midday. Fair amount of snow out Qualisch way and plenty of wind. Doing canteen accounts after returning from Qualisch and no letter cards again today, three weeks missed. Usual daily rations. News items: Plenty of mud on Russian Front. Germans pushing heavy in Italy. Our bombers busy everywhere. Fairly fine day, with plenty of wind and snow about.

Monday 14th February, 1944
Prisoner of War in Sudatenland. Three gangs out today, there being 8 to Bodisch, 8 to Halbstadt and 11 at Olberg, all on snow shovelling jobs, and home at 1715hrs. Plenty of snow fighting on the job and easy days work. No time to do much but wrote out a few canteen orders and little reading. Issued with Canadian food parcel and 50 cigarettes. Potatoes, thick porridge and bread ration. German news: Successes practically everywhere and protests about cultural interests being bombed by our planes. Russians still pushing well and 10 German divisions chopped about. German Air Force trying to get supplies, but not much chance now, neck and neck race for another important part in Russia. Fairly mild day, trying to snow and rain.

Tuesday 15th February, 1944

Prisoner of War Bodisch. Eight men Bodisch, eight Halbstadt and ten to Olberg. Myself with three others on another party at Halbstadt and unloaded two trucks of coal. Finished midday and had showers and ready to go to camp at 1500 hrs, rang up for Postern, and 'Rat' grabs him, and sends him to Olberg to get those down there, so it was usual time when we got back to camp. Reading and writing in evening. Roll call changed now to 2100 hrs instead of 2200 hrs. Usual daily rations. Not much in the news tonight. Fairly mild day, trying to snow again and some wind.

Wednesday 16th February, 1944

Prisoner of War in Sudatenland. Five men to Bodisch ten at Halbstadt and myself with fourteen others go to Hottensdorf-Johnsdorf. Did not get to job till after eight, as did not know last night as to whether we had to go on early train or not. Only about four hours work, shovelling and back in camp at 1500 hrs. One civvie got annoyed because we were sitting in the waiting room, while the civilians were standing up. On return to camp writing out poems and also during evening. Potatoes, meat and gravy, usual bread. News: fairly good with the usual Jerry successes, and practically no losses. Our planes still fairly active. Fairly cold day especially during afternoon.

Thursday 17th February, 1944

Prisoner of War Bodisch. 15 men to Johnsdorf, which included myself and rest at Braunau. To work out Johnsdorf on 0550 train. On arrival had to go to another place, so had to walk back about two miles. Snow shovelling and fairly easy day, having an hour for dinner, and getting back in camp at 1500 hrs. A little writing and reading during evening and also played crib. Air raid practice this evening. Mail up and received eleven letters. One from home, first for three months, 2 from Mrs Walker, 2 from Nurse H, one from Sigrid, one from Mrs Forrest, one from Merle, 2 from Jean and one from Verna. Usual daily rations.

News: Heavy fighting in Italy. Russians still closing in on cut off divisions, and advancing in the North. 400 Russian planes over Helsinki. Heavy fighting in Burma, also Green Island, now thoroughly secured, and bombing by our planes in New Guinea. A very cold morning, with a small amount of snow falling, bitterly cold wind.

Friday 18th February, 1944
Prisoner of War in Sudatenland. Eight men at Bodisch, some at Halbstadt, and fourteen others with myself at Ober-Addersbach, shovelling snow and a fair swine of a day, snowing and strong winds, causing it to drift, take two shovels full out, then couldn't see where you had been. Back in camp 1500 hrs. Not feeling too good so in bed early tonight. Porridge with potatoes, usual bread. News: Ten divisions now finished off, capturing many men, and planes, many tanks were lost in trying to get them out. Jerries also admit evacuations of another town. Fairly heavy fighting in Italy with a lot of help from our planes. Very cold, snowy and windy day.

Saturday 19th February, 1944
Prisoner of War near Bodisch, Sudatenland. Should have been a day off for practically everyone today but owing to snowfalls, six were called to Halbstadt, fifteen to Addersbach, and four others with myself, shovelling snow around the Lager. In afternoon with five others went to Qualisch to get false teeth, returning again at 2000 hrs. Potatoes, sausage meat and bread. No news of any kind tonight and a little snow in morning and some wind.

Sunday 20th February, 1944
Prisoner of War Bodisch. In camp today and for a wonder nobody called out to work, and being a cold frosty morning made the most of the old cot. Had a church service at 1100 hrs. No letter cards again today, being a month now without issue. Did a little writing, reading and playing cards. Chadwich gave a talk in evening of the trawlers at work

in England, but did not hear it myself as was crook and went to bed. Potatoes, meat, goulash, bread and weekly margarine issue. G News: Many of our planes over Leipzig area more of our ships sunk, and pushing the Russians back and also doing well for themselves in Italy. A very cold day, starting off with a heavy frost about and 15 degrees below at 0700, plenty of sunshine but no warmth in it.

Monday 21st February, 1944
Prisoner of War at Bodisch, Sudatenland. Six men home, ten at Halbstadt, and myself with fourteen others, at Ober-Addersbach, shovelling snow from railway line. Home on 1500 hr train. Did some writing and doing up canteen book. Usual rations for the day. G News: More of our planes over Leipzig and also Stuttgart. Jerries still resisting attacks by the Russians, and holding strongly in Italy. Fairly cold morning, otherwise mild day.

Tuesday 22nd February, 1944
Prisoner of War Bodisch. Fifteen men at Ober-Addersbach including myself, and the rest of the party at Halbstadt. Shovelling snow from railway line and in camp at 1500 hrs, then did some washing, mending and writing. A bit of wrestling going on in the snow and like Polarbears by the time they are finished also snow fights and shovels used to throw the snow about. Rations as usual. News: E.3500 American planes over Hanover, Stuttgart, Berlin and another place, and 500 over France. 1000 over Italy in action. Russians still pushing forward steadily, and fairly severe fighting in Italy, not advancing much but holding their own. Jerry news: contradicts practically all of the Russian advances, pushing them back with heavy losses. Fairly mild day with a little snow falling.

Wednesday 23rd February, 1944
Prisoner of War in Sudatenland. With fourteen others at Ober-Addersbach, rest of them at Halbstadt shovelling snow clearing railway

line. In camp 1500 hrs. During evening doing canteen book, and some reading. Potatoes, meat, goulash and bread. News: Another town evacuated by the Jerries in Russia. Heavy fighting in Italy some of our troops encircled there. Our planes still active doing over the Junkers factory at Leipzig. Russians bomb Helsinki again. Fairly cold morning, later plenty of sunshine, and being fairly nice day, and set in cold again in the evening.

Thursday 24th February, 1944
Prisoner of War stationed near Bodisch. Woke up this morning to the heaviest frost we have had this winter, being 25 degrees below on the job. Myself with fourteen others at Hottendorf, shovelling snow and back in camp at 1500 hrs, and the rest of the party at Halbstadt. Most of us at Hottendorf got sunburnt faces from the sun striking and reflecting from the snow. Mending and reading during the evening. Rations as usual. 3000 planes over Germany doing Schweinfurt, Leipzig and other places over, the previous day Pilsen in Zceckoslavakia was bombed, 500 over Holland and 300 over France. Russians still continuing their advance, our encircled troops in Italy pressed closer in and Jerry now claims 400 prisoners. Since last Saturday since the big American raids started over Germany I/C of American Air Force says they will continue till success is achieved. Germans claim more rediculous successes against the Russians. Very cold morning, a heavy frost, being down to 25 below around here, but beautiful sunny day followed.

Friday 25th February, 1944
Prisoner of War Bodisch, with fourteen others shovelling snow at Ober- Adderbach, and in camp again at 1500 hrs others at Halbstadt and home 1615. Reading, marking clothes and playing cards. All the civvies stare at us at stations unable to make out why we have such fat faces, and fairly good clothes. Vermicilli soup tonight with potatoes and bread. News: Much the same as last night. Fairly mild but very dull day.

Saturday 26th February, 1944

Prisoner of War in Sudatenland. Only seventeen men out today including myself all go to Halbstadt, six unloading cinders and the rest of us shovelling snow from lines around the engine shed. Managed to get shower and in camp by 1215 being half day. Reading, writing and played 17 games of euchre and 5 of five-hundred. Some of the band gave a few musical items during the evening. Some mail up and received one from Jean and 1 Lil and Tom. Potatoes, sausage meat and bread as rations. News: Churchills son with Tito in Yugoslavia. Our bombers busy again over one or two places and also the messerschmidt factory. 48 planes being lost. German planes over England. In Italy 15000 German dead and 400 prisoners. German plane production down as the result of our raids, 40 per cent fighters, 20 per cent light bombers and heavy bombers by 25 percent. No G News. Fairly mild but dull day.

Sunday 27th February, 1944

Prisoner of War Bodisch. No work today, so slept in till late. Reading, and writing and playing cards. No letter cards again today, 5th week now. Three of the boys here leaving tomorrow for another party and three from that party coming here. Nothing doing in the newstonight. Days rations potatoes, meat, goulash, bread and weekly marg ration. Cold morning later coming out nice sunny day with cold evening. Talk in evening by Irwin Alty NZ on cheese making.

Monday 28th February, 1944

Prisoner of War in Sudatenland, with fourteen others to Weckelsdorf-Felsen shovelling snow, started work at 0630 and finished at 1230 hrs and back in camp 1500 hrs. Three hotels in this place now used for German wounded. This is also a popular holiday resort in peace time, there being a bit of a lake in the hills about 500 feet up about 5/8 mile long, and not quite so wide, also one rock that used to be the stronghold of bandits 400 years ago, and remains are still there. 4000 visitors in two days in peace time scenic day. Rest of the party were working at Halbstadt. Three men for the other party did not leave today now probably tomorrow. Writing, reading and playing cards on return to camp. Seems to be plenty of food parcels and bulk about for prisoners of war have parcels here now for four months, and possibility of bulk arriving. Same daily rations. E News: Things reasonably quiet, except for a bit of bombing by our planes on artillery in Italy. Pacific-our planes bomb Jap naval base and cause heavy damage, also sink six other ships. Troops surrounded in Burma now free, and going strong. Indians flocking to the colours against the Japs. G News: not much, the usual fantastic claims. Fairly mild day conditions being wet as snow thawed out.

Tuesday 29th February, 1944 (extra day being Leap Year)
Prisoner of War at Bodisch, Sudatenland. Fourteen others and myself at Weckelsdorf-Felsen shovelling snow. Fairly easy day. Starting about 0630 hrs and finishing at 1230 and in camp at 1500 hrs. Dished out canteen goods on return. Rest of the party at Halbstadt and returned at 1615 hrs. Three new chaps arrive from the job at Trautenau today, two of them being Tommies and one from New York. New U/Officer here tonight to take over for ten days while the present one goes on leave to be married. Nothing doing in the way of news tonight. Semolina porridge, potatoes and bread as rations. Very mild day, with sun shining and thawing out.

Wednesday 1st March, 1944
Prisoner of War at Bodisch. All of us go to Halbstadt today, shifting snow from in front of station and off the roof. Gave us all a firearm job to finish 1600 hrs but after dinner whipped a couple away on coal, and they did not get in camp till 1745 hrs. Reading during the evening. Potatoes, meat, goulash, bread and weekly marg ration. Our warships shelling Germans a little in Italy. Plane activity very quiet. Russians still pushing forward to Scoff. Many Germans giving themselves up.

Russia dictates terms to Finland as in 1939 and waiting for acceptance of terms. Mild day and thawing out, and a little snow.

Thursday 2nd March, 1944
Prisoner of War on railway party near Bodisch in Sudatenland. All in Halbstadt, again today, ten men being on coal and twenty two on snow, shifting away from the station and on the roof. Finished and in camp at 1615. Doing canteen book and reading during the evening. No news tonight. Usual daily rations. Fairly mild day with some snow falling, but thawing out quickly.

Friday 3rd March, 1944
Prisoner of War Bodisch Two tears since job started. All at Halbstadt, except myself and three others helped welders fixing up broken rail at Mittelsteine. I did not get in camp till 1745 while the others were at home at 1615 hrs. A little mail up and some parcels. Received no mail myself. Personal parcels received by Dalziel, Gillon and Ellsmore. Cigarettes by Smith G, Smith F, Balsarini 2, Pedersen 2, Heggie 2, Lunam 2, Early, Barker and myself. Nohing doing in the way of news tonight, everything seeming to be very quiet. Fairly mild day, with a cool night.

Saturday 4th March, 1944
Prisoner of War Bodisch. At Halbstadt where on arrival 16 men go straight onto coal unloading, while the rest of us were shifting heaps of snow. At 1000 hrs another eight of us went to unload 20 ton truck of coal by bathhouse. 32 ton load of briquets come in, but refused to unload them, having done our amount for ½ days work. To camp at 1210 hrs. At 1500 hrs myself with nine others had to go and unload the 32 ton truck of briquets. Finished had baths and in camp 1745 hrs. In the evening had a concert that lasted till nearly 2200 hrs then had supper and lights out 2300 hrs. Plenty of plane activity around here from 2200 hrs until midnight. Reading for a while during evening. No

news. Potatoes, bread, sausage meat. Mild day, with sunshine in late aftrnoon.

Sunday 5th March, 1944
Prisoner of War in Bodisch, Sudatenland. No work today, so nobody out too early. Did some reading during the day and washed-out socks and handkerchiefs. Gave a talk in the evening of my first visit up the desert and back. No cards yet for writing, being about seven weeks without any. Potatoes, meat, goulash, bread and weekly margarine issue. News: Planes over Munich, two Australian squadrons praised, planes also over Berlin, and bombing of aerodrome being used as bases to bomb London. Free French advance a little in Italy. Russians advance in one sector doing well, 3000 dead and many prisoners. Americans land in Admiralty Islands, killing 5000 Japs in hand-to-hand fighting. Amercans losing only one tenth of their number and claimed it as one of the hardest battles yet fought around these parts. Chinese also doing well. Cold morning but fairly bright day

Monday 6th March, 1944
Prisoner of War in Sudatenland. Five men on coal at Halbstadt, the rest of us go to Halbstadt, but owing to there being no abeit zug, went to Olberg on the next train, shifting snow and unloading metal. It being nearly 1000 hrs before any work was done, and returned to camp at1745 hrs. Issued with Canadian food parcel and 50 cigarettes. Heard that the plane activity of Saturday night was our planes over. Reading during evening. Potatoes, meat and gravy with bread ration. Fair swine of a day with driving wind and snow.

Tuesday 7th March, 1944
Prisoner of War near Bodisch. Eleven men to Halbstadt, and nineteen others with myself go out the other line to shovel snow at Johnsdorf, after yesterday's wind which had caused it to drift, train and snow plough bogged out there yesterday. Home at 1500 hrs and playing cards and

reading during the evening. Potatoes, swede soup and bread. News items: big raid over Berlin loss of about 80 planes. Planes also over Holland and Belgium doing aerodromes over, Jerries attempt to cut off bridgehead in Italy, but pushed back after losing 1000 dead. Russians doing well, having now cut off the main line from Germany and leaving ½ million men in precarious position. New Zealand's in Fleet Air Arm sink some ships of Norway. Very gusty day with mist and very moist air causing snow to thaw out.

Wednesday 8th March, 1944
Prisoner of War Bodisch. Nineteen men and myself at Johnsdorf shovelling snow off line towards Hottendorf, no Freistig knocking off early for dinner. Rest of the party at Halbstadt and Mittelsteine. Home at 1500 hrs. Played cards and reading during the evening. Potatoes, meat and goulash with usual bread and margarine. Big Russian offensive begins. Fifth Army Front active in Italy. Planes do Calais over. Misty, foggy day with cold wind.

Thursday 9th March, 1944
Prisoner of War in Sudatenland. Eight men to Mittelsteine stomping, six men Bodisch cleaning out drains, and eighteen others and myself at Addersbach shovelling snow from railway line. Home 1500 hrs. Evening: reading and playing cards. Chadwich goes to a Civvie hospital near Gratz today. Potatoes, swede soup and bread. News: Holland done over. Big concentrated attack on Berlin. 2000 bombers and 1000 fighters, 40 bombers lost and 16 fighters. Over 100 German planes shot down, besides some damaged on the ground. Big ball bearing factory wiped out. Italy 5th Army front advance three miles yesterday. In past week on bridge head 500 tanks destroyed and evidently getting more troops together for more attacks. In Russia everything going well, advanced in one part to Lemberg 80 miles inside General Government border. Odessa seriously threatened. Very mild day with sun shining and snow thawing out very well. 'Cut again in spud ration.'

Friday 10th March, 1944
Prisoner of War in Sudatenland. Eight men to Mittelsteine, six at Bodisch and seventeen including myself at Johnsdorf shovelling snow. Easy day home by 1500. Being home tomorrow washed out pullover, trousers, socks, handkerchiefs and had a bath. Reading during evening. Some mail up and received letter from Lil, with one enclosed from home and unknown photo in them. Potatoes, barley porridge, bread and weeks sugar and jam ration. Fred went shopping today but can get practically nothing these times. Ian Gillons birthday - 28th, and had barrel of beer to celebrate it. Letter cards arrive today so will be able to write this Sunday for first time in seven weeks. A few bets and dates being predicted when our troops will make the invasion. Only Jerry news tonight and they admit certain evacuations. Mild day with fog coming up later, but thawing out.

Saturday 11th March, 1944
Prisoner of War near Bodisch. Had morning off today, as result of last Saturday afternoons work, so slept in till 0900 hrs. Writing out poems on getting up until midday. Eight men working Bodisch and the rest at Mittelsteine. Six men go to Qualisch to dentist, but had trip for nothing as dentist was not home. Afternoon playing cards and reading. Not much news tonight. Russsians still doing well. Eisenhower says everybody will have to pull their weight to win the War. 96000 Welsh miners on strike. Florence bombed. America sends three times as much food to Russia last year, as she did in 1941. Potatoes, sausage meat, bread and weekly margarine ration. Potato ration cut to 400 grammes a day. Fairly mild day with some snow falling at intervals during the day.

Sunday 12th March, 1944
Prisoner of War stationed at Bodisch. Nothing doing till the afteroon when seven men and myself were called to Halbstadt at 1230 hrs to unload coal, finished in an hour, had showers and came home on 1445 hrs goods train. Today had first writing material for seven weeks and

wrote letter card home and to Sigrid, and cards to Guy M and Donald. Reading, writing during parts of day and had whist drive in evening. Usual daily rations. News: Calais done over by Maurauders, no opposition and all returned. Toulon bombed heavily, and sub base hit. Hamburg bombed and big factory of 150 acres done over. West coast of France being heavily bombed, all three fronts active in Italy. Florence bombed again, and marshalling yards hit, 66 German planes lost in Italy to our 14. Fairly quiet Russian Front. In Pacific heavy bombing going on, American marines make landing on some island and Japs panicked and took to boats, six of these being sunk, other places of Japs being cut to ribbons. Germans state planes over Munich and not much damage done. Mild with some snow falling.

Monday 13th March, 1944
Prisoner of War Bodisch in Sudatenland. 14 men at Misselsteine and myself with eight others between Olberg and Mittelsteine and myself with eight others between Olberg and Heinzendorf; shovelling earth over bank and had easy day, having two hours for Freistig, and 2 ½ hrs midday meal, knocking off at 1535 hrs doing only 2 ½ hrs work for the day. Issued with Canadian food parcels and 50 cigarettes in evening. U/Officer returns from his leave. Reading during evening. Semolina porridge, potatoes and bread our rations. No news tonight. Gusty windy day with snow, sleet and rain.

Tuesday 14th March, 1944
Prisoner of War Sudatenland. Eight men at Bodisch and nineteen others with my self at Ober-Addersbach shovelling snow from railway line. One train snowed in here yesterday for nearly six hours and some of the men did not get home till 2200 hrs. Home today at 1500 hrs and doing some writing till the evening meal and reading during the evening. Swede soup, potatoes and bread ration. News: Planes continue to bomb coast of France heavily and also do Frankfurt over, no

opposition over France – 5th Army Front in Italy active. 35 German planes shot down in Italy and Mussolini's mouth piece killed in plane accident. Everything fairly active on Eastern Front, one place 10000 dead and 3000 prisoners. IRA declares war on England. A windy day with snow falling practically throughout.

Wednesday 15th March, 1944
Prisoner of War Bodisch. Ten men at Bodisch, nineteen others and myself at Ober-Addersbach shovelling snow. Fairly good day and at home 1500 hrs. Writing during rest of afternoon and reading during the evening. Parcels up today and received by personnel Barker, Hampton, Thorpe, Armstrong, Check, Chadwick. Cigarettes by Hampton, Hunter, Barker, Check, Stevenson 2, Balsarini, Templeman and myself one 200 and one of 600 from Godfrey Phillips, through the Red Xross and De Reske. Potatoes, meat, goulash and bread. Nothing much doing in the way of news. Mild day with sunshine and snow thawing out.

Thursday 16th March, 1944
Prisoner of War near Bodisch. Ten men working here and nineteeen others and myself at Ober-Addersbach, shovelling snow. On the fire job today so did not shovel much snow. Five Russian women working near here and wanted to carry five of us away to where they were working. In camp at 1500 hrs. Writing till tea time and resting after tea. Bull here during the afternoon. Potatoes, barley porridge, bread and sugar ration. News: Planes active over France and Germany, 3500 over Germany. Italian Fronts active. Two breakthroughs near bridgehead. In Casino 3500 tons bombs dropped and tanks then advanced under smoke screen. Battle in English Channel and four torpedo boats sunk. Russian Front very active, railway to Odessa cut in three places, and 14 divisions in some other places cut about. Mild snow morning with snow and sun at intervals with sun finally coming through about midday.

Friday 17th March, 1944

Prisoner of War near Bodisch in Sudatenland. Eight men at Bodisch, and twenty of us at Hottendorf shovelling snow and back in camp at 1500 hrs. Fred and Mac go into Stalag today with Hall who is staying there. Mail up today and received five myself. Two from Verna, one from Sigrid, one from Merle, and one from Carmel with very nice photo also. Reading during the evening. Potatoes, semolina porridge and bread. News: Bombers still active over France and Germany. 12000 pound bomb now being used and scored on Michelin Tyre factory. Heavy fighting in Cassino sector in Italy. Nothing much to report Eastern Front. Mild day with some snow falling at intervals.

Saturday 18th March, 1944

Prisoner of War Bodisch. In camp today for working last Sunday afternoon. Writing and reading during the day and did canteen book. Few of the boys working here, and some at Johnsdorf and they went through to Halbstadt to showers on the return train and in camp at 1615 hrs. Eight men to Qualisch in afternoon to dentist and return 2000 hrs. Fred and Mac return from Stalag bringing some nugget, tooth brushes, razor blades, cricket bat and ball, and musical instruments. Rations: potatoes, sausage meat and bread. News: Our troops now in ¾ of the town and coming in on the flanks. Jerries pressed into one corner (presume Cassino), still getting supplies into the bridgehead. Planes still doing France over and Australian and NZ squadrons do over parts of Germany last night. Workers in two factories in Turin and Milan go on strike, managers interviewed but remain with the people. Russians pressing strongly many divisions cut about and 6th Army practically routed, on Bessarabia border. In ten days thousands dead and thousands of prisoners, small raids over London but few casualties. Parachiute troops land in Burma- Japs throw in the sponge Solomon Islands. Very mild day with sun shining and snow thawing out.

Sunday 19th March, 1944
Prisoner of War in Sudatenland. No work today, so not up too early. Reading, writing and marking clothes during the day. Wrote letter cards to Ethel and Carmel, and cards to Poppy and Bernice. No news of any kind tonight. Potatoes, meat, goulash, bread and margarine for a week. Very mild day with sun shining and snow thawing out heavily.

Monday 20th March, 1944
Prisoner of War Bodisch. Eight men to Halbstadt, and twenty including myself at Johnsdorf shovelling snow and back in camp 1500 hrs and filled in the rest of the day reading. Issued with Canadian food parcel and 50 cigarettes. Usual rations for the day. News: 8000 planes left Italy on bomblng raids, parts of Yugoslavia and Munich. Calais being bombed heaavily day and night, also some planes over Western Germany. Russians still pushing forward crossed the Dneiper in three places and wiped out two Rumanian and four German divisions, also pushed forward between Rovno, and Lembergh. Practically on Bessarabian border. Heavy fighting in Cassino, Germans getting reinforcements. Americans occupy all islands in the Admiralty group. Mild day interspersed with heavy snow, wind and sunshine, thawing out heavily.

Tuesday 21st March, 1944
At Bodisch, Sudatenland as a Prisoner of War. Fourteen men at Mittelsteine cleaning out ditches and fourteen including myself between Heinzendorf and Olberg shovelling over bank of railway track. Fairly easy day in camp 1745 hrs. Sanitor visits Chadwick in hospital today. Had operation for appendicitus. A little reading during the evening. Potatoes porridge and bread. News: War Office declaring south coast of England out of bounds to all civilians from Saturday week. Planes bomb Munich, Vienna Stuttgard and Sofia and French coast still being done over. Six ships sunk in Suda Bay by Wellingtons.

Dedoconese also bombed. Russians still busy, and bulgarians starting to resist Germans. Hitler has ordered their mobilisation. Successful attacks at bridgehead in Italy, and doing fairly well in Cassino. Fairly mild day, with bit of snow falling and some sunshine.

Wednesday 22nd March, 1944
Prisoner of War on railway working party in Sudatenland. Eleven men at Mittelsteine, six home on coal and fourteen including myself on same as yesterday between Olberg and Heinzendorf and easy day. In camp 1745 hrs. Five parcels up and received by personnel Akester, Galletly. Cigarettes by Davis SE; Music book and myself books from London and book and games from Virgilia. Rations of potatoes, meat, goulash and bread. News: Bombers still doing French Coast over especially Calais, also over Munich, Vienna, Manneheime and aerodromes in Yugoslavia. Coastal guns fighting duel over the Channel. Things fairly good in Cassino sector in Italy, chasing Jerry out of house to house in bayonet fighting. Russians still coming forward and 15 miles from Rumanian border. First indication of Germans occupying Hungary were parachutists landing on aerodrome and taking them over. 150 members of the Government arrested. Finland refuses peace offers. Mild day with some snow falling and cold wind and little sunshine.

Thursday 23rd March, 1944
Prisoner of War in Sudatenland. Six men in Lager shifting coal, five shovelling snow at Bodisch and twenty including myself at Ober-Addersbach shovelling snow. Trains snowed in as far as Weckelsdorf and as trains late we're here till 1230 hrs when special train with arbeit zug took us home at 1630 hrs. Reading during the evening and putting post cards in a book. Usual daily rations. News: Bombers active over France again, also Berlin, Frankfurt, Munich and Sofia. 19 planes lost. Hungary now in complete control by Germany. In Cassino Monastery Hill now taken and on the bridgehead Americans advance a little. Four German ships sunk off Norway. German troops pouring

into Yugoslavia evidently in support of Rumania. Russians pushing steadily foreward. Fairly mild day with snow and strong wind.

Friday 24th March, 1944
Prisoner of War in Sudatenland near Bodisch. Gangs out today of ten men to Halbstadt and twenty including myself at Johnsdorf shovelling snow from railway line, cleaning all the centre out this time. Home at 1500s hrs. Arbeit Zug also out there. "Camp" papers and mail up, receiving four myself: one from Vera, one from Doreen, one from Mavis and one from Gladys. Heard that my photo and letter were in the "Western Mail". One letter from Melbourne dated 18th January. Mending trousers and reading during the evening. Potatoes, porridge and usual bread. News: British bombers still active doing north east France day and night. Germany raided hourly. Railway junction by the name of Hants severely damaged today. Churchill and Eisenhower and other heads watch American parachutists in action in England and hope to see them doing their duty properly in the near future, Hull tells Hungarians to resist all they can against the Germans, say they came in to help Hungary against the Russians. Russians still active and fighting handy to some big naval base. Germans in disorder in places. Bridgehead in Italy quiet around Cassino stiff fighting – otherwise OK. Mild day with snow practiically all day and fairly heavy wind.

Saturday 25th March, 1944
Prisoner of War at Bodisch. Today all rail traffic held up here for some hours because of snow. All of us and extra civilians called out to clear the line. Working till 1600 hrs instead of the ½ day. Reading during the eveening. Troop train went through here today. Potatoes sausage meat and bread as rations News: Bombers still active over France, Schweinfurt, Berlin, Frankfurt and Hants. Raids around Berlin have put out of action 365 factories. One tank factory out since last November, 55000 workers there. Churchill says American parachutists

will go into action. The best equipped in the World. New Zealanders active at Cassino. Jerries occupying only 60 houses here now. Florence bombed. Russians occupy 70 Bessarabian towns. 100 mile front. Ukranian troops kill 30000 Jerries and 6000 prisoners. A fair swine of a day with strong winds causing snow to drift.

Sunday 26th March, 1944
Prisoner of War Bodisch. Was to have gone out today at 0800 hrs but luckily called off. Reading, writing, playing cards. Wrote cards home, Virgillia (Lil & Tom) and also pasted some post cards in a book. Potatoes, meat goulash, bread and weekly margarine issue. News items: Bombers active over Northern Eastern France, especially Calais, also over Berlin and Frankfurt, burning for 48 hours as the result of bombing and practically burnt out. Still resistance in Cassino. Germany fighting every inch of the way. Bandits attacking convoys going through Yugoslavia, tanks being heavily damaged. Germans now got 15 concentration camps in Hungary and sending food out of the country to Germany. England broadcasts to Bulgaria and Rumania. Russians on Rumanian border, crossed river Pruth on a 50 mile Front and occupied several towns. Fairly mild day with some snow falling and strong wind at times.

Monday 27th March, 1944
Prisoner of War in Sudatenland. Twenty eight of us leave at 0600 hrs for Johnsdorf. Plenty of wind blowing, snow covers line everywhere between Ober-Addersbach and Hottendorf. Got stuck in the snowand had to get out and dig train out. Had several attempts to get through but failed and eventually train returned to Weckelsdorf and no passenger trains ran. Snow plough and carriage out, about ten. Had civilians and Russians shovelling snow away. Eighteen of us got on the train with snowplough and went right through to Trautenau. Had to get out at Qualisch and shift bit of snow. Here it was blowing practically a gale and snow along the banks as high as the carriages, most I have seen

near and along the line yet. Arrived Trautenau 1240 hrs and left on return journey at 1500 hrs, picked up others at Johnsdorf and returned to Bodisch at 1715 hrs. Issued with 50 cigarettes and Canadian food parcel. Playing cards and reading during the evening. Potatoes, porridge and usual bread. News: Reception bad tonight. Essen done over and new places being built were hit. Artillery duels in Cassino, and patriots in Yugoslavia active. Mild day but very strong wind blowing.

Tuesday 28th March, 1944
Prisoner of War near Bodisch. Today all out btween Ober-Addersbach and Ottendorf shovelling snow from railway line and banks. No usual trains running, so went out by special and returned by special at 1630 hrs. Still a good few civilians and Russians helping to clear the line. Will be open for traffic tomorrow they say. Plenty of women out to clear the roads, which are blocked to motor traffic. Playing cards, reading during the evening. French cigarettes up. Potatoes, swede soup and bread. News: Flying Fortresses doing over oil fields. Planes over Rhineland also last night. Fourteen German planes shot down over England. Things fairly quiet in Marshalling yards bombed in Italy by medium bombers. Russians surround a town and cut off German mechanised transport, Germans fleeing into the Carpathian Mountains. Mild morning with very warm sun late in the day and snow thawing out heavily.

Wednesday 29th March, 1944
Prisoner of War in Sudatenland. Twenty nine of us at Hottendorf shovelling snow and home at 1600 hrs being an hour late today. Had row in morning going to work with "Spitfire", the blonde conductress who shed tears in her rage. An U/O threatened to pull his revolver. Playing cards and reading during the evening. Potatoes, meat, goulash, bread and weekly sugar ration. News: Nickeljev in Russian hands. Big railway junction south of Lemberg in Russian hands. Two Russian Armies converging on Odessa. Germans retreating being chased by Russian

Air Force, who use drones as they came into their hands. Stalin issues a warning to Bulgarians, Rumanians and Hungary to make up their mind now. Bombers still over France and Germany. Quiet in Cassino. Stiff fighting in Burma. Mild day with some wind and a little snow and fair amount of sunshine.

Thursday 30th March, 1944
Prisoner of War Bodisch. Twenty-eight of us out today between Hottendorf and Johnsdorf shovelling snow. Very hard this morning as the result of a frost overnight. In camp at 1500 hrs. Fred out shopping today, but did not get much. Playing cards and reading during evening. Potatoes, porridge usual bread as rations. News: Planes over France 7000 in all. Brunswick done over in Germany. In air battle lost about twenty and shot down fifty-five. Fairly quiet on the Italian Fronts. Discovered Germans had new secret weapon. Russians still coming forward at the foot of the Carpathian Mts, 25 miles from Odessa. Yugoslavia patriots capture small island of Spit, and take 150 prisoners. Fighting broken out in more places in Yugoslavia. American troops march past King today, everything including a procession 3 1/2 miles long. Slight advances in Burma. Frosty morning followed by warm sunny day.

Friday 31st March, 1944
Prisoner of War Bodisch in Sudatenland. Florrie's birthday. Twenty-nine of us at Johnsdorf shovelling snow, very hard to start as a result of frost. Reasonably easy day, and in camp 1500 hrs. Few English letters up, but no Colonial mail. Received order for all our spare trousers and jackets to go to Stalag, evidently more prisoners arriving there, leaving the majority of us with only one pair of trousers and jacket each. Playing cards and reading during the evening. Potatoes, porridge, and usual bread. News: Bombers active over Germany and France, Calais as usual. In night raids on Nuremberg. 92 planes lost, Jerry sent up everything they had. Few bombings in Italy. Long range artillery shelling

bridgehead, and artillery duels at Cassino. Russians still closing in on Odessa, not much to report elsewhere. Everything fairly well in hand in the Pacific. Germans claim successes, and also say Japs is doing well. Frosty morning, with sun coming out very strongly and snow thawing out.

Saturday 1st April, 1944
Prisoner of War ar Bodisch near Sudatenland. No work today having the day off for working last Saturday afternoon. Spent the day playing cards and reading and putting photos in book. Eight men go to Qualisch to the dentist at 1350 and return at 2000 hrs. Some to showers at 1500 and return at 1615. Potatoes, sausage meat, and bread. News: bombers still active and and claim raid on Nuremburg of previous night great success. Planes over South Eastern Germany and Western Germany. Fighting broken out against Casino and the bridgehead in Italy. Some height taken twelve miles north of Cassino. Raids also over Italy. Armies closing in on Odessa, one twelve miles away and the other 15 miles. Not much in the Pacific. German news claims about 250000 tons of shipping for March and say thet Americans admit loss of eight units of Navy in Mediterranean. Fairly mild day with sunshine and some snow.

Sunday 2nd April, 1944
Prisoner of War of the Germans working on the railway working party at Bodisch in Sudatenland. Party E388 and attached to Stalag V111A. Nothing doing today until 1230 hrs when five men wainted for coal at Halbstadt and return at 1400. Reading, playing cards and wrote letters to Clarrie. Florrie, Mrs Forrest and Gladys. Potatoes, meat, goulash, bread and margarine till Wednesday. News: bombers still active. Places done over in Yugoslavia from Italy, and also raids in Italy. Italy fronts very quiet. Germans setting fire to Odessa Russians closing in. Four more towns captured over Rumanian border by Russians. Very mild day with sun shining and thawing out of the snow.

Monday 3rd April, 1944

Prisoner of War near Bodisch. Twenty-eight of us to Johnsdorf shovelling snow by station, and back in camp at 1500 hrs. Issued with food parcel and 50 cigarettes playing cards and reading during the evening. Usual potatoes, meat, goulash, bread as todays ration. News: Bombing activity over France again, and 6000 over Germany yesterday. Few raids over Italy, Sofia and Belgrade. Italian fronts fairly quiet. Russians 25 miles inside Rumania. One line from Odessa open and Russians 5 miles from it and taking charge will enable them to cut off German troops in Odessa, which the Russians are now ten miles from. Fighting around Kovel and Stanislau. Frosty morning with warm sunny day, causing snow to thaw out heavily.

Tuesday 4th April, 1944

Prisoner of War on railway working party Bodisch. Twenty six of us at Radowenz today shovelling snow. Finished work at quarter to twelve and in camp 1500 hrs. Very easy day and plenty of snow fights going on. Chadwich returns today from having operation for appendicitis. Playing cards and reading when return to camp. Wrote letters. Potatoes, porridge and bread. News: Planes still active over France and Germany. During March American planes dropped 27,000 tons of bombs. British planes dropped 28,000 tons. Over Berlin six times. Sofia and Budapest bombed, nothing to report in Italy. Railway cut to Odessa and troops there now cut off. Another sixty towns taken in Rumania – Area retaken by Russians 16,000 squarre miles and killed 100,000 Germans and 14 Armoured Divisions and two Hungarian Divisions. Mines dropped in the Danube – Germans claim to get in on a convoy with subs and sank fourteen destroyers and one corvette. Mild morning and coming out sultry and trying to rain during the afternoon.

Wednesday 5th April, 1944

Prisoner of War stationed at Bodisch. Twenty eight of us go to Radowenz, but no tools or gaffir until after nine o'clock, and was nearly ten o'clock then we got started and then were stomping joins on railway between Radowenz and Qualisch. Finished at 1220, then went back to station had dinner, and waited for train, getting in camp at 1500 hrs. Playing cards and reading during evening. Usual daily rations. Only German news tonight and the usual fantastic claims. Foggy morning but mild and later the sun came through.

Thursday 6th April, 1944
Prisoner of War at Bodisch. Fifteen men at Halbstadt on arbeit zug and fifteen including myself cleaning out a drain, between Tuntchendorf and Mittelsteine. Knocked off about three and home at 1740 hrs. Fairly easy day. Playing cards and reading during evening. Two weeks of "camp" paper up today. Usual rations of potatoes, porridge and bread. News: Planes over France as usual, fighters over Berlin and Munich straffing the streets, railway yards and railway engines and dromes. Rumanian oil wells bombed, said to be place where Germany gets 1/3 of her oil. Russians practically in Odessa, Germans still have a few strongholds in Cassino. Telephone communiucations cut off between Ireland and England. Mild day with sunshine.

Friday 7th April, 1944 (Good Friday)
Prisoner of War at Bodisch. Eight men at Weckelsdorf, ten at Halbstadt and twelve including myself between Tuntchendorf and Mittelsteine cleaning out drains and a fairly easy day. Back in camp at 1745. Playing cards and reading during the evening. Potatoes, porridge, bread and weekly sugar and jam issue. Nothing doing in the way of news tonight. Snow clearing away fairly fast now, river carrying away plenty of water. Crops showing through and feel of spring in the air with the birds twittering. Fairly cool morning, but fairly good afternoon.

Saturday 8th April, 1944 Easter Saturday
Prisoner of War at Bodisch. Eight men at Weckelsdorf, ten at Halbstadt, the rest in camp. At Halbstadt myself started loading earth then six of

us went on coal. Bit of a row about the amount we had to do, so took things quietly and they climbed down, but did not get in camp till 1400 hrs, instead of 1215 hrs. Parcels and a little English mail up, and received letter from (Lil & Tom). Personal parcels by Myers, Barker, McQuarni, Deeming, Smith F and Pedersen. Played cards during afternoon. Community tea this evening consisting of mashed potatoes, cabbage and meat roll. During evening had smoke social and sing song till about 2300 hrs. Lights out at 2359, had beer in. Not too good myself so reading during the evening. No news tonight. Mild morning with a very fine day.

Sunday 9th April, 1944 Easter Sunday
Prisoner of War near Bodisch. Not up too early today, everybody sleeping well till nearly ten o'clock. Church service about 1200 hrs. Wrote out a few poems for Fred. No cards for writing, but had a couple of spares and wrote to home and Mrs Walker. Reading and playing cards during afternoon. Diddie took a couple of snaps of us today. Some of the boys on the beer and having sing song during the evening. Played cards myself. Potatoes, meat, goulash, bread and weekly margarine issue. German news tonight says Australia lost 1/5 of the empire losses of this war. Our news: Planes over France doing over railway yards and engines. Planes over Stuttgart, Brunswich, Sofia and Munich. Germans in last line in Cassino. Tank battles in streets Jerries lose 35 and us 11. Americans advance 5.5 mile on bridgehead and inflict heavy losses. Russians bomb Rumania and three German ships in Black Sea loaded with soldiers. Russians in Odessa and heavy German losses and much material taken, Russians 25 miles into Carpathian Mts and on Zcech border and tell Zcecks they hope to fulfill all promises to them. Yugoslavia patriots want planes and not men, now they have 200 machines. Mild day but very dull.

Monday 10th April, 1944
Easter Monday. Prisoner of War in Sudatenland. Holiday today. Reading, playing cards, a little writing, table tennis snd football. Issued

with food parcel and 50 cigarettes. Potatoes, meat, goulash and bread. Nothing much in the news. Germans mention that Posen bombed in Poland. Mild day, but very dull, except for little sunshine in afternoon.

Tuesday 11th April, 1944
Prisoner of War Bodisch in Sudatenland. Sixteen men at Halbstadt, and fourteen including myself between Tunchendorf and Mittelsteine. Halbstadt gang in camp 1615 hrs ours at 1745 hrs. Fairly easy day but feeling very stiff myself from yesterdays football. Playing cards and reading during evening. Usual daily rations. News: Fairly good from Eastern Front. Important junction captured by Russians on the Krim. 4600 tons of bombs dropped yesterday. Planes over Magdeburg, Rhur and Hanover. France and Belgium bombed especially Orleans. Eisenhower inspects Air Force, and says plenty of work ahead of them in the near future. Drizzling rain throughout the day, until 1500 hrs when heavy showers wet us through, otherwise mild day, with snow in hills thawing out.

Wednesday 12th April, 1944
Prisoner of War near Bodisch. Fourteen men to Halbstadt, fourteen to Ottendorf. At Ottendorf-Kinke till midday, pulling down snow fences, eight men stay there stomping, myself with five others go to Olberg cleaning out drain, and then to Ruppersdorf on the 1535 hr train to take some shovels and forks ready for there tomorrow. Easy day and home at 1745 hrs. Reading during the evening. Days starting to draw out a little and boys get outside during evening and play musical instruments. Seems to be plenty of French people working in Halbstadt now. Potatoes, meat, goulash and bread. News: Russians still doing fairly well in the Krim. Place by the name of Hurchberg about 25 miles from here bombed yesterday. Planes well over German territory. Frosty morning but beautiful day.

Thursday 13th April, 1944
Prisoner of War Bodisch. Sixteen men at Ruppersdorf and the rest in arbeit zug at Braunau. At Ruppersdorf myself and here we were laying

stone and fine metal on the road leading from the station along to the goods shed. Everybody finished and in camp at 1615 hrs. Pasted some postcards in book, reading during the evening. Some of the boys playing table tennis. Nothing in way of news. Potatoes, semolina porridge and bread. Frosty morning attempting to rain midday but cleared, nice day

Friday 14th April, 1944
Pisoner of War near Bodisch in Sudatenland. Twelve men on arbeit zug at Braunau. Until Freistig with the rest of us helping to put in rails, joining up the points in Halbstadt. After Freistig myself and three others go to Ruppersdorf, doing up the road there. All home at 1615 hrs. Reading and playing cards during the evening. News again quiet, except for some of our planes over Hungary and Russians still pushing in the Krims. Potatoes with swede soup and usual bread. Frosty morning and turning out nice warm day.

Saturday 15th April, 1944
Prisoner of War Bodisch. Fourteen men on arbeit zug, the rest of us at Ruppersdorf fixing up road, home at 1215 hrs. Some go back at 1500 hrs to Halbstadt for showers and return 1745 hrs. Some mail up, first Colonial mail for three weeks, received four myself: one from Carmel, one from Sigrid, one from Alison and one late one from Merle. Playing table tennis and cards during evening. Cook's daughter married today. Potatoes, sausage meat and usual bread. Fred goes shopping and gets some mustard. Nothing startling in the way of news, being only Jerry stuff. Frosty morning and turned out fairly nice day, except for little wind in the afternoon.

Sunday 16th April, 1944
Prisoner of War in Sudatenland. No work today so slept in till 0830 hrs. Writing, playing table tennis and cricket during the day. Wrote cards to Jean and Verna. Air mail restricted, so cannot send any till

next week. Two personal parcels up and received by Chadwick and Armstrong and food parcel by McBean. Potatoes, meat, goulash, bread and weekly margarine issue. Only Jerry news this evening and the usual fantastic tales. Mild morning later turning out fairly warm day.

Monday 17th April, 1944
Prisoner of War Bodisch. Twelve men at Halbstadt on arbeit zug and home at 1615 hrs rest of us at Qualisch leaving at 0550 hrs and home on arbeit zug at 1715 hrs. Helped to load truck of firewood sleepers and then pulling down snow fences. Very muddy on ploughed ground, otherwise easy day. Issued with food parcel and 50 cigarettes. "Camp" paper up tonight. Reading and playing table tennis during evening. Potatoes, swede soup usual bread. News: Germans now out of Cassino and Americans advancing on the bridgehead against all opposition. American bomber pilots say each time they come over Germany things getting easier. Very few Germans now fighting on the Krim. Our bombers do Belgrade Budapest and Kronestadt over. Twenty six planes over England last night and 14 shot down. Germans meet up with new RAF night fighter. Dull muggy morning and continued dull throughout the day.

Tuesday 18th April, 1944
Prisoner of War Bodisch. Twelve men at Halbstadt on arbeit zug and home at 1615hrs. Myself with sixteen others at Qualisch shifting snow fences, also loaded some old plates and screws, dogs and iron sleepers. Fairly easy day and home at 1715 hrs. Big Red X train passed through tonight. Playing cards and reading during the evening. Our news: Russians five miles from Sebastapool on the Krim. They claim to have overcome most of the obstacles placed in their way by the Jerries. Germans in Italy now feelings the effects of the 5th Army there – Raids over Budapest, Sofia and France. No person allowed to leave England so there will be no leakage of doings there. Usual rations. Dull, cold and windy day and caught most of us without overcoats.

Wednesday 19th April, 1944
Prisoner of War in Sudatenland. Twelve men to Halbstadt rest of us between Qualisch and Bosighals unloading guide rails. Finished 1530 hrs so very easy day. Shifted about 100 snow breaks. In camp 1730 hrs. Halbstadt gang home 1615 hrs. Reading during the evening. Have to sign a paper now for our French cigarettes when we receive them after the exploits of our last U/O. Potatoes, meat goulash, bread and weekly sugar and jam ration. Our News: Calais bombed again, and 3000 over Berlin and Brunswich, also over Rumania and Hungary. Russians fighting in Ternapol claim 15000 dead in six days, and Russians also now in Sebastapool. Six commando raids on France and only twelve men fail to return the last raid blowing up bunkers etc. 29 bombers shot down over England last night. Americans advance 11 ½ miles in three days in Italy, two spearheads linked up, fighters co-operating well and 38 German fighters shot down. Nothing much in the Jerry news: A wet cold and windy day with thunderstorm at 2am.

Thursday 20th April, 1944
Prisoner of War in camp near Bodisch in Sudatenland. Beginning 5th year of embarkation for overseas. Hitler's 55th birthday, and flags flying everywhere, no life in them though and we reckon this is an indication, that this will be the last birthday as Dictator of Germany. Twelve men to Halbstadt on arbeit zug and home at 1615 hrs. Rest of us at Qualisch unloading a few guide rails and taking down snow fences. Fairly easy day and home by arbeit zug at 1730 hrs. Playing table tennis and reading during the evening. Porridge, potatoes and usual bread. Nothing going in the way of news tonight. A fairly dull day with some rain.

Friday 21st April, 1944
Prisoner of War Bodisch. Twelve men to Halbstadt and sixteen of us get off at station past Petersdorf, pull down a few snow fences, then

loading some rails, six stay behind there, and ten of us go through with goods loading rails at Johnsdorf-Addersbach and Addersbach - Felsen, catching train home from here and home usual time 1715 hrs. Got word that 140 English food parcels on the way. Playing table tennis and reading during the evening. Potatoes with swede soup and bread. Nothing in the news except Jerries mention sinking of part of a convoy in Mediterranean Sea. Dull day with some rain and a little sunshine.

Saturday 22nd April 1944
Prisoner of War in Sudatenland. Ten men to Halbstadt and home at 1210 hrs - half day. Sixteen of us to Qualisch, four going down to dentist, rest of us unloading guide rails, finished job before eleven and came home on the 1130 hrs train and in camp at 1245 hrs. Went to showers at 1500 and returned at 1615 hrs. A little mail up and received two myself: one from Merle and Mrs Walker. Talking to one of the chaps from forestry job this morning from our Bn and learnt the whereabouts of a few of the boys. Played cards and reading during afternoon and evening. Usual daily rations. The oil: Russians now occupy Temberg and Tarnapol and in complete possession of Sebastapool. Russians using parachute drop in Carpathian Mountains to wipe out gun positons. 80 German tanks destroyed in the foothills. Bombing planes from France, Bucharest, Frankfurt and Hamel. Not much of Frankfurt left. Cathedral still stands. Oil refinery wiped out on the Danube. Still advancing in Italy and destroying many of the secret weapons, Goliath Tanks. Big concentration of tanks discovered inland of France, light medium bombers do them over, and fifty of our planes lost but heavy damage done and many German fighters shot down. In Yugoslavia there included 48 bridges destroyed in 24 hrs, ten miles of railway torn up, and eight trains destroyed. Everything now said to be ready for the invasion. Sherman tanks to be used. RAF to play its part and everyone fitted with the best. Reasonable morning with showers in the afternoon.

Sunday 23rd April, 1944
Prisoner of War in Sudatenland. No work today so slept in till ten. During the day played cricket, table tennis, cards and reading. Wrote letter card home and cards to Dorreen and Nurse H. Potatoes, meat, goulash, bread and margarine for a week. Have to hand in jackets at night now, as well as overcoats so the nights are pretty cool. Afraid of us attempting to escape. Only Jerry news tonight and not much to report. Fine morning, but some wind and dull in afternoon.

Monday 24th April, 1944
Prisoner of War at Bodisch. Twelve men on arbeit zug at Halbstadt, and home 1745 hrs. Seventeen of us at Qualisch and Petersdorf taking down snow fences, except for a bit of walking, fairly easy day. Played second round of table tennis in evening and beaten, also reading. Issued with Canadian food parcel and 50 cigarettes. Bulk NZ and English parcels on the way. Potatoes, porridge and bread. A bit late with the news tonight, so did not hear what there was. Dull morning, but turned out warm sunny day.

Tuesday 25th April, 1944
Prisoner of War stationed at Bodisch (Anzac Day). Twelve men at Halbstadt and home 1615 hrs. The rest of us at Qualisch taking down snow fences, finished between there and Radowenz, then walked through to Johnsdorf. Rained fair bit in morning, so had a fair amount of time off, so had a fairly easy day. Work train was late so did not get into camp till about 1610 hrs. Geneva Commission was here today with German Heads. A few parcels up and received by Strange and Stevenson personnel cigarettes by Gracie, Hampton, Earl Ross, McQuare also some more library books from Stalag and some English music. Usual daily rations. Oil: France bombed heavily, especially Dieppe, Belgrade, Mannerheim and Munich bombed. Over 100 German planes shot down over Munich. Front line in Italy and Russia quiet. Fourteen German troopships sunk between the Krim

and Rumania. Germanys cronium supplies from Turkey stopped. Tito threatens the miners of Yugoslavia, and Tito thanks British nd American air force for their help down there recently. Britain laying new type of mine in Baltic and German ships suffering badly as the result. From 27th onwards no one allowed out of Britain. Two new landings in New Guinea and claim to have cut off 100,000 Japanese. Jerry news says that prisoners of War in America on bread and water and refusing to work on Hitler's birthday. Dull morning starting to rain at 0800 and continued for some time, but reasonable afternoon although dull.

Wednesday 26th April, 1944
Prisoner of War near Bodisch Sudatenland. Twelve men to Halbstadt and home at 1745 hrs, the rest of us between Johnsdorf and Hottendorf pulling down snow fences. Easy day and home at 1715. Reading and doing up canteen book in evening. French cigarettes up. Nothing doing in the way of oil or Jerry news tonight. Potatoes, meat, goulash and bread. Dull morning attempting to rain, but turned out a nice afternoon.

Thursday 27th April, 1944
Prisoner of War at Bodisch. Twelve men to Halbstadt and home the usual time; some home mending boots and one gardening, and the rest of us at Ober-Adderbach shifting snow fences and finished them today, fairly early and doing some laying around in the sun, home at 1715 hrs. Reading and playing table tennis in the evening. No oil again tonight and usual Jerry claims of everything their way. Potatoes, porridge and usual bread. Frost early and raining a bit, but came out a beautiful day from 1000 hrs onwards except for occasional clouds.

Friday 28th April, 1944
Near Bodisch in Sudatenland as a Prisoner of War. Two men in camp, twelve to Halbstadt, and home their usual time. The rest of

us eighteen in all at Bosig Wolhotten levelling metal, and cleaning alongside of line. Fairly easy day, Civil gaffer gets annoyed with some of them. Home 1720 hrs. Farmers now busy putting crops in and fields quite busy with women working in them. Fields looking nice and green Some bulk food up today equivalent to 250 parcels to last food 8 weeks at present strength. One box missing at present containing chocolates, cigarettes and biscuits. Potatoes, pea and bacon soup from the Red X bulk and usual. No outstanding news. Very dull morning with occasional sunshine during afternoon.

Saturday 29th April, 1944
At Bodisch as a Prisoner of War. Twelve men to Halbstadt three to dentist at Qualisch and twelve of us at Bosig Welhotten, stomping and cleaning up along the railway line. Knocked off about 1230 hrs and home about 1510 hrs some continue to the showers and return 1615 hrs. Reading, playing cards and table tennis in the evening. 140 English food parcels arrive today. Usual rations. Bit of oil tonight. Still plenty of air activity by our planes, ground straffing in France. Berlin done over by 850 of our bombers, escorted by the same number of fighters. On the bridgehead in Italy, now 31 miles inland. Toulon raided by bombers and heavy damage done to submarine base. Germans now occupy one aerodrome on the Krim and this was bombed by the Russians, and German transport caught that could not land because of damage. 10 German ships sunk between coast of Krim and Rumania also ten ships sunk off Skager Rocks by our submarines. Japs getting pushed back in Burma and New Guinea. Bitterly cold wind today there being rain, snow and sunshine.

Sunday 30th April, 1944
Prisoner of War near Bodisch. No work today, so slept in till 0900 hrs. Cut bit off working trousers being bit too long. Reading, playing cards and table tennis and writing during the day. Wrote letter cards to Gladys, (Lil & Tom). Parcels and mail up. Mail received by Ross, Pierce, Gracie. Cigarettes by Pedersen, Davis, Pierce, Hunter, McBean,

and myself 2. Mail received two from Verna, one from Mrs Walker, none from home again. Some music also for the camp from the Stalag. The Bull here tonight and put on two guards at night now; have also to hand in our caps at night. Usual rations for the day. The oil: Yesterdays raid over Berlin. 63 of our planes lost, and 140 German planes shot down. Toulon and Calais bombed. 58 German planes shot down over Italy. Rebels still very active in Yugoslavia and claim their greatest successes, doing heavy railway damage. Naval battle going in Channel 0 at 1800 hrs. 2 German destroyers and 9 German submarines sunk and one Canadian destoyer lost. Air activity over England last night at great heights, 14 planes shot down. Canadian pilot shooting down four. The evening cold wind blowing with sunshine and snow throughout the day and cool evening.

Monday 1st May, 1944
On railway working party at Bodisch in Sudatenland, once part of Zceckoslakia which Germany annexed in 1938. Had holiday today for May Day. Filled the day in reading, playing cards and table tennis. 50 cigarettes and bulk issue today, not enough of each issued to go round, so get some this week and next week, get the missing articles made up. Potatoes, meat, gravy and bread. Usual German fantastic claims. April shipping figures: 115,000 tons sunk, 2000 tons damaged, 17 destroyers sunk, 8 speed boats damaged. Perfect swine of a day, cold wind with scattered showers.

Tuesday 2nd May, 1944
Prisoner of War at Bodisch. Twelve men to Halbstadt and home at 1615 hrs: two home washing and the rest of us at Qualisch. Loaded truck of earth and unloaded in morning. Afternoon loaded ½ truck earth and some old sleepers. Very easy day and home at 1730 hrs. Playing table tennis and reading during evening. Potatoes, pea and bacon soup (Red X issue) and bread. No news tonight. Dull morning, but fairly warm with some light showers in afternoon.

Wednesday 3rd May, 1944
Prisoner of War Bodisch. Twelve men to Halbstadt and home at 1745hrs. Seventeen of us at Qualisch loading and unloading earth. Easier day than yesterday. Home 1730 hrs. Bit too windy for table tennis tonight so playing cards and reading during the evening. Jerry military doctor here this afternoon, and Jerry Feld Wabel here this evening who could speak English. Potatoes, meat, goulash and bread as rations. Nothing in the way of news tonight. Fairly fine day but very windy and trying to rain.

Thursday 4th May, 1944
At Bodisch as a POW. Twelve men to Halbstadt and home at 1715 hrs. Nineteen of us at Qualisch loading earth by station, but did not get home till 1815 hrs because left Qualisch late. No engine until 1500 hrs so had to push the trucks all the time. Heard from Stalag today about the extra clothes and the C/O German had no right to call in our extra suit of clothes. Potatoes, barley, porridge with the usual bread etc. Nothing doing in the way of news again tonight and no Jerry news. Swine of a day with some sunshine, strong wind and attempts to snow.

Friday 5th May, 1944
Prisoner of War stationed at Bodisch. Twelve men to Halbstad and home from work at 1210 hrs and nineteen of us at Qualisch loading and unloading earth also loaded some points, plates, screws etc. Fairly easy day again only doing about three hours work altogether home at 1730 hrs changed over parcel issue day to Friday instead of Monday and received English food parcel and fifty cigarettes tonight. A little mail up but received none myself. Played table tennis during evening. Potatoes, porridge and usual bread. Only Jerry oil tonight and nothing much of note. Reasonably fine day with cold wind and a little rain.

Saturday 6th May, 1944
Prisoner of War stationed at Bodisch. Twelve men at Halbstadt and home from work at 1210 hrs being half day and sixteen of us at

Weckelsdorf Mkt loading points finished about 1000 hrs and walked over the hills to Bodisch township, and to camp here at 1100 hrs. To showers at 1500 and returning again at 1615. During the sfternoon playing table tennis, cards and a little reading, and doing canteen book. Collins, Butler and Mc Bean received word to go to Herschberg on Monday. Potatoes, sausage meat and bread. Bit of oil tonight. Everything seems to be going well in Italy. 50 mile in from bridgehead and Jerries evacuating all civilians. Bombers active over France, Budapest and Berlin also over the Rumanian oilfields – 2nd largest in the world, claimed to be on fire with several others. 100 fighters and 60 bombers lost on the raid and Germans lost 100 fighters on the first raid & opposition weaker since. The Krim practically now in Russian hands and several Jerry transports sunk in Black Sea. Russians pushing into Rumania and Rumanians now handing out flags "Down with Hitler". Warehouses bombed on the Danube and several fires seen after fairly accurate bombing. Nothing mentioned of the Pacific. Dull day with a little sunshine and some rain, but fairly warm.

Sunday 7th May, 1944
Prisoner of War Bodisch in Sudatenland. No work today so not up too early. Filled the day playing cards, table tennis and reading. Wrote letter cards to Alison and Aunty Em. Jack and Ian went for a walk during the afternoon. Potatoes and pork meat with goulash and bread. News much the same as last night. Changeable weather with sunshine, rain and fair amount of wind.

Monday 8th May, 1944
Prisoner of War in Sudatenland. McBea, Collins and Butler leave today for Herschberg, leaving the strength of the party at 32. Eleven men to Halbstadt and sixteen to Qualisch. Halbstadt gang home at 1745 hrs. Fairly easy day at Qualisch loaded 19 rails and unloaded ten rails and in camp at 1715 hrs. A little reading during the evening. Potatoes, meat, goulash with usual bread and weekly jam and sugar

ration. No oil again tonight. Bitterly cold and dull day with some attempts to snow and very windy.

Tuesday 9th May, 1944
Prisoner of War stationed at Bodisch. Twelve men to Halbstadt and home 1745 hrs seventeen of us at Qualisch loading and unloading rails, also loaded some iron sleepers, plates, bolts stc. Fairly easy day again and home 1720 hrs. Some parcels up today and received by personnel Lunam, Ellsmore, Heggie, Smith G, Davies and Balsarini, mostly chocolate, tobacco and cigarettes by Early 2, Davies 2, Xmas 3, Gillon, Armstrong and Pedersen. Believe the Russians at Braunau getting bad treatment, Jerries using pick handles on them. Fairly quiet evening with a little reading. Potatoes, porridge usual bread. Nothing in the way of oil or Jerry news tonight. Farmer goes to Coy tonight and Diddle taking over in the Under Officers absence. Fairly fine day with sunshine but fairly cold wind blowing at times.

Wednesday 10th May, 1944
Prisoner of War Bodisch. Twelve men at Halbstadt and home 1615 hrs and sixteen of us to Johnsdorf -Hottendorf, doing a little stomping and putting in a few sleepers in place of broken ones. Easy days work. Home 1715 hrs, Halbstadt gang at 1615 hrs Days starting to lengthen out now and it is 2015 before sunset. Forest groves now looking green with the silver birch, and other trees coming out in bud and grass growing very quickly. Reading during the evening. Potatoes, meat, goulash with usual bread. Nothing in the way of news. A very nice and hot day, being practically a cloudless day.

Thursday 11th May, 1944
Prisoner of War in Bodisch. Twelve men at Halbstadt 1615 hrs and seventeen of us at Johnsdorf unloading 20 metre rails. Very old rails being three sections joined together some being as old as 1888, and had a machine for helping to unload them. Very easy day doing practically

nothing and home1715 hrs. Played piker in evening and won 15 marks. Potatoes, pea soup, spinach and bread. No oil again tonight. Fairly changeable day cloud and sunshine.

Friday 12th May, 1944
Prisoner of War stationed at Bodisch. Twelve men at Halbstadt a home usual time and seventeen of us to Johnsdorf. Ten men unloading 20 metre rails, and six others and myself replacing old sleepers and a bit of stomping. Reasonable day and home at 1715. Saw two Ukranian girls today the fairest I have ever seen from these parts. Had two guards with us today. Playing poker again this evening, but no luck at the game tonight. Mail and 'camps' up, received letters from Alison, Doreen and Verna. Bulk issue Red X food and 50 cigarettes. Usual daily rations. Only Jerry news tonight and the usual successes of theirs. Overcast with some sunshine and fairly windy, but condition really warm.

Saturday 13th May, 1944
Prisoner of War stationed at Bodisch. Mums 49th birthday today. Twelve men to Halbstadt and home early and thirteen of us at Johnsdorf, nine men unloading rails, and three others with myself replacing old sleepers in line. Easy morning, left Johnsdorf 1335 hrs through Bodisch at 1500 on to Halbstadt for showers and returned at 1615 hrs. Played cards during the evening but no luck again tonight. Usual rations for the day. Bit of oil tonight: Starting Friday night 12" 3000 RAF bombers were continuously doing over the coast of France until daylight, when American bombers took over and continued all day. 20 German speed boats sunk off the coast of France. Back to previous item Americans shot down 250 German fighters and destroyed many bunkers. Russian front quiet. 3000 of our parachutists landed behind German lines in Italy and cut off 5000 German troops and since then more have been landed. Tito's crowd in Yugoslavia busy and they claim they are twice as strong as they were nine months ago. Germans send out warning

that this bombing is probably the prelude to the invasion. (A fair number of Landwach jokers poling about with shot guns). Another ruling that no guards go out with us, having to stay here on duty. Civilian postens to come and get us and bring us home. A dull day but fairly warm.

Sunday 14th May, 1944
Prisoner of War in Sudatenland. No work today so had lie in till 0800 hrs and had an easy day, did some mending, reading, playing cards, cricket, table tennis, and also some writing. Wrote letter cards home, and Merle. Sent them both airmail as restrictions on use of airmail lifted. The usual daily rations. No oil. Fairly changeable day with clouds, sunshine and rains.

Monday 15th May, 1944
Prisoner of War at Bodisch. Six men go to Halbstadt and the rest of us out the other line, nine men at Johnsdorf, and eleven of us to Qualisch. At Johnsdorf gang stomping sleepers and myself with the gang at Qualisch fixing up crane for shifting rails, and then digging out on the side of the railway line in continuation of last years work. Easy day but time dragged. Home 1720 hrs. Playing quoit tennis and cards during the evening. Potatoes, pea soup, spinach and usual bread. Nothing doing in the way of oil and German news of nothing much. A rather miserable day, raining during the morning and fairly cold, but no rain in the afternoon.

Tuesday 16th May, 1944
Prisoner of War at Bodisch in Sudatenland. Dad's 60th birthday today. Six men to Halbstadt and twenty two to of us on the other line, eight being at Johnsdorf and fourteen of us at Qualisch, seven of us unloading rails and seven digging out. Fairly easy day and home at 1715 hrs. Myer as one of the postens today and had rifle. Six new chaps arrive today from Gorlitz, including one from the 2/28 Bn. Seventeen parcels

up today being received by personnel Dalziel. Cigarettes by Myers 2, Barker, Galletly, Earl, Armstrong, Deeming, Pedersen, Balsarini, Hunter, Templemen, Smith G and Davis SE. Porridge, potatoes and bread. No news. Fairly dull day. Cold and no sun or rain.

Wednesday 17th May, 1944
Prisoner of War Bodisch. Eleven men at Halbstadt and twenty three out the other line, eighteen getting off at Hottendorf for stomping and the rest of us to Qualisch, some unloading rails and some digging out. Took things easy and no complaints. Halbstadt gang at home at 1615 hrs and our line 1715 hrs. A little reading and packed away a few things in preparation for a search by the Gestapo. Trains running behind schedule this evening. Potatoes, meat, goulash, usual bread and jam and sugar ration. News: fairly heavy fighting in Italy and very few planes over Germany. A very dull day but reasonably warm with a few showers of rain.

Thursday 18th May, 1944
Prisoner of War at Bodisch in Sudatenland. Eight men to Halbstadt and twenty-five of us to Qualisch unloading rails and digging out. Fairly easy day and in camp at 1715 hrs. Armstrong goes to NCO's Stalag today. Feeling a bit tired during the evening so went to bed early. Potatoes, noodle soup and bread. News: still fairly severe fighting in Italy. Germans admit evacuation of Cassino and for the third day practically no planes over Germany. Fairly dull day throughout with little rain.

Friday 19th May, 1944
Prisoner of War stationed near Bodisch. Eight men to Halbstadt and twenty-five to Qualisch, some unloading rails and the rest of us digging out, twelve sleepers between two men and finished about 1400 hrs and back in camp 1715. Issued with 50 cigarettes and Canadian Red X parcel in the evening. Feld-Wabel here this evening to question

some of the Halbstadt gang about writing on railway wagons. Quoit tennis and reading during the evening. Potatoes, pea soup and bread. German news mentions heavy fighting in Italy still going on. Warm and sunny day.

Saturday 20th May, 1944
Prisoner of War at Bodisch. Eight men to Halbstadt and home 1350 hrs, nineteen of us at Qualisch and not home till 1500 hrs some continuing on to showers and back again by 1615 hrs. Weckelsdorf inspector out this morning and not much work done, when he said we could not go home till 1330 hrs. Also says we have to do seven metres per man next week so can see a bit of fun coming up next week. Bull here in afternoon and searched a few of the kits. He says if we have contract work, must have a train to bring us home when we are finished. 'Camps' up but no mail. Reading and playing poker in evening. Potatoes and usual bread as rations. Good oil tonight: Russians commence their drive towards Poland and Rumania and our troops advance in Italy. Germans taking up positions six miles behind the Hitler line. 25 German planes shot down to our 40. Fairly heavy bombing over Germany and France. Commando raids on French coast. Three ships sunk off Crete. Plane opposition over Germany very quiet. Fine morning but came up very dull in afternoon.

Sunday 21st May, 1944
Prisoner of War in Sudatenland. No work today. Doing a little mending, reading, playing cards and writing, also quoit tennis. Wrote cards to Sigrid, home, Mavis and Mabel. Going to play cricket in afternoon but it rained. Potatoes, meat, goulash, bread and margarine ration for a week. German news: mentions heavy fighting in Italy. Six of our planes shot down over Germany, a couple of Russian supply dumps bombed and the Russian Front quiet. Very nice sunny morning but came up thunderstorm and heavy rain in afternoon and continued throughout the night.

Monday 22nd May, 1944

Prisoner of War near Bodisch. Eight men to Halbstadt and home 1615 hrs, seven to the Doctor and nineteen of us to Qualisch, 3 digging out and the rest of us loading and unloading rails, picking them up between Qualisch and Radowenz and unloading them at Johnsdorf. Afternoon to Petersdorf, picking up some plates, on to Parsnitch to allow train to Pass and unload them on return them at Johnsdorf. Afternoon to Petersdorf, picked up some plates, on way to Parsnitch to allow a train to Pass and unloaded them on return between Qualisch and Petersdorf. Home at 1715 hrs. Three parcels up of cigarettes Davis SE, Hampton and myself and books from Stalag for the library. Reading and playing quoit tennis in the evening. Potatoes, porridge and usual bread. News: Eastern front quiet, heavy fighting on the defensive in Italy, reminding battles of Verdin and Somme in the last war. Our transport bombed there last night. Our planes over Rhine and Westphalia. German planes bomb east coast of England. A very wet morning, but cleared a little in afternoon.

Tuesday 23rd May, 1944

Prisoner of War Bodisch in Sudatenland. Six men to Halbstadt and home 1615 hrs. Six men to Doctor and to return to Stalag tomorrow. Twenty three of us to Qualisch digging out. In afternoon three others and myself went on arbeit zug, doing odd jobs till knock off time. Home at 1715hrs. During the evening reading and playing quoit tennis. A little mail up today but received none myself. All received an extra rug from the Reichbahn today and needed too as the nights are somewhat cold now, we do not have our overcoats. The usual daily rations. News: Fairly heavy fighting still in Italy our artillery and planes, shelling and bombing all night. Russian Front quiet. Germans bomb Russian dumps. Some of our planes over Germany a few shot down and German planes over England. A reasonably fine day except for a cold wind blowing and attempting to snow.

Wednesday 24th May, 1944

Prisoner of War stationed at Bodisch. Six light arbeiters of last week return to Stalag today, as no suitable for the heavy railway work. Six men to Halbstadt and home usual time. Twenty three of us to Qualisch six with myself on arbeit zug, doing odd jobs and the rest digging out. Easy day. Home at 1715 hrs. Reading, doing canteen book and playing quoit tennis in evening. Parcels up to day and received by personnel Check, Xmas, Galletly, Gillon, Barber, Hampton, Myers 17 Feb NZ cigarette parcels by Davis SE and Akester. Potatoes, meat, goulash, with usual bread and sugar ration. Still heavy fighting in Italy, Russian Front quiet. Our planes active over Germany or occupied territories. Very dull day with cold wind blowing.

Thursday 25th May, 1944

Prisoner of War Bodisch in Sudatenland. Six men Halbstadt and home their usual time of 1615 hrs and twenty three of us to Qualisch. Eight men including myself on arbeit zug, unloading rails and the rest digging out. Gaffirs beginning to get a bit anxious about go slow policy. Easy day unloading only 28 rails besides putting up and taking down the cranes. Quite a few of the Jerries not too optimistic about winning the war. Things tightening up more with certain things. Playing quoit tennis and doing up canteen book in evening. Rye porridge, potatoes and usual bread. News: very heavy fighting still continuing in Italy and Germans say our advance is costing us a great number of men. Russian Front quiet. Our planes over Germany, Berlin and Vienna day light raids and Americans at night raids over 100 planes shot down. 'Camp' papers up and a book on Jews of public life. Leaders of England and Empire (German Propaganda). Another cold dull day with cold biting wind and temperature fairly low, wind coming from Snow Koppe.

Friday 26th May, 1944

Prisoner of War stationed at Bodisch. Six men to Halbstadt and the usual times and twenty three go to Qualisch. Seven others with myself loading earth and unloading and the rest digging out. Solid going while working, but had a fair time off. Home at 1720 hrs. Bulk issue of food tonight and 50 cigarettes. Another propaganda sheet given to us tonight calling for volunteers to join the British Free Corp, which is supposed to be formed to fight against the Russians. Playing quoit tennis and reading during the evening. Farmer returns as guard today and the short one leaves us. Potatoes, pea soup and bread. Still heavy fighting in Italy and Germans admit one small break through. Russian Front quiet except for a little local fighting. Our planes over Western Germany and Western Europe about fifty shot down. Another very dull and windy day, but conditions a little warmer.

Saturday 27th May, 1944
Prisoner of War in Sudatenland stationed near Bodisch. Usual six men to Halbstadt and nineteen of us at Qualisch, digging out. Finished work about 1200 hrs. Left Qualisch 1330 hrs at Bodisch 1440 hrs and some of us continued onto Halbstadt to showers and returning at 1615 hrs. Reading and playing quoit tennis during the evening. Six barrels of beer up for the weekend, being a long one, Monday being free for Whit Monday. Potatoes and usual bread. News: Heavy fighting going on in Italy. Around the Dniester and Carpathian Mts local fighting. A few single bombers of ours over and a fair number shot down. Very dull morning but a nice afternoon.

Sunday 28th May, 1944
Prisoner of War near Bodisch in Sudatenland, Whit Sunday. Today reading, playing quoit tennis, a good many games, and lost more perspiration in one match than I lost at work all week. Cricket in afternoon also and wrote cards to home, Nurse H and Ethel. Passenger trains well crowded out today. Potatoes, pea and bacon soup per Red Cross bread and weekly margarine. News: Heavy fighting, still in Italy, hundreds of our tanks being thrown in. Local fighting on Russian Front. Our planes over Kiel, Mannerheim, Ludwigschafen, Arion, and

one other place and German planes bombed south of England. A very warm day with a few clouds in afternoon.

Monday 29th May, 1944
Whit Monday, a holiday. POW near Bodisch in Sudatenland. Writing, reading, playing quoit tennis. Afternoon had a race meeting of ten races and few barrels of beer. Potatoes, porridge and usual bread. Still heavy fighting in Italy. 400 Canadian panzers used in one sector. Our planes over a good many places in Germany. Snow reads out an article of the treatment of our bombers and fighters and inhuman methods from German newspaper. A very fine day and hot day practically cloudless.

Tuesday 30th May, 1944
Prisoner of War in Sudatenland. Usual six men to Halbstadt and home 1615 hrs. Eighteen men to Qualisch, three men digging out and the rest of us loading and unloading guide rails, shifting them from one place to another. Fairly easy and quiet day and home 1720 hrs. Fair amount of air activity out here today. Swimming pools in favour against Adersbach Felsen and Weckelsdorf Mkt, there being a fair crowd at each tonight. Reading and playing quoit tennis in evening. Potatoes, pea soup and usual bread. News: Still heavy fighting in Italy. Russian Front quiet (Jerry news: our planes machine gunning fields and civilians etc in Italy, Holland and France). Our bombers over northern, middle and southern Germany visiting in day light Leipzig, Posen, at night Hanover and one other place. Fair number shot down. A perfect day with hot sun and practically cloudless.

Wednesday 31st May, 1944
Prisoner of War in Sudatenland. Six men to Halbstadt and twenty two Qualisch. Myself and seven others loading and unloading earth by station and the rest digging out between Qualisch and Radowenz. Home late tonight being 1815 hrs. Greasy and the Inspector on the job today

and kept the boys digging out a bit late. A little reading during the evening. Potatoes, meat and gravy and usual bread. Heavy fighting in Italy, Germans withdraw to a new line north ward. Waves and waves of panzers used. Bridgehead now evidently joined up with main Front. 42 planes shot down over Germany yesterday, and planes over Rhine and Westphalia last night. Japs put in some terrible claims for the 2 1/2 years they have been in the war practically impossible to believe. Fairly hot day again coming up windy and cloudy in the afternoon, but clearing again by evening being cooler than usual.

Thursday 1st June, 1944
At Bodisch as a POW. Three years since the capitulation of Crete. Twelve men to Halbstadt today and home at 1745 hrs. Fifteen of us to Qualisch and being no arbeit zug all on digging out, and home by 1500 hrs leaving the job at 1300. Reading and playing quoit tennis. No news tonight because of wireless being cut off on account of thunderstorm. Potatoes, porridge, usual bread with fortnights jam and sugar ration. Very muggy morning, later coming out fine, but in afternoon came up very cloudy, and had an electric thunderstorm in evening, but not much rain though.

Friday 2nd June, 1944
On railway party E388 as a POW near Bodisch in Sudatenland, being attached to to Stalag V111A Gorlitz, and previously Stalag V111B. Lamsdorf. Gang of twelve to Halbstadt and home usual time 1615 and fourteen of us at Qualisch, eight digging out and myself with five others loading and unloading earth by station in the morning and unloading screws in afternoon. Fairly easy day and home at 1715 hrs. Reading and playing quoit tennis in evening. Issued with NZ food parcel and 50 cigarettes. Mail up and received three myself, one from Verna, Gladys and Merle including a snap. Photos returned today from Stalag that were sent in for censorship. Potatoes, porridge and usual bread. Gerry news: still heavy fighting in Italy and local scraps in

Russia. Months loss of planes by England well over a thousand and fair bit of Navy shipping as well. Dull morning with some sunshine about 1000, but with heavy rainstorm about 1330 and then fined up for the rest of the day.

Saturday 3rd June, 1944
Prisoner of War near Bodisch. Twelve men to to Halbstadt and twelve to Qualisch. Halbstadt gang home midday and we left Qualisch at 1330, and continuing on to Halbstadt from Bodisch 1500 hrs for showers and returning at 1615. Reading and playing quoit tennis in evening. 'Camp' newspaper up. No parcels for ten days. Two potatoes and usual bread ration for the day. News: much the same with heavy fighting in Italy. Rye crops beginning to come out in ear now. Fairly cool morning, but came out a little warmer in afternoon.

Sunday 4th June, 1944
Prisoner of War Bodisch. No work today so filling in the day with a little mending, reading, writing and playing deck tennis. No cricket today as no posten to take us. Wrote L Card to Virgilia and cards to home, Joyce C and Gladys. Snowy Myers reads out article from German paper of the possibility of the coming invasion and its effect on our people and theirs. Potatoes, meat, goulash, usual bread and weeks margarine. News tonight: Germans admit big break through near Abino Mountains, and are now ten kilometres east of Rome, and 50 kilometre front there. Four of our ships sunk and some prisoners taken at Spit. Germans capture some heights around Gassy and important ground elsewhere. Our planes last night over Mannerheim and Ludwig-Sehapen. Fairly cool day with clouds and sunshine.

Monday 5th June, 1944
Prisoner of War at Bodisch. Twelve men to Halbstadt and home 1745 hrs and thirteen of us to Qualisch. Early morning nine digging out and four which included myself unloading screws between Radowenz

and Johnsdorf and on returning at 1145 hrs picked up five more men and unloading rails, but did not finish them though and home 1720 hrs. Reading during the evening. Potatoes, pea soup and usual bread. Germans mention fighting in the streets of Rome because an American panzer was said to have been see in the streets. Rumanian and Germans fighting against strong Russian forces, but drove them back. Dull morning with an attempt to rain, but eventually turned out a very nice day.

Tuesday 6th June, 1944
Prisoner of War in Sudatenland. Twelve men to Halbstadt and home usual time, while thirteen of us were at Qualisch. Four men on digging out and nine of us on unloading rails between Radowenz and Johnsdorf. Finished one truck of twelve rails and put cranes on another truck and unloaded a dozen rails between 12 and 1 o'clock. After that period unload a couple of boodies where the boys are digging out. Home at 1715 hrs. Reading during the evening. Potatoes, porridge and bread. German radio says after months of preparation Canadian and English troops invaded France by parachute and boats after heavy bombing. Claims that we have had heavy losses. Landed between Cherboug and Le-Havre and a few minor places of divisional strength. Germans and Rumanians pushing the Russians back near Gassy, supported by Rumanian and German planes. Things a little quieter in Italy. Five planes over Germany and two shot down. Looks like the invasion we have been waiting for is on. Very dull day, with some fairly heavy rain.

Wednesday 7th June, 1944
Six men to Mittelsteine and home 1745 hrs and twenty-two to Qualisch with twelve digging out and the rest of use unloading rails till 1130 hrs at Johnsdorf and then to Qualisch and loaded some bolts and washers and took down to the civvie gang. Home 1720 hrs and reading and doing canteen book in evening. Potatoes, meat, goulash and bread.

Germans claim tonight that we have had heavy losses in our invasion so far, and not gained much and claim that they have cleaned out practically all the parachutists that we landed. Admit a couple of heavy breaks through in Italy. Local fighting around Gassy. Bandits in Yugo-Slavia during May were killed 17,000 and 9,000 prisoners. Our planes over Mannerheim last night and American planes over Southern Europe. Dull cold day with some heavy rain 1610 hr but cleared a little later.

Thursday 8th June, 1944
Prisoner of War at Bodisch. Six men to Halbstadt and home 1745 hrs and twenty-two of us at Qualisch way, there being fifteen digging out and six of us and the sanitor doing odd jobs, picking up old plates, screws, sleepers, loading and unloading some earth and went to Johnsdorf and stacked some sleepers. First ride in the cab of a railway engine. Home at 1715 hrs. Reading during the evening. Bit of the good oil tonight: Main Front 80 miles long and twenty-five deep. Le Harve 3,000 bombers continuing to bomb positions and fighters machine gunning positions. 10 subs sunk in the Channel and 25 motor boats and 1500 prisoners taken. Tivoli in our hands in Italy. Eisenhower will speak on the situation on Saturday. Ahead of schedule (usual rations). Fairly dull day with a little sunshine and attempt to rain.

Friday 9th June, 1944
Prisoner of War Bodisch. Six men to Halbstadt and twenty-two to Qualisch, where fourteen men were digging out and nine of us on arbeit zug. In morning loading and unloading some metals, and the afternoon went to Johnsdorf and erected cranes on wagon of rails ready for unloading tomorrow, then returned to Qualisch and back in camp 1715. Reading and playing quoit tennis in evening. Bulk issue of food and 50 cigarettes issued in evening also. About a dozen letters up but received none myself and 'Camp' newspaper also in. Pea soup, potatoes, and bread for the day. German news: admits our troops able to strengthen their bridgeheads. Near Orne River our troops advancing.

West of Orne River attacking and advancing. Forty five of our planes lost. In Italy west of Tiber River no great success to us. Heavy Soviet attacks around Gassy unsuccessful. Fairly dull day with some rain.

Saturday 10th June, 1944
Prisoner of War stationed at Bodisch. Six men to Halbstadt and home at midday. Six to dentist and home 1245 hrs. Eight of us at Johnsdorf, unloading rails, six at Qualisch digging out, us fourteen on reaching Bodisch 1500 hrs continued to Halbstadt for showers before returning to camp at 1615 hrs. Reading and playing deck tennis. A little more mail today receiving a letter from Alison and Nurse H. Potatoes and usual bread. German news: mentions heavy fighting on the invasion front, in some places all of our troops cleaned out, and heavy losses in ships and landing craft, planes and panzers. Gained a little more ground in Italy. In Gassy and Carpathian Mts local scrapping. Bandits suffer losses in Yugo-Slavia. Few of our planes over Berlin. and American planes over Hanover. Dull day with scatttered rain and sunshine, a bit of a thunderstorm in evening.

Sunday 11th June, 1944
Prisoner of War in Sudatenland. No work today and being somewhat wet, not out of bed too early. Reading and writing during the day. Wrote cards home to (Lil & Tom) and letter cards to Alison and Carmel. Potatoes meat, goulash, bread and weeks margarine ration. German news: mentions our position strengthened near River Orne. Near Cherbough our attempts failed. Fair number of transporters sunk and 68 of our planes shot down. In Italy our troops pushing forward slightly. Not much mention of Russian Front. Miserable day with rain practically all day.

Monday 12th June, 1944
Prisoner of War stationed at Bodisch. Six men to Halbstadt and twenty of us out Qualisch way, eight men on arbeit zug, and the rest digging

out. No work myself as had crook stomach. Arbeit zug to Petersdorf and loaded iron sleepers in morning and afternoon unloading guide rails. In camp 1745hrs. In bed early tonight. To enquire about money put in the bank by some of the boys. Porridge, potatoes and usual bread. German news: does not mention much of the invasion front tonight but that they are still bashing us about. Gaining a little in Italy and quiet on Russian Front. Dull day with a little sunshine.

Tuesday 13th June, 1944
Prisoner of War stationed Bodisch. Six men to Halbstadt and twenty two of us Qualisch way. Eight started digging out and fourteen of us to unload guide rails, but owing to artillery shooting could not go down the line, so eight of us went to Johnsdorf to pick up iron sleepers and others went digging out. Returned at 1100 and then loaded some poles by railway line, where the boys are digging out. In afternoon unloaded bit of earth and in camp 1715. A little reading during the evening. Outside news Sunday night. We have a coast line of 125 miles by 35 miles deep. 60 miles north of Rome (last night). Now have 5000 prisoners in two days and shot up 600 tanks. Hardly a minute of the day and night that there are none of our planes over the invasion front. Major offensive in Finland. A few of our boats lost. German news: Nothing of note on the invasion front except for heavy losses (to us) and fortified positions holding us up, sinking many ships and shot down 68 planes and cleaned out Americans who landed by parachute on Friday night. Munich raid Friday night done by negroes and heavy cultural losses. American planes over some towns in Rumania. In Italy gained a little more ground, and Soviet offensive around Gassy and Carpathian Mts repelled, and around Narva attacks at several points all repelled. Dull in early morning but later turned out a very nice day.

Wednesday 14th June, 1944
Prisoner of War near Bodisch in Sudatenland. Usual six men to Halbstadt and twenty three of us out to Qualisch. First thing nine

men digging out and fourteen on us unloading guide rails. Finished these at 0900 hrs. Then eight of us went and to Johnsdorf to unload rails and others went digging out. Two trucks of 15 metre rails arrive and unloading them from Hottendorf towards Johnsdorf. In camp 1715. Reading during the evening. Potatoes, meat and goulash, usual bread and jam and sugar for a fortnight. Bit of oil. Parachutists dropped in Ruven, and fair amount of coastline. German news: mentions heavy fighting in invasion front but meeting with no success to us. More ships sunk in the Channel. Heavy fighting also in Italy, but not much ground gained. Russian front quiet and up in the Peninsula near Finland heavy fighting. American planes over Munich yesterday 37 shot down and single British planes over Munich and Rhine and Westphalia last night and few shot down. British soldiers complaining of short ration of food. Dull sultry morning, coming out fairly warm for a while but set in with rain at 1500 hrs.

Thursday 15th June, 1944
Prisoner of War at Bodisch. Six men as usual to Halbstadt and twenty two of us out Qualisch way, nine of us at Johnsdorf unloading rails and the rest digging out. Home at 1715 hrs. Not too good in evening so too bed early. No lights tonight owing to power being cut off somewhere. Potatoes, macaroni and bread. German News: Fighting around Tilly, Caen, Bayardy. Around Calmont a few districts retaken. Panzer attacks and heavy losses to us. West and North West of St Glies we advance a little. 14 transporters and 2 destroyers sunk. In Italy pressure by us on both sides Bolsini Sea unable to hinder their withdrawal. Russian front quiet. American planes over Budapest. RAF planes over Rheinist and Westphalia last night. Dull day with a little rain in afternoon, heavy shower and hail storm in evening.

Friday 16th June, 1944
Prisoner of War Bodisch. Usual gang of six to Halbstadt and twenty two of us out other line, nine of us at Johnsdorf unloading rails and

thirteen at Qualisch digging out. In camp 1715 hrs. Reading and playing deck tennis in evening. Issued with Canadian food parcel and 50 cigarettes. Potatoes, Jerry pea soup and bread. Gerry news: Sth East of England and London done over with new heavy type of E bomb, causing heavy damage and said, 'to have caused quite a stir in England'. Successful counter attacks and retook part of the bridge head with heavy panzer attacks. Heavy attacks in Italy and our troops advance a little. Russia fairly quiet. Hanover done over by American planes. Foggy morning and turning out a dull day with attempts to rain.

Saturday 17th June, 1944
Prisoner of War at Bodisch. Six men to Halbstadt and home midday, five to Qualisch to dentist and fourteen of us at Qualisch digging out. Finished about ten, but could not leave for camp until 1330 and through Bodsich 1500 hrs and continuing on to Halbstadt for showers, returning at 1615. Reading and playing deck tennis in evening. Potatoes, and usual bread. Recent oil. Fighting fairly heavy in France, but our boys still holding their own. Mention of the Atlantic Wall what Jerry spoke so much about is no good against the warfare of today. 3 German destroyers sunk in the Channel. Roeon in our hands now for three days. Mention of Bordeoux but unable to grasp details. Jerry news: Our troops still getting pushed back in most places a little advance in one sector. Our troops pushing steadily onwards in Italy despite heavy German resistance and Russian front quiet. Heavy fighting on Finnish Peninsula. Some of our planes over different parts of Germany and fair number shot down. New type of pilotless plane which dives to earth and explodes when a fighter approaches and causes great damage, a new secret weapon they call it. Dull day with misty rain in morning reasonable afternoon and wet evening.

Sunday 18th June, 1944
Prisoner of War near Bodisch in Sudatenland. No work today, so filled in time reading, playing deck tennis and cards. Wrote cards home,

Verna, Cousin Joyce and Mrs Walker. Bag of parcels up today and received my personnel Ellesmore 2, Stevenson, Galletly. Cigarettes by Pedersen, Balsarini 2, Thorpe, Galletly, Heggie, McQuarne, Dalziel, Pierce, Gracie 2, Davis SE 2, Gillon 2, Deering, and myself. Stevenson book parcel and two Red X boxes of books for the library from the Stalag. Potatoes, meat, goulash, bread and a weekly butter ration. News: Our troops 5 miles east of Rueon and shot up 100 panzers there. German troops around Cherboug cut off. Another landing made near Calais, and heavy fighting going on. Italy our troops still steadily pushing northwards. Toulon bombed by 2000 American bombers. Parachutists dropped in Turin. Gerry news: Our troops still getting hiding and getting pushed back, because of loss of troops. Russian front quiet and fighting still going on heavily around the Finnish Peninsula. The new secret weapon still doing a lot of damage in England. Dull and wet practically all day, except from about 1600 hrs onwards.

Monday 19th June, 1944
Prisoner of War at Bodisch. Usual six to Halbstadt and home 1745hrs, and twenty one of us out to Weckelsdorf line, twelve being at Qualisch digging out and nine of us unloading rails near Johnsdorf and later in the day towards Ober Addersbach. Home 1715 hrs. Reading and playing deck tennis in evening. Majority of farmers around here now cutting the first crop of grass hay, the best I have seen since I have been in the country with most of them. Potatoes, porridge, bread and a few lettuce thrown in. News: near Genoa 20 German speed boats damaged and twelve being sunk. 1000 bombers over Bremen last night. Heavy fighting in Russia in place called Petrosovagrad. German news: troops in Cherboug peninsula now cut off, but Cherboug still in German hands. Transporters and destroyers sunk in Channel by Air Force. German secret weapon plane still pounding London and Sth East England and causing heavy damage. Our troops advance slightly in Italy. British planes over Western Germany, Hamburg, Hanover and

Bremen and 16 shot down. Jap news: In ten days in Honun province claimed to have destroyed 30 divisions, and smashed 20 up, that could not be able to reform. Dull day very windy, fairly good evening though.

Tuesday 20th June, 1944
Prisoner of War Bodisch in Sudatenland. Six men Halbstadt, and in camp at 1615 hrs. Twenty three of us out the Weckelsdorf line, twelve being between Qualisch and Radowenz digging out, and nine of us at Johnsdorf. Ready to start when engine was recalled to Weckelsdorf. Went to Qualisch on the 0900 train and loaded ninety sleepers. Returned to Johnsdorf 1145 hr and unloaded between Hottendorf and Ober-Adderbach. 1500 hrs returned to Qualisch on the engine and unloaded some sleepers. In camp 1715. Reading and play deck tennis in evening. 'Camp' newspapers up today. Porridge, potatoes, and usual bread. Tonights oil: Single unit have now pushed down to Bordeoux. New troops landing at Cherboug and Le Havre. Turkey cuts off all relations with Germany. (Other news suspect). Our troops suffer heavy losses and attacks repelled. Claim to be closing in on the bridgehead over Europe and invasion front. 26 planes hot down. On the island of Elbe Germans inflicted heavy losses on our troops, and last night were all evacuated to the mainland. Heavy attacks in Italy but no progress. Russians fighting around Vitish. In pacific around Mariana Islands heavy fighting. Germany claims to have larger, heavier and faster tanks than the Tiger tank. Sultry and windy day with clouds in afternoon, a little rain in evening.

Wednesday 21st June, 1944
Prisoner of War stationed at at Bodisch. Usual gang of six to Halbstadt, finishing and home 1745 hrs. Twenty three of us out Weckelsdorf line, twelve being between Qualisch and Radowenz digging out and eleven on arbeit zug, at Johnsdorf unloading rails in the morning and went to Radowenz in afternoon and unloaded a truck of sleepers. In camp1715 hrs. Reading and playing deck tennis in evening. French

cigarettes up today. Potatoes, meat, goulash with usual bread. German news: not much mentioned except for the amount of ships sunk since the invasion started. Front in Italy 140 kilometres long. Nth American bombers over Hamburg, Hanover and a couple of other places. 58 shot down. Japs claim several big American ships and aircraft carriers sunk. Dull sultry morning and continued throughout the day.

Thursday 22nd June, 1944
Prisoner of War stationed near Bodisch. Three years today since Germany and Russia went to war. Usual gang of six to Halbstadt and twenty two out to Weckelsdorf line, thirteen being between Qualisch, Radowenz digging out and nine of us at Johnsdorf unloading rails. Finished here today and in the afternoon took crane to Qualisch ready for unloading guide rails tomorrow. In camp 1715 hrs. Reading, playing deck tennis and cards in evening. Potatoes, semolina porridge and usual bread as rations. Not much in the news except that Germany says the secret weapon being used, London has now been under it for 160 hours, and that five divisions of soldiers are being used to fight the fires and clean up damage. Our troops still advancing slightly in Tarnapol and Vitish local fighting. Heavy bombing and many planes shot down. A fairly changeable day of sunshine and heavy clouds.

Friday 23rd June, 1944
Prisoner of War in Bodisch Sudatenland. Six men to Halbstadt and twenty one on Weckelsdorf line. Twelve digging out between Radowenz and Qualisch and nine of us at Qualisch unloading guide rails further down the line. Cleared the line at Parschnitz-Ost, the midday period being about two hours off the line. Finished the wagon and erected crane on another wagon ready for tomorrow. Issued with English food parcel and fifty cigarettes. Reading and playing deck tennis in evening. Potatoes, pea soup and bread. Heavy fighting going on in the 'Cherboug' area and peninsula. One or two spearheads cut off. Still progressing steadily in Italy. Heavy fighting commences along the

Russian front. Americans planes over and a good many shot down. England still under bombardment of the secret weapon. A changeable day of heavy clouds and fairly cool with bursts of sunshine.

Saturday 24th June, 1944
Prisoner of War in Sudatenland. Five men to Qualisch to dentist at 0800 hrs return 1230 hrs. Six men working Halbstadt and home 1350 hrs being half day. Seven men digging out between Radowenz and Qualisch and eight of us at Qualisch unloading guide rails. Did two trucks and home on 1320 train, continuing through Bodisch 1500 hrs to showers and back in camp 1615. Mail up today and received two from Alison, one from Sigrid, Verna and (Lil & Tom). Playing cards, deck tennis and reading during the evening. News: Cleaning out Cherboug Peninsula continues, and 16000 prisoners were taken. They were not told until they had been cut off for 24 hours about being surrounded by our troops. Fairly strong fighting going on all fronts in Russia. German news: In Italy our troops advance at night, after an all day battle for a few kilometres. All attacks repulsed in Russian attacks. Our bombers over a good many places and fair number shot down. Potatoes, pea soup and bread with a little sausage meat. Dull day with some rain and a little sunshine.

Sunday 25th June, 1944
Prisoner of War at Bodisch. No work today. Filled in the day reading, writing, playing cards and doing canteen books and also playing deck tennis. Wrote cards to home, Alison and letter card to Allan. OIL: Cherboug now in our hands and mopping up operations continue. Russians attacking strong and advancing. Few more districts given up in France by the Germans. (Germans News: We are still getting a hiding on the invasion front, and advancing slightly on the Italian Front). In Russia the Russians widen their breakthroughs and also in Finland the Russians pushing forward. Our planes over several districts and some shot down. Big attack by Americans on an Island near

the Mariannis group and Japs expect heavy fighting there. Potatoes, meat, goulash bread and weekly margarine ration. Frost in morning with fairly fine day, except for a few heavy clouds at times.

Monday 26th June, 1944
Prisoner of War stationed near Bodisch. Usual gang of six to Halbstadt and twenty one out Weckelsdorf line. Twelve digging out between Radowenz and eight of us at Johnsdorf unloading some iron rails near Radowenz first thing, then picking up old sleepers between Hottendorf and Ober-Addersbach. Fairly easy day and in camp 1715 hrs. Parcels up today and received personnel Davis SE 3, Thorpe, Strange, Chadwick and cigarettes Davis SE 3, Heggie 3, Galletly 2, Strange 2, McQuarne 2, Deeming 2, Check 2, Hunter 2, Barker 2, Xmas, Smith F, Gracie, Gillon, Chadwick, Myers, Lunam. Reading and playing cards in evening. Porridge, potatoes, and usual bread. News: Cherboug Peninsula still being cleaned out and to date 18,000 prisoners being taken. Progress fair on other fronts. In Russia Vitesh fallen and Russians advance 125 miles in three days and broke through all the recent defences in that sector. In Italy 200 miles north of Rime. Germans claim successes in most instances of their battles, despite strong enemy resistance and attacks. Planes over Germany. A fairly warm day with very strong wind blowing.

Tuesday 27th June, 1944
Prisoner of War at Bodisch. Usual gang to Halbstadt and home usual time. Out Weckelsdorf line twenty two of us, thirteen digging out between Radowenz and Qualisch, and nine of us on arbeit zug. Morning down to Petersdorf picked up some iron sleepers and on returning laid them out between Radowenz and Qualisch. Afternoon returned to Qualisch and loaded a truck of old point sleepers. Home as usual at 1715 hrs. Everywhere in the field are people cutting, turning, raking and carting in grass hay, and hoeing the potato crops. Reading and playing cards in evening. Potatoes, pea soup and bread as rations.

Germans say we entered the ruins of Lilly, but still getting worst of the deal on the invasion front. In Italy managed to push forward little in the evening after an all day battle. In Russian front heavy fighting going on and Russians getting pushed back slightly. Germans bomb dumps at Smolenski and elsewhere. Planes over Germany and occupied countries. Dull morning with some fairly good weather. Later in the day started to rain about 1815 and between 1900. At 2000 hrs electric thunderstorm with heavy rain set in.

Wednesday 28th June, 1944
Prisoner of War Bodisch. Usual gang to Halbstadt and returning at 1745 hrs and out on the Weckelsdorf line twenty one of us, twelve on digging out between Radowenz and Qualisch and nine of us on arbeit zug. Picking up iron sleepers at Petersdorf and unloading near Radowenz and usual working hours. Inspector from Weckelsdorf and other Inspectors out today. Reading and playing cards in evening. Potatoes, goulash and usual bread. Germans say that no German have given unconditional surender yet to us, when all their ammunition is gone they use the bayonets. Heavy fighting in all sectors and we are losing many men and materials in counter attacks. Still damage and big fires in South of England by the secret weapon V1. In Italy advancing slightly. Heavy fighting in Russia. Germans admit evacuation of Vitesh and another town to another defence line. Our planes over many places and also North American bombers and a fair number shot down. Finns have to give up a few more districts. A fairly warm day throughout.

Thursday 29th June, 1944
Prisoner of War in Bodisch at Sudatenland. Usual gang to Halbstadt, and twenty one of us on Weckelsdorf line with twelve on digging out between Radowenz and Qualisch and the rest of us on arbeit zug – to Petersdorf to pick up some iron sleepers and unloaded them near Radowenz. Metal train through and had to help with the unloading

of it and also loaded some metal shavings to be unloaded tomorrow at Parschnitz. In camp 1715 hrs. 'Camp' newspaper in. Reading and playing cards in evening. Potatoes Red X soup, bread and three lettuce each. News: practically as yesterday so no details given. Fairly warm day with heavy clouds and sunshine.

Friday 30th June, 1944
Prisoner of War Bodisch. Same gang to Halbstadt and home 1615 hrs and twenty one out on the Weckelsdorf line. Twelve on digging out and the rest of us on arbeit zug. Unloading metal screeings on crossings down to Parschnitz and picked up five concrete blocks for culverts. Afternoon unloaded and picked up a few iron sleepers. Thunderstorm set in with heavy rain and knocked off for dinner. In camp 1715 hrs. Issued with NZ food parcel and 50 cigarettes. A little reading tonight and no cards as lights had failed. Potatoes, porridge, usual bread, sugar and jam ration, also some cheese. Still some of the Germans holding out around Cherboug and fighting against superior odds. Ships attempted to come in the harbour, but coastal batteries forced them out again. Around Caen and Tilly breakthrough widened but German force now closed it with counter attacks. In Italy around Benshina Sea after us having heavy losses, did not attack again till the evening. In Russia fairly heavy fighting on all fronts. Bandits behind German lines in Russia. Germans destroy bunker dumps, killing 77,000 and taking 5,000 prisoners. Planes over Maxiberg, Dittenberg and Vienna. Japs claim to have sunk two battleships, two aircraft carriers damaged, and one battleship. Foggy till about 0700, cleared up then came over cloudy, breaking into a thunderstorm and heavy rain at midday for about 1 1/2 hours and slight rain throughout the rest of the afternoon.

Saturday 1st July, 1944
Prisoner of War on railway working party near Bodisch in Sudatenland ex Stalag V111B, but now attached Stalag V111A, and working party

E388. Same gang as usual to Halbstadt and home midday. Four men to Qualisch to the dentist and eight men digging out between Radowenz and Qualisch and seven others with myself at Weckelsdorf, loading point sleepers and finished at 1010 hrs, and walked home over the hills, getting there 1120 hrs. At 1500 hrs to Halbstadt for showers and returning at 1615 hrs. Playing deck tennis, cards, a little reading, and a little washing. Potatoes and usual bread ration. Nothing startling in the news. The usual claims by the Germans pushing us back or advancing slightly with heavy losses. In Russia still heavy fighting going on and the latest months figures on our shipping losses. Planes over Hungary Rhine and Westphalia. Japs usual fanatical claims. Foggy morning turned out warm day, although very dull at times.

Sunday 2nd July, 1944
Prisoner of War near Bodisch. No work today. In the morning a little reading, and playing deck tennis. Wrote cards to home. Florrie, Merle and Doreen. Had an early dinner and party went for a walk towards the Protectorate, through pine forests and rocky ridges to a place where is a fairsized guest house called "Resturation Stein". Saw some marvellous views of the country below us. Up about 1800 feet. About six miles there and back. On the way back had a barrel of beer. Evening playing cards after an enjoyable afternoon. Potatoes, pork and goulash, bread and weekly margarine. News: Germans admit to the loss of the Cherboug Peninsula and slight advances in another sector, but at great cost. Germans claim to have withdrawn to a new line and we advance slightly. In Russia fairly heavy fighting all sectors. Nothing else much of note except for a few planes over. Dull warm day with a few spots of rain at 1215 hrs.

Thursday 6th July, 1944
Prisoner of War near Bodisch. Twenty nine men at Weckelsdorf line and digging out between Radowenz and Qualisch. Easy day no arbeit zug engine today, so had to go home on passenger train, getting home

at 1455 hrs and had a enjoyable cup of tea. Doing canteen books and reading on return also playing deck tennis and cards. Potatoes, rolled oats and usual bread. Still heavy fighting on on invasion front, and some terrorists also cleaned up in Southern France. Slight advances in Italy, Germans say they are shortening their lines. Heavy fighting in middle Russia and Russians making breakthroughs with heavy losses. A few planes over and some shot down. A very hot day with practically no clouds till late afternoon.

Friday 7th July, 1944
Prisoner of War Bodisch in Sudatenland. Twenty nine men at Weckelsdorf line, digging out between Radowenz and Qualisch. Finished at midday and picked a few wild strawberries in the hills and home at 1715 hrs. A fair number of Zcheck children on train this afternoon. A little mail up and received one from Verna. Bulk issue of Red X food tonight and 50 cigarettes. Reading and playing cards in evening. Pea soup (Red X) potatoes and bread. Heavy fighting in France, but our troops now being pushed back after one breakthrough. In Italy nothing much of note, except for heavy fighting on East Coast. Sabotage troops landed in France cleaned up. Heavy fighting in Russia pushing on towards Vilna, the capital of Lithuania. Planes over Kiel day time and Rhinish Westphalia at night. Heavy fighting around the Bonin Islands 1,000 kilometres from Japan. A very hot day with scattered clouds in afternoon.

Saturday 8th July, 1944
Prisoner of War stationed at Bodisch. Four men to dentist at Qualisch and and twenty three of us on Weckelsdorf line digging out between Qualisch and Radowenz. Finished fairly early and went gathering strawberries and blue berries until time to catch the train at 1345 hrs. At Bodisch 1500 hrs but continued on to showers at Halbstadt and being in camp 1615 hrs. Reading, playing deck tennis and cards. "Camp" newspaper up. Potatoes, cabbage and bread. Heavy battle

going on around Caen and locally, breakthrough by our troops, but get pushed back. Heavy bombing in one sector and Jerry expecting big attack here. In Italy attacking all along front, but only made a slight advance. Terrorists and parachutists sabotage troops to the extent of 300 cleaned up in France. In Russian heavy attacks and fighting in the streets of Vitna and southwards advancing towards the capital and attacking strongly elsewhere another place evacuated by the jerries, or as they say from the ruins, but without pressure. Planes over Upper Silesia and Leipzig. Over the invasion and Germany 183 planes shot down yesterday. Another very hot and fine day.

Sunday 9th July, 1944
Prisoner of War near Bodisch in Sudatenland. No work today. Put the day in sleeping, reading, playing deck tennis, wrote card home and letter card to Sigrid. Power for lights and wireless cut out about midday so were with out lights and to bed at 2100 hrs instead of 2200. Potatoes, meat, goulash with usual bread and weekly marg ration. Last night heard a fair number of planes about, but of course could not tell whose they were, but had an idea they were ours. Passenger trains crowded today, even standing and sitting on the steps and platform, and also in the guards van. No news. Came out very Warm and muggy and thunderstorm with a few spots of rain during the afternoon, but rained heavily later in the night.

Monday 10th July, 1944
Prisoner of War at Bodisch. Twenty nine men out Weckelsdorf line digging out between Radowenz and Qualisch. Shifted boody to a new place ready for erecting tomorrow. Saw two poisonous snakes today. Home at 1715 hrs. Pay day. Stewart Davis to go to hospital with sprained arm. Playing deck tennis and reading. No power again tonight so an early night again and no news. Potatoes, macaroni and bread. A cloudy warm morning with scattered showers and in afternoon some

very heavy rain fell but cleared up a bit for the evening, although still very warm.

Tuesday 11th July, 1944
Prisoner of War on railway working party Bodisch Sudatenland. Davis SE goes to hospital this morning. Twenty six of us on Weckelsdorf line digging out between Qualisch and Radowenz. Home 1715 hrs. Finished on job early, so picked a keable of blue berries and a few strawberries. Reading and doing canteen book in evening. Power on again tonight. Potatoes, porridge and bread. Some news: heavy fighting on invasion front around Caen. Heavy artillery and bombing panzers and infantry being carried out, but did not breakthrough much. In Italy reckon Churchill says the going will be slower now as they have met up with some of the German defences. In Russia heavy fighting on the middle sector, pushing towards the Prussian frontier. Our planes over several places and some shut down. Dull morning with a few light showers and clearing up a little in the afternoon.

Wednesday 12th July, 1944
Prisoner of War stationed at Bodisch. Twenty one men on Weckelsdorf line, digging out between Qualisch and Radowenz. The going a bit heavier today, but managed to finish out the usual time and picked a few berries. Back in camp usual time. Reading, playing deck tennis and cards in evening. Parcels up and received by personnel Hunter and Ross. Books Ellesmore. Cigarettes – Pedersen 2, Davies, Ellesmore 2, Davis SE 2, Smith G 2, Chadwick 2, Check 2, Gillon, Myers, Lunam and myself and a little gear from Lamsdorf from when I was in there sick. Potatoes, meat, and goulash, cabbage and bread with fortnightly sugar and jam ration. News G: Still heavy fighting on the invasion front. In Italy advanced slightly in one sector. Eastern sector quiet. In middle Russia fairly quiet and nothing much of note, and southern sector very tame. Planes over Munich and about 25 shot down. A rather changeable day of cold, sunshine and slight showers.

Thursday 13th July, 1944

Prisoner of War stationed at Bodisch. Twenty nine men at Weckelsdorf line digging out between Qualisch and Radowenz. Reasonably easy day. Picked quite a few strawberries today. Home 1715 hrs. "Camp" papers up and also a piano accordion arrived today from the Red X, but lack a player for this instrument. Reading, playing deck tennis and cards during the evening. Potatoes, porridge and usual bread. Not much to mention in the news, except for a fairly heavy fighting everywhere by us, and the Soviets, but no success as usual. 27 planes shot down over Germany and invasion front. V1 still bombing England with heavy damage. A warm day, dull and tried to rain.

Friday 14th July, 1944

Prisoner of War near Bodisch in Sudatenland. Twenty six men working on Weckelsdorf line between Radowenz and Qualisch. Job a little heavy today being a fair amount of earth between sleepers, but managed to finish about eleven. Picked quite a few strawberries again today. In camp at 1715 hrs, a little mail up and received one from Alison. Playing deck tennis and cards during the evening. Issued with Canadian food parcel and 50 cigarettes. Potatoes, pea soup Red X and usual bread. Heavy American attacks around St Lo on invasion front, but no breakthroughs achieved. Slight advance of no importance in Italy. Southern Russia front slight attacks, Middle East front heavy Russian attacks, Vilna evacuated and some other town. American bombers over Munich, 25 shot down, and RAF over Rheinist and Westphalia. Mostly dull day with little sunshine and attempts to rain. Fairly warm.

Saturday 15th July, 1944

Prisoner of War stationed at Bodisch. Three men to dentist at Qualisch and twenty three of us on Weckelsdorf line between Qualisch and Radowenz digging out. Left work 1315 through Bodisch 1500 hrs and continued on to Halbstadt for showers and back in camp 1615 hrs.

Very amusing scenes this morning at Weckelsdorf, train absolutely packed out with berry pickers and on changing trains, old woman, buckets and kids were coming through the window in hurry to get out and get seats. Reading and playing deck tennis in evening. Potatoes and bread as rations. Still heavy fighting on invasion front, but nothing of any importance gained. Germans in Italy withdraw slightly in one sector to a prepared German line, fighting on both sides of the Tiber. Southern sector in Russia beginning to get active, and middle sector slight gains. American planes over Budapest by daylight, RAF over Hanover at night. Fairly warm morning, but came out dull.

Sunday 16th July, 1944
Prisoner of War at Bodisch. No work today. Reading, playing deck tennis and cards. Wrote card home and to Nurse H and letter card to Alison. Parcels up today and personal parcels to Pierce. Food McBean and cigarettes McBean 3, Ross 2, Pierce, Barker, Hampton 2, Ellesmore 2, Balsarini 2, Templeman 2, Dalziel 2, Smith F, Stevenson, Strange, Chadwick, Deeming 2, Gracie 2, Earl Smith G 2, and myself. Balsarini also received a pack of cards. Was to have gone for a walk today, but owing to one of the boys having a bad foot postponed it. Jack B caught outside the barracks today in the forest, but the guard said nothing to the U/Officer and cost Jack a tin of tobacco. Potatoes, meat, goulash, bread and weekly marg ration. Attempted breakthroughs on the invasion front healed over and heavy losses to us. In Italy we advance slightly and Germany withdraws slightly to new positions. In Russia southern sector heavy fighting still going on middle sector fighting west of Vilna. American planes over Rumania and bomb Polsk. RAF at night over Berlin Rheinish and Westphalia. Fine early morning and then a little rain early afternoon, fine again and some rain in evening.

Monday 17th July, 1944
Prisoner of War stationed at Bodisch. Twenty six men to Weckelsdorf line, digging out between Radowenz and Qualisch. Fairly heavy going because

of rain, but finished before dinner. Afternoon picked a few strawberries for supper. Plenty of people still picking berries and it was quite a scramble to get into the carriage on changing at Weckelsdorf. Some of the farmers ploughing up the land for next years crops. Home at 1715hrs. Reading and playing cards in evening. Potatoes, porridge and usual bread. Heavy fighting in France, a few breakthroughs, but these healed over, except where heavy fighting is in progress. Fifty seven Panzers shot up. In Italy fighting on each side of the Tiber and advancing slightly in another sector one town evacuated. Russia heavy fighting around Tarnapol and the Bug, and fairly heavy fighting in the middle sector, one breakthrough of no consequence, and planes over Saabrucken, Munich and Vienna and a few shot down. Dull morning with heavy rain about 0900 hrs till 1030, then cleared up slightly with some sunshine but not too warm.

Tuesday 18th July, 1944
Prisoner of War at Bodisch in Sudatenland. Two men to Halbstadt to sift coal, and twenty seven of us to Weckelsdorf- Trautenau line, digging out between Qualisch and Radowenz. Finished fairly early, then picked some strawberries and blueberries, having them for supper with some sugar and powdered milk mixed up for cream. In camp at 1715 hrs. Potatoes, pea soup (RC) and usual bread. Train again crowded today with berry pickers. Reading and playing cards in evening. Heavy fighting around St Lo and Caen with the use of land and ship artillery one breakthrough. More terroists cleaned up in France. In Italy slight gains by our troops but of no importance. Southern sector in Russia, fighting still around the River Bug and middle sector of Vilna one breakthrough here not yet healed over. A few planes over Berlin last night. Cold dull morning with attempts to rain but came out nice fine afternoon.

Wednesday 19th July, 1944
Prisoner of War stationed at Bodisch. Two men in camp unloading coal and twenty six of us on Weckelsdorf line near Radowenz. Finished in good time and picked the usual tin of strawberries and blueberries

for supper. Qualisch station master gets a bit annoyed because I picked a few by the station on the bank. Home usual time. English speaking civvie here this evening, making a control visit. Reading playing cards during evening. Potatoes, meat and salad with usual bread. Heavy fighting around Caen by British troops. One big breakthrough of eight kilometres here and attempting to widen it. In Italy still pressing onward Germans retiring to new positions. More terroists cleaned up in France. In Southern Russia heavy fighting, pushing on towards Limberg, and middle sector heavy battles many panzers being destroyed. Planes over the Rhur district, Berlin and other places over Germany and over invasion front over hundred planes shot down. Borin Island in American hands, and three big heads captured fighting to the last man. Fairly dull day and cool.

Thursday 20th July, 1944
Prisoner of War Bodisch in Sudatenland. Twenty six men on Weckelsdorf-Trautenau line digging out near Radowenz. Finished early and filled in some time picking berries. Afternoon ten of us walked to Qualisch to help with the unloading of metal train and stayed at Qualisch till time to come home and camp reached 1720 hrs. Plenty of thunder in distance today. "Camp" papers up today. Reading, playing cards during evening. Potatoes, soup with usual bread. An attempt to assassinate Hitler today, but failed, some of the heads of the general staff were wounded. Invasion front St Lo evacuated. Heavy fighting around Caen, supported by artilllery and bombing. In Italy fighting in the streets of one town the harbour being evacuated. In Russia fighting east of Limberg, and middle sector nothing much to report. Planes over Munchen, Sarbrucken and two or three other places. Night fighters account for fair number on invasion front. Fairly fine and warm day with few spots of rain. Thunderstorm elsewhere.

Friday 21st July, 1944
Prisoner of War Bodisch. Twenty seven men on Weckelsdorf-Trautenau line digging out near Radowenz, also a few sleepers

loaded at Qualisch. Could have finished by 0830 hrs this morning, but left a bit till after dinner. Picked a few berries. In camp at 1720 hrs. Issued with 50 cigarettes and English food parcel tonight. Some mending and playing cards in evening. Potato soup, potatoes and bread. Still heavy fighting around St Lo and Caen, nothing of importance gained. In Italy heavy attacks on east coast, but no successes. On southern and middle Russian sectors fairly heavy battles and one breakthrough at present. Several spearheads cut off. American planes over Ludwig, Schafen, Hamburg and elsewhere. English formations over Hamburg and elsewhere. 39 shot down. Destroyer sunk and some damaged off Brest. More sabotage terrorists cleaned up in France. Cold foggy morning, turning out a reasonable some what cloudy day.

Saturday 22nd July, 1944
Prisoner of War stationed at Bodisch. Twenty five of us out today on Weckelsdorf line got off at Johnsdorf and fitted up cranes for loading rails, which we had unloaded six weeks before – Arbeit engine came on 0845 passenger train and ten of us including myself stayed behind to load the rail and other fifteen went on to Radowenz and continued digging out. Loaded 42 rails and were finished. All home on 1350 train from Johnsdorf, going through Bodisch 1500 and some of us continued on to Halbstadt for showers, returning at 1625 hrs, train running late today. Reading and playing cards. Thunderstorms here between 1100 and 1300 but at Johnsdorf and Radowenz we had no rain. No mail or parcel up this week, so things a bit slow. Potatoes and bread. Heavy fighting still around St Lo and Caen, but nothing gained by our troops. More terrorists cleaned up today. Nothing much mentioned on the Italian front. South and middle sectors Russian front heavy battles and any breakthroughs were covered over. Nth American planes over many places and 69 being shot down, which included Mannerheim, Ludwigschafen, Munchin and Schweinfurt. RAF at night over Nth West and Sth East Duetschland six being shot down.

Fine morning, but later camp up thunderstorm and rain set in during afternoon and night.

Sunday 23rd July, 1944
Prisoner of War on railway working party at Bodisch in Sudatenland. No work today so slept in till 0900 hrs reading, writing and mending during the day. Wrote cards home and Jean. Some of the boys went for a walk in the afternoon to get mushrooms. Potatoes, meat, and goulash with bread. Heavy fighting still going on invasion front and no successes gained. In Italy Germans retreat at little to better their line after severe fighing. More bandits cleaned up in Sth Eastern France. On Russian front in Sth and Middle sectors, heavy battles, breakthroughs still open in northern sectors two more towns evacuated. In Pacific in big battle, Japs claim to have cleaned up 6,000 Americans. American planes over Rumania town and 28 shot down. At night few planes over. Rained early in morning until about 1000 when it cleared up and turned out a rather nice day.

Monday 24th July, 1944
Prisoner of War at stationed at Bodisch. Twenty seven men on Weckelsdorf-Trautenau line digging out at Radowenz, except four of us, doing a little stomping. Very easy day. In camp at 1715 hrs. A little mail up but received none myself. Reading and playing cards in evening. Potatoes, porridge bread, an extra ration tonight. News fairly quiet tonight, except for heavy fighting and counter attacks on Russian front. Very wet and warm morning, clearing slightly in afternoon.

Tuesday 25th July, 1944
Prisoner of War stationed at Bodisch. Twenty nine men on Weckelsdorf-Trautenau line, six being at Petersdorf loading old sleepers and rest of us at Radowenz digging out. Picked quite a few berries again today and in camp at 1715 hrs. Reading and playing cards in evening. Jerries say we have to hand in old leave passes that we have, but they are not

getting mine. Invasion front around Caen and St Lo heavy battles, but our troops not gaining anything. In Italy slight gains. Southern sector in Russia street fighting in Lemberg, and evidently Lublin surrounded as all there are fighting on the inside. Nthern sector around Kauen and Brest Litousk and other places heavy battles and one breakthrough still open. Not much mention of air activity. Hitler gives order that everything is now commandeered by the Jerry, evidently in a last effort to try to pull things together a bit. Potatoes, porridge and usual bread. A fairly fine and warm day.

Wednesday 26th July, 1944
Prisoner of War at stationed at Bodisch. Twenty nine men out today, six being at Petersdorf in morning loading sleepers and afternoon at Radowenz doing a bit of stomping, and the rest of us at Radowenz digging out, fairly easy day, and could have finished by 0900 if I had wanted to. Picked a fair few berries today for tonights supper. Some of the cockies and station masters moaning about us wandering about picking berries and talking to a Russian girl. Reports gone in. Two extra trains through this line today and had some evacuees from Eastern Prussia and this caused us to have to wait on these engines to get home making us very late, it being nearly 1830 hrs on arrival. Invasion front Nth West St Lo heavy American defences against German Third line of defence and broken through and heavy fighting. 110 more terroists cleaned up. In Italy heavy attacks south of Florence commenced slight advances. New attacks on Adriatic coast and heavy fighting going on. Russian front, Russians driven away from the town of Leberg slightly, slight advances near Lublin, elsewhere attacks unsuccessful. Planes over south and sth east Germany doing over Stuttgart, Berlin and areas and eastern Prussia. Pacific zone Americans make landing on new island in Marianne group and strengthen their positions. Potatoes, meat, goulash with cabbage extra and bread. Fairly fine and warm day with some clouds.

Thursday 27th July, 1944
Prisoner of War at Bodisch. Twenty nine out today on Weckelsdorf-Trautenau line, eight being at Qualisch in morning loading sleepers and afternoon stomping near Radowenz, and rest of us digging out at Radowenz. Reasonably easy day. Did not pick so many berries today and in camp 1715 hrs. Potatoes and vegetable soup with bread. Heavy attacks on invasion front, but no material gains. In Italy slight gains. In Russia: In Lemberg-Stanislau area heavy attacks but no break throughs. In northern sectors a couple of breakthroughs still open. Planes over Stuttgart, Berlin and other places. Fair number shot down. Fine and warm day.

Friday 28th July, 1944
Prisoner of War stationed at Bodisch Sudatenland. Fred goes into Stalag today. Twenty seven men out, eight being at Qualisch loading sleepers, and the rest of us at Radowenz, digging out. No berry picking today as too wet. In camp at 1715 hrs. Bulk issue of Red X food tonight and 50 cigarettes. New chap arrives from the Stalag today and brings out news sheet which states Russians doing extremely well on Sunday only 60 kilometres from Warsaw. Lamberg finished and several other places. Evacuation and harbour installations destroyed on Baltic coast and Nth Prussia. Not far from Konigsberg. Many German troops giving themselves up. Heavy bombing also here by Russians. Stalin tells the Jerries if they give up now there will be some Germany left after the war, otherwise there will not. On older border of Czecko and part of Slavakian. In Italy pushing well forward and Florence said to have fallen. Everything going well on the invasion front. Montgomery says war will not last many months. Been quite a few executions as the result of the attempt on Hitler. Said to be slight riots of unrest in Berlin, Hamburg, Hanover and town in Austria. Heavy bombing being carried out by planes and in one day 11,000 planes over Germany. German news: Americans pushing southward of St Lo, and heavy battles near

Caen. In Italy pushing forward. In Russia heavy fighting all fronts, and Germans admit evacuation of certain places to straighten out their line because of the Russian pincer movements. Our planes over as usual. Potatoes, vegetable soup and bread. Raining in morning at six o'clock, fine then till 1200 and thunder and lightning and heavy rain set in for about two hours and cleared up for a while more rain in the evening.

Saturday 29th July, 1944
Prisoner of War stationed at Bodisch. Twenty four men out today on Weckelsdorf line at Radowenz four men stomping, and the rest of us digging out. Easy morning, hardest part of the day was to fill in time. Left the job at 1345 hrs and through Bodisch 1500, and some continued on for showers and back in camp 1615 hrs. Fred returned from Stalag and brings back a few letters but not for myself. Reading and playing cards in evening. Fred tells us a few details of his visit to the Stalag. New German order comes in last night – no calling out Halt now, but shoot, escaped prisoner on being brought back has to be shot. Germans now want us to give up our paybooks. New potatoes, cabbage and bread. Dull warm morning with some rain coming up in afternoon and late evening.

Sunday 30th July, 1944
Prisoner of War at Bodisch. No work today, so slept in till 0800 hrs. Reading, writing and playing cards during the day. Wrote letter cards to home and Betty. A little mail up today and received one from home, the first for twenty weeks one from Betty and one from Bernice. Snow read out an article from the German newpapers. No news this evening as bad weather and did not have the wireless on. New potatoes, cabbage meat and goulash with usual bread. Reasonably fine until about 1600 hrs, when it came up thunder and some heavy rain during the evening.

Monday 31st July, 1944

Prisoner of War at Bodisch in Sudatenland. Twenty six men out Weckelsdorf-Trautenau line, ten being at Petersdorf, and Qualisch loading sleepers, seven at Radowenz digging out and myself with eight others at Qualisch unloading rails for the bends of the lines we are to build. Cranes not working too well, so did not finish them. In camp 1715hrs. Reading and playing cards in evening. Those who had pay books have to hand them in. Potatoes, macaroni and bread. Invasion front two fair size breakthroughs and heavy fighting now goes on. Italy battle towards Florence continues quietly and little local scrapping. On all Russian fronts fairly heavy fighting exists. OIL: fighting in streets of Warsaw. Fairly heavy air raids and fair number lost. A little rain during morning, but came out warm afternoon.

Tuesday 1st August, 1944

Prisoner of War on railway working party at Bodisch in Sudatenland. Working party E388 originally ex Stalag V111B Lamsdorf, but now attached to Stalag V111A, Gorlitz and POW number KRETA 4538. Twenty nine out at Weckelsdorf line digging out, except for three others and myself went to Parschitz-Orb to meet up with metal train, and returned with it, helping to unload metal between Qualisch and Radowenz. Fairly easy day and in camp at 1715 hrs. Tonight told that our party may be shifting down to the other one at Konigshan nearer Trautenau and not relishing the changeover been here so long and things coming to a close. This party also came out the same day as us when we came to Bodisch. A little reading and cards in the evening. Potatoes, and vegetable soup, cabbage and usual bread and weekly sugar and jam ration. Invasion front fairly large breakthrough and heavy fighting in an attempt to cover it over. Italy attempted a breakthrough on Florence fails. Heavy fighting on all Russian fronts and another town evacuated. Nth American bombers over Bucharest, Munich and three other places. Months shipping losses not as high as usual. Fairly fine morning with a little rain in afternoon.

Wednesday 2nd August, 1944

Prisoner of War stationed at Bodisch. Twenty eight men out Weckelsdorf-Trautenau line, digging out at Radowenz. After Freistig eight of us go to Qualisch to unload some rails. Moving camp so went home on 1345 train, getting in camp at 1500 hrs. Busy packing up gear. Late night, lights not being out till midnight. U/Officer says a few words. Potatoes, meat, goulash, cabbage and usual bread. News: much the same as yesterday except for attacking a transport convoy in the Mediteranean. Set in with rain at 0900 and continued practically all day.

Thursday 3rd August, 1944

Prisoner of War at Bodisch. Moving out today so busy packing Red X food and other goods in wagon. Cleaned up Lager and had dinner about 12.30 and went down and got on wagons the 1350 train hooking us up and came through to Trautenau arriving 1530 hrs. Waited here for some time and left again for Konigshan, the new Lager at 1615 hrs. Had to walk about 25 minutes to the Lager. Thirty four men already here, so everything a bit upset with our gang arriving, busy till about 2100 hrs bringing stuff up from station and getting settled in. Conveniences very bad here after the place we have just left. Macaroni, loaf bread, did not worry about potatoes today. No news tonight except for a few rumours floating around. A fairly fine day and warm evening.

Friday 4th August, 1944

Prisoner of War now stationed at Konigshan after the change over yesterday. Queens 44th birthday today. First days work on new party. Leaving here about 0645 to march to station, 20 minutes walk. Caught rain at 0710 and got out at Parschnitz Ort where digging out and wanting a fair bit done, but wanting to get home at 1400 hrs to fix things up a bit in the Lager so did it today, but will be a bit different tomorrow. Issued with Canadian food parcel and 50 cigarettes. These to do us for ten days to get back to the Monday issue of this party. Things terrible here and plenty of complaints. Potatoes, soup with bread. Nothing much to mention in the news except for heavy fighting on practically all fronts. A fairly fine day except for heavy clouds.

Saturday 5th August, 1944
Prisoner of War stationed at Konigshan in Sudatenland. At Parschnitz-Ort again today digging out started us off with five sleepers wanted them finished by 12.30 but adopted a go slow policy then cut us down to four and still continued going slow, some of us doing only two sleepers but went home on 13.15 from Parschnitz, getting in camp at 1400 hrs. No showers to go to here so have to take it in turns of rooms at a time in a bath in the basement so did not get ours today. A little reading. Not sleeping too well lately as have a cold. Soup and potatoes. Nothing much in the news. Fairly warm day with a little rain falling.

Sunday 6th August, 1944
Prisoner of War stationed at Konigshan. No work today so not up too early. Had bath in morning and did washing, being practically midday before I was finished. During the afternoon doing up the canteen book and paying out the accounts to the boys as the Canteen now broken up. Wrote cards home, Joyce H, Donald and Mrs Walker. Sent letter card by Fred to Stalag to Bernice. Also went to play football in afternoon but after about four minutes play the ball busted. A few women hanging around about the place here, and some of them have caused trouble at sometime or other. Put the wireless in today and going fairly well, but heard no news as yet. Porridge for breakfast. Potatoes, cabbage soup midday and usual bread. A very nice day practically cloudless.

Monday 7th August, 1944
Prisoner of war at Konigshan. The gang broken into three parties today some working at Parschnitz-Ort myself with others one stationed past Trautenau called Aldstadt, and others one station beyond us. On the party I was on carting a bit of metal on small wagons, clearing a

bit of grass along railway line. Easy day and knocking off about 1515 hrs, and getting home about 1730 hrs. Saw mill party alongside where we were working and they told us BBC news, and everything going fairly well. Americans breaking through and Poles take Warsaw. Fred Earl, McQuarne, McBea, Check and Smith G returned to Stalag today. Soup, potatoes, usual bread. Nothing much to report in the German news. Evening spent quietly. A very hot day with a few clouds. Air raid alarm here today and heard A/ACK in distance.

Tuesday 8th August, 1944
Prisoner of War stationed at Konigshan. Same parties as yesterday and home at same time, except for party beyond us moved back to Parschnitz-Ort at midday. Playing monopoly in the evening, and a little reading. Mixed soup, potatoes, usual bread and margarine. Heard that Black Hammer was the place of yesterdays raid. Another very hot day with thunderstorm somewhere in the afternoon.

Wednesday 9th August, 1944
Prisoner of War at Konigshan. Two gangs today the party I was on being in usual place and the one beyond us being Parschnitz-Ort. Half day and fairly easy day. Knocked off 1120 hrs and walked to Trautenau to catch 1210 express which stops at Parschnitz and Konigshan. Other party came home on late train, being in camp about 1400 hrs. A little reading and writing durng the afternoon and evening. Potatoes, vegetable soup, bread and marg. Also got some preserved tomatoes about twelve months old. Nothing much to mention in the news except for fairly heavy fighting on invasion front. A fairly warm day but came up a heavy thunderstorm at 2000 hrs and some very heavy hail fell.

Thursday 10th August, 1944
Prisoner of War stationed at Konigshan in Sudatenland. Parties same as yesterday being Parschnitz-Ort and Ober-Albstadt. At the latter place myself and unloading metal, spreading out metal, cleaning grass away and straightening line a bit with crowbars. Back in camp 1730 hrs.

Reading during the evening. Potatoes, soup, usual bread and marg. News seems to be fairly good. German news mentions new places on invasion front. A fairly cloudy day, but very warm.

Friday 11th August, 1944
Prisoner of War stationed at Konigshan in Sudatenland. Teams at the same place as yesterday, myself being with the gang at Ober Aldstadt. Fairly solid days work today, doing stomping all day. In camp at 1730. Hampton, Balsarini and Dave return to Stalag today. A little mail up today, but none myself being mostly English mail. Reading during the evening. Potatoes, soup, bread and marg. Nothing much in the way of news except that the American troops seem to be doing fairly well. Another very hot day with a few clouds.

Saturday 12th August, 1944
Prisoner of War stationed at Konigshan. Two gangs out again today, one at Parschnitz Ort and Ober-Aldstadt. At the latter place myself, had to unload a few trucks of metal, one of the boys got his finger squashed in the buffer. Half day and in camp about 1400 hrs. The copper broke down, so only a few managed to get a bath. Have to do our washing again this weekend, but next week will probably be done for us. Some parcels up for us ex Bodisch boys. Templeman getting personal parcel, myself books. Cigarettes Stevenson 2, Abester 2, Dalziel 3, Hunter, Pierce, Ellesmore and parcels for those returned Hampton, McBean, Pedersen and Lunam. A little tired tonight not feeling too good. Heard tonight that American troops are now 57 kilometres from *(unreadable)* so evidently been a fair move on that front. Nothing much to report elsewhere except for the Russians to make a fair move again soon. Dull morning but later cleared and came out fairly warm day.

Sunday 13th August, 1944
Prisoner of War stationed at Konigshan. About twenty eight of the party have to work at Parschnitz-Ort today, putting in points and a long day for them, not getting home before 1800 hrs. Reading, writing,

bathing and washing clothes also helped to fix up the bulk ready for tomorrow night. Wrote card to Virgilia thanking for cigarettes and Sigrid for book parcel. Reading during the evening. Nothing much of importance in the news, except Germans still holding out in St Malo, and several breakthroughs elsewhere on the invasion front. Nothing to mention in Italy. Russian front attacking strongly in several places including ten crack divisions in one place repelled. Morning started out fine but rained about 1000 and in afternoon set in very heavy. Still overcast at night with fairly warm evening.

Monday 14th August, 1944
Prisoner of War stationed at Konigshan. One party at Parschnitz-Ort. Myself with about twenty others at OberAldstadt and another six beyond us unloading stone. The party I was on we unloaded two trucks of stone and did some planeering. Fairly easy day and finished at 1510 hrs getting home about 1730 hrs. Issued with bulk Red X food and 50 cigarettes tonight, and had the job myself of cutting up the cheese, and dishing out the sugar. A little reading during the evening. Heard that Paris is supposed to be surrounded and fighting in St Germain, near Paris. Americans pushing very strongly everywhere. British General supposed to have said France will be Germany's Dunkirk. Russians also appear to be attacking strongly again. Potatoes, soup, bread etc. Sultry morning, but turned out hot day.

Tuesday 15th August, 1944
On railway working party as a POW stationed at Konigshan. Some of the boys home today for arbeiting on Sunday. Eight men at Lampersdorf and myself with the rest at Ober- Aldstadt. Fireman today, so had easy day. Boys finished work at 1500 and home 1730. Reading during the evening. Potatoes, vegetable soup, bread & marg. News: Heard that our troops made another landing in France, being southern France near Toulon and Marseilles. Landing air borne, and troops by sea said

to be 14 thousand by air and 16,000 by other means, said to be 800 boats and other craft used. Big encirclement in France and said to be about 20 German divisions cut off for a depth of 45 miles deep. Russian and Italian fronts quiet. Tito, Churchill and Churchill's son meet in Rome. British general says there will be great things happening this week. Jerries cigarette ration next week two cigarettes a day. Very cold morning, slight frost, but turned out very warm day, except for a few clouds.

Wednesday 16th August, 1944
Prisoner of War stationed at Konigshan. One party at Parschnitz-Ort and myself with fifteen others at Ober-Aldstadt. Levelling out of metal and cleaning away grass and easy morning and a half day getting in camp at 1400 hrs. Did a little reading and some washing on return. Potatoes, soup and usual bread. Evening playing monopoly. News: Landing in Sth of France was preceeded by a French General and 100 others who were landed about a week before and held on there. Other parts of France our troops doing fairly well, more places being evacuated. Italian front quiet, and in Russia heavy fighting on practically all fronts the usual Russian attacks being repelled with heavy losses. Forty kilometres from Paris. A fairly hot day.

Thursday 17th August, 1944
Prisoner of War at Konigshan. Usual parties today and same place as yesterday. Cleaning grass away today and a fairly easy time, finished 1500 hrs and in camp at 1730 hrs. A little reading during evening. Potatoes, soup and usual bread, marg and sugar ration. News: on invasion front sounds reasonably good by the German news, several more places being given up. Italian front still very quiet. In Russia heavy fighting continues on the part of the Russians, but without success. Raids north and nth west Germany in daylight and Berlin at night. Rained while going to work, then cleaned up and came up very hot.

Friday 18th August, 1944

Prisoner of War Konigshan. One party at Parschnitz-Ort and myself with other other party at Ober Albstadt. Unloading metal, and cleaning up grass alongside of railway line. Reasonable day. Finished work at 1510 and in camp 1730. A little mail up and received one from Verna and one from England being 11th July. Two of the boys leave here today and go on saw mill party at Ober-Albstadt. Reading during the evening and usual rations for the day. Nothing much in the news except for another attempted landing in sth of France, but all repulsed. Attempt to cross some river in Italy but thrown back and nothing much to mention on the Russian front. Foggy morning and fairly warm day.

Saturday 19th August, 1944

Prisoner of War Konigshan in Sudatenland. One party at Parschnitz and myself with the other party at Ober-Albstadt. Doing up sides of line with metal, and also unloaded some. Finished 1215, left for camp at 1240 and in at 1400. During afternoon and had bath and did washing. Evening reading and playing monopoly. Potato soup, bread and marg. German news: says our troops strengthened and widened their bridgehead south of France and armoured vehicles feeling their way further north. USA troops take position of Orleans St Malo gives mention heavy fighting in Arsentan. Heavy fighting in breaking out again in Italy. River Dneister, Rumanian troops repelling Russian attacks and elsewhere heavy attacks opening up again. Russian planes bomb town in Norway. American and British planes also active (OIL: 30 divisions given up in France. Sth France 7000 officers and men give in). Very warm day throughout.

Sunday 20th August, 1944

Prisoner of War Konigshan. In camp today and slept till nine o'clock. Morning reading and writing. Wrote card home and letter card to Verna. In afternoon went for a walk up to a fair sized hill, not far from the Lager, and saw some wonderful views, especially of Lubau railway junction and town and elsewhere around the district. Porridge for breakfast, potatoes, cabbage, gravy and bread midday ration. Jerry news admits some of our troops crossed the River Seine in France and tanks also across. Heavy fighting near Chatres – Advancing slightly in southern France, heavy Russian attacks but no successes. A fine and very hot day.

Monday 21st August, 1944
Prisoner of War stationed at Konigshan. One party at Parschnitz and myself with other party at Ober-Albstadt. A little planeering and stomping today, finishing 1500 and in camp at 1715. Issued with NZ food parcel and 50 cigarettes. Potatoes soup, usual bread and marg. Nothing much in the news tonight. Fighting close to Paris and Marseilles. A fine day one of the hottest for some time.

Tuesday 22nd August, 1944
Prisoner of War stationed at Konigshan Sudatenland. One party at Trautenau and myself with others at Ober-Albstadt, doing stomping, cleaning grass away from line and tightening up rail joints etc. In camp usual time 1715. Potatoes, soup, bread and jam. German news heard heavy fighting around Toulon and the place where they crossed the Seine, also other places heavy defensive battles going on. In Italy heavy fighting but no successes. Fighting flares up in Southern Russian sector around the Carpathian Mts and elsewhere heavy battle but no success. Fine and very hot day hotter than yesterday.

Wednesday 23rd August, 1944
Prisoner of War stationed at Konigshan. One gang at Parschnitz and myself with other party at Ober-Albstadt and another gang at Trautenau. On our party cleaning away grass from line, doing odd jobs and shifted the boody past the station. Finished at midday and in camp 1400. During afternoon reading and resting, also some reading during the evening. Potatoes semolina porridge double bread ration

and marg. German news mentions being heavy fighting in France, but our troops not gaining much ground. In Sthn France a little ground gained. In Russia fairly bitter fighting all sectors. In Italy nothing of importance gained. 'OIL' Russians break through into Rumania on 170 kilometre front. Our troops said to be 60 kilometres past Paris. A few clouds about today and weather slightly cooler than yesterday.

Thursday 24th August, 1944
Prisoner of War stationed near Konigshan. Gangs out today of five at Parschnitz, fifteen at Trautenau and myself with others at Ober-Albstadt. Cleaning away grass, some stomping and other odd jobs. Finished at about 1420 hrs and went for a wash and some for a swim. In camp 1730 hrs. Saw Red X train go through this morning, and an air raid alarm here today from 1130 to 1330 and heard that Hirselberg had been done over. 'Camp' papers up. Reading during the evening. The Bull here today and wants some drastic changes to take place. Potatoes soup and usual bread. German news says heavy fighting around Toulon and on the cross over of the River Seine, also drove German rearguard south of Paris towards the Seine. In Italy nothing of importance to mention. Heavy fighting near Bessarabian border, being fought back by Rumanian and German troops. Air raids over Hungary and Ober-Silesia. Heard this morning as rumours go, that Rumania has packed in and declared war on Germany at seven o'clock this morning, also that Paris had fallen at 1430 hrs yesterday. Another fairly warm day but slightly cooler in evening.

Friday 25th August, 1944
Prisoner of War stationed near Konigshan. Ten men to Parschnitz, ten to Trautenau, and myself with another gang at Ober-Albstadt, cleaning away grass stomping tightening up plates on railway line. Fairly easy day, just kept moving thats all. Finished 1500 and in camp 1715, saw Carlo today go by in train, and also Noel Lumby, 2/11Bn and talking to him. Reading during the evening. Potatoes, soup and usual

bread ration. Heard today that our troops thrown back to the River Seine. Southern France Toulon and Marseilles still holding out and Germans retreating northward are hampered by terroists. In Italy everything quiet. Heavy motorised units in South Russian pushing forward. Numerous attacks Nth East Warsaw repelled in heavy fighting. USA planes attacked places near Vienna, 28 planes lost. British planes and Soviet planes raided Petsama in Finland, and the town of Totsit and 29 planes lost. 2000 planes raid over Czeck territory yesterday and did heavy damage to railway yards. Another fairly warm day, but a cool evening.

Saturday 26th August, 1944
Prisoner of War in Sudatenland. One party got off at Parschnitz and myself with other party at Ober-Albstadt. First thing cleaning away grass and after Freistig, arbeit zug came out late with stone and also had the other party on from Parschnitz. Knocked off at 1210 and in camp 1400, being half day. Bathing and washing in afternoon and reading during the evening. A little mail up and received one from Carmel, the first for four months. Potatoes, soup and bread. Germans claim successful counter attacks on our forces in Nthn France. Toulon and Marseilles still holding out but other troops pushing forward to the north. In Italy all fairly quiet. In southern Russian front mentions some of the Rumanian troops throw down their arms and refuse to fight against the Soviets and repelling the Soviets in the Northern sector. Another very warm day. Lights out early reckon there is an air raid alarm.

Sunday 27th August, 1944
Prisoner of War at Konigshan. No work today so slept in 31st birthday today. Reading, writing, resting during the day. Wrote cards to Merle, Carmel and Aunty Em. Porridge for breakfast, potatoes, soup, cabbage and bread midday. News as such: Toulon and Marseilles still holding out fighting on street outskirts of Paris pushing stilll further

north from the south, fast motorised units hampering German units. Feeble attacks in Italy. Russia pushing ahead slightly in Bucharest and outskirts traitorus Rumanian clique fighting against the germans. Fighting heavy around Ducal pass. Heavy attacks against bandits coastal shipping costs the bandits 140 ships of all types and sizes. OIL Some of our troops on Belgium border. Bulgarians disarming German troops. Ducal pass into Slavakia in Russian hands. Eisenhower has warned the people of Luxemburg, Rhine and Saar districts to evacuate as this area will be a battle ground before long. Fairly warm day with plenty of wind throughout the day.

Monday 28th August, 1944
Prisoner of War stationed at Konigshan. No 1. room stay home today, to do out their room, scrubbing beds and pointing it out etc. One party at Bernsdorf a few at Trautenau, and myself with the other party at Ober-Albstadt planeering and unloading stone. Finished about 1500 and in camp at 1715 hrs. Issued with bulk food and 50 cigarettes. Potatoes, soup and usual bread. Nothing doing in the way of news tonight, as there was a storm in the air and wireless not too good and there was no news-paper. Heard that about 500 thousand Germans were disarmed in Bulgaria and Rumania. Wind in morning but fairly warm and came up with thunderstorm in evening.

Tuesday 29th August, 1944
Prisoner of War stationed at Konigshan. One gang to Parschnitz and one at Ober Albstadt, including myself planeering and unloading stone. Finished at 1510 and home 1715 hrs. Sam Blee returned to the Stalag today. Cleaning the room out a little tonight in preparation for tomorrow's cleaning out and painting, also a little reading during the evening. Potatoes, soup and bread. German news: mentions several rearguard actions with our forward troops pressing onwards. Fighting in streets Paris. Brest garrison refuses to give in. Marseilles still holds out. Counter attacks around the Seine. Heavy sea fight West

Coast of France and Holland. Reconnaissiance activity in Italy only. Hungarian and German troops resisting attempts by Soviets of gain onto Hungarian Territory. Rumanian section nothing much mentioned. Raids over Kiel. Konigsberg, Hamburg and Berlin. Dull warm morning. In afternoon coming over real cloudy and some rain set in with a little thunder and warm evening.

Wednesday 30th August, 1944
Prisoner of War stationed at Konigshan. Nobody in our room went out today having to stay in pulled beds down and scrubbed and had the room painted out. Some of the boys home at 1400 and the rest as usual at 1715. Porridge, potatoes, usual bread, marg and a sugar ration. German news seems to give quite a few admissions in our favour. Paris given up to the superior force of our troops. Marseilles still holding out in a confined space. Still pushing northwards from the south, elsewhere gains mentioned but too many places to write down. In Italy on Adriatic Coast slight ground gain. In Russia and Rumania on all sectors heavy fighting and one town mentioned as given up to superior forces. Rouen given up in tonights wireless news. Raids over Vienna, Hungary and other places. Fighters over West Germany (OIL) Arras fallen, at one point troops twelve miles from German border. A very cool day witth a spot of rain.

Thursday 31st August, 1944
Prisoner of War at Konigshan. Some of the boys at Parschnitz, some at Trautenau and myself with gang at Ober-Albstadt, planeering and unloading stone. Finished and in camp at 1715 hrs. A little mending and reading during the evening. Potatoes, bread and marg. German news admits Rouen given up and our troops pushing forward in all quarters. Marseilles still holding out. Nothing much doing in Italy. Russian front activity on all sectors. Raid over Konigsberg and Stettin, also Hungary raided Hamburg and Berlin. (OIL: Greece, Crete and YugoSlavia being evacuated and some of the Zcecks rising up in

arms. Rumania asks Bulgaria to state her intentions of fighting with the Germay or Russia, 20 miles from German border at some points. Tank superiority of 30 to 1. Germany said to have gas ready for use on Dutch-Belgium borders) Cool morning coming out warm about 1000 and afternoon dull with some rain.

Friday 1st September, 1944
Prisoner of War on railway working party at Konigshan in Sudatenland, previously at Bodisch and attached to Stalag V111A Gorlitz and previously V111B Lamsdorf. One party at Trubenwasser, and myself with other party at Ober-Albstadt. In morning planeering and unloading stone. In afternoon cleaning away grass, as more stone arriving tomorrow. Finished about 1500 and at camp at 1715. In evening reading. No paper today, so got no news, except at 2000 announced the fall of Amiens. Five parcels up but did not get the names. Potatoes, soup, bread and sugar ration. A very dull morning, coming out warmer about 1000 and continuing to be a reasonable day.

Saturday 2nd September, 1944
Prisoner of War on party at Konigshan. One party to Trubenwasser and myself with other party at Ober-Albstadt. Clearing away grass and unloaded five trucks of stone and on finishing went straight to Trautenau on arbeit train and caught the 1212 express from Trautenau and in camp 1315. Afternoon washing and bathing and reading during the evening. Potatoes, soup, bread and marg. No oil, but German news mentions of our forward troops in the south being harassed by their rearguard actions. Heavy fighting for Brest and our attacks being thrown back. Italian front on Adriatic coast, but no success. On Russian front from the Carpathians to the Finnish Sea heavy fighting in all sectors, but no gains. Raids over West and Nth West Germany. A very dull morning, but coming out warm and sultry later in the day.

Sunday 3rd September, 1944

Prisoner of War stationed at Konigshan. Beginning of the 6th year of war with England and Germany at 1100 hrs. Twenty seven of us including myself had to go out for half a days work unloading stone at Ober-Albstadt. Wanted us to clear some grass away first of all but set in with heavy rain, and none of us would do anything. I went straight under a tree and copped a bit of abuse. Eventually went out of rain and waited for stone train. Finished at 1130 then went to Trautenau and caught express to Konigshan, getting in camp at 1315 hrs. Afternoon a little sleep, reading and wrote cards to home, Florrie and Alison. In evening reading. German news: Wireless bad tonight but mentions the evacuation of Warsaw in Poland and Lyons in Sth France. OIL: Finland capitulates and Tournai in Belgium captured. Potatoes, cabbage, soup, usual bread and a jam ration. A very wet morning and dull day throughout, except a little clearer in afternoon.

Monday 4th September, 1944

Prisoner of War stationed at Konigshan. Everybody forty three in all at Ober-Albstadt. Cleaning away grass from railway line and some of us unloading stone. Train late for connection at Trautenau this morning, so had to walk from to Ober-Albstadt, bit of an arguement as they did us out of our Freistig. Finished work at 1510 and in camp 1715. Issued with 50 cigarettes and each pair had Canadian and English food parcel. Potatoes, soup, usual bread and marg. OIL Germany has 14 days to get her troops out of Finland. Brussels supposed to have fallen. G <u>News: Heavy</u> fighting between Arras and Verdun and our troops coming from the Sth are harassed by the German troops. Heavy fighting on the Adriatic coast in Italy, but only small breakthrough. Nth East Warsaw heavy fighting and elsewhere along the front. Planes over Bremen at night. Potatoes, soup, usual bread and marg. Dull morning but came out fairly good day later, especially the afternoon.

Tuesday 5th September Friday,1944
Prisoner of War stationed at Konigshan. Eight men at Trautenau, some at Trubenwasser and myself at other party at Ober-Albstadt, planeering and some stomping. Finished and in camp at 1715 hrs. The Jerries want us to work tomorrow and because they promised us Wednesday morning off for Sundays work we kick about it. U/Officer says we will not be going out tomorrow on returning home. Reading during the evening. Chap going through from Stalag today says from next Monday will be on half parcel a week. Potatoes, soup usual bread. German news: Brest still holding out and some fort gives in after heroic fighting and troops from the south push northwards but hampered by German flank security forces and Nthn France pushing forward in all sectors. In Italy heavy fighting on Adriatic coast, but we gain only slight breakthroughs. Nothing much from the Russian front. Rumanian sector no mention at all. OIL: Our troops said to be fighting in the Rhineland, Mitz in Alsace-Lorraine in our hands. Antwerp fallen, and also the Hague in Holland in British hands. Rumours: Nazi Party ready to get out of it. Rumour says parachutists landed in Hills, and Jerries out after them but only half of them return. Fairly cool morning but came out very nice day.

Wednesday 6th September, 1944
Prisoner of War at Konigshan in Sudatenland. Only one party out today the rest of us, including myself at home today for working last Sunday morning. Did not get out till 0800, did some washing, mending and reading during the day. Porridge for breakfast for those in camp, and potatoes, soup, pork chop and usual bread. The fall of the Hague is only false we learned tonight. Another town in Alsace Lorraine has fallen to our troops by the name of Akon. Other news: Our forward troops now fighting in Antwerp and Brussels while from the Sth still moving forward harassed by German flank security troops. In Italy slight break-through in heavy fighting 200 tanks destroyed. In Russia consistent attacking with no success. Planes over a couple of places.

Radio tonight somebody chipping in and practically giving reverse of German news. A fine and fairly warm today.

Thursday 7th September, 1944
Prisoner of War stationed at Konigshan. One party on the Lampersdorf line and myself with other party at Ober-Albstadt. On the fire job today so had it easy. Miller not in a too good a mood. Finished about 1500 and in camp 1720. Potatoes, soup, bread and marg. German news: German troops move from the area of Antwerp to the Albert Canal zone. Troops from the Sth still harassed by German Security Troops. Still fighting at Brest. Our troops attack the fort of Le-Harve but no success. In Italy a little ground gained. Russian front mentions Hungarian and German troops repelling Russian attack. Low flying planes do over 60 railway engines and two complete trains. Bombers in daylight over Mannerheim, Rudwigschafen, Karlsrubr and one other place. At night over Hanover and 31 planes shot down. No oil tonight. Cool morning but came out fairly warm day.

Friday 8th September, 1944
Prisoner of War stationed at Konigshan. One party out Lampersdorf line and myself with other party at Ober-Albstadt, on getting to work were told we had to work 10 hours a day and could not get home till 1800 hrs. Had the cheek to expect contract on 10 hr day, but howled it down immediately and as a result the days work dropped considerably. Finished about 1650 and home at 1830 hrs. Reading in evening not much time though. Potatoes, goulash with usual bread and marg. German news: heavy attacks by the Americans on Brest also heavy fighting still around Antwerp and other places. On the Italian front and French passes heavy attacks with Moroccan troops, but nothing gained, also heavy losses as the result of our attack on the Adriatic coast. Russian front Hungarians fighting heavily against the Rumanians, also heavy attacks around the Warsaw area. Bombers over Hungary and Serbia, also Emden and NW Germany. At night over

Hamburg. OIL Hungary declares War on Rumania. German division gets mixed up with Canadian division in Belgium. German General picked up in one of our convoys. 30,000 prisoners taken in Russia and 10 Generals. Belgium Govt returns to Brussels from England. Goering to go to second line of defence to be manned by Hitler Youth Arbeit Corp. German students have to work in factories. The trial of the Mayor of Leipzig who made the attempt on Hitler commences tomorrow. Heavy rain between 0630 and 0800 and then gradually cleared up and very warm day.

Saturday 9th September, 1944
Stationed at Konigshan in Sudatenland as a POW. One party at the Lampersdorf line and with other myself at Ober-Albstadt, owing to the extra hours to be worked, did not finish today till 1500 hrs, instead of 1200, getting in camp at 1715 hrs. As the result not much work was done, and the boss got a bit annoyed and threatened to bring the Army out. On returning had bath, doing some reading during the evening. The U/Officer and Major create bit of a stir in evening by being worse for drink. U/Officer puts his fist through a couple of windows, when they wouldn't let him put a bullet through them. Control Feldwabel here also this evening. Potatoes, soup, usual bread and margarine. No OIL tonight. German news: Our forces attack Brest heavily, but repelled. Troops from south continue forward, harassed by the German rearguard. Northern France attacks failing and at Antwerp heavy fighting. In Italy heavy attacks by us but nothing gained, heavy losses and some tanks. Rumanians and Hungarians fighting strongly against each other, but the Hungarians fight strongly. Nothing much of importance on the rest of the Russian front. Several places raided by day and night. Very cool morning, but came out warmer during the day, and turned cool again in the evening.

Sunday 10th September, 1944
Prisoner of War in Sudatenland. Was one of a party of twelve to go out working today at Ober-Albstadt having to unload four wagons of stone

by midday and was told could have the rest of the day free, as we to have worked the whole day, getting home at 1315 hrs and have tomorrow free so actually gained half a day. In the afternoon resting reading and writing. Wrote card home and letter card to Jean and Gladys. Potatoes, soup, cabbage and double ration of bread and jam issue. Heard that Bulgaria had declared war on Germany, otherwise no OIL. German news: In Northern France attacks against Brest, Bologne and Dunkirk were repulsed. In Flanders rearguard German Army in heavy fighting. Attacks of our troops from bridgehead at Antwerp were wrecked. Heavy fighting around the Citadel of Luttick and North West Metz. Troops still moving back from the Sth, with our forces attempting to break through. In Italy heavy fighting in the Adriatic with heaviness that climbed to great heights. Our troops attempted to get through on six occasions, but one breakthrough narrowed down, our lines lying with great losses. Southern Russian front German and Hungarian troops repelling heavy attacks. In the northern sectors everything fairly quiet. USA planes made terror attacks against Karlsruke, Mainz, Mannerheim and Ludwigschafen outstanding damage and personal losses, 22 planes shot down. At night British planes over Nurnberg. A very cool and fine morning, later comimg over dull and some rain about midday, but otherwise fine.

Monday 11th September, 1944
Prisoner of War stationed at Konigshan. Gang on Lampersdorf line and some at Ober Albstadt. Myself with eleven others stayed in for working yesterday (Sunday morning). During the day did washing, reading and dished out the bulk food to be issued tonight. Issued with half the usual bulk food today and 25 cigarettes. Great excitement here today 200 of our bombers went over heavily escorted by fighters. Every plane in formation and no sign of German fighters or ACK/ACK. First time have seen planes over this part of country and the biggest formation of British planes I have ever seen. Supposed to have done over Ober-Silesia. Porridge for breakfast, potatoes, soup and usual bread. OIL supposed to be fighting in the middle of the

Seigfreid line and tanks also penetrated there. 25 divisions said to be cut off in Greece and Yugo-Slavia. Heavy attacks broken out again on Russian front a 1,000 guns used in the defence area. In Italy said to be going well. German news: Vienna, Stuttgart, Berlin and other places bombed by American and our planes. A very cold morning, later coming out fine and fairly warm with a cool evening.

Tuesday 12th September, 1944
Prisoner of War at Konigshan in Sudatenland. One party on Lampersdorf line with myself the other party at Trubenwasser and four men at Freihest in morning and afternoon at Trautenau. Long day again, getting in camp at 1830 hrs. The Germans call this their total war effort, another air raid alarm at midday today but did not see or hear any of our planes but saw one German fighter hedge hopping as fast as he could go. A little reading during the evening. Potatoes, very watery soup tonight and bread. No oil. German news: still fighting near Brest, one little peninsula lost. Fighting around Albert Canal. Still pushing foreward from the Sth. Fighting on the passes of the Italian-French border. Numerous other places mentioned. In Italy on Adriatic coast heavy attacks repulsed. Strong fighting on most of the Russian front, but no success gained by the Soviets. Air raids over Sth and Western Germany, Berlin, Stuttgart, Vienna, Mannerheim and other towns mentioned. Fairly heavy frost this morning and during the day sunshine and dull clouds being fairly cool at times. May be winter coming early.

Wednesday 13th September, 1944
Prisoner of War in Konigshan. One party on Lampersdorf line, four in Trautenau stomping, and myself on party at Trubenwasser, stomping and planeering. A long day getting back to camp at 1830 hrs. A little reading during the evening. A new U/Officer comes today to take the place of the one who was drunk over the weekend and is going to the front. New one had at Bodisch in May 1942. Soup, potatoes and bread

as rations. German news: heavy fighting on all sectors in France especially against Brest, Le Havre and Dunkirk. Forward troops from the South still contacting German rearguard. French-Italian passes still fighting for, in Italy heavy fighting going on and our troops getting the worst of it. Russian front heavy scrapping in all sectors and small breakthroughs healed over. Heavy bombing raids on a good many places including Brux on the border of the Protectorate and at night on Berlin. OIL: Said to be on 140 kilometres by 10 deep near Aaken on German border and said to be doing well in Italy. Le Havre fallen after being done over by 3000 bombers and 400 infantry take 7000 prisoners. Goering said to be missing. Some of the Hitler Youth said to have been captured and sent back again to their own side. Frost in morning then came out fine but a little dull in the afternoon.

Thursday 14th September, 1944
Prisoner of War stationed at Konigshan in Sudatenland. Usual party on the Lampersdorf line, four at Trautenau and myself with the other party at Trubenwasser, stomping and cleaning away grass and other jobs. Home at 1855. Quiet evening with no reading. Soup, potatoes, usual bread and margarine. German news: Le Havre fallen. Brest still holding out, also attacks on Calais, 142 tanks and armoured cars shot up in big fighting around Achen. Still heavy attacks going on around Arras and a couple of other places. In Italy German rearguard fighting our forward troops. Heavy fighting flared up again around Warsaw and attacking with tanks and battle planes achieved a breakthrough which has since been narrowed down. Raids on Munich, Munster, Mannerheim and many other places. Frost in morning and then came out fairly warm day and cool in evening with a breeze blowing.

Friday 15th September, 1944
Prisoner of War stationed at Konigshan. One party out on the Lampersdorf line, four men at Trautenau, and myself with party at Trubenwasser. Stomping, clearing away grass, and other odd jobs.

Went slow on the stomping today and Miller the gaffir was pretty annoyed, in fact just about boiling with rage at some times, and home in camp usual late time. Mail up and received one from Gladys. Potatoes, soup usual bread, marg sugar and jam ration. Issue also meat four to a tin. German news: Still heavy fighting in Italy and coming under the heavy defensive fire of the enemy we received heavy losses. Still fighting in Brest, Dunkirk and Calais. A fair number of places mentioned it seems as if our troops are pushing forward to the German border. Heavy battles on all sectors of the Russian front and nothing gained by breakthrough near Warsaw area. Raids at night over Berlin, day time Sth and Western Germany fair number of towns mentioned and about 90 planes lost. Cool morning, being slightly cloudy but very warm later in the day.

Saturday 16th September, 1944
On railway working party as a POW at Konigshan, Sudatenland. Brother Jacks 30th birthday. Party out on Lampersdorf line, four to Trautenau and another party with myself at Trubenwasser until 1000 then moved up to Freiheit, two stations further on, and we're taking out old sleepers and replacing with new ones. Shorter day today, getting in camp at 1715 hrs. Too late for our room to have baths. Reading during the evening. Potatoes soup, usual bread and marg. German news: mentions our troops fighting in the forward positions of the West Wall. Germans still holding out in Brest, quite a few other places too numerous to mention of heavy battles fighting. In Italy our troops under heavy defensive fire. Still strong battles going on Russian front but no breakthrough is achieved. Rumour has it that Germany is to have a 100 hour bombardment. Cool morning but later came out very warm and continued till evening when a cool breeze sprang up.

Sunday 17th September, 1944
Prisoner of War stationed at Konigshan. No work today for a change and did not get out of bed till 0900 hrs, chopping wood, washing and

bathing up till midday. Afternoon reading, writing and playing football. Wrote cards home, (Lil and Tom Eng) and letter card to Virgilia. In evening reading. Potatoes, soup, cabbage and double issue of bread. Heavy fighting around Aachen with infantry and tanks, but only able to win a little ground in a breakthrough Nth East via Stolberg. 27 tanks destroyed. Sth of Aachen in the area of Nancy. Heavy attacks by us but no successful gains. Still holding out in Brest. Harbour towns in south England under fire from coastal batteries. In Italy slight breakthrough at heavy cost, despite stronger measures. Adriatic German troops hinder attempts to break through upon Rimini. In Russia strong attacks beaten back by German and Hungarian troops. Soviet troops in East Carpathian wrecked. Nth East Warsaw breakthrough attempts were thrown back by SS and Hungarian troops. Several other attacks with tank and battle planes were frustrated by divisions of our troops and Lettlandish volunteer brigade. British bombers raid Keil and Berlin at night. V1 reported from London to have operated early hours of Saturday morning. A very nice and sunny day.

Monday 18th September, 1944
Prisoner of War stationed at Konigshan. Usual party to Lampersdorf, four at Gabensdorf and one party at Freiheit and myself with five others got off at Trautenau, and unloaded seven sets of wagon wheels. Also loaded 16 double sleepers on the wagon. After finishing this joined party at Freiheit and put in the rest of the day stomping. Went very slow and Miller rings up Starkey and Starkey refers to the Coy with the result a couple of Coy captains, came to see the guards at Trautenau tonight. Miller also had a couple of trucks of stones to be unloaded, and said they must be unloaded today and we told him we were not on contract and there was no such word as must, so he left the stone till tomorrow. Home at 1840 hrs. Issued with 25 cigarettes and half English Food parcel and some NZ parcel between 2. Potatoes, soup, usual bread and margarine. No German news tonight. OIL 40 kilometres from Colognne. Invasion on Holland and 1200 planes used. Also

rumours of landing in Denmark. Hitler has a week to get out and big riots in Austria. Fairly cool morning but came out a very warm day.

Tuesday 19th September, 1944
Prisoner of War stationed at Konigshan. One party on Lampersdorf line, four men at Gabensdorf and the rest of us at Freiheit, stomping and unloading metal, go slow policy again today and old Miller still annoyed about it. In camp at 1840, potatoes, soup, bread and marg. Nothing in the way of OIL. German news: some German troops still holding out in the ruins of Brest, also fortifications of Bolognne attacked and wrecked as they were at Dunkirk. Heavy fighting in around Aachen and towards Nancy, but nothing of importance gained. Landing in Holland by our troops after heavy air attacks, three places mentioned, and another attempt near Antwerp to link up with parachutists troops. Heavy fighting Nth and Nth East of Florence, but nothing of importance gained and on the Adriatic fighting towards Rimini checked with heavy losses. Heavy attacks in most sectors of the Russian front but nothing gained. Raids on Budapest and other places at night. Raid over town in Hungary. Late item for us at Lager. Fred Earl returns here today, possibly to take over from the Sgt Major who has been ordered by the Coy to return to Stalag because of being drunk here one weekend. Fairly cool morning and dull day throughout.

Wednesday 20th September, 1944
Prisoner of War stationed at Konigshan in Sudatenland. One party on Lampersdorf line, eight men at Gabensdorf, and myself and the other party at Freiheit, stomping and replacing sleepers and only did three for the whole day, and in camp at 1835 hrs. Plenty of fruit and vegetables coming into Freiheit the last couple of days. Played crib during the evening. Potatoes, soup, and usual bread (OIL) More troops landed by air into Holland, behind German lines, fair number cut off and 2nd and 3rd Armies moving up to help, doing 80 kilometres in 2 days. Aachen surrounded. Spolberg fallen and Brest finished.

German news: German troops out of Brest to another place on the peninsula. Little ground gained by our troops in Holland in heavy fighting. Also little ground gained near the area of Aachen. In Italy our attacks around Florence failed and elsewhere in Italy pushing without much gain. In Russia on all fronts attacking without success. Raids in Budapest and Hungary and other places in Germany. Cool morning and fairly warm day.

Thursday 21st September, 1944
Prisoner of War on working party as a POW near Konigshan. Eight men at Gabensdorf, party out on the Lampersdorf line and with others myself on the Trubenwasser job, stomping and doing other jobs. Had another row with one of the postens today and he went white and shaken with rage. Home at 1830 hrs. Playing crib in evening. Potatoes, soup, usual bread. Oil. Bolognne fallen. 60,000 prisoners taken in the fall of Brest. German news: In Holland the air landed troops areas were further narrowed down. Near Eindhoven our tanks pushed to the North East. North West Aachen able to widen our bridgehead with strong tank forces. Heavy fighting in the Nancy, Luneville areas. Nancy lost to our troops. Much of Calais, Bologne and St Nagaire were wrecked. Big battles on Adriatic Coast in Italy, reached highest point and German troops move to new positions to hinder our breakthrough. Enemy attacks at North and North East Florence were wrecked. Heavy attacks in Russian front were wrecked. Russians attempting to cross river under cover of mist were broken up. Raids over North and North West Germany especially the town area of Coblenz, building damage and civilian losses. At night Gladbach, Munchen and Budapest. Cool morning, but a reasonably warm day.

Friday 22nd September, 1944
Prisoner of War stationed at Konigshan. Usual party on Lampersdorf line, eight men at Gabensdorf, and myself with the other party at Trubenwasser and stomping the points there. Did not do much, and

in camp usual time of 1830 hrs. Pierce, Myers, Trickett and the Major return to the Stalag today. A little mail up, received one from Lil and Tom. Played crib during the evening. Potatoes, soup, bread also weekly jam and sugar ration. German news: In Holland air landed troops of ours were compressed closer in, and 2,800 prisoners were taken with Divisional Commander. Brest now finished. Calais, Bologne attacks wrecked. In heavy fighting around Aachen nothing of importance gained. In Italy heavy attacks on both fronts and breakthroughs achieved with strong ship artillery and battle planes. In Russia heavy attacks especially in Lettland and Estonia where the Russians lost 600 tanks. Day raids on Budapest. Ruab and Pressburg. A night raid on Trier and caused heavy personal losses. Very dull day with a little drop of rain.

Saturday 23rd September, 1944
Prisoner of War stationed at Konigshan in Sudatenland: Party on Lampersdorf line, eight at Gabensdorf and with myself, sixteen of us at Trubenwasser on stomping; and also six men in camp carting potatoes. Finished work 1500hrs and in camp 1715hrs. A little washing on return and played crib during the evening. A little mail but none myself. Potatoes, soup, bread and margarine. (Oil) supposed to have taken 600,000 prisoners since the invasion started. Did not read the German news sheet tonight. A fairly dull day with a few spots of rain.

Sunday 24th September, 1944
Prisoner of War in Sudatenland stationed at Konigshan. No work today, except for those who were carting potatoes yesterday, still had a few to finish off. Put out the bulk food this morning ready for tomorrow, also had bath during the morning and did washing. Wrote card home to Sigrid. Reading and doing odd jobs in evening. Potatoes, cabbage, soup, and double issue of bread. German news: Western front in Holland our troops suffering high lossses, but gaining nothing. South East of Aachen our troops repulsed in heavy fighting. German

counter attacks throw our troops back. North East of Echlernach 5 American tank divisions suffered heavy losses. Area of Luneville heavy fighting. On the upper Mosel changeful fighting – near Remeremont and Epinal. Fortified harbours of Bologne, Calais and Dunkirk lay under heavy fire and rolling air attacks.

Italy north of Luca Pistoca tank conducted thrusts being unsuccessful, North of Florence heavy attack by us. In heavy fighting of superior forces attacks repulsed. Russia heavy attacks everywhere but no successes. Central sector South of Memel local thrusts of the enemy were unsuccessful. Fighting in Northern sector climbed to great hardness. All Soviet breakthrough attempts defended. Disengaging movements North of Estonia proceeded according to plan. Raids by day attack against Munich and Kassel. 15 planes shot down. Afternoon 20th September United States of American forces attacking Aachen received heavy losses, and had to call for an Armistace to collect wounded, and on resuming Americans were thrown back. Very wild and windy morning, and a thunderstorm in afternoon about 1530hrs and storm in evening at about 2100 hrs to 2300 hrs and heavy rain.

Monday 25th September, 1944
Prisoner of War stationed at Konigshan. One party at Schatzler, eight men to Gabensdorf, and myself with the other party at Trubenwassers stomping and doing odd jobs. Finished 1645hrs and in camp 1830hrs. Issued with half parcel of bulk and 25 cigarettes. Potatoes, soup and usual bread. (OIL) Supposed air landed troops in Holland said to be 3 kilometres inside German border. No paper tonight for German news. Very dull day with some showers of rain.

Tuesday 26th September, 1944
Prisoner of War stationed at Konigshan. One working party at Schatzler, eight men at Gabensdorf and with myself other party at Trubenwasser on stomping and in camp at 1830hrs after the days work. Played crib

during the evening. Potatoes, soup, bread and weekly jam ration. German News mentions of compressing air landed division in closer space, and also disengaging movement in Holland.

In Luneville continues heavy fighting. In Aachen and other areas heavy attacks but our troops gaining only little ground. Italy our forces pushing forward slightly, as German troops withdraw to straighten their line. Heavy attacks on practically all sectors on Russian front. Reval evacuated. In Estonia the German disengaging movement continues without hindrance from the enemy. Fair number of raids including Munich and also over Sudatenland. 32 shot down. (OIL) Supposed speech by Eisenhower tells foreign workers not to attack Nazi party but to await events. Dull heavy day with rain starting about midday, and falling steadily practically rest of day.

Wednesday 27th September, 1944
Prisoner of War in Konigshan Sudatenland. One party at Schatzler, eight at Gabensdorf, and myself with the other party stomping sleepers and other jobs. Home usual late time of 1830hrs. Played crib during the evening. Potatoes, soup, bread and margarine. (OIL) Supposed news of our troops said to be in Cologne – and also 1st Air Division reinforced by 2nd Air Division, and 15 kilometres over the German-Dutch border. (No German news except that they claim to have wiped out 1st Airborne Division in Holland taking 6,400 prisoners by wireless news 2000hrs) Cold morning with fog, and fog drifts coming up till midday when it brightened up.

Thursday 28th September, 1944
Prisoner of War stationed at Konigshan. Myself with party at Trubenwasser, one party at Schatzler, and eight at Gabensdorf. Our gang on stomping till 1000hrs, then with eleven others took small wagon and went picking up rails between Trubenwasser and Trautenau. Had two derailments, and the second one left them where they were and Max done his block with a couple of the boys. Caught 1310hrs

train back to Trubenwasser, and then raised line in bridge and after dinner cleaning up a few stones. In camp 1835hrs. Played crib in evening. Potatoes, soup and usual bread.

German News: Confirmed in paper of finish of our 1st Airborne Division with 6,400 prisoners, 1,000 gliders and 100 planes destroyed, beside anti-tank guns and other material. Between Aachen and Mitz heavy fighting by our troops with no results, also on all other fronts on the Western area we had heavy losses. Guns from Channel coast bombard English coast, and still holding out in Calais. In Italy gained little ground at the expense of heavy losses. Fairly active on all Russian sectors, but breakthroughs and attacks repulsed, and disengaging movement from Riga continues. Raids over good many towns and 53 planes lost for two days. OIL: Division landed in Albania. Withdrawn from 1st Airborne Division area, leaving 800 wounded behind. Land Army reached there a day late. Cold morning but came out fairly good day.

Friday 29th September, 1944
Prisoner of War stationed in Sudatenland at Konigshan. Usual party at Schatzler, eight Gabensdorf and the rest of us at Trubenwasser on stomping till 1030hrs, then all of us there, and tools moved to Trautenau. During the rest of the day shifting plates, bolts, screws, and laid few lengths of rails by engine shed. Fairly easy day and in camp at 1830hrs. "Camp" papers up and played crib in evening. Potatoes, soup and usual bread. OIL: Speech by Churchill says his Generals cannot accept victory this year with any certainty. Probably early next year. The loss of the Airborne division was a set back for all. German News: Heavy fighting without our troops gaining any success - except heavy losses men and material in Holland. Around Aachen all attempts to go forward repulsed. In Italy heavy fighting and slight gains by us on both sectors. Rebels cleaned out of Warsaw. Fairly heavy fighting on all sectors of the Russian front, but no gains of importance all attacks being repulsed. Fair number of towns bombed and 32 planes lost. Dull frosty morning, but came out warmer in the day.

Saturday 30th September, 1944

Prisoner of War stationed at Konigshan. Party of workers at Schatzler, and the other party with myself at Trautenau putting in rails near the place where the engine coal up. Started out on contract with the intention of coming home at 1300hrs, then they piled more on, so I went slow, and did not finish the job, and came home 1615hrs and getting in camp 1715hrs. Had a bath and did washing in evening. A very nice tea dished up tonight, being mashed potatoes with spinach, pumpkin and meat and gravy, usual bread, issue cheese and apples. (OIL:) Supposed to have taken the capital of Albania, 2nd Airborne division said to be 15 kilometres over the German-Dutch border and things going very well for us in Italy. German News: Attempts by us with heavy airborne troops to gain ground over the Maas and Rhine-Hendems in Holland and go around the West Wall between Ernden and Munster to break through to Germany were wrecked.

English 2nd Army now the small attacking point, via Eindhoven upon Nimwegan West of Venlo. Our attacks between Antwerp and Herzogen Busche livened up. Our troops thrown back by counter attacks from the break through area North of Luneville. Americans started counter attacks North of Nancy, only little gains with heavy losses. In one part our troops forced the Americans east of the line. Fortified coastal batteries still holding out. In Italy gains but meeting with heavy defensive measures. In Russia fairly heavy fighting on most sectors and disengaging moment continues in Lithuania.

In Central Kroatia. Kroatian troops fight shoulder to shoulder and take backtown of Banja-Luka and link up with the occupants, who were cut off for a day. Counter attacks by German-Hungarian troops on the Hungarian and Rumanian border between Sveged and Groswardien makes good progress. Town of Newmarkt given up on the Moros sector. Air raids on Kassell, Madgeburg, Essen and several places in the area of Leipzig-Halle. During the night Brunswick done over and 75 planes shot down. Heavy frost this morning and very cold wind blowing, then came up fairly warm day except for the breeze which got cooler again in the evening.

Sunday 1st October, 1944

Prisoner of War on railway working party stationed at Konigshan in Sudatenland and previous party at Bodisch E388 ex Stalag VIIIB Lamsdorf, but now attached to Stalag VIIIA Gorlitz. No work today so slept in till nine. A little washing and mending. Wrote card home. Some mail up but mostly English, and received none myself. Porridge for breakfast with soup, potatoes and carrots midday and double issue of bread. No Oil, but German news as follows: In Holland our troops pressing on all fronts but no gains. Aachen to Nancy only local attacks and successful counter attacks by the Germans – Area of Luneville and Chateau – Salini our troops in embittered fighting took back high positions and forest areas. Fortifications of the channel report artillery fire and local fighting. V1 on London. Italy state heavy losses received by us day before, we did take up our attack yesterday. On Adriatic 8th Army fighting around Savigriena. Russia fighting on Danube sleeve both sides Eiserrin-Tores with new forces thrown in on both sides continues. Germans and Hungarians with fighter planes push Soviets back towards the border. Between the Duna and Riga bay the attacks of the Soviets have abated. Disengaging movement on the North front, the Navy has repeatedly by the sea assisted in a short time, strong troop formations with weapons and materials. Anglo-Americans continue terrorizing the West German populations with bombers and fighter formations on the 29th. Outstanding civilian losses on the left Rhine area. Night of 29th planes dropped bombs in the area of Karlsrupe. Pacific after 70 days of heroic fighting the Marianne Islands, Guam and Tinian fell to the Americans. The Japanese defenders have fallen to the last man. Fairly fine day coming up dull and windy in the evening and rain setting in lightly at 2030hrs.

Monday 2nd October, 1944

Prisoner of War stationed at Konigshan. Party working at Schatzler, seven at Gabensdorf and myself with the rest digging out on No 3 line at Trautenau station. Set a length between four men to do, but very slow work and only about half was done. Home at 1835hrs, and was practically dark when we finished work at 1700hrs owing to the clocks being put back an hour at midnight. A quiet evening doing a little sewing. Big Red X train with wounded came into Trautenau today, and one of them shook his fist at some of the boys. Issued with ½ Red X food parcel and 25 cigarettes. (OIL) American Army making big attack on Seigfried line near Aachen and British Army making big attacks in Holland. Island of Sylt of Holland taken by us. Calais fallen and 70,000 prisoners taken. A kind of rocket ship used against Calais and now being turned on Dunkirk. In fighting in Holland the Germans fighting like fanatics and penetrating right onto British lines, where cleaning up operations are continuing. Germans using flame throwers. In Holland three big pro Nazi's taken, one being shot, one sentenced to 16 years and one about ten years.

In France in old mine shaft complete Messerschmidt factory discovered, Germans getting out in such a hurry that everything was left complete; they were forcing French and Russians to work in it. French troops under De Gaulle have taken 120,000 German prisoners in France. In Italy nothing much mentioned. Two islands of Greece taken by our troops. Russian troops have now linked up with Tito's in Yugo-Slavias and only 13 kilometres from Belgrade. Russians also said to have broken through some pass into Czeckoslavakian, and in Hungary 130 kilometres of Budapest. Estonia and Lithuania practically finished and Russians making big attack near Warsaw. Finns capture an important railway junction from the Germans in Finland. British have warned anybody they catch who are Pro-Nazi's will be put in concentration camps. A dull cool morning which continued all day with slight rain falling, being a fairly heavy shower about 1800hrs.
P.S. Max the help posten gets told off by Starkey today for attempting to draw his revolver on us.

Tuesday 3rd October, 1944
Prisoner of War stationed at Konigshan. Party at Schatzler, eight at Gavensdorf and other party with myself at Trautenau digging out very slow work, and bosses moaning because nothing is getting done,

threaten to keep us out till eight o'clock, but eventually knocked off at 1715hrs and in camp at 1835hrs. A little reading in evening.

Saw Chris today going out from Stalag to Weckelsdorf. Says plenty of parcels arriving in Stalag and that our Army getting all the big stuff at the front for a big push. Potatoes, soup, usual bread and margarine. Fighting still going on fairly heavy on all sectors of the fronts in Europe, and nothing much gained by us except for heavy losses. Cape Griz Nez fortified area falls to our troops. Night raids over Brunswick and Rhine Westphalia area. A very dull cold morning and continued fairly cool until after midday when the sun shone for a while.

Wednesday 4th October, 1944
Prisoner of War stationed at Konigshan and everybody goes to Trautenau today on the digging out of the main line by the station. Plenty of slow work again today and Maxie says he will report our stopping as sabotage. Fred went to see the inspector about getting a contract job. Kept us working until 1730hrs, and then kicked up a fuss, because some of us went to get our bags and coats before we put the tools away. In camp at 1830hrs. Seven parcels up, and of the Bodisch gang Dalziel received clothing and Grace cigarettes. Reading during the evening. All money belonging to Lager collected tonight to be changed into proper German money. Mashed potatoes, marrow, spinach, meat and gravy and plenty of it, also usual bread. No paper today, so no German news except that black guard reckons our planes were all over Germany bombing last night. A very frosty morning, but fairly fine day. Snow seen on snow koffe this morning.

Thursday 5th October, 1944
Prisoner of War stationed at Konigshan. All of us at Trautenau again today, and given a contract job to do – and go home. Finished about 1145hrs and to camp on the 1212hrs train, and arriving there at 1315hrs. No work myself today as was on the fire making job. Quiet afternoon and evening with little reading. Potatoes, soup, bread and

marg. Received our Lager money back today in German money, also pay day and now have 345 Reichmarks. No OIL except that heard Belgrade supposed to have been evacuated. German news. Fairly heavy fighting still going on in Holland and around Aachen and other places, but very little ground gained by us and fairly heavy losses. In Italy a little ground gained. Soviets fighting at some town on the Rumanian – Serbian border and fairly consistent but unsuccessful. The Island of Dafoe fighting there by our troops and the occupants. Raids over Halle and Kamm, and at night on Brunswick and 31 planes lost. Very heavy frost and fine day until about midday, when started to cloud over again.

Friday 6th October, 1944
Prisoner of War stationed at Konigshan. All at Trautenau again today, digging out earth loading and unloading and putting in stone where earth was dug out. Fairly heavy days work, but came home on 1618hrs train and in camp at 1720hrs, instead of catching the 1735hrs train. A little mail up but received none myself again. Saw a couple of Aussies today in Trautenau who had been to the holiday camp near Berlin for a month. Quiet evening with a little reading. Potatoes, soup, usual bread weekly jam and sugar issue. OIL. Greece said to be invaded by us on 1,000 kilometre front. That Patros has already fallen capitulating with 1,000 German prisoners. Said to be 3 kilometres from Cologne. Cloudy cool morning, but came out a little warmer during the day and cooled off again in evening with cold wind.

Saturday 7th October, 1944
Prisoner of War stationed at Konigshan in Sudatenland. All at Trautenau again today, some on helping put in line where we had finished, and the rest of us digging out, loading up and unloading. finished at 1215hrs today instead of 1600hrs, so home at 1400hrs. During the afternoon scrubbing out room, bathing and washing clothes. In evening reading and sewing. One of the boys was talking to a Jerry Officer today whose Mother was English and Father German. Mother

living in Vienna. Parcels up. Mashed potatoes. marrow, meat and gravy with bread and marg. German News: On the Holland and Aachen sectors very heavy fighting, but very little ground gained by us, owing to successful German counter attacks. Four officers and some prisoners in one sector. In Italy our troops attempting push their way through the mountains towards Bologna, but very little ground gained. Russian front mentions fighting at good many places without success, also North East of Belgrade. Raids over Coblenz, Wilhelmhaven and two or three other places in daylight, in evening a few bombs dropped on Berlin and the Saarbrucken area. A few planes lost. Cool cloudy morning, but with some sunshine later in the day and warm.

Sunday 8th October, 1944
Prisoner of War stationed at Konigshan. No work today, not getting up till 0900hrs. Passed the day reading, writing and a little sewing. Wrote card home and letter card to (Lil and Tom). Issued with bulk food and 25 cigarettes, and meats went into the kitchen to be dished up on Tuesday and Thursday. In the evening playing cards. Potatoes, cabbage, meat and gravy usual bread. No paper today for any news. Germany supposed to have received heavy bombing last night including Breslau. Very dull misty day.

Monday 9th October, 1944
Prisoner of War stationed near Konigshan. Twelve men at Gabensdorf, and the rest of us at Trautenau but owing to no stone available, not digging out at station, but on the Hohenelbe line about 600 yards from the station. Doing from the side to the rail. Doing from the side to the rail, and about six inches under the sleeper, a length of 15 metres between 2 men finished myself about 1500hrs. Home on 1618hrs train, instead of 1735hrs train. 2 more get orders to return to Stalag today, bringing our Bodisch group down to 16. A little reading during the evening. Potatoes, soup, usual bread, marg and jam issue. NO OIL. about. German news: Heavy attacks on Dutch-Belgium border and around

Aachen and many other sectors on the Western front, but very little ground gained by us, owing to successful German counter attacks. In Italy on the Florence Bologna sector fighting against Italian mountain positions, but no gains. Also bandits cleaned up in the Balkans, fighting North East of Belgrade fairly heavy, and many other sectors, but attacks repelled by German counter attack-raids. American terror bombers make attacks over Berlin, Hamburg, Stralund, and Stettin. British formations over the Rhine Westphalia area, and night attacks on the living quarters of Dormund and Bremen, also over Berlin. Over Germany and Western front 72 planes shot down. Very dull day with showers setting in with a steady rain about 1600hrs and continued – Weather warm though.

Tuesday 10th October, 1944

Prisoner of War stationed near Konigshan. Twelve men to Gabensdorf, and the rest of us at Trautenau, digging out on Hohlenelbe line, also unloaded a couple of trucks of plates, bolts and lashings, and finished about 1500hrs. Worked a bit harder today and in camp at 1720hrs. A quiet evening playing a little table tennis. Potato soup. Red X stew and usual bread etc. German News: Heavy fighting on all sectors of the Western front and some ground gained despite strong German counter attacks. In Italy our troops fighting against strong forces South of Bologna and the River Rubikon, but pushing forward steadily. In Russia Russians pushing strongly, but German counter attacking strongly especially around the passes to Slavakia and around the area of Belgrade. Strong disengaging movements being carried out. Finns fighting against the German withdrawing movements in Finland. OIL. Further forces landed by sea in Holland and advanced 4 miles inland. Ireland of Sylt flooded and strong force of Germans cut off. Encircling movement continues around Aachen, also around the Mertz area. In Italy advancing steadily. Budapest-Belgrade railway cut preventing supplies from coming in that sector. 2,000 planes in Saar area. Greece, Corinth is now in our hands and guerilla tactics on the

Athens-Salonika railway sector, 1,000 prisoners taken, 200 killed and 200 transport shot up. Germans having to use sea routes to get out, and being hampered by our Air Force etc. Russians 30 miles south of Memel and 20 miles from Prussian border. Churchill Eden, Field Marshall Brooke, Stalin etc. at meeting in Moscow. Dull warm morning, later turning out fairly warm sunny day.

Wednesday 11th October, 1944
Prisoner of War stationed at Konigshan. Twelve men to Gabensdorf and the rest of us at Trautenau, continued on at the station today with No. 3 line digging out. Fairly easy day finishing at 1455hrs myself, home on 1614hrs train and in camp at 1715hrs. Parcels up today, received a personal one myself sent in July, the third one since being a prisoner, Reading during the evening. Mashed potatoes, cabbage, roast pork and soup with usual bread and marg.

The inhabitants said to have been given a time limit to get out of Aachen. 65 kilometres from Budapest. German news mentions fairly consistent attacks by us on all sectors in Holland and Western front and some ground gained at heavy cost. In Italy fighting in the mountain areas of Florenz and Bologna, but nothing of importance gained. Nothing mentioned of Greece. Fighting around Belgrade and passes near Hungarian border, heavily defended against Russian attacks. Disengaging movement in Northern sector. In Finland Finns attempt to hamper, German withdrawal movement, and were wiped out. Fair number of Air R,aids, but as usual only civilian losses etc. over 100 shot down. A dull morning early with some rain, but later turned out a fairly nice day.

Thursday 12th October, 1944
Prisoner of War stationed at Konigshan. Gang of twelve men to Gabensdorf and the rest to Trautenau digging out, loading earth and unloading. Finished about 1545hrs, on 1612hr train for camp and there at 1720hrs. Reading during the evening. Soup, Red X stew with

potatoes and bread. No OIL. The Western front, Italian and Russian sectors practically the same as yesterday, and not worth noting. Fair number of air raids and usual damage done. Heavy mist during morning, turning into a very nice day.

Friday 13th October, 1944
Prisoner of War in Sudatenland stationed at Konigshan. Twelve men to Gabensdorf rest of us at Trautenau and fairly easy day. 4 others and myself cut out our section of work by 1000hrs, and could do nothing until the others finished their sectors, so did nothing more until 1445hrs. In camp at 1725hrs. Air raid alarm today but no planes were seen or heard. Reading during the evening. Heard this morning that some place in Czecko was done over yesterday at 1500hrs. Potatoes, mashed with pumpkin and cold roast pork, bread and margarine and weekly sugar ration. Fairly misty morning and fairly cool, but turned out fairly warm later. German News: for this report see next page (separate page).

GERMAN NEWS: Friday 13th October, 1944 (as previously stated) In Holland in the last few days, further heavy fighting continues on the bridgehead, Sth of the Wester Schelbe. The enemy landed East of Breskens, received through artillery fire and counter attacks heavy losses. The land bridge leading to Sth Beverland that was blocked by strong Canadian attacks was again fought free. In the battle around Aachen our counter attack forced the American formations on to the defensive. Nth of the town, East of the town the enemy after a hot srtruggle was able to gain ground. In the forest of Roetgen, the strong repeatedly attacking enemy forces were thrown back. Also in the front section of Metz and East of Epinal local attacks, partly supported by tanks here repulsed. East of Remiremont continues the hand fighting with Algerian and Moroccan formations that have pressed into our positions. Before our coastal bases the autumn weather limited the fighting to artillery duels and reconnasiance activity. The V1 was again laid on London. Italy, the fighting in the Alps climbed to great heaviness during the day both sides of the route Florence-Bologna.

The enemy attacks on a broader front were broken. Only a mountain position that changed hands three times was in the hands of the enemy in the evening hours. Russian front: On the Balkans the Soviets have strengthened their pressure between Zetecar and Belgrade and the lower Morawa. Escort vessels of the Kriegs marine, shot a British speedboat in flames in Agean Sea and damaged a further ship by artillery fire in the same sea area. Ships anti-aircraft defended a troop ship convoy and shot down 5 planes out 16 unsuccessful attacking bombers. An enemy submarine was badly damaged. Heavy fighting Sth Hungary with advancing enemy that has crossed the Thiess and are moving to the West. A Hungarian Cavalry formations threw the enemy over the river to the East that had advanced on Kecskemet Sth of Debrecen further embittered fighting. After a hard fight our troops from the area of Klausenberg withdrew to the Nth in orderly manner. Sharp advancing enemy were thrown back. Nth of Warsaw our troops achieved full defensive success against the attacking Soviets. Also Sth of Rozan and by Wilkowischken strong attacks of the Soviets remain unsuccessful. The heavy fighting Nth of Tilsit and in the Memel district continues further 42 enemy tanks were destroyed. Attempts of the enemy to squeeze out our bridgehead around Memel were knocked by tough resistance of the occupants. By Riga the enemy attacked with several infantry and armoured formations. The attacking Soviets of the Peninsula of Sworbe were repulsed and a landing attempt from the West was frustrated. On the ice sea front defended our mountain troops the encircling attacks of the superior enemy forces and destroyed an enemy battalion. The enemy landed on the Fischer Peninsula were caught up. American terror flyers dropped bombs on Vienna, Cologne and Coblenz. A few British planes attacked Berlin during the night. 11 bombers and 2 fighters were shot down.

Saturday 14th October, 1944
Prisoner of War stationed at Konigshan. Eleven men today at Gabensdorf, rest of us at Trautenau. First thing went out unloading earth on Hohenelbe line, then came back and continued digging out

on Hohenelbe line until 1230hrs, and brought tools back and caught the1301hr train to camp instead of 1618hrs. In afternoon bathing, washing and *(unreadable)* reading and also reading in the evening. Another air raid alarm today. Olly Hunter returns from Stalag, after being gone only a day and half, cannot fix his teeth yet. Soup, potatoes, carrots, usual bread. Athens said to be in our hands. German news: Much the same as yesterday, but slight admissions in our favour. Fairly cool, dull morning but came out warm about 1100hrs, and continued through the day.

Sunday 15th October, 1944
Prisoner of War in Sudatenland. No work today, so in bed till 0900 hrs. Reading, writing and sewing. Wrote letter card home, and card to Alison. Parcels up, mail and "Camps". Played crib in evening. Received cigarette parcel, but no mail. Potatoes, soup and cabbage with the usual bread. No paper for German news today. Hungary said to be asking Russia for peace terms. Issued with the bulk today and 25 cigarettes instead of tomorrow and fairly cool morning and reasonably cool throughout the day.

Monday 16th October, 1944
Prisoner of War stationed at Konigshan. Party at Gabensdorf and the rest at Trautenau, digging out No. 3 line, and filling in with stone. Home in camp at 1720hrs. Saw Wally Pedersen this morning, one of the ex original Bodisch gang, and a few more Aussies going to the holiday camp near Berlin. Two air raid alarms today. Reading during the evening. Soup, potatoes, usual bread and extra marg ration. Rommel said to be dead, and Hungary said to have capitulated. No German news again tonight because of no paper. Fairly dull day with occasional bursts of sun and came up a cool evening.

Tuesday 17th October, 1944
Prisoner of War stationed near Konigshan. Twelve men to Gabensdorf, and the usual gang of us for Trautenau. Went to Lampersdorf first to

unload some earth, going to Trautenau on the 1340hr train and then taking up old rails and sleepers. Knocked off at 1550hrs, and in camp at 1715hrs, so had very easy day. Air raid alarm again today. A quiet evening. Soup, Red X stew, potatoes, bread, and marg. German news: On Western front heavy fighting goes on, but little gains to us. Some of the forts on the Atlantic coast and Dunkirk still holding out V1 again on London. In Italy fighting towards Bologna in the mountains at a place called Vergator. On Russian front throughout heavy attacks continuing and withdrawing movements by the Germans. Air raids Vienna, Cologna and Coblenz visited, also fighters machine gunning. Dull cold day with some slight rain.

Wednesday 18th October, 1944
Prisoner of War stationed near Konigshan. One party at Schatzler, twelve to Gabensdorf and the rest of us at Trautenau, taking up old line and sleepers, unloading metal and stomping. In camp 1715hrs, and starting to get dark earlier now. Reading during the evening. Mashed potatoes and marrow with gravy, bread and weekly jam issue. German news: Still heavy fighting going on around Aachen and a pass to Alsaiee-Lorraine but nothing of importance gained. In Italy heavy defensive battles assisted by parachutists. Through traitorous Rumania and Bulgaria, Germany admits withdrawing from Greece because of their rear positions being threatened. Athens evacuated without fighting. On all sectors of the Russian front heavy battles, but not much ground gained. Fair number of air raids on Rhineland and Upper Silesia, Cologne and Coblenz, also dropped indiscriminately on Brunswick. Very dull day with occassional slight falls of rain, setting in heavy about 1600hrs.

Thursday 19th October, 1944
Prisoner of War stationed at Konigshan in Sudatenland. Today six men at Schatzler, and the rest of us at Trautenau working on No. 3 line on stomping and also unloading metal on Hohenelbe line. Finished 1600hrs and in camp at 1715hrs. Reading during the evening. A

lieutenant inspects here during the evening. Soup, potatoes, Red X stew, bread and margarine. List of rations put up, as to the amount you are allowed in your possession each day. No German news as no paper available. Said to have broken through the Seigfried line in five places. Dull, warm day with some heavy rain setting in at 1600hrs.

Friday 20th October, 1944
Prisoner of War stationed at Bodisch. Only four men to Schatzler today, and the rest on to Trautenau where the Gabensdorf gang stomping on No. 3 line near the station, and the rest of us on the Hohenelbe line digging out ends of sleepers and finishing about 1500hrs. Left Trautenau at 1615hrs and in camp 1720hrs. Reading during the evening. Potatoes, soup and usual bread. Said to be half way through Greece. Budapest in Russian hands. German News: Says after fifteen days bloody fighting the flanking encircling movement around Aachen has united. Other parts of the Western front nothing of importance gained. In Italy attempts to press on towards Bologna proceeding slowly. On Russian front heavy attacks and some breakthroughs of previous day closed or practically closed over with heavy losses to Russians. Also movement to shorten line in one area carried out successfully. In Finland objective reached after going over bad roads and hindrance by the Finns. Raids over Vienna, Cologne, and Upper Silesia, 36 planes shot down. Late German News: Big battle going on the East Prussian border. Another town evacuated in Greece. Phillipine Islands invaded by Americans Tuesday morning. Heavy fighting continues around Aachen. Dull wet morning, coming out fairly warm about 1000hrs and about 1430hrs overcast and some slight rain and again in the evenings.

Saturday 21st October, 1944
Prisoner of War stationed near Konigshan. Everybody at Trautenau this morning, some being in Trautenau yard, and myself with others at Hohenelbe line digging out and unloading stone. Finished at midday, and in camp at 1410hrs. During afternoon bathing and washing.

In evening a little reading. "Camps" and some mail up received letters from Sigrid and Jean. Everything fairly dry at home. Mashed potatoes, marrow, meat and gravy with usual bread and a jam issue. No Oil but German News mentions fighting in the streets of Aachen going on very heavily and elsewhere on the Western front. Fair sized battle for mountain positions in Italy on Florence-Bologna road, but our troops receiving heavy losses. Fighting around Belgrade and towards Hungarian border and in the North by Prussian border, a raging battle going on, but being successfully defended by the German troops. In Finland Germans reach their base successfully. Raids over Cologne, Vienna and other places. 30 planes shot down. Big battle going on in landing on Phillipine Islands and Manilla Island bombed by 270 planes. Dull, cold, foggy morning with a little sunshine about midday and came up a cold wind in afternoon.

Sunday 22nd October, 1944
Prisoner of War stationed at Konigshan. No work today, so in bed till 0900hrs. A little washing, reading and odd jobs during the day. Wrote card home and a letter card to Guy Moulton. 9 personal parcels up and received a May personal parcel myself. Dusting receives October and December 1943 parcels, and Gozelle also personal. Bulk food issued out today and 25 cigarettes. Soup, potatoes, cabbage and usual bread and porridge for breakfast. (OIL) Aachen said to have fallen. Cologne in ruins. Attempting to push forward through Greece to Vienna. Russians said to be in part of Czecko. Some Germans interned by Turkish authorities in attempting to get out of Greece by crossing Turkish Territory. Fairly cold morning with practically no sun and came up very cold again in the evening.

Monday 23rd October, 1944
Prisoner of War stationed near Konigshan. Twelve men at Bernsdorf, rest of us to Trautenau digging out on Hohenelbe line and unloading stone. Finished at 1500hrs left Trautenau 1620hrs, and in camp

1715hrs. Two air raid alarms today, and in the distance could hear the bombing and ACK/ACK. Reading during the evening. Soup, potatoes, double issue of bread. Said to have been 10,000 prisoners taken at Aachen and a big battle raging in Holland. German news: Heavy fighting still going on in the streets, and around Aachen man to man fighting. In Holland heavy fighting goes on with no success to ourselves. In Italy fighting around Vergato, but nothing of importance. Russian sector Belgrade evacuated by Germans after all military conveniences destroyed. In Hungary Soviets able to gain some ground. On East Prussian border heavy fighting still continues, and Soviets gain a little ground. In Finland encircling movement broken down. Regensberg bombed and low diving planes attack civilian population in West, South Western Germany. Kids of 16 being called up for medical examination. Dull morning and continued throughout day but reasonably warm.

Tuesday 24th October, 1944
Prisoner of War in Sudatenland stationed near Konigshan. Twelve men to Bernsdorf, and rest of us at Trautenau digging out on Hohenelbe line. Finished myself about 1430hrs, and home early train getting in camp at 1720hrs. Reading a little during the evening. Soup, potatoes, Red X stew usual bread and margarine. During past six days Russians said to have taken 260 villages and towns in East Prussian push, including four major towns. German News: Much the same as yesterday except for admitting a fair number of breakthroughs on the Russian front. Air raids as usual, and night raids over West and South Western Germany. A dull, cold and misty day with some rain.

Wednesday 25th October, 1944
Prisoner of War stationed at Konigshan. Seventeen men to Bernsdorf, and the rest of us to Trautenau digging out on the Hohenelbe line. Home in camp at 1715hrs. Rogers returned to Stalag today, and Fred makes a trip to the Stalag also. Reading during the evening. Mashed

potatoes, cabbage, meat and gravy with usual bread quota. No OIL. German News: mentions nothing of Aachen, but heavy fighting going on in Holland. In Italy small breakthrough against heavy defensive fire. Russian front fighting still going on around North Belgrade and around Hungarian. Rumanian and Soviet encircled group cleaned up. North Russian front heavy battles going on in several breakthroughs. More bandits cleaned up in Slavakia fighting in Spain near French border between the Reds and others using British-American arms. 3,000 said to have beeen killed. A cool morning and fairly dull day with heavy mist.

Thursday 26th October, 1944
Prisoner of War stationed near Konigshan. Sixteen men to Bernsdorf, the rest of us to Trautenau digging out on Hohenelbe line. George and I finished our quota by midday, and all finished their work today. 6 men go to Freiheit in afternoon and did not get home till 1830hrs, whereas the rest of us were in at 1715hrs. Fred returned during the evening and said mail and parcels are on the way. No Red X parcels in Stalag. Soup, potatoes, Red X stew and usual bread. Supposed to have been big railway accident between Kuhbank and Loubon. 120 killed. German news: Still heavy fighting and attempted breakthroughs in Central Holland, but nothing of importance gained. In Italy quiet on Adriatic coast, also Italy the other sector meeting against defensive fire. In Russia heavy fighting going on in Northern sectors and in Finland. Jerries getting pushed towards the Norwegian border, otherwise other sectors reasonably quiet. The usual air raids and low flying planes harrassing civil population in the Rhineland. Cold morning with a little sunshine about 0900hrs, but otherwise dull, cold day and cool evening.

Friday 27th October, 1944
Prisoner of War stationed near Konigshan. Twelve men to Bernsdorf, four at Parshnitz and the rest of us to Trautenau digging out on

Hohenelbe line. George and I finished at 1300hrs. In camp 1715hrs. No OIL, and the only news of German is of successful Japanese attacks on American Navy and their landing on the Phillipines, many aircraft carriers and warships sink. Reading during the evening. To bed fairly early. Soup, potatoes, usual bread, margarine, also jam and sugar ration. A wet foggy morning, coming out a little sun about 1100hrs, but otherwise a bitterly cold day, with a cold wind.

Saturday 28th October, 1944
Prisoner of War stationed near Konigshan. Twelve men to Bernsdorf, and the rest of us digging out on the Hohenelbe line near Trautenau. Started us off with five for the two of us, but some of the boys kicked up, so knocked it down to four, being half day. Finished just after midday and back in camp at 1400hrs. Afternoon bathing and doing washing. Reading in the evening. Bulk food dished out today and cigarettes instead of Monday. Mashed potatoes, meat and gravy, also cabbage with the usual bread and marg ration. No OIL. Heavy fighting still going on in Holland around Antwerp and strong German counter attacks throwing us back. Heavy losses to us. In Italy our troops slightly moving forward to Imola and one other place, not very far from Bologna. In the Balkans bandits and Bulgarian troops being cleaned up. Other Russian fronts heavy battles and one or two places captured, and also another couple of places evacuated, Pelsama being one, but Germans claiming to be inflicting heavy losses on the Russians. Raids over a good many districts, but no mention of plane losses. Japs claim to have the show in hand around and on the Phillipines. A wet morning, but very warm, and a little sun about midday, but otherwise a very overcast day.

Sunday 29th October, 1944
Prisoner of War stationed at Konigshan. No work today, so in bed till 0900hrs. Fifth Sunday in the month, so no cards or lettercards for writing today. Reading and sewing during the day. "Camps"

and parcels up, received cigarettes myself and six books from Mrs Forrest. Meat and gravy with potatoes and cabbage and usual bread. German NEws: Heavy fighting continues with the whole of the front in Holland with high losses to our troops. One town was taken by our troops though. In Italy on account of heavy rain, quiet except by surprise attack captured a high position from us near Imola. In Central Hungary, Germans and Hungarians repelling attacks, Germans halted the Russians on East Slavakian border. In Northern sectors heavy battles raging and all attempted break throughs and encirclement by Soviets were repulsed with heavy losses especially to armoured divisions. Pacific Americans lose 108 ships, and troops on Island unable to make headway. Spain Spanish Reds occupy a dozen local towns and captured the Republic of Andora. A dull, miserable day throughout with showers of rain.

Monday 30th October, 1944
Prisoner of War at Konigshan in Sudatenland. Six men to Schatzler, and the rest of us to Trautenau, some digging out, some unloading stone and some unloading rails. Finished about 1245hrs myself, home on 1618hr train and in lager at 1720hrs. Reading during the evening. A little mail up and received a letter from Gladys. Potatoes, soup and Red X stew with usual bread and marg. No OIL and no paper so no German news tonight. Started off a wet morning, cleared a little about 1100hrs, and later in the day came up wet again otherwise fairly warm day.

Tuesday 31st October, 1944
Prisoner of War stationed at Konigshan. Everybody at Trautenau today, some digging out on Hohenelbe line, some unloading rails, and four loading coal for Lager. Only did about two hours work because of rain so easy day. In camp at 1720hrs. Two more New Zealanders arrived on party today, making the strength 50 of us. Reading in the evening. Potatoes, soup, Red X stew with usual bread etc. Heard the

Yanks and Canadians had carried out a big encirclement movement in Holland and heavy fighting going on. Around the battle of Formosa Yanks claim to have destroyed 90% of the Jap fleet engaged there. No paper again tonight, so no German news; so dont know how anything is going on. A very wet and dull day throughout but fairly warm.

Wednesday 1st November, 1944
Prisoner of War working on railway party at Konigshan in Sudatenland and Ex party E388 Bodisch attached to Stalag VIII A Gorlitz and previously Stalag VIII B Lamsdorf. Prisoner of War No KRETA 4538 having been taken prisoner on the fall of Crete to the Germans. Everybody at Trautenau today, first of all unloading stone, then twelve of us went to load some concrete pipes, while the other were digging out. Very dirty and heavy job loading the pipes, finishing at 1520hrs, and in camp 1725hrs. Reading in evening. mashed potatoes, pumpkin, meat and gravy with usual bread. No paper again tonight, but hear the Germans are expecting a big offensive any time on the Western Front. The biggest ever attempted, otherwise news quiet everywhere. Fairly cold day being overcast with a sprinkle of rain practically throughout the day.

Thursday 2nd November, 1944
Prisoner of War stationed at Konigshan. All at Trautenau again today, some unloading metal, by engine shed and cement pipes at Gabensdorf, some unloading rails, and myself with the other party unloading metal and digging out on Hohenelbe line. Finished work at 1500hrs and home in lager at 1715hrs. Some mail up this evening and received five myself, one from Lil and Tom, Carmel, Ethel, Nurse H and Guy Moulton. Reading during the evening. Potatoes, soup, Red X stew and usual bread. German news mentions heavy attack by us in Holland and breakthroughs which they were unable to prevent. In Italy only local scrapping, but mentions bandit losses in Northern Italy, 3000 killed and 8000 prisoners, beside heavy material. In Greece Larissa and area has been evacuated and attacks of no importance in

rest of Balkans, and still heavy fighting around the Prussian border in Northern Sector. Planes over Cologne, Munich and Hamms and low flying planes among the civil population of South and South Western Germany. Very cool morning, warming up later, but very overcast, snow gradually creeping down the foothills.

Friday 3rd November, 1944
Prisoner of War near Konigshan. Everybody at Trautenau again today, some loading old sleepers, and a bit of stomping by engine shed, myself with others digging out on Hohenelbe line. Rain delayed work so did not finish till after1500hrs and in camp by 1720hrs. Quiet evening with no reading or anything tonight. Potatoes, soup and Red X stew with usual bread and marg and weekly sugar issue. No OIL. German News: Heavy fighting going on in Holland and small breakthroughs achieved by our troops with heavy losses and heavy counter attacks by German troops throw us back in any achievement. In Italy very slow fighting and nothing of any importance gained. Many bandits killed and taken prisoner. In Greece Larissa and Salonika evacuated, a couple of islands landed on by our troops and fighting going on. In the rest of the Balkans Soviets getting thrown back in attempted breakthroughs, and in Northern Russian front heavy battles, losses without success to the Russians, and heavy loss of materials. Raids on Cologne, Hamburg, Berlin and other districts. Pacific area. Tokio received raid of Anglo-American bombers, second of the war. They were intercepted by Japanese fighters. Wet and overcast in early morning, clearing up slightly later on from rain, but continued dull.

Saturday 4th November, 1944
Prisoner of War in Sudatenland and stationed near Konigshan. Everyone to Trautenau again today, some doing odd jobs and myself with other party unloading metal and digging out on Hohenelbe line. Half day and in camp 1400hrs. During afternoon chopping and sawing wood, washing and bathing. Evening reading and playing cards.

Mashed potatoes, cabbage, meat and gravy, Red X stew and usual bread. German News: Mentions heavy fighting and breakthroughs in Holland and on some of the islands there. In Italy everything reasonably quiet except for defensive actions. Fighting in islands west of Rhodes, and fighting still going on in the island of Malos, the other one our troops cleaned up. Landing by our troops on Dalmation coast near Spit. In the Balkans fighting creeping towards Budapest. In the Northern sector the Russian attack over Prussian border has somewhat abated. Anglo-American bombers raid Naval bases in Norway, Vienna, Hamm, Rhineland and numerous other places raided with a fair number of planes shot down. Fairly cold morning, being a heavy frost, but no rain of anything to mention.

Sunday 5th November, 1944
Prisoner of War stationed at Konigshan. No work today, so in bed till 0830hrs. During the day reading, writing and other odd jobs. Wrote lettercards to Mrs Forrest and Carmel. Potatoes, soup, cabbage midday with Red X stew and double issue of bread at night, marg, and had porridge for breakfast. OIL: Near Aachen our troops advanced towards Schmidt, but because of mine fields and German artillery, retired and planes cleared the area and advanced again. French occupy a town on Alsoce-Lorraine. Our troops pushing well in a big breakthrough in Holland and forced Germans into a new position.

Four out of every five landing ships destroyed in landing on island by Dutch coast. Heavy rains around Budapest, Russian troops nine miles on South side from Capital advancing closer on the North evidently with the intention of encircling it. In Prussian sector Russians doing well. Practically continuous air aids from Bochum to Karlscrube on troop concentrations being 3000 American and 1000 English planes. V1 on London, many shot down though and a Henkel plane. Fairly fine but cool day with a little sun in afternoon.

Monday 6th November, 1944

Prisoner of War stationed at Konigshan. All at Trautenau in morning, but some at midday to return to Schatzler to do a job, rest of us odd jobs in yards and some of us digging out on the Hohenelbe line. On fire making job myself today. In camp 1720hrs. Reading during the evening. Soup, potatoes, Red X stew, usual bread etc. German News: Few more breakthroughs in Holland, but counter attacks by Germans successful. Around Alsace-Lorraine fairly quiet. In Italy nothing of outstanding importance. In the Balkans heavy fighting on around Budapest and Germans making successful attacks against breakthroughs. Prussian front battle goes on, disengaging movement in Finland and continues unhampered by the enemy. Small raids on Munich, Vienna and Berlin. Munition train American blows up result unknown causes, only nine of forty wagons saved. Fine cool morning with some sun at midday, but set in with rain at 1600hrs, getting heavier at 1700hrs and fairly rough night ensured.

Tuesday 7th November, 1944

Prisoner of War stationed near Konigshan in Sudatenland on railway working party. Melbourne Cup Day. Four men at Schatzler, rest of us to Trautenau, some in the yards and myself on party digging out on Hohenelbe line. As a result of rain practically throughout the day, only did about one and a half hours work. In camp at 1720hrs. Reading during the evening. Soup, potatoes, Red X stew, bread and marge. OIL. Stalin supposed to have said war will be over by Christmas. German news: Heavy fighting continues on the islands around and in Holland and some breakthroughs. On the Alsace-Lorraine area in a surprise attack recapture a certain area and materials. Italy nothing of note. In the Balkans heavy battles near Budapest continues and all breakthroughs successfully counter attacked with high losses to the Russians. In Prussian area Goldlap recaptured from Russians and elsewhere battles continue. Raids over most parts especially Vienna being heavily hit. 48 planes shot down. Rained practically throughout the day, being very heavy about 1530hrs to 1600hrs.

Wednesday 8th November, 1944
Prisoner of War stationed in Sudatenland. Eight men to Bernsdorf and the rest of us to Trautenau, some doing doing odd jobs about the yards, but changed their minds again. Where digging out now has to be stopped as building with new rails will not go on because lack of materials, this was in reference to the digging out in station yards. Home at the usual time and put in a quiet evening. Soup, mashed potatoes, cabbage, steak and onion rissoles with usual bread and weekly jam issue. Said to have been 200 out of 400 German planes shot down in big battle over Holland. Dunkirk said to be finished, also Antwerp, and rumoured Budapest. Out of Schatzler, population 2000, 148 has been killed in this War. German News: Heavy fighting continues in Holland and supply bases around Aachen attacked by bombers and night fighters. In Italy nothing of importance to mention. In the Balkans troops surrounded by Germans cleaned out or taken prisoner. In the Russian sector heavy attacks and counter attacks going on. Commissioner for the Middle East Lord Moyne murdered. Hungerford bridge destroyed as the result of a V1 bomb. Bombing continues over a good many places. Snow on the ground this morning, but cleared away after about 1000hrs and turned out fairly decent sort of day. First snow for the winter this area.

Thursday 9th November, 1944
Prisoner of War stationed near Konigshan. Five years today since marched into Northam Camp to join A.I.F. Eight men at Bernsdorf, and some later return from there to Lampersdorf, the rest of us at Trautenau digging out on Hohenelbe line and finished about 1450hrs and in camp at 1720hrs. Reading and playing crib in evening. Soup, potatoes, Red X stew, usual bread and margarine. No paper today, so no German news. Heard that the Stalag had received invoice for

15000 food parcels Canadian and bulk food. A cool morning with a little sleet about 1100hrs, got heavier and continued until about 1600hrs when it came up cooler again. Roosevelt said to have been returned again as President of United States of America.

Friday 10th November, 1944
Prisoner of War stationed at Konigshan. Eight men to Lampersdorf, rest of us to Trautenau on the Hohenelbe line digging out. Job cut down to six sleepers to day, instead of seven on account of some not finishing yesterday. Partner and myself finished about 1250hrs and in camp at 1720hrs. Mail and parcels slack. Heard that personal and cigarette parcels still arriving in Stalag, also heard the following two German prisoners spoke over the radio from England last night on the English News in German our troops said to be smashing through everything, as Germans have no petrol to move anything on the Western front. German News: Things seem to be well on the move on Western front, and looks as if we can expect big things anytime now. In Italy things very quiet. In Balkans attempted breakthroughs all broken up by counter attacks and heavy losses to Bulgarians and Russians. In the Prussian sector Germans claim to have the upper hand, pushing the Russians back. A fair number of raids being carried out, but not many planes lost. Potatoes, soup, Red X stew, usual bread and weekly sugar issue. A reasonably fine morning but later came on to snow, clearing at 1600hrs.

Saturday 11th November, 1944
Prisoner of War stationed at Konigshan. "Armistace Day". Eight men to Lampersdorf, and the rest of us Trautenau way digging out on the Hohenelbe line. Given three sleepers between two and finished my lot by Freistig (morning tea) and caught the 1212hr train, getting in camp at 1315hrs and the others at 1400hrs being half day. During afternoon washing and bathing. Issued with parcel between 2 and twenty five cigarettes. During the evening playing crib, mail and parcels up, but

received none of either myself. Mashed potatoes, cabbage, meat and gravy, Red X stew and usual bread. OIL: Our troops pushing forward well in Holland, in one place said to be 8 miles from Saarbrucken. Around Metz area, double line of forts here, and Germans have all retired behind these and evidently intend to defend it from there. In Italy a slight movement forward, In the Balkans Russians said to be half way between Budapest and Vienna. Prussian sector quiet. 400 Liberators bomb Bachom and in the Rhineland. Oil plants bombed. In Burma evidently a big do going on with Indian Division, and many English divisions having the Japs bottled up somewhere. Subs in and abound Pacific sunk 45 vessels. Nanking bombed by Super Fortresses. Fairly decent day, except for fine melting snow.

Sunday 12th November, 1944
Prisoner of War stationed near Konigshan. No work today so in bed till 0830hrs. Reading, mending and odd jobs. Wrote cards home and to Mrs Walker. Black guard came in and took some group photos today. Potatoes, cabbage, mince meat, soup and double issue bread. OIL: Big going on around Saarbrucken and Metz, pushing over the German border. Prisoners taken. Also big happenings on the Phillipine Islands. Late OIL: Our troops 15 miles beyond Metz on one side and 20 miles on the other, and morning well towards Saarbrucken. First counter attack for some time near Metz pushed our troops back 2 miles. Lights on again in some places in England. Also heard that Red X Food parcels on the way. P.S. Churchill given the freedom of the City of Paris, and extract from speech enemy will be beaten in six months. German News: Strimiski Valley evacuated in the Balkans. On the island of Milos our troops getting pushed back. In Italy street fighting in Forti. In the Prussian sector only local battles but big preparations getting under way evidently for a big battle. In Alsace-Lorraine slight advances to us, and in Holland our troops suffering heavy losses, but gained some ground. A dull day with some snow and fair amount of wind.

Monday 13th November, 1944

In Sudatenland near Konigshan as a P.O.W. Party at Trautenau digging out and in camp at 1400hrs, and two parties Schatzler and home at 1715hrs, and myself in Lager cleaning up and scrubbing doors in readiness for Swiss Commission coming on Wednesday. Playing crib and a little reading in evening. Soup, mashed potatoes, Red X stew, bread and margarine. OIL: Metz surrounded and 40000 Germans said to be in the circle. No German news tonight. A miserable day with snow and very strong wind, there being a fair coating of snow now on the ground.

Tuesday 14th November, 1944

Prisoner of War stationed at Konigshan. Party at Schatzler, one near Konigshan and the rest to Trautenau. In lager myself, helping to scrub out rooms and other jobs. All home by 1720hrs. Playing crib in evening. Soup, potatoes, Red X stew, and bread. No German News. OIL: Circle around Metz pierced and three miles from the town. In Italy successes to the Army there around Forti and Bologna of great importance. Fighting in the streets of Budapest. Forty bombers carrying 6 ton bombs sink 45000 ton ship Admiral Turpin. Plenty of food in England and all getting special treat for Christmas. In Burma Mountbattens troops gaining successes, and in the Phillipines, Japs strengthen with another five divisions. A fairly cool day with some wind but no snow fell, but plenty lying about.

Wednesday 15th November, 1944

Prisoner of War in Sudatenland. Six men Konigshan, eight at Parschnitz and myself with other party at Trautenau digging out on Hohenelbe line and loading earth. In camp 1720hrs. Swiss Commission were here today as per schedule visit. Parcels at station. Early to bed tonight. Potatoes, soup, Red X stew with usual bread and weekly jam ration. OIL: Our troops 1 ½ miles from Metz on one side and two on the other, looks as if they do not intend to make a fortress of it after all. In Holland between Vilno and some other town, which is 20 miles from the Rhine. In Italy pushing forward on the Bologna Road. 500 planes drop 650 tons of food to Tito. Russians and Slavs pushing forward near Slavakian border. Cruiser sunk in Norweign Fiord. In Burma Indian division pushed forward and linked up with our troops. town not easy to pronounce – 2 cruisers and 11 destroyers of Jap Navy sunk near Phillipines. Later OIL. Our troops 3 miles over the River Maus and two or three new places in our hands. Innsbruck and a couple of other places bombed today, objectives petrol making plants. Question of as to who will fight in the Japenese war. New insurance bill passed and waiting for Kings signature. Fine cool morning, a little snow about 1000hrs, fine drizzle after midday and snowing steadily at 1700hrs.

Thursday 16th November, 1944
Prisoner of War stationed at Konigshan. One party at Schatzler, also Konigshan and myself with other party at Trautenau loading and unloading earth in the morning and afternoon helped unload three coppers weighing ½ ton each. In camp at 1720hrs. Everything going very well this week with Maxie out of the road. A little reading and playing cards in the evening. Mashed potatoes, cabbage, soup, usual bread and marg. OIL: Everything going very well in Holland, several breakthroughs uniting, and forming one solid front, pushing towards the Rhine. Around Metz south ward group, pushing towards the North. Jerry makes a counter attack, and recaptured one of the forts taken yesterday. Things progressing well along the Bologna Road in Italy. In Hungary heavy fighting going on around Budapest. In Burma another town captured from the Japs, and Americans make a landing on island 150 miles north of New Guinea, also some bombing done on the main arterial roads feeding the Japs from China. P.S. Results of Swiss Commissioners. Visit. British strongly advise against escaping at the present time. Nobody allowed to take part, or be partisans in anyway in this country, otherwise will be courtmartialled after the

war. Fine snow in morning, and a fine misty rain, otherwise a fair day with cool evening.

Friday 17th November, 1944
Prisoner of War on railway party near Konigshan in Sudatenland. One party at Konigshan, and the rest of us to Trautenau, some doing odd jobs, and myself with party digging out in the station yards. Finished at midday. In camp at 1730hrs. Reading and playing cards in evening. Potatoes, soup, Red X stew, bread, margarine and weekly sugar ration. Some good OIL around today. Six Armies said to be advancing on the Western front on a 400 mile front from Switzerland to the coast in Holland. One Army captures 5 towns in the last 12 hours. Around Metz a five mile place where the Jerries can get through. In Italy pushing towards Ravenna. Still fighting about Budapest 1500 heavy and light bombers used in the action today. Still doing well in the Phillipines and Burma. Air raid alarm today, and Breslau station said to have been done over. German News: Mentions themselves in heavy defensive action but able to gain ground over our troops, and still with drawing in the Balkans, and also in Finland going as foreseen. A fairly nice day with some sunshine and a cool evening.

Saturday 18th November, 1944
Prisoner of War stationed at Konigshan. Five men Konigshan and the rest of the party at Trautenau. Three men helping dig out foundation for a building and the rest of us were unloading rails and a bit of earth and were able to catch the 1212hr train express, and getting in camp at 1315hrs. Half day. During the afternoon bathing and doing washing, also making a bag for carrying dinner in etc. In evening sewing, reading and playing crib. Issued with bulk Red X Food and 25 cigarettes. Mashed potatoes with soup, cabbage, and again in evening horse flesh or so it seemed. No mail up this week and no OIL tonight. German news as follows: Mentions heavy battles around Aachen again and practically along the whole of the Western front.

In Italy our forces facing the German Grenadiers and standing under defensive fire. In the Balkans marching, but according to plan and around Budapest the battle goes on with heavy losses to the Soviets, and in the Prussian sector things reasonably quiet. Marching out according to schedule in Finland. V1 and V2 over London and Antwerp. Japs sinking more ships around the Phillipines. A wind blowing practically all day with some snow falling, and wind practically at gale force, evening and the night.

Sunday 19th November, 1944
Prisoner of War stationed near Konigshan. No work today so in bed till 0900hrs. During the day reading, sewing, washed out a few articles and writing. Wrote cards home and to Ethel. Everything fairly quiet. Potatoes, cabbage and soup with Red X stew at night and usual bread quota. OIL: On the Western front practically havoc everywhere, Germans in retreat, only five forts left out of the double circle of forts around Metz. French covered 20 miles in three days around Belfor and Stolberg. Night fighters pick up convoys in retreat from the front created great havoc. Munster attacked by 900 planes today, and other places in Eastern Germany looking for oil plants. In Italy our troops meeting with hard resistance, as no sooner is ground taken than the Germans counter attack strongly. British troops fighting with Tito in the Balkan States. Street fighting in the capital of Albania. Snow in the Balkans and Tito appeals for food and clothing, as the population are starving and dying of cold. These will be carried by Yugo-Slav ships. Two year Anniversary since the Russians started the Germans on the retreat from Stalingrad, and in two years has come through to Budapest. Guns fired in most places to commemorate the event. No Middle east troops will be home for Christmas, as no convoys leaving before the New Year. Pipe line running from Calcutta to China. Another town captured in Burma. Post in Borneo bombed, battle ship damaged and cruiser sunk. A reasonably fine day with fair amount of sunshine and thawing out, but very boisterous wind blowing.

Monday 20th November, 1944

Prisoner of War stationed at Konigshan. Six men at Konigshan, the rest of us in Trautenau unloading earth on Hohenelbe line up till 1000hrs, and after Freistig, some loading earth, and some digging out in railway yards. Finished myself at 1500hrs and in camp at 1720hrs. To bed early tonight. Potatoes, soup, Red X stew, bread and weekly jam issue. Bit of OIL: In last 24 hours our troops have captured 22 towns and advancing steadily. In one place French on the Rhine and 30 miles from it on another place. In last month German casualties have amounted to one million, and the amount of iron being put over per medium of artillery mortars etc amount to 6 million tons. Air raid alarm at Trautenau today. More German troops leave Trautenau for the front. A cool morning, but turned out a reasonable day and as usual some rain in the evening. Dark in the morning now when going to work at seven, and starts getting dark again about 1600hrs.

Tuesday 21st November, 1944

Prisoner of War in Sudatenland stationed at Konigshan. Six men working at Konigshan, the rest of us to Trautenau. One gang getting ready with the Czecks for laying on Hohenelbe line, and myself with other gang digging out in railway yards and loading earth. Finished at 1400hrs, and went to boody except for helping with a couple of small jobs. In camp at 1715hrs. See another mob of boys about fourteen or fifteen being called up for Arbeit Corp for the front. Fair number coming in lately. Quiet evening with a little reading. mashed potatoes, cabbage, and steak and onion rissoles with usual bread and marg. OIL: Said to be German S.S. General captured. Our troops advancing steadily. The French building a bridge over the Rhine. No German news. A wet morning with some sunshine later conditions being reasonably warm.

Wednesday 22nd November, 1944

Prisoner of War stationed at Konigshan. Five men at Konigshan and the rest of us to Trautenau. One gang being with the Czecks laying rails, and myself with the other party digging out and loading earth near the station. Finished about 1230hrs myself, and in the boody for the rest of the day till time to go home, and in camp 1720hrs. A little reading during the evening. Room photos received tonight, but not the best on account of the dull conditions when taken. Potatoes, soup, double of issue of bread. OIL: Our troops still advancing steadily several places mentioned. French also doing very well. Big battle going on around Aachen and German throw in nine divisions in an attemp to hold us, but to no good purpose. Metz has been freed. Heavy rain going on the front near Budapest. Island captured near Riga will be used as depot for Russian front. Planes still active doing over roads, railways and other communications very few planes being lost. Slight fall of snow during the night, with some wet snow about 0830hrs, which later turned to fine rain, but cleared up about midday and came out fairly cool again in evening.

Thursday 23rd November, 1944
Prisoner of War in Sudatenland stationed at Konigshan. Five men at Konigshan, the rest of us to Trautenau, some being on the gang on the Holenelbe line laying rails, and myself with other gang unloading earth, and digging out in railway yards. Finished at 1245hrs myself and in camp at 1720hrs. A little reading during the evening. Mashed potatoes, cabbage, soup, Red X stew, bread and marg. OIL: Fighting in the streets Strazburg and between Stolberg and Velno the main part of the attack at present, also some town 10 mile past Aachen. 1500 Fortresse's doing over communications etc continuously. In Italy 5th and 8th Army doing fairly well. Most German troops now out of the Balkans, despite still heavy rain in Hungary. The Russians continue to attack and threaten the gateway in Czecko. Big convoy today landed troops and materials in Salonika Greece, through one of the heaviest minefields ever seen without losing a ship. Troops doing well in Burma and the Americans in the Phillipines. German news: Mentions heavy fighting everywhere, and their usual repulsing of all attacks. Vienna

and other places bombed. About 40 planes lost. A very dirty day with fine misty rain falling throughout.

Friday 24th November, 1944
Prisoner of War stationed near Konigshan. Five men to Konigshan putting up snow fences, and the rest of us to Trautenau, one party laying rails on the Hohenelbe line, myself with others working in yards digging out loading earth and loading sleepers. Finished work about 1545hrs and in camp at 1730hrs. Reading and darning some socks in the evening. Soup, potatoes, Red X stew, bread, marg and weeks sugar issue. 'Camps' up today and no mail in for a fortnight. Red X parcels supposed to be in Trautenau awaiting distribution to various working parties. Also saw a chap from Stalag says two truck loads of personal parcels recently arrived in Stalag. O.I.L.: Our troops still doing well on The Western Front. Strazburg fallen. 27 Armoured divisions of Jerries badly mauled by English and Americans. French Army doing well and Military Governor appointed for that area. Approaching The Rhine on a 120 mile front. Planes still doing over synthetic oil plants. Tito's mob doing well and captured town over Austrian border. A dull and miserable day with drizzling rain at times and turned out fairly warm evening.

Saturday 25th November, 1944
Prisoner of War stationed near Konigshan. Five men at Konigshan and the rest of of us to Trautenau, some being on the job laying rails, and myself with other party digging out, loading earth and loading some sleepers. Finished 1230hrs and caught a 1301hr train, and in camp 1400hrs being half day. Afternoon bathing and washing. Issued with 25 cigarettes, and the last of the bulk, so unless parcels arrive next week no food parcel next Saturday. Bit of reading during evening and playing cards. Bit of a stir this evening as Fred and Alec are missing at Roll call and U/Officer still waiting up for them at midnight. Potatoes, cabbage, soup midday, with Red X stew at night and bread ration. O.I.L.: French and American troops cross the Rhine and Pattons troops in the Rhur

and advancing on the Rhine. Around Aachen – Kerben heavy battles continue and Germans throw in another 12 divisions. 1000 American planes doing over transport and oil installations behind the German lines. Planes from Italy doing over Munich, Innsbruck and places in Hungary. Another town captured in Italy. German troops in Czecko. Further successes in Burma; and in the Phillipines Japanese troops coming to the assistance of the beleagured garrison of Leyte. 30 ships were attacked by planes and all set on fire, also destroyer sunk and one damaged. Bevin says owing to American slackening off production of shells after the fall of France, there would probably be a shortage of shells, but the British would continue output to the utmost. A very wet miserable morning, but cleared slightly in afternoon.

Sunday 26th November, 1944
Prisoner of War stationed near Konigshan. No work today so in bed till 0900hrs. A little reading and resting during the day. No cards to write. Mail up but received none myself again. Fred and Alec in again this morning and U/O passes the incident over evidently with the intention of covering himself up. Played cards in evening. Porridge for breakfast, potatoes, cabbage, soup midday and Red X stew at night and bread. No O.I.L., but German news mentions heavy losses to us, and Americans in men and materials, and successful in the majority of their counter attacks. Reasonable sort of day with fair amount of sunshine, but very cold wind in early morning.

Monday 27th November, 1944
Prisoner of War stationed near Konigshan. Four men at Konigshan and the rest to Trautenau, one party on rail laying on Hohenelbe line and myself with the other party digging out and loading earth, and finished my section by 1245hrs, and sat in the boody for the rest of the day till leaving for camp and arriving at 1720hrs. A quiet evening. Fred and U/O go to Hohenelbe today to pick up a couple of chaps for here, but not returning till tomorrow. One chap from Gabensdorf

arrived here today. Played cards in evening. Potatoes, soup, Red X stew, bread and weekly jam issue. No O.I.L. or German news tonight. Frost in morning, otherwise turned out a fairly nice day with the sun shining freely.

Tuesday 28th November, 1944
Prisoner of War in camp near Konigshan. Four men at Konigshan and rest of the gang to Trautenau one party laying rails on Hohenelbe line and myself with the other party, digging out and loading earth in the railway yards, finishing at 1330hrs myself and in camp 1720hrs. Fred returned this morning with a Sergeant and Corporal from Hohenelbe, but they may not stay here long. Reading during the evening. Potatoes, soup, Red X stew, bread and margarine. O.I.L.: Our troops still steadily advancing on all fronts in the West. Recco planes pick up troop concentrations today, they were heavily bombed. New bomb out weighing 5 ¼ ton. New type of bombsight said to be one of the greatest of the British inventions of the War, makes no difference whether it is cloudy on a darkest night. Progressing steadily in Italy. Russians in Czecko and partisans hindering German retreat, Burma going well. Last battleship in Italian-German hands in Mediteranean sunk by two man torpedo 18 guns. One person now a prisoner and the other one missing. One gets D.S.O. and the other D.S.M. Frost again this morning, but it turned out a beautiful sunny day and perfect evening, with a practically full moon shining. P.S. Saw a big train of refugee children from the Rhinelend go through Trautenau today towards Hohenelbe.

Wednesday 29th November, 1944
Prisoner of War stationed at Konigshan. Four men at Konigshan, and rest of the party to Trautenau, one party being on rail laying on the Hohenelbe line, and myself with the other gang in station yards digging out and loading earth. Finished 1300hrs myself and in camp at 1720hrs. Quiet evening with a little reading. Mashed potatoes, cabbage, Jerry meat and gravy with bread and marg. Tonights OIL: Fighting in

the Saar Basin well over the Rhineland area. On the Cologne and going over the Dutch border. Verilo being shelled. French doing well. 2000 American bombers operating behind German lines, and R.A.F. during the night. Heavy rain in Italy, Russian troops capture town in Czecko. At Burton-on-Trent big underground bomb explosion, 100 killed and fires still raging. Churchill makes statement that people must not expect an early finish to the war, and King said victory would be ours in the near future. Dull cold frosty day, frost not leaving the ground all day and misty evening.

Thursday 30th November, 1944
Prisoner of War stationed near Konigshan. Five men to Schatzler, putting up snow fences, and rest of us to Trautenau, with one party laying rails and taking plates off old sleepers on the Hohenelbe line, and myself with other party in railway yards digging out and loading earth. With the help of the boss, I finished at 1230hrs. A bit of grumbling by the boys because I finish too early so doing a bit of threatening if I do not ease up. In Lager at 1715hrs. Quiet evening with a little reading. 13 parcels up tonight mostly cigarettes. Heard the 7000 bulk units arrived in Stalag on Tuesday. Soup, potatoes, Red X stew, bread and marg. Big doings again on the Western front with advances everywhere. 20 miles north of Metz, big doing near Verilo progressing into Saar Valley. French and American Armies 40 miles apart from joining up and this is serious threat to Jerries in that area. New divisions thrown in to try and hold things up a bit. Super Fortresses do Tokyo over. Churchill 70 years old today. Frosty morning and cold bleak day throughout.

Friday 1st December, 1944
On railway working party as a Prisoner of War stationed at Konigshan in Sudatenland and previously working party at Bodisch and then attached to Stalag VIII B. Lamsdorf, but now to Stalag VIII A at Gorlitz and P.O.W. number KRETA 4538 having been taken by the

Germans at the fall of the Island of Crete in June 1941. Twelve men at Lampersdorf, and the rest of us to Trautenau. One gang unplating sleepers on Hohenelbe line and myself on party digging out in railway yard. Finished my quota at 1300hrs. In camp at 1720hrs. Quiet evening. Potatoes, soup, Red X stew, bread, marg with weekly sugar issue. OIL: Our troops still pushing forward, and advancing strongly towards Cologne, and expecting a big attack here anytime. French cut off from Jerries, and now mopping them up. Americans over the Saar River. Speech broadcast to the foreign workers in the Saar, Rhur and Rhineland areas. Things progressing steadily in Italy. No mention of Hungary. In Burma steady movement. German News: mentions high losses for us practically everywhere and successful counter attacks against the majority of our movements forward. Raids over Hamm, Dortmund and Hanover, and disturbance raids at night. P.S. A bit of an argument in evening with Taaffe about the boys clearing outside at night. Probably to do with his getting out of barracks at night, and sleeping with German woman over the road. Another frosty morning with an attempt to snow in the morning but otherwise reasonable day.

Saturday 2nd December, 1944

Prisoner of War stationed at Konigshan. Twelve men to Lampersdorf, and the rest of us to Trautenau one party digging foundations for building, myself on the party digging out and loading earth in the railway yards. On the boody job myelf, so no work today. Finished work 1250hrs and in camp at 1400hrs being half day. Air raid alarm in Trautenau today from 1200hrs to 1310hrs, but saw or heard no planes. In afternoon washing and bathing, and in evening did some reading and mending and playing cards. Boys give us a bit of music in the evening also. Cabbage, minced meat in soup, at 1400hrs, and at night Red X stew, bread and weekly jam ration. No parcels or bulk in stock, so no issue this week but received 25 cigarettes. Expecting bulk or parcels this coming week. No news of any sort either way. Reasonably mild morning with some wind early and fairly good afternoon.

Sunday 3rd December, 1944
Prisoner of War stationed near Konigshan. No work today so in bed till 0830hrs. During day reading and sewing. No mail up this week and no letter cards to write again. Porridge for breadfast, with potatoes, cabbage, and soup midday, with Red X stew at night and bread. O.I.L. Patton Army on 15-mile front on Rhine or Ruhr (Forgot which). Germans retreating over Rhine, and blown up four bridges. Big battle around Venlo, army call on bomber command and 2000 planes bomb Venlo and planes report heavy artillery duels. 8th Army move over two more rivers in Italy. In Hungary Russians capture important railway junction, north of Budapest and movement also in the South African Corp capture place in Burma, said to be the gateway to Central Burma. Tokyo done over for the fourth time in a week. German News: Mentions counter attacks all places and successful in giving us heavy losses. The usual raids, some planes shot down. Some minister in Lower House in England says that Britain should annex Tripoli and Benghazi for safe guarding the Mediteranean after the war is over. Some snow during the night, cold wind early, fairly fine morning, and reasonable afternoon except for an attempt at trying to snow.

Monday 4th December, 1944
Prisoner of War stationed at Konigshan. Six men to Schatzler, and the rest to Trautenau, one party digging foundations for building, and myself on other party, loading a little earth, unplating sleepers, where some of them were laying and carting the plates away. Finished about 1530hrs and in Lager at 1720hrs. Reading during the evening. Wilson returns from hospital at Schatzler today. Nothing in the way of griff tonight as wrong bloke on the job. Boots and socks fairly wet on return to camp tonight, because the snow was very slushy today. Potatoes, soup, Red X stew, bread and margarine. Snowing on going to work, later turning to rain, and this caused the heavy snow fall in the early hours of the morning to become very wet and conditions somewhat wet underfoot otherwise a reasonable day.

Tuesday 5th December, 1944

Prisoner of War in Sudatenland at Konigshan. Six men to Schatzler, rest of us to Trautenau, one gang digging foundations for building, and myself on other party, loading a little earth, unplating sleepers, and carting sleepers and plates etc. for rail laying, and taking away old plates and bolts after old sleepers unplated. Fairly easy day and finished work 1540hrs and in Lager at 1720hrs. One chap went to Co'y this morning because he wasn't going to work, but returned again, and on Thursday going to N.C.O. Stalag. Mail up today and received one from Sigrid one from Betty. 18 weeks and none from home. Potatoes, soup, Red X stew and usual bread. OIL: Six miles from Saarbrucken, bombers well in action behind front line in Germany, doing over Hann Karlsruhre and another town and also Berlin, dropped 3 ½ thousand tons of bombs, using 5 ½ ton bombs over Berlin in trying to get at underground factories. Ravenna latest place taken in Italy. Russians still moving forward in Hungary, and coming up from South. Bad riots continue in Athens. German <u>News: Heavy</u> losses as usual to us everywhere, and little gained out of it all. Usual long distance shelling of London and Antwerp by V1 and V2. Mild morning with attempts at snowing, otherwise fairly good day with a patch of sunshine.

Wednesday 6th December, 1944

Prisoner of War stationed at Konigshan. Six men to Schatzler, and the rest to Trautenau area, except for six at Freiheit. One gang digging out building foundations and one gang helping with the relaying of track including myself, helping cart sleepers, plates, lashings and carting away the old plates, bolts and screws from the pulled up line. Finished about 1530hrs and allowed ½ an hour for dinner today. In camp at 1720hrs. Control Feld Wabel here this evening. Received November cards for writing tonight, so wrote card home, letter card to Sigrid and Mr Doust. Mashed potatoes, cabbage with Jerry meat and gravy and usual bread etc. Still waiting on food parcels, other lagers around here received some or received notes that parcels are coming. OIL:

Several more crossings of the Saar River. Jaar Union in our hands and now only three miles from Saarbrucken. Steady advances elsewhere on Western front. 800 bombers escorted by 800 fighters bomb Leipzig today doing over oil refineries. Our troops cross two more rivers in Italy. Russians making move in Hungary. Riots in Athens getting worse. All well in Burma. Australians to go into action in Phillipines under General Blamey. Island in the Agean Sea shelled by four destroyers and small boats. A very mild day but somewhat cloudy.

Thursday 7th December, 1944
Prisoner of War stationed in Sudatenland. Five men to Schatzler, six to Freiheit and the rest to the Trautenau area. One party laying foundation for building huts, myself on the other gang, taking some sleepers up the line and resorting and stacking some old stacks of sleepers in yard. Fairly easy day and in camp at 1720hrs. A quiet evening. Still no personal or Red X Food parcels up. The old cigarette question beginning to talk now, blokes being short, and want to sell things to you, as tonight offered a pair of slippers, but have only a few left myself, and keeping these for the bread racket if possible. Soup, potatoes, Red X stew, and bread. OIL: Our troops still fighting around Saar Union and two or three other Saar places, especially around Saarbrucken. Heavy fighting between Aachen and Cologne. French still pushing the Jerry. 1350 planes over Germany today, mostly over Leipzig. 8th Army in Italy on a 6 mile past Ravenna and on a 20 mile front on some rivers there. Russians pushing southwards and Northwards around Budapest, and in one sector on the South 45 miles from the Austrian border. A fairly mild day with strong wind at times, and snow lying on ground thawing out.

Friday 8th December, 1944
Prisoner of War stationed at Konigshan. Everybody at Trautenau today, there being about four different parties, doing odd jobs about the yards. Myself started off restacking sleepers, and later went

unloading barracks. Did very little work after 1400hrs, and in camp at 1720hrs. Mail up again today and a couple of 'Camp' papers. Received eight letters myself three from Verna, two from Sigrid, one from Ethen H, one from Bernice and one from Gladys, also received three photos. One letter very old, being May, cant understand why none comes from home. Pay night tonight. In photo tonight did not know some of them, having grown up so much. Always arguments going on in this room for some reason or other. Potatoes, soup, Red X stew, bread weekly jam and sugar issue. No griff tonight and German news mentions their usual successes against our troops, and the attacks of our terror planes on the civilian population, fair number of towns bombed. Very mild day being fine till about 1200hrs, then set in with heavy rain for rest of afternoon. Heavy wind this morning though.

Saturday 9th December, 1944
Prisoner of War stationed at Konigshan. Six men to Schatzler, rest of us Trautenau way, being split up into four gangs, doing different jobs, myself with five others doing some stomping on the Hoheneble line, between the points and the first bridge out. All finished at midday and caught the 1212hrs express, and being in camp at 1315hrs. Reason for knocking off an hour earlier was a Christmas meeting for dinner for members of the Reichbahn. Sewing, washing and bathing during afternoon and playing cards in evening. Usual arguments in the room again tonight, about the mucking in spirit and bringing home coal and wood for fire. No bulk issue again this week, but had the last of the cigarettes, there being 19 each. Still hoping on some food parcels or bulk arriving before Christmas. Mashed potatoes, cabbage, soup midday with Red X stew at night, bread and marg ration. OIL: Everything going well on Western front, pushing the Jerries back in one sector to the fringe of the Seigfreid line. 400 bombers do over Stuttgart. In Italy advance steadily towards Fairizi. Everything now quiet in Athens, a ring being placed around there and guerillas attempting to get through.

In Hungary in one place Russians make big push of 37 miles on a five mile front and North and South of Budapest strong activity. Still pushing towards Austrian border. Snow during early hours of morning, and also continued a little after daylight, but came out fairly nice day after 1100hrs, and turned out fairly cool evening. Air raid alarm.

Sunday 10th December, 1944
Prisoner of War in Sudatenland stationed near Konigshan. In bed till 0830hrs. During the day little mending, reading and writing. Wrote letter cards to Aunty Em, Gladys and Merle, card to Bernice. Four parcels up today, personal for Galletly, cigarettes Strange, Houston and Hall. Porridge for breakfast, soup, cabbage, potatoes midday and soup again at night with bread etc. OIL: Trouble in Athens getting worse, we are using 25 pounders, and they replied with French 75's we also bombed them. Patton crosses the Saar River in another two places. Another big attack around Aachen starting 15 miles North and 15 ½ miles South East. 500 bombers do over behind Seigfried line. Slight advance in Italy. In Hungary Russians still advancing and Jerries in chaos not knowing where they are. Quiet elsewhere. German News: says that in last twelve months against Japanese, Americans have lost 224,000 men. The British 70,000 and their losses as 168,000 killed and wounded. A fairly nice day with plenty of sunshine but a cold wind blowing.

Monday 11th December, 1944
Prisoner of War stationed at Konigshan. Six men to Schatzler, and the rest to Trautenau, one party on rail laying on Hohenelbe line, some on putting up foundations for buildings, myself on party of six unloading and stacking sleepers. Finished at 1545hrs, and had fairly easy day, being in camp at 1720hrs. 'Camp' paper up tonight, and received word that bulk to the extent of 246 parcels on the way, also heard that bag of personal parcels at Johanisbad for us, having gone there by mistake. Plenty of arguments again tonight, this time about the way things are being run in England. Potatoes, soup, Red X stew and usual bread. Air

raid alarm today about 1010hrs. No news of any sort tonight. Heavy frost which later turned out to a very nice sunny day, but not enough to clear all the frost off the ground and a cool evening.

Tuesday 12th December, 1944
Prisoner of War stationed at Konigshan. Four men at Schatzler, rest of us to Trautenau area. One party on Hohenelbe line rail laying, and the rest of us digging out on No 4 line by railway station. Fairly solid going and did not knock off till 1550hrs, and in Lager at 1720hrs. Air raid alarm this morning about 1010hrs until 1105hrs. Packed extra clothing tonight that has to go into Coy H.Q. Soup, potatoes, Red X stew, usual bread and marg ration. OIL: Fairly good progress being made on Western front. Saarbrucken now being seriously threatened. 4000 bombers operating over Germany yesterday. Bases of V2 bombed in Holland, as the result of enemy action over England last month. 716 being killed and over 1000 injured. Slight advances in Italy. the trouble in Athens gets worse, there being about 25000 rebels, operating 2000 being killed and 2000 taken prisoner, all wearing English uniform and battle dress. Dull morning bit milder, but turned out reasonable day with some wind at night.

Wednesday 13th December, 1944
Prisoner of War in Sudatenland stationed at Konigshan. Six men at Schatzler, six get off at Parschnitz, but follow on to Trautenau later to join us there. Split up into two or three parties, myself on the party digging out on No 4 line by station also loading the earth. Finished about 1445hrs myself. In Lager 1720hrs. Parcels from Johanisbad not here yet, probably been returned to Stalag. Air raid alarm again today between 1300hrs and 1345hrs. A quiet evening. Mashed potatoes, cabbage, German meat and gravy with usual bread. OIL: Troops still pushing towards the Rhine and the awkward point of putting bridge over, must now be concentrated on as the river flows at about 6 miles an hour, and is dammed further up, also floating mines can be sent

down and it can be bombed. Big battle going on between Aachen and Cologne. Bombers active behind German lines Colblenz and Carlsrube being done over. Advances in Italy enabling a mile front to be made in one place. Trouble getting worse in Athens. Russian front fairly quiet around Budapest concentrating on pushing towards the Austrian border. Things going fairly well in Burma. Japanese troops being conveyed Leyte sunk Naval or Air Force action. Position relieved around Chungking and Chinese in a better position. Dull morning, but reasonably warm day and brighter about 1000hrs, came up with some rain at 1500hrs and fine snow fallng during evening.

Thursday 14th December, 1944
Prisoner of War stationed at Konigshan. Six men Schatzler, rest of us to Trautenau, and being in about four parties, one rail laying, one on building, some loading rails, and myself on party digging out and loading earth on No 4 line by the station. Fairly easy day. In camp at the usual time. Parcels up there being five clothing and four cigarettes. Still no bulk arrived yet. Potatoes, soup, Red X stew, bread and weekly jam ration. OIL: Nothing of any importance to mention on the the Western front. In Italy Canadians widen their bridgehead of the previous day. Russians practically completed their circle around Budapest, which will then mean the finish of Budapest, and still pushing towards the Austrian border. Events in Athens a little quieter than yesterday. More successes in Burma. More transporters sunk off the coast of Norway. Snow during the early hours, dull and cold on going to work and continued fairly dull throughout with snow again in evening.

Friday 15th December, 1944
Prisoner of War stationed near Konigshan. Six men to Bernsdorf doing a little stomping, rest of us to Trautenau, some on rail laying, one party picking up rails, another on building foundations, and myself on party shifting sleepers to uncover rails and lay them along the track for the picking up gang, and also loaded some metal, thereby having a

fairly easy day, and in camp at 1720hrs. Air raid alarm about 1230hrs. Bulk arrives today and also nine cigarette parcels. Will receive bulk issue tomorrow for this week and next week, actually being a full issue, but nothing startling in the issue. Potatoes, soup, Red X stew and usual bread. OIL: Steady fighting going on the Western front, one place in the South seven miles from Karlsruke but the Rhine and Seigfried line in between here. Bombers active behind the German lines. Steady advance in Italy. Russians tightening their grip around Budapest, and Germans putting in new divisions to stem the attack but not too successful. A dull day with fine snow falling practically throughout the day and at times was very cold on the ears.

Saturday 16th December, 1944
Prisoner of War stationed at Konigshan. Six men Schatzler, rest of us to Trautenau, being split up into four parties – myself for party picking a bit of stone on Hohenelbe line, and unloading on No 4 line by station where we dug out, also little digging out to fill in time. Finished work about 1200hrs. Train held up by Red X train, so were half an hour late getting in, it being 1430hrs instead of 1400hrs for half days work. Issued with 25 cigarettes and fortnights bulk, being for last week and the coming week. Bathing and a little washing in afternoon and evening playing cards. mashed potatoes, cabbage, Jerry meat and gravy at midday, with Red X stew in evening and bread and marg issue. No OIL tonight, but the German news mentions heavy losses everywhere for us and very little ground gained. Snowing during the night and fairly cold morning, which continued throughout the day with some wind.

Sunday 17th December, 1944
Prisoner of War stationed at Konigshan. No work today so slept in till 0900hrs. In morning making bag for carrying coal. Afternoon playing cards for a couple of hours. Some mail up today and received three myself two of them being October, one from Merle, one from Carmel and one from Mrs Stephens informing me of Mrs Walkers

death last February. Received word from Stalag of full bulk issue for Christmas, and twenty five cigarettes only instead of fifty and also a notice classing Australian troops here as under the British Army and being regarded as visiting troops to England. Only one card for writing today, but had a spare one so wrote card home and lettercard to Mrs Stephens. Potatoes, cabbage, soup and usual bread with porridge for breakfast. Nothing in the way of OIL., and German news the usual nothing gained by us. Frosty looking day with cold wind blowing.

Monday 18th December, 1944
Prisoner of War in Sudatenland near Konigshan. Six men to Schatzler line putting up snow fences, rest of us around Trautenau in three or four parties, doing various odd jobs, myself on party digging out loading earth and unloading. Unloading none too easy this morning as the earth was frozen to the bottom and sides of the wagon as well as frozen on top to a depth of about four inches. Otherwise fairly easy day and in camp at usual time of 1720hrs. Air raid alarm today. Some sewing during the evening. Soup, potatoes, usual bread and marg. OIL: Germans started big counter offensive on Belgium. Luxemberg border on a thirty mile front and throwing in everything they have. Mentions a case of do or die, have gained considerable ground to date, but have taken a fair number of prisoners. We have Armies on both sides of the Army pressing forward in the counter offensive. 1500 bombers operating behind the lines. Munich, Hamm, Coblenz and some other place being concentrated on at present. Slight advances in Italy, near Bologna. Faenza finished. Affair in Athens has stiffened, and our troops managed to get stuff from Pireous to Athens. Circle completed around Budapest and pushing forward in other sectors, another town captured near Czeck border. All going well in Burma. Third largest town in Japan, and Hankow occupied by the Japs were bombed. Broken down horses being unloaded for meat. Fairly cold morning, being dull all day, but fairly warm evening.

Tuesday 19th December, 1944
Prisoner of War stationed near Konigshan. Six men to Schatzler line, rest of us to Trautenau area being in about four parties, some unloading barracks, some on stomping, myself on party digging out on No 4 line in station yards loading earth and unloading. Fairly easy day with Miller doing his usual whining, and in Lager at usual time. Air raid alarm again today. Soup, potatoes, Red X stew and bread. OIL: German counter offensive said to be advancing being twenty miles into Belgium, otherwise advances also by us on Western front. American Army said to be getting pushed back in the counter offensive and support to have been organized by the Fuhrer himself at his own head quarters. Slight advances on the Italian front. Joe said to have taken three more villages in Czecko. Fairly mild morning with some wind otherwise continued mild and dull throughout the day.

Wednesday 20th December, 1944
Prisoner of War stationed at Konigshan. Six men on the Schatzler line, and the rest of us to Trautenau area, being about four parties. Myself on party digging out and loading earth, also unloading some fine stone on line last done by the station. Took things fairly easy and finished about 1545hrs and in Lager at 1720hrs. Two wagons of old bones being loaded in Trautenau today and looked to be quite a few old horses heads amongst them. Mashed potatoes, soup and usual quota of bread and margarine, and weekly jam ration. OIL: German counter offensive evidently getting very serious being about twenty miles into Belgium and for security reasons no communique of the situation has been given for 54 hours, but troops and materials are being rushed up in an attempt to stem the breakthroughs. In Italy New Zealanders evidently making successful attacking movement. In Slavakia Joe captures important railway junction in a new drive. Insurgents in Greece given till 9 o'clock tomorrow morning to give in or we will go in with everything we have including artillery, naval guns, Airforce and rocket planes. Germans claim tonight to have taken 10,000 prisoners, 200

planes and 200 tanks and armoured wagons. Very nice day with plenty of sunshine, but turning very frosty in evening and freezing.

Thursday 21st December, 1944
Prisoner of War in Konigshan. Sudatenland usual six to Schatzler line, and the rest of the party to Trautenau, in different groups, some stomping, some unloading barrack frames, some on buillding foundations for the barracks, and myself on gang of four digging out and loading earth. Very solid picking the earth, as frozen to a depth of about six inches, as the result of frost, otherwise reasonably easy day and in camp at 1720hrs. Played cards in evening. Potatoes, soup, Red X stew and bread. Not much in the way of OIL tonight, except that some Army of ours have pushed the Jerries back in one sector of their counter offensive. Jerries land parachutists somewhere and were wiped out. Germans claim more prisoners. Cool frosty morning ground frozen, but turned out nice sunny day, but not strong enough to cast the frost out of the air, and frosty again in evening.

Friday 22nd December, 1944
Prisoner of War stationed near Konigshan. Six men to Bernsdorf today, and the rest in about four parties at Trautenau, some stomping, some unloading barracks and some building foundations for the barracks, myself on party started digging out, and then had to go and loosen earth in wagons that had frozen, ready for unloading, going out at 1210hrs andr returning 1340hrs from unloading earth and till knock off time, picking and shovelling bit out that had been left in the wagon. Have never seen earth so hard in winter, as the result of four frosts, had frozen complete in wagons and were using hammers and wedges to break stuff up, with picks could only pick off about a table spoon at a time. Finished 1545hrs and in Lager at usual time. Tonights news gives one a bit more confidence for the Christmas period. Potatoes, soup, usual bread and margarine with weekly sugar ration. OIL: Eisenhower in order of the day told the soldiers and people to

stand firm and resist the present attack with a stout heart, as they had got the Jerry out in the open where they wanted him, away from his bunkers, had made four breakthroughs, and three had been checked, and if they carry this out successfully would go down as one of the gretaest victories of the world and one of Germany's worst defeats. Parachutists landing were practically cleaned out, before they got into action. After having got over the first shock of it all, the stuff that was brought up to the scene was done with amazing thoroughness. The *(unreadable)* being used as the infantry were too slow for the tanks. Bad weather rain and fog hindering our troops with plane support. Stettin and two other places bombed today. Stettin having one of the two biggest oil refineries in Germany. Troops well away in Italy evidently got the Germans in retreat on the plains. Trouble in Athens eased as no shots fire since 9 o'clock yesterday morning, 3,000 insurgent prisoners taken away and another 1,000 waiting to go. Old Joe pushing North of Budapest towards Czecko border and doing well. Heavy frost with cold wind blowing, a little sunshine, but did not get very warm and ground frozen to a depth of nearly nine inches.

Saturday 23rd December, 1944
Prisoner of War stationed at Konigshan. Five men on Schatler line, and the rest of us at Trautenau, doing odd jobs, being half day. Myself one of seven changing 20 metre broken rail on Freiheit line. Everybody finished about 1215hrs, caught 1301hrs train home and back in the Lager at 1400hrs. Bathing and washing during the afternoon. Playing cards during the evening. A few letters up but received none myself. Full parcel issue for Christmas, but only 25 cigarettes given out today. Potatoes, cabbage, soup, usual bread. Nothing much in the way of OIL: German counter offensive continues, weather clearer and 400 bombers and 700 fighters operating behind German lines and our troops. Joe still pushing towards Czecko border and elsewhere. Advancing in Italy still. Civil War in Greece between rebels and Royalists, the latter calling on Scobie for assistance, otherwise quiet. Further successes

in Burma and Americans closing in on Japs on Leyte Island. Very frosty morning with cold wind but sunny day and 19 below at night at 2000hrs.

Sunday 24th December, 1944
Prisoner of War on railway working party at Konigshan in Sudatenland. No work today. A little washing in the morning, made cake today with rolled oats, Canadian biscuits, chocolate sugar, margarine, raisins, prunes, egg powder and Klim powdered milk, put icing on top and looks alright, but the proof will be in the cutting tomorrow. Passed the afternoon away quietly and in the evening had a sing-song and a few barrels of beer. Roll call 2300hrs also played a few games of crib during the evening. Few letters up again today, received two myself, but very old, being a March one from Sigrid and August one from Verna. Soup, potatoes, cabbage, bread and margarine. German News: mentions breaking out from St Naziare of the German troops and capturing 80 square kilometres of new ground, also things going heavily against us in the counter offensive in Belgium. OIL: All breakthroughs being held in the German counter offensive, planes been active behind the German lines. In Italy everything progressing very well, also old Joe continues steadily onward. Things seem to be quieter in Greece. In Burma further successes to us, and in Leyte Japanese left there being further closed in on by American troops and Jap Islands around Japan being heavily bombed. Very frosty morning with sunny cloudless day and cold night with thirteen below at 2000hrs and getting colder.

Monday 25th December, 1944
Christmas Day. My fifth Christmas as a Prisoner of War. Stationed at Konigshan in Sudatenland. Slept in till 1000hrs today, and had cup of tea in bed for the first Christmas in my life. During the day reading, writing and odd jobs. Wrote letter cards to Home and 'Virgilia'. Porridge for breakfast with potatoes eggs and sausages. Midday meal mashed potatoes, cabbage, peas, sausages with pudding and custard

at night. Not quite the same sort of Christmas we had the previous two when stationed on the party at Bodisch. Musical programme in evening. Afternoon Fred heard Kings speech, OIL: Morning missed Western front, but other fronts Joe still moving forward, and also the boys in Italy. Evening news: Western front looks like big battle coming up, with plenty of materials on both sides coming up, and Germans breaking out again in one sector. 700 bombers and 700 fighters operating behind the German lines. Snowing in Italy, so only patrol activitiy. Joe going forward in Czecko and circle around Budapest and closing in. All well in Burma. Navy and Air Force bombing islands in Japanese hands in Pacific. Heavy frost but nice sunny day.

Tuesday 26th December, 1944
Boxing Day. Prisoner of War near Konigshan. Holiday today, so slept in till about 0900hrs. Bit of reading, sewing, odd jobs and playing poker in afternoon and reading. Potatoes, Soup, Red X stew in evening, bread and margarine with weekly jam issue. OIL: Western front Germans continuing to push forward slightly in one sector of their counter offensive, but in the sides our troops holding out. Bombers and fighters fairly active behind German lines. In Italy fairly quiet. Old Joe still active around Slavakian border, in the ring around Budapest 2 miles from the city on one side. Churchill and Eden fly to Greece for conference at 1600hrs today. All going well in Burma. The island of Leyte fighting now finished, costing the Americans 12000 troops and Japs over 100,000 men. Very heavy frost this morning, being 23 degrees below followed by sunny cloudless day and some wind.

Wednesday 27th December, 1944
Prisoner of War Prisoner stationed near Konigshan. All of us go to Trautenau today, and being split up into about four parties, doing different jobs, myself being one of seven who changed rail in yard by station up till Freisteig time. After early dinner and then went to Parschnitz by 1300hrs train, picked up rail and went down line

between Gabersdorf and Parschnitz to change badly broken rail. On arriving found the keys we had taken were too big and had to wait until the 1420hr train from Trautenau went through bringing the necessary tools. In the mean time had to cut the rail and bore a couple of holes. Had to finish the job in the dark with the aid of lanterns, it being nearly 1900hrs on arrival in camp. Miller tried to blame us for not having the necessary tools, saying that we had left a couple of keys behind. A little reading during the evening. Soup, potatoes, usual bread. OIL: Things still fairly stiff in the West, and Germans still pushing slightly forward. In Italy our troops pushed back a little. Fighting in the streets of Budapest, otherwise nothing of importance. Germans claim to have the V1 on Manchester now. Heavy frost again this morning followed by beautiful sunny cloudless day, and perfect moonlight night, still with a fair amount of wind. Ground now frozen very hard.

Thursday 28th December, 1944
Prisoner of War stationed near Konigshan. All at Trautenau again today, except six others and myself who got off at Gabersdorf, to finish off job we were on yesterday, having to bore four holes in new rail and put bolts in, and a little stomping. Finished about 1310hrs and caught the 1320hr train from Parschnitz being half a day, on account of the late hour last night. Just managed to make the train by half a minute before it pulled out. Had everything gone alright during the morning, would have had plenty of time, but boring holes did not go too good. In Lager 1400hrs. Air raid alarm about midday and heard planes and bombing exceptionally distinctly today being three or four very severe rumbles. Three years ago today since the party of us at Tymbakion on Crete, started packing up and leaving for Germany. Soup, potatoes, Red X stew usual bread and margarine. OIL: The German counter offensive halted on practically all sectors, or being pushed back. 600 planes lost by Jerry since counter attack started, and many tanks destroyed, some tanks captured because of no petrol to get them away.

Our planes flying over aerodromes to get the German planes up, but refuse the bait. Still fighting in the streets of Budapest, the Jerry's making every house a nest of soldiers but artillery and tanks getting them out of it. Russians practically at the pass that leads into Austria. Conference in Athens Greeks say that they want a monarchy for the country and will help matters. So Churchill to approach the late King George of Greece. Everything progressing in Burma satisfactorily. Another landing in the Phillipines. Japanese ships coming to the Japs assistance set on and three destroyers sunk, and the rest clear out. Early very dull and terribly cold wind, attempting to snow, just before midday, sun came out a little later, but continued very cold and some snow falling slightly in evening.

Friday 29th December, 1944
Prisoner of War stationed at Konigshan. Six men on Freiheit line, rest to Trautenau on different jobs and myself with six others got off at Parschnitz and changed a rail in the yards, then went onto Trautenau, and after midday loaded sleepers on the Hohenelbe line and then came back and unloaded some of them. Fairly easy day. About 1530hrs goods train derailed where new line had been laid on Hohenelbe line, axle on tender broken, and practically broad side on the line, three lengths of line and sleepers torn about. First of all thought that we would have to stay behind late, but were allowed to go at the usual time, and in camp at 1720hrs. Soup, potatoes, usual bread and weekly sugar issue. OIL: All Jerry attacks of their counter offensive broken up and the counter offensive now taken by us. Many tanks and trucks captured by us as the result of no petrol for Jerry to get them back. Many Jerries on the way walking back to their lines picked up. Plenty of plane action on our side. In Italy everything fairly quiet. Heavy fighting going on in Budapest and other sectors there. All well in Burma, Phillipine Islands action, island of Mindora fell today, and one aerodrome on one of the islands, American planes destroyed over 100 Jap planes on the ground. Dull, cold windy morning with snow falling, and falling finely

throughout the day, although had periods of sunshine and wind kept up all day.

Saturday 30th December, 1944
Prisoner of War stationed at Konigshan. Six men to Trubenwasser, rest of us to Trautenau area, doing different jobs. After Freisteig six men go down the line to the Protectorate area to change a broken rail. On the boody job myself. Half day, but just on going home called for six men to unload some logs and stone and I was one of them. After waiting in boody all afternoon for engine to bring the stuff where we are to load it, went up usual time at 1618hrs, also the six men from the line changing came home with us, and get next Saturday morning off. On getting in Lager bathing and washing clothes occupied the evening interspersed with a little reading. Six men to go out in morning now for the job we were supposed to do. Line all cleared Hohenelbe way again, and traffic running as normal, although big congestion of goods line in main yard, this morning as the result of the hold up on the line. Issued with ½ bulk parcel and 25 cigarettes. Mashed potatoes, cabbage, Jerry minced meat and soup, bread and marg.

OIL: German counter offensive still failing, being pushed back 15 miles, and the widest point in the South now 12 miles wide. Heavy loss of vehicles by Germans, and 1300 bombers operating practically day and night over and behind the German lines. Italy fairly quiet. Big battle continues around Budapest and in the town tanks being used in the streets to a great extent trying to hold out, and prolong the situation, here as long as possible. Elsewhere Joe still plodding steadily onward. Cleaning up still going on in Athens, and Archbishop in Greece, has accepted the Regency, so things fairly quiet, and both parties have thanked Churchill and Eden for their help. German News: mentions raid in Protectorate and machine gunning of trains, 38 being killed and 105 wounded, the towns of Pardubitz and a couple of others mentioned, also terror raids over German civilians and living quarters suffering. Fairly cool morning and turned out very nice day.

Sunday 31st December, 1944

Prisoner of War stationed at Konigshan. Last day of 1944. Six men go to work this morning to unload poles and stones which were not done yesterday as a result of not being in place on time. Out bout 0800hrs and doing some washing and odd jobs before breakfast. Nine parcels up today, but none came to our room. During the afternoon and evening played cards. Lights did not go out till midnight being New Years Eve and to welcome in 1945. Soup, potatoes, cabbage and usual bread. A little OIL: Everything going fairly well on the Western front. Bombers and fighters operating very freely. Owing to bad weather in Italy patrol activity only. Heavy fighting continues in and around Budapest. Russians still pushing along the Slavakian border towards Austria. Progress still being maintained in Burma. The fighting on Leyte cost Japs 117000 men. Cold windy day with snow falling slightly.

Year of 1945 Survivor and Liberation

Private Vic Petersen has been in German hands since June, 1941. He is about to add another 6 months.

Monday 1st January 1945
New Year's Day and we wonder what the year will bring. Prisoner of War of the Germans working on railway party in Sudatenland, now stationed at Konigshan, but previously of party E388 at Bodisch in Sudatenland now attached to Stalag VIII A Gorlitz, but previously of Stalag VIII B Lamsdorf. Holiday today, slept in till 0900hrs. In morning do odd jobs. In afternoon race meeting held which occupied till 1630 hrs and in evening played cards but luck still out, the same as the whole weekend. Potatoes, cabbage, peas, usual bread, margarine and weekly jam issue. News: practically the same, nothing unchanged, except for more bombing being carried out. Cold windy day with steady snow falling.

Tuesday 2nd January 1945
Prisoner of War stationed near Konigshan. Six men on Freiheit line, rest of us in three parties at Trautenau, myself on party stacking sleepers first thing, and then helping to unload three wagons of stones, where we had been digging out. Reasonably easy day. In camp at 1720

hrs. Quiet evening with a little reading. Potato soup, red X stew, usual bread. OIL: Things going fairly well on Western front. Bombers active on synthetic oil plants etc doing heavy damage. Italy patrol activity only owing to bad weather. Still heavy fighting in and around Budapest. Bishop of Greece who took over Regency forming new Government. 2/3 of Athens cleaned up. Fairly cold morning, but came out very nice day with plenty of sunshine but turned cold again 1500 hrs.

Wednesday 3rd January 1945
Prisoner of War stationed near Konigshan. Twelve men to Freiheit line, rest of us to Trautenau in three parties, myself on party of eight started stacking sleepers then caught 0900 hr train to Konigshan and on Arbeit Zug unloading coal at the signal boodies between there and Parschnitz and also shovelled a little snow at Konigshan. Back in Trautenau at 1500 hrs then had to cart 60 firewood sleepers from stack to workshop. In Lager at 1720 hrs. Some mail up tonight and received three myself: one from Jean, one from Ethel H and one from Merle. Heard something of a present from Australian Government, containing some small articles, also heard of Chrisrmas parcels on way, and will get one when they arrive and 75 cigarettes. Crib tournament commenced this evening and played my first round being beaten 2 – 1. Mashed potatoes, cabbage, minced meat, soup, usual bread and marg. Big battle going on in Western front. Jerries got tanks dug in and using the guns for artillery. Big activity behind these, Jerry evidently trying to withdraw back to Seigfried line and Pattons Army attempting to prevent them from getting back, Jerries also attempting to break through by French and American bombers and 700 bombers doing over behind German lines from Karlscruke to Cologne. 8th Army in Italy progressing again. In Hungary Budapest finished, and also Pest believed finished now as celebrations in Warsaw today, also big battle 50 miles north of Budapest. House to house cleaning up in Athens continues and over 2/3 now in our hands. In Burma advanced 75 miles in 14 days. Japan being bombed by Super fortresses

from Saipan. Tokyo a big steelworks place and some other towns heavy damage being done over the last week. Very heavy wind at Konigshan practically a gale, but very mild at Trautenau and continued rough at Konigshan evening.

Thursday 4th January 1945
Prisoner of War stationed near Konigshan. Twelve men to Freiheit line, and the rest of us to Trautenau on various jobs. Myself, party stacking sleepers unloading stone and loading old sleepers by side of railway line. In Lager at 1720 hrs. Reading during evening for a while and to bed fairly early. Potatoes, soup, Red X stew and bread. German News: claims heavy losses and set backs for us everywhere also Antwerp and London still under V1 fire, and our bombers doing heavy damage to housing & civilians. Nothing doing in way of OIL. Fairly windy day again but fairly calm in Trautenau, some sunshine otherwise fairly mild day.

Friday 5th January, 1945
Prisoner of War stationed near Konigshan. Six men on Freihteit line, six men down Protectorate way rest of us in Trautenau some loading coal, some putting up barracks. Myself picking up old sleepers by track of Hohenelbe line. Easy day again and in camp at usual time. Little reading during the evening. Potatoes, soup, usual bread and marg with weekly sugar ration. OIL: Everything Western Front going very favourably. Montgomery in charge on one sector from Holland and another general in charge of the sector from the Swiss border and evidently helping considerably in our plans. The usual bombers and fighters in action over and behind German lines. In Italy progressing favourably. Athens still continues to be getting cleaned up. Budapest about finished despite heavy resistance of the Germans. Big battle contiinues still north of Budapest, Jerries throw in troops from Czeckoslavakia, tanks and aeroplanes regardless of cost. Fairly cool morning on Konigshan but much milder in Trautenau but came over like as if it was going to snow heavily in the evening.

Saturday 6th January 1945

Prisoner of War stationed at Konigshan. Six men home from work of previous Sunday, six men Freiheit line, rest of us to Trautenau, unloading sleepers. Finished work 1145 hrs but would not let us home before the 1301 hr train and in Lager 1400 hrs. Bathing and washing clothes in afternoon. Played crib and poker in evening. New orders about water not allowed to get any after dark so unable to get any griff today, or probably will not be too easy to get it now. Mashed potatoes, cabbage, mince meat, soup and usual bread. Jerries claim usual successes and us losing plenty of material. Fairly mild morning but came up misty and frosty in afternoon.

Sunday 7th January 1945

Prisoner of War stationed near Konigshan. In Lager today and slept till 0845hrs. Doing odd jobs throughout morning. Afternoon and evening reading and playing cards, also wrote card to Lil and Tom. Porridge for breakfast with potatoes, cabbage and soup midday and usual bread, and margarine. No OIL again tonight. Fairly cool day with mist being frosted on the trees and looking a marvellous sight.

Monday 8th January 1945

Prisoner of War stationed at Konigshan. Six men Freiheit, rest of us to Trautenau area on different jobs. Six men go home at 1300hrs for extra work of nine days ago. Myself on job of unplating sleepers first thing, then had another job of carrying bricks, slack and sand. Took things fairly easy. In Lager at 1720hrs. Starkey going on the deep end, because of too many pranks, and says he will send them to the Coy military Dr. Jerrie issue of tobacco up and it comes from Russia and enough sticks in it to light a fire. With race meeting on New Years Day and donations collected 1000 marks for the Red X. Potatoes, soup, usual bread. No OIL again tonight. Fairly mild day with a little snow falling.

Tuesday 9th January 1945
Prisoner of War stationed at Konigshan. Six men Schatzler line, rest of us to Trautenau on various jobs, myself on carrying sand, slack and cement. Came home on 1301hrs train for work of one Saturday ten days ago, so in Lager at 1400hrs, and the rest usual time. Reading during the evening. Potatoes, soup, usual bread and margarine. Search party here today. No OIL again, so don't know how anything is going. Jerry claims usual success, supposed to have gained 25 miles of ground in Hungary. V1 still on London and Antwerp. Our bombers over Berlin, Munich and done damage to living quarters. Fairly cool morning with snow falling, but sun came through about 1100hrs, and fairly good day, coming up cool again in evening.

Wednesday 10th January 1945
Prisoner of War stationed at Konigshan. Six men to Schatzler line, six men Freiheit, rest of us Trautenau on different jobs. Myself with four others unplating and stacking sleepers. Fairly easy time, just kept moving to keep warm. In camp at the usual time. Played crib match in evening and beaten 3 – 0, also reading. Mashed potatoes, cabbage, minced meat, soup with usual bread. No OIL yet. Fairly cold morning, snow in Trautenau but warmed up later and coming up cold again in evening.

Thursday 11th January 1945
Prisoner of War stationed near Konigshan. Six men to Schatzler line, and through train being late to Trautenau, nobody went to Freiheit, so rest of us on different jobs at Trautenau, myself with five others unplating and stacking sleepers in station yard. Saw Jack Barker and Ian Gillon today, who have left Weckelsdorf party and gone to the sawmill party at Oberalstadt. In camp at usual time. Did some reading early part of evening, and to bed early. Potatoes, soup, Red X stew, bread and marg. No OIL again and German news as claims still heavy losses for us, and any little gains have cost us much material and manpower.

Planes over South West, South East and Southern Germany not many shot down though. Fairly mild day with a little snow falling, and at one stage started to rain, sun shone for an hour and snowing again in evening.

Friday 12th January, 1945
Prisoner of War stationed at Konigshan. Six men to Schatzler, rest of us to Trautenau on various jobs, myself on party unplating sleepers, and stacking to freistig, and then four of us went by passenger train to Freiheit, and then back to Youngsback on Arbeit Zieg to unload coal, then returned to Freiheit, and going by passenger train to Trautenau again, and having dinner and after that unplating more sleepers. All got caught tonight with our bags of coal and told train would not go home until they were emptied. No one moved and police were called, and finally emptied them in station yard, and which constituted a heap a kangaroo would have had trouble jumping over, but the funny part of it to see the eyes of the civilian population at what was going on, and finally on our way home and have heard no more about the incident. We presume one of the local population must have dobbed us in, as we had done this many a time going home with bags of coal for our room fires, and eventually in camp usual time. Potatoes, soup, usual bread and weekly sugar ration also some cheese. Reading during the evening. Heard from yesterday a bit of OIL: All well on the Western front, Southern sector of Russian front more villages gained by Joe's boys and indications of a big push starting in the Northern sector, otherwise nothing much. Germans with more fantastic claims, and very little ground gained by us anywhere, except of heavy losses in everything. Fairly cool morning, but later turned out a reasonably nice day.

Saturday 13th January 1945
Prisoner of War stationed at Konigshan in Sudatenland. Six men Konigshan today and the rest of us Trautenau way, myself on party

unplating sleepers and stacking them. Finished work 1240hrs and being a half day in Lager at 1400hrs. Bathing and washing during the afternoon. Evening a little reading and playing crib and poker. A little mail up but received none myself. Stalag rumour says Christmas parcels arriving, and three wagons of personal parcels mostly Colonial. Bulk issue of ½ parcel and twenty five cigarettes. German news: mentions Turkey opening up the Dardanelles to the Allies, thus allowing supplies to be taken through by our ships to Russia. OIL: Mention of our practically complete withdrawal of Ronstadts Army in the West, evidently with intention of trying elsewhere. Patrol activity in Italy only. The 'Cease Fire' signal in Greece takes place at one minute past twelve Sunday midnight. Only one fort now holding out in Budapest. Jerries send reinforcements to help them out, and out of 100 tanks 37 shot up, and 1000 men killed. Our planes attack U boat bases in Northern Norway with 12000 lb bombs. In Burma still going forward. In Pacific on the Island of Luzon capture junction of 5 roads leading to Manilla. Convoy of reinforcements attacked by plane, over 20 sunk and 17 damaged. During last month over England 300 killed and 800 injured as a result of enemy action. Mashed potatoes, cabbage, mince meat, soup, usual bread and marg. Cold morning, but turned out a nice day with cold evening.

Sunday 14th January 1945
At Konigshan as a Prisoner of War. No work today, so slept in till 0830hrs. During morning mending and odd jobs. In afternoon playing cards. Wrote cards to Florrie Jean, and Doreen. Reading during the evening. Potato soup, Red X stew, porridge for breakfast and usual bread issue. OIL: Joe starts big push towards Krakou. Rumoured this afternoon that Jerries are commencing to evacuate Ober. Silesia – 600,000 fresh troops on Western front. New type of fighter also used on Western front. Berlin received heavy bombing last night. Supposed to be 2,000,000 out of work in Germany, as result of bombed out factories. Very heavy frost this morning, but turned out nice day, but came out frosty evening.

Monday 15th January 1945

Prisoner of War stationed near Konigshan. Five men to Schatzler, six at Freiheit, and the rest to Trautenau and myself on job of unplating and stacking sleepers, finishing at 1515hrs and in camp at 1720hrs. Reading during the evening. Potatoes, soup, Red X stew, bread and marg. OIL: Joe said to have broken through 60 kilo's wide and 40 deep and making good progress. No enemy news tonight. Heavy frost but came out rather dull early, and cleared slightly later in the day, coming up frosty again in evening.

Tuesday 16th January, 1945

Prisoner of War stationed at Konigshan. Gazelle goes to Stalag today, after his operation for rupture and Dick also goes in, but returning in a couple of days. Five men to Bernsdorf, and rest of the gang to Trautenau doing different jobs and myself on stacking sleepers, and finishing at 1530hrs and in camp at 1720hrs. Coal for Lager arrived today, also some person tells bloke in charge of rations that the cooks are giving around new potatoes at night, so our ration cut down tonight to the correct amount. Reading during the evening. Soup, Red X stew and usual bread. OIL: Fairly good news on Western front. Both sides of our Army closing in, but American and 7th Army receiving heavy pressure from the Jerries. 700 fighters operating practically without opposition, and bombers doing over oil refineries and factories heavily.

Joe's new offensive going very well, and 20 miles from Krakou. Warsaw Kraukou railway line cut and communications with Breslau seriously hampered, many tanks, guns and other material captured and many dead. American figures for the German counter offensive recently states 40,000 men mostly taken prisoner and Germans lost 50,000 dead and wounded, besides many prisoners. In Burma successes all the way, not meeting with much resistance, and must count, as one of the Japs worst defeats here, some of the fastest going in history. In the island of Luzon, American planes straff Jap aerodrome near Manilla causing heavy damage. Hong Kong raided, and one or two other places. One Jap convoy completely wiped out. Frosty morning, but nice sunny day, and turned cold again in evening. Air raid in vicinity today as heard ACK/ACK and bombs exploding.

Wednesday 17th January 1945
Prisoner of War stationed at Konigshan in Sudatenland. Five men at Konigshan and the rest of the party to Trautenau, and all on barracks job except for four men, helping to dig out trench about 18 inches wide and six feet deep. Heavily frosted to a depth of about two feet, and very hard picking, broke two picks, did not shift a square yard of earth all day. Walking up and down a fair bit of the time to keep feet warm. Had row on job because fire was put out to prevent us going to warm our feet, guard puts a bullet in breech of rifle, and another bloke goes to draw his gat. In Lager usual 1720hrs. Mashed potatoes, cabbage, soup, meat and usual bread. Germans admit heavy battles West and Eastern fronts, but very little ground gained by us or Joe. OIL: Heavy battle by English troops in Holland and tanks advanced through fog to within 3 miles of the German border. Still pressing in on both sides of the Lower sector of the Western front, and Amerian 7th Army still being pressed. Bombers over Breslau, Dresden and Brux, the latter place in the Protectorate. Fighters up and meeting with little opposition. Another 2 million Yanks arrive in France. Quiet in Italy and Greece. Old Joe pushing forward very quickly, captured 1300 towns and villages now practically no front line here now, as all wiped out on a 200 kilometre long front and 100 deep, only 37 miles from German borders and not far from Krakou. 14 Armoured divisions bottled up and being cut up. Advanced over one river 15 miles before they knew he was over. Still going ahead in Burma, and on the island of Luzon, now meeting first Jap resistance, but no aircraft and our planes taking full advantage and doing heavy damage everywhere and bombing places on Indo-China coast. Fighting broken out in Northern province of

Norway between Norwegians and Germans, and all Germans cleaned out of this province. Place being fixed for meeting of Stalin, Roosevelt and Churchill. Heavy frost with gusterly winds, and continued very cold all day with heavy wind still blowing in evening.

Thursday 18th January 1945
Prisoner of War stationed at Konigshan. Five men to Bernsdorf, and rest of us to Trautenau, but eleven of us returned to Bernsdorf by arbeitzug with rail to replace broken one, already taken out by five men there, and only here about half an hour and returned to Trautenau again, getting back at twelve, and very cold ride in open wagon, and had dinner on getting back. In afternoon digging out trench of new barracks. Sharkey sniffing around in afternoon. In camp usual time. 'Camp' papers up and reading during the evening. Potatoes, soup, Red X stew and bread. Churchill made big speech today and Fred gave us an account of it, and proved very interesting. OIL: Very good. Warsaw in Russian hands, and the whole front from here to Budapest going forward with the Germans in complete route, and no natural defences from here to Berlin, just open plains, and only 20 miles from the border in one place, in an Easterly line from Brelau, possibly Krakou in Russian hands, but not admitted by the B.B.C. On Western front all going well except by sector of American Army. Going forward slightly again in Italy. Still fighting in Budapest. In Burma three Armies converging on Mandalay, the capital of Burma, and not very far from there Americans continue their victorious march towards Manilla and the Phillipine Islands will soon be in American hands, and this is only a forepart of the doom awaiting Japan. Heavy frost again this morning but wind not quite as bad as yesterday and coming up cold again at 1700hrs.

Friday 19th January 1945
Prisoner of War in Sudatenland stationed near Konigshan. Five men to Schatzler, rest of us to Trautenau on different jobs. Myself on barrack

party digging trench for water pipe. Fairly easy day. In camp at 1735hrs as train was late leaving Trautenau and had to wait for Red X Train, with soldiers, women and children at Parschnitz. Heard that engine had been derailed on Weckelsdorf line, and fireman was killed, and two coaches went over the side. Potatoes, soup, Red X stew, bread, margarine and weekly sugar and jam ration. OIL: Joe still pushing and fighting taking place at Lodz and Krakou, at one point last night 12 miles fom German border. Fighting still going on in Budapest, 59000 prisoners being taken here, not much holding out now. On Russian front police and Volkstrumen being used. Western front still advancing in Holland and on other parts of the front, no changes. Plane still active bombing behind the lines. In Italy everything pointing to another big offensive coming off. In Burma and Phillipine Islands tonight all quiet. Churchills speech gets great prominence and being broadcast to the German people, telling them to throw in while the going is good. Cold morning with very strong gusterly wind, that was still blowing tonight and fairly cold with it.

Saturday 20th January 1945
Prisoner of War stationed near Konigshan. Six men to Schatzler and the rest of us to Trautenau on different work, myself on barrack job filling in trench that was dug for the laying of water pipes. Easy morning and a half day being in Lager at 1400hrs. Mail up mostly English, received none myself. None from home now for 25 weeks. Washing and bathing during the afternoon. Played poker in evening. Mashed potatoes, cabbage, minced meat, carrot soup and Red X stew with usual bread. OIL: Russian advance continues and now in Ober Silesia over the German border, said to be 100 kilometres east of Brelau. Kakou fallen and Lodz also in Russian hands – German news mentions fairly freely of the Russian advance, although having heavy losses in materials. Warsaw given up and also the towns of Tschentoclau, Tomaschau and Zichenau evacuated, and elsewhere heavy breakthroughs. On

Western front Americans still meeting with losses in men and materials. Fairly calm morning here and Trautenau, but slight snow fell in Trautenau most of the morning and sun broke through in afternoon.

Sunday 21st January 1945
Prisoner of War stationed near Konigshan in Sudatenland. In camp today and slept in till 0830hrs. During morning mending gloves, and afternoon and evening played poker, and also wrote card home and letter card to Carmel. Potatoes, carrot soup, Red X stew at night also had porridge for breakfast and usual bread and marg. Everybody pleased again with Joe's movements, another town taken in Prussia, and another on Czecko border, and in his march towards Breslau was 50 kilometres away when heard at 0900hrs and tonight at 2100hrs, 30 kilometres away at a place called *(unreadable)*, so should be close in on Breslau by tomorrow. French pushing forward in South of the Western front. Frosty morning and fine sunny day and came up cool again in the evening.

Monday 22nd January 1945
Prisoner of War stationed near Konigshan. Six men to Schatzler, and the rest through to Trautenau. First job on myself, filling in trench over water pipe, but at 1100hrs with three others went to Parschnitz to load old plates, bolts, lashings etc, and had fairly easy day. In Lager 1720hrs. Trains from Ruhbark and running late today. New orders out civilians not allowed to travel anymore than 75 kilometres. Supposed to be evacuating woman and children from Breslau. Burgcher, Weaver and Prentice transfer to Ober – Allstadt party today and three others came and from there to here in their places. Guards on duty with rifles at Trautenau. Reading during the evening. Potatoes, soup, Red X stew, and bread. OIL: Very good. Russians victorious drive continues, all spear points of the Northern sector now in German territory.

Tuesday 23rd January 1945
On the South of the West front French still going forward. All going well in Burma and in the Phillipines not far from Manilla, and captured big airfield there. Planes from aircraft corner do over the island of Formosa, and planes also do over the big industrial island where Tokyo stands. Units of the American Navy patrolling in Pacific have sunk over 500000 tons of shipping and shot down 400 planes without sighting one unit of the Jap Navy. Frosty morning with very cold wind, but turned out fairly good day with attempts ay trying to snow.

Wednesday 24th January 1945
Prisoner of War near Bodisch in Sudatenland. Four men to Schatzler, and the rest of us at Trautenau on different jobs. In morning on party of four sorting out and counting lashings, plates, bolts, screws etc. Afternoon digging out trench at barracks. Easy day and in Lager at the usual time. Dunstan returns from Stalag today. Railway line from Ruhbank to Trautenau taxed with evacuee trains, as well as the usual trains. Two trainloads of railway workers from the Eastern area pass through here today, said to be on the way to Dresden. Stalag news says Tseken evacuated and 8000 on foot for Gorlitz, nationality as yet unknown. No parcels or cigarettes in Stalag. Mashed potatoes, soup and usual bread. No OIL about tonight. German News: Fairly good admissions of the fighting on the Eastern front, but does not give much away on the Western front. V1 still shelling London and Antwerp. Cold windy morning and continued same throughout the day in Trautenau, except for no wind and some snow falling in late afternoon and evening.

Thursday 25th January 1945
Prisoner of War stationed at Konigshan. Four men to Schatzler and rest of the gang to Trautenau, except that thirteen of us went to Freiheit to load trucks of sleepers, and returned Trautenau 1245hrs. During afternoon sorting out and tying up lashings with wire, and

finished at 1530hrs, and in camp at 1720hrs. Plenty of evacuees still arriving at Trautenau, said to be 7000 going to Scholtze, and about 400 around here. One train load of soldiers in Trautenau this morning, with all clothing, equipment and war stuff, and had about 300 dogs with them, and about a dozen horse carcases for feeding the dogs. All dogs heavily muzzled and being mostly Alsatians. Still plenty travelling by roads and a good many on foot. Reading during the evening. Potatoes, soup, usual bread, margarine and weekly jam issue. OIL: Joe still continues forward Posen, Oppeln and Konigsberg fallen, 4 miles from Breslau and 180 from the Posen area to Berlin. Unable to give details of all that is happening in the different sectors. Area around Gleiwitz said to be encircled. Another push from the Hungarian end and advanced twelve miles. Has taken another 1300 towns and villages. On the Western front all is going well, and bombers active all sectors. Italy quiet. In Burma meeting heavy Jap resistance as nearly the town of Mandalay. The island of Luzon have now captured what is is known as Clarke's field, being about five aerodromes here, and now forty five miles from Manilla the capital of the Phillipines. Fairly mild morning and throughout the day with some snow falling in the afternoon.

Friday 26th January 1945
Prisoner of War stationed near Konigshan. Usual 4 men to Schatzler, with the rest of us going on to Trautenau on odd jobs. Myself and 3 others shifting plates, lashings and screws etc, tying up and stacking. Exceptionally easy day, and in camp usual time. Coming home tonight saw a party of Jewesse's, who had been out with picks and shovels under armed guard to dig defences and also the local froggies, and local inhabitants cutting down timber for the making of tank traps. Was after dark when they were going back to their lager. Still plenty of stuff being evacuated by rail and road. Told tonight in the event of us moving only allowed 30 k of clothing. Soup, potatoes, Red X stew and bread. OIL: Gleiwitz fallen and unconfirmed report of fighting in the

streets of Breslau, otherwise nothing of interest. Mild morning and continued throughout the day, with some snow falling in the evening.

Saturday 27th January 1945
Prisoner of War stationed near Konigshan. Eight men Lampersdorf and the rest of the gang to Trautenau, train running late, so no work before 0900hrs. Myself with three others shifting stones and stacking them. Did very little though ½ day and in camp at 1400hrs. Owing to the shortage of coal in Trautenau, and cut off from supplies, only two passenger trains, running from Konigshan to Trautenau next week, so will be going to work at 0700hrs, and will probably be after seven before we get home at night. Another order in tonight that only allowed 30 lbs to carry, instead of 65 as told last night in the event of moving, so during the afternoon, sorted what will be leaving behind. Unfortunately, will have to leave many things behind I wanted as souvenirs. Also washing during the afternoon. Still hundreds and hundreds of evacuees' going past here in wagons and other conveyances many being from Kreuzberg, the other side of Oppeln. Jewesee's working out here again today. Tank officer had the cheek to ring Coy Commander to have us tomorrrow for digging the tank ditch, but the Coy says there is nothing he can do about it. Reading during the late evening. Mashed potatoes, horse meat, soup, usual bread and Red X stew in evening. Issued with the last of the bulk food and 25 cigarettes. Still a few cigarettes left and think we have seen the last of it now. No definite OIL: but rumour of Danzig in Russian hands, fighting in streets of Breslau also Liegnitz west of Breslau being evacuated. A fairly mild morning and came out a real fine afternoon, but a cold evening with heavy frost.

Sunday 28th January 1945
Prisoner of War at Konigshan in Sudatenland. No work today, so slept in till 0830hrs, and in the morning bathing and doing odd jobs.

Afternoon and evening reading, a little writing, and finished packing clothes in the event of a sudden move. Wrote cards home and to Mavis, but do not expect them to get through. Potatoes, carrot soup midday with Red X stew and bread. Had porridge for breakfast. No definite news, but Russians said to be advanced as far as Glugau on the line between Breslau and Berlin, and Brieg between Oppeln and Breslau fallen. All hoping here that Russians encircle us before they can move us out, which will mean marching and going goodness knows where. Heavy frost this morning, with some snow falling later, and sunny during part of the day, but turned cold again in evening. The temperature being 16 below at 1700hrs and 19 below at 1900hrs, and at 2130hrs 21 ½ below, so looks like heavy frost in morning.

Monday 29th January 1945
Prisoner of War stationed near Konigshan. Eight men Lampersdorf, and the rest of us catch combined passenger and goods train to Trautenau and doing odd jobs. Myself on party of six picking out ice between the lines in front of station. Fairly easy day throughout. Caught goods train from Trautenau to Konigshan at 1605hrs, otherwise no passenger train till about 1900hrs. Two big trains of evacuee's go through Tratenau on way to Reichenberg, and to see the state of things, one wonders why they carry on. Soup and bread given out at Trautenau, and the men as bad as the kids in effort to get it. Evidently railway have not much for us to do, so Coy have given orders for us to be used digging defences or roadwork between here and Bernsdorf. Nothing definite done yet, so will go on railway work as usual tomorrow. German News: Mentions breakthroughs on the East and West fronts, but achieved at heavy losses, and their own troops fighting bravely to stem the enemy advance. A bit of OIL: Germany: fate will be decided within the next eight days. Posen not yet fallen, but Russian troops beyond it. Memel fallen Russians over Polish border and 20 miles into Germany proper. Germany suffering heavy losses, and

another 30 divisions cut off somewhere and being mopped up. Cold frosty morning with some wind blowing, and later in the day snow falling and coming up bitterly cold again in the evening.

Tuesday 30th January 1945
Prisoner of War stationed at Konigshan. Ten men to Lampersdorf, and the rest of us to Trautenau on various jobs. Myself on the boody job. Home to Lager on same time train as yesterday, being in about 1720hrs. Still plenty of evacuee's travelling through Trautenau by train, and plenty still going through Konigshan by road in wagons and some of them looking very tired on it. Reading during the evening. Nothing more said about going off the railway job this week. Russians said to be 75k past Posen, and elsewhere said to be going steadily forwards, and said to be coming up fast through parts of the Protectorate in the State of Moravia, and looks as if we may yet get encircled, which I hope does happen and save us shifting. Potatoes, soup, Red X stew and usual bread. Cold frosty morning with snow falling otherwise fairly mild day until 1600hrs.

Wednesday 31st January 1945
Prisoner of War stationed in Sudatenland. Eight men to Lampersdorf the rest of the gang to Trautenau on about four different jobs. Myself on party chipping and shovelling ice away from the rails by the station. Easy day, and home same as previous two days. Still plenty of evacuee's by train, did not see so many travelling by road today. One evacuee been in Australia for four years, about ten years ago, and spoke English. Also speaking to a Jerry Dr who had been a P.O.W. in Australia for two years and had been repatriated. Big load of lorries and cars came in this afternoon by train, evacuated from Glatz, so looks as if old Joe must be getting close to there. Reading during the evening. Nothing in the way of griff, except that Joe supposed to be 140k from Berlin. Potatoes, minced horse meat, soup and usual bread and marg. Very strong cold wind blowing this

morning, but otherwise not such a bad day and strong wind again in evening.

Thursday 1st February 1945
Prisoner of War stationed near Konigshan Sudatenland on railway working party, and previously of working party E388 at Bodisch in Sudatenland, and now attached to Stalag VIII B Gorlitz, but previously of VIII B Lamsdorf where we arrived from Island of Crete when taken P.O.W. by the Germans in June 1941. Ten men at Lampersdorf, and rest of us to Trautenau on various jobs, myself on party picking out ice from rails near railway station, and fairly easy day. Another big evacuee train went through to Reichenberg today and packed to the limit. Saw a party of our boys today, who came to Trautenau by train to go to the hospital, having come from Oppeln and marched for ten days, and these fell out through bad feet. Some Jerries came in today, whose feet looked to be in a terrible state, one bloke was being carried and others were shuffling along. Big train load of hospital staff arrived in Trautenau, evidently some hospital evacuated, fair number of nurses arrived also. Reading during the evening. Rumoured that Joe 63k from Berlin and his line follows down the full length of the Oder. Breslau still under shellfire. Joe evidently made landing somewhere in the North, but seems a bit fantastic to be true. Potato soup, Red X stew and bread. Strong mild wind blowing, and later heavy fog came up, and about 1600hrs rain set in, and big thaw now set in and the ground very slushy.

Friday 2nd February 1945
Prisoner of War in Sudatenland near Konigshan. Eight men to Lampersdorf, rest of us at Trautenau on different jobs, myself with three others on chipping ice away between rails by station, but having crook stomach which have had for three or four days, came back to Lager at midday. Rest in Lager at 1710hrs. 'Camp' papers up. Heard that another ten men arriving here tomorrow, also heard that Joe 62 kilometres from Berlin and that the Americans and English are on

the move again on the Western Front, also R.A.F. blew up eighteen bridges over the Rhine. More evacuee's leaving for Reichenberg today, pretty big train load. Roads quiet today. Plenty of arguments about the rooms tonight as to where the ten men coming tomorrow are going to fit in. Potatoes, soup, Red X stew, usual bread and marg, with weekly sugar ration. Strong wind blowing otherwise conditions fairly mild and heavy thaw continues.

Saturday 3rd February 1945
Prisoner of War stationed at Konigshan. Eight men to Parschnitz, rest to Trautenau and being ½ day, home at 1400hrs. Myself in Lager with bad stomach. Was to have gone to the Dr, but guards had to go for the other ten men, and during the morning got bad pains in the back and unable to lift any weight. The ten men were some who had come into Trautenau the other day from being on the march for 10 days, they are in a terrible state. Mail up today and received four being from Bernice, Mavis, Doreen and Alison, but luck still out in the mail from home. Froggies receive chit today for personal parcels, so maybe we will get some yet. Received 25 cigarettes today, but no food stuff as finished this last week. New restrictions around here, big German orders. Iron control over coal and food rations to do five weeks instead of the usual four. OIL: No communique for last 24 hours from Russian or Western fronts, but the latest was 2 ½ miles from Frankfurt 60 from Stettin, and elsewhere going well. Western front and British Armies said to be 2/3 of the way through the Western Wall. Montgomerys tactics said to have completely baffled the German Command. Between 70 and 80 wagons of evacuee's go past here today towards Trautenau. A little reading during the evening and to bed early. Mashed potatoes, horse meat, soup, with Red X stew in evening and usual bread. Fairly mild day with some sunshine in afternoon.

Sunday 4th February 1945
Prisoner of War stationed at Konigshan. In bed most of the day with bad back. Dr visits here today to see the ten men who arrived yesterday

and have all got this coming week off, having to go and see him again at the end of the week, also saw him myself and got six days off. Plenty of Army tracks on road this morning, also good many Jerry soldiers going by on push bikes and other conveniences. Reading most part of the day. Wrote card home and letter card to Alison. OIL: Joes mob starting to surround Berlin, and also pushing on towards Hamburg. Berlin also received heaviest amount of bombs in one raid last night, otherwise everything very tame. Porridge for breakfast, potatoes, soup midday with Red X stew at night and usual bread and margarine. Fairly mild with some wind, but otherwise reasonably nice sunny day.

Monday 5th February 1945
Prisoner of War stationed at Konigshan in Sudatenland. In camp today with bad back. About forty men being out to work mostly in Trautenau. Quite a few Army trucks went past here this morning towards Trautenau. Plenty of civilians still travelling past here towards Trautenau also, about 60 wagons going past today. Boys home a bit later than usual tonight, being 1730hrs before they got in. Myself spent the day fairly quietly reading and a little writng. German news: Mentions fairly heavy fighting in majority of places, but nothing much gained except at heavy loss. Fair number of air raids. Extract from Roosevelt, Stalin and Churchills meeting calls for giving up of all arms and unconditional capitulation and will be humanely treated by the Victors. (Griff) Big tank battle going on near Berlin. Heavy fighting along the whole of the Western front. Saarbrucken coming into news again, otherwise all quiet. Some talk of having to put away 80 loaves of bread aside for emergency cases. Potatoes, soup, Red X stew and usual bread. Fairly mild day with some wind and thawing out slightly making conditions wet.

Tuesday 6th February 1945
Prisoner of War at Konigshan, and in camp again today with bad back, and slept in till nearly midday. Reading, had a bath, and a little washing in afternoon. Rest of the gang at Schatzler, and Trautenau. Still plenty

of evacuee's going through in all types of vehicles. No German News, and nothing being in the way of OIL, so everything quiet. Potatoes, soup, Red X stew, bread, marg and weekly jam issue. Fairly mild day with some rain and thawing out heavily.

Wednesday 7th February 1945
Prisoner of War at Konigshan. In camp again today with a bad back, and passed the day away with reading and some washing. Eight men go to Schatzler and the rest to Trautenau. Some parcels up today and received 2 cigarette parcels, and Christmas parcel myself containing 1 kilo tin of jam, roll cake, fork & spoon, mirror, soap container, razor and razor blades, tooth brush and tooth brush container. No German News, but supposed to be big battle going on between Frankfurt and Berlin, things livening up again around Breslau. In the Stettin sector of the West front activity, middle sector fairly lively and the Northern Sector well into the Seigried defences, and heavy bombing going on. Still some activity of Army trucks going past here, and still a few civil evacuee's going past. Heard some rumbling in the distance today. Minced horsemeat, soup, potatoes with usual bread. A very mild day and thawing out.

Thursday 8th February 1945
Prisoner of War stationed at Konigshan. Still in Lager with bad back. Six men to Konigshan and the rest to Trautenau on various jobs. Home late again tonight getting in at 1745hrs. Still evacuee's going through by road, and also a big train load went through. Fair number of soldiers went past here on foot, some of horseback, and some in buggies and wagons, and still some Army trucks going past. No German News, but what OIL we hear was fairly good. Heavy fighting still going on towards Berlin, being over the last river and 56 kilo from the capital. One of Joe's spearheads pushing from the South towards Walderberg, another through the Protectorate, and another one further South. Result of Churchills, Roosevelts and Stalin's conference regarding Germany after the War. Russia take the Eastern portion

America the South Western portion and England the Northern part, and the finish of the war is imminent, so means that Germany will be cut up into three parts, and all leaders agreed on all parts of the conference. Potatoes, horsemeat and carrot soup, Red X stew and bread etc. Fairly cold wind blowing this morning, otherwise mild day, some sunshine and rain.

Friday 9th February 1945
Prisoner of War stationed in Sudatenland at Konigshan. Still in camp with a bad back, playing cards and reading otherwise quiet day. Six men to Konigshan and the rest to Trautenau on various jobs. Home at 1730hrs. At 0500hrs Volkstrumn holding a practice of putting up barracades across the road 100 yards from the barracks. More evacuees go past today, but somewhat quieter than yesterday, most of them from the Scholmz around the Breslau West area. Germans mention fighting around Leignitz area, but not confirmed by the BBC or Moscow. OIL: Heavy fighting between Frankfurt and Berlin. Place near Stettin by the name of Regnitz heavily bombed, big oil refineries here, and Russians only thirty kilo away. Railway line towards the Danzig and Prussian area cut. Big doings started on the Western front this morning and the first bulletin stated that they had advanced 4000 yards. Heavy bomber support flying practically wing tip to wing tip in front of our forces and no ACK/Ack or fighter opposition. Berlin bombed again and also supporting the Russians. On the Western side of the Rhine in the Southern Sector all German resistance practically ceased. Roosevelt, Stalin, Churchill discussions continue, says that Germany will pay for this war in money and goods, even if it takes generations, thus wiping out the military ideas of trying to be top dog. All going well in Burma. In the Phillipines Manilla is finished and fighting elsewhere on the island of Luzon on which Manilla stands. Late news Germans say the forts of Dunkirk and St Lorient still holding out and VI fire on London continues. Potatoes, soup, Red X stew, bread and weekly sugar ration. Fairly mild day with a little snow.

Saturday 10th February 1945

Prisoner of War stationed near Konigshan. Six men to Konigshan, rest of us off to Trautenau on various jobs, myself with three others unloaded some iron and wooden sleepers off wagon from Parschnitz, and then stacked some of them. Easy morning and being only a half day in Lager 1400hrs. Evening reading and playing cards. Early morning hours a lot of motor traffic passed through here, and continued to hold out practically all day and still plenty of evacuees going by in wagons and also by trains. Said to be a big battle going on in the West in the Northern sector, and in the Southern sector German resistance ceased on the West side of the Rhine, all left being pushed over to the East side. Still big battle between Frankfurt and Berlin going on with Joe advancing his front wider towards Stettin. Reported that Russian tanks have been seen on the other side of the mountains behind Landeshut which is not very far from here. Evidently our raid somewhere today as the railway signal alarm was out. Mashed potatoes, dumplings and soup midday, with Red X stew at night, usual bread and ten to a pound of marg. Mild morning trying to snow, and came out a nice afternoon.

Sunday 11th February 1945

Prisoner of War in Sudatenland stationed near Konigshan. No work today and in bed till 0800hrs. During the day reading, wrote card home and taking things quietly in general. Still evacuees pouring past here, and still plenty of Army trucks also, evacuee trains, and Army trucks going by train. Still big battle going on in the West, and rumoured that Jerry admits Leignitz fallen, otherwise nothing of note. Potato soup, Red X stew, and usual bread. Very mild day with plenty of sunshine for most part of the day.

Monday 12th February 1945

Prisoner of War stationed near Konigshan. Six men at Konigshan, and owing to the fullness of the usual train, could not go till after 1000hrs to Trautenau, so cleaned away a little snow and had Freistig in the meantime. This train also crowded, but managed to get us on and in Trautenau 1100hrs. Up till midday stacked some sleepers, and after dinner went down line towards Parschnitz and cleaning out drain by railway line and finished work about 1515hrs, so had an exceptionally easy day. Big convoy of Air Force gear and trucks came into Trautenau by road this afternoon, being about 150 and 200 trucks and cars in all. Also more and more evacuees by road and train coming from over many parts of Germany. Trains packed with trucks, pontoon bridges, boats and rafts and to the limit with evacuees. Two Red X trains through here today – and Gorlitz supposed to have been evacuated and other places around here have orders to be ready. Joe still going ahead and many more towns captured and pushing towards others. Breslau surrounded. Five big battles going on in the West in preparation for the final do, after the Churchill, Stalin, Roosevelt conference in Black Sea. Twenty-five Froggie cigarettes up. Potatoes, soup, and usual bread, marg with weekly jam issue. Mild day with fair amount of sunshine.

Tuesday 13th February 1945
Prisoner of War stationed at Konigshan. Six men to Schatzler, and rest of us to Freiheit and Trautenau. Myself at Trautenau and on same job as yesterday, cleaning out ditch between Trautenau and Parschnitz. Easy day again and finished work about 1515hrs. In Lager about 1740hrs. More and more evacuee wagons on the road again today, also many on foot and bicycles, and also trucks and cars of the Army by the dozen, and extra trains for evacuees, also some standing in open truck coal wagons. Two Red X trains also arrive in Trautenau again this afternoon. Trucks still going past here at 2000hrs, and plenty of congestion about the roads with the continuous stream of traffic. OIL: Joe still pushing onward, and more towns captured, pushing past Gorlitz towards Dresden, and now 100 kilometres from Dresden. Around Frankfurt and towards Stettin, the front being broadened and

strengthened. A couple of spearheads also going South East of Berlin. On the West front few more towns taken, and many groups being encircled and mopped up, taking 5000 prisoners in one lot. In Burma still fighting around Mandalay, Phillipine Islands, Manilla practically cleaned out, while those in the centre of the island being compressed and practically cleaned out. Churchill Stalin and Roosevelts conference finished and all agreements reached as to the future of Germany after the War, also the smaller states Poland and Greece question. The Army, Navy, and Air Force will be completely demobilized, and not allowed to rise again, while all war industry factories will be broken down for other purposes, and all Nazi Officers will be brought to justice after the war, and Germany must be completely democratic. Big meeting of all nations to be held in America on April 26th for the fostering of good feeling and fellowship etc. Reading during the evening. Potatoes, soup, Red X stew usual bread. Very mild day with some snow falling and heavy fog in afternoon.

Wednesday 14th February 1945
Prisoner of War stationed at Konigshan. Six men at Lampersdorf and rest of us of about thirty six working on a drain near Konigshan and Schatzler, because of both work trains to Trautenau were too overcrowded with passengers and evacuees. Did not start work till about 1100hrs and finished at 1545hrs, and came back to camp practically straight away, being in camp at 1630hrs. Train loads of evacuees going past again, and many in open coal wagons, and by wagon on the roads, continuous stream all day, at one period they moved about a ¼ mile in an hour and a half, having to up a bit of a hill, and road not the best, as they have to make a detour through Lampersdorf now leaving the main road to the Army traffic. From 1230hrs heard continuous rumbling in the direction of Herschberg. Sounded like bombing, but some say it was the mountain artillery there. OIL: Joe still pushing towards Dresden, and the RAF and American Air Force now co-operating with him, and Dresden bombed for the first time with 800 planes,

and no opposition met and oil refineries at Magdeburg also done over by 600 planes, and also oil refinery at Leipging, 16 planes lost in these operations. In the Southern section two spearheads making towards Vienna. In the West cleaning out pockets. Phillippine naval base captured 15 miles from Manilla, otherwise news fairly quiet. Mashed potatoes, minced horsemeat, soup and dumplings, usual bread and marg. Mild morning with sleet and rain but cleared away except for a few spots of snow and wind blowing continued mild throughout.

Thursday 15th February 1945
Prisoner of War stationed at Konigshan. Managed to get to Trautenau this morning by the early train, everybody going there except for two at Parschnitz, some unloading coke, some working on the barracks, and myself with ten others cleaning out drain along the railway line between Parschnitz Ort and Trautenau. Easy day throughout finishing at 1515hrs, and in Lager at 1720hrs. Air raid alarm today. Still plenty of evacuees going through Trautenau by rail and road, and lots of other goods by rail. Saw three tanks today. Some more of our boys passed through the march today from Blackhammer, been on the road for a month, were on the way to Gorlitz, but now think they are going to Reichenberg. OIL: Joe pushing forward to Dresden through Gorlitz and many other towns, also coming towards the Ruhbank area, not such a great distance from here. Encirclement of Berlin continues today making towards Cottsburg, and said to be 29 Panzer divisions there, this place was also heavily bombed by RAF. Dresden done over again also Leipzig and only six planes lost. Budapest finished and having taken 123000 prisoners. Spearheads towards Vienna continue. Said to be only 50 kilometres from Braunau this morning. In the West all going well, Jerries losing enormous amount of material and manpower. In the Pacific America making a big Naval Base of Guam, which is near to Japan and will now be used as base for future operations. Quiet evening. Potatoes, soup, Red X stew. Very mild day with a little rain.

Friday 16th February 1945
Prisoner of War in Sudatenland. Eight men to Lampersdorf, two at Parschnitz, and the rest to Trautenau, some unloading coke, some working on barracks, and myself with six others cleaning out drain by railway line, have been on it about four days and nothing to show for it yet. Finished at 1515hrs and in Lager about 1745hrs. Still an endless stream of evacuees going through Trautenau, more than ever walking, but railway a little quieter today. Two of the boys saw a couple of postons who had brought some of the boys from Lamsdorf to Gorlitz, and said that many of the boys had died on the way for the lack of food etc. Heard that 300 evacuees travelling in open trucks had died through cold and exposure to the open air. Still fair bit of Army stuff going by road. Saw an amusing incident today when General got hold of a Feld Webel and nearly shook him to pieces. Nothing going in the way of griff tonight, but heard at Trautenau that Joe's spearhead forty kilometres from Braunau. Heard planes over last night, and also heard gunfire in the distance this morning. Quiet evening. Potatoes, soup, Red X stew, usual bread and marg, also a Quark cheese ration. Fairly mild morning, but came up cold later in the day and cool evening.

Saturday 17th February 1945
Prisoner of War at Konigshan in Sudatenland. Six men to Lampersdorf, rest to Trautenau on different jobs, myself and eight others cleaning out drain between Trautenau and Parschnitz. On the boody job myself. Half day, knock off 1230hrs to catch 1301hr train, and in Lager about 1410hrs. Afternoon washing bathing and darning socks, also some reading during the evening. Still an endless stream of evacuees going Trautenau by roads on all modes of transport, and still a fair number by rail. Big hospital train went through today. Saw some of our boys on the road today from Glatz area, this being their fourth day, knew one of the chaps from the 28 Bn. OIL: Joe sixty kilometres from Danzig and on all other sectors progressing favourably assisted

at places by RAF and American Air Forces, and broken through one place at Breslau and street fighting going on. One aerodrome captured with 700 planes, as no petrol to get them out. Joe bring tanks by rail practically to the front line, and unloads them there. Western front all going well, in one sector 7000 prisoners taken and Canadians occupy 16 kilometres of the Rhine. Also Canadian Army and English Army going forward to occupy to evidently important places to Jerry, as he is fighting strongly there, and in another place 8 more divisions brought in but to not much affect. Dresden still being bombed and Frankfurt on Maine, also by Air Force 1800 goods wagons shop up, and also 200 engines, and many miles of railway bombed. Nothing much in Italy. 133000 prisoners now taken to date in Budapest. Submarine Porpoise been lost. Australians cleaning up in New Guinea and Solomon Islands. Tokyo, Yokohama, and another place Southern Japan bombed from planes off Aircraft Carriers, and practically no opposition. Mashed potatoes, soup, dumplings midday with Red X stew at night, and usual bread. Fair mild morning and turned out fairly nice afternoon. (Hear guns in distance day and night)

Sunday 18th February 1945
Prisoner of War stationed at Konigshan. In Lager today and not out of bed till 0830hrs. During morning fixing up kitbag in case of having to go on the march. Afternoon reading and wrote cards home and to Mrs Stephens, but don't think it much use writing them. Everybody voicing their opinion today, as to whether we will shift this week or be here next Sunday. Everyone practically got all their gear packed up ready in the event of a move. Nothing in the way of griff tonight, so hope we get some tomorrow. Roads past here a lot quieter as far as evacuees are concerned today, also not much military traffic. Macaroni for breakfast, soup and potatoes midday, Red X stew at night, usual bread, marg and weekly jam issue. Fairly mild day throughout, with some sunshine during the day. Fair amount of aircraft about during last night, and early morning hours. No sounds of artillery in the distance today.

Monday 19th February 1945
Prisoner of War at Konigshan. Six men to Lampersdorf, and the rest of us about forty at Trautenau on different jobs. Myself with ten others working one drain between Trautenau and Parschnitz Ort. Fairly easy time, finishing about 1500hrs. Late home tonight, because of other trains on line and running out of steam, nearly 1830hrs before in Lager. Still an endless stream of evacuees by road, the number that is walking now is amazing, also railway trains packed to the limit, and open wagons also in use. Saw some big artillery guns come in by rail today, and also cars and trucks, and fair amount of ammunition. Also saw two lots of our boys today from the Blackhammer area, having been on the road for a month. Could hear the rumble of guns from here tonight, and after dark could see the gun flashes and very lights in the air. Fair amount of aircraft over again last night, but think they are mostly Jerry troop carriers by the sound of them. OIL: Another landing on some Pacific Island, there being 800 American ships used in the operation. In Burma fighting on both sides of the river by Mandalay. Breslau being supplied by Air. Some big ammunition dump was to have been destroyed by Jerry, but captured by Joe's boys. Mannheim and Berlin bombed otherwise everything quiet. Reading during the evening, potatoes, Soup, Red X stew and usual bread. Fairly cold morning with biting breeze, but came out lovely sunny day and turned cool again in evening.

Tuesday 20th February 1945
Prisoner of War at Konigshan. Six men to Lampersdorf and the rest to Trautenau on various jobs, myself with eleven others between Trautenau and Parschnitz cleaning out drain by side of railway line. All the work that was done was harmless, finishing at 1525hrs. Train held up again by other trains and 1815hrs before reached Lager. Nothing doing in the way of griff from anywhere. Road a little quieter today with evacuees, but railway still busy and plenty of war material being moved about. To bed early tonight as not feeling too good. Potatoes,

soup and the last of the Red X stew, usual bread and marg. Fairly cool morning, but it came out a beautiful sunny day and followed by a cool evening again.

Wednesday 21st February 1945
Prisoner of War in Sudatenland stationed at Konigshan. Most of the boys at Trautenau today, and home a little earlier than last night. Myself went to the Dr and got four days off, having to walk there and back again getting in Lager at 1045hrs and spent most of the day in bed. (Couple of bombs dropped in Trautenau today by unknown plane.) OIL: Heard fighting going on in Breslau. Joe's spearhead pushing towards Vienna in South. Nothing much to report on the Western front. Dusseldorf, Dortmund, Mannheim and Berlin bombed. Island of latest American landing 600 miles from Japan, and have cut the Japanese forces in halves there. Churchill and Roosevelt having conference in Cairo with Hail Selassie, the heads of Egypt, Syria and Arab states. Potatoes, soup, bread and margarine. Cold morning, but nice sunny day until 1100hrs when came up dull and some snow falling during the evening.

Thursday 22nd February 1945
Prisoner of War stationed at Konigshan. In Lager with cold and bad back myself. 6 men working at Lampersdorf, rest at Trautenau. Home late tonight being 2100hrs, having waited for some reason or other at Parschnitz for three hours. Resting and reading during the day. Fair number of evacuees about again today, and roads also busy with Army trucks and cars, and tanks went up by rail past here today. OIL: Town captured by Joe 30 kilometres west of Gorlitz. Fighting continues in Breslau, being bombed at night by Russian Air Force, and heavily shelled by artillery. West front corridor between Rhine andd Maas cleaned out of Jerry troops, and in the Saar area progress being made. In Italy some success but fairly quiet. Fair number of divisions landed on the island and 600 miles from Japan. (Heavy bombing being

carried out in Western area of Germany, Berlin and Nurnberg being two places). Potatoes and soup with usual bread and marg. Fine early but later came over very dull and some snow fell.

Friday 23rd February 1945
Prisoner of War in Sudatenland stationed near Konigshan. In Lager myself with cold and bad back. Washed out a few clothes and reading. Six men to Lampersdorf, and rest to Trautenau. Still evacuees passing here, and plenty of military traffic about again. Heard that Herschberg was being evacuated, and that people around here were to prepare their carts ready in case of having to evacuate. OIL: Fighting North West of Berlin. Cottbuss under heavy shellfire. News of the Western front fairly quiet and elsewhere. Heaviest days raiding of the war took place yesterday from the Saar to Berlin. Communications, oil refineries, 9000 planes being over. Potatoes, soup, usual bread, marg and weekly sugar issue. Fairly dirty day being wind snow and rain.

Saturday 24th February 1945
Prisoner of War stationed at Konigshan. In Lager myself with cold and bad back, and those out working all at Trautenau unloading coke and coal. ½ day and in later at 1400hrs. Myself did a little washing, had a bath and some reading. OIL: Turkey declares war on Germany and Japan and puts 22 divisions in the field in Hungary, but does not commence hostilities until 1st March. Fierce fighting going on in Breslau, Posen fallen, and despite the orders of fighting to the last man gave in with enough food and arms to carry on for four months. Pushing towards Stargard in the North Western sector near Stettin. On Western front 1st and 9th American Armies under the temporary command of Montgomery are advancing and have captured eleven new villages and towns. Canadian Army pushing forward. Around Luxemborg area Jerries being cleaned out. Heavy bombing still being carried out and places too numerous to mention. Food situation in Holland bad and supplies to go in as soon as area cleaned out, and 30000 of the worst

cases to go to England for treatment. Midday thin soup and potatoes, at night meat and goulash, bread and weekly jam ration. Fairly dirty day with rain, snow and wind making conditions very wet underfoot.

Sunday 25th February 1945
Prisoner of War at Konigshan. No work today, slept in till 0830hrs. Reading most of the day and wrote card home. Heavy battle going on not far from here, by the sound of gunfire this morning, and plenty of plane activity overnight and early morning. Also fair amount of military traffic going by rail, and fair bit on the roads. Not so many evacuees about today. No OIL today, but heard this morning that Egypt and Palestine declared war on Germany, otherwise nothing else. Macaroni for breakfast with soup, potatoes midday, and meat and goulash in evening and usual bread. Fairly fine day, some wind and sunshine.

Monday 26th February 1945
Prisoner of War stationed at Konigshan. Train too crowded to go to work to Trautenau this morning, so waited in waiting room till 1030hrs and then decided 18 men to do a couple of jobs and the rest of us go home. Was fortunate enough to miss out on work and in Lager at 1115hrs. For the rest of the day reading and resting. OIL: Still heavy street fighting in Breslau, now being in Hindenburg square, also around the North West area of Berlin. Around the circle of Danzig 2000 more Germans killed and Konigshan another 1000 and some prisoners. Prisoners taken say it is terrible for the Army to see the way the civilians are carrying on. Says that German workers are carrying out their part of slowing up traffic in Germany successfully. Western front Goch now in Canadian hands and American 3rd Army only 15 miles from Cologne and say that there is no chance of German counter attacks now as our strength is far superior to the enemy's, and pity help them if they should attempt one. Heavy raids still going on, and big underground oil refinery between Munich and Nurnberg blown

up. General Alexander been in consultation with Tito in Yugo-Slavia, and looks like a big do about to commence in Italy. Still some evacuees going past by road, and fair number by rail, also some military traffic going up to the front. Soup, potatoes, usual bread and margarine. Cool windy morning with some rain and continued rough throughout the day, and rain in evening.

Tuesday 27th February 1945
Prisoner of War Sudatenland. All go to Trautenau today, some in yards unloading coal and coke, and myself with ten others cleaning out drain by railway line between Trautenau and Parschnitz Ort. Finished work at 1520hrs, and in Lager at 1750hrs. Fair amount of military traffic going about by train today and also evacuees, still plenty also going by road. Saw some more of our boys on the road today from Glatz and going to Arnau, and one of the original Bodisch boys Jack Horsburgh being amongst them, and some said they were going to Schatzler. Rumour of about 1200 English to make a lager at Schatzler, and also rumoured that German Administration from our Stalag VIIIA being established there, which is not very far from here. OIL: Still heavy fighting in Breslau. On Western front activity continues on practically all sectors in our favour. Heavy bombing of Berlin by American Air Force dropping 1200 tons of bombs and half a million incendiary bombs, bombing heard by Russian Army and Mosquitos over today, said big fires were still raging. Counter attacks of Jerries repulsed in Italy. Big speech by Churchill today which included all of what went on in the meeting of Churchill, Roosevelt and Stalin in the Crimea and what points we heard proved very interesting. Soup, potatoes, usual bread and marg. Dirty morning with some light rain, but fining up and some sunshine till about 1500hrs, when came over dull and raining again.

Wednesday 28th February 1945
Prisoner of War Konigshan. Eight men at Konigshan, six at Gabersdorf and the rest of us to Trautenau on different jobs. Myself first of all

went to the dentist and then came back and digging out ditch from maintenance line by barracks into the inside of the barracks. Home late again tonight being 1830hrs on arrival at Lager. Trautenau station very busy with getting evacuee trains away, and war material and troops. Some of the evacuees said to be going to Prague. OIL: Bishop of Beslau refused to evacuate and his palace said to be full of others who also refuse to leave. Gekov's Army in the Northern sector fairly active again and have cut the railway line between Stettin and Danzig, also near Danzig and pushing towards the Baltic Coast. On the Western front 1st and 9th American Army pushing well, also 3rd Army and the Canadians doing well, 15 kilometres from Cologne. Heavy bombing still being carried out, Berlin being done over for the 8th day and night in succession and also marshalling yards, before Bremner Pass done over. Archbishop in Greece speaks to 100000 people in Salonika. A little reading during the evening. Potatoes, soup, bread and marg. Very dull morning early, but later came out very nice sunny day.

Thursday 1st March 1945
Prisoner of War stationed at Konigshan in Sudatenland on railway working party and attached to Stalag VIII A Gorlitz, and originally of Stalag VIII B Lamsdorf, having been taken POW on Crete June 1941. Twelve men to Konigshan, eight at Gabersdorf, and the rest to Trautenau some unloading coal, others digging ditch by barracks nearly coalyard including myself. Finished at 1520hrs, and home a bit earlier tonight, but had to ride in open wagon and was none too warm. Evacuees by the hundred going through Trautenau by road and rail. Two special evacuee trains out today, and one more came in tonight, also big Red X train of civilians at Hersehberg. Still plenty of war material of all kinds including trucks, guns, tanks, ammunition and troops. OIL: Fighting still carrying on in Breslau around Neisse. In the North bit the Baltic coast, 140 miles from Danzig, having driven in from three points, and many troops surrounded. In the West everything going well 7 miles from Cologne, and in other sectors practically

through the West Wall, and broadening the fronts for future operations. 100 trucks captured in one place, also 11500 prisoners taken yesterday. New method of tank attack called the Blackout methods. Still heavy bombing being carried out. In the Pacific Manilla Harbour now open to American shipping. Latest island landed on, fighting in the main town and aerodrome captured, and Marines fighting further north. Spokesman in Japan says today that Japans position is serious and owing to success of operation in Burma plans have been altered somewhat. A little reading during the evening. Potatoes, soup, and usual bread. Fairly mild day, but very dull throughout.

Friday 2nd March 1945
Prisoner of War stationed at Konigshan. Twelve men at Konigshan, eight at Gabersdorf and the rest of us at Trautenau, some unloading coal, and myself and six others digging ditch by new barracks near Froggie Barracks. Had an argument today about old clothing or overalls for digging out these ditches in the wet. Home fairly late again tonight, getting in Lager at 1830hrs. Still plenty of evacuee trains leaving Trautenau, and fair numbers travelling by road, also plenty of military traffic going through, and railway yards, so congested, hardly knows where to shunt the stuff, while they make up the trains. Plenty of road blocks being built about the countryside here, where there are narrow places to pass through on roads or gullies between the hillsides. Said to be 400 of our boys started work at Lampersdorf mine yesterday. No OIL about tonight, so looking forward to some tomorrow. Potatoes, soup, usual bread and weekly sugar and jam ration. Cold morning with very heavy wind, snow falling at intervals throughout the day, with occasional burst of sunshine.

Saturday 3rd March 1945
Prisoner of War stationed at Konigshan. Twelve men to Konigshan, six Gabersdorf, and the rest to Trautenau. First of all myself to dentist to get false teeth, so did not start work until about 1045hrs, and finished

at 1230hrs being half day. Digging out ditch at barracks. Train held up, so did not get into Lager at 1420hrs. Afternoon had a bath, and did washing. Evacuee traffic at Trautenau shows no signs of dwindling yet and road seemed a little busier again today, and railway engines seem to have their work cut out getting the stuff clear of the yards. There being engines here now from Leignitz Breslau & other places, some out of order through numerous breakages. OIL: Very good. Jerries in full retreat on Western side of the Rhine and all Armies doing well, place not far from Dusseldorf taken, and many other places said to be 8 kilometres from Cologne. 7000 sorties over the West wall yesterday, which is practically made useless now. Heavy bombing also being carried out. German Air Force up yesterday and 67 shot down and thirty seven destroyed on the ground. VI damage in London, but good many shot down. Big artillery duels in Italy. Heavy fighting continues in Breslau and some of the Volkstromn lay down their arms. Big lot cut off in the Danzig, Stettin, Konigsberg area and fair numbers killed yesterday, otherwise eastern front news quiet. All going well around Phillipines and the new landing 600 miles from Japan. Thin soup at midday, with meat and goulash in evening with usual bread. Very windy morning and snow falling, which continued practically all day, despite the fact of the sun breaking through occassionally.

Sunday 4th March 1945
Prisoner of War stationed at Konigshan. In Lager today and slept in till nearly 0900hrs. A little sewing and reading most of the day, also wrote card home and one to Gladys. Had a meeting tonight to consider the new ration period, and will have to go on 1/8 loaf bread instead of 1/5 from Wednesday onwards. No griff today, but heard that our troops are completely through the West wall and that Finland has declared war on Germany. A little military traffic goes towards Liebau direction today, otherwise everything fairly quiet. Could hear artillery fire in the distance again today. Rations poor today, having no porridge, only one soup and potatoes with usual bread and

marg. Fairly fine day with some sunshine and a little snow falling in afternoon.

Monday 5th March 1945
Prisoner of War near Konigshan. Eight men Konigshan, eight to Gabersdorf and the rest of us to Trautenau, some unloading coal and some carting sleepers for new barracks and myself with six others loading a few sleepers till freistig, and from then till knock off time unloading some timber and finished work at 1530hrs, but got home very late, the train leaving Trautenau late and having to wait at Parschnitz for ½ hour, and got in Lager at 1915hrs. In open wagon and very cold. Ten chaps go away from here today, and ten others come in their place, there being one Aussie in the party. Quiet evening. OIL: Very good. Eastern front Zukov's army doing well in all the Northern sectors, and many German divisions cut off. On the Western front our troops pushing forward in all sectors, being all round Cologne and Germans in retreat in many places. Heavy bombing still being carried out. Eisenhower broadcasts to German civilians to keep off the roads, and in the cellars until our troops come along. 14th Army in Burma closing in on Mandalay. Still plenty of evacuee traffic about by road and rail, also military traffic by rail going backwards and forwards. Heavy rumbling heard in the distance again today. Trautenau railway yards very congested at present, and some very big railway engines knocking about, and railway workers from everywhere running around with nothing to do. Potatoes, soup, bread. Fairly cold morning and continued fairly cool throughout the day, and tried to snow once and came up very frosty in the evening.

Tuesday 6th March 1945
Prisoner of War stationed at Konigshan. Twelve men to Konigshan, eight to Bernsdorf, and the rest to Trautenau, some unloading coal, and myself with seven others digging out ditches for water pipe. Fairly easy day. Finished at 1530hrs, and home earlier than last night, getting

in at 1750hrs. Cologne completely surrounded, and 1/3 of it in our hands, and heavy fighting going on about the old Rhine river, and also pushing forward from Bonn. 17500 prisoners. Heavy bombing still going on everyhere. Eastern front nothing much mentioned and the 14th Army in Burma going well, having cut off 35000 Japs from their base. Reading during the evening. Hear the rumble of guns again today. Saw a few truck loads of mines go past when coming home tonight. Railways as busy as ever. Potatoes, soup, usual bread and marg. Frosty morning and fairly cold, but sun came through fairly early, and a little snow fell, otherwise passable day.

Wednesday 7th March 1945
Prisoner of War in Sudatenland near Konigshan. Eight men Konigshan, six Parschnitz, six to Freiheit, some at Trubenwasser and thirteen of us at Trautenau digging out trenches by barracks for water pipes. Finished at 1520hrs and in Lager at 1740hrs. Six more of the boys leave from here today going to Trubewasser, from there they are supposed to be going by hospital train to Bavaria, either tomorrow or Friday. Still evacuees going through Trautenau by train and also by road. Eastern front Joe's mob still pushing in the Northern sector around Danzig, and the Baltic coast. Western front all armies pushing forward, some near Bonn, and some towards Coblenz. In one sector advance 60 kilometres in 48 hrs. Jerries getting across the Rhine in ferries and any boats available, as most of the bridge area cut off. Still plenty of air activity on oil refineries and other important targets. Potatoes, soup, usual bread and marg. Heavy snow overnight, and still snowing this morning at 0900hrs, and plenty of wind, but at 0900hrs, sun came out and turned out real nice day.

Thursday 8th March 1945
Prisoner of War at Konigshan. Eight men to Konigshan, four Lampersdorf, six Gabersdorf, and the rest to Trautenau, and myself being with nine others digging out ditch by barracks. Finished

at 1520hrs but home late, not getting in lager till 1900hrs, taking 50 minutes from Parschnitz to Konigshan. Cologne finished, and Pattons Army advancing well, 3 miles from Bonn. On one bridgehead of the Rhine in Northern sector, Jerries giving heavy resistance and British Army advancing fast to help them. Usual bombing. Joe's army doing well Stettin practically surrounded, and 19000 prisoners taken yesterday, also away again on the Oder bridgehead. In Burma Mandalay being closed in on. Potatoes, soup, bread down to 1/6 loaf instead of 1/5 and usual marg and weekly jam issue. Frost this morning and later started to snow being dull throughout with the sun trying to get through. (Argument with one of the boys about the lights last night).

Friday 9th March 1945
Prisoner of War stationed at Konigshan. Some working at Konigshan, some at Gabersdorf and rest of the gang to Trautenau, myself being on party digging trench by barracks. Easy day again, but home late again, although knocking off at 1520hrs, not in camp till 1905hrs, being held up by trains. Still big evacuee trains going through Trautenau, also saw some big artillery guns in the station today. Heard heavy rumbling about 1250hrs today, shaking the boody, and then the sound of heavy gun fire throughout the whole afternoon. No (OIL) tonight. Potatoes, soup and bread. Frosty morning with some snow during the day, and fairly cold again at night.

Saturday 10th March 1945
Prisoner of War stationed at Konigshan. Twelve men at Konigshan, six to Gabersdorf, and others at Trautenau filling in and digging trench at barracks. Easy morning finishing at 1220hrs, being half day, catching 1301hr train home, but train late and did not reach camp till 1430hrs. Afternoon washing clothes, had bath and other odd jobs and in evening played cards. (OIL: very good. Joe's front 5 mile from Stettin. In the sectors Danzig and the Baltic, the cut of divisions have been further cut in half being cut up. 4000 killed yesterday and many prisoners

being taken. For security reasons nothing given of the middle east sector. On the Western front troops now over the Rhine, and taking out the detonators before Jerry could blow up the bridge, beating the Jerries to it, and now have 250 guns across and shelling Essen. Pushing on all other sectors, and shelling the Ruhr, also many prisoners being taken. A new type of weapon out, being used on the Sherman tanks, 200 men now doing the work of 2500. Still plenty of air raid activity in all sectors doing heavy damage with bombing. German Air Force refuses to come up during the day and comes up at night. Big columns seen coming down from North and they say wherever he weakens his forces he will pay dearly. In Burma everything going well, and the island not far from Japan, successes here also. Heard heavy gunfire again this morning. Thin soup and potatoes midday with meat and goulash in evening usual bread. A wet drizzly morning, but came out fairly fine afternoon, but heavy wind which increased to practically gale force at night.

Sunday 11th March 1945
Prisoner of War in Sudatenland. No work today, so fairly lazy day, reading and playing cards. No cards to write today, and no news so a somewhat dragging day. Thin soup, potatoes, midday with meat and goulash at night and bread, also had macaroni for breakfast. Fairly fine day throughout with some sunshine and came up cool again at night.

Monday 12th March 1945
Prisoner of War stationed at Konigshan. Twelve men working Konigshan, eight to Gabersdorf and the rest of the gang to Trautenau, myself being on party digging trench and some filling in for water pipes and slop water. Everything went very quietly with very little work, finishing at 1520hrs, but late home on account of waiting for trains, getting in camp at 1825hrs. German News: today says of counter attacks, and take back 28 places from the Russians, including Laukan,

Gorlitz, and Leignitz. OIL: Nothing much except for heavy bombing, and widening the bridge head on the Rhine, which is now three mile deep and nine mile wide. Forty seven enemy bombers attempt to destroy the bridge but gave up when half of them were shot down. Said to be heavy losses for us at the bridgehead. Essen one of the places heavily bombed and said to be 35000 civilians killed. 114000 prisoners recently taken. German prison camp South Wales all escape and said to be armed and an area 100 square miles surrounded by troops and air force co-operating. Reading during evening. Potatoes, soup, usual bread and marg. Fairly mild morning with some wind, but turned out reasonably warm day with some sunshine.

Tuesday 13th March 1945
Prisoner of War stationed at Konigshan. Twelve men Konigshan, seven Gabersdorf, and the rest of Trautenau on various jobs, first of all till 1000hrs unloading cement pipes, and after digging out ditch by barracks for drain water. Miller away most of the afternoon, so not much work done. Some of the boys managed to get into a wagon of flour today with some busted bags, and of course some of it returned to the lager, also plenty of traffic done in the old bread trade these days. In lager again late tonight being 1815hrs. Still plenty of evacuees about Trautenau. Bridgehead over the Rhine being widened, and still plenty of bombing being carried out, and elsewhere other armies pushing forward and taking many prisoners. The so called Volkstromm only too pleased to hand over their arms and be done with it all. Around Danzig and Gardinia area Joe pushing well, and some place near Stettin has fallen, and in Hungary by some lake heavy fighting goes on, otherwise other Eastern front news scarce. Big raid by super Fortresses on some part of Japan, shows an area of 40 square miles burnt out, which included the largest aircraft factory in Japan. Americans make landing on another island in the Pacific. Potatoes, soup, 1/6 loaf bread and marg. Fairly mild this morning and continued same thoughout the day.

Rumour from Gabersdorf party of 300 Red X food parcels around for camps in this area, which will not amount to much.

Wednesday 14th March 1945
Prisoner of War in Sudatenland. Eight men Lampersdorf, seven Gabersdorf, and fourteen to Trautenau, and myself with fifteen others went on to Trubenwasser, also the Zcek gang here, and are relaying an old line from the points, Freitheit end across a field to a factory there, which is probably going to be used as a storage for ammunition, there being seven loads of bomb there now, and some wagons of ammo. Helped to unload a slack wagon, and pushed a couple around, otherwise did practically nothing, finishing at 1445hrs, as had to walk to Trautenau to catch train back to Lager, which was late again tonight, having to wait at Parschnitz for other trains for an hour and in lager at 1900hrs. Could hear the sound of gunfire again today. No Oil tonight. Reading a little during the evening. Soup, meat, potatoes, bread and marg and weekly jam issue. Mild morning which continued the same throughout the day with a cool evening.

Thursday 15th March 1945
Prisoner of War stationed at Konigshan. Eight men Lampersdorf, seven Gabersdorf, fourteen Trautenau, and the rest of us including myself at Trubenwasser on continuation of job of yesterday. Carrying sleepers today about 50 to 60 yards, and did not feel much like work, and had rows with the Gaffir and the Postern, telling him the time we get in at night and not much grub. He also said he had to do 14hrs out, but told him he did no Arbeit and he didn't like it. Had to walk to Trautenau again to catch the train leaving at 1445hrs, and took us a full hour and only just made it. Home a little earlier tonight, not having to wait at Parschnitz so long getting in at 1745hrs. (Pattons Army pushing towards Coblenz, and bridgehead over the Rhine widened to eleven miles and elsewhere pushing well. Still plenty of bombing being carried out and using a ten ton bomb for the first time. Aroung Stettin and Northern sectors Joe

carries on, otherwise nothing much mentioned, except that Churchill hoped to have us out by the end of the summer. Meat, soup, meat, potatoes and usual bread. Mild morning with a little fog, which later turned into a beautiful sunny day and nice evening. Heard the sound of ack/ack fire and bombing in the distance today.

Friday 16th March 1945
Prisoner of War stationed at Konigshan. Eight men Konigshan, seven Gabersdorf, twelve Trautenau and nineteen including myself at Trubenwasser in continuation of previous two days job. Carted few sleepers, rails and unloading slack. Finished about 1430hrs as had to walk to Trautenau again for home train. Had easy day. Managed to catch empty evacuee train home tonight and in camp 1720hrs. Reading during the evening. Planes kicking about today and leaflets said to have been dropped at Leibau telling Jerry to pack in. Except one of these days to get raid around here with the amount of rail traffic about. Heard the sound of gun fire, and bombing again today. OIL:Joe busy again between Gorlitz and Frankfurt and around Stettin. Said to be over the West of the Oder. In the sector around the Baltic all going well. Western front French pushing from the South, 3rd Army from the North, and another from the middle getting Jerry in a triangle, and said to be making things awkward for Jerry. Bridgehead widened. Ruhr said to be cut off from everything now. Rail and road communications being bombed. 6000 planes over Germany yesterday, and Berlin bombed day and night for the 26th day in succession. Oil refineries bombed and many railway coaches, and motor transport vehicles done over. Potatoes, soup, 1/6 loaf bread and marg, with weekly sugar ration. Fairly mild morning with some fog in Trautenau, and came out a beautiful day again with plenty of sunshine and snow now practically disappeared, and a beautiful moonlight night.

Saturday 17th March 1945
Prisoner of War in Sudatenland. Eight men Konigshan, seven Bernsdorf and rest of us Trautenau. On boody job myself. Half day,

so in lager at 1400hrs. Air raid alarm at Trautenau at just after midday. Afternoon bathing, washing clothes and cleaning up in general. Evening reading and playing cards. OIL: good. Western front pushing on practically all fronts, and have the Jerries in a triangle of the Mosel and the Rhine. Bridgehead widened. Still plenty of air raids being carried out and much railway and transport wrecked. Eastern front plenty of activity most sectors and along Baltic coast, another wedge driven in. Konigshan covered with smoke from fires. Sabotage and Norway, and transport difficulties getting bad in Norway. S. S and Volkstrom in Austria get mixed up with each other. Pacific zone – Aussies cleaning out New Britain, Caroline and other islands. Georgina Island in American hands, and proved the costliest operation to date for the Americans. Heavy air raids on Japan and eleven subs sink 75 ships in recent patrol. Potatoes, soup midday, with meat and goulash at night and usual bread. Mild morning with sprinkling of rain, which set in heavier at midday and continued showers during the afternoon.

Sunday 18th March 1945
Prisoner of War stationed at Konigshan. No work today, so slept in till 0830hrs. Reading and resting most of the day, as not feeling too good. Nothing much in the way of oil, except that Coblenz is supposed to have fallen, and 50 k from Frankfurt on Main. People of Frankfurt-on-Main to stop in their cellars or else also Ludwigschafen. Had another row with Taffe (The Welshman this afternoon – boys play music for cigarettes.) Soup midday with potatoes, and meat and goulash in evening, bread and marg. Fairly mild day throughout with some rain and sunshine.

Monday 19th March 1945
Prisoner of War at Konigshan. Six men Konigshan, six Bernsdorf, twelve Trautenau, and with myself eighteen of us at Trubbenwasser continuing work on branch line from points. Not feeling too good and did not do much work. Goods train to Freiheit today, so returned by it instead of walking, getting there about 1520hrs. Train home running

fairly well tonight and in lager at 1745hrs. A little reading during the evening. OIL: Eastern front around the Baltic coast and Stettin Joe pushing strongly. Western front Coblenz fallen, and bridgehead widened and pushing on practically the whole front. Planes very active and Berlin done over for 27th day and night in succession; and fighters escorting bombers went on and gave Joe a hand in fighting operations. Potatoes, soup, 1/6 bread and marg. Margarine ration cut down to practically nothing. Mild morning with a dull day, but fairly warm.

Tuesday 20th March 1945
Prisoner of War Sudatenland. Men at Konigshan, Bernsdorf, Trautenau. Stayed in camp myself as not too good, and day passed terribly slow, so will be glad to get out tomorrow I hope. Air raid alarm in Trautenau today and a couple of planes seen high up. Russian planes said to have been around last night. OIL: Joe pushing around Stettin, and around Konigsberg, and Danzig in plenty of smoke and blazing ruins. West front bridgehead widened and deepened and 7th American Army pushing forwards, yesterday taking 8000 prisoners. Still plenty of bombing and Berlin visited for 28th day and night. Raid from Italy on place not far from Munich. Bremer Pass and surroundings done over, say that Italy has been cut off through here for 51 days. Food situation in most of Europe getting bad. In Burma North of Mandalay, another town taken and Mandalay some of the big forts taken. Americans make another landing on Island in the Phillipines group, also Super Fortresses raid main postmain port of Japan. Big discussion of Air Services etc after the war held in South Africa, and Britain building planes of 110 tons to carry 100 passengers. Potatoes, soup, usual 1/6 loaf of bread and marg and weekly issue of jam got honey in its place. Fairly mild day throughout with some sunshine and strong winds.

Wednesday 21st March 1945
Prisoner of War stationed at Konigshan. Seven men to Bernsdorf, nine to Konigshan and the rest of us to Trautenau, myself on barracks

party digging out trench for slop water drain. Very easy day finishing at 1520hrs, and train home fairly well to time, and in lager at 1750hrs. Big evacuee train goes through Trautenau today out Hohenfels way with trucks, troops and telephone equipment, and also fair number of Jerries leaving by train tonight. OIL: Saarbrucken finished and several other places fallen now 7k from Ludwigschafen, and have just about cleaned out the triangle having taken 30000 prisoners. On the bridgehead at Remagen centre span broken down, but fixed up again and everything going well. Jerry resistance weakening at the bridgehead and troops moving back being machine gunned from the air. Berlin done over for 29th night in succession, and 15 towns East of the Rhine, have been warned by Eisenhower to get out. Refineries and tank factories in Austria bombed from Italy. East front around Stettin Joe closing in on the town and Danzig and Konigsberg being closed in on. In Burma Mandalay is now finished. In big attack on part of the Jap fleet amongst some of the islands near Japan many warships were damaged and sunk, also many freighters, these operations being carried out by planes from aircraft carriers, and the fleet. Japs also lost 200 planes, and American losses 43 planes and one warship heavily damaged. A little reading during the evening. Potatoes, meat, soup and usual bread. Dull day throughout with attempts at trying to rain and fairly cold wind blowing.

Thursday 22nd March 1945
Prisoner of War at Konigshan. Men at Konigshan, Bernsdorf, one party at Trautenau, and myself on Millers party of twelve stomping between Trautenau and Parschnitz Ort. Reasonable day and knocked off about 1520hrs. Left Trautenau very late tonight, and then had to wait on shunting at Parschnitz, and it was 1940hrs before we got into the lager. Air raid alarm goes twice today and saw 20 of our planes go over, and also heard the sound of bombing, the heaviest I have heard it yet. Rumour heard today that there are supposed to be 85 wagons of Red X Food parcels on their way from Geneva to Arnau or are already there. Evidently some clothing getting through as Fred has to

go to Trautenau tomorrow to pick some up. OIL: Very good tonight. American tanks go straight through Ludwigschafen to try and reach bridgehead on Rhine before Jerry blew it up, but failed to get there in time. Saargemund also fallen, and one or two other places. In the Rhine – Mosel triangle 54000 prisoners now taken. Bridgehead widened and deepened to the extent of 40 by 13 miles. Jerry officers and men giving themselves up by the thousand, the officers with their best uniforms and suitcases packed saying that the show is finished, and 16 mile convoy picked out by air and completely destroyed. Heavy damage everywhere by bombing and machine gunning, and planes been over practically since daylight yesterday morning and in Northern Germany portion of the Rhine practically every town is in flames, and with the smoke screen of Montgomery preparations, there is nothing but a fall of smoke. Oil refineries in Leipzig bombed and Berlin again a target. 20000 foreign workers released as the result of our advances. Eastern front still fighting in Breslau and receiving bombing by Russians. Danzig and Konigshan closing in and 4000 killed in one place yesterday. Kopenhagen bombed and 500 Gestapo said to have been killed, they have been badly persecuting the people for refusing to work. In Burma Mandalay said to have been the biggest supply depot of that area for Burma and Rangoon bombed. In Pacific latest island landed on, capital taken. Two destroyers and freighter destroyed off Japan. Japanese spokesman says loss of the latest island dealt Japan their greatest blow, talk of maybe a landing on the mainland of Japan to follow shortly. Quiet evening. Meat, soup, potatoes and bread. Mild morning followed by a practically cloudless sunny day and beautiful mild evening with the moon shining.

Friday 23rd March 1945
Prisoner of War in Sudatenland. Some at Konigshan seven Bernsdorf, eight to Parschnitz and rest of the gang to Trautenau, some on barracks job, and the rest of us stomping between Trautenau and Parschnitz-Ort. Fairly easy day till 1520hrs, when Miller and Starkie came out

with that we had to work till 1630hrs, so finished up arguing about it all till 1600hrs and nothing done, so knocked off and marched to station, only to see the train disappearing out, and had to catch the 1645hr train which got to Parschnitz 1705hrs and then had to wait here for 2¼ hrs for four trains from Konigshan to come through, one being coal train, passenger train, and two trainloads of transport with troops going through the Protectorate, and evidently got to lager at 2030hrs, and all have refused to go to work tomorrow, us who were at Trautenau 23 in all. Air raid again today and heard the sound of bombing, the heaviest have heard the sound of yet, and did not seem to be very far away. OIL: Very good. Joe away again in the area not far from Neisse around Neustadt and has advanced quite a few kilo's and now in the Protectorate, taking many prisoners, guns, trucks and tanks. Also the Danzig, Konigsberg, Stettin area carries on with success. In the West fighting in Ludwigschajen and another place fallen and many prisoners, guns and transport captured in the Rhine and Mosel triangle. Montgomery preparing for a big attack under cover of a heavy smokescreen, which is to be compared with D Day and more or less have Jerry guessing as to when and where they will strike, as they can come off equally as well as in about four places. Heavy bombing activity still being carrried out all over Northern Germany and dense clouds of smoke everywhere. German E boats attack convoy, and four E boats shot up without damage to our convoy. Danish people thank the R.A.F. for their raid on the Gestpo Head Quarters in Copenhagen. Eisenhower asks workers in area already knocked about not to move to other areas, and help prolong the war, as it will not do any good, as they are in the last weeks of the war. In Burma moving towards Rangoon and Americans make another landing on one of the Pacific Islands. 3 Jap ships sunk off Japan, and Australian Prime Minister says Japan has a lot to answer for her treatment of Australian Prisoners of War. Potatoes, soup, bread, marg and sugar issue. Sight frost this morning which turned out to be a practically cloudless and beautiful sunny day and cool moonlight evening.

Saturday 24th March 194

Prisoner of War at Konigshan. Only about twenty three go out to work this morning as twenty three of us who last night said we were not going, did not go, although guards came up and told us we were to go, so Fred, Feld'Wabel and Voight are away to Trautenau to see the Coy & Starkie about it all, so will not know the verdict of it all before 1400hrs. They say we are likely to get nine days straff, but this is not worrying us one bit. During morning washing clothes, had bath, and played five games of crib. In the afternoon resting and reading, and in the evening played poker. OIL: Montgomerys Army breaks out over the Rhine this morning with artillery, tank, and airborne support. 51st Highland Regiment one of the first over. Artillery barrage the biggest in history 1500 prisoners taken and resistance weakening. Bradley over the Rhine by Mainze, pushing steadily towards bridgehead at Remagen; and pushing steadily outwards. Bridgehead at Ramagen lengthened and widened. Joe still closing in on Danzig, Konigsberg, Gardinia and Stettin, also pushed over the Oder in drive towards Berlin, and in Hungary broken out again in a drive towards Marie. Ostrov in the Protectorate. Churchill with Montgomery in the attack, and since February 7th Germany has had a ¼ million casualties. Lancasters used to transport the Air borne troops. In Burma English 14th Army pushing towards the South and have advanced 75 miles. Soup, potatoes, midday with meat and goulash in evening and usual bread. Frosty morning with perfect sunny spring day and cloudless moonlight evening.

P.S. Received some clothing and boots from Lamsdorf. Result of visit to Starkie and Coy Head Quarters this morning, say we have to do 54 hours a week, and if we have done them by Friday night, do not have to go to work on Saturday, time to include walking to station to and from the lager. Starkie wanted to straff us five marks, but Coy said 'No' as we had right on our side, by stopping home this morning.

Sunday 25th March 1945

Prisoner of War at Konigshan. No work today, so slept in till 0800hrs. During the day resting, reading or playing cards. No letter cards etc for writing. OIL: Good. Joe pushing on 100k wide and 75k deep by the Platten lake in Hungary and the latest was 30k from the Danube in his drive towards Vienna, also in the sector towards the Protectorate still going steadily forwards, and in the Danzig or Northern sector still going well. Western front news excellent. Montgomery Army pushing strongly and taking 8000 prisoners to date, many of them standing in groups waiting to be taken, and some of them crying. 10000 sorties made yesterday and the bombing is terrific everywhere, 3000 heavy planes escorted by 2000 fighters. Heavy Halifax planes dropped their supplies 30 metres from the ground, and all German aerodromes were heavily bombed to prevent German Air Force attempting to come to the attack. In the Patton area 18000 prisoners taken yesterday, and everywhere going steadily forward. In Burma 14th Army take another town, also Americans land on another island between Formosa and Japanese mainland. Porridge for breakfast with soup and potatoes midday, followed by goulash at night and bread ration. Very nice sunny day, but fairly strong wind blowing, spoilt the day.

Monday 26th March 1945

Prisoner of War in Sudatenland. Five men Konigshan, seven Bernsdorf, eight Parschnitz, four Trubenwasser and rest of gang to Trautenau, one gang at barracks, and myself and eleven others stomping between Trautenau and Parschnitz-Ort. Fairly easy day but not allowed to catch the 1553hr train, with the result it was 1925hrs before we got home. Those of us who were at Trautenau, but the rest home by 1715hrs. OIL: Everything still going well on the Western front, still taking many prisoners, and bombing still being carried out, and resistance being not too heavy, and pushed crack German parachutist division back 3k. In Eastern front in Hungary Joe pushing strongly towards the knee of the

Danube. Around Konigberg this is the only place left in East Prussia. In Pacific Americans sink two Jap destroyers, one escort vessel as well as three transport vessels, and heavy bombing carried out over Japan today. Quiet evening. Potatoes, soup, bread, marg and jam issue. Fairly warm morning, and also fairly warm sunny day throughout except for a few clouds.

Tuesday 27th March 1945
Prisoner of War stationed at Konigshan. Usual gangs at Konigshan, Bernsdorf, Parschnitz, and the rest to Trautenau, some being on the barrack job, and myself with eleven others stomping between Trautenau and Parschnitz-Ort. Easy day and instead of walking to Trautenau did a quick walk to Parschnitz and caught the 1553hr train and in camp at 1730hrs. Montgomery still continues to widen and deepen his bridgehead in the Northern Western front, and on the Middle western front Patton is going very strongly, and elsewhere on this front everything going well. In Southern Hungary Joe pushing strongly toward the Austrian border and in Danzig still closing in. In Burma in the push south towards Rangoon another town taken. Southern Islands of Japan strongly bombed. Many ships sunk in Rangoon in last few days. Lloyd George dead. A little reading during the evening. Potatoes, soup, usual bread. Dull day throughout with very little sunshine.

Wednesday 28th March 1945
Prisoner of War at Konigshan. Usual gangs at various places, and at Trautenau some on barracks job, while myself and eleven others between Trautenau and Parsccnitz-Ort on stomping and changing broken rail in Trautenau yards. Every day taking things very easy, as do not get enough rations these days to feel like work. Have to work till 1630hrs and not allowed to catch the train, until the one that leaves at 1645hrs, which tonight did not leave Trautenau until about 1815hrs with the result did not get home till 1930hrs. A quiet evening.

Everything on Western front going well, all Armies pushing forward. Pattons army being 200k over the Rhine and 150k from the Czeck border, and Montgomery going well over the new bridgehead, many thousands of prisoners being taken. At the present rate of lorries and transport going over the Rhine equals about 50000 a day. Hodges with tank Army says he hopes to meet up with old Joe before Pattons Army. Still heavy bombing being carried out. S/S fighting against us in street fighting in Frankfurt-On-Main. In Hungary Joe's Army still going steadily ahead to the Austrian border and in Danzig further closing in. Commentator says it will be lucky if there is any German resistance by May 1st. Potatoes, meat, soup, bread and marg. Dull day with attempts to rain, which it finally did, set in at 1500hrs, still raining at 1930hrs.

P.S. Caught taking sugar from wagon today, and had the railway police on to us, and made put it back.

Thursday 29th March 1945
Prisoner of War at Konigshan. Usual gangs at various places, and the rest of us to Trautenau, one gang on unloading timber and myself on party replacing broken rail. More arguing today regarding the work and time we knock off, and Starkie would listen to none of us, and says travelling time does not count and tonight Miller wanted rails shifted on knock off time, so walked off and left him and had the railway police on us again today, making two days in a row. Caught Zceck train from Trautenau to Parschnitz and managed to get the earlier train, than supposed, which was still waiting at Parschnitz and getting in lager at 1830hrs. News still good, many prisoners being taken, and towns too numerous to mention, meeting no resistance in South anywhere. Past Numberg where the boys went to, so maybe now they are out of it. Frankfurt finished. Sabotage going on in Austria, and some big bug been shot. Some German Nazi already have fled to Switzerland. Planes able to operate over both fronts now practically within ½ hour

flying time. Joe pushing on Southern front over Austrian border, 75k from Vienna. Bridge blown up by entrance to Kopenhagen Harbour and a German convoy evidently for Norway is unuable to get out. Food questions in Europe – some serious thinking, especially in Holland where things are very critical. 900000 tons have already come into Europe. France receives loan of hundred million pounds. American Air Force when finished in Europe to be used for the crippling of Japanese industries. Potatoes, soup, usual bread. Practically dull day throughout, except for little sunshine after midday and cool evening.

Friday 30th March 1945
Prisoner of War at Konigshan. Seven men Bernsdorf, four Konigshan, eight Parschnitz, four Freiheit and the rest to Trautenau, some unloading timber, and with five others myself, replacing broken rails until 1220hrs, when had to leave the job and all called out, including Zceck gang from Parschnitz, to repair line where trucks of coal had come off the line, and tore up the track for about a chain. Finished work ourselves at 1700hrs, on train at 1710hrs, but it was nearly 1900hrs before we left Trautenau, eventually reaching lager at 2015hrs. More arguments with Starkie, about the time we have to work and the late hours. Actually us Trautenau gang had put in our number of hours by Friday night and do not want to go to work tomorrow, but Jerry Feld-Wabel says we cannot stay in, unless have a written order from the Coy, so going to work tomorrow, in the hope of something being done next week. Fred went to Trautenau today to see if he could get some vegetables and was lucky enough to get some swedes and carrots, also dried onions and cabbage, costing in all 234 Marks or equivalent to about 15 Pound, this is on the black market, but hopes to get some more next week. OIL: Very good again tonight. Our tanks rolling through Germany practically all western front with not much resistance, and taking thousands of prisoners. Bombing continues in Northern sector. On Eastern front in Southern sector Joe has pushed over the Austrian border taking many prisoners and not very far from Vienna. Northern

sector Danzig and Gardinia finished. In Pacific more air raids over Japan. Potatoes, soup, usual bread, marg and a weekly sugar issue. A dull day with some rain coming on during afternoon and evening.

Saturday 31st March 1945
Prisoner of War at Konigshan. Usual gangs at various places, and main party to Trautenau. On starting out this morning Feld-Wabel told us Trautenau workers, that we would have Tuesday off, so will have a long weekend, as have Easter Monday off as well. On boody job myself this morning, and half day coming home on 1310hrs train and in camp at 1400hrs. Bit of a scare in Trautenau and area about 1100hrs, as some Russian fighter planes circled over Trautenau, have never seen the guard or railway blokes move so quickly, cleared out of railway yards. Our guard grabbed his rifle and off without a word to us. Planes did not stay long though. Eight of the boys leave here today and twenty one others come in their place making things very overcrowded here now, there being sixty six of us here now. Had meetings in evening to consider the ration question and buying of more vegetables. Changes takes place in cook-house, also Christmas goes in and Ted Wicks comes out. Afternoon washing clothes and had a bath. Even playing poker. No OIL today. Soup midday with potatoes, meat and soup at night and bread ration. Mild morning with sunshine and clouds and a few spots of rain at midday.

Sunday 1st April 1945
April Fools Day and Easter Sunday. No work today, slept till 1100hrs and during the afternoon and evening playing cards. OIL: Good. On the Western front still rolling on, taking many prisoners, and a fair amount of war material. Army in the South with the French pushing further Southwards, evidently with the intention of linking up with Joe's mob in the South. Joe broken through at the Ratibar area. Eisenhower issues ultimatum to the German Army about packing in and how to go about it. In Holland Jerries getting out as quick as they

can. Americans make another landing on island between Formosa and main land of Japan. Potatoes, soup midday, with meat, soup at night and bread. Fairly dull and windy day with a little rain. P.S. A little mail in today.

Monday 2nd April 1945
Easter Monday. Prisoner of War stationed at Konigshan in Sudatenland on railway working party, having previously been on a railway party at Bodisch near Weckelsdorf, and attached to Stalag VIII A Gorlitz and previously VIII B Lamsdorf and taken prisoner on fall of Crete June 1941. No work again today, being Easter Monday, so out of bed late again today. During the day reading and playing cards. Clock goes forward one hour at midnight. Nothing much happened today, being fairly quiet, and nothing outstanding in the OIL, except that all fronts seem to be going reasonably well, and many prisoners still being taken, the front on the Southern east sector closing in towards Vienna. Potatoes, soup midday with soup again at night and usual bread. Fairly dull windy day with some rain.

Tuesday 3rd April 1945
Prisoner of War stationed at Konigshan. Some of us in the lager today including myself for overtime worked last week, otherwise gangs out at all usual places, and all home early tonight for a change. Fred managed to get some more rubens today in the way of vegetable. Nothing startling in the way of news tonight, except for prisoners still being taken, Glojau finished and 8000 of the garrison gave themselves up. Also fairly quiet in the Pacific zone. Potatoes, soup and usual bread. Dull cloudy day with strong wind and some rain.

Wednesday 4th April 1945
Prisoner of War at Konigshan. Four men Konigshan, seven Bernsdorf, twelve Parschnitz, and about thirty five to Trautenau, some on barracks job, and myself on party replacing sleepers at the joins of the

rails. Easy day except kept working till nearly 1700hrs and caught the Zceck train to Parschnitz and then catching goods from there to Konigshan and in lager about 1845hrs. OIL: Fairly good. Montgomerys Army pushing towards Hannover. 300k's from the Russians and 200k's from Berlin, also around Gotha and Erfurt and in lower section of the West 100k's from the Zceck border, 30k's of railway seized between Gratz and Trieste, one of the supply lines to Italy. Russians fighting in the suburbs of Vienna, Nuestadt fallen and still closing towards Presburg. Keil and Hamm bombed and needed 850 fighters to escort them. Three train loads of S/S trying to get out of Karnin were done over by the Air Force. One lot of S/S from the Russian front brought to the West fighting without tanks. One Army Southern sector had made arrangements to surrender, but a fanatic Major appeared and made them fight including woman and girls and boys. Americans rubbing it into the people and Eisenhower says why not throw in. Fairly quiet in Italy. In Pacific Americans make landing on island 50 miles from Borneo and Tokyo bombed. A lot of wheat trucks, tractors, railway engines and wagons also coal being sent to France. Quiet evening. Mashed potatoes, cabbage, meat, soup and usual bread. A very changeable day, being a little snow, rain, black clouds, cold and at times brilliant sunshine.

Thursday 5th April 1945
Prisoner of War at Konigshan. Ten men Konigshan, eight Bernsdorf including myself, fifteen Parschnitz and rest at Trautenau. On our job finished 1600hrs and in lager 1730hrs, others in about 1830hrs. Fairly easy day taking out old sleepers, and putting new ones back. Air raid alarm at 1000hrs today. OIL: Western front still pushing forward on all sectors. Gotha, Erfurt, Bayreurth and many other places fallen pushing towards Hanover and meeting some resistance in the North. In Southern Russian front Presburg fallen, and pincer movement closing in on Vienna. Planes flying over housetops and machine gunning German movements. More bombers over and many fighters

needed to escort them. In Italy some movement. Since Montgomery crossed the Rhine, have averaged 20000 prisoners a day. Destroyer patrol sinks two ships and damages one off convoy for Norway without damage to themselves. Another landing on the last of the islands of the Phillipines group. Japanese cabinet resigns. Potatoes, soup, usual bread. Another day of very changeable weather being very cold at times with brilliant sunshine and attempts to rain.

Friday 6th April 1945
Prisoner of War stationed at Konigshan. Ten men Konigshan, myself on party eight Bernsdorf, fifteen Parschnitz and about twenty six Trautenau. Us working at Bernsdorf and Parschnitz in camp at 1800hrs, but those at Trautenau did not get in till 2030hrs. Fairly easy day having to change three sleepers between two men. Gaffers say we have to work all day tomorrow, but Feld-Wabel has told guards to knock us off at midday and get in at 1400hrs. Fred goes to Trautenau today and buys beetroot, carrots, parsnips and dried onion and cabbage costing 281 marks. News: Joe pushing steadily all round Vienna in Southern sector and also not far from Jerries Head Quarters in Yugo-Slavia, also Tito not far from important place on Adriatic coast. Western front advancing steadily towards Hannover and Bremen. Fair number of planes taken in Holland and no bridges blown over the canals, enabling fair progress to be made. Usual heavy bombing being carried out escorted by many fighters. In Italy troops behind Jerry lines doing well. In the Kattegut German convoy attached five transporters sunk, one convoy vessel left sinking. Eisenhower still appealing to German Army to give in and save the useless slaughter. Potatoes, soup, usual bread, marg, weekly sugar and jam ration. Dull day with fair amount of rain falling steadily throughout.

Saturday 7th April 1945
Prisoner of War stationed at Konigshan. Ten men Konigshan, fifteen Parschnitz, rest to Trautenau, except for eight of us at Bernsdorf. Were

to have worked all day according to Starkie, but Army said we come home at midday, so only had half day. In at 1400hrs, rest of afternoon washing clothes and had bath. In the evening reading and playing cards. OIL: Still coming forward on Westerrn front, on all sectors Americans release 5000 of our boys from imprisonment. Usual bombing being carried out. In the raid over the Kattegut we lost seven planes. Joe still pushing in South sector of East front, also driving toward German Head Quarters in Yugo-Slavia. Couple of big places in Japan bombed. Soup and potatoes at midday with soup minced meat at night and bread. Fairly fine day with occasional clouds, but very cold wind blowing.

P.S. Police and Volkstromm out this morning.

Sunday 8th April 1945
Prisoner of War at Konigshan. No work today. Slept in till 0930hrs. During the day a little mending, reading and playing cards, and also wrote any cards we had in hope getting them away, and also played cards in the evening. OIL: Joe closing around Vienna, three sides hemmed in, only the Northern sector open to getting out and heavy fighting in the streets, Western front, not far from Hannover, and Bremen and also moving towards Madgeburg, a little resistance now being shown in Northern sector, and in Holland still pushing forward. In Southern sector numerous places mentioned. Usual bombing. A big hoard of bullion discovered including French money and English notes and American dollars. Greek government resigns said to have too much sympathy with the Reds. Japanese suffering heavy losses in Burma. Places in Japan bombed. Latest Japanese warship of 45000 tons sunk, also a cruiser and two destroyers. Took three torpedoes and eight bombs to sink the warship. Americans lost seven planes. Potatoes, soup midday, with meat, soup at night and bread. A very nice sunny spring day with a fairly cool breeze.

Monday 9th April 1945
Prisoner of War at Konigshan. Parties at Konigshan, Bernsdorf, Parschnitz and Trautenau. Myself stayed in today to help with the

clothes washing, as one of the usuals doing some carpentering. Started 0830hrs and finished at 1130hrs and so reading most part of the day. Boys in early being in by 1730hrs. OIL: Good. Joe battling against Konigsberg and harbour side taken with 15000 prisoners. Around Vienna the cirle being drawn closer in, and three of the four main stations in Joe's hands, and also the arsenal. Towards the North Vienna pushing over some river on a broad front and in the Protectorate having taken one town. Planes from Italy assisting Joe in the South. In the West going far in all directions. 7th Armoured Division go 130k's in 24hrs and 300 in the last eleven days. In Holland parachute troops landed 25k's in front of Canadian Army, and who have now linked up. This in Northern Holland, Hannover, Bremen, and several other places under fire. Stuttgart in French hands. Schweinfort fallen. 4000 French officers released yesterday from prison camp, and also a survivor from what they called a torture camp, saying about 6000 had died of hunger in recent months. Heavy bombing still being carried out. Skirmish in North Sea between our forces and Germany's, enemy losing five and us two. Prince Bernhardt arrives in Holland and well received. Refugees arriving in Denmark from Germany by the thousand and 30000 waiting to disembark, but will not allow them, also German Luftwaffe landing in Sweden and calling themselves refugees. In Italy a little fighting being carried out. New Greek cabinet sworm in last night. Jap's have lost 305 planes in last five days in sea battles. New Japanese minister 77 years of age. Potato soup, vegetable salad, usual bread and marg. In last fortnight have bought for ourselves costing 40 pound on the black market or 600 German Marks. Dull morning but fairly fine afternoon but cool breeze blowing.

P.S. A little mail but none myself.

Tuesday 10th April 1945
Prisoner of War stationed at Konigshan. Ten men Konigshan, nine including myself Bernsdorf, some at Parschnitz and Trautenau. Home early again tonight, getting in the lager at 1710hrs. Easy day. Sifting

earth from metal by railway line. Reading during the evening. Nothing startling in the OIL.. On the Western front Canadian Army still going well in Holland. Around Bremen and Hannover, still under fire, some of the crack German troops defending here. In the middle and Stettin sectors pushing steadily forward. The Eastern front Vienna completely encircled now and more prisoners and municipal places taken. Konigsberg finished and 42000 prisoners taken, being subjected to a heavy 48hr bombardment. In Yugo-Slavia Tito's troops kill 5700 and 6000 taken prisoner. News of offensive started on the whole front in Italy from both coasts. Some ships sunk in the Kattegut. Sweden has ordered all refugees out of the country, and Switzerland refuses to allow refugees in the country. Potato soup, beetroot and usual bread. Fairly cold day with very heavy fog till 1030hrs, when lifted and turned out a beautiful day and a perfect evening. 2000hrs before the sun set.

Wednesday 11th April 1945

Prisoner of War in Sudatenland. Ten to Konigshan, myself one of nine at Bernsdorf, some at Parschnitz and the rest to Trautenau. Easy day as usual of late, just as well thse days, as none of us have any energy for work. Home early train getting in lager at 1720hrs. Reading during the evening. Some mail today and received one from Sigrid dated 5th November 1944. News: Western front Hannover fallen and troops many K's ahead of there already. Bremen Hamburg, Madgeburg, and Brunswick mentioned as closing in towards three places. Canadian capture more territory in Holland. Erfurt in middle sector completely surrounded. Nothing much mentioned in Southern sector. Said to be 80k's from Zceck border, Eastern front more places captured. In Vienna practically all important places taken. Total prisoners from Konigshan now 92000 inlcuding four generals and about 40000 were killed. Steady progress in Italy. Sabotage in Denmark and Norwegian U boat bases. Americans capture the last island of group next 500 miles to the mainland of Japan. Big chain of islands around Borneo now all in American hands. More heavy losses inflicted on Japs in

Burma on drive from Mandalay to Rangoon. Mashed potatoes, sauerkraut, meat, soup, usual bread. Cold morning, but turned out beautiful day, except after midday clouds came up, and some wind and looking like rain again. Farmers now busy with seeding operations.

Thursday 12th April 1945
Prisoner of War in Sudatenland. Gangs at Konigshan, Parschnitz, Trautenau, and myself on party at Bernsdorf. Planeering and changing sleepers. Easy work and home by early train, but a little later than usual getting in at 1745hrs. Reading during the evening. News: Western front Canadians still pushing forward in Holland to the North. Hannover finished and tanks racing ahead of there. Bremen under fire, and charging towards Leipzig and Madgeburg, also fighting in Brunswick. Third Army in middle sector advancing under a cloud. No news of Vienna or any other Eastern front news. Usual bombing being carried out. In Italy steady fighting and airborne troops landed behind German lines. Potatoes, soup, usual bread, marg, and weekly jam issue, probably the last. Very dull and in the afternoon a little rain started to fall, otherwise a fair sort of day.

Friday 13th April 1945
Prisoner of War stationed at Konigshan. Myself on party at Bernsdorf, other gangs to Konigshan, Parschnitz and Trautenau. Replacing old sleepers today finishing at usual time, but in camp at 1700hrs, as train managed well to time tonight. Fred goes to Trautenau today and gets more vegetables, including some fresh leeks. Reading during the evening. Boys at Parschnitz did well today in the corn racket and the old coffee grinder busy tonight. OIL: In Holland and Northern German sectors still going forward. Three bridges over some river on the way to Hamburg. Bremen under heavy artillery fire. About 40k's North of Leipzig and about 40k's south west of Leipzig, 3rd Army racing over the last 50k's to the Protectorate, 40000 prisoners taken yesterday. Vienna not quite finished, and on parts freed old Austrian National Flag is

flying. Usual bombing Berlin done over three times last night. In this month Germans have had 2500 planes shot up on the ground. Surprise raid on aerodrome yesterday and shot up 78 planes. Italy going along quietly. Roosevelt died yesterday at the age of 63 with clot of blood on the brain. 14th Army in Burma capture another railway train on way to Rangoon. Japs lose 188 planes in raids on American invasion fleet, said to have been bit of a revolt in German Air Force and 90 officers and one general shot. Potatoes, soup, usual bread and marg. Dull day with some rain setting in at 1700hrs, and first thunder of the season tonight.

Saturday 14th April 1945
Prisoner of War stationed at Konigshan. Twenty six men at Konigshan today including myself stomping on the new line put in. Some at Parschnitz and the rest to Trautenau. Us Konigshan gang in at 1345hrs, Trautenau gang in at 1415hrs, but the Parschnitz gang did not get in till 1700hrs, having to go down towards the Protectorate, where there had been a train collision between work train and another one. Jewesse's working on the Arbeit train, and some having had their arms and legs cut off. During afternoon bathing and washing clothes. In evening playing cards. OIL: Canadian Army still pushing forward and closing towards Bremen. On a 160 kilometre front over the Elbe pushing towards Hamburg. Fighting in Madgeburg and tanks reported 60k's from Berlin, by passing Leipzig which has been practically surrounded, and going towards Dresden, being 60's, and also 18 miles from the Protectorate. Still cleaning up the Ruhr, and taken 114000 prisoners. Million French prisoners released, and also an English Offlag, releasing 2000 offficers and 400 other personnel. Around Vienna Joe still pushing towards the Protectorate, and Tito starts new offensive in Yugo-Slavia. Bombing being carried out on Kiel, said to be ships from Konigsberg and others of the North Sea sheltering there, also big liner sunk in Kattegut, probably with troops from Norway. Nothing much to report in Italy. American Foreign and War Policy to stand same as when Roosevelt was President. More raids

on Tokyo. Japs lose 118 planes in raid on British fleet during the shelling of Formosa. Potatoes, soup, midday, soup again at night and bread. Very dull cold morning with fairly fine sunny afternoon.

Sunday 15th April 1945
Prisoner of War at Konigshan. No work today, except that I cut up the beetroot for the cooks. Reading, mending, playing cards, and wrote home. OIL: Joe starts new push on Oder bridgehead by Frankfurt-On-Ode. From the Vienna area stilll pushing through the Protectorate, and taking more villages, and going west moving towards Linz only 100 miles separates our troops and the Russians. Hitler split Germany into two parts North and South, and each part under separate Generals. Canadians still pushing towards North coast in Holland despite the many canals. Fierce resistance about Madgeburg and towards Hamburg. In the middle western sector still moving towards the Protctorate and in a Southern sector still steadily onward. In the Ruhr Count Von Papen taken with son in law and his wife. 140000 prisoners to date in this area. 43000 taken yesterday. New bridge over the Rhine to be called Roosevelt Memorial bridge, planned two years ago, and taking ten days to build. Usual bombing being carried out. – assisting French at the mouth of some river in France, where Jerries are still holding out, also assisted by planes dropping a type of fire bomb, with a covering distance of 60 yards and over 400000 of these dropped. 13000 planes took part in this. In Italy nothing much of note. Japs lose more planes in raid on British Fleet. 14th Army in Burma still on their way to Rangoon, and Bangkok bombed by Air Force. Roosevelt buried today. Potatoes, soup midday and at night with usual bread. A cold night and morning with fair mount of sunshine in morning followed by cold wind and some dull clouds in afternoon.

Monday 16th April 1945
Prisoner of War at Konigshan. Twenty four of us at Konigshan including myself, stomping the new line put down 'firearm' job and

finished at 1415hrs and in lager at 1445hrs. Others at Parschnitz and Trautenau and in at 1730hrs. Reading for the rest of the afternoon when came in. OIL: Canadians reach the coast of the North Sea in Holland and a fair force of Jerries now cut off. Still pushing towards Hamburg. Heavy fighting around Bremen still. Army ready for a big offensive on Berlin. Still heavy fighting in Madgeburg, heavy opposition here. Around Leipzig big oil refinery works captured that have received so much bombing lately, and also Junkers biggest aircraft factory captured. Aerodrome South of Leipzig taken with 38 planes on the ground. 15 miles from Numberg, and also 15 from Protectorate. Big concentration camp taken where 60000 have died during the course of the war. Daladier, Mayor of Prague was also here, but was taken away. Wappertel taken in the Ruhr, only one big town left here now. French and Americans going well in the South. Eastern front Joe still pushing from Vienna side through the Protectorate, and more towns taken, also still driving towards Linz. Usual heavy bombing being carried out and another German ship sunk off the Baltic coast. Fighting at the mouth of the Duron in France, still continues with the Jerries being compressed into a narrow area. Navy silences the coastal batteries. In Italy advancing on the whole of the front, and about 30 divisions in here with no chance of getting out. Tokyo, Yokohama, Canton and Shanghai bombed by Super Fortresses. Mention on German news of a big offensive started by Joe on Silesian front and told by Hitler to be held at all costs. Potatoes, soup, usual bread and marg, with monthly cheese ration. Cold frosty morning with very nice sunny day and a cool breeze at times, and setting in again with a fairly cold night.

Tuesday 17th April 1945
Prisoner of War at Konigshan. Myself with others at Konigshan, stomping and bumping new line into place, being 'firearm' job finished at 1310hrs and in camp at 1400hrs. Others at Parschnitz and Trautenau and in camp at 1720hrs. Not feeling too good myself today,

having had bad stomach last night, and today eating very little. News: Canadians still pushing towards Emden, where fairly heavy fighting is taking place, also around the area of Hamburg, heavy resistance, but showing signs of breaking. Still closing towards Numberg and Dresden in the middle section. Leipzig surrounded. 3rd Army on the Czeck border. In the South fighting in the hills of the Black Forest, 20000 Allied prisoners released in the North of Germany recently. Heavy bombing still going on. Germans at the mouth of the Duron in France compressed in closer. Two German ships give themselves up in Norwegian waters. Eastern front, Joe still pushing northwards from Vienna in the Protectorate area, closing towards Brunn and going westwards further towards Linz. In the East Prussian area, only one place left and these being compressed to the sea where large force is hoping to get way, but the harbour is being continually being bombed by Russian planes. Nothing from Moscow, but German reports says Joes guns can be heard from Berlin and only 45 kilometres from there. Reports of hunger riots in Berlin and also Nazi's lost control in Southern Germany and riots going on. In Italy still moving forward slowly. Poles in the Army there said to be doing good work. 14th Army in Burma progressing well towards Rangoon, and place on large mainland island of Japan heavily bombed. Reading during the evening. Potatoes, soup, usual bread. Cold frosty morning with fairly fine day and some wind.

Wednesday 18th April
Prisoner of War at Konigshan. Parties at Konigshan, Bernsdorf, Parschnitz and Trautenau. Went to Dr myself this morning with bad stomach, and got four days, no arbeit, and so no work till Monday. Filled the day reading, doing odd jobs of cooking for the boys when they come home etc. A fair cut in the rations to be announced tonight especially in the bread owing to the overdrawing of meal since the beginning of the year. Meeting held regarding rations and find out that

we have to go on to an 1/8 loaf of bread for the next ten days, with no sugar, marg or jam or soup meat and in the next period still owe back some overdrawn meal, so many say they are not going to work on these rations, as they are hardly enough to exist on without working. Anyway going to see the Coy about it and working till Saturday, and if nothing done by then no work Monday. Canadians clean out North of Holland area and Jerries left fleeing westward to Amsterdam and getting out by boats, ships and barges whatever is available and being continually harassed by the Air Force. Still pushing towards Hamburg, Leipzig, and Murnberg surrounded, Leipzig nearlly cleaned up, and still fighting in Madgeburg. Ruhr cleaned up, and 309000 prisoners taken here, some Field Marshall commits suicide, who in any case was one of those down to be shot after the war for his atrocities in Latvia. Hamburg, Berlin, Dresden bombed. Our forward troops towards Dresden, practically on the rear lines of the Jerries facing the Russians. At the mouth of the Duron some big Admiral and his staff and 600 prisoners taken yesterday, this area practically cleaned up now. Eastern front Joe pushing well into the Protectorate from Vienna northwards, more towns taken and 20 miles from Brunn, also progressing westwards, still towards Linz. No mention of Berlin sector but Jerry news admits attacking from five points and only 30k's from Berlin. Steady progress in Italy. We lose 508 planes this month and destroyed over 2000 Jerry planes on the ground and in the air. Concentration camp, 5000 of the worst cases to receive invalid food right away and to be attended to by American Red X. Round up of some of the Jerry civilians and show them through the place to show what their people have done. In Burma steady progress by 14th Army towards Rangoon. Attack by Super Fortresses on one of the mainland islands of Japan, Japs lose over 100 planes in suicide raids on invasion fleet, among the islands there. Reading during the evening. Mashed potatoes, cabbage soup snd 1/8 loaf bread, no marg. Dull morning with clouds and a little rain but afternoon fairly fine and strong wind blowing.

Thursday 19th April

Prisoner of War stationed at Konigshan. In lager myself with bad stomach and filled in the day, after sleeping in till 1000hrs by some mending, washing jacket, pressing trousers and a little reading. Parties at Konigshan in at 1720hrs and at Bernsdorf, Parschnitz and Trautenau, and in a little late owing to train holdups being 1800hrs. News: Madgeburg finished and 15k's from Hamburg. Still heavy fighting in Leipzig and Nurnberg, but some parts of the town captured. Canadians pushing towards Amsterdam in Holland and only 20k's from there meeting little resistance. 17 polish women who were in the Warsaw uprising last year, and when they came to the camp were standing guard with tommy guns. 3rd Army 3 mile over the Protectorate border, and spearhead had to turn back, because they had gathered too many prisoners to handle. Heavy bombing carried out on Berlin and Helogoland, the reason for Helogoland is because of the coastal batteries, submarine, E boats and other warships to prevent our shipping from coming into Emden and Wilhelmshaven when there places are ready. Eastern front Joe still does not mention Berlin sector, but German newspapers say they have through some of the defences and 30k's from the city, and the fires can be seen from the lines caused by our bombers over Berlin. Still pushing westwards from Vienna, more places taken, 15k's from Brunn, and closing in on Marie-Ostrov. Steady progress being made in Italy. Message to German merchant seamen asking them to prevent sabotaging of the ships, as they will be required after the war, to bring supplies in for them, as the Allied shipping will not be available. Americans make another landing on island in the Pacific. Captain Pasha from the Coy here today on an inspection. Potatoes, soup, and 1/8 loaf bread. If it was not for the vegetables, we have brought to put in the soup these days, it would be water, and as have no soup meal. Very dull first thing this morning, with some rain, but afternoon came out reasonably fine, except wind blowing practically at gale force all the afternoon. P.S. Fair amount of air activity here this morning, but unable to say whether they were German or Allied forces as visibility bad.

Friday 20th April 1945
Prisoner of War stationed at Konigshan. Five years today since embarked on the "Nevassa" at Fremantle and hit Hitlers birthday today, but do not notice any happy cheering anyway today. In lager again today with a bad stomach, so slept in till 1000hrs, and filled in the day, having a bath doing washing, and ground some corn and reading. Few letters up this evening and received one myself from Cousin Don. Parties at Konigshan, Bernsdorf, Parschnitz and Trautenau. Parschnitz gang in at 1400hrs, having half day for extra work last Saturday. Konigshan gang in at 1640hrs and Bernsdorf, Trautenau gangs in at 1730hrs. Nothing much in the news Halle and Leipzig fallen. 1 ½ k's from the suburbs of Hamburg, and Joe's and our Armies converging on Dresden. Fred went to Trautenau today, but was unable to get any vegetables. Fields beginning to look nice and green now, and the farmers working long hours to get their crops in. Potatoes, soup, 1/8 loaf of bread, little marg, and some of our bought beetroot. Cool morning, but very nice sunny day with cold breeze blowing and fairly cool evening. P.S. Plenty of planes over here last night, being practically a continual stream, evidently the Jerries taking stuff to the occupants of Breslau.

Saturday 21st April 1945
Prisoner of War in Sudatenland. In lager again today with bad stomach, being my last day off. Reading most of the day. Boys working at Konigshan in at 1300hrs others at Bernsdorf, Parschnitz and Trautenau, and being half day in at 1420hrs. Washing clothes and bathing occupied the rest of the day. Very little news. Bremen and Hamburg being shelled by Artillery. Our troops and Russians 40k's apart in the Dresden area. Russians in Brunn and Marie-Ostrov and German reports Russia shelling outskirts of Berlin. Potatoes, Vegetable

soup, midday, with meat and very little soup at night 1/8 loaf bread. A very cold dull day throughout with some rain.

Sunday 22nd April 1945
Prisoner of War at Konigshan. No work today; up for breakfast 0845hrs, then to bed till 1130hrs. Reading and playing cards during the day. In ten o'clock news nothing startling. The meeting of our forces and Russians between Dresden and Gorlitz is iminent. Pattons Army between Ajer and Asch in the Protecorate. Bremen and Hamburg still under artillery fire, as also German reports of centre of Berlin under Russian artillery fire. French and Americans doing well in Southern sector. Southern most island of Japan bombed. Tauffe spends the day away. A few moans going about concerning the bread and Fred copping a lot of abuse on the quiet, also myself quietly, reckon not cutting bread up fair enough. Potatoes, soup, midday with soup again at night and 1/8 bread. Dull cold day with rain, ice and snow falling different parts of the day.

Monday 23rd April 1945
Prisoner of War stationed at Konigshan. Working lager myself today, helping with the washing, as one of the usuals crook. Started about 0915hrs and finished at 1130hrs, then had shave and wash down. Parties at Konigshan, Bernsdorf, Parschnitz and Trautenau. Boys home late tonight, did not get in till 1920hrs. Ration situation still unaltered and still on 1/8 loaf bread. News: Russian tanks in the streets of Berlin, and command about 2 miles of the main streets of Berlin, being 2 ½ miles from the centre of the city, and all big buildings being heavily pounded by artillery also between Berlin and Dresden. Joe moved strongly forward, and all this area at any time likely to be met by the American and England forces. Bremen and Hamburg still under heavy artillery fire and well to the North above Wilkelmshaven to a place called Cuxhave. Canadians pushing towards Rotterdam and Amsterdam still. In the middle sector Nurnberg has fallen and

other towns mentioned. In the South French and Americans pushing onwards and now 80k's from Munich. Kiel, Hamburg and Berlin bombed. In Italy 40k's past Bologna and 2 from Ferrara and Germans fleeing northwards. The French also coming in from the French-Italian border. Tito captures port on Adriatic coast by the name of Fume. 47 nations to be represented at San Fransisco Conference. 14th Army in Burma, steady progress towards Rangoon. On lastest island Americans landed in Pacific, Japs suffer heavy losses. Reading during the evening. Potatoes, soup 1/8 loaf bread. A very dirty day, with wind hail, rain and snow and fairly cold.

Tuesday 24th April 1945
Prisoner of War stationed at Konigshan. Four years ago today since the Bn fought rear guard action at Braylos pass in Greece. Parties at Konigshan, myself with eight others get off at Gabersdorf walk back to Golden – where four of us pulled down signal and four others digging hole about 400 yards further down the line to put it in. Finished about 1500hrs, thereby having an easy day, and other gangs at Parschnitz and Trautenau, home late being 1830hrs on getting in. Meeting in evening considering the bread question and still on 1/8 loaf to the end of the month, and probably next month will be 1/7 loaf, but hoping won't have to see that month out on that. No griff tonight, except that Germany has supposed to have told England through Switzerland that they will be unable to move any more prisoners. A little reading during the evening. Potatoes, soup, 1/8 bread. Another dirty day, the same as yesterday.

Wednesday 25th April 1945
Prisoner of War in Sudatenland. Anzac Day, thirty years since the landing of the Anzac's at Gallipoli. 4 years since out Bn was lying off the Greek Coast among the olive trees waiting to go on board boat, evacuating from Greece. Parties at Konigshan, Parschnitz, and Trautenau, and myself with seven others, same place as yesterday, shifting and

putting up signal posts, supporting signal wires and in fact very easy day, knocking off at 1530hrs to go to catch train. All in lager at same time, being early tonight at 1700hrs. Reading during the evening. Fair number of planes about today and 500 bombers with 500 fighters said to have done over the Skoda armament works also partisans very active in the Protectorate. OIL: Half of Berlin in Russian hands, and heavy fighting going on still. Germans attempt to get through to the Russian rear lines by the underground tunnels, but Joe takes artillery down to stop them. Only the river Elke is between our troops and Russians linking up one place. Lager of 11000 men led by the Commandant of the camp and hand over the troops to Patton. Bremen and Emden still under fire. Pattons Army 70k's from Pilsen and French Army in the South 70k's from Munich. In Italy naval station of Sheguu in the west taken and on the Adriatic sector Medino and Ferrara fallen, and our troops advancing over the plains. 14th Army in Burma capture big oil place on way to Rangoon. Americans land on more islands between Formosa and mainland of Japan. Fred goes to Trautenau today to get some vegetables but only able to get four crates of beetroot. Potatoes, soup and some of the beetroot we recently bought and 1/8 bread. P.S. Some of the Todd organization fellows we have seen the last couple of days pleased that Hitler and Goebels are in Berlin, and reackon the war will be over in a fortnight, so lets hope they are right. Heavy frost this morning, but fairly nice sunny morning with clouds coming over during the afternoon, but still nice and warm though.

Thursday 26th April 1945
Prisoner of War stationed at Konigshan. Four years ago today since left Greek shores in the evacuation and landed in Crete. Gangs today at Konigshan, Bernsdorf, Gabersdorf, Parschnitz and Trautenau. Myself on Bernsdorf party, going to Konigshan with the small wagon first to pick up sleepers, and returned to Bernsdorf, and unloaded them, then did a little planeering till dinner time and afternoon carted old sleepers and the tools to the station in prepartation for working this

in the morning. All home reasonably early getting in at 1725hrs. Some leaflets fell in the area today warning the Germans about the treatment that prisoners of war are getting. Reading during the evening. News: Steady progress still in the fighting in Berlin. Russian artillery now in the main streets, and the place is entirely surrounded now, with no chance of anybody getting out. Fierce fighting around Hamburg and Bremen and our troops pushing Northwards still. Russians and our troops feeling their way cautiously around Dresden ready for linking up, as there are a lot of prisoners in this area giving themselves up. In the South French now 60k's from Munich, and more towns in this area fallen. In Northern sector another 14000 of our boys recaptured. Pillau in East Prussia now finished. Berlin and power station near Munich bombed. Italy all going well there.

In Burma 14th Army capture another town and Fortresses do over mainland of Japan. Another concentration camp found near Leipzig. Potatoes, soup and 1/8 loaf bread. Cold morning, but turned out a nice day with overcast sky in afternoon.

Friday 27th April 1945

Prisoner of War stationed at Konigshan. Gangs at Konigshan, Bernsdorf, Gabersdorf, Parschnitz and Trautenau. Konigshan party home 1700hrs. On Bernsdorf party myself with eight others, and walked home as train was late getting in at 1750hrs, and the other three gangs in at 1845hrs. Easy day at Bernsdorf replacing three sleepers for two of us. Reading during the evening. OIL: Very good today. Practically the whole of Italy has capitulated, and many places fallen with the aid of Partisans, many generals and others give themselves up. American and Russian troops met yesterday afternoon and great rejoicing in Moscow tonight, meeting somewhere in the Dresden area. Joe's troops in the protectorate around area of Marice-Ostrov and Brunn doing well, as also their drive towards Linz. Stettin in Russian hands. The fall of Berlin going very well Germans now left with an area of 10 miles by 6. Partisans also active in here and have captured one station. Regensburg fallen in the South, and only 50k's from Munich. The Burgomaster of Munich shoots himself and several other Nazi heads commit suicide. Eger taken by Patton on the edge of the Protectorate, and now converging on towards Pilsen, as is also part of Joe's Army. Fui-shoo island of Japan bombed. Potatoes, soup, 1/8 bread and beetroot. Fairly warm sunny morning with cold wind and clouds in afternoon and about five minutes of rain about 1730hrs.

Saturday 28th April 1945
Prisoner of War in Sudatenland. Gangs at Konigshan, Bernsdorf, Gabersdorf, Parschnitz and Trautenau. Half day and all in lager at 1420hrs. During afternoon had bath, washed clothes and sawed wood. In evening reading. For the first time in my life had a scrap with Taaffe in our room because he called me a German spy in British uniform, he got a blood nose and a bit of skin off his face as the result, lost no skin myself, but got a couple on the jaw. All over a remark that was said when we were waiting outside to go to work, and he was dragging his feet. OIL: Very good. A host of towns fallen everywhere, Jerries also giving themselves up, and big heads being killed or committing suicide. All the German-Swiss frontier in our hands and the Italian-Swiss frontier in Partisan hands in Italy who were led by British Officers. Germany now in three portions and actually 4/5 of the country is in our hands. Our troops pushing their way well to the North Coast and more of our prisoners released here. Many thousands of Jerries give themselves up in Italy, and German forces left now split in two. Partisan activity in Munich led be former strong Nazi man. 2/3 of Berlin in Russian hands, and definitely said to be right that Goebels and Hitler are here. Expect the leaders to be if these fall, Kesselring or Bromberg and maybe they will give in. Report from San Fransico conference that Himmler offered unconditional surrender to England and America only, but the Allies would not listen to these terms. Old Joe says fight on and get it finished with. Soup and potatoes midday

with soup at night and 1/8 bread. Dull cool morning coming up colder in evening and some rain fell. P.S. A few letters up but none myself.

Sunday 29th April 1945
Prisoner of War near Konigshan. No work today, so slept in till nearly 1100hrs, and then had easy day reading and playing cards. Everyone in fairly good mood today because news is fairly good. Big eats in the weekend with wheat porridge, and cakes, scones and bread made from flour sifted after the grinding down. OIL: Americans and Russians now holding together an 80k's front and close to closing in on more ground. Heavy fighting going on around Hamburg. Harbour of Bremen being prepared ready to receive our shipping. Fierce fighting in Berlin with about 2/3 of the city in Russian hands. Underground railway dynamited killing thousands of Germans, and dead laying everywhere in the streets. From Stettin Russians pushing towards Lubeck and other Northern places. South West sector French still advancing towards Munich. 100000 prisoners now taken in Italy. Since D Day on the Western front our troops have taken 2,500,407 prisoners. Mussollini tried before tribunal in Milan and already executed. In Burma 14th Army in a rapid advance of 90k's in 24hrs have cut off Japs from their bases and are now only 100k's from Rangoon. Potatoes, soup midday, soup at night and 1/8 loaf bread. Dull morning but it turned out nice sunny afternoon with cool breeze.

Monday 30th April 1945
Prisoner of War at Konigshan. Working gangs to Konigshan, Gabersdorf, Parschnitz and Trautenau. First thing eight others and myself went to Bernsdorf to the two small wagons, and bring them back to Konigshan, getting back at 1020hrs, had freestig, then combined with the other gang already there on stomping, and tighening up bolts and screws etc. Easy day finishing at 1530hrs on account of rain and hail, and then brought home to lager, getting in at 1630hrs. Parschnitz gang in at 1720hrs, and other two gangs at 1800hrs. A little

reading during the evening. OIL: Still heavy and fierce fighting in Berlin and Russians now 800 to 1000 metres from the Reichstag ansd Chancellery, the head quarters of Hitler in Berlin. Scenes of ruin and desolation in Berlin 51000 prisoners taken yesterday Hamburg being by-passed in the North, and our troops and Russian Army making for the North to cut off any chance of Jerries from getting out of Denmark. Georing, Goebels, Ribbentrop said to have left Hitler, who is supposed to be dying in Berlin. In the middle sector steadily forward, in the South French going ahead and three American divisions in Munich and Stalag VII A Moosburg has been released, there being 27000 POW's released. Venice now in English hands, and many prisoners taken here. 250 tons of food stuff dropped over Holland yesterday, and the same going on today. In Burma monsoonal season approaching and a race ensuring whether our troops reach Rangoon before the season breaks. Ammunition, aircraft factories, and fields bombed in Japan. Potatoes, soup, 1/9 loaf bread and marg. Cold morning with cold wind, which finished up with icy snow and rain this afternoon but came out a fine evening. P.S. A little mail up but none myself.

(This page is missing)

Thursday 3rd May 1945
Hamburg declared open city and our troops to march in today at 1300hrs. Our troops and Russians linked up between Rostrov and Lubeck, only the Northern part with Kiel, the main part left here now. More food dropped in Holland. More Allied prisoners released. Prague declared a hospital city; so will be no fighting there. Admiral Doenitz said to be in Copenhagen. In Denmark Jerries still capitulating to the Danish people, and in Norway. Generals want troops to fight, but soldiers say no. In Italy General in charge has unconditionally surrendered all troops involving about a million men, which includes part of the Tyrol in Austria. (Speculation still rife as to whether they will fight on or surrender before the week is out). In Burma our troops in Rangoon as the result of the sea and air landing of yesterday.

Australians make landing on island on North of New Guinea. Southern Island of Japan bombed. Potatoes, soup, 1/8 loaf bread. Cold morning with wind and later came out with rain and snow, but cleared up late afternoon.

Friday 4th May 1945
Prisoner of War in Sudatenland. Gangs at Konigshan which included myself, stomping planeering and changing sleepers, finishing 1305hrs and came home in lager at 1410hrs. Gabersdorg gang in at same time. Parschnitz and Trautenau parties in at 1710hrs. A bath and did washing on returning to lager and reading in evening. News: Good. In Northern Germany still capitulating, and in one area occupied 15 kilometres of troops. Our troops over the Danish border. German ships getting away from Denmark, 35 sunk and 178 damaged. Hamburg quietly taken over, and people told to obey the curfew, otherwise the occupying troops will let their presence be felt. One Army through the Bremner pass, and not far away from the 5th Army in Italy. Big newspaper editors visiting concentration camps in Germany. Austria finished and the collaboration of the people asked for. Linz under artillery fire. On the outskirts of Pilsen 20 more generals taken prisoner. Two Russian Generals leading two free divisions of Germans. Rangoon finished. Aussie's doing well on recently landed island. South Island of Japan bombed again. Fred goes to Trautenau and managed to get a bag of onions, leeks and three boxes of beetroot. Potatoes, soup, 1/7 bread, beetroot, period issue of cheese, issue of sugar and some margarine. Fairly cool morning, with the sun shining at times, and very nice afternoon but cold wind. P.S. Expecting hourly to hear that the Jerries have all packed in, and everybody giving the day, hour, when it will be over.

Saturday 5th May 1945
Prisoner of War near Konigshan. On party myself at Konsigshan stomping and 'firearm' job, and being half day in lager at 1300hrs. Others at Gabersdorg, Parschnitz and Trautenau in at 1425hrs. Afternoon

and evening, a little washing, reading and playing cards. News: Still armies capitulating and still places holding out. Montgomery going to Copenhagen. Czeck Army rise up, and have taken half of Prague and calling on England for air support. Rangoon finished. Australians still doing well on recently landed island, also Southern island of Japan bombed. Everybody practically on edge waiting to hear of the work of that they have surrendered this area around here and to hear it is all over. Soup, potatoes midday, with meat goulash at night, 1/9 loaf bread and period jam ration for three weeks, 3 ½ spoonfuls. Cold morning but came out sunny about 1000hrs, but after 1400hrs came over dirty and was wet.

Sunday 6th May 1945
Prisoner of War in Sudatenland. No work today, slept in till late and during the day reading and playing cards. Still waiting for the finish of it all as conflicting evidence going about, it is worse now than about six months ago, when we were not so anxiously waiting to hear the finish, as we now realise it can be finished any hour. (Prague still fighting 3 more German Armies give themselves up. Tension between us and the Russians at San Fransisco Conference very high.) German reports of Russian tanks in Waldenburg and Lieben and Landeshute declared free towns. Also supposed to be an ultimation for the protectorate, all arms to be handed in by the Germans at 1200hrs today, but as yet no confirmation of all the rumours. Porridge for breakfast with soup and potatoes midday, meat and goulash at night and 1/7 bread, marg also beetroot today. Dull cold wet morning, coming out fair afternoon with some sunshine, but clouded over in the evening.

Monday 7th May 1945
Prisoner of War near Konsigshan. Everyone of tiptoe this morning, as there seems a tension in the air. On party at Konigshan myself and at 1235hrs told to pack in as going to lager, as work for us was finished. Others at Parschnitz and Trautenau, home in lager at 1400hrs. On

getting in, informed that that had to pack up as the Coy had given orders that we were to be taken to the Protectorate and handed over to the Americans, but Fred got us together and said we would remain here and wait for the Russians, as they were said to be coming through, but of course if the Coy forces us to go with the rifle we will have to go. 1530hrs says that German radio Admiral Doenitz has unconditionally surrendered to the three powers, so Fred says we will be stopping and later reports says that they are still fighting the Russians and pushing them to the sea. Waldenburg and the Jerry. *(A little section here faded and unreadable)* and so with conflicting reports we don't know what is to be done, but are ready to move anyway. Plenty of evacuees going towards the Protectorate area, and yet army supply wagons with hay for horses still going towards the front at Waldenburg. Joe and Franz here and the stuff that was given them was enormous. Ikey said a few words and broke down, they both want us to write to them after the war. At 1600hrs everything fairly quiet here, and just waiting on orders as to a definite move. French, Italians, Poles and all nationalities streaming along the road. Big bus loads of people still going past and also fire engines. 1800hrs heard that it is definitely over to the three powers. Boys outside roaming around as if they owned the country now. Have heard also that if we go we leave at 0900hrs tomorrow for Trautenau and not Protectorate as first stated. Some mail up today, but none myself and our last as a POW's I guess.

Note: Vic ceased writing on May 7, 1945. He stayed with the train that took him west towards Munich. The Americans and British were liberating all and sundry and sending them to London by aeroplane.

Private (Vic) Petersen was interrogated in Eastborne before he was sent home to Western Australia. The war for him was over, he had offered five and a half years of his life and should be recognised for this sacrifice.

Trials & Tribulations

The Story of My Life by Vic Petersen
DRAFT COPY 2 April, 1993
Mr CAGV (Vic) Petersen
6 Sarre Street, Gosnells. WA. 6110.

© Copyright CAGV Petersen 1993. No part of this story may be copied, reproduced or transmitted in any form whatsoever, without written permission of the author or upon his death from his family.

This story starts when I can start to remember things between four and five years of age, when at that time we were living in a place about two or three miles out from Bridgetown on the road to Manjimup and known as Devil's Hollow, with the railway line to Manjimup on one side and bounded by a hill on the other which had a permanent creek running along the foot of it.

I was born at Bridgetown August 27th 1913; and as I was born premature weighing two and a half pounds and was christened at home, and was given the names of Charles Amos George Victor Petersen, my parents being Charles and Alice Petersen.

The farm we were on had some fruit trees, and quite a few tomatoes were grown there, and had cows and pigs and also an enormous passion vine, which produced hundreds of passionfruit. I also remember my father used to boil up buckets of wheat for the pigs of which my two eldest brothers and myself used to help ourselves to.

I can just remember a little of the war and my two uncles, George and Bill Nash going away, George returning home and Uncle Bill being killed in France.

About the beginning of 1919 I started school at Bridgetown, going with our neighbour's children Stan and Lorraine Shepherd and of course a walk of between two and three miles. Had not been going to school for long, when I was pushed by a cousin of our neighbours from the school steps and had my right arm broken in two places, and I remember being taken by two of the bigger boys at the school up to the hospital to have it put in splints and Dad came and took me home in the cart. This put me out of schooling for a while in Bridgetown, and then Dad leased a place out of Bridgetown on the road to Nannup belonging to a Mr. Bagshaw, which was mostly fruit.

From here went to another school, where the Blackwood River was the boundary of Bagshaws place and a William Wheatley, and here used to have to walk about three miles. In the winter months when the Blackwood River was in flood I used to be rowed over on Monday and boarded at Mr. Wheatley's place and returned home by boat on Friday for the week end.

The Wheatley's farm had a fairly big orchard and they also milked a good many cows and which was my job on helping out while there.

While at Bagshaws Mum and Dad had their fifth child in the family, there now being four boys and a girl. I was the eldest 1913, Jack 1914, Clarrie 1916, Florrie 1918 and now Bill 1920.

Towards the end of 1920 or early 1921 we left here and moved to a place about a mile from Mayanup on the Jayes Road in the upper Blackwood District, having bought the place off a Mr. Charlie Thompson, being about 740 acres, being bi-sected by the Jayes Road and Scotts Brook flowing through it. The place was known as Red Hill, as on one side of the property was a big red granite hill.

Our main neighbours were the Edward Lee Steeres of Jayes, a Mr. Charlie Hales, Mr. Alf Unstead, and a Mr. Ernie Moulton. The property had about a five acre orchard, sheep, a few milking cows, and cereal crops of wheat and oats.

Here again started school known as the Scotts Brook school my third in about three years, and started off by going with our neighbours children Bill and Doug Unstead and as usual about a three mile walk. My teacher was a Miss Wallbank, and there were about twenty three children of boys and girls from infant class to seventh grade, and during later years my teacher was a Mr. Harry Crocos.

There were children from the Lee Steere family, Hales family, Henderson family, Sinnott family, Forrest family, Unstead and Fuller families.

While living here, one year we had the experience of a terrific bushfire going through the district, when we had only about forty acres of feed left, and much damage to fences. Also in the district in the early 20's were a lot of Italian sleeper cutters, and during our dinner hour at school we used to watch them in the Unstead paddock joining the school ground.

In early 1927 I left home to go and help friends of ours on a farm near Kenninup, and once again to another school.

At the farm owned by a Mr. Albert Jolliffe an English migrant from the War, I was helping out with his wife on milking cows and going to school during the day, while Mr. Jolliffe was away working on the roads of the Upper Blackwood Road Board and came home during the week ends.

Towards the end of August, my birthday being during the school holidays, and coming up 14, and being unable to go away to High School, I left school on the Friday night and Saturday morning started work on the farm for the big sum of' ten shillings a week and keep, and with cows concerned, seven days a week.

During November 1927 I left here and went to a place about four miles from Wilga, where there was a timber mill, and worked in a boarding house owned by a Mr. Gill Hales.

Early 1928 I left here and returned home to Dad's farm at Mayanup, and then not long after I went out to a farm about five miles away owned by Nix Bros. Cecil and Bert Nix.

While working here in the April I had a serious accident in a fall from a horse, which happened while I was going around to the chaff sheds on the farm, to see if the chaff was free falling into the troughs for the sheep, and all the Nix family were away at a neighbours funeral, when the horse bolted after crossing a creek bed, and ran into a post, about five in the afternoon, and I was not found till nearly eight o'clock at night.

I could see the car lights going around the paddocks looking for me, but I could not call out, when I heard somebody call out "here he is", and when they picked me up, I will never forget these words as long as I live, God we have just been to a funeral and it looks like another one, and at the same time I vomited over his nice navy-blue suit.

I was taken up to the house, given a drop of whisky. I had practically all the skin taken off one side of my face, a big clot of blood on the top of my head, and quite a large fracture on the front of my head. This happened on a Tuesday, and on the Thursday Dad came and took me home. On the Saturday I complained of pains in the head, could hardly stand to hear a pin drop, when a neighbour who was there said to Dad "if I were you I would get that boy to hospital," and on the Sunday night all the family were at the hospital, as they did not expect me to pull through.

I finished up in hospital for twelve days before returning home.

After being home for a while I returned to work again on the farm where the accident had happened.

About October 1928 I left this place to go and work for a Mr. Wilfred Moulton on a place about a mile from Mayanup and back to milking cows. Mr. Moulton sold his property towards the end of 1928, and I promised to go with him wherever he moved to, and so loaded on to the Boyup Brook carrier Mr. Herb Hiscock we set off one Sunday morning and headed off, and finished up at a farm just past Waroona, and as the carrier wanted to get back about four p.m. we unloaded the goods on to the verandah of the house. During the night, something we never had at Mayanup, a strong easterly wind blew up, and a lot of the things were up by the South West Highway next morning a quarter of a mile away, and what a night we spent, eaten alive by bed bugs, as the place had been owned by an Italian bachelor and was not too clean, so it was into Waroona early next morning to get disinfectants to clean the place out.

Commenting on the winds the Italian chap said "sometimes wind blow so hard tops of trees touch the ground", and I quite believed him after living there for a while.

Not long after leaving Mayanup, my father also sold out and in 1929 bought a dairy farm at Wokalup, not far from Harvey.

After the cows were dried off for the summer months there was nothing to do, and so left here and went for a while to a Mr. Hayward Clifton's property at Cookernup where my brother Jack was working. From here later on I moved to Boyanup to a farm about four miles out of Boyanup on the road to Bunbury, belonging to M.L. Clifton & Son, the mother and the brother of Hayward Clifton, and also here was a Miss Katherine Layman a daughter of Mrs. Clifton's previous marriage.

Part of the farm had the Preston River as its boundary, and most of the land near consisted of orchard, and they also had a dairy and ran pigs. The property was bi-sected by the road from Boyanup to Bunbury.

I worked here for a few years, one winter going home to Wokalup to help on my father's place, and it was in 1933 when I finally left here going back to the Upper Blackwood District where I spent most of my time till the outbreak of the war.

My first job here in 1933 when a friend of ours a Mr. Eric (Jack) Cross had a bad accident from an Aladdin lantern blowing up in his face, and the while he was in hospital I helped out with his wife in milking the cows for the big sum of seven and six pence a week, but on returning from hospital he asked me to stay on at that, I said "no thanks" and moved on. I was here for seven weeks.

From here out of work I went over to Mayanup where they were putting in a new bridge over the Scotts Brook, and saw a Mr. Lea Moulton of M.F. Moulton and Son and got a job straight away on their farm which was a fairly large one, with sheep, dairy cows and cereals, and extended about a mile along the road to Kojonup, back to Mayanup with a boundary line on the road to Boyup Brook.

Always keen on cricket and tennis, although not brilliant at either, as in those days you taught yourself the best way you could, unless you had the good fortune to go to High or Public School.

I played cricket for the Jayes Cricket Club, and tennis for Maybrook Tennis Club, a little way from Mayanup, and was secretary of the latter for twelve months. Due to my going to cricket one Saturday afternoon and being home late to milk the cows, had a dispute with Lea Moulton, which led to me giving a week's notice on the Sunday, having been offered another job with no cows to worry about.

This was November 1934, and I went to work for a Mr. W.E.J. Pearce on the Jayes Road towards Bridgetown, who ran quite a few sheep, but his main interest was cropping, as he had a large chaff contract selling to the group settlers around Bridgetown, Greenbushes and even towards Nannup.

It was like a home to home working here as Mr. and Mrs. Pearce had known my mother and father before they were married. I was here till about January 1936, when Mr. Pearce got me a job in Bridgetown, but did not stay long, because he was English, and you were the worker attitude.

Heard of a job going over at Dinninup in the Upper Blackwood about twelve miles from Boyup Brook on a big fruit orchard owned by the Chidzey Bros. of Percy, Bert and Vern Chidzey, the orchard being 160 acres the second largest in W.A., and here I put in fruit picking, till the season finished in May. There were many varieties of apples, pears, peaches and plums, a lot of it being export and going overseas.

I put my name and address in on a case of fruit and it finished up in Northern Ireland and I corresponded with a girl from the fruit shop where it finished up till the outbreak of the war when I lost contact.

At the end of the fruit season I stayed on here during the winter months when we did quite a bit of rabbit-proof fencing. The rabbits were very bad here then, also did ploughing in the orchard and digging around the fruit trees.

One of my jobs, after proof fencing a paddock, and had set poison for the rabbits, was any that were left in burrows I used to set rabbit traps, and except for going around about eight at night, the morning and afternoon rounds were done in my working hours and I was allowed to keep the skins to sell. Also, during the fruit season used to make fruit cases till nearly midnight every night and also in spare time in the week end for the sum of six shillings a hundred which meant a few extra shillings at the end of the season.

About the end of October moved to Wokalup at my father's place, and then for the next six to eight weeks put in digging potatoes for various people, getting mostly 9d and a shilling a bag, and this was some of the hardest work of my life on the old back. We used to start in the morning at practically daylight, and would not finish till you could hardly see at night. Fortunately, the job was not a seven day one, as we had to work in the week ends to get the potatoes to the Fremantle wharf by a certain time for shipment to the eastern states.

On completion of the potato digging I gave up work for a while and went for a trip to the Eastern States, having been invited for a holiday by my great-aunt in Adelaide. I left just before Christmas on the interstate boat Kanimbla, and travelled second class to Adelaide for £7.10.0, and spent Christmas with my relations in Adelaide.

One of my main reasons for this holiday was to see the Centenary Celebrations of South Australia and with the re-enactment of the landing at Glenelg Beach and the signing of the Proclamation under the old gum tree 100 years before.

Also my interest in cricket was to see the last three Test Matches of the 1936-37 season between England and Australia, so this took me through Mt. Gambier and the Victorian coastline to Melbourne, arriving a couple of days before the end of 1936, and I got a room in King Street for ten shillings a week, and in those days you were able to get three-course meals for 9d and a shilling.

To the Third Test Match New Year's Day 1937, and which lasted until they were finished in those days, and able to get in for 2/- and always lined up waiting for the gates to open to get a good seat, as they had big crowds in those days, and in this one which Australia won, saw Don Bradman score a double century. England had won the first two played in Brisbane and Sydney.

From here I went back to Adelaide for the Fourth Test Match with Australia again winning and making the series two all, and then finally back to Melbourne for the Fifth Test Match, which Australia also won and winning the series three matches to two, and again had the chance of seeing Bradman make another double century, and during these three matches never missed seeing one ball bowled.

After the cricket was over visited various places in Victoria, meeting penfriends whom I had been writing to including Korumburra where I stayed for about ten days, my penfriend's father being a policeman and visited various local towns.

On leaving here I went up past Shepperton where there is a big fruit preserving factory known as the S.P.C. and they had millions of tins of fruit stored there for export, and finally to a place called Waaia in the wheatbelt, where I had a job for a while, driving ten and fourteen horse teams in the plough, scarifier and harrowing.

My first job before breakfast was the grooming and harnessing of the horses, and never missed a breakfast of sausage and eggs, and the rugs on my bed consisted of washed-out super bags.

Eventually left there and decided to come back to W.A., but on reaching Melbourne decided to look around a little longer, so had a job on a dairy farm not far from Melbourne at a place called Broad Meadows not far from the main Melbourne aerodrome, where with the foggy conditions that existed in June, could hear the planes flying around to try and land, and also there were big rejoicings when King George V1 and Queen Elizabeth were crowned.

After working on the dairy farm, got a little money together and headed for Adelaide, and then booked my berth back by train to Perth. Just before I was to leave a cousin came down from Monash, from around the soldier settler s farms on the Murray River, and persuaded me to cancel my ·booking for a while, which I did, and go back with him for a while, his place having sixty six orange trees, and grapes of the currant, sultana, raisins, and also grapes for producing wine, and while there helped with the picking of the oranges and some fencing.

Finally left Monash, returning to Adelaide, where my great-aunt informed me I had another brother called Allan, born seventeen years after the last one.

Left Adelaide for Perth on the 23rd August in the evening, arriving Perth on the 26th, and caught the train to Wokalup to my father's place on my birthday, being my twenty-fourth, and I had been away travelling and working over East just on 8 months.

Did odd jobs till November came around, and then on to the potato digging, when towards Christmas I went down to Mr. Pearce's place on Jayes Road to help with the hay harvest again, and in February over to Dinninup to help Chidzey Bros. with the fruit season again, and helping out with other jobs till spring, and I worked on these three jobs for years 1938 and 1939, until I was called into Northam Army Camp on 9th November 1939 having enlisted in the A.I.F.

On finishing the potato digging season in 1938, I had got fed up with riding the old pushbike around, and was going to Perth to get a motor bike, but my Father howled me down on this, and said "why not spend a little more and buy a second hand Austin 7 utility which were going cheap at that time, and was I glad I took his advice, as I really did not like motor bikes, and what fun I had with it until I went into the Army. Wherever I worked the boys would pay for the petrol, and we would go off somewhere, but the corrugated roads were terrible for such a small vehicle.

Was digging potatoes at Benger November 1939, when got my notice to go in the A.I.F at Northam, and all the way up from the South West we had boys joining us at nearly every station, on what was known as the midnight horror from Bunbury, and when we got off at East Perth station to await our train to take us to Northam what a collection, some in uniform, including a Lieutenant Shanahan who worked in the railways at Bunbury, and we spoke to each other on the station, and he eventually became my first platoon commander, and then to Northam where we marched out to the Army Camp up 9th November 1939.

Here I became WX571 Pt. Peterson, C.A.G.V., and into a Company of the 2/11 Bn. A.I F. with my platoon Commander P.M. Shanahan, and my original section leader was a Fred Roberts from Bunbury, and if necessary would have followed this man to the end of the earth. A really wonderful chap.

The first few weeks were taken up with plenty of marching and drill exercises, and needles, which not being used to made me have fainting and giddy turns, sickness was something I knew nothing of till I joined the Army.

Just before Christmas was given a few days leave, and got the German measles, and then we boarded the interstate boat Duntroon at Fremantle, and as we passed through West Perth early in the morning on the train from Northam all the brothel girls in Roe Street came out waving to us, and wishing us luck.

After boarding the Duntroon, where we were on our way to Sydney to continue our training, we were treated as passengers and meals and waited on at the table, and really enjoyed the trip.

On reaching Sydney boarded a train, and went north through some lovely countryside, through Newcastle, Maitland in the famous Hunter River valley, and to a place called Greta, a small coal mining town, which was our camp over Christmas and New Year, and were then joined by the other half of the Bn. who had been camped at Rutherford, having come over a week ahead of us.

Here things started getting a little heavier and busier in our training over the Hunter River valley and hills and exercises at night.

Over Christmas Day and Boxing Day many of us had invitations to Christmas dinner and night, held by many organisations in Newcastle, and I was one of those entertained by 2KO, a local wireless station, and it made Christmas worthwhile.

New Year's Eve 1939 a chap from South Australia and I were in one of the local cafes having a cool drink, when a married couple walked in and asked us what we were doing for the evening, and we said "nothing much" so they invited us to their place for the evening, where we met all the family, and saw the Old Year out and the new one in 1940, before returning to camp. We had been invited by Mr. Swan and his wife, and he was a returned man from the First World War.

Early in the New Year we were taken out to the local rifle range for shooting practice, and as the wind was blowing towards us, many of us were very sick the next day from cordite fumes, and we were given castor oil to take, which made some of us worse.

While in the camp, the couple who had befriended me on New Year's Eve, invited me down to tea on a couple of occasions, when we left here to go to Ingleburn, after the N.S. Wales contingent had moved out to go overseas. I wrote to the family thanking- them for their hospitality, and it fell to their daughter Merle Swan, thirteen years old at High School at that time to answer my letters, and which I continued to write to all the time I was overseas, and of course she had to c all me Mr. Petersen. More on that later, as you never know what life has in store for you.

On moving to Ingleburn training was intensified, not so very far from Sydney. The two main railway stations being Ingleburn and Liverpool where we used to- catch the train to Sydney when on leave.

While in this camp I went to the pictures in Liverpool to see a film called " Sixty Glorious Years" based on the reign of Queen Victoria, and it was a really great picture.

I really enjoyed my Army training here, especially the marchcs and field exercises, took you to different parts of the countryside, and also to the Liverpool Rifle Range for shooting exercises, and a really big rifle range.

During March I had an attack of not feeling too well when out on exercises, and hated to miss them, but finally my Company Commander ordered me to the R.A.P., and next morning had blood all over the floor from a bleeding nose, and I said to the orderly "I have red spots all over me," and was immediately rushed to the Infectious Diseases Hospital in Sydney, The Prince Henry, as I had a bout of the real measles this time, and I was so sick I did not care what happened, as I found out after being in there ten days, that besides the measles I also had bronchitis. I ate hardly anything for ten days, when they were just about to poke it down my throat, when I suddenly came good and ate like a horse.

I was still not quite the best, when a few of us who were there were suddenly bundled back to the camp on a Friday. Saturday was in camp and early on the Sunday morning we had to march to the railway station at Ingleburn to board a train for W.A. for embarkation leave prior to going overseas. I was so weak from being in hospital that on arriving at the station I had to change my shirt and underclothes, as I was soaked with sweat and just about doubling up at the knees.

On returning to W.A. for our embarkation leave, I wrote back to the sisters and nurses of the ward I was in, and thanked them for looking after me while I was thereby, and thereby gained another pen-friend for the period of the war, a Nurse Hamilton answering my letter.

After my leave, during which time I went down to the South West to say goodbye to relations, school mates and sporting organisations to which I belonged, cricket, tennis, football and golf', and many whom I worked with and some of them later joined the Bn. as reinforcements and other Bns., we were stationed at the Claremont Showgrounds, and was able to get night leave from there to go to Perth.

On Friday we the 2/11 Bn. and also known as the City of Perth marched through Perth, and was given a great reception, and next morning the 20th April 1940 we embarked at Fremantle on an old coal-burning ship of about 10,000 tons and taken out into Gage Roads from the Harbour, and here we were anchored for the week end. The name of the boat was the Navassa, and used in peace time by the British government for transporting troops from England to India, and the only ventilation to below was big canvas funnels, which on the trip to Columbo were useless as there was so little wind you could have rowed a rowing boat to Columbo.

While in Gage Roads for the week end, ships from the Eastern States came with more troops, and they were allowed ashore for week end leave, which did not please us.

We left Fremantle on Monday 22nd April with many ships in the convoy, and what a rough trip past Rottnest, the boat really rolled and at least fifty percent on board were seasick. Our Company drew the bottom deck below the water-line, and how we sweltered, and at night a lot of us used to take a hammock up on deck, as it was the only way we got any sleep. The only trouble we had to be off deck by five a.m. in the event of any enemy action.

April 25th 1940 Anzac Day somewhere in the Indian Ocean, and ships of the Royal Navy on escort duty honoured us by circling our convoy, one of' the escorts being the battleship Ramilies.

Did not stop at Colombo very long, but time for a little shore leave, while they took on supplies, and then it was on to Aden, the Red Sea, and down the Suez Canal, where we anchored in Bitter Lakes, as each ship went on to El-Kantara to dispose of the troops, and where we eventually disembarked on to a train through the desert of' sandhills and sand to Gaza, and at a place called Kilo 89 we left the train and into camp here, being one big tent city, and being May 19th 1940, and this place became our home till we moved to Egypt towards the end of the year.

While in Palestine we continued our training over sandhills and the desert, and instead of the three other Bns. we had trained with 2/9 Queensland, 2/10 South Australia and 2/12 Tasmania, and with our Bn. we were known as the 18th Brigade, but while on the way overseas they had cut the Brigade down to three Bns. and the other three Bns. finished up in England, still as the 18th Brigade, while we the 2/11, the 2/4 Bn. from the 16th Brigade, and the 2/8 from the 17th Brigade, became the 19th Brigade under the command of Brigadier Robertson, known as Red Robbie.

Managed to get leave to Tel Aviv and Jerusalem. My first time to Tel Aviv was on picket duty when the first lot went on leave, and I met a Jew who had lived in Geraldton and Pemberton, he had a newspaper business, and when I was to come on leave to Tel Aviv he was going to show me around the settlements, but the Italians spoilt that leave by coming into the war.

On the way back to camp our bus was involved in a roll-over by a vehicle coming- around a bend on the wrong side of the road. Fortunately nobody was hurt.

I had a week's leave in Jerusalem and visited Bethlehem, Jericho, and the Dead Sea, the latter said to be so salty you can't sink in it, and hundreds of feet below sea-level, and visited many other historical places while on this leave.

Also in August managed to get a week's leave in Cairo, there being quite a party of us, and I arrived in Cairo at 1.30 a.m. 27th August, the day of my 27th birthday, and what a week's holiday I had, going on all the tours available and seeing many historic places and churches, and when I described the trip home, it took me two letters of about ten pages in each.

Arrived back in Palestine to join in the end of a march and bivouac through the Hebron Hills, which ended up on a Saturday at a place called Berbera where a horse-race meeting was held, and then back to camp a couple of days later.

About October we had a big five-day bivouac around the desert country, no shaving, no washing, exercises at night, with hardly any sleep at times, and so we were a bedraggled group when we got back to camp with a forced march of two hours with our respirators on the last morning of getting in, but we had done a good job, and were now ready for action.

One of' my hobbies was letter writing, and nearly every night after tea I headed for the YMCA and wrote to quite a few relations and friends back home, and enjoyed receiving their letters in return. My money was spent on stamps instead of beer, gambling and cigarettes, and many a 10/- or pound was borrowed from me, when the boys went on leave, as they all seemed to know I had a few shillings in my paybook.

Anyway just before Christmas 1940 we left Kilo 89 and went to Burgel Arab in Egypt, and here we carried on with more exercises, and here we were lucky to have two Christmas dinners.

It was said we were going on a sea landing action somewhere before Christmas, so had an early Christmas dinner, and actually got down to the wharf for the operation when it was called off, and back to camp for another Christmas dinner on the actual day.

After Christmas and before the New Year we were on the move, and went through Mersa Matruh, Sidi Barrani, and over the escarpment into Libya near a place called Fort Capuzza, where we camped.

From here started the actions where the Australians, 6th Division, went into action, and resulted in the fall of Bardia, Tobruk where our Bn. did 22 miles that day, and the fall of the two places ended in many thousands of Italian prisoners being taken. Then on to Derna and past Benghazi where the English 7th Armoured Division had cut off the retreating Italians, and we then came back to a place called Tocra on the coastline, some of the boys going on leave to Benghazi while here, and also received a visit from Mr. Menzies while here.

We then moved back to an aerodrome not far from Tobruk, and then eventually to Tobruk on guard duties.

From here we eventually moved back to Mersah Matruh, and met up with the 2/28 from our State of the 9th Division, who were on their way to Tobruk, and who with many other Allied Bns. became known as the Rats of Tobruk, an Association which still lives today in 1991.

While here the two Bns. engaged in an Australian Rules football match, which resulted in for years after the war an annual cricket match, and then on to bowls.

Again moved from here to a place not far from Alexandria, and where had leave to that place from the camp there, and there was a big day of all the Bns. in a big sporting day of all events, of which Findlay Campbell of our Bn. won the broad jump and pocketed a few handsome bets for some who knew of his capability in that event.

After a short stay here our Bn. embarked for Greece, where we landed at a port called Piraeus near Athens, and after landing in all our gear except for needy things and our Army equipment, things which we did not see again, we were put on a train and somewhere through Greece to a place called Larissa, and then on trucks up to the Greece-Yugoslavia border, where we soon came in contact with the German Army, and soon we were retreating back the way we came with the dreaded Stuka bombers on to us, and here for the first time I saw the real effects of war, with the Greek population pushing and carrying whatever they could along the roads, getting machine-gunned and bombed, and we could do nothing to help them.

At one stage we were caught in a maze of about eight S-bends in the road, and for about two hours one lot of bombers would be over, and then machine-gunned us, till the next wave of' bombers, almost praying we would be hit, to get out of the misery of it all.

Eventually we moved on again, and got redirected on to a wrong road, until we met English troops coming back, and they told us we were heading for the enemy, and we found out on our return that was the enemy fifth columnist who had taken control and directed us that way.

Anyway we did not reach our Bn. lines that night but camped on the sides of Mt. Olympus, and reached our lines next morning tired and hungry.

We next moved to Mt. Braylos, and here we fought our last rearguard before heading somewhere for the coast, where on Anzac Day 1941 we hid among the olive trees till nightfall, and moved onto a boat for embarkation, at the time did not know where, so our stay in Greece was very short.

On the day of the 26th off the coast of Greece, and we were bombed by the Germans, and although not a direct hit on our boat, the plates were sprung, and we were taking on water, and we headed for Suda Bay on the island of Crete, and disembarked during the afternoon, and in the harbour saw sunken ships and a British cruiser that had been sunk by enemy action.

Camped in the hills near Suda Bay that night, and next day weary and footsore, no trucks here we marched on to a place called Georgeiopolus, and then lost count of days, and moved to Retimo, and here we were told to dig in to await eventualities, which was expected to be an invasion of Crete by the German Army.

Days went slowly by, during which time Crete was being heavily bombed, and sometime in May they believed that Crete would be invaded by parachutists, and which on 20th May actually took place, planes landing them around Malame and Suda Bay area in the morning, also by gliders, and in the afternoon Heraklion and Retimo were the targets, and what a sight it was to see all these men floating down, but I did not envy them the job they had, as many were killed before they reached the ground and hundreds wounded and killed before they got out of their planes. We captured many prisoners that afternoon, including the Commander of that area, who said it "wasn't cricket" because we fired on his men before they landed.

Must mention we also had the N.S. Wales 2/1 Bn. fighting ·alongside of us, besides Greek troops. During the first night of the battle, the Germans who were left managed to regroup, and proved to be a thorn in our side, as they holed up in an old factory, and without artillery could not shift them.

Well eventually the Germans took the aerodrome at Malame and landed tanks and more men, and we were finally overrun at the end of May, and told to smash our rifles and take to the hills, and some of us made for the other side of the island, where some were being evacuated, but we missed the place, and hid in the hills, but managed to outfit a barge, which eventually got away with some mixed troops, and found out at the end of the war, that they had landed at Mersah Matruh on the beach in Egypt

Well the Germans finally caught up with us at a place nearby called Timkakion and we became "Prisoners of War" on the evening of 6th June 1941, and then I with many others was marched through the hills till midnight and nothing to eat.

While on the march they took us through Heraklion and on to Retimo, where they camped us for the night, and the area where I had been fighting during the Battle of Crete.

During the night I woke up with a stinging feeling on my neck, and eventually I was screaming with pain and could not get the guards to take any notice, when I suddenly collapsed at their feet, and I became paralyzed and could not use my arms or legs, so they rushed me to the Retimo hospital, where they discovered two puncture marks on the side of my neck, saying I had been bitten by a snake, which they froze and lanced, and the doctor said "another three minutes and we could not have saved you." I had already thrown in the sponge, thinking of all the snakes in Australia I had to come here to be bitten by one. During the night I had oxygen and needles to keep the old ticker going, and during the next two days had serious relapses. The medical orderly came in and said "Your life was saved but it was very difficult," so I had great respect for German doctors and orderlies.

I was told later by the boys when I was taken to hospital that you could have heard me screaming about five miles away that night.

The boys had also been told when they marched through Retimo next day, that they had done all they could for me, but that I had died, and many were the looks of seeing a ghost when I eventually met up with some of them.

I was in hospital about twelve days, and then put in a compound with Greeks and a few of our troops, who with myself were taken back past Suda Bay and a big P.O.W. camp near Malame, and here remained for some time, and had the care of our own W.A. 2/7 Field Ambulance, especially when I started having giddy turns, with the tent rolling around which they said was through the effects of the bombing etc. I had been through.

It was fully three months before I started to feel good, and the poison out of my system from the snakebite.

About the end of August 41, a party of about 200 including myself was told to pull down tents and pack them up as we were going to another camp on the island, and the tents and us were loaded onto a boat at Suda Bay.

Were told we were going by boat to Heraklion, not a very long way from Suda Bay, but on the way had a bit of excitement in which I did some cursing as I could not swim, in the way of one of our submarines had a go at us, and missed us by about six yards, and the guards all got worked up, and ordered a count and found one missing. He had got off the boat in the harbour, and was immediately branded as a spy, as having warned the submarine that we were coming out.

They had a submarine chaser and a plane escorting us, and dropped depth charges which shook our boat up a bit, and said "that they had got the submarine. Anyway we eventually reached Heraklion, and were going to leave us on the boat that night, but decided at the last moment to take us off, and we were bundled into the same barracks, of about three months before when we were on the march after just being captured, and hardly room to stand up in.

About an hour after being taken off the boat, there was a loud explosion in the harbour, and evidently the submarine they were supposed to have sunk had come into the harbour and torpedoed the boat which we had been on.

Confusion reigned, and the guards had been on the plank, so for the rest of that night we did not get treated too kindly, and in the morning having to go down and work on the boat, discovered where the torpedo had hit was the hatch that we would have been on had we stayed on board. Two lucky escapes in one day.

Eventually got away from Heraklion on trucks, and I discovered that we were headed out the way we had come from when first captured, and it proved that we were going into a camp not far from Tymbakion and which we had to put up all our tents on arriving, but which was already fenced with barb wire about six foot high, and our water supply was a channel inside the fence, coming down from the hills.

Well for the next three months, being one of the few level places left on the island, our job was to grub out olive trees, some eighty to a hundred years old, and prepare for the making and laying of an aerodrome. Times were hard, very little food, boiled lentils being the main course at night, and had it not been for the Greek and Cretan population, on leaving food at night in the holes where we were grubbing out the olive trees, and on special church days coming down from the hills with big containers of dried beans, being done in olive oil, and whatever other food they could spare, things would have been a lot worse.

The Germans stopped it at first, but realised they were helping to feed us, and allowed it to continue, and little items of clothing.

Knowing what work we were doing was against the Genova Convention, we had a strike, but the Germans would not listen to our story, and pulled out ten of the boys and said "work or else," and so work continued and they had the whip hand.

Towards Christmas 41 things started getting very cold here, with hardly any clothing, snow on the mountains and not being able to wash our clothes, it was only natural that the old lice took a hand, and plenty of scratching was done.

Christmas went by quietly, with a little extra food found from somewhere; but the authorities evidently realised at the rate we were working that it would be ten years before the drome was finished, and told us we were going to Germany, and leaving the Greeks and Cretans to finish the job, as without us being there, could make them work as they wished.

Anyway, we were eventually put on trucks, and taken through Heraklion, Retimo, and to Suda Bay, a little quicker way than when we came when first captured near Tybakion, and coming through Heraklion noticed that the boat that brought us there was still sunk tied up to the wharf.

At this stage of my P. O.W. life I was beginning to look a bit like a broomstick, having dropped in weight from eleven and a half stone to eight stone, and conditions getting much colder with snow down to the water's edge at Suda Bay, which had not been seen for a few years, which we found out later when we really got to Europe.

Put on a boat here, and left about 1st or 2nd of January 1942, and arrived at Piraeus near Athens, where we off-loaded on to a Bulgarian boat, and taken down through the Aegean Sea to Salonika, where most of the coastline you could see was snow, and got stuck on a sandbank somewhere, but managed to free itself eventually.

At Salonika, what conditions, and in charge of the Allied troops going through was a British sergeant major, and what a bastard, he was worse to his own troops than any German had ever been.

Anyway, while here we did get a Red Cross food parcel between two of us, and how nice to get a real cup of tea. I shared my first parcel with a friend of mine, Ray Blechynden f'rom Bridgetown and of the 2/11 Bn. also.

Snow, snow and more snow, and eventually about the middle of January hundreds of us were bundled into cattle trucks, forty at a time, and put on a train, bound for somewhere. All cutlery was taken from us, straw on the floor of the truck and one rug, and six foot of snow outside, and off we went, getting some food occasionally and now and again out for toiletries, and when troop trains or other emergencies we were bundled on to a side line, and so after travelling through parts of Greece, Yugoslavia, Austria, and except at one big town where they marched us to a Red Cross soup kitchen, such was our home for fifteen days and sixteen nights, till we finally came to a place called Lamsdorf, and a big P.O.W. stalag known as V111B.

This became my home for the next few weeks, but the greatest relief was the first week here, was that we had to shave all the hair off our body, including thirteen weeks head of hair that I had, and through the delouser to get rid of the lice on our body, and then to be given completely new clothes, and no more scratching, but my head was so cold that I had to pull some old socks to pieces to make a cover for it, and as it was Europe's coldest winter for twenty one years, one can understand why we felt the cold, and having not much fat in one's body because of our skinniness, I think that if it had not been for the Red Cross food parcels to boost up the food, which was received from the camp ration, it would have been hard for survival.

There were thousands of prisoners here from the different Commonwealth nations and our other Allied troops, and were at times allowed into other compounds, and with troops going out on working parties and some coming in through sickness were able to gather to a certain extent what was going on in the world and conditions on working parties which were of varied occupations.

Also was able to meet many of my Bn. mates, and hear of their stories of being over here after the fall of Crete, and had been here six months earlier.

Eventually the time came when I was to be sent out on a working party, in which we were searched before leaving, and on the day two parties of about fifty men went out to Sudetenland, and arrived at a place called Bodisch where our party got off, and the other one to Konigshan.

Not much room to move, our beds were three tiers high, with a straw mattress and one rug, and part of this room was also our messing room. Found out that we were on a railway working party, and being still winter with plenty of snow about, our first job was to be shovelling snow from the railway line to keep the trains running, and standing in snow all day was not the warmest of jobs, especially when the temperature is twenty five degrees below, and you are getting icicles in your moustache.

The food was not the best for working conditions, being very watery with no body in it, potatoes and swedes and turnips that sometimes needed an axe to chop them up, and fish cheese which you could always smell before you reached the camp. The bread was the only solid part, and not enough of it unfortunately, so it was with the help of the good old Red Cross food parcels that we struggled on, sometimes getting one per person per week or maybe a parcel between two, according to supplies on hand, and nearly always fifty cigarettes a week as well.

Mail and food and clothing parcels from home and friends were one of the main things we looked forward to, and although I received letters from other relations etc. I did not receive my first letter from home until I had been a prisoner for eighteen months. To many of the boys one of their greatest receivals was a cigarette parcel, and although I received quite a few they did not worry me, except for bartering with, my cigarettes for food, and on every food article was a fixed exchange rate, so it was fair and above board, and even came in handy outside at times

Finally the snow cleared and all crops came through, and the sowing of potatoes, beet and other foods, but it meant harder work for us, as we had to take out the earth between sleepers of the railway line, and putting back metal in its place, to eventually pulling up the old railway line, and putting in new sleepers and rails. To see some parts of the railway line after the snow cleared made one wonder how the trains over stopped on them.

The first time we started on this, were given seven sleepers to dig out between and under for two men as a days' work, and many were the rows that first day, as saying we would not be allowed to go back to camp till they were all finished, but we were all so weak could hardly lift a pick, let alone swing it, so there 'were many unfinished jobs that first day. It took my mate and I three days to finish our seven sleepers.

As time went along we managed to get some of our strength back, and things got easier, being able to get into the swing of it, but we refused to over-exert ourselves, and many were the threats levelled at us by the guards, bosses and the engineers, till finally they put us on a contract job, do a certain amount and when finished could go back to camp.

Forgot to mention on the party were English, New Zealanders, Australian, a couple of Spaniards, and a Christian from Pitcairn Island, and the party was known as E.388 ex Stalag VIIIB.

Well time came and went, some of' the boys leaving to go elsewhere, and others replacing.

The person in charge of our party was a chap from Mount Lawley in W.A., was a sergeant major, and had been a prisoner in the First World War, and again in the second. He was Jewish and his name was Sol Burcove, which he changed to Burton when he became a prisoner this time.

He left us and we had an English sergeant in the medical corps in charge, and spoke the German language, and he became to me one of the finest English chaps I met during the war. His name was Sgt. Casson, and another fine English chap I was friends with was an Eric Thorpe.

Christmas 1942 and 1943 went by, and two occasions I will always remember, as the way we all got together and made a Christmas of it with the help of the guards of our camp, who because of' the way we did not cause them much trouble, they made things easier for us, as between Christmas 42 and New Year 43 we had six barrels of beer in camp over that period, and there were many other occasions when we were allowed to have beer in the compound.

In this part of Sudetenland there was some beautiful country, of rock formations, the pine plantations, and the lovely formations of snow on the trees in the winter time when they were frozen. Of the friendly times with the guards during the springtime when the wild strawberries, and blueberries were ripe in the hills, and we had finished our contract job for the day, I used to wander half a mile from the job picking them, the guards saying "don't care where you go as long as you are here when the train goes to camp," so many a lovely meal I had, and on one occasion on a Sunday when all the raspberries were ripe near the camp, they allowed us to go out and pick them to make jam for ourselves.

Of course there was a lot of bribery went on between the guards and ourselves, getting them accepting and smoking our cigarettes, as we had them where we wanted them if they got too nasty, but taken right through most of them had been in the front line and were fairly good to us, except for the local station master, who complained to higher up, and so between us and the guards we got him caught with English cigarettes in his pocket, got nine months gaol, stripped of his war ribbons and kicked out of the Nazi Party.

Towards the end of 1944, owing to the fact that they could not get reinforcements for our working party, and none for the other one -further down the line, which came out from Stalag VIIIB the same day as ours, we were transported to the one at Konigshan, and here the barracks were in upstairs and downstairs, with different rooms for sleeping, and we all got split up into other rooms, and here things were somewhat tighter, as there had been many attempted escapes, end even when I was there one Welsh bloke went out nearly every night, and slept with a German woman over the road, and back again before morning.

He was in the same room as myself, and one of our windows used to face across to where she lived, and one night as he was shaving by the window she was looking over, and behind his back I waved to her, and she must have told him about it, and he told me not to do it again, and I told him I'll wave to whoever I like, and naturally for some reason or other did not get along too well, when one morning while we were waiting out in the snow for him to come and get to work I remarked about him always being last out, and being Saturday we were back in camp, just after midday, and he remarked on the fact of what I had said, so I said "if the cap fits that's O.K. with me" whereupon he remarked that I was a German spy in British uniform, and as I had let him get away with various other insinuations, and going by the looks of the other boys in the room, it finished up with a fight, my first and only one in my life. I got a few bruises, but he had a bit of skin taken off his face, so don't know what his girl friend said to him that night.

Well, dragging on towards Christmas 1944, and going by what news we were getting and the attitude of the local population that things were going a little our way, and perhaps only months away when we could see our freedom coming, and things were getting tough, as they were not being able to get the Red Cross food parcels through to us, which meant such a lot.

Christmas 1944 was not the same here on the party at Konigshan, aks were the two previous ones of 42 and 43 held at Bodisch, and was a very low-key affair, but one thing in our favour, the winter was not quite as bad as the previous ones, being somewhat milder.

After January 1945 things were tightening up a little, they were wanting more work for their total war effort, and the rations were getting less, and our sergeant in charge, a Fred Earl, a big bloke from New Zealand, started going to the local markets with a guard and buying food for us, in the vegetable line only, and on the black market we were paying up to three times what they were worth, but they were helping to keep us going, and as we said, "the reichmarks will probably be worth nothing after the war."

Coming up April 45, we could see things were not going too well for the Germans, as the railway lines were working to the utmost in getting war material back from the fighting zones to elsewhere and more people were being evacuated, and one of the main junctions, Trautenau, where we worked, was so full of traffic at times they did not know where to start their shunting of the trains and trucks to get moving.

From the middle of April it was really chaotic, they had a job at times to get us to work, and sometimes two hours late getting to camp at night, and to see the cluttering of the roads with civilian traffic, hardly room to move, and every kind of transport it was possible to find, and on the trains a lot of people were just in open trucks, and although I probably should not say it, it made us feel good to see what they were going through, as no doubt they had done to countless millions in the countries they had invaded or overrun during the war.

May 1945 came and we could see the end was getting close, and they had us working right up to the 8th May, when the guards finally said "you can put your tools away, arbeitfertig", work finished, the war is over.

From here we were marched over to some barracks near Trautenau, where quite a few other working parties from around here were also brought in, and to await transport eventually to England.

We were here for some time, and got our first glimpse of Russian soldiers, or which we were not very impressed. The local population were scared of the Russians, and at night they would come to our barracks to get us to go and sleep at their houses for the night, and on one occasion a chap from the 2/32 Bn. and from Northam W.A., and myself were at this house when a Russian soldier came in early one morning and demanded cigarettes and wine, we were in the double bed and the woman had slept in a single bed at the bottom of ours, when told she had none, he started opening drawers, and when he saw us, and on discovering what our nationality was he left the room, but one wonders what would have happened had we not been there, and on another occasion we were invited to stay at a farm house for a night.

Well after quite a few days here, beginning to wonder whether we were ever going to get away, finally on Sunday 20th May we boarded a train which took us to Prague, and from here the Americans picked us up in trucks, and took us to a big Air Force place near Pilsen, and here we stayed for a few days, and the barracks we stayed in were bug-ridden, and a few sleepless nights were spent here before we finally went by American Dakota planes to Rheims in France, a big American established base, went through showers etc., our old clothes taken from us and we were practically rigged out in American clothing, given a big Yankee kit bag and other items of American clothing.

While at the base for one night, had we had the articles of German swords, cameras, field glasses, and any article of German clothing, we could have made a fortune, as the Yanks would have paid any price to get these as souvenirs of the war.

Just on dusk 26th May when we thought we would be spending another night, after a brief storm we finally boarded a Lancaster bomber on the last leg to England, and arriving at some Air Force base spent the night here.

Next day were all sorted out, English, Australian and New Zealanders, and our Australian contingent of various units left by train, going through London and down to Eastbourne near the east coast of England, and finally drafted off to our various Battalions, and so back under military control again. I called it the end of my P.O.W.

days, being eighteen days from when the war finished till we reached England, and about ten days short of being a P.O.W. for four years.

It was nice to receive some really up to date mail from home, relations and friends, and to send a cablegram home, letting them know I was here and well.

While recuperating at Eastbourne I was given leave, and went to Edinburgh in Scotland, and visited the home where Sgt. Casson was living with his parents, and whom after the war I kept in touch with his parents every Christmas, and also with Sgt. Casson until his death, and then his wife who passed away about eighteen months later, and now in touch with his sister Betty, and also visited the other English chap whom I liked very much, Eric Thorpe and his wife, and also still keep in touch at Christmas. Now 1991.

Also visited various places around London and went to a cricket match at the Lords Oval, between the R.A.F. and R.A.A.F.

Had about ten days' leave, and could have had more, but was more interested in returning home, and all who were leaving at that time were told, well you know there has been a war on, so don't expect anything elaborate to go home on, and I thought not something like the old tub we came overseas on, and imagine my surprise when I got to Liverpool and found out I was coming home on the 42,000 ton Mauretainia.

There were about two thousand troops on board, being Australians and New Zealanders, and there was a Scottish major in charge of us, and as the troops liked gambling, especially the old two-up, well he tried to ban it, but he got nowhere, and at times there were thousands English pounds waged in the centre at the toss of the coins, with the result that on reaching home, some had plenty and some had none.

Came home through the Panama Canal which was an experience coming through all the lochs on the Canal, and jungle vegetation on each side, and to Pearl Harbour, where you could still see some of the damage done by the Jap raid in June 1941.

Some of the boys had leave, but I was not too well the first day, so did not go and missed out, as on the second day for some reason or other we had to hurriedly leave and I missed out, and quite a few of the boys got left behind, overstaying their leave the first day.

From here our next destination proved to be Wellington in New Zealand to unload the New Zealanders, and we had a days' leave there, and I was picked up by a f'amily by the name of Clarke, and taken to their home and entertained for the day.

Leaving New Zealand, our next port of call was Sydney, where all of us disembarked, more so the West Australian members, as the Mauretania was too big to enter Fremantle Harbour, and what a welcome home we received as we went into Sydney Harbour from all the boats blowing their whistles, and even the trains were blowing their whistles.

Luckily for me on disembarking at Sydney, had to come down, and with all equipment and stuff I was bringing home, clothing, tobacco, chocolate, as I would not have been able to walk upstairs with it all.

On leaving the boat we were all taken out to the Sydney Showgrounds to be our camp for a couple of days. On arrival at the Showgrounds was a letter from Nurse Hamilton, the one who·had answered my letter of appreciation when I was in hospital at Prince Henry Hospital in March 1940, and asking me to come out to her parents' home in Burwood if I had any leave, and which was granted while we were at the Showgrounds.

On arriving at their home I was made very welcome, and they filled the bath half full of nice hot water, and I had the best bath for many a long day.

The next day Nurse Hamilton took me over through Manly, and showed me around, and evidently while I was away overseas she had trained as a missionary and was going overseas to Africa, and asked me if I would like to go with her, but unfortunately after the years I had just been away I did not think I would like to go.

After the break here in Sydney on the train, on our way home to the West going through Albury, Melbourne and to the Adelaide Showgrounds.

Were not to be here for long, but managed to wangle a couple of hours leave to visit great-aunts and cousins, through the Red Cross, and told us the train would be leaving again at quarter past twelve, or so we thought, but on arrival back at the Showgrounds cliscovered it had left at a quarter to twelve.

Consternation reigned, as the train's·first stop was Port Pirie and all my gear and equipment was on the train, so got in touch with the transport officer and explained to him my predicament, so he got in touch with authorities at Port Pirie, and had my equipment all sent back to Adelaide, where I picked it up that night, and luckily it was all there, as I·thought it could easily have been rifled, as I had pounds of tobacco and hundreds *of* cigarettes in it which I had been buying on the way since we left England, although I did not smoke myself. Thinking of those at home.

Well, having sorted that all out, and as the result had a few extra days leave in Adelaide, and enjoyed visiting my relations, including one of my brothers who was in the transport section of the Air Force, and here had the distinction of witnessing V.J. Day, the end of the war with Japan, and the throngs of people who let themselves go that day.

Finally left Adelaide by passenger train for Perth, there being about twelve P.O.W's on that train, and through some mistake my parents had not been notified I was coming.

Eventually a chap in Red Cross uniform by the name of Ron Tynan, after finally sorting out other commitments said "1 will take you home", which was out to Armadale twenty miles from Perth.

On getting to Armadale, being a new area to me, and getting directions from various people, eventually arrived at my father's place, and imagine the surprised look on Mum and Dad's face when they saw me as they had not been told I was coming home on today's train from the East.

Most of all, they were so pleased to see me looking so well, as they had seen some of the P.O.W's who had come home and were not looking well, and heard various tales of some of them, and after a cup of tea and sending off Mr. Tynan with a big bag of oranges for his trouble of bringing me home, and whom we remained friends with for a good many years.

Then it was round to tell of all my experiences since I had seen them last on 19th April 1940.

For the first few weeks of being home I visited friends and relatives around close to Perth, as I had made up my mind after being a P.O.W. for so long that I was not going to do any work before the New Year.

Of course I had a few weeks leave before I went back to camp at Point Walter for examinations, and finally to Karrakatta where I was discharged and paid off by the Army on 20th September 1945, about seven weeks short of being six years in the Army.

After being discharged I went down to the South West and visited more relatives and friends, whom I had not seen since 1939, and also found the loss of some of my school and sporting mates as the result of the war.

Had Christmas at home in 1945, and a very nice occasion after the previous four, and after the New Year 46, I left for Adelaide, and then up on the River Murray to my cousin's place Allan Harvey at Monash, as I had promised to go and help him to pick his grape crop that season, owing to the shortage of labour.

Also helped one of his neighbours with some grape picking, and at the end of the grape picking season I stayed on and helped with some of the pruning.

Leaving here I went to Sydney, then Newcastle, and Greta to see the Swan family who had befriended me when I was in the Army there, and also their daughter Merle who had corresponded with me during the war years.

From here I went back to Sydney and Melbourne, where I visited relations, then on to Adelaide and home again to Perth and Armadale.

For a few weeks up till Christmas 46 I got a job at a local vineyard called the Derry-Na-Sura, managed by a German of German/East African descent, and he really proved to be one with his treatment. Was bottling up wine and packaging it for Christmas orders.

In the New Year of 1947, I went down to the South West on to a farm where I had worked before the war, now being run by Cecil

Rodway, whom I had also worked with on the farm, which was previously owned by W.E.J. Pearce. After a few weeks here helping out, I went to Bridgetown to help picking apples during the fruit season for a Mr. Mitchell.

There were two big fruit packing sheds in the town, and most of the fruit in the district was being exported overseas, and in the evening for two or three hours to earn some extra money I used to help with the wiring- up of the packed fruit cases.

While working at Paterson & Co's shed, the manager was a Mr. Harold Armstrong who had gone to school with my Mother, and he wanted me to learn the aspects of the packing and other things concerned with fruit, but the season was coming to a close, so he told me to go and see the manager of P. & Co. at Fremantle and get a job there, but they had nothing.

The next job I nearly went out into the wheatbelt to help on a farm, but happened to notice an advertisement for workers in a timber mill at Jarrahwood out from Busselton, and not far from Nannup, and I finished up here helping to stack timber.

One week and I happened to go to Bridgetown and ran into Mr. Harold Armstrong, who was surprised to see me, as he said "I thought you were working at Fremantle" and I told him they had had nothing for me, and I was working at Jarrahwood.

About ten days later I got a surprise when I received a letter from Paterson & Co. at Fremantle, asking me to call as they had something coming up that might interest me, and so I left the job at the timber mill, and headed for Fremantle, where I was asked to start in about a fortnight's time.

I advertised in the paper for board and lodgings at Fremantle and had about six replies, when I discovered a cafe in Pakenham Street which took in boarders, and I could leave at two minutes and start work at eight, and very convenient to work, which it later proved too inconvenient for the work coming up.

On first starting work I was busy packing vegetables for the export market to Singapore which Paterson & Co. were involved with at that time, and also in the putting together of John Deere tractors, which came in big wooden crates.

With the start of the crayfishing season in November 1947 and Paterson & Co. involved with the export to America of crayfish tails, I became involved with three or four others in the processing of the crayfish, and working down at Robb's Jetty, and as Paterson & Co. had fishermen working out from Lancelin Island, and they were transported live by truck from there, and when a load arrived down, any time of the night, we were called out to process them, so at times we had some very irregular hours.

Well Christmas 1947 went by, and into the year of 1948, and reverting back to other work when the cray-fishing season finished.

Then on to November 1948, and the start of the new crayfish season, and working at Robbs Jetty, and working there on Melbourne Cup day 1948, when I had taken my wireless to listen to the Melbourne Cup, when I had the wireless on for the news at 12 30pm when an item came over that consternation reigned at the Quay

Cafe where I boarded, that a ticket in that day's lottery draw, with "Day of Luck" c/- Quay Cafe had won first prize, and I said to the boys "that's me" and I had won £3000 for 2/6d, but I still was not too sure till I got back to Fremantle and ducked up to my room to check, and so it proved to be one of the lucky days of my life, but had to borrow five pounds from the foreman that night to shout drinks for the boys, and even the managing director said "I won't be able to live up to you now," but one of my first thoughts was "New Zealand here I come" as I had made up my mind one day to get there to meet the boys I was associated with in the P.O.W's camps.

I left Paterson & Co. just before Christmas, and left for Adelaide in time to have Christmas there with my great Uncle and Aunt, and their descendants, and what a houseful there was.

From here I continued on to Melbourne, and then over by plane to Hobart and doing various trips from there by bus, which included Port Arthur, and I also visited a pen-friend who I had been corresponding with since about 1930.

Was in Hobart about middle of January when they had their wettest January day for about twenty years and their coldest for the same period with there being snow on Mt. Wellington, what a contrast for summer.

On the return trip a party of us did a car trip up the east coast of Tasmania and visited many historical and beautiful places up to Launceston, from where I flew again to Melbourne.

From here I went by train to Sydney, and made arrangements to go on the boat Wangonella to Auckland in New Zealand, and where I spent the next five months.

On arriving there, and going to the bank, discovered that the money I had transferred to New Zealand had not arrived, and I was without money, so went to the railway yards and enquired of a Fred Earl who worked in the railways, and luckily found him on duty, and what a surprise he had when he saw me, one of my P.O.W. mates, and I explained my predicament and he lent me £5 till the next day when my money had arrived from Australia, 200 pounds Australian for 160 New Zealand, being on the British currency rate. How would that go today, 1991?

After seeing Fred Earl again the next day and paying my debt after my money had come through, I visited another of my P.O.W. mates, Arthur Davies, in Auckland, and on the Saturday with one of his mates, took me on a fishing trip, where I had the misfortune on throwing my line out on one of the occasions, I don't know what happened, but no line went out as I had the hook embedded in one of my fingers, and had to go to a doctor to get it cut out and a couple of stitches in it, and so spoilt their fishing day, and had the stitches taken out on my trip somewhere ten days later. Luckily for me it all cost nothing as they had a free scheme somehow, despite the fact that I was only a visitor to New Zealand.

From Auckland went up north to see another mate by the name of Alec Gracie at a place called Dargaville, but he had moved south of Auckland, so returned south again on to town called Hamilton, where I met four more of the boys by the name of Pierce, Myers, Hunter and Peterson, and a very nice place on the banks of the Waikato River.

From here I visited another one of the boys by the name of Charlie Clarke, who had a butcher's shop there, then on to a place called Cambridge, and then on to Rotatua, a place of hot and cold springs, hot boiling mud and geyers shooting water in the air, and the air with sulphuric acids giving an unpleasant smells.

My next visit was to a chap by the name of Jack Kirkpatrick who had a dairy farm not far from here, I think the place was called Te-Whaite, and then a visit to Lake Taupo, 1172 feet above sea level, and what an enormous expanse of water, and this is where the Waikato River has its source and is New Zealand's longest river, and also from Lake Taupo many hundreds of tons of trout are caught each year.

I next moved on to the Hawkes Bay area to Napier, a town severely devastated by an earthquake just before World War 2, and then down to Hastings and to a small place called Otane where I met another one of the P.O.W. boys called Rae Templeman, where he was farming sheep and cattle.

I then wandered down through various towns to Wellington, and then I caught the ferry across Cook Straights to Picton and the South Island, and I then went by bus to Nelson and then to Westport on the west coast, and to Greymouth, Hokitiki, and from here down to the Fox and F'ranz Joseph Glaciers, an awesome sight of great masses of ice, and at that time there were three hundred and sixty five bends in the road between Hokitiki and the glacier, and at that time had to go back to Hokitiki, as the road did not extend beyond there in 1949.

I then returned over the Southern Alps and to Christchurch, where I met with four more of the boys of P.O.W. days by the name of Hamilton, Armstrong, Dalziel and Dumurgue, and meeting up with all these chaps was really making a wonderful holiday.

From Christchurch south to Ashburton, Timaru where I met another one of my mates by the name of Ian Gillon, and on to Dunedin, where walking down the street, to the surprise of both of us I ran into Stuart Davis, another one of my P.O.W. mates who had a farm not far from here. Also in Dunedin met Lunam, H. Davis, and a Len Blee. I then came down to Milton, then inland to Gore and Lumsden, and to Lake Wakatipu at Queenston high in the mountains, hundreds of feet above sea level, and even a hundred and twenty feet below sea level, a really magnificent area.

Returned back to Lumsden and up to Te-Anau, where saw the beautiful Lake Te-Anau and Lake Manapouri, and was hoping to got to Milford Sound, but the tunnel that was being built under the Alps had been closed by a big avalanche that had fallen from the Alps.

Back through Lumsden to Winton, Riverton and to Invercargill, where I called on another mate, and while there I took a boat trip to Stewart Island, south of Invercargill, where on the return trip my luggage went astray for a couple of days before it turned up, and I had to borrow some of his things for a couple of days.

From here I returned to Christchurch, and the Canterbury Plains to a place called Culverden, where I met Noel Ross, and then on to Waiau, where I met a Sandy Galletly who had a farm there, and then up the coast north to Kaikoura, Blenheim, and to Picton, where I again caught the ferry to Wellington to the North Island.

From Wellington I went up the west coast of the North Island to Otaki, Levin, to Palmerston North, Fielding, and to Wanganui where I met another one or the boys by the name of Rueb Check, and then to the Taranaki District, a big dairying area with cheese factories everywhere, and here at Eltham I met another one of the boys who worked in one of the factories by the name of Irwin Alty, whose nickname was "Teapot."

Continuing on to New Plymouth, back through Rotorua and over to the Bay of Plenty area to Tauranga, where I met Jack Barker and Len Christmas, and then on to Matamata where I met - Buckley, another one of the boys, and on the way from here to Auckland I met Alec Gracie who had moved down from Dargaville up north, and out of this trip to New Zealand I met twenty nine out of thirty of my N.Z. P.O.W. mates of Greece and Crete and our days in Germany.

In June, on my return trip to Australia, I travelled by flying-boat to Sydney by T.E.A.L. known as Tasman Empire Airways Limited.

From Sydney I went up north to Newcastle, where I met my friend Merle Swan, and we went out to Maitland and her parents place at Greta for the week-end, and at that time the Hunter River valley was in flood and we were on the last train from Newcastle to Maitland before the line was closed because of floodwaters.

The river really came down in flood with Maitland awash, and in the railway station nearly all you could see was about a foot of the top of the railway carriages, and to get back to Newcastle after the week-end was to travel by bus detours inland, and I then returned to Sydney to catch the train to Melbourne for the following week-end.

The reason for wanting to get to Melbourne was that there was a big interstate football match between W.A. and Victoria.

The Melbourne ground was a quagmire and what a thrashing Victoria gave us. In those days we had a big over six foot player by the name of Merv McIntosh, and he played in the ruck, and the pictures in the paper on the Monday of him standing about a foot deep in mud, and trying to get out to punch the ball from the bounce downs at the centre. This was played in June 1949.

After visiting relations and friends in Melbourne I continued my homeward journey by train on to Adelaide, and stayed here for awhile visiting my great-aunts and uncles and my many cousins.

At last I decided about July it was time I returned home, and got back to work again, after having been away on holidays nearly eight months, and no work and spending all my money.

I went and saw my previous employers of Paterson & Co. which had now been taken over by Tropical Traders, and became known as Tropical Traders and Paterson, and I was taken back into their employ.

Around about this time just before Christmas I was getting fed up with life around the city, and had noticed in the papers where they were calling for workers at the Wittenoom Asbestos Mine, so had actually applied for a job, and was to go on a certain day, when one of the bosses said "I believe you are leaving us", and I stated why, so he said "We are going to start a cray fish factory at Geraldton, what about going up there for us," so I said "that suits me, it's away from the city," so a chap by the name of Bill Brooks and I went up there to work on getting the factory going, and going up by the "Nord Star" fishing boat owned by the Aberstrom brothers.

Just a few days before I left I had made arrangements to purchase one of the new A40 utilities; being sold by Winterbottoms, and to pick up on a certain day, and the firm said you leave by the boat on a certain morning, so had to make a mad dash to the Commonwealth Bank, and draw out seven hundred pounds, and put it in a little box and register it to my father in Armadale for him to pick it up and take out home for me to pick up when I could get down from Geraldton.

The hotel to which Bill Brooks and I were booked into belonged to a John Shea, whom I had first met at Waroona when he had the hotel there in 1928-29, and he had a son Jack Shea who played cricket for W.A.

After getting the factory started, I went on the "Nord Star" out to the Abrolhos Islands on processing the crayfish caught there, and when the hold was filled would bring them back to Gcraldton to go in the freezer there.

I enjoyed working out there, in the clear waters seeing the fish swimming around amongst the coral below, and the Aberstroms were wizards of dishing up fish meals with spaghetti, but I did not enjoy the trips each way, and got very squirmish, although never really seasick, with the boat being below the waves one minute, and way up on top of them the next.

My one real experience of being seasick was on an occasion coming from Port Gregory to Geraldton when we ran into a southerly buster, and on reaching Geraldton one of the meat inspectors from Robbs Jetty was there, and he said, "I have heard of ghosts, but this was the first time had seen one", I was so white.

A couple of hours after and getting cleaned up, went down town to have a meal, and the restaurant was; just rolling around. It took me about three days to get over the effects of the sea-sickness.

Also did some processing of crayfish on the boat while in Geraldton, picking the fish up from the boats and going outside the harbour to process them, and would take turns at fishing from the boat while processing, and as quick as you threw your line in you had a fish, and during this time I was living on the "Nord Star."

About March during- a couple of quiet days on the processing I managed to slip down to Perth one night on the train, and pick up my Austin A-40 utility, and return during the following night, and it came in handy to have a look around at places.

The crayfishing season eventually closed for the year, so returned back to Fremantle, and on various jobs, helping to instal fridges, which were being brought over from the Eastern States at the time. I think they were called the Holstrom, and also as the firm knew I could drive, I used to have to go to the West Perth markets and pick up apples, and take drums of molasses from the sugar refinery to their depot in West Perth.

The year was now 1950 and creeping around to the opening of the Fremantle and coastline upwards towards Lancelin Island from November onwards, and Tropical Traders & Paterson built crayfish processing factory at Lancelin, and with one of the bosses, I was in charge of fourteen men during the season, and what long hours we put in sometime, especially when the white crayfish came in for the day. You would start at one o'clock for the day, and finish at six the next morning, having at times to get the fishermen's wives to help us pack them to get them into the freezers, and finishing at six, hardly had time to have breakfast, a little sleep, dinner and at it again at one o'clock. We practically prayed for rough weather sometimes so the fishermen could not go out and pull their pots.

I was the head grader, and there were five different sizes, they had to be graded into, and a pink and white flesh which had to be packed separately, so by the time the night was over you were seeing all colours.

Came May 1951 and the season closed, and had six months up there and during that time did not go home for Christmas or New Year 1951, the only break I got was when the fishermen did not pull their pots.

At the start of the season we were paid so much a week and keep, but the boys were dissatisfied with that arrangement and the firm finally came up with overall processed weight at 3d a pound to be paid between us.

On returning to Fremantle I decided that I wanted to invest some or my money in land and do something for myself, and so left the firm during May. Dad and I looked around at various pieces of land for sale, and I finally settled for fifty seven acres in the Southern River area of Gosnells.

A bachelor by the name of Charlie Lander had the place, a little old shed on it, and a small cement-floored house, a well, and a couple of rainwater tanks, and a few big pines planted in 1927, and partly fenced. The property had a gazetted road but unbuilt running through by the name of Bradley Street, with six five-acre blocks one side and three nine-acre blocks on the other side, and I paid £2300 for it.

As I had not had a break for six months, I decided I would go for a trip in my Austin A-40 to Queensland, and I set out on the 1st June 1951, staying with friends the first night at Kellerberrin, then a night at Southern Cross and on to Kalgoorlie for a night, and Norseman where just on entering the town I had a blow-out, and as I only had the one spare, I purchased two more tyres and tubes, and stayed here a couple of nights.

Where I purchased the tyres, the chap asked me if I could take a big truck tyre to a chap stranded at Eucla. I was well loaded up, but said "I will see what I can do", and squeezed it in.

After leaving Norseman it was just a dirt road through the bush, and in places tracks everywhere, where you took which you thought the best, and so there was some very rough travelling.

The first night out I camped in a shelter of a shed and tanks, just past Balladonia, having a stretcher with me which I set up under the shed after getting a bit of wood, and a nice bonfire going, being winter time and a little on the cold side.

On the second day went through Caiguna, Cocklebiddy, and stayed at Madura Pass, and some pretty rough travelling, as all the big interstate trucks, what there were, had tracks like furrows everywhere, and once you got in one it was hard to get out, and then on to Mundrabilla and the W.A./S.A. border at Eucla, and here I handed over the truck tyre I had brought from Norseman to the chap stranded there. He was from Melbourne, and had had fifteen tyre blow-outs up to here.

From Eucla on to a place called Ivy Tanks where I stayed a night, and on today's run I was driving up a slight incline, and as usual when climbing you have that little extra speed, and on reaching the brow of the hill was about a two yard ditch which I had no hope of avoiding, as it was right across the road, and what a jolt, landed about :five yards further on, and thought I had broken every spring in the vehicle, but except for shaking everything around in the ute, everything was O.K. much to my relief.

On towards Penong and Ceduna, where had another unpleasant sensation, as on a very corrugated section of road, heard a noise engine-wards, and immediately stopped, and found the nut must have come loose holding the air cleaner must have come off, and the air filter was two inches of going through the fan and radiator, and managed to wire it down till I got to Ceduna, and double-locked it with screws.

From Ceduna onwards through a number of small towns, mostly farming areas, and to Port Augusta where I stayed a night, the largest town I had seen since leaving Norseman in W.A., and then on to Port Pirie the following day, and then Adelaide to the great-aunt's place, where I washed off all the Nullarbor mud that I had collected.

Only in Adelaide a couple of days, when I headed up to the Murray valley to Monash to visit the cousin whom I had helped to pick his grape crop in 1946, and then on to Mildura, a big soldier settlement area of the First World War of vineyards and citrus fruit. From here to Bendigo, and down to Melbourne, where I was to go to a cousin's 21st birthday party which had been on my list of engagements when I left home on the 1st June.

After visiting a great-aunt, various cousins and a penfriend in Melbourne, I went on to Sale to visit more cousins, then on towards the ranges, which were just starting to·show the effects of winter with a little snow, and then on to Albury where I visited a cousin, daughter of the great-aunt I had seen in Melbourne.

From Albury down towards Sydney, which I by-passed going up to Newcastle, Maitland and Greta to visit my friends, who had befriended me during the war, the Swan family.

Then on northwards up through Armidale, Tamworth, and to Tweed Heads near the Queensland border, and passing through some varied and interesting country, and many different venues of farming.

Over the border at Coolangatta into Queensland, and on to Brisbane, where I went out to meet a penfriend in one of the suburbs, and stayed two or three days.

Onwards to the north of Queensland, up through Nambour, Gympie and to Maryborough, where I met people by the name of Truran, who were relations of the people Richardson whom I boarded with in Fremantle when working for Tropical Traders & Paterson, and who were engaged in the timber business on Fraser Island off the Queensland coast.

From here along the Bruce Highwy through a town called Gin Gin, and along the Bruce Highway are planted hundreds of bougainvilleas, and then on to Gladstone and Rockhampton.

From here I could not follow the coastline road any further because of landslidea up near Mackay, I had to go inland to Emerald and Clermont, where from then on to Charters Towers, a gravel road used during the war years, and through cattle country which this night I was driving, and all of a sudden there were a hundred and one little lights on the road in front of me, and had to stop as a herd of cattle were camped on the road, and had to wait for them to move, and this delayed me getting into Charters Towers, and managed to get a beer down before the hotel closed, to wash the dust down after my long days drive, and book in for the night, it being 10 p.m.

From Charters Towers I headed back to the coastline by the town of Townsville, and here I stayed a couple of days, and did a boat trip out to Magnetic Island while here. Up though the towns of Ingham and Tully, these areas being mostly cane growing country, and Tully is reputed to be the wettest place in Australia, an average of 422 inches a year.

On through miles and miles of sugar cane country to Innisfail, Babinda, Gordon Vale, and to Cairns, which was my target when I left home, and as Dad had said "you'll never do it" I went fifty miles further on to Mosman, which was as far as the bitumen road went in those days, and on one part of the road were rocks and trees that had been washed down some time before by twenty inches of rain in twenty four hours, but luckily one could get through.

Back to Cairns, and then inland to Mareeba, up through the mountains to Atherton and the Atherton Tablelands, where I said "if ever I left W.A. this is where I would come," a really lovely place of Queensland where you could grow anything all the year round.

From Atherton down one of the windiest roads I had ever been on, to Ravenshoe, where at one section traffic had to come down, and then stopped, while the traffic went the other way, and then back again to the coast at Innisfail, and then again to Townsville. Here I had intended to go to Charters Towers again and inland to Hughenden for a change of scenery, but was advised the roads were not in very good condition, so finished up down the coastal highway, and through the section that I could not get through before, because of road blockages.

So from Townsville down through lots of sugar cane country, and the towns of Ayr, Bowen, Proserpine, Mackay and eventually·again to Rockhampton. From here leisurely down the coast through Gladstone, Bundaberg, Maryborough, Gympie and to Brisbane. A few days stay with my penfriend here, and then on the way again, this time out through Ipswich and Warwick, an area of beautiful rich black soil, Stanthorpe over the Queensland/New South Wales border, to Tenderfield, Lismore down the coast road of northern N.S.W. to Grafton, Coffs Harbour, Taree, and back to my friends at Greta near Maitland and Newcastle.

Here a few days, and now going on to Sydney, but while here, one of the sons of Mr. and Mrs. Swan wanted to come back West with me, so made arrangements when I was to leave Sydney would come down by train and meet me in Sydney.

On us leaving Sydney, went out through the Blue Mountains area to Bathurst and on to Orange, and a small town of Blayney, where we stayed the night, and what a cold night, having to scrape about half an inch of ice off the windscreen of my vehicle next morning.

Continuing on from here on to Cowra, Grenfell and to West Wyalong, where l called in to see a cousin working in the Post Office, through Rankins Springs, Goolgrow and on to Hay. I intended going on through here to Mildura, but found out could go no further that way because of floods. So it was a case of through the outback on some very rough, gravelly and wet roads to Booligal, Mosquiel and Ivanhoe, and eventually to Wilcannia, and travelling through here with all the new feed saw hundreds of kangaroos and thousands of rabbits.

From Wilcannia on to Broken Hill to visit a cousin, Reg Harvey, who was running the Willyama Hotel, one of the few early hotels in Broken Hill and run by the Harvey family, being owned in the early days by my great-Uncle and great-Aunt Phil and Emily Harvey.

From Broken Hill I continued on to Adelaide, where Kevin Swan and I boarded at a boarding house, and from here I visited aunts, uncles, cousins and friends, while Kevin visited the Adelaide Royal Show which was on at that time.

Eventually left Adelaide on the last long stage of my return home across the Nullarbor to home in W.A., staying at Port Pirie, Port Augusta, Ceduna and a couple of places before through Eucla at the W.A./S.A. border, Madura and after a very rough trip to Norseman, the last day being very hot and humid and not helped by having three punctures during the last day, and on getting to Norseman accommodation was a problem as there was a big cycling carnival on for the week-end, but my friend and I washed the dust down with a few cold beers.

From here on to Coolgardie, Southern Cross, and many more wheatbelt towns to Northam, over the Darling Ranges to Midland Junction, and home to Armadale after being away just over three months, and having done a few thousand miles, and except for a few punctures, blow-outs, and only one occasion trouble with the engine of my Austin A-40 which I rectified myself, I had a very enjoyable trip, and saw quite a lot of Australia that had only heard and read about before.

After a couple of days in Armadale it was time to move to my own property about 2 ½ miles out of Gosnells West, the Southern River area where I had bought my property before leaving on the trip east, and doing something about developing it, and this was about the first week in September 1951.

Although the house was not a first-class one, it was liveable, having been built by the previous owner, a Mr. Charlie Lander, there were two fairly big rooms, kitchen, couple of smaller rooms, and the bathroom, and the floors were of cement.

There was a wooden stove for cooking purposes, and of course the old kerosene lamp for lighting, there being no electricity in those parts then, and there was no scheme water, but there were three big tanks for water, and also a small well and overhead tank, and an old fashioned engine for pumping water for garden purposes, and also for the house if needed, but no good for cooking purposes as the water was brown.

And so it was to settle down to batchelor days, and get things going, and not being a working man at that time, it was a case of with mattock, axe and shovel that I set to to clear some of the land and get some kind of pastures going, the timber being mostly banksia, she-oak and red gum, except for some swamp area which was very thick with tea tree.

As the easterly winds blew very strongly here, one of the first things I did was to plant a Victorian tea tree hedge to make a bit of a windbreak around the house and also for the garden of which I was always very keen on.

By the time Summer came I had quite a few acres of land cleared, and by doing some fencing for one of my neighbours, he promised in repayment to rotary hoe my cleared land for me.

After buying super, oats, clover, rye grass, I set to work about May 1952 in the old-fashioned way with the dish around my shoulders and throwing out the seed and super by hand, and on doing this I was helped out by a very good neighbour by the name of A.B. Facey who loaned me a horse and harrows to harrow it in with, and over the years till he left he was a very good friend to me, and later my wife.

Also during this stage I had to do quite a bit of fencing as some of the boundary fencing had had it, except where joining onto neighbour's fencing, so had to buy quite a lot of posts and fencing material, and so for the first eight months the days were long and hard, and except for Mr. Facey getting me to join the local Progress Association, there was not much time for social activities.

In June 52, funds were starting to get a bit low, as having not done any work since June 1951, and so was more or less looking for something to do, when Mr. Facey, whose son worked on the local Road Board, suggested I try there, as they were looking for someone to work with him on the sanitary round, and I said "I will give it a go for a week," which I thought would be as long as I would last, but to my surprise I finished with 26 years on the local council.

The first night I started early June was a cold wet winter's night and started about 1.15 am., so it was something different to usual working hours, and used to be finished by about seven a.m. Took turns week about on driving, Joe Facey doing the first week, so one week you did one side of the truck and next week the other side, and on the first week's change over I went where I thought Joe said and opened up a gate and shone the torch in, and all I could see was about twenty little lights glowing at me, and it was a goats' pen, but one soon got used to the places, but could not get used to the East Cannington run for a long time, as we always seemed to be going around in circles, and the job had its laughs, especially if you ran into the clothesline and your torch flew out of your hand and went out, and much groping around before you found it, and on two occasions got bogged and had to wait for the other workers to start at 8 a.m. to get a truck or something to come and pull us out, and this made our shift somewhat late, and on another occasion when the round got to daylight hours, I was told to report to the office as some chap had reported me for pulling the pan out while his wife was, on the toilet, so the job had its laughs, but Joe and I got on very well for the years we worked together.

In March 1952 Merle Swan whom I mentioned earlier of my Army days in Greta N.S.W. with a friend came over to Western Australia, and was working at the Mount Hospital, and then the Hollywood Hospital, and we saw each other at times, and on January 1st 1953 we became engaged, and February 14th, Saint Valentine's Day, we were married, and if anybody would have said I would marry this 13-year old High School girl thirteen years later, I would have said "you are mad," but it happened.

Had a short honeymoon at Denmark, and then Merle and I decided to go in for a little farming, as well as my working job. Bought a couple of cows to start with, and increased it to half a dozen, bought a separator, and began sending cream to the Watsonia factory at Spearwood.

Also bought little pigs to use up the skim milk, after the calves were fed, and at the Midland weekly stock sales had the distinction of getting top price for porkers one week, also went in for poultry and used to send eggs to the Egg Marketing Board.

Milking of the cows on working days was after I got home from work at seven a.m., and then again about five in the afternoon, so they were busy days. Also in my love for gardening I grew lots of vegetables and flowers, and one time had two thousand gladioli growing and selling the blooms, and also had quite a big strawberry patch.

A few years into the dairying, with a little hot weather to help, I got a couple of cans of second grade cream, and the inspector came out and inspected things. and said "I had to do this, and had to do that", and I told him I did not have the money, and I would let the calves run with the cows, and just milk a little for ourselves and make butter, and a little cream for our own use.

As we did not have the electricity here, and local Progress Association fought to get it to the local area, but I had to pay ninety pounds, this in 1956, to get the line brought about a quarter of a mile to the corner of my block, which in later years when other people joined on to it I was reimbursed, but with no interest after years they used my money.

After getting the power to the corner of the block, I had to get it two hundred yards .to the house, meaning about four poles and six wires, the reason for the six wires being at this time I had a bore put down and a stand and overhead tank, and of course with the electricity was able to instal an electric motor.

To go back a little, after being married in February 1953, Merle and I had our first child born in November 1953, a son called Phillip Lawrence, and in August 1955 our second, a son called Colin Victor, and being nearly forty when I got married decided that two would be enough to educate on the wages in those days.

With the advent of the electricity and the bore this was when I really started getting into the garden, as by putting in pipes I was able to irrigate it all. I joined the local Horticultural Society, and in their Spring Show held every year I took many prizes for flowers, fruit and vegetables, and never missed first prize for potatoes for ten years, and one year held the Gerry Wild trophy for twelve months for the most points over the whole Show.

During the 1969's the local council bumped the rates on the land I held about three hundred per cent in one hit, and as a working man on wages it was a bit too much, so had to sell some of my land, and finally all of it, and kept my own five acre block on which the house stood.

The five acre blocks I sold for about seven hundred and forty dollars, and in the late 1980's was sold for just over fifty six thousand dollars. What a contrast.

With only the five acres to look after I grew quite a. few daffodils and also a lot of iris's as well as the gladioli, and one year sold six and a half thousand iris blooms, in those days 40 cents a dozen.

In the meantime, work was still going on with the local council, and eventually with a government decree brought in, all householders had to put in septic tanks, so gradually the pan system was phased out, but also about this time a rubbish service was instituted, so Joe Facey and I used to have week about on the sanitary round and rubbish service till finally only one was needed for the sanitary round and eventually this faded out.

The first place the nightsoil tip was located was close to Gosnells, corner of Corfield Street and close to Verna, which eventually closed, and today is known as Robinson Park, and the tip moved out four miles from Gosnells, out Southern River Road towards Ranford Road.

Worked on ·the rubbish round for years, and saw many types of' vehicles being used for the service, and our various dumping grounds were a couple of places in Maddington where clay had been dug out for making bricks, and a couple of brick pits in Kenwick near the Kenwick cemetery, a place in Cannington near the river, at Riverton where a mound was built up at the local sports ground, and a lot was dumped near the river in Wendouree Road in Cannington, and eventually the final place at Kelvin Road in Orange Grove.

During the 1970's I had my own council vehicle to do the duties of cleaning out public halls and the toilets of the various sports grounds, and then to doing the round of all the street bins around the area and sports grounds.

During my years on the council I saw the offices shifted from Maddington to Gosnells, near the Canning River, and also from a Road Board to a Council and Town and finally to a city in 1978, and many changes to new road and large developments of land into big new housing areas, and also industrial projects.

I finally retired from working with the City of' Gosnells on 22nd September 1978, having reached the age of sixty five the previous month, when at which age they say out you go.

In November 1978 I became involved with the Addie Mills Senior Citizens Centre as a volunteer driver, and drove the bus for ten years, bringing the senior citizens in to lunch and then returning them home afterwards, and one always had an offsider to open the door and help the people in if needed, and at the age of seventy five, in fairness to myself and the passengers I gave up driving, and became an offsider myself, and these two jobs I did the job once a week except when away travelling on holidays.

I had a Villa Nova van which was jacked on to my ute, and most of the travelling with my wife was done this way and we stayed mostly in caravan parks at night, and the van has paid for itself time and time again instead of staying in hotels and motels. One trip about 1982 we went across the Nullarbor to Port Augusta and up through Coober Pedy, the place of opals, to Ayers Rock which I climbed and left my name in the record book on top, to Alice Springs, Katherine and Darwin.

Returned via Katherine and Victoria River, Timber Creek, and to Kunnunurra, Wyndham, Halls Creek, Fitzroy Crossing, Derby, Broome, Port Hedland, Carnarvon, Geraldton and home.

In 1983 did a trip by railway bus to Geraldton, and from here by a tourist bus to Carnarvon, Gascoyne Junction, part of the Hamersley Ranges, staying at a couple of cattle stations, on to Cue, Mt. Magnet, Yalgoo, Mingenew, and back to Geraldton then home again by West Rail bus.

In September 1984 went to Sydney, by Ansett-Pioneer bus, a three-day trip over the Nullarbor to Adelaide, Broken Hill, Dubbo and then Sydney, and then went by Qantas to New Zealand where my wife and I hired a two-berth pop-up vehicle and did a month's trip touring both islands of New Zealand, and meeting up with many of my P.O.W. mates, but many had since passed on since I was there for the P.O.W. re-union in 1965, and visited the cities of Auckland, Wellington, Dunedin, Christchurch, and many important tourist places including Rotorua, Milford Sound Glaciers, and beautiful lakes up in the mountains.

In August 1986 my wife and I left on our longest trip over with the Villa Nova, travelling up the North West coastline road through places we had been before, to Katherine in the Northern Territory, and then down south to a place called Three Way, a few miles north of Tennant Creek.

From here we headed to Camoweal in Queensland, on to Mt. Isa, a big mining town, then on to Cloncurry, then up to Normanton, and out to Karumba, a big fishing place where boats head out into the Gulf of Carpentaria for fishing.

Back to Normanton, and over some very rough roads to Blackbutt and Croydon, the latter an old gold-mining town, and to Georgetown, Mt. Surprise and to Ravenshoe on the Atherton Tablelands, one of my favourite spots. Through the town of Atherton, Mareeba, and then out of the mountain country to Mosman, and to Daintree which is as far as the bitumen road went in 1986, and a place where there was a lot of controversy about a road going through the forest country.

Returned back to Mosman, and down to Cairns, a big tourist town, where went for a trip out to one of the islands and saw parts of the coral reef, and thousands of fish that are protected here.

From Cairns down through a lot of cane growing country to Innisfail, Tully, Ingham and to Townsville, Ayr, Bowen, Mackay, and to a small place called Sarina, and during part of this trip we paid a visit to the second largest sugar mill in the world, and the largest in Australia, and saw the processing of the sugar cane until it was in the bags ready for distribution.

From the town of Sarina we went inland over winding and mountainous roads to a place called Moranbah, where there is a big opencut coal mine, and we were lucky enough to be shown around, through meeting up with people who were friends of the Anglican priest who had come to Gosnells from here, just before we left on our holiday.

On leaving Moranbah we went a little further inland and came to Clermont, more coal-mining country around here, and then to Emerald, and through Blackwater, more coal mining country, to Duaranga and to Rockhampton.

From Rockhampton we followed the coastline down to Gladstone, Bundaberg, Maryborough, where I met a chap from my trip there in 1951, and so down through pineapple country to Gympie and Nambour.

On arriving at Caboolture, not far from Brisbane, we turned inland again and through to Kingaroy, and there is some very rich and fertile country around here.

On leaving Kingaroy travelled to Dalby, Chinchilla, Miles, and to Roma, where we turned south to St. George, Goondiwindi, Toowoomba and to Brisbane. After a few days here, came across to Warwick, and then to Southport on the Gold Coast, which was to be our home for the next ten days, the reason for our trip being a Prisoner of War Reunion at Surfers Paradise, being worldwide for any countries on the Allied side of' the 1939/45 war, and what a week of festivities it turned out to be, and being held in the month of October.

Continuing on after the Reunion came down over the border into New South Wales to Ballina, Lismore, Tenderfield, Glen Innes, Moree, Collarenebri, Walgett and to Brewarrina to meet a couple from Gosnells who had moved to there not long before we left, and we certainly struck some rough roads from Moree in the outback.

From Brewarrina travelled down to Nyngan, and now returning to the coastline again in northern New South Wales, and through Warren, Gilgandra, Armidale, Dorrigo and to Grafton.

Leaving Grafton and so down the coast to Coffs Harbour, Kempsey (where my wife was born), Port Macquarie, Taree and to the Newcastle area where quite a few of my wife's relations live, and stayed here for a few days.

Onwards from here back through Maitland, Singleton, and through the ranges to Mudgee, Gulgong, Dunedoo, Dubbo, Wellington, Orange, Cowra, Young (cherry picking time here), Cootamundra, Wagga Wagga (some rich country around here), Narrandera, Leeton (a rice mill here), Griffith, then to Hay, Balranald, Robinvale and

Wentworth on the N.S.W. side of the Murray River, the other side being Victoria. From Wentworth went through the outback to Broken Hill, where one of the first hotels here, the Willyama was owned by my great uncle and aunt, the Harvey family

From Broken Hill travelled to Petersborough in South Australia and to Burra, an old copper mining town and where my Mother was born, and another great uncle and aunt were Mayor and Mayoress of the town 1910-13. On this days travelling we had one of the coldest and most miserable days of our trip. It was here that my grandfather and grandmother lived and worked before going on to the mines in Kalgoorlie and eventually farming out from Bridgetown in the south west of W.A.

Leaving Burra, and not intending to go to Adelaide, we were now heading west and for home, going through Port Pirie and Port Augusta to Kimba, Ceduna, Norseman, Kalgoorlie and home to Gosnells after a very interesting trip lasting fourteen weeks and twenty thousand kilometres.

While living here in Gosnells I have been a continuous member of the R.S.L., having joined up on being discharged at Karrakatta in September 45, and was secretary for ten years and helped in many ways, and was made a life member of the Gosnells Branch about ten years ago Also have Certificate of Service from headquarters.

I have also been interested in sporting activities, having played B-Grade cricket and tennis for Gosnells in the 50's, and now play bowls for Gosnells. Although I have played about seven different sports, I have not been any champion, but have always enjoyed whatever I have played.

I also have a Certificate of Service from the City of Gosnells presented during the Sesquicentenary year 1929-1979 in recognition of services to the community.

Another fund-raising effort I was involved in after my retirement used to go out on the roads picking up bottles, and when first started it would not take long to pick up a ute load, and also visited the local football grounds after the Sunday games, and visited the roadsides of Gosnells, Armadale and Cannington during the picking up.

All the unreturnable bottles were broken up and a truck used to come and pick them up for recycling of making more glass bottles. The big beer bottles, cool drinks and flagons were taken or called for by bottle dealers. All this went to our local Anglican Church of All Saints, and was used for the welfare of Anglican centres by way of food and anything necessary, and during the last four years before moving from Southern River area to Gosnells, my wife and I raised a thousand dollars a year, but had to give the glass part of it away when we moved into Gosnells, because of the noise of broken glass would create, and now with health problems have unfortunately to give it away altogether.

And so ends the story of most of my life, written between the years of seventy seven and seventy eight, or 1990 and 1991.

C.A.G.V. Petersen 11th July 1991

Obituary for Private Charles Amos George Victor (Vic) Petersen

—m—

Private WX571, B Co, 2/11 Battalion, AIF, POW, #4538,
Born at Bridgetown, Western Australia, 27th August 1913

Vic enlisted November 1939 and commenced training at Northam Military Camp, WA. Three weeks later transferred to Rutherford, NSW and then to another camp at Greta, NSW.

On 13th January 1940 moved to Ingleburn, near Sydney, then returning to Perth in March for pre-embarkation leave before sailing to the Middle East.

Departed on 20th April 1940 on the troopship NEVAS. One of the escort ships was the battle ship RAMILIES.

After further training in Gaza and Egypt the 2/11th Bn, under General Mackay and Allied Armies General O'Connor, engaged in their first action and victory against the Italian Army. This action resulted in the capture of 90,000 Italian soldiers and regaining control of Bardia and Tobruk in Libya. Next action was against the German Army in Northern Greece.

The Yugoalav and Greece Armies collapsed against the intense German attack. Australian, NZ's and British (British Expeditionary Force) troops were continuously attacked by German Stuka dive bombers using machine guns and bombs, tanks and along with SS troops from the elite "Liebstandarte Adolph Hitler". This resulted in a retreat back down to the south of Greece and on 26th April 1941 with a nighttime embarkation to Crete. The daring escape of 51,000 allies from Greece is recorded as a major achievement of WWII, logistically being more successful than Dunkirk.

At Crete, 42,500 Allies dug in, waiting for the German Invasion.

The Germans continuously bombed Crete until 20 May, when they commenced the largest ever aerial invasion consisting of parachutists and gliders supported by 1209 aircraft, 63 small ships to carry three infantry divisions. After many fierce battles and the huge losses on both sides, the Germans captured Crete, June 1941.

Vic was forced to surrender on 6th June 1941.

Vic was one of the 12,000 allies being taken POW, his POW No is 4538. As a result of a snake bite to the neck, Vic was separated from his 2/11th Bn (who were transported to Stalags in Germany) and remained on Crete for some time, forced to dig up olive trees so the Germans could build more air bases.

Eventually he was transferred Jan 1942, to Salonika in Greece where after 14 days crammed in a rail truck arrived at Stalag VIIIB at Lamsdorf in Sudatenland, Germany.

Due to forced labour Vic and the other POW's worked on (and sometimes sabotaged) railway lines until the end of the war, May 1945, being a POW for almost 4 years.

On his release, Vic was transferred, arriving in Eastbourne, England 30th May 1945. His return to Australia was on the MAUREANIA via the Panama Canal to New Zealand and onto Sydney, Australia

In later years, Vic settled on a property in Southern River, near Perth, W.A. with his wife Merle and two son's Phillip and Collin. He was staunch supporter of the Returned Services League, 2/11 Bn Association and POW Association and kept in contact with many of his comrades in England, NZ and Australia till his death.

Vic died in Hollywood Hospital on 30th January 1995 aged 81 years.

Vale Vic
Lest we Forget
This summary was written by his wife, Merle and son, Phillip. 27th August 1998, coincidentally Vic's birthday.

Map of Vic's Journey from Perth to Palestine 1940

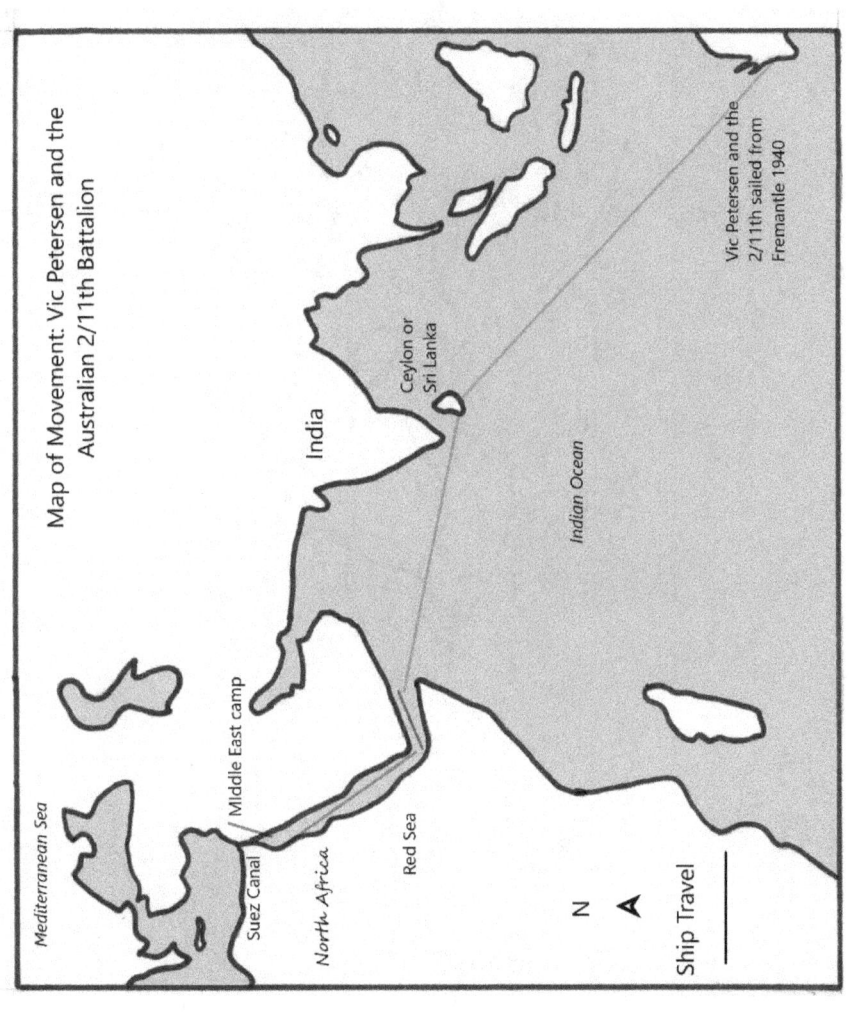

Map of Crete

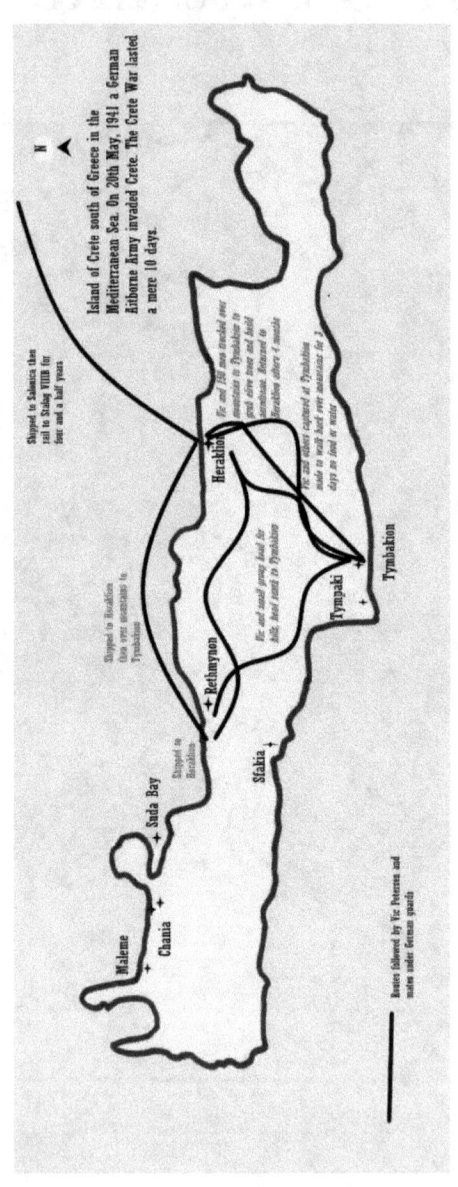

Map of Vic's Movements from Crete to Stalag VIIIB

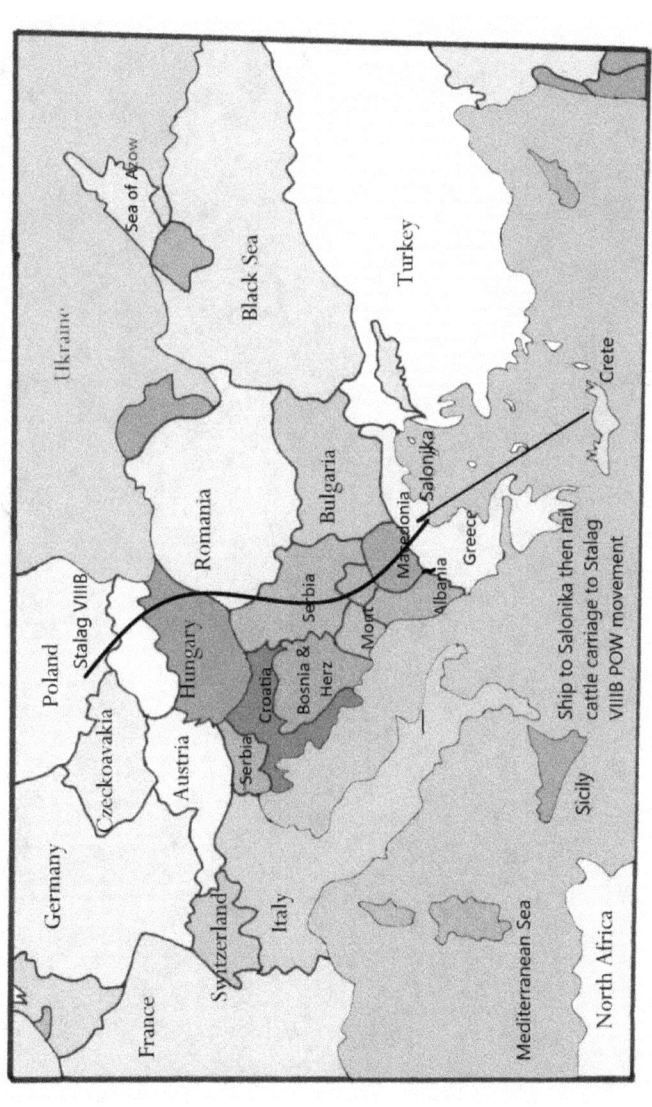

German Town Names

German Name	Post WW2	Country
Aldersbach	Adršpach	Czech Republic
Aldstadt	Staré Město (Karviná)	Czech Republic
	Stare Miasto	
Bernsdorf	Bernartice (Trutnov District)	Czech Republic
Bodisch	Bohdašín	Czech Republic
Braunau	Broumov	Czech Republic
	Bronów	Poland
Breslau	Wrocław	Poland
Freiheit	Svoboda nad Úpou	Czech Republic
	Wolnica	Poland
Gabensdorf	Trutnov	Czech Republic
Glatz	Klodzko	Poland
Gorlitz	Zgorzelec	Poland
Gratz	Grodzisk Wielkopolski	Poland
Halbstadt	Meziměstí	Czech Republic
Heinzesdorf	Hynčice (Náchod District)	Czech Republic
	Jasienica	Poland
Herschberg	Jelenia Gora	Poland
Hohenlbe	Vrchlabí	Czech Republic
Johanisbad	Janské Lázně	Czech Republic
Johnsdorf-Hottendorf	Jívka	Czech Republic
Konigsberg	Klimkovice	Czech Republic

German Name	Post WW2	Country
Konsigshan	Královec	Czech Republic
Lampersdorf	Lampertice	Czech Republic
Lamsdorf	Lambinowice	Poland
Neisse	Nysa	Poland
Olberg	Olivětín, p. of Broumov	Czech Republic
Ober Aldstadt	Horní Staré Město	Czech Republic
Parschnitz	Poříčí, p. of Trutnov	Czech Republic
Petersdorf	Gliwice, -Szobiszowice	Poland
Qualisch	Chvaleč	Czech Republic
Radowenz	Radvanice	Czech Republic
Ruppersdorf	Liberec XIV-Ruprechtice	Czech Republic
Ruttersdorf	Wyszonowice	Poland
Schatzler	Žacléř	Czech Republic
Sudatenland		Czech Republic
Trautenau	Trutnov	Czech Republic
Trubenwasser	Mladé Buky	Czech Republic
Tuntchendorf	Tlumaczow	Poland
Weckelsdorf	Teplice nad Metují	Czech Republic
Weckelsdorf	Křinice	Czech Republic

The 37 towns are where Vic worked or travelled through while in the Railway Maintenance Work Party, E 388.

Glossary

Araklian	person living in Middle-east
Arbeit Zug	small working train assisting with maintenance
Bagatelle Composition	short music piece very brief
Ballast	heavy material to keep balance
Biliousness	bad tempered, disorder of bile
Boody	small shed
Bounce	return to sender (often post or money-cheques)
Bravo Cigarettes	brand or type of cigarette
Canteen	shop for goodies for provisions in a barracks
Civvy	citizenship
Bridge	card game played in teams
Bridgehead	fort area protecting end of bridge
Briquets	compressed inflammable blocks
British Free Corps	turncoat Brits work for Germany during WWII
Buckley	idiom meaning 'no hope at all' (eg Buckley's chance)
Colonials	those living in a colony
Crib	break for workers also a card game
Deck tennis	tennis played on ship's deck using quoits
Ersatz coffee	tastes like coffee but is not

Euchre	card game played in fours.
Fat hen	weed growing by wayside
Feld-Wabel	German shoulder boards
Fertig	German for finished or ready
Firearm job	jobs related to guns of all types
Fleisch	flesh or meat
Froggies	French person
Gaffir	game character as a boss enemy
Klim Milk Powder	type or brand of milk
Landwach	land agent buying land
Lager	type of beer
Lashings	hit with a whip or lots of food
Light arbeiters	worker
marks	to cut or scribble upon Money.
Mifag Essen	Personal Leir name of good German Guard
Mifag Essen	Personal name of one POW nasty German guard
Phennig	old place of Germany.
Plating	outside of metal, sheets used in construction of machinery
Postens	post office business
Protectorate	state controlled and protected by another
Quark C	cheese
Quoit tennis	fun game like tennis except played with quoits
Reichbahn	German national railway system.
Reichbahn railway	German national railway system
Reichmarchs	German money used during Third Reich
Ruben	Food especially a sandwich
Sanitary	health and hygiene especially related to toiletry
Sanitor	cleaner of toilets and other area of uncleanliness can occur

Sauerkraut	shredded cabbage allow fermentation
Slack	lazy. Stops work too often
Strafe	shoots from aeroplane at land based soldiers.
Tommies	over the top name for British soldiers.
Unplating sleepers	removing the screws/bolts from sleepers before discarding them
Virgilia	Newspaper group during WWII. Men encouraged to have a pen friend to correspond with. Many letters published.
V1 rockets	Experimental rockets shot at London and Antwerp. Gave Germany an edge in the war.
Volksturm	Young militia used by Hitler as last ditch at the end of WWII.
Whist	Card game